Managerial Economics

Managerial economics, meaning the application of economic methods in the managerial decision-making process, is a fundamental part of any business or management course. This textbook covers all the main aspects of managerial economics: the theory of the firm; demand theory and estimation; production and cost theory and estimation; market structure and pricing; game theory; investment analysis and government policy. It includes numerous and extensive case studies, as well as review questions and problem-solving sections at the end of each chapter. Nick Wilkinson adopts a user-friendly problem-solving approach which takes the reader in gradual steps from simple problems through increasingly difficult material to complex case studies, providing an understanding of how the relevant principles can be applied to real-life situations involving managerial decision-making. This book will be invaluable to business and economics students at both undergraduate and graduate levels who have a basic training in calculus and quantitative methods.

NICK WILKINSON is Associate Professor in Economics at Richmond, The American International University in London. He has taught business and economics in various international institutions in the UK and USA, as well as working in business management in both countries.

Managerial Economics
A Problem-Solving Approach

Nick Wilkinson

CAMBRIDGE
UNIVERSITY PRESS

CAMBRIDGE UNIVERSITY PRESS
Cambridge, New York, Melbourne, Madrid, Cape Town, Singapore,
São Paulo, Delhi, Dubai, Tokyo

Cambridge University Press
The Edinburgh Building, Cambridge CB2 8RU, UK

Published in the United States of America by Cambridge University Press, New York

www.cambridge.org
Information on this title: www.cambridge.org/9780521526258

First published 2005

A catalogue record for this publication is available from the British Library

Library of Congress Cataloguing in Publication data

Wilkinson, Nick, 1953–
Managerial economics: a problem-solving approach / Nick Wilkinson.
    p.   cm.
Includes bibliographical references and index.
ISBN 0 521 81993 8 (hb) – ISBN 0 521 52625 6 (pb)
1. Managerial economics.   2. Problem-solving.   3. Managerial
economics – Decision-making.   I. Title

ISBN 978-0-521-81993-0 Hardback
ISBN 978-0-521-52625-8 Paperback

Transferred to digital printing 2009

Contents

students to analyse. However, the result of this is that the textbook problems tend to fall between two stools: they are still too difficult in some cases for students to tackle without considerable help (the first problem), yet they are too simplified and abstract for students to see how textbook methods can be applied to real-life situations (the second problem).

This book attempts to overcome the considerable obstacles above. It adopts a user-friendly problem-solving approach, which takes the reader in gradual steps from easy, very simplified problems through increasingly difficult material to complex case studies.

Pedagogical features

1 The objectives of each chapter are clearly stated at the start of the chapter.
2 Case studies are plentiful and have been carefully selected. These are designed to be global in their application and relevance, and of recent origin. They are sometimes longer than the typical case study in textbooks in order to achieve a fuller flavour of real life, and they concentrate on the managerial decision-making aspect. The cases are also integrated with the material in the text, not just in terms of relevance, but also in terms of asking specific questions, often of a quantitative nature.
3 Examples are given throughout the text of firms or situations, to illustrate principles and their real-life application; an effort is made to use examples to which students can easily relate from their own experience.
4 There is an emphasis on the interdisciplinary aspects of managerial economics; problems are addressed in all the main functional areas of marketing, finance, production and human resources.
5 Quantitative techniques are introduced only where they are relevant to the material discussed, and are then applied in that context. This is contrary to the common treatment, where many techniques are explained in the early part of textbooks, before the relevant economic theory. Teaching experience suggests that students comprehend the techniques more easily if they can immediately see their application. It is assumed in the text that students already have a basic knowledge of calculus and statistics.
6 Key terms and concepts are written in **bold**; the definitions and interpretations of these terms and concepts are written in ***bold italics***.
7 Many chapters include a section titled 'A problem-solving approach' at the end of the chapter, in order to bridge the gap described above as the first student problem. These sections include several solved problems, with the rationale for the methodology explained as well as the calculations.
8 Summaries are provided at the end of each chapter of the key points.
9 Review questions are included at the end of each chapter for students to test their understanding of the material.
10 Problems of a quantitative nature are also included at the end of chapters. These can be used by both students and instructors, as test questions or assignments.

Preface

Managerial economics, meaning the application of economic methods to the managerial decision-making process, is a fundamental part of any business or management course. It has been receiving more attention in business as managers become more aware of its potential as an aid to decision-making, and this potential is increasing all the time. This is happening for several reasons:

1 It is becoming more important for managers to make good decisions and to justify them, as their accountability either to senior management or to shareholders increases.
2 As the number and size of multinationals increases, the costs and benefits at stake in the decision-making process are also increasing.
3 In the age of plentiful data it is more imperative to use quantitative and rationally based methods, rather than 'intuition'.
4 The pace of technological development is increasing with the impact of the 'new economy'. Although the exact nature of this impact is controversial, there is no doubt that there is an increased need for economic analysis because of the greater uncertainty and the need to evaluate it.
5 Improved technology has also made it possible to develop more sophisticated methods of data analysis involving statistical techniques. Modern computers are adept at 'number-crunching', and this is a considerable aid to decision-making that was not available to most firms until recent years.

As managerial economics has increased in importance, so books on the subject have proliferated. Many of the more recent ones claim like this one to take a problem-solving approach. I have found from my own teaching experience that, in spite of this, students of the subject tend to have two main problems:

1 They claim to understand the theory, but fail to see how to put principles into practice when faced with the kind of problems they find in the textbooks, even though these are considerably simplified compared with real-life situations.
2 They fail to see the relevance of the techniques presented in the books in terms of application to real-life situations.

The two problems are clearly related. Textbook problems are simplified, in terms of the amount of data and decision variables, to make them easier for

11 Starred material is included which indicates a greater degree of difficulty; this is more suitable for MBA students, and can be omitted without causing problems with understanding the remaining material. Sometimes the starred material relates to whole sections, sometimes to subsections, and sometimes just to particular headings.

12 Throughout the book there is an effort to tie economic theory and practice together. Students should be able to see how empirical studies are conducted and the role of these in testing theories; the relevance of this process to managerial decision-making is emphasized.

Structure and content

The text is structured into parts, chapters, sections, subsections, headings and subheadings. The first four are self-explanatory; headings are titled alphabetically, while subheadings are titled numerically. An attempt is made to ensure both consistency of treatment and clarity of exposition, so that students can easily see how the various materials are related.

Part I of the text is an overview of the subject matter, and is particularly concerned with the methodology employed and the objectives of firms and managers. Part II is concerned with examining demand analysis. This involves a discussion of consumer theory, the theoretical principles of demand and the empirical aspects of demand estimation. Considerable attention is given to examining statistical techniques of estimation, much more than in the typical text. This is because of the increasing importance of the use of these techniques and the ubiquity of software packages for data analysis. Part III examines production theory and costs; the treatment is similar to the previous part, in that the principles of production and costs are discussed, and then the empirical and statistical aspects of estimation are explained. Part IV examines strategy analysis; this covers market structure, pricing, game theory, investment analysis and the impact of government policy on managerial decision-making. The coverage here is broader than a typical text, and there is particular emphasis on the consideration of non-price decisions and interdependent decision-making.

In each chapter there are three or four case studies, with questions attached. These are inserted into the text as close as possible to their points of relevance. Many chapters also include solved problems; sometimes these are embodied in the text as examples to illustrate the concepts involved, and in other cases they are included at the end of the chapter, according to whatever seems more appropriate. There are also review questions and in many cases additional problems at the end of the chapters, following the chapter summaries. The currency units involved in these problems vary, being mainly in pounds sterling and US dollars; this is in keeping with the international nature of the material in both the text and the case studies.

Acknowledgements

This text grew out of lecture material that I have developed while teaching courses at both undergraduate and graduate level, mainly but not entirely in managerial economics, over more than twenty years. During that time I have had many excellent students in my classes, who have enabled me to understand more clearly the requirements for a text of this type. Their comments and questions have contributed significantly to the style and form of the book. Other students have also contributed, in that their questions and problems have over the years led to certain methods of presentation and exposition which have, I hope, improved both the clarity and relevance of the material.

I am grateful to the anonymous referees for various pieces of constructive advice regarding structure and content. In particular I would like to thank John Mark of King's College London for his advice and encouragement. Finally, I would like to thank Yasmin, my wife, for her unending patience and support.

The majority of the material in the text has been class-tested, but I am sure that there is still scope for improvement in terms of both content and clarity of exposition. Constructive suggestions in these areas are certainly welcome.

Detailed contents

PART I
INTRODUCTION

Part I (Chapters 1 and 2) examines the nature, scope and methods of managerial economics and the theory of the firm. Chapter 1 is therefore concerned with explaining why managerial economics is important and useful as an area of study, how it relates to other disciplines, what its core areas are, and the methods of analysis which it uses. Chapter 2 examines the basic profit-maximizing model of behaviour, and its underlying assumptions, and then proceeds to relax these assumptions to develop a more complex but realistic model of firms' behaviour. The focus is on the individual and the nature of transactions, with an emphasis on agency theory. These two chapters introduce the framework of parameters and analysis that are developed throughout the remainder of the text.

1

Nature, scope and methods of managerial economics

Outline

Objectives

1 To introduce and define managerial economics.
2 To outline the types of issue which are addressed by managerial economics.
3 To explain the difference between positive and normative economics.

4 To explain the relationship between managerial economics, economic theory and the decision sciences.

5 To explain how managerial economics is related to other disciplines in business, such as marketing and finance.

6 To identify the main subject areas in managerial economics, explain how they are related to each other, and describe how they are organized and presented in the text.

7 To explain the methods used in the development of scientific theories and show their relevance to managerial economics.

8 To explain how economic theory is presented from a pedagogical viewpoint, and how this relates to the organization and presentation of the material in the text.

1.1 Introduction

What is managerial economics about? What kind of issues does it deal with? How can it help us make better decisions, in business or elsewhere? These are fundamental questions which any student may ask when first approaching the subject. It is therefore a good idea to make a start by examining a situation that has become increasingly high on the economic and political agenda on a global basis over many years; yet it is not a situation where it might seem at first sight that managerial economics is particularly relevant. We shall see, to the contrary, that the methods studied and implemented in managerial economics are vital to identifying solutions to the problems raised.

Case study 1.1: Global Warming

Part I: What to do about global warming[1]

A UN treaty now under discussion looks promising – as long as it remains flexible

How should reasonable people react to the hype and controversy over global warming? Judging by recent headlines, you might think we are already doomed. Newspapers have been quick to link extreme weather events, ranging from floods in Britain and Mozambique to hurricanes in Central America, directly to global warming. Greens say that worse will ensue if governments do not act. Many politicians have duly jumped on the bandwagon, citing recent disasters as a reason for speeding up action on the Kyoto treaty on climate change that commits rich countries to cut emissions of greenhouse gases. This week saw the start of a summit in The Hague to discuss all this.

Yet hot-headed attempts to link specific weather disasters to the greenhouse effect are scientific bunk. The correct approach is coolly to assess the science of climate change before taking action. Unfortunately, climate modelling is still in its infancy, and for most of the past decade it has raised as many questions as it has answered. Now, however, the picture is getting clearer. There will never be consensus, but the balance of the evidence suggests that global warming is indeed happening; that much of it has recently been man-made; and that there is a risk of potentially disastrous consequences. Even the normally stolid insurance industry is getting excited. Insurers reckon that weather disasters have cost roughly $400 billion over the past decade and that the damage is likely only to increase. The time has come to accept that global warming is a credible enough threat to require a public-policy response.

But what, exactly? At first blush, the Kyoto treaty seems to offer a good way forward. It is a global treaty: it would be foolish to deal with this most global of problems in any other way. It sets a long-term framework that requires frequent updating and revision, rather like the post-war process of trade liberalisation. That is sensible because climate change will be at least a 100-year problem, and so will require a treaty with institutions and mechanisms that endure. The big question over Kyoto remains its cost. How much insurance is worth buying now against an uncertain, but possibly devastating, future threat? And the answer lies in a clear-headed assessment of benefits and costs. The case for doing something has increased during the three years since Kyoto was signed. Yet it also remains true that all answers will be easier if economic growth is meanwhile sustained: stopping the world while the problem is dealt with is not a sensible option, given that resources to deal with it would then become steadily scarcer.

That points to two general conclusions about how to implement Kyoto. The simplest is that countries should search out "no regrets" measures that are beneficial in their own right as well as reducing emissions – such as scrapping coal subsidies, liberalising energy markets and cutting farm support. The second is that implementation should use market-friendly measures that minimise the costs and risks of slowing economic growth.

Part II: Hot potato revisited[2]

A lack-of-progress report on the Intergovernmental Panel on Climate Change

You might think that a policy issue which puts at stake hundreds of billions of dollars' worth of global output would arouse at least the casual interest of the world's economics and finance ministries. You would be wrong. Global warming and the actions contemplated to mitigate it could well involve costs of that order. Assessing the possible scale of future greenhouse-gas emissions, and hence of man-made global warming, involves economic forecasts and economic calculations. Those forecasts and calculations will in turn provide the basis for policy on the issue. Yet governments have been content to leave these questions to a body – the Intergovernmental Panel on Climate Change (IPCC) – which appears to lack the necessary

expertise. The result is all too likely to be bad policy, at potentially heavy cost to the world economy.

In our <u>Economics focus</u> of February 15th this year, we drew attention to (and posted on our website) telling criticisms of the IPCC's work made by two independent commentators, Ian Castles, a former head of Australia's Bureau of Statistics, and David Henderson, formerly the chief economist of the Organisation for Economic Co-operation and Development (OECD) and now visiting professor at Westminster Business School. Their criticisms of the IPCC were wide-ranging, but focused on the panel's forecasts of greenhouse-gas emissions. The method employed, the critics argued, had given an upward bias to the projections.

The IPCC's procedure relied, first, on measuring gaps between incomes in poor countries and incomes in rich countries, and, second, on supposing that those gaps would be substantially narrowed, or entirely closed, by the end of this century. Contrary to standard practice, the IPCC measured the initial gaps using market-based exchange rates rather than rates adjusted for differences in purchasing power. This error makes the initial income gaps seem far larger than they really are, so the subsequent catching-up is correspondingly faster. The developing-country growth rates yielded by this method are historically implausible, to put it mildly. The emissions forecasts based on those implausibly high growth rates are accordingly unsound.

The Castles–Henderson critique was subsequently published in the journal *Energy and Environment* (volume 14, number 2–3). A response by 15 authors associated with the IPCC purporting to defend the panel's projections was published in the same issue. It accused the two critics of bias, bad faith, peddling "deplorable misinformation" and neglecting what the 15 regard as proper procedure. Alas, it fails to answer the case Mr Castles and Mr Henderson had laid out – namely, that the IPCC's low-case scenarios are patently not low-case scenarios, and that the panel has therefore failed to give a true account of the range of possibilities. If anything, as the two critics argue in an article in the subsequent issue of *Energy and Environment*, the reply of the 15 authors gives new grounds for concern. This week the IPCC is preparing to embark on its next global-warming "assessment review" – and if the tone of its reply to the critics is any guide, it is intent on business as usual.

It is true, as the IPCC says in its defence, that the panel presents a range of scenarios. But, as we pointed out before, even the scenarios that give the lowest cumulative emissions assume that incomes in the developing countries will increase at a much faster rate over the course of the century than they have ever done before. Disaggregated projections published by the IPCC say that – even in the lowest-emission scenarios – growth in poor countries will be so fast that by the end of the century Americans will be poorer on average than South Africans, Algerians, Argentines, Libyans, Turks and North Koreans. Mr Castles and Mr Henderson can hardly be alone in finding that odd.

TUNNEL VISION

The fact that the IPCC mobilised as many as 15 authors to supply its response is interesting. The panel's watchword is strength in numbers (lacking though it may be in strength at numbers). The exercise criticised by Mr Castles and Mr Henderson involved 53 authors, plus 89 expert reviewers and many others besides. Can so many experts get it wrong? The experts themselves may doubt it, but the answer is yes. The problem is that this horde of authorities is drawn from a narrow professional milieu. Economic and statistical expertise is not among their strengths. Making matters worse, the panel's approach lays great emphasis on peer review

of submissions. When the peers in question are drawn from a restricted professional domain – whereas the issues under consideration make demands upon a wide range of professional skills – peer review is not a way to assure the highest standards of work by exposing research to scepticism. It is just the opposite: a kind of intellectual restrictive practice, which allows flawed or downright shoddy work to acquire a standing it does not deserve.

Part of the remedy proposed by Mr Castles and Mr Henderson in their new article is to get officials from finance and economics ministries into the long-range emissions-forecasting business. The Australian Treasury is now starting to take an active interest in IPCC-related issues, and a letter to the British Treasury drawing attention to Castles–Henderson (evidently it failed to notice unassisted) has just received a positive, if long delayed, response. More must be done, and soon. Work on a question of this sort would sit well with Mr Henderson's former employer, the OECD. The organisation's economic policy committee – a panel of top economic officials from national ministries – will next week install Gregory Mankiw, head of America's Council of Economic Advisers, as its new chairman. If Mr Mankiw is asking himself what new work that body ought to take on under his leadership, he need look no further than the dangerous economic incompetence of the IPCC.

This case study illustrates the variety of issues with which managerial economics is concerned. The following questions arise:

1 Is there a problem to be addressed?
2 Is there a solution or solutions to the problem, in terms of strategies or courses of action that can be taken?
3 What objective or objectives can be defined for these strategies?
4 What constraints exist in terms of operating any strategies?
5 How can we identify strategies as solutions to the problem?
6 How can we evaluate these strategies in terms of costs and benefits, particularly when these involve life and health?
7 What is the best way of measuring the relevant variables?
8 What assumptions should be made in our analysis?
9 How do we deal with the problem of risk and uncertainty regarding the future and the effects of strategies in the future?
10 How can we approach the problems of conflicts of interest between different countries and between different consumers and producers?

11 What criteria can we use for selecting strategies from among different possible courses of action?

12 How do political biases and agendas affect decision-making processes in practice?

The above questions represent steps in the decision-making process involved not just in the global warming situation, but also in any situation involving decision-making. However, many people are unaware of the breadth of issue that is amenable to the analysis of managerial economics. In particular, they sometimes regard managerial economists as being apologists for greedy capitalists, who do not take quality of life into consideration, or the long-term interests of the public. They may view markets with suspicion and doubt their ability to allocate resources efficiently, for example the creation of trading rights in pollution. They may fear deregulation, seeing it as leading to the exploitation of consumers by monopolists. They may believe that it is impossible in principle to put a money value on human life or health. They may believe that governments should not be swayed by narrow economic interests and analysis, and have a duty to exercise ethical principles which otherwise would not be considered. Such antagonistic feelings towards global capitalism have been expressed at various meetings of international politicians to discuss world trade. On a more academic level, there has for some years been huge controversy surrounding the publication of a book by Lomborg[3] taking an economist's approach to these issues.

Much of the sentiment expressed is based on an ignorance of the issues involved, a misuse of statistical information and a lack of understanding of economic analysis, its relevance and application. One major objective of this book is to explain not just the methodology of managerial economics but also the breadth of its application, and to illustrate that it can have a lot to say about the types of issue raised in the above case study. All the case studies in the text have been selected with this objective in mind; for example the following situations and issues are discussed: prize money in sport, the law of diminishing returns applied to computer software, Internet banking and competition, price discrimination in the pharmaceutical industry, issues in the National Health Service, deregulation of electrical utilities, the level of fuel taxes and subsidized car manufacturing.

1.2 Definition and relationships with other disciplines

1.2.1 Definition

So what is **managerial economics?** Many different definitions have been given but most of them involve *the application of economic theory and methods to business decision-making*. As such it can be seen as a means to an end by managers, in terms of finding the most efficient way of allocating their scarce resources and reaching their objectives. However, the definition above might seem to be a little narrow in scope when applied to the case study involving global warming. This situation involves governments, non-profit objectives, non-monetary costs and benefits, international negotiations and a very long-term time perspective, with an associated high degree of uncertainty. Therefore it needs to be clarified that managerial economics can still be applied in such situations. The term 'business' must be defined very broadly in this context: it applies to *any situation where there is a transaction between two or more parties*. Of course this widens the scope of the concept beyond the bounds that many people find comfortable: it includes taking someone on a date, playing a game with one's children in the park, going to confession in a church, asking a friend to help out at work, agreeing to look after a colleague's cat while they are away, taking part in a neighbourhood watch scheme. In all cases, costs and benefits occur, however intangible, and a decision must be made between different courses of action.

As an approach to decision-making, managerial economics is related to economic theory, decision sciences and business functions. These relationships are now discussed.

1.2.2 Relationship with economic theory

The main branch of economic theory with which managerial economics is related is microeconomics, which deals essentially with how markets work and interactions between the various components of the economy. In particular, the following aspects of microeconomic theory are relevant:

1 theory of the firm
2 theory of consumer behaviour (demand)
3 production and cost theory (supply)
4 price theory
5 market structure and competition theory

These theories provide the broad conceptual framework of ideas involved; the nature of these theories and how theories are developed is discussed in section 1.4. At this stage it is worth stating that these theories are examined and discussed largely in a **neoclassical** framework. This is essentially an approach that treats *the individual elements within the economy (consumers, firms and workers) as rational agents with objectives that can be expressed as quantitative functions (utilities and profits) that are to be optimized, subject to certain quantitative constraints*. This approach is often criticized as dated and unrealistic, but can be defended on three grounds. The first is that it is very versatile and can easily be extended to take into account many of the aspects which it is often assumed to ignore, for example transaction costs, information costs, imperfect knowledge, risk and uncertainty, multiperiod situations and so on. The implications of all these factors are considered in the next chapter. The second and third grounds of defence are explained in section 1.4 and are related to scientific method and pedagogy.

There is one main difference between the emphasis of microeconomics and that of managerial economics: the former tends to be **descriptive**, explaining how markets work and what firms do in practice, while the latter is often **prescriptive**, stating what firms should do, in order to reach certain objectives. At this point it is necessary to make another very important distinction: that between **positive** and **normative** economics. This is sometimes referred to as the 'is/ought' distinction, but this is actually somewhat misleading. Essentially positive statements are factual statements whose truth or falsehood can be verified by empirical study or logic. Normative statements involve a value judgement and cannot be verified by empirical study or logic. For illustration, compare the following two seemingly similar statements:

1 The distribution of income in the UK is unequal.
2 The distribution of income in the UK is inequitable.

The first statement is a positive one while the second is a normative one. Normative statements often imply a recommendation, in the above example that income should be redistributed. For that reason they often involve the words *ought* or *should*. However, not all such statements are normative, they may in fact be prescriptive. For example, the statement 'Firm X should increase its price in order to increase profit' is a positive statement. This is because the word 'should' is here being used in a different sense, a conditional one; there is no value judgement implied. In practice it can sometimes be difficult to distinguish between the two types of statement, especially if they are combined together in the same sentence.

What is the relevance of the above to the study of managerial economics? It is often claimed, for example by those protesting against global capitalism, that economics is of no use in answering the fundamental questions involving value judgements, like reducing pollution. Indeed, economists themselves often admit that their science can only make positive not normative statements. However, this can give a misleading impression of the limitations of economics; it can indeed be helpful in making normative statements. First, consider the following statement: *governments should make use of market forces in order to achieve a more efficient solution in terms of reducing pollution.* This might sound like a normative statement but it is actually a conditional use of the word *should* as described in the previous paragraph. Provided that the term efficiency is carefully defined, the statement is a positive one, since the concept of efficiency does not involve any value judgement.

Of course the example above only shows that economists can make positive statements that might appear to be normative statements. Now consider this statement: *world governments should aim to reduce pollution by 90 per cent in the next ten years.* This is a genuine normative statement. Economists might estimate the costs and benefits of such a policy and show the costs to vastly exceed the benefits. This in itself cannot determine policy because it ignores the distribution of these costs and benefits, both over space and time. However, it might in principle be possible to show empirically that both rich and poor countries would suffer overall from a policy of reducing pollution by 90 per cent and that future generations might not benefit either. A realization of this might then cause the maker of the statement to change their mind. The reason for this is that they are forced to revalue their values in the context of other values that they have, in the light of economic analysis. Thus the application of economic principles can help to make normative statements on which policies are based and action taken. This issue is examined in more depth in Chapter 12.

1.2.3 Relationship with decision sciences

The decision sciences provide the tools and techniques of analysis used in managerial economics. The most important aspects are as follows:

- numerical and algebraic analysis
- optimization
- statistical estimation and forecasting
- analysis of risk and uncertainty
- discounting and time-value-of-money techniques

These tools and techniques are introduced in the appropriate context, so that they can be immediately applied in order to understand their relevance, rather than being discussed *en bloc* in isolation at the beginning of the text.

1.2.4 Relationship with business functions

All firms consist of organizations that are divided structurally into different departments or units, even if this is not necessarily performed on a formal basis. Typically the units involved are:

1 production and operations
2 marketing
3 finance and accounting
4 human resources

All of these functional areas can apply the theories and methods mentioned earlier, in the context of the particular situation and tasks that they have to perform. Thus a production department may want to plan and schedule the level of output for the next quarter, the marketing department may want to know what price to charge and how much to spend on advertising, the finance department may want to determine whether to build a new factory to expand capacity, and the human resources department may want to know how many people to hire in the coming period and what it should be offering to pay them. It might be noted that all the above decisions involve some kind of quantitative analysis; not all managerial decisions involve this kind of analysis. There are some areas of decision-making where the tools and techniques of managerial economics are not applicable. For example a sales manager may want to motivate a salesperson to achieve a higher level of performance. In this case an understanding and application of behavioural and psychological principles is relevant. That is not to say that economists can ignore these, but managerial economics tends to focus more on behavioural aspects when they concern consumers rather than when they concern the behaviour of employees. A more detailed discussion of the scope of managerial economics follows in the next section.

1.3 Elements of managerial economics

1.3.1 Subject areas and relationships

The main areas are illustrated in Figure 1.1. This only shows the core topics covered; other areas, for example capital budgeting, location analysis and product strategy, are also frequently examined.

1.3.2 Presentation of topics

Since the objectives of a business form the starting point of any analysis of its behaviour, the theory of the firm is the subject of the next chapter. Traditionally, pricing has formed the central core of managerial economics, although this narrow focus is somewhat misleading in terms of the breadth of analysis that is possible. As the various topics are examined, further applications and extensions of analysis will be discussed. In order to examine pricing it is necessary to consider demand and supply forces; in managerial economics supply forces are discussed under the theory of costs, as will be explained in Chapter 6. In order to consider demand we must first consider consumer theory and in order to consider costs we must first consider production theory.

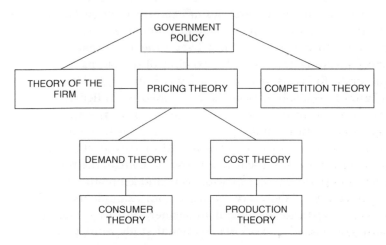

Figure 1.1. Relationships among subject areas.

Consumer theory is included in the chapter on demand theory, but a separate chapter is dedicated to production theory, since otherwise the chapter on cost theory would be too long. The main reason for this difference in treatment is that many aspects of consumer theory relate to behavioural psychology, and these are not normally discussed in managerial economics, while production theory deals more in engineering concepts which economists traditionally have been more willing to examine. The topics of demand and cost analysis both involve separate chapters on theory and on estimation, which is again a traditional distinction, but sometimes the relationship between these two aspects is not fully explained. Since it is very important to understand this relationship in order to appreciate the objectives and methods involved in managerial economics, a section on methods now follows.

1.4 Methods

It is essential for anyone studying managerial economics to understand the methodology involved. This is not just an academic exercise, it is essential for managers who have to make decisions. True, they are not generally believed to develop and test theories themselves, but in reality this is part of their job. This is explained later on in this section after the meaning of the term theory and the process of testing theories have been discussed. There are two aspects of methods that need to be explained: first, the methods that professionals use to develop the subject; and, second, the methods used to present material to students learning the subject.

1.4.1 Scientific theories

In the previous section the term theory was used extensively, both in describing subject areas and in denoting a contrast with estimation. A scientific theory does two things: it **describes or explains relationships between phenomena that we observe,** and it **makes testable predictions**. Theories are indispensable to any science, and over time they tend to be gradually improved, meaning that they fit existing observations better and make more accurate forecasts. When a theory is initially developed it is usually on the basis of casual observation, and is sometimes called a hypothesis. This then needs to be tested and in order to do this an **empirical study** is required. An empirical study is one which involves **real-world observations**. Such studies can be either **experimental** or **observational**: the former involve a situation where the investigator can control the relevant variables to isolate the variables under investigation and keep other factors constant. This is often done in laboratory conditions, for example in testing the effect of heat on the expansion of a metal. In business and economic situations this is usually not possible, so an observational study must be performed. An investigator may for example be interested in the effect of charging different prices on the sales of a product. However, it may be difficult to isolate the effect of price from the effects of promotion, competitive factors, tastes, weather and so on, which also are affecting sales. This problem, and its solution, is discussed in detail in Chapter 4. The analysis of the data in the study involves statistical techniques, such as regression analysis, and then inferences are drawn from this regarding the initial theory, in terms of its acceptance or rejection. The whole process of testing economic theories is often referred to as **econometrics**.

The procedure above is a repetitive one; further empirical studies are carried out, sometimes under different conditions, and as time goes on theories tend to become modified and refined in order to improve them. The process of the development of theories is illustrated in Figure 1.2.

It is obviously of vital importance to managers to have good theories on which to base their decision-making. A 'good' theory has the following characteristics:

1 It explains existing observations well.
2 It makes accurate forecasts.
3 It involves **mensuration**, meaning that the variables involved can be *measured reliably and accurately*.
4 It has general application, meaning that it can be applied in a large number of different situations, not just a very limited number of cases.
5 It has elegance, meaning that the theory rests on a minimum number of assumptions.

The better the theories used by managers the better their decisions will be, in terms of being more likely to achieve managerial objectives. However, it is not just a case of managers using other people's theories. Consider the following situation: a marketing manager has just received sales figures for a particular product showing a considerable decline in the last quarter. She has a meeting with the sales manager, the advertising manager, the PR manager and the production manager. The sales manager claims that sales are down because of the recent price rise of 15 per cent; the advertising manager says that advertising was cut in one of the normal media, because it was thought to be ineffective; the PR manager says that customers reacted badly to the announcement in the papers that the firm was stopping its sponsorship of a

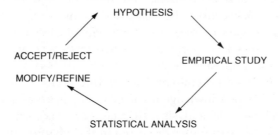

Figure 1.2. Theory development process.

local school sports team; finally the production manager admits that problems in quality control for the previous period might have put some customers off repeat purchase of the product. These are all competing theories; they may all have some element of truth, or maybe none at all. It is the marketing manager's responsibility to determine how much each possible problem contributed to the decline in sales, or whether some other factors were involved. In effect the manager has to test various theories before she can make an appropriate decision.

There is another important implication of the above criteria for a good theory: they apply very well to the neoclassical approach, as will be seen more clearly in the next chapter.

1.4.2 Learning economics

When students first study economics in introductory courses they often become disillusioned because it seems very abstract and theoretical; what do all these graphs and equations have to do with the real world? What possible use can they have, since they often seem to make incorrect conclusions? These understandable criticisms need to be addressed.

Because economics is a difficult subject area, involving complex interactions among many people and variables, the pedagogical approach to learning the subject generally involves initially making many assumptions about behaviour and relationships in order to build simple models. A **model** in general terms is a *representation of a system*, which is simplified in order to illustrate the important features and relationships involved. Economic models often involve diagrams, graphs or equations. Basic analysis is then performed with these models, and conclusions drawn. This again relates to the neoclassical approach. The first and second reasons for using this approach have now been discussed; the third reason is that it provides this very useful starting point, by making necessary assumptions. The conclusions from this simplified model often turn out to be erroneous, not because of errors of analysis, but because the assumptions on which the analysis was based were unrealistic. In order to make progress these assumptions must be gradually relaxed, thus making the situation more realistic, and allowing better theories and conclusions. However, the greater complexity of the situations being analysed requires more sophisticated models and tools of analysis, and algebraic analysis is largely used throughout this book because of its ability to show more explicitly the relationships between multiple variables. In the majority of cases these extensions of the basic model can be incorporated into a neoclassical framework.

The pedagogical approach described above will become clearer as it is illustrated well in the next chapter. The starting point, as with many other chapters, is the body of knowledge involved in any introduction to microeconomics. The framework of analysis is then developed accordingly. Case Study 1.2 illustrates the range of issues discussed in this chapter; in particular: the different perspectives and objectives of various decision-makers, factors that

Case study 1.2: Import quotas on Japanese cars

In 1980 the United Auto Workers (UAW) and Ford Motor Company petitioned the International Trade Commission (ITC) to recommend relief from import competition; during the first half of that year foreign car companies shipped 1.2 million passenger cars to the United States, an increase of 21 per cent over the previous year. The foreign share of the US new car market increased from 17 per cent to 25 per cent in that period.[4] US car manufacturers and workers faced big problems. American Motors sold out to Renault, Chrysler made huge losses and was forced to sell most of its foreign subsidiaries, Ford made even larger losses and General Motors had to borrow large sums to keep afloat. By the end of 1980 193,000 out of 750,000 members of the UAW were unemployed.

The ITC rejected the appeal, saying that the problems of the motor industry were due to a shift in demand to small, fuel-efficient cars caused by higher petrol prices, and that the industry had failed to anticipate this. The reason for the US consumers' preference for Japanese cars was debatable. One theory, along the lines of the ITC position, was that imports were perceived as having better fuel economy, engineering and durability. This was supported by a survey of 10,000 US households carried out by the Motor and Equipment Manufacturers Association. Supporters of this theory felt that imports should not be limited.

However, another theory was that price differences created by labour cost differences were the cause. The Bureau of Labor Statistics estimated that average Japanese car workers' wages and benefits in the first half of 1979 were only half those of US car workers. Those supporting this theory largely favoured taxing imports in order to raise their prices.

The arguments for protecting or aiding the US motor industry were based on two main premises. The first was that the costs of unemployment were higher than the increased costs to consumers of limiting imports, and the second was that the US manufacturers could recover and become fully competitive with imports if they were given temporary help. The first issue involved an estimation of the hardships of being unemployed, the adverse effect of their lost purchasing power on other industries, and the higher taxes necessary to support the unemployed. A *New York Times* poll[5] showed that 71 per cent of Americans felt that it was more important to protect jobs than to get cheaper foreign products. The second issue related to the past performance of US manufacturers, the possibility of achieving economies of scale and higher productivity with new plants. Ford, for example, estimated that the conversion of its Dearborn engine plant would cost $650 million but would increase productivity by 25 per cent.

Those who rejected the idea of protection, like the ITC, blamed the managers of the US companies for their bad decisions. They claimed that these managers and firms should not be rewarded at the expense of the consumer and taxpayer, who would not only face higher prices and taxes, but also suffer from limited choice. Retaliation from foreign countries was another problem that they said might ensue from any kind of protection.

The UAW was mostly concerned about maintaining jobs rather than protecting the profits of the manufacturers. They thus pushed for foreign manufacturers to produce in the United States and to have 75 per cent of their parts produced in the US. This was against the interests of the manufacturers, who were trying to produce cars globally by buying parts in many different countries wherever they could be bought cheapest. The Ford Escort for example, which was assembled in the United States, Britain and Germany, contained parts from nine countries. The UAW gathered much public support and, with opposition from consumers being largely unorganized, was successful in 1981 in obtaining a 'voluntary' agreement with Japan to limit car exports to the United States to 1.68 million units a year for three years. Japanese producers and politicians entered the agreement fearing that lack of co-operation could result in even stricter limits. When the agreement expired, Japan continued to limit exports, but by that time the major manufacturers like Honda, Toyota and Nissan already had plants in the United States and sales from these soon outnumbered imports.

The effects of the import quotas are also controversial. The US car industry did recover, but some of this was due to the economy moving out of recession. US consumers switched back to consuming more expensive and profitable cars, but this was partly an effect of the import restrictions, which gave US consumers little choice except to buy more expensive cars. The limits on Japanese imports were in quantity not in value; therefore Japanese firms redesigned their cars to make them more luxurious and expensive. During the three years of the original export agreement, the average Japanese import increased by $2,600; a Wharton Econometrics study attributed $1,000 of this to the import limits. In the same period the prices of US-made cars increased by 40 per cent.[6]

Questions

1 Explain how different theories presented in this case study are supported and how they can be tested in general terms.

2 Explain why the results of the *New York Times* poll reported above are meaningless.
3 Explain the conflict of interest between the US car manufacturers and the UAW.
4 Why would the Japanese car manufacturers be willing to co-operate with the limiting of their exports to the United States?
5 Explain how the costs and benefits of the import quotas can be estimated in monetary terms, describing any problems involved.
6 One study[7] estimated the cost of the quotas at $160,000 per job saved. In view of this, why do you think the quotas were implemented?
7 Explain the differences between the decision-making processes of the US car manufacturers and the US government.

are relevant in the decision-making process, the identification and measurement of costs and benefits, and the value of empirical studies.

1.4.3 Tools of analysis: demand and supply

The concepts of demand and supply are among the most important in all economics. They are of course not the only tools of analysis in the economist's armoury, but they allow us to identify and understand the relevant factors in analysing many economic situations. It is assumed at this point that students already have some familiarity with these concepts, but a brief review is in order here, so that we can then see their application to a situation that has caused considerable controversy in recent years, the subject of equal prize money in tennis.

a. Demand

In the economic sense demand refers to *the quantities that people are or would be willing to buy at different prices during a given time period, assuming that other factors affecting these quantities remain the same*. For reasons explained in Chapter 3 on demand theory, there is generally an inverse relationship between the quantity demanded and the price charged, and this is customarily shown in the downward-sloping demand curve, although the relationship can equally be expressed in terms of a function or equation. The demand relationship is determined by many factors, but consumer tastes are fundamental. This applies both to products and to the services of people in the labour market.

b. Supply

In the economic sense supply refers to *the quantities that people are or would be willing to sell at different prices during a given time period, assuming that other factors affecting these quantities remain the same.* When talking about the supply of products it is often the costs of production that are most important in determining the supply relationship, and generally there is a direct relationship between the quantity supplied and the price offered, with more being supplied the higher the price. However, in factor markets, in particular the labour market, supply is more complex. The availability of people with the relevant skills, the pleasantness of the work and the opportunity cost involved are all important factors.

In order to get a further flavour of what analysis in managerial economics is all about, it is useful to consider the next case study, where there have been a lot of views expressed which show a lack of understanding of economic fundamentals.

Case study 1.3: Equal prize money in tennis

A British cabinet minister has now stepped into the debate regarding equal prize money at Wimbledon, the British Open tennis championships. Patricia Hewitt (no relation to the men's winner), the Trade and Industry Secretary, announced that it is 'simply wrong' that the winner of the men's singles should collect £525,000, while the women's winner should receive only £486,000, when they had both worked equally hard.

The debate regarding prize money is not new, and has aroused some strong feelings in the last ten years. The 1996 men's champion, Richard Krajicek, commented in 1992 that most women players were 'fat, lazy pigs' who deserved to win less. This attracted a storm of protest from many supporters of women's tennis, and these supporters and lobbyists have been successful in gradually reducing the differentials in prize money. Tim Henman, the British number one player, attracted criticism in 1999 for accusing female players of being 'greedy' in demanding more prize money in 'Grand Slam' tournaments. The situation in 2002 was that in the four 'Grand Slam' tournaments the prize money was equal for men and women at both the US and Australian Opens, but interestingly the women's prize money was only half that of the men's at the French Open.

Let us consider some of the main arguments that have been put forward both for and against equal prize money:

FOR

1 Women have to train just as long and hard as men.
2 The ball is in play longer in women's matches, because the game involves more rallies and less

'serve and volley' tactics, according to research by the Women's Tennis Association.
3 Female stars are just as popular with the crowds as male players.
4 Unequal pay is an example of unfair discrimination, which in many countries is illegal.

AGAINST

1 Men have to play the best of five sets, while women only play the best of three. Therefore men play longer. Research from Stirling University shows that, on this basis, men earn less. The 1998 men's singles champion, Pete Sampras, earned £26,270 per hour, compared with £42,011 per hour received by the women's champion, Jana Novotna.
2 Competition at the top of women's tennis is less stiff, allowing female stars to compete in the doubles more easily, and win two prizes. The combination of singles and doubles prizes for women would exceed the singles prize for men.
3 Male players attract bigger crowds.
4 Women are not as good as men.

The last point has also raised argument, since it is difficult to make any objective evaluation. On a purely objective measure, the top female stars serve nearly as fast as the top male players, but obviously there are many other factors which make a top tennis player apart from a fast serve. In a recent television interview John McEnroe, never one to shy away from controversy, opined that the top female seed at Wimbledon in 2002, Venus Williams, would only rank about number 400 in the world among male players.

Adding another dimension to the debate is sponsorship income. Anna Kournikova has never won a major tournament; she is currently ranked number 55 in the world. Her career total prize winnings amounted to just under £3 million at the end of 2001. However, it is estimated that she has accumulated around £50 million in sponsorship income, mainly from Adidas, the sportswear supplier. Although sponsorship income tends to be directly related to the talent of the player, as reflected in computer rankings, there are obviously other factors that are relevant. However, one factor that is important here is that sponsorship income is determined much more by the market forces of demand and supply than is the amount of prize money in a tournament. The amount of tournament prize money at Wimbledon is determined by the management committee of the All England Club.

What do the public make of all this? In a recent television poll by the BBC the viewers calling in were nearly equally divided: 51 per cent thought the men should receive more, 49 per cent thought prize money should be equal.

Questions

1 Do the observations by Patricia Hewitt make any sense in economic terms?
2 How relevant is hard training to determining prize money?
3 How relevant is length of playing time to determining prize money?
4 Why is sponsorship relevant to the prize money debate? Is it a good idea to relate prize money to sponsorship?
5 Can you suggest any way of using economic forces to determine prize money? What about having an 'open' championship where men play women, with no distinction between men's singles and women's singles?

Summary

1 Managerial economics is about the application of economic theory and methods to business decision-making.
2 The term business must be considered in very broad terms, to include any transaction between two or more parties. Only then can we fully appreciate the breadth of application of the discipline.
3 Decision-making involves a number of steps: problem perception, definition of objectives, examination of constraints, identification of strategies, evaluation of strategies and determination of criteria for choosing among strategies.
4 Managerial economics is linked to the disciplines of economic theory, decision sciences and business functions.
5 The core elements of the economic theory involved are the theory of the firm, consumer and demand theory, production and cost theory, price theory and competition theory.
6 A neoclassical approach involves treating the individual elements in the economy as rational agents with quantitative objectives to be optimized.
7 Positive statements are statements of fact that can be tested empirically or by logic; normative statements express value judgements.
8 The application of economic principles is useful in making both of the above types of statement.
9 A theory is a statement that describes or explains relationships between phenomena that we observe, and which makes testable predictions.

10 Economic theories have to be tested using empirical studies and econometric methods.
11 Economics is a discipline that proceeds by initially making many assumptions in order to build simple models, and then gradually relaxing these assumptions to make things more realistic and provide better theories.
12 As the situations being analysed become more complex, so more sophisticated and advanced methods of analysis become necessary.

Review questions

1 Why is the subject of managerial economics relevant to the problem of global warming?
2 What is meant by the decision-making process?
3 Give some examples of transactions that are not normally considered as business transactions.
4 Explain, using the car import quota case, how different and conflicting theories can arise.
5 What is meant by a 'good' theory?
6 Explain, using examples, why it is important for managers to have good theories.
7 Why when we study economics do we tend not to learn good theories to start with?

Notes

1 'What to do about global warming', *The Economist*, 18 November 2000.
2 'Hot potato revisited', *The Economist*, 6 November 2003.
3 B. Lomborg, *The Skeptical Environmentalist*, Cambridge University Press, 2001.
4 'U.S. autos losing a big segment of the market – forever?', *Business Week*, 24 March 1980: 78–85.
5 '7 out of 10 Americans agree', *New York Times*, 6 November 1980: A23.
6 C. Collyas and S. Dunaway, 'The cost of trade restraints: the case of Japanese automobile exports to the United States', *International Monetary Fund Staff Papers*, 34 (March 1987).
7 R. Dardis and J.-Y. Lin, 'Automobile quotas revisited: the costs of continued protection', *Journal of Consumer Affairs*, **19**, no. 2 (Winter 1985): 277–292.

2

The theory of the firm

Objectives

1 To introduce and define the concept of the firm and its nature.
2 To discuss various methods for undertaking business transactions.
3 To compare the advantages and disadvantages of using the market rather than internalizing transactions within the firm.
4 To explain the nature of transaction costs.
5 To introduce the concept of the profit-maximizing model.
6 To describe the various assumptions which frequently underlie the profit-maximizing model and explain why they are made.
7 To explain the limitations of the basic profit-maximizing model.
8 To consider the nature of the agency problem in terms of how it affects firms' objectives.
9 To consider the problems associated with the measurement of profit, and the implications for objectives.
10 To consider the nature of the shareholder-wealth profit-maximizing model and its limitations.
11 To consider the implications of risk and uncertainty as far as objectives are concerned.
12 To consider multiproduct firms and the implications for objectives.
13 To summarize the strengths and weaknesses of the profit-maximizing model in comparison with other models.

2.1 Introduction

The neoclassical theory of the firm is sometimes called a 'black box'. What this means is that the firm is seen as a monolithic entity; there is no attempt to probe inside the box and explain why firms exist in the first place, or how the individuals who constitute firms are motivated and interact. Therefore, before examining business objectives, it is necessary to address these more fundamental issues. Sometimes these aspects are omitted from courses in managerial or business economics, since they can be viewed as aspects of organizational behaviour. However, we should not think of economic aspects and behavioural aspects as being two distinct areas of study. Any behaviour has economic aspects if it involves the allocation of resources. As we shall see, the motivation and decision-making of individuals are more fundamental than that of the organizations which they form.

There are six main areas of economic theory that are involved in the examination of the nature of the firm: transaction cost theory, information theory, motivation theory, agency theory, property rights theory and game theory. These are now described briefly before being examined in greater depth.

a. Transaction cost theory

This examines the costs of undertaking transactions in different ways. These include trading on spot markets, long-term contracts with external parties and internalizing transactions within the firm. Different methods are appropriate under different circumstances.

b. Information theory

This examines the concept of bounded rationality, and the associated aspects of incomplete contracting, asymmetric and imperfect information. These give rise to opportunistic behaviour, which in turn affects the behaviour of other parties and can lead to inefficiencies.

c. Motivation theory

This examines the underlying factors that cause people to behave in certain ways. In economic terms we are searching for general principles which can be used to explain and predict behaviour.

d. Agency theory

This examines the situation where one party, an agent, is involved in carrying out the wishes of another, a principal. This happens very frequently in all sorts of transactions; indeed it is the cornerstone of democracy, where people elect a government to govern on their behalf. The nature of the resulting problem is that principal and agent usually have goals that do not exactly coincide, and that the principal can only partially observe the behaviour of the agent. Therefore principals have to engage in monitoring activities and design incentives in ways that optimize their own welfare.

e. Property rights theory

This examines the nature of ownership, and its relationship with incentives to invest and bargaining power. On this basis it predicts the allocation of property rights on the basis of efficiency.

f. Game theory

This examines the strategic interaction of different agents. The key to under-standing this strategic interaction is that the behaviour of one party affects the behaviour of other parties, and the first party must consider this in determining their own strategy. Furthermore the first party must also consider that the other party or parties will also consider the first party's considerations in determining their own strategy. This area of economics has expanded greatly in the last twenty years, and, in view of its importance, a separate chapter, Chapter 9, is devoted to its discussion.

There is a lot of interaction among the six areas, and this creates some pre-sentational issues. The first five areas are now discussed in some detail; how-ever, since the relevant aspects of information economics are incorporated in agency theory, these will be discussed in a single section to avoid excessive repetition. Also, agency costs are involved in transaction cost theory, so agency theory is introduced in section 2.2, and then developed further in section 2.4. During this discussion many instances will arise where strategic interaction is involved. A more detailed and mathematical analysis of these interactions is postponed until Chapter 9, since the main applications of game theory involve both the theory of the firm and competition theory.

2.2 The nature of the firm

Managers manage organizations; therefore we must first ask the fundamental questions: what are organizations and why do they exist? The answers to these questions lead to a discussion of transaction cost theory, since by then the context and importance of transactions will have become apparent.

2.2.1 Economic organizations

Organizations occur at many different levels; the most comprehensive eco-nomic organizations are worldwide, for example the United Nations, the World Trade Organization and the International Monetary Fund. There are also many other organizations that are international, in particular trading blocs like the European Union. The economies of individual nations form the next level of organization. All of these organizations are ultimately com-posed of individuals and are created by individuals in order to serve particular purposes, which are ultimately some compromise of individual purposes. They are also managed by individuals and their performance can be evaluated in terms of certain criteria, which at this level can be difficult and controversial to determine, since they tend to involve value judgements made by large numbers of individuals.

The main types of organization that we are concerned with examining are business organizations, consisting of corporations, partnerships and sole proprietorships. In order to understand why such organizations exist we first need to consider the benefits of co-operation and specialization. In any organization different people perform different functions, each specializing in some particular activity; the advantages of such specialization have been known for a long time, ever since humans specialized in either hunting or gathering hundreds of thousands of years ago. Adam Smith gave the famous example of the pin factory, where workers specialized in pulling a wire, straightening it, cutting it to a specific length, sharpening it to a point, attaching the head, or packaging the final product. The resulting output was much greater than would have occurred if each worker had performed all the activities above.

Business organizations are independent legal identities, separate from the individuals that form them. This enables them to enter into binding contracts that can be enforced by the legal system (albeit at some cost). This means that the firm is really a legal fiction which simplifies business transactions because it enables the firm to contract bilaterally with suppliers, distributors, workers, managers, investors and customers, rather than there being a situation where each party has to enter into complicated multilateral arrangements. Thus Alchian and Demsetz[1] have labelled the firm a **nexus of contracts**, meaning that the firm can be viewed as a *hub in a hub-and-spoke system*.

In order to develop our understanding of the above concept, imagine an individual who wants to create a university. Such an undertaking requires the co-operation of a large number of individuals. In the case of a university this may have to be built from scratch, and therefore the creator may have to enter contracts with construction companies to erect the necessary buildings, once they have bought or rented the land. They have to hire various types of administrator and faculty; they have to provide catering facilities, recreational facilities, computer facilities, cleaning services, repair and maintenance services, gardening services; they have to provide communications facilities and transportation facilities; they need basic utilities such as gas, water and electricity; they need insurance to cover various types of risk; they probably want some kind of accreditation from a reputable organization; they may need finance from various investors; they also need customers, meaning students or, arguably, their parents. Many bilateral contracts are necessary here, between the university and the various other parties. However, imagine the situation if there were no firm forming a hub of the system; each faculty member would have to contract with every single student that they taught!

The discussion so far illustrates that the most appropriate level of analysis for most economic behaviour is the individual and the **transaction**. A transaction refers to **an exchange of goods or services**. Transactions can be performed in the following three ways:

1 Trading in spot markets
2 Long-term contracts
3 Internalizing the transaction within the firm.

Each of these has certain advantages and disadvantages related to the transaction costs involved. The nature and implications of these transaction costs now need to be discussed.

2.2.2 Transaction cost theory

Transaction costs are related to the problems of co-ordination and motivation. Costs will occur whichever method of transaction is used, spot markets, long-term contracts or internalization within the firm, but they will vary according to the method.

a. Co-ordination costs

These costs are sometimes referred to as Coasian costs, since Coase was the first economist to examine them in detail.[2] The following categories of costs can be determined here:

1. Search costs. Both buyers and sellers have to search for the relevant information before completing transactions. Such information relates to prices, quality, delivery and transportation; in markets this search is external, while within organizations, information held in different parts of the organization must be transmitted through the relevant channels to the decision-makers. Even in highly efficient markets like stock exchanges a large amount of resources, in terms of physical assets like buildings and computers and human assets in the form of brokers, is devoted to providing the relevant information.

2. Bargaining costs. These are more relevant when markets are involved, where negotiations for major transactions can be protracted, but even within the firm, salary and wage negotiations can also be costly in terms of the time and effort of the parties involved.

3. Contracting costs. There are costs associated with drawing up contracts; these take managerial time and can involve considerable legal expense.

b. Motivation costs

These costs are often referred to as agency costs. This area is discussed in more detail in section 2.4 on the agency problem, but at this stage we can observe that there are two main categories of such costs.

1. Hidden information. This relates to asymmetries referred to earlier. One or several parties to a transaction may have more information relevant to the transaction than others. A classic example of this is the secondhand car market, where sellers have a big advantage over buyers. This has many consequences for the market, which are discussed later, but one obvious effect is that buyers may have to devote resources to obtaining more information (for example, paying for an engineer's inspection of a car).

2. Hidden action.   Even when contracts are completed the parties involved often have to monitor the behaviour of other parties to ensure that the terms of the contract are being upheld. Monitoring and supervision are costly, and there is a further problem because this behaviour is often difficult to observe directly. This problem is known as 'moral hazard'. The situation is even more costly if legal action has to be taken to enforce the terms of the contract.

Transactions have a number of attributes which affect the above costs and therefore affect the way in which they are conducted, in particular asset specificity, frequency, complexity and relationship with other transactions. Asset specificity refers to how easy it is for parties in a transaction to switch partners without incurring sunk costs, meaning costs that cannot be recovered. For example, a firm that commits itself to building a facility designed for a specific customer will usually want to be protected by a long-term contract. Again, transactions that are repeated frequently may most easily be conducted by having a long-term contract instead of negotiating individual spot transactions, as with obtaining cleaning and catering services.

One of the main implications of transaction cost theory is that there is an optimal size of the firm from the point of view of minimizing transaction costs. Generally, as the firm increases in size and incorporates more transactions internally as opposed to transacting in the market, those costs associated with using the market decrease, while those costs associated with co-ordination increase as the amount of administration and bureaucracy increases. There is thus a trade-off situation, with the optimal size of the firm being at the point where 'the costs of organizing an extra transaction within the firm become equal to the costs of carrying out the same transaction by means of an exchange on the open market or the costs of organizing another firm'.[3]

It should be realized that the optimality situation described above is only optimal from the point of view of transaction costs. In practice there are a number of other considerations that will be relevant in determining the actual size of the firm, and these will be examined in the remainder of this chapter.

2.2.3 Motivation theory

In order to understand the nature of the firm we must first appreciate that any firm consists of individuals, and that viewpoint has already been emphasized in the previous section. In order to understand the behaviour of these individuals we must in turn examine the nature of motivation. Economists tend to assume that people in general act in such a way as to maximize their individual utilities, where these utilities are subjective measures of value or satisfaction.

Thus the fundamental pillar in the basic economic model of behaviour is that people are motivated by self-interest. This has been a feature of the economic model of behaviour since the days of Adam Smith, who famously stated: 'It is not from the benevolence of the butcher, the brewer, or the baker that we expect our dinner, but from their regard to their own interest.'[4] The neoclassical economist Edgeworth expressed the same attitude even more forcibly: 'The first principle of Economics is that every agent is actuated only by self-interest.'[5]

The resulting behaviour is sometimes said to typify *homo economicus*. However, it is not just economists who make use of this basic assumption. It has been applied in the fields of politics, for example by Downs,[6] in law, by Posner,[7] and in crime, by Becker,[8] to mention just some of the more important areas and contributions. However, some of the most fundamental contributions have come in the fields of evolutionary biology and psychology, in connection with what has sometimes been referred to as 'selfish gene' theory. This term was originated by Dawkins,[9] but there have been many other similar accounts, in particular by Hamilton,[10] Maynard Smith,[11] Pinker,[12] Ridley,[13] Trivers[14] and Williams.[15] It is not within the scope of this text to review the findings here in any detail, but we will see shortly that in many respects these contributions have helped to rescue the economic model from its critics.

The main criticisms are that the economic model is too narrow and ignores altruistic behaviour and spiteful behaviour.

a. Altruistic behaviour

Unfortunately some confusion is caused by the fact that various economists, psychologists and biologists have used the term altruism in different ways. Some economists, such as Hirshleifer[16] and Collard,[17] insist that altruism refers to motivation rather than action. However, biologists tend to view altruistic motivation as biologically impossible, meaning that it could not have evolved and survived. They therefore tend to mean by altruistic behaviour any **behaviour which confers a benefit to others, while involving a cost to the originator of the behaviour, with no corresponding material benefit** (in monetary or genetic terms). Some biologists do include genetic or material benefits in their definition of altruism when they refer to kin selection and reciprocal altruism. Examples of altruistic behaviour frequently mentioned are charitable gifts, tipping waiters and endangering oneself to help others, particularly non-relatives, in distress; helping relatives would be an example of kin selection rather than strict altruistic behaviour.

b. Spiteful behaviour

This can be viewed as the flip side of altruistic behaviour. This is **behaviour which imposes a cost on others, while also involving a cost to the originator of the behaviour, with no corresponding material benefit**. An example is vandalism, which damages the property of others, while incurring the possibility of being caught and punished. In the business context it is possible that some industrial strikes and stoppages also feature spiteful behaviour, if labour unions are prepared to forgo income in order to damage the welfare of the management.

It is true that the conventional model only considers narrow self-interest, and basically posits that people act amorally. Milgrom and Roberts[18] refer to this model as an 'extreme caricature'; it is certainly an oversimplification in some ways. However, before discarding the model on the above basis, two important points in the model's favour need to be considered. First, it is possible to extend the model to take into account both altruistic and spiteful behaviour. When the concept of utility is broadened beyond its normal material concerns to include psychic benefits and costs in terms of emotional satisfaction or dissatisfaction, then utility maximization is still consistent with the existence of altruistic behaviour. Some economists, like Sen,[19] would count sympathy as self-interest, being a psychic cost, but still want to define certain actions as non-egoistic if they involve a detached moral view or commitment. Again, biologists will have none of this, claiming that such detachment is physiologically impossible; if people believe that certain behaviour is wrong they will automatically incur a psychic cost if that behaviour is seen to exist. Thus biologists tend to believe that unselfish motivation in the broadest sense is not viable and therefore refer to altruistic behaviour rather than altruistic motivation, as mentioned earlier.

As far as the examples of altruistic behaviour given earlier are concerned, they can now be explained in terms of broad self-interest, which not only takes into account psychic costs and benefits but also a long-term time frame. People give to charity because of the emotional satisfaction it yields, which more than offsets the monetary costs. People tip waiters because they feel guilty if they do not; the guilt is an emotional or psychic cost. Likewise, people may indulge in spiteful behaviour which is costly to them provided that the psychic benefits make it worthwhile. The obvious question here is: what causes the existence of these psychic costs and benefits? This phenomenon has been explored by various evolutionary psychologists and certain economists, such as Schelling,[20] Hirshleifer[21] and Frank,[22] who have given an evolutionary explanation for the existence of the emotions involved. Frank calls this extended model of broad self-interest a **commitment model**, where *emotions are evolved commitments to behave in seemingly non-egoistic, meaning altruistic or spiteful, ways*. Therefore the existence of these emotions, while seeming to cause irrational behaviour (discussed below), may actually help us to act in our long-term self-interest. For example, feeling guilty about not returning favours may help us to gain the co-operation of others; engaging in spiteful acts may cause others to be wary about cheating us. Frank thus calls his commitment model a 'friendly amendment' to the conventional narrow self-interest model. Although this extended model is more realistic than the conventional model, it is far more complex and difficult to implement in practice.

A second point in favour of the narrow self-interest model is that it is still very useful. As with any theory, it stands or falls by its ability to explain and predict, as discussed in the first chapter. On this basis the assumption of utility maximization in the conventional neoclassical sense is still able to explain and predict a large amount of human behaviour. As Milgrom and Roberts[23] point out, even though the model may be a caricature, its predictions are not very sensitive to relaxations of its assumptions. They give the example of a bank, which has guards, vaults, security systems and audits as the model would predict, even though many honest people would not rob an unguarded bank.

There is one final objection that can be raised regarding the narrow self-interest model: by teaching that people are selfish and opportunistic it encourages socially undesirable behaviour. When people expect to be cheated they are likely to behave in the same way, as seen in more detail in the chapter on game theory. There is some evidence that this is true, in that economics students have been found in some studies to be more selfish (in the sense of showing narrow self-interest) than other students (maybe that is why they were studying economics in the first place). Against the accusation that I am corrupting public morals, I will plead first that the broad self-interest, or commitment, model is a 'better' model than the conventional economic model, and second that my purpose in writing this text is not to improve people's moral behaviour, merely to aid an understanding of it.

2.2.4 Property rights theory

This is a relatively new area of economic theory, opened up in the 1980s, with a seminal paper by Grossman and Hart in 1986.[24] The focus is on the issue of ownership; the nature of ownership and its relationship with incentives to invest and bargaining power are the key features of this model.

The institution of private ownership and the associated property rights is one of the most fundamental characteristics of any capitalist system. Its main advantage compared with the state ownership of the majority of assets found in communist countries is that it provides strong incentives to create, maintain and improve assets. However, we must ask the question: what does it mean to own an asset? This question turns out to be particularly difficult to answer for a complex asset like a firm.

There are two main issues involved in dealing with this question: residual control and residual returns. These are discussed first, before turning to the issues of efficiency and the allocation of property rights.

a. Residual control

Even for simple assets the concept of ownership is more complex than it might seem at first sight. Take a hi-fi system; you are free to use it when you want, but the noise level you are permitted to play it at is often limited by law, according to time of day. You may not be allowed to use it in certain locations. You may not be permitted to play certain material on it, particularly if it involves public broadcast as opposed to private use. Usually there are no limits on lending it out or selling the asset. However, we can now see that the owner has **residual rights of control**, in the sense that the *owner's decisions regarding the asset's use are circumscribed by law and by any other contract involving the rights of other parties to use of the asset*. Therefore property rights are limited in practice, even in a capitalist system.

As we have seen in the previous section, contracts in practice tend to be incomplete. Therefore the residual rights of control are by necessity unspecified, but relate to all those that are not explicitly regulated by law or assigned to other parties by contract. This makes the process of contracting much easier, but it can lead to ambiguities for complex assets like firms, as is seen shortly.

b. Residual returns

It is a fundamental feature of ownership of an asset that the owner is entitled to receive income from it. With some assets like cars or buildings this could be a rental income, but there would be some expenses involved, like maintenance and repair, and the liability to pay these would have to be specified in the contract. Likewise, there may be a legal obligation to pay taxes on the income. Thus, again, the returns received by the owner can be viewed as residual. We will consider the situation relating to the residual returns for firms once the issue of the allocation of property rights has been considered.

The central idea of the property rights view is that bargaining power – and the assets that confer bargaining power – should be in the hands of those people whose efforts are most significant in increasing the value of the business relationship. Giving these people more bargaining power ensures that they receive more of the rewards from investing time and energy and, thus, that they have a stronger incentive to make these investments.[25] This is a slightly oversimplified view, but it illustrates the main principles involved.[26] Decisions about asset ownership – and hence firm boundaries – are important because control over assets gives the owner bargaining power when unforeseen or uncovered contingencies force parties to negotiate how their relationship should be continued.[27]

In the model often called the classical firm, the 'boss' both has residual control and receives residual returns. Assuming property rights are tradable the market for corporate control ensures that those people who are bosses are those best suited to the position. Furthermore, since control and returns are both vested in the same person, the boss has maximum incentive to manage the firm in a profitable manner, just as the owner of a simple asset like a car has an incentive to use the car efficiently, compared to a renter, who has no such incentive. In reality there are a number of problems with this oversimplified view. In public companies there are essentially four parties who can lay claim to certain rights of ownership and control: shareholders, directors, managers and other employees.

1. *Shareholders*. In legal terms shareholders own the company, but in practice their rights are quite limited. They have voting rights on issues such as changing the corporate charter, electing and replacing directors, and, usually, mergers.

However, they have no say in other major strategic issues, such as hiring managers, determining pay levels, setting prices or budgets, or even determining their own dividends. Thus the rights of shareholders cannot be viewed as being residual; they are specified by law.

2. *Directors.* The board of directors certainly appears to have residual control, making many of the major strategic decisions of the firm, including hiring the managers and setting their pay levels. However, the directors do not have a claim to the residual returns; these essentially belong to the shareholders.

3. *Managers.* In practice the senior managers may have effective control over many of the major strategic decisions of the firm. This is because they control the flow of information within the firm and set the agenda for many board decisions; because shareholders rely on information from managers in electing the board, the managers may effectively determine board nominations. Thus there is a problem of asymmetric information in terms of managers having more information regarding the firm's operations than either board members or shareholders. There is also a problem of moral hazard in that it is difficult for either directors or shareholders effectively to monitor the activities of managers.

4. *Other employees.* This relates to non-managerial workers; again managers rely on such workers to provide them with information, and also to carry out managerial decisions. Thus, although like managers they have no residual claims on the firm, they do exercise some control. Once more the problems of hidden information and hidden action are present; in this case the other employees have more information than managers, and the managers are not able to observe their behaviour easily.

Thus the concept of ownership of the firm, particularly in the case of the public company, is fraught with difficulties. In practice there are subtle differences in the nature of ownership between different firms, according to factors like the diversification of shareholders and the nature of the production process, and these tend to lead to different organizational forms.

The situation is made even more complex by the fact that the returns to the various parties above are not simply in terms of current financial compensation. Managers can profit from obtaining experience, and from increased prestige, which often comes in the form of perquisites like company cars and expense accounts. Such returns are often in direct conflict with the residual returns to shareholders. Employees also benefit from training and experience as well as in terms of wages and salaries. They also benefit from taking leisure while working ('shirking'), which again is in direct conflict with the interests of shareholders, and also the interests of managers, if the latter can be held responsible for the resulting lack of productivity.

It can already be seen that there are a number of agency problems involved in the nature of the firm, and the implications of these will be explored more fully in section 2.4 and in case study 2.1 on corporate governance. Before doing so it is useful to examine the standard economic model concerning the objectives of the firm, the basic profit-maximizing model.

2.3 The basic profit-maximizing model

In economic analyses the most common objective that firms are regarded as pursuing is profit maximization. This is a fundamental element in the neo-classical model described in Chapter 1, and is part of the more general assumption that economic entities rationally pursue their self-interest, discussed in the previous section. Using the marginal analysis on which much neoclassical theory is based, the basic profit-maximizing model (BPM) prescribes that a firm will produce the output where marginal cost equals marginal revenue. Both concepts are explained in more detail in later chapters, but at this stage a simple diagram will suffice. Figure 2.1 illustrates a rising marginal cost (MC) curve, where each additional unit costs more than the previous one to produce, and a falling marginal revenue (MR) curve, assuming that the firm has to reduce its price to sell more units. The output Q^* is the profit-maximizing output. If the firm produces less than this it will add more to revenue than to cost by producing more and this will increase profit; if it produces more than Q^* it will add more to cost than to revenue and this will decrease profit.

Although there is much intuitive appeal in the assumption of profit maximization, it should be realized that it, in turn, involves a number of other implicit assumptions. These assumptions now need to be examined, considering first of all their nature, then their limitations, and finally their usefulness.

2.3.1 Assumptions

The basic profit-maximizing model incorporates the following assumptions:

1 The firm has a single decision-maker.
2 The firm produces a single product.
3 The firm produces for a single market.
4 The firm produces and sells in a single location.

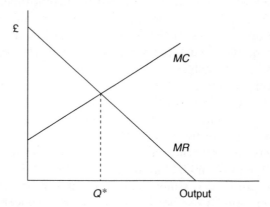

Figure 2.1. Profit Maximization.

5 All current and future costs and revenues are known with certainty.

6 Price is the most important variable in the marketing mix.

7 Short-run and long-run strategy implications are the same.

a. Single decision-maker

The meaning of this assumption is self-explanatory, unlike some of the other assumptions. It is also obvious that it is not a realistic assumption since in any firm above a small size the owner, or anyone else, is not going to have time to be able to make all decisions. Thus the decision-making process involves delegation, so that decisions of different importance and relating to different functional areas are taken by different managers and other employees, while the board of directors and shareholders still make some of the most important decisions. This leads to an agency problem, as we have seen, which is discussed further in the remainder of this chapter.

b. Single product

Again this assumption is self-explanatory in meaning, as long as we remember that the majority of products sold now are services rather than goods. It is also clear that this assumption has even less basis in reality than the first one. Even small firms may produce many products, while large firms may produce thousands of different products. Given this situation the assumption may seem hard to justify, yet all analysis at an introductory level implicitly involves it. The graphical framework of analysis measures quantity on the horizontal axis, and this can only relate to a single product, or at least similar products.

c. Single market

This seemingly simple term does need a little explanation. The reason is that economists have a somewhat different conception of a market from business-men in many cases. To an economist a **market** involves *an interaction of buyers and sellers*, and this is the interpretation that has been used in the previous chapter. Such a market does not necessarily have to involve a physical location; the Internet provides a market, as does NASDAQ and similar stock exchange systems. However, businessmen and managers often are referring only to *buyers or potential buyers* when they use the term market. It is this sense that is meant in the assumption of a single market. Thus a single market means a homogeneous group of customers.

d. Single location

While the meaning of producing and selling in a single location is clear, it is equally clear that many firms do not do this. Some firms produce in many different countries and sell in many different countries. The reason for using different locations is the differences in costs and revenues involved. The analysis of these spatial differentials is a specialized area in terms of the techniques involved and again represents a complication in the analysis.

e. All current and future costs and revenues are known with certainty

One might expect a well-managed firm to have accurate, detailed and up-to-date records of its current costs and revenues. This is necessary in order to determine a firm's cost and revenue functions, in terms of the relationships between these and output; in theory it is necessary to know these to determine a profit-maximizing strategy. In practice it can be difficult to estimate these functions, especially in a constantly changing environment. Even if these can be reliably estimated on the basis of historical data, it still may be difficult to estimate reliably what these will be in the future, next year, next quarter or sometimes even next week. This has important implications for any decision or course of action that involves future time periods, since risk and uncertainty are involved.

f. Price is the most important variable in the marketing mix

The nature of this assumption requires considerable explanation. First of all the **marketing mix** must be defined: it is normally viewed as '*the set of marketing tools that the firm uses to pursue its marketing objectives in the target market*'.[28] McCarthy[29] has developed a classification that is frequently used, the **four Ps**: *product, price, promotion and place* (meaning distribution). Not all marketing professionals agree on the components of the marketing mix, but they and business managers do generally agree that price is not the most important of these. Aspects of the product are normally regarded as the most important factor. So why then is price assumed to be so important in the profit-maximizing assumption?

There are two reasons for this. The most important concerns the general orientation of economists. In any market economy it is the price system that is responsible for allocating resources. For example, if there is a shortage of a product or resource its price will rise, causing consumers to cut back consumption and producers to increase production, motivated by profit. These actions will in turn help to alleviate the shortage and bring the price back down. This focus on price determination is the core of microeconomics. However, in managerial economics we are not primarily concerned with price determination, which essentially treats price as a dependent variable; we more often treat it from a managerial perspective, as a controllable or marketing mix variable. In this different context it does not follow that price is the most important variable. This issue can only be settled empirically, and some evidence regarding the importance of price is discussed in Chapter 4.

A further reason for concentrating on price lies in its ease of measurement. While it is true that there may be certain problems with this in practice, it is certainly a far easier variable to measure than product aspects. These problems are discussed in more detail in Chapter 3.

It is therefore fair to say that the essential reason for the focus on price is the inherent bias of economists, who tend to view price through a different lens from business managers. The implications of this practice are discussed in Chapter 10.

g. Short-run and long-run strategy implications are the same

This assumption means that any strategy aimed at maximizing profit in the short run will automatically maximize profit in the long run and vice versa. Again, as will be seen in the following sections, this is not a realistic assumption, with different strategies being appropriate in each case, but the advantage of the assumption is that it simplifies the analysis by ignoring the factor of the time frame.

2.3.2 Limitations

Some of the limitations of the standard assumptions of the basic profit-maximizing model (BPM) have already been seen. At this point we need to focus on four of these:

1 *The agency problem.* We have now seen that whenever there is more than a single decision-maker there are inevitably going to be agency costs, even if we regard managers and other agents as being honest and co-operative, rather than self-seeking opportunists.
2 *The measurement of profit.* It is important to realize that the concept of profit is an ambiguous one, since it can be defined and measured in different ways. Furthermore, it is unrealistic to assume that decision-makers should only consider a short-term horizon like a year as far as measuring profit flows are concerned.
3 *Risk and uncertainty.* As soon as we start to consider longer time horizons the existence of risk and uncertainty becomes important. As mentioned in the previous chapter, this relates not only to the measurement of profit but also to the agency problem, since principals and agents frequently have different attitudes to risk.
4 *Multiproduct firms.* The problem of analysing the behaviour of firms producing multiple products can only be partly solved by modelling the situation in terms of drawing multiple graphs (or specifying multiple equations). Problems of interactions on both the demand and cost sides still remain.

These limitations are examined in the following sections. Before doing this, however, it is necessary to discuss the usefulness of the BPM, given its obvious limitations.

2.3.3 Usefulness

There are two main aspects of usefulness to be considered. The first concerns the implications of the BPM, along with the other elements of the neoclassical model, in terms of welfare and efficiency. The second involves an aspect that has already been discussed in the previous chapter, the ability to explain and predict, combined with sensitivity to a relaxation of assumptions. These are now discussed in turn.

a. Welfare and efficiency implications

The neoclassical model is essentially a mathematical model involving consumers and producers, with both individuals and firms acting as both consumers and producers of inputs and outputs. All profits of firms are distributed to consumers in the form of dividends. The price system is seen as having the functions of co-ordination and motivation. The first function concerns the provision of relevant information to buyers and sellers, while the second is concerned with motivating buyers and sellers to act according to the prices charged. On this basis a remarkable and much-celebrated conclusion, known as the **fundamental theorem of welfare economics**, can be mathematically derived. The conclusion is that, even *if we assume in terms of these functions that (1) producers and consumers only have local information, with no central planning or extensive information-sharing, and (2) producers and consumers are motivated entirely by self-interest, then the resulting allocation of resources will be efficient*. This conclusion uses the concept of what is called 'Pareto efficiency', that *nobody can be made better off without making somebody else worse off*. There are a number of other assumptions involved in this conclusion, particularly the ignoring of the existence of market failure. This aspect is discussed in detail in Chapter 12 on government policy.

b. Ability to explain and predict

Regardless of how nice and neat a set of conclusions is, such conclusions are useless in practice if the model underlying them is unable to produce accurate explanations and predictions. This point has been made in both of the first two chapters. As was noted in connection with the narrow self-interest model, the profit maximization model also performs well in this respect. The reason is the same: the model is **robust**, meaning that it is *not very sensitive to relaxations in its assumptions*.

2.4 The agency problem

As stated earlier, agency theory examines situations where agents are charged with carrying out the desires of principals. Since we have now seen that different individuals are generally attempting to maximize their own individual utilities, there is often a conflict of interest between principal and agent. The nature of the resulting problem is a misalignment of incentives, and much of agency theory is concerned with designing incentives so as to correct for this situation in the most efficient manner. We need first to consider the nature of contracts and the problem of bounded rationality, before considering two problems related to asymmetric information: adverse selection and moral hazard. Next, strategies for dealing with agency problems are considered. Finally, the limitations of the standard agency model and alternative agency models are discussed.

2.4.1 Contracts and bounded rationality

We have seen in discussing the nature of the firm that contracts are an important method of conducting transactions. Complete contracts would specify the rights and obligations of both parties over the whole term of the contract, and would help to eliminate the agency problem since parties could be held liable in law for any breach of contract. However, it is usually impractical to draw up a complete contract that accounts for all possible eventualities. Such a contract would require the following conditions:

1 All possible eventualities must be foreseen.
2 These eventualities must be accurately and unambiguously specified.
3 In the future it must be possible to determine which eventuality actually occurred.
4 Courses of action for each eventuality must be determined.
5 The parties must be willing to abide by the terms of the contract, with no desire to renegotiate.
6 The parties must be able to observe freely the behaviour of the other parties to ensure that the terms of the contract are being met.
7 The parties must be willing and able to enforce the contract if the terms are not met.

As an example, take the situation where a firm hires a health club to supply in-house fitness facilities. Both equipment and staff may be provided under the terms of the agreement. The supplier may be responsible for the maintenance of the equipment and its safety. What happens if a user injures himself while using the equipment? What happens if the equipment is damaged by flooding? What happens if a member of staff harasses an employee? What happens if either party wants to terminate the agreement before the stipulated time period in the contract? Such problems become more complex and difficult to foresee as the period of the contract increases.

Therefore, in practice, contracts tend to be incomplete, because of **bounded rationality**. This means that ***people cannot solve problems perfectly, costlessly and instantaneously***. Incomplete contracts are sometimes called relational, in that they frame the relationship between the parties but do not lay down detailed contingencies or plans. For example, an employment contract may stipulate that the employee obtain permission in order to take other part-time employment outside the firm ('moonlighting'), but it may not specify under what circumstances such permission may be given or refused. It is implicitly assumed that employees will perform according to the wishes of their managers, and their ultimate defence in the face of unreasonable management demands is to quit, although they may have certain statutory rights regarding dismissal. The advantage to the firm of contracting in this way is that it saves costs compared with trying to draw up a more complete contract; the disadvantage is that incomplete contracts lead to the problems of hidden information and hidden action, which now need to be discussed.

2.4.2 Hidden information

The first problem relates to the existence of **asymmetric information**. Sometimes this is referred to as **hidden information**, meaning that *one party to a transaction has more information regarding the past that is relevant to the transaction than the other party or parties*. An example is the second-hand car market, where sellers have much more information about the history and condition of the car than buyers. This situation provides an incentive for **pre-contract opportunism**; this means that one party can try to take advantage of the other by *obtaining better contractual terms than they would obtain under conditions of perfect information*. Thus in the secondhand car market sellers will try to obtain higher prices than they would get if buyers had complete knowledge; this presents a strategic situation, since buyers know this and will therefore not be prepared to pay as much as they might otherwise do. In turn this leads to a problem known as **adverse selection**. This means that *only the products or customers with the worst quality characteristics are able to have or make transactions and others are driven from the market*. Such a situation is obviously inefficient.

In order to understand this phenomenon further, let us examine the second-hand car market again, and review the conclusions reached in a classic article by Akerlof.[30] According to his analysis, sellers with better-quality second-hand cars would not put them on the market, since they could not obtain a good price for them. Buyers discounted them in terms of quality because of their lack of complete information. This in turn meant that the average quality of cars on the secondhand market declined, further reducing the prices that buyers were willing to pay, driving more sellers from the market, and so on in a vicious circle. The end result was that only 'lemons', or the worst-quality cars, were put on the market. This explained the observation that secondhand cars that were nearly new were selling for much lower prices than new cars.

Adverse selection can occur in many situations, and it is not always the seller who has the informational advantage. The insurance market is an example where buyers have more information than sellers relating to their risk profile. However, the result is similar in that buyers with more risk are the most anxious to take out insurance, driving up premiums, which in turn drives the less risky buyers from the market. The end result is that only the riskiest buyers will stay in the market – if they can afford it. This is one reason why governments often intervene in the market, either providing certain types of insurance themselves (like health), or requiring buyers to have insurance by law (drivers). Government intervention, however, does not eliminate the problem of achieving efficiency, as will be seen in Chapter 12.

The examples of adverse selection given above relate to market transactions, but the problem applies equally well to situations within organizations. For example, a firm may advertise an employment position at a low salary; it is likely that only less skilled or experienced persons will apply for the position.

The question of how firms can reduce this problem of adverse selection and improve efficiency is discussed in the last subsection.

2.4.3 *Hidden action*

The problem of **hidden action** is sometimes referred to as the problem of **moral hazard**, in that *the behaviour of a party cannot be reliably or costlessly observed after entering a contract*. This, in turn, provides an incentive for **post-contract opportunism**. The insurance market is again a good example for such behaviour; once people take out insurance there is less incentive for them to take care of the insured property (including their health in the case of health insurance). The insurance company cannot monitor the behaviour of its customers easily, although in the case of large claims it may undertake thorough investigations.

As with adverse selection, the problem of moral hazard can affect organizations internally as well as in their external transactions in the market. Employees may be reluctant to put in much work effort if they know that such effort will not affect their income, and they believe that the lack of effort will be unobserved by management. This is the well-known problem of 'shirking'. Again, this is a strategic problem and is discussed in more detail in Chapter 9 on game theory. At this stage it is sufficient to observe that efficient incentives are again necessary in order for the organization to reduce the problem.

So far a clear distinction has been drawn between hidden information and hidden action; they are both aspects of asymmetric information, but the first relates to past behaviour, prior to the contract, while the latter relates to behaviour after the contract. The insurance market features both types of problems, but they have still been seen as distinct. However, in some instances it may be difficult in practice to determine which problem is applicable. Milgrom and Roberts[31] give the example of a study in Washington D.C., where it was observed that the proportion of Volvos going through stop signs at intersections without stopping was significantly higher than the proportion of Volvos in the total population of cars in the area. It could be argued that Volvo drivers were confident regarding the safety of the build of their cars, and therefore took more risks. This is a moral hazard explanation. However, it could also be argued that bad drivers tended to buy Volvos because they knew of their shortcomings as drivers. They therefore ran the stop signs because they were bad drivers, not because they drove Volvos. This is an adverse selection explanation, if it imposes costs on Volvo. Without further information it cannot be determined whether buying Volvos makes bad drivers or bad drivers buy Volvos. Maybe Volvo drivers have another explanation.

A combination of the problems of hidden information and hidden action has been observed in several firms whose actions had very wide repercussions for the US economy, notably Worldcom and Enron. There is a multitude of aspects, including political, legal and social factors, involved in these situations.

However, one of the main implications of the agency problem is that managers tend to pursue **revenue maximization** rather than profit maximization. This is because the remuneration of managers often depends more on the revenues of the firm than on its profits. There may be a profit constraint affecting this objective, in that managers may feel that they have to make a certain minimum profit to keep the shareholders content. Shareholders themselves may be aware of this situation, and may take measures to remedy it; this aspect is discussed in the next subsection.

Some of the above issues are discussed in Case 2.1 on corporate governance; others are discussed in Case 2.2, which also involves the issue of the measurement of profit, and is therefore postponed until the next section.

2.4.4 Control measures

The functions of these measures are (1) to enable the organization to operate more efficiently, both in terms of its external transactions in the relevant markets and in terms of transactions internal to the organization, and (2) to align the interests of the various constituent parties in the firm, managers and other employees, with those of the shareholders. One major decision, touched on earlier, is to determine which transactions to undertake internally and which ones to undertake externally. It should also be mentioned that the control measures discussed here are those that can be implemented by firms themselves. If market failure exists, as is the case with imperfect information, then a case can be made for government intervention. Since 2002 there has been a greater degree of government intervention in corporate governance, with the Sarbanes–Oxley Act in the United States and the Higgs Report in the United Kingdom. This aspect is discussed more fully in Chapter 12.

a. Increased monitoring

The most obvious way of reducing inefficiency is for the firm to obtain more information on the parties with which it is transacting, both in terms of their past behaviour and in terms of their behaviour after the contract is signed. Thus insurance companies can attempt to obtain more details of their customers in order to assess their risk levels more precisely. For example, drivers have to reveal all accidents in the last five years, and all motoring offences, as well as their age, occupation and residential area. They are also often asked the purposes of usage of the vehicle, annual mileage, whether other drivers are permitted to drive, whether the car is garaged, whether it is fitted with an alarm or immobilizer, and so on. Such information allows the firm to segment its market and, in this case, determine premiums more appropriately. The drawback is the increased expense involved in collecting and analysing data.

b. Screening

Screening is another way for the firm to segment its market, this time by *undertaking activities designed to result in self-selection in order to obtain the*

relevant private information. It is more commonly used internally, in the context of hiring appropriate employees, but can be used in external transactions also. An example is a firm wanting to construct a factory that includes penalty clauses in the construction contract for late completion. When the contract is put out to tender, only those construction firms which are confident of completing on time are likely to make offers. Thus private information regarding the ability of firms to complete work on time is revealed in a self-selection process.

c. Signalling

Signalling is similar to screening, in the sense that it involves self-selection, but in this case the **behaviour is initiated by the party with the private information in an attempt to reveal the private information in a credible manner**. Again this is used both internally and externally; for example, any prospective employee being interviewed wants to signal their ability and enthusiasm. The problem in any signalling situation is to achieve credibility. Taking an example of an external or market transaction, it does not benefit a construction firm bidding for an important contract to claim that it is highly competent and provides good value; any firm can do that. On the other hand, if the firm offers to pay penalties if the project is not completed on time this is a credible indication of its efficiency in this respect. Similarly, firms can also signal their good intentions regarding post-contract opportunism in certain respects; guarantees or warranties are examples of credible good behaviour, since it may cost more to honour a warranty than to renege on the contract.

d. Risk-pooling

This is an activity that can best be effectively performed by the state, since it involves an element of coercion. Health insurance is an example: everyone may be forced to pay health insurance through the tax system, and the risks of the population are pooled. This means that those who use the system most end up paying less than their actual costs, while those who use the system least pay more than their actual costs, but are unable to opt out of the system by not paying their taxes. Without the coercion element there will be adverse selection, since only the least healthy will find it advantageous to pay the premiums charged. It should be noted, however, that this combination of risk-pooling and coercion creates a problem of moral hazard. The state health system becomes a shared resource and is overused; people will visit doctors more often than if they had to pay the real costs. In order to reduce this problem, the Swedish government has recently made reforms to their health system whereby patients are charged a fee for visiting the doctor.

e. Internalization

It has already been seen in the section on transaction costs that in certain situations firms may find it preferable to internalize transactions rather than use the market, in order to reduce the inefficiencies associated with asymmetric information. Thus firms may take over suppliers if they are concerned that the suppliers may be selling them inferior materials, and if it is difficult and costly to ascertain the quality of these materials.

f. Structure of pay incentives

These should be specifically designed to align the interests of managers and other employees with those of the shareholders. Two methods are being increasingly used to achieve this: share ownership plans and share options.

1. Share ownership plans.   These have now become very common, particularly in the United States. Sometimes they apply only to managerial employees, but often all employees are eligible. In the United States there are about 11,500 firms that have Employee Stock Ownership Plans (ESOPs), covering 8.5 million persons. These essentially act as employee pension plans, whereby the firm acquires its own stock and places it in trust in the plan. Employees are allocated such shares each year, and they are held in the plan until retirement or until the employee leaves. There are considerable tax advantages in setting up such a plan in terms of the company borrowing funds. There may be other advantages for the company; it may also be in a better position to fight off hostile takeover bids if more shares are in the hands of employees. Another reason for the popularity of such plans is that during the boom period for high-tech and dotcom firms during the 1990s many such companies were not in a financial position to offer large salaries to employees. They therefore invited employees to share in the risks of the company by being compensated in the form of shares, sometimes this being the only form of compensation. Furthermore, it is possible for directors, who determine the remuneration structure, to restrict the sale of shares, so that, for example, senior executives are not able to sell shares for a period of five years from purchase. This serves to motivate executives to act in the long-run interests of the firm.

For the employees there may be some incentive effects arising from such schemes in terms of improved performance, but as mentioned above, these effects are normally very small when the typical employee holds only a tiny fraction of the total value of equity in the firm. There is an additional disadvantage of such plans, which has become more evident in recent years, and that is increased exposure to risk. When stock markets tumble, employees can find they get hit with a double whammy: they may not only lose their jobs through lack of demand or bankruptcy of the firm, but they may also lose much of the value of their pensions. There is much to be said for having a pension plan whose value is based on a widely diversified portfolio.

2. Share options.   This form of compensation has become very popular in the last two decades, particularly for senior executives and CEOs. It has been seen that in practice managerial compensation is more related to the size of the firm rather than to the size of profit. As with share ownership plans, the sale of options can be restricted to certain time limits, preventing sale within several years, to discourage short-term manipulation of the share price. One result of generous share option offerings is that some CEOs have made huge personal gains; Michael Eisner of Disney was claimed to have earned $203 million in 1993, largely as a result of option ownership. There is some evidence that share options are now becoming less popular than outright ownership, particularly after the bear market following 2001. Some employees prefer shares rather than options, since when the market falls the shares still have some value whereas the options may be worth nothing. Furthermore, directors have increasingly become aware that share options tend to encourage excessive risk-taking by executives, since there is no downside for the option-holder.

2.4.5 *Limitations of the agency model*

The model presented up to this point could be described as the standard agency model. As stated at the start of this section, it focuses on the conflicts of interest between principal and agent and assumes that agents will indulge in self-seeking opportunistic behaviour. In other words the standard model is based on the neoclassical narrow self-interest model of motivation. In recent years this model has come under attack, mainly on the basis that it ignores co-operative, or altruistic, behaviour. It is thus claimed to misunderstand and mispredict many relationships within firms involving managers as either principals or agents. For example, the behaviour of employees in teamwork may not fit the model.[32, 33] Also, the model ignores reputational effects, meaning that firms can benefit from establishing a good reputation by showing themselves repeatedly to be reliable and honest; this obviously discourages opportunism.

A particularly comprehensive version of such an alternative agency model has been developed by Hendry;[34] this model focuses on the implications of complexity of objectives and environment, combined with bounded rationality of both principals and agents. He then makes various predictions based on these conditions, assuming that agents are honest, rather than being self-seeking opportunists, in pursuing the objectives of principals, at least insofar as these objectives are specified. His conclusions are that, for the most part, organizations will behave in terms of structure and incentives in a way very similar to that predicted by the standard model. Perhaps this should be no surprise, given the point made by Milgrom and Roberts stated earlier, that the predictions of the narrow self-interest model are not especially sensitive to relaxations in its assumptions. The main difference in predicted behaviour concerns the response to asymmetric information. In the standard model, shareholders as principals will tend to respond to this situation, where there is greater managerial discretion, by basing compensation more on outcomes than on behaviour. Essentially this involves more incentives like share-owning and stock option schemes, rather than straight salaries. The opposite conclusion is arrived at in Hendry's model. Unfortunately it is difficult to test the different models based on empirical evidence, given the similarity in many of the predictions.

Now that the nature of firms as organizations and the problems of agency have been discussed, it is possible to examine a case study relating to the topic of corporate governance, which has been featured heavily in the media over the last few years.

Case study 2.1: Corporate governance

Designed by committee[35]

How can company boards be given more spine?

'Coote got me in as a director of something or other. Very good business for me – nothing to do except go down into the City once or twice a year to one of those hotel places – Cannon Street or Liverpool Street – and sit around a table where they have some very nice new blotting paper. Then Coote or some clever Johnny makes a speech simply bristling with figures, but fortunately you needn't listen to it – and I can tell you, you often get a jolly good lunch out of it.'

The blotting paper has vanished. But to judge by the crop of scandals currently tormenting American business, little else about life in the boardroom has changed since Agatha Christie wrote 'The Seven Dials Mystery' in 1929. As some of America's best-known bosses lied, swindled and defrauded their way through hundreds of millions of shareholders' funds in the effervescent late 1990s, boards of directors, supposedly the guardians and protectors of shareholders' interests, appear to have snoozed through it all.

Dennis Kozlowski, recently ousted from the top of Tyco, an ill-fitting conglomerate, stands accused of evading taxes on fine art, which his board may have lent him the money to buy. Bernie Ebbers, former boss of WorldCom, a telecoms firm, persuaded his board to lend him hundreds of millions of dollars so that he could bet on his company's share price. The board of Adelphia, a publicly owned cable company with a stock worth little, put the company's name on $2.3 billion-worth of bank loans to the founding family, which owns one-fifth of the shares. Not to mention Enron, whose board rode roughshod over its own rules in order to allow Andrew Fastow, its chief financial officer, to benefit personally from the off-balance-sheet vehicles that he set up.

Scandal leaps from company to company with bewildering speed, and as share prices collapse the lawsuits mount. Directors are in the front line. PricewaterhouseCoopers, an accounting/consulting firm, has counted almost 500 securities lawsuits filed by investors in the past year. Marsh, an insurance firm, reports that the premiums that companies pay to insure their directors against lawsuits have shot up by between 35% and 900% recently, depending on the business. Companies at greatest risk, says Steve Anderson of Marsh, could be paying $2m a year for a $10m policy – if they can find an insurer willing to underwrite the risk at all.

'What to do when you become a target of the SEC' is the topic that exercises the latest issue of *Directors & Boards* magazine. The SEC, meanwhile, is urging state and federal prosecutors to bring more criminal cases against securities-law violators, and on June 12th it voted to introduce a new rule requiring chief executives to vouch personally for their companies' financial statements. America's boards have been in scrapes before. Never, however, has their reputation sunk so low.

EUROPEAN CONCERNS

With such forces on the loose, even boards themselves have begun to understand that something needs to be done. And not only in America. Corporate governance is a hot topic around Europe too. The scandals there may not have been as great as on the other side of the Atlantic, but recent experience in America has helped to highlight an issue that has been on Europe's corporate agenda for some time.

In Britain, a former director of the Prudential insurance company, Derek Higgs, was appointed by the government in April to head a review into the role and effectiveness of non-executive directors (more or less equivalent to America's independent directors).

On June 7th, Mr Higgs issued a consultative document inviting comments on, inter alia, whether existing relationships with shareholders need to be strengthened, and on what can be done to attract and recruit the best people to non-executive roles. He is due to report by the end of this year.

One person from whom he will not need to canvass views is Lord Young of Grafham, a former trade minister in Margaret Thatcher's government. As outgoing president of the Institute of Directors, Lord Young shocked an audience in April by suggesting that non-executives can do more harm than good and should be abolished. George Cox, the institute's director-general, had to explain sheepishly that Lord Young's views did not reflect the official views of the institute. 'We believe non-executives have a valuable role to play,' affirmed Mr Cox.

In Germany, where companies have two boards – a supervisory board of non-executives and a management board responsible for running the company – a government-appointed commission issued a code of corporate governance in February. Most attention was focused on a suggestion that companies publish top managers' pay, hitherto regarded as a private matter. But the longest section of the code was concerned with turning supervisory boards into better watchdogs. They should, it suggests, contain no more than two ex-members of the management board. Their work should be delegated to small, competent committees; and no member of a management board should sit on more than five supervisory boards of unrelated companies.

In such countries as France and Italy, the issue of corporate governance has yet to come to the fore. Many of the biggest public companies in these countries – from LVMH to Fiat – still have large family shareholdings, family representatives among their senior management, and strong family representation on their boards. In France, it has been claimed that only about one director in five on the boards of public companies is truly independent.

Such a structure may help to resolve the perennial conflict between owners and managers. But it limits the role of the board as a check on management. It also leads to even greater cosiness among leading businessmen, who love to appoint each other to be external directors of their boards. For example, Bernard Arnault, chairman of LVMH, a luxury-goods group and one of the largest companies in France, sits on the board of Vivendi Universal, a media group that is also among the largest companies in the country. The chairman of Vivendi Universal, Jean-Marie Messier, in turn sits on the board of LVMH. In Italy, the high-level business and financial club of directors is known as the *salotto buono*, literally 'the good drawing-room'. It's that cosy.

EAST INDIAN ORIGINS

One reaction to the corporate scandals in America has been to seem to act tough, in the hope of restoring investor confidence. In this spirit, the New York Stock Exchange (NYSE) published on June 6th a set of proposals for new boardroom standards for its listed companies. These include everything from boardroom 'executive sessions' without the boss to mandated 'orientation programmes' (including a field trip to corporate headquarters) for incoming directors. Institutional investors, corporate-governance activists, regulators, corporate lobbies and Congress are all jostling for position with ideas for reform.

Working against this, meanwhile, is a countervailing impulse to protect the best bits of the existing system from poor, or unnecessary, regulation. The periodic worry that America may be asking too much of its boards has begun to return. Headhunters such as Spencer Stuart and Korn/Ferry say that, as the legal risks rise, emptying chairs around the boardroom table are getting harder to fill. Others warn that shackling the boss with an interventionist board may threaten America's entrepreneurial business culture.

The origins of the board lie in the 17th century among early forms of the joint-stock company, notably the British East India Company. After merging with a rival, it organised itself into a court of 24 directors, elected by and reporting to a 'court of proprietors', or shareholders. America has dabbled with other models of governance from time to time. In the 1920s, the chairman of General Electric, Owen Young, pushed the idea of stakeholder boards. But since the rise of pooled investment savings in the 1940s and 1950s, the trend has been towards the East India Company model, with the board accountable to shareholders. Corporate law, the courts and activist institutional investors such as Calpers (which began publishing lists of 'underperforming' boards in the 1980s) have further entrenched the shareholder model.

One strand of history traces a push by shareholders for greater board independence. In the 1970s, many shareholders became particularly upset by public companies whose boards were beholden to powerful private interests, often the founding family. These sorts of tension still linger. Bill Ford, the boss of Ford, did not get his job on merit. And until last month, Adelphia's board accommodated no fewer than four members of the Rigas family – the company founder, John Rigas, and his three sons. 'There should never be more than one Rigas on any board,' comments Dennis Block of Cadwalader, Wickersham & Taft, a Wall Street law firm.

Modern problems of board independence tend to be more nuanced than this, although not hugely so. In America, the chief executive tends to chair the board. In good times Americans heap praise on the strong business leadership that such a system cultivates. But during bad times, they fret about the worrying lack of spine elsewhere around the boardroom table – the 'nodders and yes-men', as the author P.G. Wodehouse once called them.

This matters particularly in America, where the tyrannical corporate leader is a well-established figure. John Patterson, once boss of NCR, a computer company, fired an underperforming executive by removing his desk and chair, parking it in front of the company's factory, and having it soaked in kerosene and set alight in front of the poor man. Armand Hammer, when boss of Occidental Petroleum, kept signed, undated letters of resignation from each of his board directors in his desk. Among Jack Welch's top tips for bosses: never put an academic in charge of your compensation committee. They are more susceptible to envy than rich old men.

Sure enough, in the midst of the latest corporate-governance disasters stand the usual feudal-baron types – such as Mr Kozlowski of Tyco, Mr Ebbers of WorldCom and Gary Winnick, the founder of Global Crossing, a bust telecoms firm. These burly ex-sports jocks get things done quickly. But they also tend to bully their boards into meek docility. The symptoms are clear: egomaniacal corporate strategies and extravagant personal rewards. IBM's board recently rewarded Lou Gerstner on his retirement from the chair not with the stereotypical gold watch but with $100m-worth of company stock.

Most people reckon that one of the board's most important duties should be to plan a replacement for the boss should he die or need to be jettisoned. Yet many boards seem to lack the backbone even to raise this topic. 'It is surprising and distressing how few boards have a clearly thought-out process,' says Don Gallo of Sibson Consulting Group. 'I think it's a huge failing in their fiduciary duties towards shareholders.'

Tyco and other companies have chosen to bring back former chief executives when they have lost their bosses, a clear sign (if not conclusive proof) that their boards had no plan for succession. Nell Minow of The Corporate Library, a watchdog website, recalls talking to board directors of a public company who got into a shouting match with the boss about succession. 'His policy was: "I'm not going to die",' says Ms Minow.

Reformers start with the way in which directors get elected. 'The CEO puts up the candidates, no one runs against them and management counts the votes,' says Ms Minow. 'We wouldn't deign to call this an election in a third-world country.' In theory, shareholders can put up their own candidates, in what is known as a proxy contest. But proxy fights are exorbitantly expensive. The recent tussle at Hewlett-Packard between its boss, Carly Fiorina, and Walter Hewlett, a dissident board director, may have cost the company's shareholders $150m.

As the incumbent management has the corporate coffers at its disposal, this expense tends to make proxy fights one-sided affairs: even the smallest of Hewlett-Packard shareholders reported receiving 20 or more calls from the company. As a final blow to shareholder activists, the courts in Delaware, where the majority of American companies are incorporated, found insufficient evidence that Ms Fiorina had unfairly coerced a big shareholder, Deutsche Bank, despite hints to the contrary. Proxy contests happen at less than 1% of public companies each year in America.

The British and Canadian solution to the overbearing boss is to split the role of chief executive from that of chairman of the board, a post that can then be filled by a 'lead' independent director. This idea has found some support in America. Harold Williams, a former chairman of the SEC, championed it in 1978. Institutional investors, says Roger Raber of the National Association of Corporate Directors, are keener than ever before to split the roles. But support among companies, says Mr Raber, is going the other way. They say they fear conflict in the boardroom, threatening precious 'collegiality'.

The NYSE is thought to have toyed with the idea of a separate chairman, but it does not appear in its published proposals. The exchange is, however, proposing new standards for director independence, along with a requirement that all boards contain a majority of these newly defined independent directors. (Almost all American boards already have a large majority of non-executive directors.) The NYSE's proposed executive sessions without the boss ought to give directors a chance to escape the perils of 'groupthink', intimidation and what Victor Palmieri, a crisis-management expert in the 1980s, called a 'progressive loss in the collective grasp of reality'. Companies seem to hate the idea of executive sessions – which might mean they could actually work.

Some embrace these reforms as part of a creeping 'professionalisation' of the board. This need not mean that the job becomes full-time. But it does mean raising and standardising the qualifications for joining a board. Part of the NYSE's answer to the proliferation of accounting scandals among listed companies, for instance, has been to set clearer and more detailed qualifications for board directors who serve on audit committees.

A DIRECTOR'S LOT

To get the right people, consultants say, their pay may have to rise. Outside the top 100 companies in America, whose directors typically earn $250,000–300,000 a year, the rest make do on $50,000–75,000. The consultants point out that exchanges, regulators and Congress have been heaping extra burdens on the board for years. Boardroom committees, for instance, have proliferated. Even audit committees were uncommon 20 years ago. Now any board worth its salt needs a compensation committee, a nomination committee, a finance committee, a public-policy committee and now a governance committee as well.

This creates unrealistic expectations among investors, say critics. No director can be expected to catch sophisticated fraud by company insiders. The head of Enron's audit committee, Robert Jaedicke, is a professor of accounting at Stanford University, who could hardly have been more qualified for the job.

'Shit happens,' says one Wall Street financier. He calls the NYSE proposals 'a lot of nonsense'.

The most powerful catalyst for change ought to be the big institutional investors that have their own fiduciary duty to protect their investors. Right now, these institutions are busily blaming boards for recent wrongs. But this seems rather convenient. One of the more interesting features of the assorted revelations now scandalising the market is that many of them are hardly news. Everybody suspected that America's energy-trading companies inflated their revenues. Software-contract accounting was an acknowledged black art. And the fact that telecoms firms bought from each other to boost their numbers has shocked nobody but neophytes. The big institutions knew who the cheats were. But life was good, and they nodded and winked and chose to go along with it. In many ways, they now have nobody to blame but themselves.

As part of its reforms, the NYSE proposes to give shareholders more opportunity to monitor and participate in governance. This includes allowing them to vote on stock and stock-option plans for bosses, and making companies disclose codes of business conduct and ethics on their websites. In Delaware, judges seem more willing to put their faith in the judgment of sophisticated institutions, and may increasingly throw open contentious issues to a vote. When it comes – as it inevitably will – the next wave of corporate scandals might put institutions, not boards of directors, in its crosshairs.

Questions

1 What is the problem of the CEO being chairman of the board, as is common in the United States?
2 What is the role of non-executive or independent directors?
3 What are the problems of having a more active board?
4 What is the purpose of having executive sessions without the CEO being present?
5 What could be the role of the institutional investors in changing corporate governance?
6 Why has corporate governance not become an issue in France and Italy?
7 Could the burning of an executive's desk and chair in front of the factory be described as a spiteful act? What other motivation might there be for such an act?

2.5 Measurement of profit

There are a number of problems with defining and measuring profit in practice. Some of these are discussed in Chapter 6, in the context of cost theory, since they are not relevant to the present discussion of objectives. There are two main problems that need to be discussed in the current context:

1 ambiguity in measurement
2 restriction to a single time period.

These are now discussed in turn, before examining the concept of the efficient markets hypothesis and the implications.

2.5.1 Nature of measurement problems

a. Ambiguity in measurement

This problem was strongly highlighted in 2001 by the bankruptcy of Enron, the biggest business collapse in history. There are a multitude of issues involved in this case, but problems in measuring and reporting profit are certainly among the most important. As well as affecting business objectives, ambiguities in the measurement of profit can lead to serious problems in terms of efficiency and the allocation of resources, particularly when they are compounded by agency problems and moral hazard.

It is noteworthy that Enron is not alone; since 1998 over 1,200 American firms have restated their earnings, admitting in effect that they have previously published wrong or misleading figures.[36] Although the number is far smaller in Europe, some big names have been involved: Vivendi, ABB, Credit Lyonnais, Marconi, and Royal Ahold of Netherlands, the world's third largest food retailer. The US firms also include some very large corporations, particularly in the telecoms and energy industries, with names like Global Crossing, Adelphia, Qwest, Dynegy and Tyco hitting the headlines. In 2002 two giants, Xerox and WorldCom, reported overstated earnings. In Xerox's case, revenues were overestimated over a five-year period by possibly as much as $3 billion; in WorldCom's case, $3.8 billion of operating costs were wrongly classified as capital expenses over a five-quarter period. The number of firms restating their earnings will inevitably increase as the Securities and Exchange Commission pursues more actively firms that have used creative accounting procedures. We must now ask: why and how have such abuses arisen?

Accounting profit is an ambiguous term that can be defined in various ways: operating profit, earnings before interest, depreciation and tax, pro-forma earnings, gross profit and net profit are some of the more frequently used measures. Many of these definitions involve estimates rather than precise measures for a number of reasons, some of which are briefly described here:

1 *Depreciation.* This cost can only be estimated by assuming an economic life for an asset, which is subject to much uncertainty. Also, tax laws in different

countries allow firms to treat depreciation in different ways, thus allowing considerable flexibility in the measurement of reported profit.

2 *Bad debts*. This flexibility is also important in the writing off of bad debts; firms can defer reporting these losses for considerable time periods.

3 *Stock option offerings*. In the United States there is currently no requirement to account for these in reporting profit, as there is in some other countries.

4 *'One-off' losses*. There has been an increased tendency to identify certain losses as 'extraordinary items', and remove them from the body of the accounts; they end up as footnotes, explained in complex legal technicalities.

5 *Off-balance-sheet finance*. The use of this has been another important loophole for many firms that utilize a lot of physical assets; for example, many airlines lease their aircraft, and so such assets are not included on the balance sheet.

6 *Human and other intangible assets*. These are traditionally not accounted for in any financial reports.

There is obviously scope for managers to manipulate the firm's accounts in ways that shareholders will not be able to comprehend easily, if at all; this is an example of hidden action. The incentive, as discussed in the previous section, is to overstate earnings so as to boost the share price and the personal earnings of the managers, particularly the CEO and Chief Financial Officer. There is definitely a clear case here of an agency problem combined with moral hazard. In theory there are checks in the system in the form of auditing procedures, which are supposed to protect shareholders and potential investors. As seen clearly in the Enron case, and probably also in the case of WorldCom, these checks failed because of another conflict of interest. Auditing firms not only supply auditing services, but also supply consultancy services, a much more lucrative business. Thus there is a reluctance on the part of auditors to question the reports prepared by managers, for fear of losing consultancy fees. It should be noted that Andersen, the auditor of both Enron and WorldCom, has not been the only one of the big five accounting companies to be found wanting in this respect. Other accounting discrepancies have been found in firms audited by PricewaterhouseCoopers, Deloitte and Touche and KPMG. This situation has important implications for government policy, and is further discussed in Chapter 12. Both the US Congress and the SEC, as well as governmental institutions in other countries, are currently working on a regulatory solution.

b. Restriction to a single time period

The major problem with the concept of profit that is relevant in the current context is that it is normally related to a single time period, such as a year. As was stated earlier, the BPM assumes that short-term and long-term profit maximization amount to the same thing in terms of the strategies involved, and therefore it is not necessary to distinguish between these concepts.

This is obviously a highly simplistic approach. Any owner of an asset is going to be interested in the stream of earnings or benefits from that asset, not just the benefits in a single time period. The value of a firm can be measured in the same way as the value of any asset. Thus it is more appropriate to consider the long-run profits of a firm, or more precisely the present value of the expected future cash flows, discounted by the required rate of return. This equates to the value of the shareholders' wealth and is expressed as

$$V = \frac{\pi_1}{(1+k)} + \frac{\pi_2}{(1+k)^2} + \frac{\pi_3}{(1+k)^3} + \cdots = \sum_{t=1}^{N} \frac{\pi_t}{(1+k)^t} \tag{2.1}$$

where π_t represents profits expected in different time periods in the future, and k represents the rate of return required by the shareholders. This concept of present value assumes that the reader is familiar with the concept of discounting future values. By considering the whole stream of future earnings it is also possible to see how the share price of the company can be determined, by dividing shareholder wealth by the number of outstanding shares.

The result of the above analysis is that it may be more realistic to consider that shareholders want to maximize their wealth, meaning the current share price, rather than just maximize profit in the current time period. Such a model of behaviour is referred to as a shareholder-wealth maximization model (SWMM). One important implication of this is that managers, if they are acting as true agents, may pursue strategies aimed at long-run profit maximization, for example a **market penetration** strategy. This generally involves *entering a market with a low price in order to achieve a substantial market share, and then later raising the price, relying on brand loyalty to maintain market share*. In the short run such a strategy will not maximize profit; in fact it may even result in losses if the price is so low that it does not cover costs.

The factors that determine a firm's share price in the SWMM can be explained in more detail by examining the efficient markets hypothesis (EMH). A discussion of this now follows, but the material tends to be more important in financial economics and it is not necessary for the general under-standing of the above material; thus the following subsections are starred.

2.5.2 Efficient markets hypothesis[*]

The determination of share prices has been a controversial topic in finance for decades, and the discussion has centred on the various forms of the efficient markets hypothesis. In order to give a flavour of the situation, we can recall an old economist's joke about two economists walking down the street. One sees a hundred dollar bill lying on the pavement and bends down to pick it up. 'Don't bother,' says the other, 'if it was real someone would have already picked it up by now.' This seemingly warped logic gives an important insight into the nature of the EMH.

In its weak form, investors' expectations of share prices are based solely on past and current prices. In the more commonly discussed semi-strong form, *the share price and value of the firm incorporate all the information that is publicly available regarding the firm's prospects*. The mechanism that achieves this result is the usual self-interest acting through perfect markets. Speculators pounce on even the smallest informational advantage at their disposal, and in doing so they incorporate their information into market prices and quickly eliminate the profit opportunities that gave rise to their speculation. If this occurs instantaneously, which it must in an idealized world of frictionless markets and costless trading, then prices must always fully reflect all available information, and no profits can be made from information-based trading (because such profits have already been captured). The only way to consistently beat the market under these conditions is to have inside information. The strong form of the EMH assumes that inside information is widely available, in which case *the share price and value of the firm incorporate all the information that is available regarding the firm's prospects, whether such information is publicly available or not.*

There are various implications of this version of the EMH. For one thing it means that it is not necessary to distinguish between maximizing long-run profits, the value of the firm or shareholder wealth; these will all be identical. Also, it should not be possible for managers of publicly owned firms to pursue short-run goals because of their own individual agendas. If such behaviour does occur, and it is expected to harm long-run profits, then the current share price of the firm will fall and such managers can be expected to pay the penalty for this. Another particularly important implication concerns risk and uncertainty: expected future profits are discounted by a required rate of return, and this reflects the risk involved in the strategies of the firm. The more risks the managers take, other things being equal, the more future earnings will be discounted and the lower the value of the firm and the share price. The issue of risk and uncertainty is further discussed in section 2.6.

The model involving the efficient markets hypothesis highlights one other problem with the concept of profit. The model uses the concept of cash flows rather than profits. Most of the ambiguities discussed earlier can be avoided by using the concept of cash flows, with the result being that the shareholder wealth maximization model is consistent with the maximization of the present value of economic profits.

2.5.3 Limitations of the EMH*

Criticisms of the EMH have tended to come on two different fronts: empirical evidence and agency problems. These are discussed in turn.

a. Empirical evidence

Over the last few decades there have been many tests of the different versions of the EMH. Different conclusions have been reached, depending on the nature of the study and the form of the hypothesis tested. Findings have been sensitive to such variables as the time frame of the study, the nature of external variables, the nature of government policy, the type of econometric methods used and individual interpretation.

As far as the weak form of the hypothesis is concerned, there is no consensus regarding its general validity. Using the London Stock Exchange and FT-30 as an example, one study found no evidence for the weak form,[37] while another, using the same data, found that there was some evidence for it.[38]

As far as the stronger forms are concerned, the stock market crash of 1987 destroyed much of the confidence in the EMH; there seemed to be no fundamental change in conditions that could have caused a more than 20 per cent change in valuation over a weekend. In the crash, or slide, which began towards the start of 2000 there was again little evidence of any change in economic fundamentals. Such an event could not really be claimed until the terrorist attacks on the United States in September 2001. By mid-2002 the value of the NASDAQ index had fallen over 70 per cent from its peak two and a half years earlier, while the less sensitive S & P 500 had fallen over 30 per cent. The US economy, however, was still growing at 4 per cent a year over the same period. Yet pundits are claiming that the markets are still generally overvalued in the United States, in terms of price/earnings (p/e) ratios. One problem here concerns the measurement of earnings, discussed earlier; p/e ratios are highly sensitive to different measures. Using some measures they were, in mid-2002, as low as the high teens, whereas according to more realistic measures they were in the low forties, compared with a long-term average in the United States of 16.

However, before writing off the stronger forms of the EMH, it must be remembered that it is not just the expected cash flows that determine the valuation of shares. The required rate of return is also important, and, furthermore, share values are highly sensitive to relatively small changes in this return. The required return is related to the **equity premium**; this represents *the interest rate differential which shareholders require in excess of the interest rate on long-term government bonds in order to compensate for the greater risk of holding shares*. Historically this premium has been in the 6–8% range, but currently it is only 3%. It has been estimated that if this premium were to rise to only 4% the effect would bid share prices down by about 25%.[39] This current overvaluation is also supported by analysis using **Tobin's Q** measure; this is a *ratio of market share prices to the replacement cost of corporate assets*. Again this suggests that, in July 2002, US shares should fall by 25–30%. Thus it may be that market sensitivity and deviations from the EMH predictions are caused by volatility in the perceived equity premium. Obviously the debate regarding the validity of semi-strong and strong forms of the EMH is going to continue for some time.

b. Agency problems

The criticism here is that unless the strong form of the EMH is valid, which we have now seen is unlikely, managers and shareholders will not necessarily want to maximize shareholder wealth, measured in terms of the current share price. The agency problem arises because managers will have inside information that is not reflected in the current share price, while shareholders and outside investors will not have access to this information. The behaviour of managers will then depend on the structure of their compensation. If their compensation is based on share-price performance, as is now often the case for senior executives, then such managers will have incentives to act in ways that are dysfunctional for the shareholders' long-term interests. The reason is that it is generally easier for investors to obtain information relating to short-term performance, such as current market conditions and strategies, than it is to obtain information relating to long-term performance, like research projects. Thus share prices will be more sensitive to short-term performance factors than long-term ones. Assuming the compensation of managers is linked to the share price, this in turn induces managers to behave in ways that favour short-term performance at the expense of long-term performance, a criticism that has been frequently levelled at US managers. This aspect of behaviour leads into the whole issue of incentives and performance-related pay; it is sufficient to note at this point that incentives have to be carefully designed in order to align managers' interests with those of the shareholders, or they may distort performance in unexpected and undesirable ways from the principal's point of view.

Case study 2.2: Enron

Badly in need of repair[40]

Enron and others have shown how easy it is to manipulate companies' financial statements. Can it be made more difficult?

Bodo Schnabel, the boss of Comroad, a navigation-technology company listed on Germany's Neuer Markt, treated his accounts with wild abandon. In 1998 the company invented two-thirds of its total revenues and backed them up with the name of a non-existent client in Hong Kong. By 2000, 97% of Comroad's revenues came from the imaginary company, the existence of which its auditor, KPMG, did not bother to verify.

Comroad is just one of a series of accounting scandals that have badly damaged investors' confidence in financial statements. Companies such as Waste Management, Cendant, Xerox and, of course, Enron, have lied wholesale to investors who have now become suspicious of all accounts. The share price of General Electric (GE), the world's biggest company by market capitalisation, has fallen by some 23% this year, due in part to concerns about its accounting methods. Blacklists have circulated round the City of London and Wall Street. One listed all companies whose chief financial officers had been recruited from one of the Big Five accounting firms.

Many investors now believe that companies can manipulate their accounts more or less at will, with the aim of producing profits that increase steadily over time. Provisions are bumped up in good years and later released, or the value of an acquisition is slashed; there are plenty of tricks. In the dotcom years, finance directors resorted to so-called pro-forma numbers, which strip out negative items from the income statement.

The primary purpose of financial statements is to show the underlying economic performance of a company. The balance sheet provides a snapshot, at a moment in time, of the assets, liabilities and capital of the business; and the income statement, or profit-and-loss account, shows the difference between total revenues and total expenses. The auditors vouchsafe that these present a fair view, acknowledging the subjective nature of some of the measures behind the accounts. The independence of the auditors guarantees, in theory, that 'fair' is just that.

Somewhere along the line, though, things seem to have gone wrong. 'Our financial reporting model is broken,' said Joseph Berardino, former head of Andersen, Enron's auditor, last year. Designed in the 1930s for an industrial age, financial statements, he argued, look backwards to historic costs; they give investors little clue about the future. Companies cannot include internally produced software, drugs or brands in their balance sheets because they are intangible assets. That has led to an increasing gap between the value of companies as measured by the stockmarket and the value measured by their accounts (their book value), although the difference has contracted of late along with the market values of technology companies.

OFF-BALANCE-SHEET HOLES

Accounts certainly rely too heavily on historic costs. But what concerns investors far more is the stuff that lurks beyond the balance sheet. Although numbers recorded on the balance sheet are often misleading, investors can adjust them by using information that companies are obliged to disclose elsewhere. The worrying thing about so-called 'off-balance-sheet' items is that they can appear suddenly out of nowhere, without warning. There may be clues in the footnotes, but few people pay close attention to these impenetrable bits of legalese.

Special-purpose entities (SPEs) are a sort of non-consolidated, off-balance-sheet vehicle that have some legitimate uses, such as, for example, the financing of a research and development partnership with another company. They can, however, also be used to shove nasty liabilities and risks into corners where, with luck, nobody will see them. At the moment, investors are assuming that they are being used mostly for the latter purpose.

In November 2000, Enron restated its financial statements, reducing its profits by $591m over four years and increasing its debts by $628m. Most of the restatement came from the consolidation of two SPEs. America's standard-setter, the Financial Accounting Standards Board (FASB), points to Enron's restatement as evidence that it was the energy trader's disobedience that was the problem, not the rules on special-purpose entities.

Another of Enron's special-purpose vehicles, however, called LJM2, stayed off its balance sheet in accordance with FASB standards. And there are many more SPEs out there, notably off the balance sheets of companies which securitise (ie, repackage and sell on to investors) large chunks of their assets.

Another example of off-balance-sheet deceit is the dry-sounding yet potentially dangerous phenomenon of commitments, a variety of contingent liability. A company commits itself to a future contingent payment but does not account for the liability. Telecoms-hardware manufacturers, for example, often guarantee bank loans to important customers in return for buying their products. That is fine so long as the business is healthy, but if a company enters into such a transaction purely to lubricate its own cashflow, the commitment can become a risk. At the moment, according to American, British and international accounting rules, many varieties of commitments are mentioned only in footnotes since there is, in theory, only a low probability that they will crystallise.

Operating leases, through which a company agrees to rent an asset over a substantial period of time, make up most off-balance-sheet financing. Airlines use them to clear their accounts of large numbers of aircraft. The practice helps to avoid tax, but it also results in a drastic understatement of the airlines' debt, according to Trevor Harris, an accounting analyst at Morgan Stanley Dean Witter. In 1997, one-third of the aircraft of the five biggest American airlines were treated as operating leases rather than as assets.

Needless to say, this is all done in accordance with accounting rules. Standard-setters have come up with hundreds of pages of rules on operating leases, but they have failed to get companies to admit what any analyst knows: that airlines reap the economic risks and rewards of their aeroplanes and ought to treat them as assets.

Unlike off-balance-sheet financing methods, most of which date from the last 15 years or so, the trick of recognising revenue too early (or booking sales that never materialise) is an old one. Global Crossing, a bankrupt telecoms-equipment company now under investigation by the Federal Bureau of Investigation and the Securities and Exchange Commission (SEC), is accused of swapping fibre-optic capacity with a competitor as a way to manufacture revenue. And according to the SEC, Xerox, a photocopier company, wrongly accelerated the recognition of equipment revenue by over $3 billion. Standard-setters admit that no country has adequate rules on the recognition of revenues. A solution in the meantime may be to look at cash, which is far harder to disguise or invent. Comroad duped its auditor about its revenues, but it could not conceal the fact that its cashflow was negative.

A different sort of problem lies in the very nature of American accounting standards. Companies always think of new ways to get round the rules, and the standard-setters' job is really an unending attempt to catch up. But the body of accounting rules in America has become both too detailed and too easy to circumvent. Until the 1960s, standards were simple and based on broad principles. With the advent of class-action lawsuits against companies whose share prices had tumbled, however, audit firms demanded detailed, prescriptive rules to help them in court. As a result, accounting standards in America have multiplied into vast tomes.

America's web of accounting rules, or generally accepted accounting principles (GAAP), date from the 1930s and are now produced by FASB, a private-sector body staffed by accountants. Elsewhere, accounting standards are set by private-sector groups or, in some cases, especially in Europe, directly by governments. Accounting rules outside America lean more towards principles, particularly in Britain, where the importance of providing a "true and fair" view of a company's performance overrides specific rules.

Fights over new accounting standards do not usually grab headlines. But companies care a lot about changes to accounting rules, since at one swoop their numbers may fall under a far harsher light. They lobby intensively behind the scenes, often with the help of one of the Big Five audit firms. Whether or not a standard-setter has the ability to withstand pressure depends on its legal status, the independence of its funding, and the country's overall culture of corporate behaviour and influence.

FASB is under attack over Enron's demise. Its efforts to sort out consolidation accounting, an issue directly relevant to the energy-trader's downfall, had been going on for 20 years, or for a large part of its 29-year history, with no conclusive result. The argument centres around when a company must add all the assets and liabilities of a related entity into its books. Harvey Pitt, the chairman of the SEC, has criticised FASB for taking so long to make up its mind.

The board has tried hard to address off-balance-sheet abuses. Too many times, though, it has run up against corporate pressure applied through Congress, not least in the case of special-purpose entities, the trick that Enron used. In 1999–2000, FASB was moving towards a concept of effective control rather than ownership to determine whether or not a special-purpose entity should be consolidated into a company's accounts. If the more subjective idea of control is used for standards on consolidation, as it is in Britain and elsewhere, it is easier for an auditor to exercise his judgment and insist that an entity be brought on to the balance sheet.

But FASB's initiative would have created difficulties for companies that rely on such entities. Richard Causey, Enron's former chief accountant, wrote in to object. So did Philip Ameen, head of Financial Executives International, a corporate lobby group, and a top financial officer at GE, itself a heavy user of SPEs. In January 2001, nine months before Enron went bankrupt, FASB announced that it was putting the project on hold.

In the 1970s, Congress mostly left FASB alone, with one big exception: oil and gas accounting. In 1978, the oil and gas industry persuaded it to stop the SEC from forcing any company to use an unflattering method of accounting for drilled holes. Congress became involved in accounting issues again during the savings-and-loan crisis of the late 1980s. The result was that the industry's bad-debt problems dragged on for longer than they might have done.

In recent years, the most blatant political intervention in the standard-setting process has been over the stock options that many companies grant to their employees. In 1993, FASB proposed that companies should account for stock options as expenses. The following year, Congress threatened to take away its standard-setting powers if it did not water down its proposal. In the end, FASB settled for footnote disclosure. Under heavy pressure, says Lynn Turner, a former chief accountant of the SEC, 'they had no choice but to fold, like a cheap tent'.

Another problem, says Mr Turner, is that a lot of standard-setting power has been given to the Emerging Issues Task Force (EITF), an offshoot of FASB whose mission is to respond quickly to new accounting problems. The EITF was set up in 1984 with a membership drawn from industry and the accounting profession. Whereas a key part of FASB's mission is to serve the public interest, the EITF has no explicit duty to shareholders or the public.

As far back as the late 1980s, the SEC asked the EITF to look at special-purpose entities, worried that they might lead a company to become overly leveraged without investors realising it. At a meeting in 1990, the group voted unanimously to do nothing to change the status quo. After an appeal from the SEC's chief accountant, Edmund Coulson, three EITF members agreed to change their vote.

The outcome, eventually, was a rule by which a company can keep a special-purpose vehicle off its balance sheet as long as an independent third party owns a controlling equity interest equivalent to at least 3% of the fair value of its assets. That number, post-Enron, is now judged to be too low, and FASB may raise it to 10%.

Mr Turner believes that the EITF should be given an explicit mandate to serve the public interest. Its rulings should be approved by FASB as a matter of course. At present, part of FASB's controlling board of trustees comes from industry groups and its funds from audit firms, industry and financial groups. A new bill from Congressman Billy Tauzin, aiming to boost the independence of FASB, would hand the responsibility for its funding to the Treasury, which would levy compulsory fees on companies and accounting firms.

In Britain, a series of business scandals in the 1980s, most notoriously Polly Peck, a conglomerate which manipulated its foreign-exchange earnings, convinced the corporate world that accounting rules had to get better. The Accounting Standards Board (ASB), set up in 1990, declared war on off-balance-sheet chicanery. It produced a new rule, FRS5, which requires the substance of an entity's transactions to be reported in its financial statements, regardless of legal form.

The ASB has recently enraged businesses in Britain with a new standard, FRS17, which will force them to disclose and recognise the full effect of pension-fund gains and losses. Companies hate the standard because it will bring the volatility of financial markets into their earnings. They have tried hard to get politicians involved, says Mary Keegan, the standard-setter's chairman, but the ASB has not come under

government pressure to scrap or change the standard.

A new private-sector standard-setter in Japan, the Financial Accounting Standards Foundation, gives investors some hope of better standards there. Its predecessor, the Business Accounting Deliberation Council, appeared powerless to pass any standard that would damage the suffering Japanese economy. Japan's accounting rules contain loopholes that allow companies to hide the economic substance of their performance. For instance, the recent guideline on fair-value accounting, which decrees that companies must show equity holdings at their market value, also contains a provision that allows them to avoid writing down shares if they think that they will soon recover in value.

DO THE RIGHT THING

If accounting standards are to improve, it is probably the International Accounting Standards Board (IASB), originally established in 1973, which will lead the way. America does not yet recognise its rules; companies that wish to raise capital in American markets must still reconcile their accounts with GAAP. But the IASB gained a lot of influence in 2000 when the European Commission decided that all companies in the European Union must report according to its standards by 2005.

When he was head of the ASB, Sir David Tweedie, now chairman of the IASB, successfully fought off attempts by business to influence the standard-setting process. He is determined to do so again. He believes, for instance, that the effect of giving stock options to employees should be counted in companies' accounts, not just mentioned in footnotes, as they are at the moment. The IASB will soon publish a draft proposal for a global standard on stock-option accounting. Like FASB, it will face strong opposition, including, crucially, from the European Commission, which wrote this January to say that it would prefer the IASB to concentrate on better disclosure of stock options rather than a new conceptual approach.

Sir David also wants to bring in a new international standard on pensions, similar to FRS17. Like FASB, however, the IASB would be better positioned to push through high-quality standards if it did not rely on business and big audit firms for its funding. Earlier this year it was badly embarrassed by an e-mail showing that Enron expected to be able to influence its standards in return for cash.

If accounting standard-setters have their way, financial statements are likely to become far more volatile in the future. Representatives from some of the world's most influential bodies – including those of America, Australia, Britain, Canada and the IASB – have published proposals to value all financial instruments at market value rather than at cost. Bank loans and deposits, as well as traded financial instruments with easily obtainable prices, would be marked to market. Because changes in balance-sheet values would be passed through the income statement each year, this would be sure to make corporate results far jumpier.

Proper accounting for pension schemes, along the lines of FRS17, would have the same effect. The IASB is working on the recognition and measurement of intangibles, as is FASB. Again, if intangible assets are recognised on balance sheets, they will add volatility to income since, on the whole, their value tends to fluctuate more than that of tangible assets.

Changes such as these are the ultimate answer to people who criticise accounts for being industrial and irrelevant. Standard-setters have already started to crack down on off-balance-sheet abuses and they have more backing to do so, post-Enron. Companies will fight against either sort of change. They want their earnings to move gradually upwards, not to jerk around, and they do not want the fact that they use volatile financial instruments to be reflected in their results, even if the volatility is real. Standard-setters should take the views of companies and governments into consideration. But if future Enrons are to be avoided, they must be given the freedom to force companies to reveal far more economic reality in their accounts than they do at present.

Questions

1 Explain the different types of conflict of interest that are evident in the Enron situation.
2 Explain the discrepancies that arise in comparing the measures of book value and market value.
3 Why do SPEs and off-balance-sheet items represent a problem?
4 Why has the past accounting treatment of stock options represented a problem?
5 Explain why future regulations may cause more volatility in reported accounts.

2.6 Risk and uncertainty

The basic profit-maximizing model ignores risk and uncertainty by assuming all costs and revenues are known in the future. While the shareholder-wealth maximization model does take risk and uncertainty into consideration by incorporating a required rate of return, aspects of this now need to be considered in more detail. First of all the distinction between risk and uncertainty needs to be clarified. Although the two terms are often used interchangeably, there is a technical difference between them. When there is certainty in a situation there is only one possible outcome. *In a risky situation there are several possible outcomes, and each can be assigned a probability of occurring. In an uncertain situation the possible outcomes are not fully identified, and they cannot therefore be assigned probabilities*. In practice many of the implications of risk also apply to uncertainty, but there are some additional implications that are examined more fully in Chapter 9 on game theory. We will now consider attitudes to risk; then the impact of risk on objectives will be discussed; finally, the relationship between risk and the agency problem will be examined.

2.6.1 Attitudes to risk

The concept of risk again relates to bounded rationality. Since we cannot perfectly foresee events in the future, the values of possible outcomes are called **expected values**. Although the student should already be familiar with this concept a brief review will help to lead us on to the aspect of risk aversion. Say that it has been estimated that one particular action has a probability of 0.6 of yielding an outcome of $1000 and a 0.4 probability of yielding an outcome of $500. The expected value of the action is given by $\sum p_i x_i$ in general terms. In this case the expected value is given by:

$$EV = 0.6(1000) + 0.4(500) = \$800$$

However, this expected value is not certain; it is a mean value of expected values, but there will be a distribution of values involved, with some variance around the mean. The value of the variance is given by $\sum p_i (X_i - \bar{X})^2$ or $\sum p_i (X_i - \sum p_i X_i)^2$ in general terms. Since the expected value is the sum of two other expected values, $600 + $200, we have to add the variances of each of these in order to obtain the variance of the expected value of $800. Thus the variance is given by:

$$\text{Variance} = 0.6(1000 - 800)^2 + 0.4(500 - 800)^2 = \$60,000$$

The decision-maker may have a choice between taking the above action and taking some other action, which has a certain outcome of $800. If the decision-maker is indifferent between the two alternative actions he is said to be **risk-neutral**. This means in general terms that *the individual is indifferent between a particular expected value and its certainty equivalent* (in this example, $800). Many individuals are **risk-averse**; this means that they *prefer the certainty equivalent to the expected value of the same amount*. Such people are willing to pay a **risk premium** to avoid taking the risk involved. This premium is *the difference between a certainty equivalent and the expected value*. In the above example, if the person is indifferent between receiving $700 with certainty and taking the action with the expected value of $800, the risk premium is $100. Alternatively we can say that the risky outcome of $800 has a certainty equivalent of $700. Other individuals may be **risk-seeking**; this is the opposite attitude to risk, meaning that such people prefer the expected value to the certainty equivalent. Someone might be indifferent between receiving $900 with certainty and receiving the expected value of $800.

We should not think that individuals display constant attitudes to risk. These attitudes depend on the amount of money involved and the circumstances. For example, the same people who take out insurance (showing risk aversion) may also gamble on the lottery (showing risk seeking).

2.6.2 Risk and objectives

Managers frequently have to choose between strategies where risk and return are positively correlated. An example will illustrate this situation: a firm is

considering launching a new product onto the market, something significantly different from any current product, rather than just a modification of
an existing product. This could be a new soft drink, a new type of phone, or a
microscooter. The firm may have carried out a consumer survey and discovered that consumer attitudes were generally favourable to the new product. At
this point it may have to decide whether to **test-market** the product or go
straight for a national launch. Test-marketing involves *selling the product on a
limited basis in a selected sample of locations, usually designed to be representative of the firm's total market*. The advantage of test-marketing is that the
costs are limited, so that if the product fails the losses will be relatively small
compared with a national launch, where large initial costs are involved in
equipping facilities, hiring and training workers, and promotion. Thus test-
marketing can be viewed as a low-risk strategy compared with going straight
for a national launch. However, one problem with test-marketing is that it
alerts competitors to the new product and they will make efforts to imitate and
improve the product, reducing the firm's competitive advantage. When it is
considered that it often takes a fair time, maybe several months, to obtain
reliable results from test-marketing, the firm may decide that the loss of profit
may be too great to do this; this applies in particular to firms introducing
products involving new technology, like many electronic appliances involving
IT. Thus we can say that test-marketing, while low-risk, is also a low-return
strategy.

The above example is just an illustration of a choice between strategies
involving different degrees of risk where the difference in risk is obvious. In
reality, any choice between different strategies or courses of action will
involve some difference in risk. The significance of this is that many firms,
or managers, are risk-averse; it has been seen in the previous subsection that
such individuals do not like to take much risk. Managers may fear for their job
security if they take excessive risks that do not pay off, preferring to maintain
the status quo. The implication of this attitude to risk, as far as the theory of the
firm is concerned, is that no firm will aim to maximize profit, since that would
be too risky. Instead they will tend to **satisfice**, that is make a *satisfactory
rather than a maximum profit*. There are a number of different reasons for
satisficing behaviour, which are again related to agency problems.

2.6.3 Risk and the agency problem

It was stated earlier that principals and agents frequently show different
attitudes to risk. For example, investors with widely diversified portfolios
may be risk-neutral regarding a firm's strategy, while managers, as agents,
may be risk-averse; they have more to lose (their jobs) if things go wrong.
Similarly, employees may be more risk-averse than managers; again they may
have more to lose if a particular venture goes wrong.

As has been seen above, managers who are risk-averse may be inclined to
satisfice. However, other managers may be risk-seekers. This may happen if

managers have asymmetric information and are in a position to distort the reported profit of the firm in the short term, in order to make a quick gain and then quit the firm leaving the shareholders to suffer the long-term losses. Such differences in attitudes towards risk aggravate the nature of the agency problem, since it becomes more difficult to design efficient incentives to align the interests of principal and agent. However, some of the incentives discussed under control measures earlier can help to reduce the problem.

2.7 Multiproduct strategies

In practice most firms produce a variety of different products, often with many different product lines in their overall product mix. It was stated earlier that this complicates the analysis because there are frequently both demand and cost interactions among these different products. By demand interactions we are referring to the situation where a firm produces a **product line** of similar products, for example Casio calculators. These products are to some extent **substitutes** for each other, meaning that they have *similar perceived functions or characteristics*. Therefore the demand for each of the firm's products depends to some extent on the demand for its other products; if Casio introduces a new model the demand for this will automatically reduce the demand for some of its existing models.

The example of Casio calculators also serves to illustrate the relevance of cost interactions. Many products may be produced using the same resources: different models may be produced in the same factory, using the same equipment and labour. These shared overhead costs can be allocated by accountants on some notional basis like machine-time in order to perform full-cost accounting, but if some product is added or dropped from the product line this will then affect the costs of the other products, reducing them in the first case and increasing them in the second. This is because, in the first case, the new product will share some of the overhead costs, thus reducing their burden for the existing products. The reverse is true for the case of dropping products, where the overhead cost burden on the remaining products is increased.

Given these demand and cost interactions, how do such firms seek to maximize profits? There are two main strategies that need to be discussed here: product line and product mix profit maximization. While there are some similarities between these strategies, there are certain important differences that necessitate separate discussions of each.

2.7.1 Product line profit maximization

The example of Casio calculators was given earlier to illustrate a product line. This time the example of car manufacturers will be used. All major car firms produce a variety of different models. Volkswagen for example have the Lupo, Polo, Golf, Beetle, Passat and Sharan. Each model in turn comes in different forms, with different engines and other equipment or trim. On top of these model forms there is a variety of optional equipment that a customer can order, which does not come standard with that model. This can include air-conditioning, heated seats, electric windows, a CD player and so on. A recent TV campaign for the Volkswagen Polo featured many different advertisements, all with the common theme of low price. The goal was simply to get potential customers to visit the showrooms, attracted by the low price. In such a situation it is common practice for the salesforce to try to persuade the customer to buy a more expensive model or model version. This is sometimes referred to as a **bait-and-switch** tactic. In this case the firm is not trying to maximize profit on each and every model and model form that it produces; the price may be too low on the most basic model forms to make significant profit, and indeed losses may be incurred here if the price is particularly low. However, if the firm is successful with its bait-and-switch tactic, it may be able to maximize profit on the product line taken as a whole, by persuading people to buy more expensive cars with a much higher profit margin. Any firm selling a product line, not necessarily products from the same manufacturer, can attempt to use this tactic, although it tends to be more common with the more expensive consumer durables and with services.

2.7.2 Product mix profit maximization

The **product mix** of a firm refers to the ***total range of products offered by the firm***. Whereas products in a product line tend to be substitutes for each other, products in a product mix are often **complementary**, meaning that they are ***consumed together*** in some way. This 'togetherness' can operate in various ways: obvious examples are bread and butter, cars and petrol, mobile phones and service networks. However, the togetherness does not have to be so direct, as the following illustration demonstrates. Supermarkets sell thousands of different products in different shapes, sizes, forms and containers. Many of these chains regularly have a sample of products on special offer and advertise them using direct mail and other means. When a consumer sees a special offer for, say, a two-litre bottle of Coke, they may decide to shop at that store rather than a different one; but while they are there they will usually pick up a number of other items, at the normal price, that they might have bought anyway, but not necessarily at that store. Thus the firm will not be maximizing its profit on each and every item, since some items may be sold at below cost, but it may be maximizing profit on the whole product mix by attracting customers into the store who would not ordinarily shop there. Such an approach could be called a **bait-and-add** tactic. The products being added are complementary products, and while it may not be immediately obvious that Coke and dog-food, say, have a complementary relationship, they are still complements in that they are purchased together.

The difference between bait-and-switch and bait-and-add is not always distinct. In the earlier example of car sales, instead of the bait-and-switch tactic of persuading customers to buy a different, more luxurious model, the salespeople may instead try to persuade customers to add a number of items of optional equipment, such as climate control, electric seats or satellite navigation. This is now a bait-and-add tactic. The objective of product mix profit maximization is further examined in the following case study.

Case study 2.3: PC World

PC World is a major retailer of computers and related equipment in the United Kingdom, calling itself 'the computer superstore'. The market features much heavy advertising by different types of seller: Time, Tiny and Gateway, who put together their own packages of components under their own names; Dell, which produces custom-made packages as well as standard offers; and retailers like Dixons and Comet which sell a variety of appliances. However, PC World probably out-advertises them all with its regular full-page spreads in the major national newspapers. Because of the nature of the product most of the advertisements feature packages at a special sale price. These packages often include a variety of software, and sometimes items like printers and scanners. The featured computers are highly competitive in terms of price, and include most major manufacturers, like Compaq, Packard Bell, Advent, Hewlett Packard, Apple and Sony. The company has been expanding in terms of size and profit for several years.

While many customers have been very happy with the deals that they have obtained from PC World, some of them claim that the end cost has considerably surpassed their initial expectations. There are several reasons for this.

1. Some of the add-ons that they want to buy are not available with the deals on offer; sometimes the add-ons in the special offers include low-quality or obsolete items, causing one to suspect that the firm is just trying to get rid of these items by packaging them with others, since nobody would want to buy them separately. Similarly, the packages often do not include the most desirable software. Thus, even with a seemingly complete offer, the buyer may end up having to buy several additional items to obtain the system they really want.

2. The firm tries to hard-sell its extended warranty scheme. Depending on the package purchased, this can increase the cost by 5–6 per cent. This tactic is by no means exclusive to PC World. Several electrical appliance retailers in the UK, particularly Dixons and Argos, are currently under investigation by the Monopolies and Mergers Commission because of their alleged excessive profits in this area of activity.

3. The credit terms can be misleading. Often a lengthy period of interest-free credit is offered, like nine to twelve months. It is highly attractive to many buyers to buy something costing over £1,000 and not to have to pay anything at all for such a long period. These credit terms are offered through HFC Bank. The problem is that people are not notified at the end of the interest-free period, and they then become liable to pay interest on the whole purchase price from the date of purchase at a high interest rate, close to 30 per cent annually. The result is that the unwary consumer can end up paying about twice the original purchase price over a period of four years.

Questions

1 Describe the various complementary products, both goods and services, that a consumer may consider in buying a computer system.

2 Compare and contrast the situation of PC World with that of a supermarket chain, as far as product mix profit maximization is concerned.

2.8 Conclusion

It has been seen that the basic profit-maximizing model, and even, to a lesser extent, the shareholder-wealth maximization model, have certain limitations.

There are also certain other aspects relating to these models that need to be discussed, and they are now examined before returning to the BPM.

2.8.1 *The public sector and non-profit organizations*

The profit motive does not apply, at least in the same way, to non-profit organizations.[41] They tend to pursue a different set of objectives because of the nature of their funding and the nature of the product they supply. Such objectives may include:

1 Utility maximization of the contributors
2 Utility maximization of the administrators
3 Maximization of the quantity or quality of output subject to a cost constraint.

In the case of the public sector the contributors are taxpayers, who to some extent exert control in terms of their voting power. The particular factors relating to the objectives of the public sector are discussed in detail in Chapter 12.

The class of non-profit (NP) organizations includes a wide variety of types: voluntary organizations, co-operatives, credit unions, labour unions, churches, charities, hospitals, foundations, professional associations and some educational institutions. Their objectives may vary accordingly, but one general pattern can be observed. The greater the proportion of their funding from external contributors, the more will the first objective above be emphasized, the maximization of the utility of the contributors; this means that the behaviour of the organization will resemble more closely that of the profit-maximizing firm. This would be the case for many co-operatives, credit unions and labour unions. As the organization relies less on external contributions so the second objective may become more important. This can also have serious implications for the public sector; it is often assumed that this has the third objective above, but the second objective may be more important if external contributions become taken for granted. Once again, an essentially neoclassical framework of analysis can be used to examine the behaviour of all these organizations.

2.8.2 *Satisficing*

Two reasons for satisficing behaviour have already been explained, the existence of risk and uncertainty and the agency problem. However, it was also mentioned that there are other reasons for such behaviour, and these now need to be discussed. One problem is the transaction costs with which managers are increasingly faced as they try harder to maximize profit; these involve, in particular, the costs of obtaining more information in order to improve decision-making. Related to this problem is the issue of diminishing returns to managerial effort. As managers work harder and longer to maximize profit, they are forced to explore avenues of activity that are less and less fruitful. Not only that, but there is an increasing opportunity cost to their efforts; they lose more and more leisure time, the marginal value of which therefore increases.

There is an additional factor involved in satisficing. Firms are organizations of different managers, often in different and in some ways competing departments. These managers and departments compete for resources, in particular the firm's budget. Since the compensation, power and prestige of managers often depends on the size of their department and budget, this competition can be intense. It also means that managers, particularly those of cost centres as opposed to profit centres, have incentives to spend as much as they can, not just on perks, as we have already seen; there is the additional factor that, if they underspend their budget, it may well be cut in future. This obviously reduces efficiency within the firm and necessitates top management monitoring performance, adding further agency costs.

2.8.3 Surveys of business objectives

Many surveys have been carried out at different times and in different countries asking senior executives what their business objectives are. It should come as no surprise that trying to maximize profit does not top the list; moreover it is rarely mentioned. Such executives often refer to increasing or maximizing market share, providing customer satisfaction, providing a high quality service, or improving the firm's image and reputation. They may also mention more personal objectives, like achieving prestige, fame, wealth, or a sense of achievement. Superficially this may seem to provide evidence against any profit-maximization theory of the firm. However, it is not surprising that executives do not admit to a profit-maximizing objective, for to do so would seem to be selfish and greedy in the eyes of many consumers, and cause a loss of the firm's reputation. It might also alienate the firm's workforce, making them feel exploited. Finally, it might attract unwelcome attention from various regulators and government agencies.

There is another factor in the consideration of stated objectives by business-owners and managers. Sometimes means are confused with ends; thus maximizing market share or providing consumer satisfaction may merely be a means to the end of profit maximization. Alternatively, profit maximization may be a means to the end of personal objectives like the achievement of status and prestige. Further justification for these possibilities will be provided in the concluding part of this section. First it is necessary to consider one more objection to the profit-maximization assumption.

2.8.4 Ethics

Firms in recent years have seemed to become much more concerned with ethics than previously. They often claim that they are concerned not just with profit but with treating customers, workers and local communities fairly and being a responsible contributor to society generally. This involves a wide variety of different activities: sponsoring local events and communities, giving aid to charities, increasing people's awareness of social problems, providing ancillary services to workers and their families and so on. Such activities are often related to the stated objectives of business executives described earlier. The concern with ethics can be summarized in the concept of **societal marketing** popularized by Kotler,[42] which states that 'an organization's task is to determine the needs, wants and interests of target markets and to deliver the desired satisfactions more effectively and efficiently than competitors in a way that preserves or enhances the consumer's and the society's well-being'.

However, it is one thing to say that one is concerned with ethics and another to act in such a way. In view of the discussion above regarding statements of objectives it might seem to be difficult to establish the real objectives of firms and their managers. The only real test is to perform an empirical study on the actual behaviour of companies to see whether their concern with ethics is altruistic or merely a cover for profit maximization. This might seem to be a difficult task but an ingenious study by Navarro[43] has shed some light on this issue; this study concluded that charitable giving by corporations was explained by profit-maximizing motives rather than altruistic behaviour by managers.

2.8.5 Profit maximization revisited

The discussion in this section teaches us to be cautious before rejecting the profit-maximization assumption, for two reasons. First, we cannot accept statements of objectives by business executives and managers at face value. Second, and more generally, an economic theory like the profit-maximization assumption can only really be tested by empirical study, not by theoretical objections like those raised earlier. Another example can illustrate this. An objection to the profit-maximization assumption discussed earlier was that managers do not have access to accurate and detailed up-to-date information regarding costs and revenue functions, and certainly have difficulty with forecasting. It was suggested that this would lead to satisficing behaviour. However, a couple of studies by Day[44, 45] have shown that such information, to a large extent, is not necessary for managers to achieve profit maximization. Day introduced a simple learning model wherein managers adjust output from one period to the next on the basis of changes in output and profit in the previous period. He demonstrated that profit-maximizing behaviour can emerge in this situation, even without a knowledge of cost and revenue functions. Thus satisficing can in practice closely approximate to maximizing. An analogy can be drawn here: a bird does not need to know the laws of aerodynamics in order to be able to fly. A more general analogy can be made with the Darwinian law of natural selection, or 'survival of the fittest' as it is often called. Dawkins[46] has dubbed this process of nature 'the blind watchmaker'; similarly, managers can be blind to cost and revenue information but the forces of competition may force them to maximize profit regardless, while managers who make bad decisions will ultimately force their firms out of business.

Therefore we can conclude that, whatever the theoretical objections to the profit-maximization assumption, provided that it can make reasonably accurate predictions of the behaviour of firms and managers, it is still a useful and sensible theory with which to work. Thus the neoclassical approach can be vindicated.

Summary

1 In order to understand the nature of the firm we need to consider five main areas of economic theory: transaction costs, motivation, agency, information costs and game theory.

2 Transaction costs consist of co-ordination (Coasian) costs and motivation (agency) costs.

3 Transactions have four main dimensions: asset specificity, frequency, complexity and relationship with other transactions.

4 According to Coasian theory there is an optimal size for the firm, since as the firm becomes larger the costs of transacting in the market decrease while the costs of co-ordinating transactions within the firm increase.

5 The ownership of a complex asset like a firm is a difficult concept since four parties have different types of claims regarding control and returns: shareholders, directors, managers and other employees.

6 The conventional economic model of motivation is that individuals try to maximize their utilities; this assumes that people act rationally in their self-interest.

7 The nature of the agency problem is that there is a conflict of interest between principal and agent.

8 The agency problem is aggravated by the existence of asymmetric information, leading to adverse selection and moral hazard.

9 Adverse selection means that only the products or customers with the worst quality characteristics are able to have or make transactions; others are driven from the market.

10 Moral hazard is sometimes referred to as the problem of hidden action, in that the behaviour of a party cannot be reliably or costlessly observed after entering a contract. This, in turn, provides an incentive for post-contract opportunism.

11 There are various control measures that firms and shareholders can use to combat agency problems in their internal and external transactions: increased monitoring, screening, signalling, risk-pooling, internalization and the structure of pay incentives.

12 The basic profit-maximizing model (BPM) is useful because it enables managers to determine strategy regarding price and output decisions; it thus enables the economist to predict firms' behaviour.

13 The basic model involves many other assumptions that do not appear to be at all realistic.

14 Agency problems arise because of conflicts of interest between shareholders and lenders, between shareholders and managers and between managers and other employees.

15 There are various problems in measuring profit. Managers can take advantage of various legal and accounting loopholes in reporting profits, which are in their interests and may boost the share price, but are against the interests of shareholders.

16 The shareholder-wealth maximization model (SWMM) is a superior model because it takes into account profits in all future time periods, not just those in the present. As such it represents a long-run profit maximization model.

17 The SWMM also has the advantage that it takes into account risk and uncertainty, by discounting future profits by a required rate of return.

18 The SWMM has certain limitations because it ignores the fact that managers tend to have better information than shareholders and investors.

19 In order to understand the behaviour of multiproduct firms we need to consider the concepts of product line and product mix profit maximization, and the associated strategies to achieve these.

20 The public sector and not-for-profit organizations pursue different objectives depending mainly on the nature of their funding.

21 Satisficing behaviour by managers can arise for a number of reasons: risk aversion, transaction costs, diminishing returns to managerial effort and conflicts of objectives between different managers.

22 Claims regarding ethical behaviour and altruism need to be closely examined; empirical evidence does not support the existence of these if they conflict with maximizing profit.

23 The profit-maximization assumption cannot be rejected on purely theoretical grounds. It must be tested by empirical study, and when this is done the assumption proves to be a good working theory in terms of predicting the behaviour of firms and managers.

Review questions

1 Explain why the concept of the ownership of a public corporation is a complex issue.

2 Explain the differences between profit maximization and shareholder-wealth maximization. Which assumption provides a better model of a firm's behaviour?

3 Explain the implications of risk and uncertainty for the theory of the firm.

4 Explain the implications of the agency problem for the theory of the firm.

5 Explain how managers can take advantage of the problems in measuring profit.

6 Explain what is meant by the various forms of the EMH; what are the main criticisms of the EMH?

7 Discuss the reasons for satisficing behaviour by firms.

8 Explain the role of empirical studies in terms of the theory of the firm.

Notes

1 A. Alchian and H. Demsetz, 'Production, information costs and economic organisation', *American Economic Review*, **62** (1972): 777–795.

2 R. Coase, 'The nature of the firm', *Economica*, **4** (1937): 386–405.

3 Ibid., 403.

4 A. Smith, *The Wealth of Nations*, Modern Library edition, New York: Random House, 1937 [1776].

5 F. Y. Edgeworth, *Mathematical Psychics*, London: Kegan Paul, 1881.

6 A. Downs, 'An economic theory of political action in a democracy', *Journal of Political Economy*, **65** (1957): 135–150.

7 R. A. Posner, *The Economic Analysis of the Law*, 2nd edn, Boston: Little, Brown and Co., 1977.

8 G. S. Becker, 'Crime and punishment: an economic approach', *Journal of Political Economy*, **76** (1968): 493–517.

9 R. Dawkins, *The Selfish Gene*, New York: Oxford University Press, 1976.

10 W. Hamilton, 'Selfish and spiteful behaviour in an evolutionary model', *Nature*, **228** (1970), 1218–1220.

11 J. Maynard Smith, 'Optimization theory in evolution', *Annual Review of Ecology and Systematics*, **9** (1978): 31–56.

12 S. Pinker, *How the Mind Works*, New York: Norton, 1997.

13 M. Ridley, *The Origins of Virtue*, London: Penguin, 1996.

14 R. Trivers, 'The evolution of reciprocal altruism', *Quarterly Review of Biology*, **46** (1971): 35–57.

15 G. C. Williams, *Adaptation and Natural Selection: A Critique of Some Current Evolutionary Thought*, Princeton University Press, 1966.

16 J. Hirshleifer, 'The expanding domain of economics', *American Economic Review*, **75** (1985): 53–68.

17 D. Collard, *Altruism and Economy*, New York: Oxford University Press, 1978.

18 P. Milgrom and J. Roberts, *Economics, Organization and Management*, Upper Saddle River, N. J.: Prentice-Hall, 1992.

19 A. K. Sen, 'Rational fools: a critique of the behavioral foundations of economic theory', *Philosophy and Public Affairs*, **6** (1977): 317–344.

20 T. C. Schelling, 'The intimate contest for self-command', *Public Interest*, no. 60 (September 1980).

21 J. Hirshleifer, 'On the emotions as guarantors of threats and promises', UCLA Economics Dept. Working Paper 337, August 1984.

22 R. H. Frank, *Passions within Reason: The Strategic Role of the Emotions*, New York: Norton, 1988.

23 Milgrom and Roberts, *Economics, Organization and Management*.

24 S. Grossman and O. Hart, 'The costs and benefits of ownership: a theory of vertical and lateral integration', *Journal of Political Economy*, **94** (1986): 691–719.

25 M. Berlin, '"We control the vertical": three theories of the firm', *Business Review*, 2001, no. 3: 13–21.

26 D. De Meza and B. Lockwood, 'Does asset ownership always motivate managers? Outside options and the property rights theory of the firm', *Quarterly Journal of Economics*, **113** (May 1998): 361–386.

27 B. Holmstrom and J. Roberts, 'The boundaries of the firm revisited', *Journal of Economic Perspectives*, **12** (Fall 1998): 73–94.

28 P. Kotler, *Marketing Management: Analysis, Planning, Implementation and Control*, 7th edn, Englewood Cliffs, N. J.: Prentice-Hall International, 1991.

29 E. J. McCarthy, *Basic Marketing: A Managerial Approach*, 9th edn Homewood, Ill.: Richard D. Irwin, 1981.

30 G. A. Akerlof, 'The market for "lemons": qualitative uncertainty and the market mechanism', *Quarterly Journal of Economics*, **84** (1970): 488–500.

31 Milgrom and Roberts, *Economics, Organization and Management*.

32 D. Hansen, 'Worker performance and group incentives: a case study', *Industrial Labor Relations Review*, **51** (1997): 37–49.

33 C. Prendergast, 'The provision of incentives in firms', *Journal of Economic Literature*, **37** (1999): 7–63.

34 J. Hendry, 'The principal's other problems: honest incompetence and the specification of objectives', *Academy of Management Review*, **27** (January 2002): 98–113.

35 'Designed by committee', *The Economist*, 13 June 2002.

36 'An economy singed', *The Economist*, 20 June 2002.

37 N. Al-Loughani and D. Chappell, 'On the validity of the weak-form efficient markets hypothesis applied to the London Stock Exchange', *Applied Financial Economics*, **7** (1997): 173–176.

38 A. E. Milionis and D. Moschos, 'On the validity of the weak-form efficient markets hypothesis applied to the London Stock Exchange: comment', *Applied Economics Letters*, **7** (July 2000): 419–421.

39 'Calling for the band to strike up', *The Economist*, 22 June 2002.

40 'Badly in need of repair', *The Economist*, 2 May 2002.

41 B. A. Weisbrod, *The Nonprofit Economy*, Cambridge, Mass.: Harvard University Press, 1988.

42 Kotler, *Marketing Management: Analysis, Planning, Implementation and Control*.

43 P. Navarro, 'Why do corporations give to charity?' *Journal of Business*, **61** (1988): 65–93.

44 R. H. Day, 'Profits, learning, and the convergence of satisficing to marginalism', *Quarterly Journal of Economics*, **81** (1967): 302–311.

45 R. H. Day and E. H. Tinney, 'How to co-operate in business without really trying: a learning model of decentralized decision-making', *Journal of Political Economy*, **67** (July–August 1969): 583–600.

46 R. Dawkins, *The Blind Watchmaker*, London: Longman, 1986.

PART II
DEMAND ANALYSIS

Part II (Chapters 3 and 4) examines the topic of demand. The demand for a firm's products determines its revenues and also enables the firm to plan its production; thus a thorough understanding of demand by managers is fundamental to a firm's profitability. Chapter 3 is concerned with the factors that determine demand, both those that are controllable by the firm and those that are uncontrollable, or environmental. The sensitivity of demand to these factors is examined, and also how knowledge of this sensitivity is useful to managers. Chapter 4 is concerned with the estimation of demand, examining techniques for estimating and interpreting demand relationships, and using such relationships for forecasting purposes. The use of statistical methods is explained in particular. Finally, important results from empirical studies are discussed.

3

Demand theory

Objectives

1 To explain the meaning of demand and how it can be represented.
2 To interpret demand equations.
3 To explain why the demand curve is downward-sloping.
4 To identify the factors that affect demand.
5 To examine the ways in which the above factors affect demand.
6 To distinguish between changes in demand and quantity demanded.
7 To explain the concept of elasticity and different elasticities of demand.
8 To explain the different ways of measuring elasticity.
9 To examine the factors determining different elasticities.
10 To explain the uses and applications of different elasticities.

3.1 Introduction

It is of vital importance for any firm to have an understanding of the demand for its products. Demand relationships determine revenues and indirectly affect output and costs; they thus have a fundamental impact on profits. An understanding of demand is also relevant for planning purposes, involving production, transportation, inventory, sales, marketing and finance functions. The identification of factors affecting demand and the precise effects that these have is therefore a core element in managerial economics.

3.2 Definition and representation

3.2.1 *Meaning of demand*

Unfortunately the word 'demand' can be used in a variety of senses, which often causes misunderstanding and errors of analysis. We can talk about demand curves, schedules, functions, equations, relationships or points. When economists use the single word 'demand' they are referring to the relationship that is frequently called the demand curve. In this sense, demand

Table 3.1. Demand table

Price of Coke (pence per can)	Quantity sold (cans per day)
30	120
40	100
50	80
60	60
70	40

refers to **the quantities that people are or would be willing to buy at different prices during a given time period, assuming that other factors affecting these quantities remain the same**. It is worth noting that this definition incorporates three important concepts:

1 It involves three parameters – price, quantity and time.
2 It refers to quantities in the plural, therefore a whole relationship, not a single quantity.
3 It involves the *ceteris paribus* (other things being equal) assumption, which is a very common one in making statements in economics.

The second of the above concepts, in particular, tends to cause misunderstandings, since it is common in both business and marketing to refer to demand as a single quantity. For example, consider the following statement: the demand for Coke is 80 cans per day at the price of 50 pence per can. First of all there are issues of definition and measurement. Whose demand is being considered? Does 'Coke' include Diet Coke and different flavours? What is the size of the can? How do we include bottles? However, even if these issues are clarified, the statement is still technically incorrect from an economist's standpoint. The statement refers to a quantity demanded, not to demand. As will be seen in section 3.4 it is vital to distinguish between these two concepts, as otherwise errors in analysis will occur. It is now useful to consider the different ways of expressing the demand for a product since this is helpful in illustrating this distinction.

3.2.2 Tables, graphs and equations

a. Tables

These are the simplest method of representation. An example of a demand table or schedule faced by a retailer is given in Table 3.1. The table shows the general 'law of demand', that less is demanded at higher prices. It should be noted that the original statement above relating to a quantity demanded is included in the table as one of the five pairs of values. Although they are simple to understand the main problem with tables is that they are not very useful for analytical purposes.

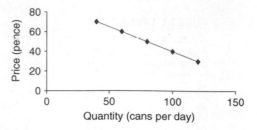

Figure 3.1. Demand graph.

b. Graphs

These are much more useful for analysis, and indeed most analysis in introductory microeconomics involves the use of graphs. A graph relating to the
above demand schedule is shown in Figure 3.1. It can be seen that the demand
relationship in this case is both inverse and linear. At this stage both of these
characteristics are assumed, but later on both of these assumptions will have
to be examined. Again the difference between the concepts of demand and
quantity demanded is illustrated: the former relates to the whole demand
curve whereas the latter relates to a single point on the curve.

Although graphical analysis is very useful in economics its main disadvantage is that it essentially involves a two-dimensional framework. Thus it is
mainly limited to examining two-variable relationships. Demand relationships
often involve many variables and although the effects of these can be shown
on a graph, as seen in section 3.4, they are difficult to measure.

c. Equations

These are the most useful method of representation for analytical purposes
since they explicitly show the effects of all the variables affecting quantity
demanded, in a concise form that at the same time reveals important information regarding the nature of the relationship. Taking the demand curve in
Figure 3.1, we can estimate the equation relating to it in various ways. The
general form of the demand function in terms of price and quantity demanded is:

$$Q = f(P) \tag{3.1}$$

This is the most general way of describing the relationship since it does not
involve any specific mathematical form. It can obviously be expanded by
including any number of variables that might affect quantity demanded on
the righthand side of the equation, for example:

$$Q = f(P, A, Y, P_s, \ldots) \tag{3.2}$$

where A represents advertising expenditure, Y represents average income of
the market and P_s represents the price of a substitute product.

In the two-variable case the demand function can be expressed in a linear
form:

$$Q = a + bP \tag{3.3}$$

The coefficients a and b can then be calculated for the demand schedule in Table 3.1. One way of doing this is to use simultaneous equations and substitute any two pairs of values in the table to solve for a and b. However, it is more insightful to calculate the value of b first, using the mathematical concept that b represents $\Delta Q / \Delta P$. Again any two pairs of values can be used to establish that $b = -2$. For example, if the first two pairs of values are taken, $b = -20/10 = -2$. Then any pair of values can be used, substituting the value of b, to calculate the value of a. If the first pair of values is taken the following expression is obtained:

$$120 = a - 2(30)$$

Thus $a = 180$ and the demand equation can now be written:

$$Q = 180 - 2P \qquad (3.4)$$

The advantage of this approach is that the value of b can more easily be interpreted as a **slope** coefficient. The value of a in turn can be interpreted as an **intercept**.

At this point we encounter a problem: the slope of the demand curve on the graph in Figure 3.1 is *not* equal to -2, nor is the vertical intercept equal to 180. Why is this? The reader may have noticed that there is an inconsistency or lack of correspondence in terms of the treatment of the dependent and independent variables in the exposition above. In the graph the price variable is treated as the dependent variable, with quantity as the independent variable, while in the equation it is the reverse. This is the most common way in economics of representing both the graph and the equation but it raises the question: why is there such an inconsistency? The easiest way to explain this is to start with the equation. It is logical here to treat the quantity demanded as depending on the price, and other variables if we want to include these in the equation on the righthand side. Thus all the independent variables in the situation are on the righthand side of the equation.

What about the graph then? As with understanding so many things in life, we have to consider the origins and evolution of this type of representation. Marshall[1] was the first economist to develop this method, at the end of the nineteenth century. However, the purpose of his analysis was different; he wanted to show how equilibrium prices were determined in markets, in terms of the interaction of both demand and supply. Thus he wanted to show how much consumers were prepared to pay for certain quantities, and compare this with the prices that suppliers wanted to receive in order to put such quantities onto the market. In this context it is logical to treat price as a dependent variable; both price and quantity are simultaneously determined by demand and supply, but Marshall and other neoclassical economists were primarily concerned with price determination, since the price mechanism was seen as the key to allocating resources in the economy.

In conclusion we can say that either method of representing the graph or equation is correct, meaning that either price or quantity can be treated as the dependent variable. However, the student needs to be able to switch from one method or treatment to the other, according to convenience; the importance of this will be seen as more material is covered.

Returning to the graphical interpretation of the coefficients, the value of b represents the slope of the demand curve and a represents the vertical intercept *if the graph is drawn with the Q variable on the vertical axis*. If we switch the equation around we obtain:

$$P = 90 - 0.5Q \tag{3.5}$$

In this case the value of -0.5 represents the slope of the demand curve and the value of 90 represents the vertical intercept if the graph is drawn in the customary way, with P on the vertical axis.

3.2.3 Interpretation of equations

In the analysis above the coefficients in the linear two-variable equation have been interpreted in graphical terms. They also have economic interpretations. The value of a represents the maximum sales that will occur if the price is zero. While this interpretation obviously has limited practical application, the interpretation of b is of much greater practical importance. It represents the **marginal effect** of price on quantity demanded. This means that *for every unit the price rises, the quantity demanded will rise by b units*. In the context of the demand equation the value of b will normally be negative. This interpretation can be extended to multiple-variable equations; each coefficient of a variable represents the marginal effect of that variable on quantity demanded. Thus in the equation:

$$Q = a + bP + cY \tag{3.6}$$

the value of c represents the marginal effect of Y (income) on Q.

So far it has been assumed that the demand relationship is linear. This is not because the linear relationship is most common in practice but because the analysis and interpretation of such relationships is the easiest to understand. In reality the demand relationship may take a number of mathematical forms, a topic explored more fully in the next chapter, but a particularly common form is the **power form**. The two-variable expression of this is:

$$Q = aP^b \tag{3.7}$$

This is shown graphically in Figure 3.2; it can be seen that the slope of the demand curve decreases from left to right, as quantity increases. The shape is the same if the axes are reversed, with the slope decreasing as price increases. As with the linear form, the function can be extended to include other variables; in this case the function is multiplicative:

$$Q = aP^b Y^c \tag{3.8}$$

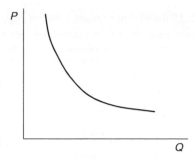

Figure 3.2. Demand graph of power form.

The values of b and c represent elasticities; more specifically, b represents the **price elasticity of demand,** and c represents the **income elasticity of demand**. In the case of the price elasticity of demand this means that *for every 1 per cent the price rises the quantity demanded will rise by* **b** *per cent*. In the case of the income elasticity of demand this means that *for every 1 per cent the income rises the quantity demanded will rise by* **c** *per cent*. This interpretation is explained in greater detail in section 3.5.

Since the interpretation of marginal effects and elasticities is often a source of confusion for students, it is worthwhile at this point to summarize the interpretations of the linear and power forms:

Linear: $Q = a + bP + \ldots$
  b and other coefficients of variables are *marginal effects*.
  For every 1 *unit* P increases Q increases by b *units* (b is normally negative).
Power: $Q = aP^b \ldots$
  b and other coefficients of variables are *elasticities*.
  For every 1 *per cent* P increases Q increases by b *per cent* (again b is negative).

We can also compare and contrast the interpretations of the linear and power forms of demand equation in the following way:

Linear – *constant marginal effects, varying elasticities*
Power – *varying marginal effects, constant elasticities*

There is one other point of interpretation that requires clarification at this stage. Economists talk about **demand curves** and **demand equations**; this sometimes confuses students, who tend to think of a demand curve in purely graphical terms. A demand curve refers not just to a line on a graph but also to a relationship between price and quantity demanded, assuming other things remain equal. Thus it is a particular type of demand equation.

3.2.4 *Demand and revenue*

The demand curve for a firm automatically determines its revenue function, since revenue is simply price multiplied by quantity. As we shall see later in the chapter and elsewhere, the concept of marginal revenue is also very important;

Table 3.2. Demand and revenue relationships

Quantity	Price	Total revenue	Marginal revenue
40	70	2,800	50
			40
60	60	3,600	30
			20
80	50	4,000	10
			0
100	40	4,000	−10
			−20
120	30	3,600	−30

this was introduced in the last chapter with reference to the profit-maximizing model, being defined as the additional revenue derived from selling an extra unit. We can now rearrange and expand the information in Table 3.1 to show how total and marginal revenue can be measured. The table is rearranged because revenue and marginal revenue are normally considered as functions of quantity rather than price, as explained in more detail in Chapter 8. It should be noted that marginal revenue can be calculated in two different ways, which must not be confused:

1 $\triangle R/\triangle Q$ – Thus when quantity changes from 40 to 60

$$MR = (3600 - 2800)/(60 - 40) = 40.$$

These values are given in bold in Table 3.2 and inserted between the quantities of 40 and 60.

2 dR/dQ – This is the derivative of the revenue function.

$$\text{Since} \quad P = 90 - 0.5Q$$
$$R = PQ = 90Q = 0.5Q^2$$
$$MR = 90 - Q$$

These values are given by substituting the value of Q into the MR function and are written directly opposite the relevant values of Q in the table. The graphs of total and marginal revenue functions are illustrated in section 3.5.

3.3 Consumer theory

This area of economic theory is concerned with explaining why consumers behave in certain ways, in particular with how the variables of price and income affect what consumers buy and how much. While it may be true that managers and business-owners are often not interested in this theoretical background and analysis, being more concerned with demand responsiveness to changes in different variables, this theoretical framework is still useful in explaining both motivation and behaviour. Some of the conclusions and implications in terms of economic welfare are particularly relevant for government policy. As in the previous chapters, a largely neoclassical approach is taken here, and this is the traditional approach taken in both microeconomics and managerial economics textbooks. However, it will be seen that this can be extended to apply to a broader range of situations. At the start a basic model is presented.

3.3.1 Assumptions

The most basic assumption of the neoclassical model is that consumers have the objective of **maximizing their total utility**. Utility is defined in terms of value or satisfaction. This is derived from consuming combinations of different products. These products are purchased from what is assumed to be a fixed amount of money available; thus there is a **budget constraint** on consumers' purchasing, which is largely determined by current income, although other factors like past saving, expectations of future income and the availability and cost of credit are relevant. Thus the general situation from a consumer's viewpoint is an optimization problem subject to constraints.

The initial analysis of this situation involves using graphs and **indifference curves**. The use of graphs limits the analysis to a two-variable situation, a helpful initial assumption. An indifference curve shows *combinations of two products between which the consumer is indifferent because they give the same total utility*. It is worth noting that with this approach the concept of utility does not have to be measured in **cardinal** terms, only in **ordinal** terms. This means that we do not have to use an **interval** scale for measurement, as with price or quantity; with an interval scale the difference between 4 and 5 units is the same as the difference between 9 and 10 units in absolute terms because the interval is the same. With an ordinal scale values are simply ranked in order, without saying anything about the differences between the values. In terms of indifference curves, one combination of products may be preferred to another, but no attempt is made to measure the amount of the difference. This avoids the problem of trying to measure utility; although utility can be measured in money terms this is not totally satisfactory because of the non-constant relationship between utility and money (for example, having twice as much money does not necessarily give twice as much utility).

A graph showing three indifference curves, I_1, I_2 and I_3, is shown in Figure 3.3. Each indifference curve can be regarded as an 'iso-utility' curve; this means that any combination of products on I_1, for example, gives the same total utility to the consumer. It is assumed that consumers prefer more of a product to less; therefore, indifference curves that are higher and to the right represent greater total utility. Thus combination C gives more total utility than either A or B, both of which give the same total utility. The indifference curves shown represent only a sample of such curves for the consumer; there is an infinite number of curves that could be drawn in principle, each with a slightly higher

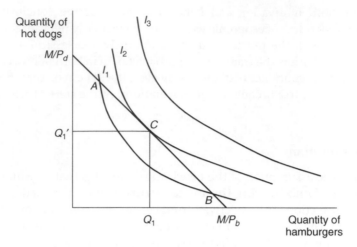

Figure 3.3. Indifference curves and consumer equilibrium.

level of total utility than its neighbour to the left. A graph showing such a sample is often referred to as an **indifference map**.

In drawing the indifference curves above it may be noted that they possess three main properties; these are now explained, along with the relevant assumptions regarding consumer behaviour:

1. *Negative slope*. This follows from the assumption that consumers prefer more of a product to less, as stated above, so that in obtaining more of one product a consumer can afford to give up some of the other product to maintain the same level of total utility. This assumption is sometimes referred to as **non-satiation**, but it should be realized that there are exceptions to this: garbage and nuclear waste are examples, and such products are sometimes called 'bads' as opposed to goods.

2. *Convexity*. This means that the slopes of the curves are decreasing as one moves to the right. The absolute value of the slope is given by the **marginal rate of substitution** of one good for another, in this case of hamburgers for hot dogs, or in general, MRS_{XY}. The **MRS_{XY} is the marginal rate of substitution between X and Y and refers to the amount of Y that a consumer is prepared to give up to gain one more unit of X**. It has to be said that there is a certain amount of confusion in the textbooks regarding this expression. Some texts omit subscripts completely, while others mistakenly refer to MRS_{YX} in the above context. The confusion is understandable since we can refer to either giving up Y for X or substituting X for Y, meaning the same thing. Thus the assumption implies that people are willing to give up less and less of one product to gain more of another. This in turn follows from the **law of diminishing marginal utility** which states that *as people consume more of a product within a given time period, eventually the increments in total utility will begin to fall*. This law is demonstrated in Figure 3.4: the consumer is willing to give up three hot dogs to get one more hamburger when they only

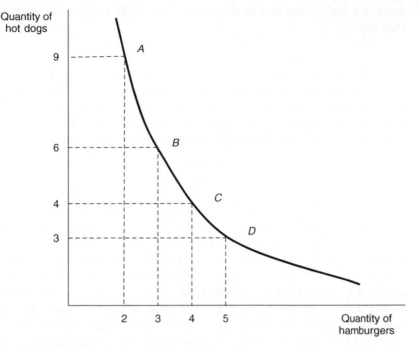

Figure 3.4. Indifference curves and convexity.

have two hamburgers (MRS_{XY} is 3 in moving from A to B), but they are only willing to give up two hot dogs to get one more hamburger when they already have three hamburgers (MRS_{XY} is 2 in moving from B to C); they are only willing to give up one hot dog to get one more hamburger when they already have four hamburgers (MRS_{XY} is 1 in moving from C to D).

3. *Non-intersection.* Indifference curves can never intersect as this would violate the principle of **transitivity** of preferences. Transitivity means that if combination F is preferred to combination E and combination E is preferred to combination D, then combination F must be preferred to combination D. An example of non-transitivity is the paper–rock–scissors game; rock beats scissors and scissors beats paper, but rock does not beat paper.

This now concludes the section regarding assumptions; in order to explain the remaining features of Figure 3.3 it is necessary to move on to the analytical aspects.

3.3.2 *Analysis*

a. *Consumer equilibrium*

In order to find the consumer's equilibrium point in Figure 3.3, where total utility is maximized, it is necessary to combine the indifference curve map with the consumer's **budget line**. A budget line shows *the maximum combinations of products that can be purchased with a fixed sum of money, given fixed* *prices for the products.* The equation of the budget line is in general terms given by:

$$M = P_X X + P_Y Y \qquad (3.9)$$

where the budget of the consumer is given by M. If the consumer spends the whole amount on hamburgers they will be able to buy the quantity M/P_b. Similarly, if they spend their whole budget on hot dogs they will be able to buy the quantity M/P_d. The budget line will therefore be linear and have negative slope; the absolute magnitude of the slope is given by:

$$\frac{M/P_d}{M/P_b} = P_b/P_d \qquad (3.10)$$

In general terms the budget line has the slope P_X/P_Y. In order to maximize utility the consumer must be on the highest indifference curve possible for a given budget. Thus, although with budget M the consumer could just afford to consume at point A or point B on I_1, they will be better off consuming combination C on I_2. This will represent their equilibrium point, where their budget line is tangential to the indifference curve.

The slope of an indifference curve can also be derived. When the consumer moves from point A to B they gain utility from consuming more hamburgers given by $\Delta Q_b \times MU_b$ where ΔQ_b represents the increase in number of hamburgers purchased, and MU_b represents the marginal utility of the additional hamburgers. The consumer also loses utility from consuming fewer hot dogs given by $\Delta Q_d \times MU_d$. Since the points are on the same indifference curve and therefore must give the same total utility, the gains must equal the losses, thus

$$\Delta Q_b \times MU_b = \Delta Q_d \times MU_d \qquad (3.11)$$

Since the slope of the indifference curve is given by $\Delta Q_d / \Delta Q_b$, and from (3.11) we can express ΔQ_b as $\Delta Q_d \times MU_d/MU_b$, we can now express the absolute magnitude of the slope as:

$$\Delta Q_d/(\Delta Q_d \times MU_d/MU_b) = MU_b/MU_d \qquad (3.12)$$

In more general terms this slope is given by MU_X / MU_Y.

The consumer's equilibrium can now be derived as follows. At equilibrium the slopes of the budget line and the indifference curve are equal, thus:

$$P_b/P_d = MU_b/MU_d \qquad \text{or generally} \quad P_X/P_Y = MU_X/MU_Y \qquad (3.13)$$

This means that a consumer should spend their budget so that the ratio of the prices of the goods should equal the ratio of the marginal utilities of the last units purchased. This is easier to understand if the expression is rearranged as:

$$MU_X/P_X = MU_Y/P_Y \qquad (3.14)$$

The interpretation of this is that *a consumer should spend so that the marginal utility of the last unit of money spent on each product is the same*. This

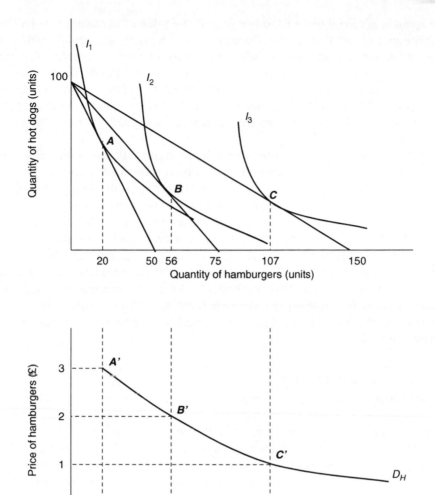

Figure 3.5. Derivation of demand curve from indifference curve analysis.

interpretation can easily be extended to the more realistic situation where a consumer is allocating a budget among many competing products.

b. Derivation of the demand curve

We have seen in section 3.2 that a demand curve describes the relationship between prices and quantity demanded per time period, other things remaining equal. At that point it was assumed that the curve was downward-sloping, but we are now in a position to prove this and derive the demand curve using indifference curve analysis. In Figure 3.5 it is assumed that the price of hot dogs remains the same whereas the price of hamburgers changes. The budget to be spent is assumed to be £150 per year. If the price of hamburgers is £3 the maximum number that can be afforded is 50 (with no hot dogs purchased), but the consumer will maximize their total utility at point A, representing 20 hamburgers. If the price is reduced to £2 the consumer can afford a maximum of 75 hamburgers, but will achieve equilibrium at point B, representing 56 hamburgers. If the price is further reduced to £1 the maximum number that can be purchased rises to 150, but the equilibrium is at point C, representing 107 hamburgers.

It can now be seen that as the price of hamburgers falls so the quantity that the consumer wants to buy will increase, which confirms the law of demand stated earlier. The graph in Figure 3.4 applies to a single individual; in managerial economics we are normally more interested in the demand curve for a firm or market. In principle this can be obtained by adding together all the quantities demanded by the different consumers at each price. Thus if Smith and Jones constitute the market for hamburgers, and at the price of £3 Smith wants to buy 20 hamburgers while Jones wants to buy 30, the quantity demanded by the market at £3 is 50. This method of derivation (sometimes called the 'market build-up' method) is tedious if there are a lot of customers in the market; in this case the methods of estimation described in Chapter 4 are more appropriate.

c. Income and substitution effects*

When the price of a product changes there are actually two different effects of this on the quantity demanded. In most cases these will reinforce each other by acting in the same direction. Thus when the price of hamburgers falls both the substitution and income effects may cause quantity to rise. The use of indifference curve analysis enables these effects to be separated from each other to see the direction and relative importance of each one. This aspect may be of little importance to most managers or business analysts, but it does have some important welfare implications that can affect government policy, as seen in Chapter 12.

The **income effect** of a price change arises because the real income, in other words purchasing power, of the consumer is affected. With a price fall, the income effect is that the real income of the consumer is increased; if the good is a **normal good** they will *consume more of that good when their income increases*, thus causing a negative relationship between price and quantity demanded. Economists refer to goods as being 'normal' if more is consumed when income increases and vice versa. However, there are some products, referred to as **inferior goods,** where *consumers buy less of the good when their income increases*; in this case they are switching to buying better quality products. Examples from empirical studies include bread, margarine, beer and public transport, although it should be stressed that these products are only inferior in certain situations, not generally. In the case of inferior products the income effect is positive, as a price fall reduces quantity demanded.

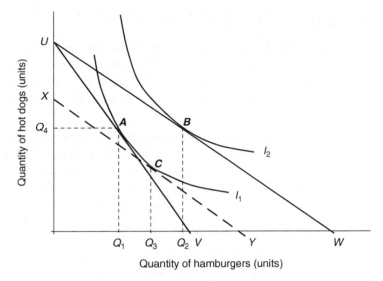

Figure 3.6. Income and substitution effects.

The **substitution effect** on the other hand is always negative. Consumers will always switch to buying more of the product if its price falls, other things including income being equal. The method of separating the income and substitution effects of a price change is to draw a **compensated budget line**. The approach is illustrated in Figure 3.6. In this case the price of hamburgers is falling (while the price of hot dogs stays the same), thus causing the consumer's budget line to rotate counter-clockwise from UV to UW. The original equilibrium at point A, corresponding to Q_1 hamburgers, now shifts to point B, corresponding to Q_2 hamburgers. Thus there is a total increase in quantity demanded of $Q_2 - Q_1$.

Now the income effect of the price reduction can be compensated for by shifting the budget line to the left, keeping it parallel to the new budget line UW. There are two different approaches to doing this: the more common one, used in Figure 3.6, compensates the consumer by maintaining their total utility at the original level, shown by indifference curve I_1. This is sometimes referred to as the Hicks[2] approach. In this case the compensated budget line is shown by XY, which is *parallel to the new budget line UW* and *tangential to the original indifference curve* I_1. The alternative approach, associated with Slutsky, is to compensate the consumer by allowing them to buy the same combination of goods as originally purchased, thus maintaining their real income constant; in this case the compensated budget line would still be parallel to UW, but pass through point A.

Using the Hicks approach it can be seen that the substitution effect involves a movement along I_1 from A to C; thus the substitution effect is given by $Q_3 - Q_1$. The shift from C to B represents an income effect; thus the quantity $Q_2 - Q_3$ is an income effect.

3.3.3 Limitations

The approach to consumer theory taken so far in this section has many advantages. It explains a number of features of behaviour that are observable in practice and it makes possible many testable predictions, at least in general terms. However, there are some serious shortcomings of the model, particularly in its basic form:

1 *Concentration on price.* This is the same problem as with the basic model of the theory of the firm. Other aspects of the marketing mix are ignored. In fact the model predicts that advertising should not affect demand, since consumers are rational and have perfect information regarding products. Furthermore the model ignores the importance of product quality in affecting demand.

2 *Search costs.* Consumers have to obtain information regarding price, quality and availability of products and there is a cost attached to this. For inexpensive products that are bought frequently habit formation is important, since this reduces search costs. In other situations, consumers may use price as an indicator of quality, particularly in the absence of other quality cues, again to reduce search costs and uncertainty.

3 *Rationality.* It is sometimes argued, particularly by behaviourists, that humans rarely make the relevant computations that are necessitated by the neoclassical model, particularly with practical time constraints. Instead behaviour is impulsive and satisficing. This aspect was discussed in Chapter 2, in connection with the concept of bounded rationality.

In view of the above criticisms it is worth considering some alternative approaches to the traditional model.

3.3.4 Alternative approaches*

Two approaches will be reviewed here: the first is concerned with the first limitation above, while the second is concerned with the last two. Both approaches are described only briefly; to do them both justice would require at least another two chapters, but some of the main scholars in each area are mentioned for reference purposes.

a. Characteristics approach

This was originally developed by Lancaster;[3] he argued that consumer preferences are based not on goods as such but on characteristics of those goods. It can be summed up by a pithy quotation attributed to Revlon: 'in the factory, we make cosmetics; in the store we sell hope.' Since Lancaster, many marketing scholars have taken up the theme in various ways, notably Howard and Sheth,[4] Green and Wind[5] and Myers and Alpert.[6] Most of these approaches involve identifying and measuring product attributes in various ways and developing models with different criteria for consumer choice between products. For example, an **expectancy value** model predicts that consumers will favour a product that maximizes the sum of the weighted attribute scores. Other criteria for evaluating and selecting products involve 'ideal brand' models, conjunctive, disjunctive and lexicographic models. It is not appropriate to discuss these here, but they are explained in any good marketing text.

Lancaster's original approach was somewhat different in that it emphasized the importance of attributes from the point of view of the firm launching new products, particularly in terms of pricing strategy. A firm had to determine first of all what constituted the main competitive products; then it had to identify the relevant product characteristics and measure these compared with those of its own proposed product. Finally it could calculate what prices it needed to charge in order to dominate these other products, i.e. be superior in at least one characteristic without being inferior in any other. The firm could also estimate **implicit prices**: these are *the prices consumers have to pay to gain an additional unit of a characteristic*. Thus Lancaster's approach was particularly useful in identifying competitive products, determining pricing strategy and determining the feasibility of new products.

b. Irrationality theories

There are a number of different theories in the area of irrationality. One example is **prospect theory**. This was originally developed by Kahneman and Tversky[7] and is based on various findings of psychological research. As seen in Chapter 2, the main claims of this theory are that people do not measure risk consistently and regularly miscalculate probabilities. In particular they have asymmetric attitudes to gains and losses, being **loss averse**. This means that they obtain less utility from gaining £100, for example, than they would lose if they lost £100. This affects the demand for gambling and insurance. People also tend to **compartmentalize**, meaning that they tend to view decisions in isolation, rather than as part of a whole framework; this can lead to inconsistency in decision-making.

A considerable body of research, by both psychologists and economists, has shown that much decision-making involves the emotions, which can seemingly lead to irrationality. Frank,[8] in particular, has examined this connection. In various experiments, like the 'ultimatum bargaining game', people were found to act irrationally if their sense of 'fairness' was offended. In this game John is given £100 in cash and told to share it with Jim. John must say how much he intends to give Jim and, if Jim refuses the offer, neither person will get anything at all. If Jim accepts the offer, then he gets the amount John has offered. The 'rational' action for John, assuming he thinks Jim is also 'rational', is to offer Jim a tiny amount, like £1, and keep the remaining £99. Jim, if he is 'rational', should accept the £1, since if he refuses the offer he will get nothing. In practice Frank found that not only do very few people in John's position make such a small offer, but also even fewer will accept such offers in

Jim's position. The most common offer made was £50. Frank concluded that a sense of fairness was involved here, and that John had to show that he was committed to being a fair person and therefore should be trusted in any transaction.

There is another dimension to this situation to be considered: John offers Jim £50 because he knows Jim will refuse a lower offer. Jim refuses a low offer because he does not want to be perceived as a 'soft touch'. Therefore, although it might seem to be in Jim's short-run best interest to accept a low offer as being better than nothing, it may not be in Jim's long-run best interest to do so since others may try to take advantage of him in the future. This type of situation is discussed in much more detail in Chapter 9, in connection with game theory.

Thus consumers may act 'irrationally' if they feel they are being 'gouged' by sellers, i.e. they might not buy even if the marginal utility of consumption exceeds the price. Furthermore, various researchers like Elster and Damasio[9] have concluded that emotions are a necessary part of our psychological make-up; without them we become indecisive, depressed and social misfits. In Frank's model they are necessary to ensure commitment, to convince other people that we are trustworthy, so that they will engage in transactions with us.

3.3.5 Conclusions

Some of the main objections to the neoclassical model have now been explained and alternative approaches discussed. However, it was seen in the previous chapter that the neoclassical model can be very versatile in the sense that it can be extended to overcome many of the initial shortcomings of the basic model. This again applies in the context of consumer behaviour.

Taking the characteristics approach first, although the neoclassical model places an undue emphasis on price, the expectancy value model is very much in keeping with the utility-maximizing tradition. The criticisms relating to rationality are harder to deal with, but a number of economists are now incorporating 'irrational' behaviour into their models. Becker,[10] for example, has claimed that a downward-sloping demand curve can still be derived on the basis of irrational behaviour.[11] Other economists have even extended this analysis to animal behaviour, showing that a downward-sloping demand curve applies in this context also.

Indeed, much modern research into motivation and behaviour is now coming from biologists and evolutionary psychologists. Important relationships between Darwinian natural selection or modern 'selfish gene' theory and neoclassical economics are not difficult to find. Many economists are now taking the approach that much behaviour that was previously seen as irrational, like tipping a waiter that you never expect to see again, or doing charity work, is indeed rational if seen from a broader viewpoint, in other words considering our evolutionary history. For example, Smith[12] has introduced some developments and variations on Frank's ultimatum bargaining games and concluded that a rational reciprocity underlies people's motivation. This indicates that it pays to have morality and emotions, because the resulting 'irrational' behaviour is actually in our rational self-interest in the long run. The challenge is to be able to model these more complicated patterns of behaviour.

3.4 Factors determining demand

This section is concerned with identifying the factors which affect the quantity demanded of a product, describing the nature of these factors, examining how they can be measured, and examining the relationship with quantity demanded. These factors can be considered in terms of a demand function:

$$Q = f(P, L, A, D, Y, \ldots) \tag{3.15}$$

where each symbol on the righthand side denotes a relevant factor. P refers to price, L to quality, A to advertising spending, D to distribution spending and Y to the average income of the market.

It is useful from a managerial decision-making viewpoint to distinguish between controllable and uncontrollable factors. Controllable in this context means controllable by the firm; the distinction in practice between what can be controlled and what cannot is somewhat blurred, as will be seen. The relevant factors are summarized in Figure 3.7.

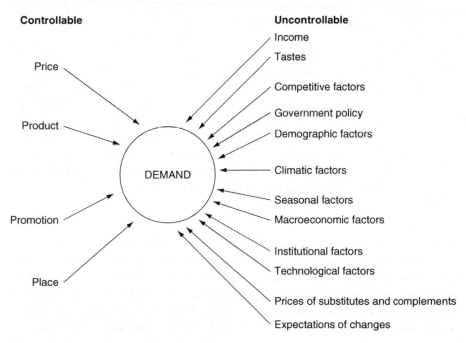

Figure 3.7. Factors determining demand.

3.4.1 Controllable factors

These correspond to what are often referred to as the marketing-mix variables.

a. Price

The nature of price has been discussed above, in terms of how it can be measured and how it affects the quantity demanded. A further aspect of the nature of price, as an indicator of quality, will be considered in Chapter 4, in terms of the implications of empirical studies. The firm may well be a multi-product firm, in which case the prices of its other products are also relevant, since they are often substitutes or complements. This factor is discussed in the context of 'uncontrollable factors'.

b. Product

It is the perceived quality of the product that affects quantity demanded. In practice there are two problems of measurement. The first of these is subjectivity: different consumers perceive quality differently. The second is multidimensionality which is now discussed at greater length.

Products often have many different attributes, as was mentioned in the previous section. This is particularly obvious for expensive and hi-tech products. With mobile phones, for example, a consumer may be looking for a good design, small size and weight, multiple features, a good complementary network, a good brand name, a good warranty, and so on. Even with an inexpensive product like toothpaste, consumers may be looking not just for something to clean their teeth, but also something that whitens their teeth, smells fresh, prevents decay and plaque and comes in a convenient dispenser. Marketing professionals and researchers often make use of multidimensional scaling in this situation. Consumers are asked to rate a product on a range of characteristics, giving a score for each one. Such questionnaires have to be carefully designed in order to include all the relevant factors; they also involve assumptions regarding the relative importance of the factors in terms of their weighting. Sometimes the unit cost of production is used as an approximate measure of quality; this again may not be an accurate indicator of quality, since it may be more a reflection of the efficiency of the firm.

c. Promotion

This refers to communication by the firm with its intended customers, ultimately aimed at persuading them to buy the product. The main components of the promotion-mix are customarily identified as: advertising, personal selling, publicity and sales promotion. Sometimes other elements are included separately, like direct marketing or packaging. These are usually measured in terms of expenditure and there is a direct relationship with quantity demanded.

d. Place

This is not a very apt description of what is involved here. It refers to distribution strategy, in particular the selection of distribution channels. This is again measured in terms of expenditure and again there is a direct relationship with quantity demanded.

In summary, the last three components of the marketing mix can all be considered as costs, while price is the only component that contributes directly to revenue; its relationship with revenue depends on price elasticity and this is examined in section 3.5.

3.4.2 Uncontrollable factors

These generally are external or environmental, and include a wide variety of factors whose relative importance varies from one product to another.

a. Income

This is a very important factor affecting quantity demanded for the majority of goods. Although it is expressed numerically there are a number of measurement problems. First of all, economists measure income in a number of different ways. The measure that is usually the most relevant to determining demand is personal disposable income (PDI). Although most governments or governmental agencies publish reliable figures relating to this on a regular basis, these are on a national basis and are therefore only strictly applicable to firms that have national markets. It is the average personal disposable income of the market for the firm that is relevant. There is thus a measurement problem if the firm has only a small market, because of the difficulty in obtaining relevant information; this is easier for national markets, or at least regional markets. In the situation where a firm has a small market, or one that is difficult to identify in terms of geographical area or otherwise, some proxy income variable may have to be used. For example, a shop selling products to just a small area or customer base within London may have to use average income in London as a proxy variable. The relationship with quantity demanded can be direct or inverse depending on whether the product is normal or inferior, as discussed in the previous section.

b. Tastes

These are difficult to define and measure, because they relate to subjective preferences and are multidimensional, just like perceived quality, which they influence. They can vary considerably both **intertemporally** and **interspatially**. *Intertemporal variations are variations over time*; these apply especially to products whose demand is affected by fashion. This refers not just to clothes, but to other consumer products like entertainment, food and sports. Examples of products where fashion has caused big increases in demand are micro-scooters, teletubby dolls (Barney dolls in the United States), computer games, adventure sports and Viagra. Of course, demand for these products can also fall rapidly when they go out of fashion, like a yo-yo (another good example). These trends in fashion may be recurrent over time.

Inter-spatial variations are variations from place to place, especially from country to country. Good examples of products where tastes vary from country to country are beer, Coke, ketchup, TV programmes and Marks & Spencer (see Case 3.1). Much of this variation arises because of socio-cultural factors. Of course, tastes are not an entirely uncontrollable factor; firms try to influence tastes through their advertising. Cigarette advertising is an example of this, and this is one factor that causes governments to regulate it. This leads us straight into the next factor.

c. Government policy

This has both micro- and macroeconomic effects. The first of these are considered here. Governments often want to discourage us from buying certain products and sometimes to encourage us to buy more of other products. The reasons for this are examined in Chapter 12. Examples of the first category are cigarettes, alcohol, many other drugs (as opposed to medicines, which are in the second category, even though in practice the distinction may be very difficult to draw), weapons, products whose consumption or production causes environmental damage, and sometimes pornography and foreign goods. Goods in the second category are often their opposites. There are many policy instruments in either case: bans, indirect taxes/subsidies, health warnings, promotion regulations, licences, age restrictions, restrictions on times and places of consumption. It is important to distinguish between policies primarily affecting supply, like the first two, and those affecting demand. The fact that indirect taxes (or subsidies) do not affect demand is explained in the next subsection.

d. Competitive factors

This refers to the marketing mix of competitors. Price is not the only relevant factor here because firms often compete in other ways. This non-price competition occurs particularly in oligopolistic markets, for reasons that will be explained in Chapter 8. An example of this is the competition between Coke and Pepsi, who have a virtual duopoly of the cola market. The competition between them occurs mainly in terms of promotion and distribution.

e. Demographic factors

These refer not only to the size of population, but also to its structure. In particular the ageing of the population affects demand in many ways because older people demand more health services and pensions. This has important implications for government policy and the taxpayer.

f. Climatic factors

Weather, rainfall, temperature and also terrain are important. In Canada, for example, there is a greater demand for snow shovels, snow tyres and chains, salt for the roads and rust-proofing for cars.

g. Seasonal factors

These refer to any regular, repeated pattern in demand. Many products have a demand that varies according to season of the year, like air travel, hotels, car rental, jewellery and restaurants. The latter also has a monthly pattern (more people eat out at the beginning of the month when they have more cash), a weekly pattern (more people eat out at weekends) and a daily pattern. Many products have a daily pattern in demand, for example public transport, electricity, telephone calls and health clubs. This also has implications for pricing; many firms use peak and off-peak pricing. This will be examined in more detail in Chapter 10.

h. Macroeconomic factors

These include income, discussed earlier, and also interest rates, exchange rates, inflation rates and unemployment rates. If interest rates fall, for example, this may affect demand for two reasons: many homeowners have mortgages and the falling interest rate will increase their **discretionary income**. This is the income that they have available to buy non-necessities. Thus they will buy more of most (normal) goods. In addition, the demand for consumer durables will be increased, since these are often bought on credit and will therefore be in effect cheaper. Government policy obviously affects these macroeconomic factors to some degree.

i. Institutional factors

These include a wide variety of effects; the physical infrastructure of roads, railways and telecommunications is relevant, so are political systems, legal systems, education systems, housing systems, religious systems and family systems. For example, a country that has a poor transportation infrastructure will have a low demand for cars; a country with low literacy levels will have a relatively low demand for newspapers and magazines.

j. Technological factors

These primarily affect supply but also affect demand indirectly; this is best explained with an example. Mobile phones will again serve this purpose. Before the 1980s the concept of a truly mobile phone was still in the realm of science fiction, because the technology was not available. Thus consumers had not taken time to consider the potential of such a product and there was no real demand. As advancing technology made possible smaller, lighter, more effective and cheaper products, consumers had a true chance to evaluate the potential of the product and then demand began to increase accordingly.

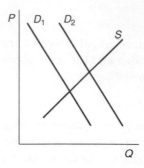

Figure 3.8. Change in demand.

k. Price of substitutes and complements

A substitute is a product with similar perceived functions or attributes; cars and public transport are substitutes. If the price of public transport were to rise this would increase the demand for cars, other things being equal. Complementary products are consumed together in some way; cars and petrol are complements. If the price of petrol were to rise this would reduce the demand for cars, other things being equal. Thus in the case of substitutes the relationship is positive, while in the case of complements the relationship is negative.

l. Expectations of changes in any of the above factors

If any factor, controllable or uncontrollable, is expected to change in the future, this can affect current sales. For example, it has been estimated that car sales in the UK in 2000 were 300,000 units lower than they otherwise would have been because prices were expected to fall. Similarly, expectations of changes in income, climate, government policy and competitive factors can all affect current demand.

3.4.3 Demand and quantity demanded

As already mentioned in the first section of this chapter, the failure to distinguish between these is very common and causes errors of analysis. The following explanation, graphs and example are intended to clarify this distinction.

a. Type of change: demand

    1 *Graphical Representation*: Shifts in the demand curve (Figure 3.8)
    2 *Cause*: Changes in any factor affecting the quantity demanded apart from price.

b. Type of change: quantity demanded

    1 *Graphical representation*: Movements along the demand curve (Figure 3.9)
    2 *Cause*: Changes in price, which are in turn caused by changes in costs and supply.

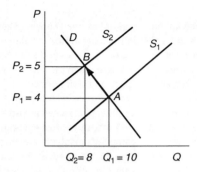

Figure 3.9. Change in quantity demanded.

A good example illustrating the difference between the two cases is the effect of an indirect tax. It is sometimes claimed that a tax on cigarettes will reduce the demand. This is untrue; such a claim would relate to the first case above (a change in demand), but with the demand curve shifting to the left, *reducing* the price. In fact we know that the price increases. This is because the increase in an indirect tax falls into the second category above (a change in quantity demanded). It increases the marginal costs of production, thus shifting the supply curve upwards and to the left. This increases the price (from P_1 to P_2) and reduces the quantity demanded (from Q_1 to Q_2).

Case study 3.1: Marks & Spencer

Does M&S have a future?[13]

The country's most famous retailer Marks & Spencer's big store in London's Kensington High Street has just had a re-fit. Instead of the usual drab M&S interior, it is now Californian shopping mall meets modernist chrome and creamy marble floors. Roomy walkways and designer displays have replaced dreary row after row of clothes racks. By the end of the year M&S will have 26 such stores around Britain – the first visible sign that the company is making a serious effort to pull out of the nose-dive it has been in for the past two years.

Things have become so bad that M&S, until recently a national icon, is in danger of becoming a national joke. It does not help that its advertisements featuring plump naked women on mountains – the first-ever TV ads the company has produced – have met with an embarrassed titter; nor that, last week, the BBC's Watchdog programme savaged M&S for overcharging and poor quality in its range of garments for the fuller figure.

As the attacks grow in intensity, so do the doubts about M&S's ability to protect its core value: a reputation for better quality that justified a slight price premium – at least in basic items, such as underwear. It is a long time since any self-respecting teenager went willingly into an M&S store to buy clothes. Now even parents have learned to say no. Shoppers in their thirties and forties used to dress like their parents. Now many of them want to dress like their kids.

M&S's makeover comes not a moment too soon. Compared with the jazzy store layouts of rivals such as Gap or Hennes & Mauritz, M&S shops look like a hangover from a bygone era. The makeover aims to bring it into the present.

People tended to join M&S straight from college and work their way slowly up the ranks. Few senior appointments were made from outside the company. This meant that the company rested on its laurels, harking back to 'innovations' such as machine-washable pullovers and chilled food.

Worse, M&S missed out on the retailing revolution that began in the mid-1980s, when the likes of Gap and Next shook up the industry with attractive displays and marketing gimmicks. Their supply chains were overhauled to provide what customers were actually buying – a surprisingly radical idea at the time.

M&S, by contrast, continued with an outdated business model. It clung to its 'Buy British' policy and it based its buying decisions too rigidly on its own buyers' guesses about what ranges of clothes would sell, rather than reacting quickly to results from the tills. Meanwhile, its competitors were putting together global purchasing networks that were not only more responsive, but were not locked into high costs linked to the strength of sterling.

In clothing, moreover, M&S faces problems that cannot be solved simply by improving its fashion judgments. Research indicates that overall demand for clothing has at best stabilised and may be set to decline. This is because changing demographics mean that an ever-higher share of consumer spending is being done by the affluent over-45s. They are less inclined than youngsters to spend a high proportion of their disposable income on clothes.

The results of M&S's rigid management approach were not confined to clothes. The company got an enormous boost 30 years ago when it spotted a gap in the food market, and started selling fancy convenience foods. Its success in this area capitalised on the fact that, compared with clothes, food generates high revenues per square metre of floor space. While food takes up 15% of the floor space in M&S's stores, it accounts for around 40% of sales. But the company gradually lost its advantage as mainstream food chains copied its formula. M&S's share of the British grocery market is under 3% and falling, compared with around 18% for its biggest supermarket rival, Tesco.

M&S has been unable to respond to this competitive challenge. In fact, rather than leading the way, it has been copying rivals' features by introducing in-house bakeries, delicatessens and meat counters. Food sales have been sluggish, and operating margins have fallen as a result of the extra space and staff needed for these services. Operating profits from food fell from £247m in 1997 to £137m in 1999, while sales stayed flat.

Perhaps the most egregious example of the company's insularity was the way it held out for more than 20 years against the use of credit cards, launching its own store card instead. This was the cornerstone of a new financial-services division, also selling personal loans, insurance and unit-trust investments. When, in April this year, M&S eventually bowed to the inevitable and began accepting credit cards, it stumbled yet again. It had to give away around 3% of its revenues from card transactions to the card companies, but failed to generate a big enough increase in sales to offset this. Worse, it had to slash the interest rate on its own card, undermining the core of its own finance business. And this at a time when the credit-card business was already becoming more competitive, with new entrants offering rates as low as 5%.

If shrunk to its profitable core, M&S may become an attractive target for another big retailer. At the moment, however, while its food division may be attractive to the likes of Tesco, the clothing side represents a daunting challenge. Why take the risk now, when the brand may be damaged beyond repair?

Questions

1 Identify the main factors affecting the demand for M&S products.
2 Analyse the weaknesses and threats on the demand side of M&S, relating these to controllable and uncontrollable factors.

3.5 Elasticity

Elasticity in general terms is concerned with *the responsiveness or sensitivity of one variable to changes in another*. Demand elasticity is concerned with how the quantity demanded is responsive to changes in any of the factors described in section 3.4. Essentially elasticities are an alternative way of measuring responsiveness to the marginal effects discussed in the first section of this chapter; however, they have the advantage that they allow more meaningful comparisons between different products because they are measured in relative terms, meaning percentages, rather than in absolute units. Theoretically we could discuss elasticities for all the different controllable and uncontrollable factors affecting demand but in practice there are four main types of elasticity that tend to be measured and examined, corresponding to four particularly important factors in the demand function: **price, promotion, income** and the **price of a related product**:

$$Q = f(P, A, Y, P') \qquad (3.16)$$

Each of the above elasticities needs to be analysed in terms of:

a. definition
b. measurement
c. range of values
d. determinants
e. use and applications.

3.5.1 Price elasticity

a. Definition

PED is the *percentage change in quantity demanded in response to a 1 per cent change in price*. In symbols we can write:

$$PED = \%\Delta Q / \%\Delta P \qquad (3.17)$$

b. Measurement

The reader should be warned at this point that the following material will appear highly abstract at first, and for many people will only start to make sense when it is applied to the kinds of problem discussed later on in the chapter.

The definition in (3.16) is the easiest one to use for measurement. Referring to Figure 3.9, in the previous section, if price is raised from 4 to 5 units (the units do not matter):

$$PED \text{ from } A \text{ to } B = -20/+25 = -0.8.$$

The interpretation of this value is that for every 1 per cent rise in price there is a 0.8 per cent fall in the quantity demanded. However, there is a measurement problem here, because if we now reverse the price change and reduce the price to 4, the calculation is as follows:

$$PED \text{ from } B \text{ to } A = +25/-20 = -1.25.$$

Therefore this measure of PED (termed the **simple** PED) is *inconsistent*; later on it will also be shown to be *inaccurate*. The reason for this is the *changing* *base* for the percentage calculation. It is therefore better in terms of consistency and accuracy to use a measure involving average prices and quantities. Thus

$$\%\Delta Q = \frac{\Delta Q}{(Q_1 + Q_2)/2} = -2/9 = -22.22$$

and

$$\%\Delta P = \frac{\Delta P}{(P_1 + P_2)/2} = 1/4.5 = 22.22$$

Therfore in the above example $PED = -1$, both from A to B and from B to A; this measure of PED is termed the **adjusted** PED. The procedure above can be simplified by deriving the formula:

$$PED = \frac{\Delta Q}{\Delta P} \times \frac{P_1 + P_2}{Q_1 + Q_2}$$
$$= \frac{-2}{1} \times \frac{4 + 5}{10 + 8} = -1 \text{ (as before)} \tag{3.18}$$

It can easily be verified that the same result is obtained if the price change is from 5 to 4 units.

The above measures, both simple and adjusted, are called measures of **arc elasticity**, because they *apply between two points or values*. Sometimes we want to measure elasticity at a single point or price, and this is appropriate when we are considering the effect of a very small price change. This can be done using a **point elasticity**, and involves the concept of limits and derivatives. The relevant formula becomes:

$$PED = \frac{\partial Q}{\partial P} \times \frac{P}{Q} \tag{3.19}$$

where $\partial Q/\partial P$ represents the **partial derivative of Q with respect to P**. This mathematical concept of a partial derivative has an important economic interpretation, which follows from the material in section 3.2: it represents *the marginal effect of price on quantity, assuming other factors affecting demand remain the same*. Normally this partial derivative is calculated by differentiating the demand function, in this case:

$$Q = 18 - 2P$$

Therefore at A:

$$PED = -2 \times 4/10 = -0.8$$

and at B:

$$PED = -2 \times 5/8 = -1.25$$

This shows that the PED varies along the linear demand curve.

Table 3.3. Range of values for PED

|PED|	Demand	Interpretation
>1	Elastic	Consumers responsive to price changes
<1	Inelastic	Consumers not very responsive to price changes
=1	Unit elastic	Intermediate case
∞	Perfectly elastic	Infinitely responsive (buy nothing if price rises)
0	Perfectly inelastic	Totally unresponsive (buy the same if price rises)

With the power form of demand curve we can again use either arc or point elasticity but in this case we can prove that they are the same. If we apply the point PED formula to the power form $Q = aP^b$ we obtain the following from (3.19), using partial differentiation:

$$PED = baP^{b-1} \times \frac{P}{Q} = baP^{b-1} \times \frac{P}{aP^b} = \frac{baP^b}{aP^b} = b \qquad (3.20)$$

This is a very important result: it shows that for any power form of the demand curve the power represents the PED, which will be constant for all prices along the demand curve. This in turn means that the arc and point elasticity must be the same, as stated earlier. Furthermore, the result can be generalized to apply to any elasticity; *for any power form the power of a variable represents the elasticity of the dependent variable with respect to that independent variable*. This concept will be applied in many situations as we continue our analysis, not only in this chapter.

c. Range of values

This can be seen from Table 3.3. It should be noted that the PED is always interpreted in terms of its absolute magnitude when we are referring to whether demand is elastic or inelastic; its negativity is simply because of the inverse relationship between price and quantity demanded. We shall see, however, that in performing calculations involving the PED, it is important to include the sign.

d. Determinants of PED

There are three main factors that affect the price elasticity, of which the first is the most important.

1. Availability of substitutes. The more close a substitute(s) a product has the more elastic is its demand. An example is the demand for cigarettes: this demand is inelastic because such substitutes that exist (like cigars, pipes, chewing tobacco, other drugs, nicotine patches and chewing gum) are not very close in terms of their perceived functions and attributes. However, a single brand of cigarettes may have elastic demand, depending on brand loyalty. In this case we are referring to a different issue; instead of asking what will happen when the price of *all* cigarettes changes we are asking what

Table 3.4. Estimates of price elasticities

Product	PED
Airline tickets (USA–Europe), economy	−1.30[14]
Auto repair	−0.36[15]
Beef	−0.65[16]
Beer (consumed at home)	−0.84[17]
Bread	−0.09[18]
Cheese	−1.16[18]
Chicken	−0.65[18]
Chicken (not free range)	−0.13[18]
Cinema tickets	−0.87[15]
Coffee (instant)	−0.36[19]
Coffee (regular)	−0.16[19]
Dental visits (adults)	−0.72[20]
Electricity (household)	−0.13[15]
Fruit juices	−0.80[18]
Furniture	−3.04[21]
Health club memberships	−0.87[22]
Household appliances	−0.64[15]
Housing	−0.23[23]
Legal services	−0.61[15]
Medical insurance	−0.31[15]
Milk	−0.18[18]
Milk	−0.49[16]
Potatoes	−0.27[16]
Restaurant meals	−1.63[15]
Shoes	−0.73[15]
Taxi service	−1.24[15]
Telephones	−0.10[24]
Tobacco products	−0.46[15]

will happen when the price of one brand changes *while the price of other brands stays the same.* In this situation the PED will depend on whether other brands are seen as substitutes; hence the importance of brand loyalty in affecting PED. If there is a great amount of brand loyalty, other brands will not be seen as substitutes and demand will be less elastic than would be the case if there were less brand loyalty. Generally speaking, the more narrowly a product is defined the more elastic its demand will be, for example food, breakfast cereals, cornflakes and Kellogg's cornflakes have increasingly elastic demand.

2. Proportion of income spent on the product. The higher this is, the more elastic the demand, other things remaining equal. This is because the income effect of the price change is greater. Thus the demand for sugar will tend to be inelastic while the demand for cars will be more elastic.

3. Time frame. Demand tends to be more elastic in the longer term, because it may take time for consumers to switch to different products. An example of this was oil in the 1970s, when the price quadrupled. The demand was inelastic in the short run because it was difficult for households and firms to cut back on their consumption. As time went on consumers could switch to other forms of heating and more fuel-efficient cars, and firms also switched to other firms of energy, such as electricity and gas-turbine generators. Habits are easier to change over a longer time period. Two further examples relate to electricity and cinema tickets. The

Table 3.5. PED relationships with revenue, costs and profit

Demand	Price	Quantity	Revenue	Costs	Profit
Elastic	↑	↓more	↓	↓	?
	↓	↑more	↑	↑	?
Inelastic	↑	↓less	↑	↓	↑
	↓	↑less	↓	↑	↓
Unit elastic	↑	↓same	same	↓	↑
	↓	↑same	same	↑	↓

↑ = increases; ↑more = increases by a larger proportion; ↑less = increases by a smaller proportion; ↑same = increases by the same proportion; ↓ = decreases; ↓more = decreases by a larger proportion; ↓less = decreases by a smaller proportion; ↓same = decreases by the same proportion; ? = unknown without further information

PEDs of − 0.13 and − 0.87 respectively, as reported in Table 3.4, are short-run estimates; the same study estimated the long-run PEDs at − 1.89 and − 3.67.

These examples of short-run and long-run estimates illustrate a very important point, one that is emphasized throughout this text: theory alone cannot predict exactly what the PED for a product will be; it can only provide some indications of the general size and sign of the value. We need to measure elasticities using empirical studies (this methodology will be explained in Chapter 4) to confirm (or refute) any theoretical considerations. Table 3.4 shows selected results for a wide variety of different products from a number of different studies in different countries. Two products, chicken and milk, are included in the table twice because different estimates have been obtained in different studies.

e. Use and applications

Firms want to know the PED for their products in order to charge the right price and to make forecasts. The 'right' price is the price that achieves the firm's objectives, for example profit maximization or revenue maximization. Some important relationships are shown in Table 3.5, which shows the effects of price changes on other variables, given different values of the PED. At this stage the topic of costs has not been covered, but because the table is very general in terms of examining the directions of the changes rather than their precise sizes, it is sufficient to note that costs (meaning total costs) are directly related to output. It is assumed here that this output corresponds to the quantity that people want to buy, implying that firms maintain fairly constant levels of inventory.

The above information can also be illustrated graphically. Figure 3.10 aids in understanding the relationships between the variables and the implications involved. Note that a linear demand curve is assumed, with an equation corresponding to the graph in Figure 3.9; this is given by $Q = 18 − 2P$, which readers should verify for themselves. Table 3.6 shows the relationships in Figure 3.9 in numerical form, ignoring costs. It should be noted that the marginal revenue can be calculated either from taking the differences in total revenue between

Table 3.6. Linear demand, PED and revenue

Q	P	TR	MR	PED
0	9	0	0	$-\infty$
2	8	16	7	-8
4	7	28	5	-3.5
6	6	36	3	-2
8	5	40	1	-1.25
10	4	40	-1	-0.8
12	3	36	-3	-0.52
14	2	28	-5	-0.29
16	1	16	-7	-0.125
18	0	0	-9	0

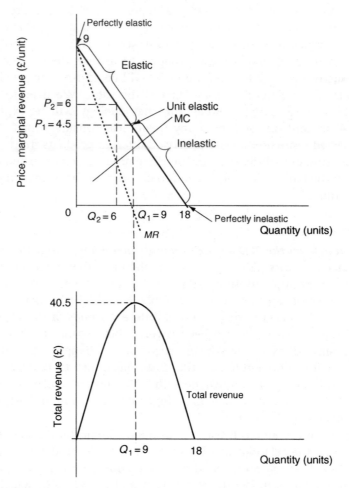

Figure 3.10. PED, revenue and profit.

each pair of prices or by taking the derivative of the revenue function; the latter method is used in Table 3.6.

Tables 3.5 and 3.6 and Figure 3.10 show three things of particular importance:

1. The arc elasticity using average prices and quantities is correct. If revenue stays the same when there is a price change, demand must have unit elasticity; revenue at A and B in the earlier example was the same, at £40. This can be shown more formally by having a power form $Q = aP^{-1}$; this can be rewritten $Q = a/P$, where a is a constant representing revenue.

2. Firms will always maximize revenue by charging a price (P_1) where demand is unit elastic. This is proved mathematically in Chapter 8. In this situation $MR = 0$. It can also be seen that the MR curve has twice the slope of the demand curve. Thus the output Q_1 is halfway between the origin and point B, the horizontal intercept of the demand curve. This is proved as follows:

$$\text{The demand curve has equation } P = a + bQ$$
$$\text{Revenue}, R = PQ = (a + bQ)Q = aQ + bQ^2$$
$$\text{The } MR \text{ curve has equation } MR = \frac{dR}{dQ} = a + 2bQ \qquad (3.21)$$

The interpretation of the MR curve and its shape is considered in more detail in Chapter 8.

3. Firms will always maximize profit by charging a price (P_2) where demand is elastic. This can be explained in terms of Figure 3.10 by seeing that $MC = MR$ (the condition for profit-maximizing output) at an output less than Q_1, since MR must be positive in this situation. Therefore at this output (Q_2) the price must be higher than P_1, so demand must be in the elastic range. In order to determine the exact price that maximizes profit, more precise information regarding the demand and cost functions must be known; this is examined in Chapter 8.

As far as forecasts are concerned, the firm can estimate the effects on sales of a change in price if it knows the PED. These effects are shown in detail in the worked problems.

In the above analysis we concentrated on the importance of the PED from the viewpoint of the management of the firm. Governments are also interested in price elasticities as a guide to various aspects of policy, for example the determination of levels of indirect taxes and import duties, and competition policy. These aspects are considered in Chapter 12.

3.5.2 *Promotional elasticity*

Promotional elasticity is now discussed; this is not because it is seen as being next in importance to price elasticity, since that position usually is taken by income elasticity, but because, like price, it is a ***controllable variable***. Since, in practice, promotion often refers to advertising, the term 'advertising elasticity' will be used from now on.

a. Definition

Advertising elasticity (AED) can be defined in a very similar way to PED; AED refers to the ***percentage change in quantity demanded in response to a 1 per cent change in advertising***. This means just changing the last word of the definition of PED to advertising (measured as expenditure). In symbols:

$$AED = \%\Delta Q / \%\Delta A \tag{3.22}$$

b. Measurement

As with PED both arc and point elasticities can be used. The **simple** measure of elasticity, using the formula above, should again not normally be used, unless the changes in advertising are very small, because it is **inconsistent** and **inaccurate**. The formulae for arc and point elasticities are similar to the formulae for PED, with the variable A substituted for P. Thus we have the following:

$$\text{Adjusted } AED = \frac{\Delta Q}{\Delta A} \times \frac{A_1 + A_2}{Q_1 + Q_2} \tag{3.23}$$

$$\text{Point } AED = \frac{\partial Q}{\partial A} \times \frac{A}{Q} \tag{3.24}$$

where $\partial Q/\partial A$ represents the partial derivative of Q with respect to A. This partial derivative has a similar economic interpretation to that involved in price elasticity; in this case it represents the marginal effect of advertising on quantity, assuming that other factors remain constant. With the power form of demand equation $Q = aP^b A^c$, it can be shown using partial differentiation that the advertising elasticity is given by c. We can see that all elasticities in a power form are given by the powers of the relevant variables and are constant; thus the power form is sometimes known as the **constant elasticity** form.

c. Range of values

AED is expected to be positive, since we would expect consumers to react positively to promotion or advertising.

d. Determinants

The ***effectiveness*** of the firm's advertising is important and so is the ***amount spent*** on advertising. As the firm spends more and more the market may become saturated (diminishing returns) and AED may decrease. There are no widely published results of empirical studies relating to promotional elasticities, and it would be difficult to generalize any conclusions even if there were.

Table 3.7. Range of values for YED

YED	Demand	Interpretation
> 1	Income elastic	Luxury products
0< YED< 1	Income inelastic	Staple products
<0	Negative elasticity	Inferior products

e. Use and applications

Firms want to know the AED for their products in order to spend the right amount on promotion and to make forecasts. The details of how to optimize promotion are given in Chapter 10, in the section on pricing in the marketing mix.

3.5.3 Income elasticity

a. Definition

Income elasticity (YED) is defined similarly to the above elasticities; it is the **percentage change in quantity demanded in response to a 1 per cent change in income.** Again just the last word is changed, to 'income'. In symbols:

$$YED = \%\Delta Q / \%\Delta Y \tag{3.25}$$

b. Measurement

This is also the same as for the above elasticities; there are three measures, simple, adjusted and point, but the first should not normally be used unless the changes in income are very small. Thus the adjusted and point elasticities are:

$$\text{Adjusted } YED = \frac{\Delta Q}{\Delta Y} \times \frac{Y_1 + Y_2}{Q_1 + Q_2} \tag{3.26}$$

$$\text{Point } YED = \frac{\partial Q}{\partial Y} \times \frac{Y}{Q} \tag{3.27}$$

where $\partial Q / \partial Y$ represents the partial derivative of Q with respect to Y. The power form of the demand equation would be extended to become $Q = aP^b \, A^c \, Y^d$.

c. Range of values

Income elasticity can be positive or negative, depending on whether the product is normal or inferior. Normal products can be further divided into **luxury** products and **staple** products, according to whether the income elasticity is **more than one** or **less than one** respectively. This is summarized in Table 3.7.

d. Determinants

As can be seen above, the **type of product** is the main factor determining the income elasticity. The **level of income** in the market is also relevant; for

Table 3.8. Estimates of income Elasticities

Product	YED
Airline tickets (USA–Europe), economy	1.38[14]
Alcohol	1.54[15]
Apples	1.32[16]
Beef	1.05[16]
Bread	−0.25[25]
Butter	0.42[15]
Car travel	1.23[23]
Chicken	0.28[16]
Clothing	1.47[23]
Cinema tickets	3.41[15]
Coffee	0.00[15]
Dental visits (adults)	0.58[20]
Flour	−0.36[15]
Furniture	1.48[21]
Housing (low-income renters)	0.22[26]
Housing (owner-occupied)	1.49[15]
Margarine	−0.20[15]
Medical insurance	0.92[15]
Milk	0.50[16]
Potatoes	0.15[16]
Restaurant meals	1.40[15]
Shoes	1.10[15]
Tea	−0.56[25]

example, products that are staple goods in developed countries, like telephones and radios, might be luxuries in a developing country. As with price elasticity, theory alone cannot tell us whether a product is in a certain category; we need empirical studies to confirm this. Table 3.8 shows selected results for a wide variety of different products from a number of different studies in different countries.

e. Use and applications

Firms want to know the income elasticities for their products in order to select target markets and make forecasts. Note that income is not truly a controllable variable, but a firm can gain an element of control by selecting from different target markets with different levels of average income.

3.5.4 Cross-elasticity

a. Definition

This refers to the **percentage change in the quantity demanded of one product in response to a 1 per cent change in the price of another product**. This can be expressed in symbols:

$$CED = \% \Delta Q / \% \Delta P'$$ (3.28)

b. Measurement

The same methods and principles apply as for the other elasticities. Thus:

$$\text{Adjusted } CED = \frac{\Delta Q}{\Delta P'} \times \frac{P'_1 + P'_2}{Q_1 + Q_2} \qquad (3.29)$$

$$\text{Point } CED = \frac{\partial Q}{\partial P'} \times \frac{P'}{Q} \qquad (3.30)$$

where $\partial Q / \partial P'$ represents the partial derivative of Q with respect to P'.

The power form of the demand equation would be extended to become $Q = aP^b \, A^c \, Y^d \, P'^e$.

c. Range of values

CED can be **positive** or **negative** according to whether the other product is a *substitute* or a *complement*. For example, if the price of Pepsi rises, the quantity of Coke demanded should also rise, as people switch from Pepsi to Coke. Note the importance of the assumption of other things being equal, in particular that the price of Coke stays the same.

d. Determinants

As well as the above, the *degree of substitutability or complementarity* is important. The greater this is, the larger the absolute value of CED. Thus, in the example above, the closer Pepsi and Coke are seen as substitutes, the more people will switch from one to the other. Again, it is important to test theoretical considerations by empirical studies. For example, the CED between electricity and natural gas has been estimated to be only 0.20 (US data);[27] the same study estimated the CED between butter and margarine to be 0.67 (when the price of margarine changed), while another study[28] estimated this CED to be 1.53 (when the price of butter changed). The last two products are much closer as substitutes than gas and electricity.

Studies have also measured the CED for complementary products. For example, food has been found to be complementary to both clothing[29] and entertainment.[30] In the first case the CED was found to be − 0.18, while in the second it was − 0.72, indicating that food and entertainment are more complementary. In this case it does not mean that food and entertainment are actually consumed together (although this may be true); because food involves a relatively high proportion of income there is a substantial income effect when the price of food changes. When food prices rise, real incomes fall and this in turn causes a fall in spending on entertainment.

e. Use and applications

Firms want to know the CED for their products in order to see what their main competition is and determine strategy accordingly; sometimes the 'other products' involved are in the same product line or product mix of the firm itself. In this case, information relating to CEDs is important for product planning purposes. The information is again useful for making forecasts, when the price of a related product changes, as shown in the solved problem SP3.3.

3.6 A problem-solving approach

There is a world of difference between 'knowing' the principles of demand theory and being able to apply them to practical managerial problems, even of a simplified kind. Even though all problems in this area are essentially concerned with how different variables affect quantity demanded, this gulf between theory and application is greater with this topic than with most others since problems can come in many different forms and guises. Students are often bewildered by the problems and do not know how to start, even though they claim to know all the principles. The following approach is therefore recommended as an aid.

Three questions need to be asked, in the following order:

1 *Does the problem involve marginal effects or elasticities?* Sometimes this is explicit in the question, but in other cases the different interpretations of these different concepts, in terms of **units** or **percentages**, have to be applied to the data in the problem to see which is relevant.

2 *Which type of marginal effect or elasticity is relevant?* Again this may be specified in the question, but in other cases it is not, so the student has to decide which of the four variables is relevant: **price**, **promotion**, **income** or a **price of related good**. It is possible that a different variable may be involved, or that more than one variable is involved, for example in the solved problems SP3.2 and SP3.3.

3 *Which measure of elasticity is involved?* This obviously only relates to elasticity questions, since there is only one way of measuring marginal effects; however, elasticity can be measured using either **arc** or **point** methods. The main criterion is to see whether there is a **change** in the relevant variable, or whether it stays **constant**. In the first case the arc method is used, while in the second the point method is appropriate. In some questions either method is feasible (see SP3.2 and SP3.3), but there are advantages and disadvantages of each, as will be explained.

Once the above questions have been answered it is recommended that the student write down the **relevant formula in general terms** rather than trying to substitute the numbers in the data immediately. This tends to eliminate a number of mistakes.

This approach is now illustrated in the following four solved problems.

SP3.1 Interpretation of elasticities

Midwest Cable TV has estimated the demand for its service to be given by the following function:

$$Q = 9.83P^{-1.2}A^{2.5}Y^{1.6}P_0^{-1.4}$$

where
Q = monthly sales in units
P = price of the service in $
A = promotional expenditure in $'000
Y = average income of the market in $'000
P_0 = price of 'home movies' in $

The current price of Midwest is $60, promotional expenditure is $120,000, average income is $28,000, and the price of 'home movies' is $45.

Indicate whether the following statements are true or false, giving your reasons and making the necessary corrections.

a. If Midwest increases its price this will reduce the number of its customers.
b. If Midwest increases its price this will reduce its revenues.
c. People's expenditure on the cable TV service as a proportion of their income will increase when their income increases.
d. If Midwest increases its price this will increase the sales of 'home movies'.
e. 'Home movies' are a substitute for cable TV.
f. A 5 per cent increase in income will increase demand by 16 per cent.
g. A 10 per cent increase in price will reduce demand by 12 per cent.
h. Current sales are over a million units a month.
i. The demand curve for Midwest is given by: $Q = 9.83P^{-1.2}$
j. Midwest's sales are more affected by the price of 'home movies' than by the price of its own service.
k. If Midwest increases its price this will reduce its profit.

Solution

a. **True**; customers and quantity demanded are synonymous in this case, and there is an inverse relationship between Q and P, as seen by the **negative price elasticity**.
b. **True**; **demand is elastic**, since the PED is greater than 1 in absolute magnitude. Therefore an increase in price causes a greater than proportional decrease in quantity demanded and a fall in revenue.
c. **True**; this is because the YED is greater than 1, indicating that cable TV is a luxury product. Note that the statement would be false if the good were a staple. For staples, although expenditure on the product increases as income increases, expenditure as a proportion of income falls, since expenditure rises more slowly than income.
d. **False**; the two products are complementary, shown by the CED **being negative**; therefore an increase in the price of one product will reduce the sales of the other. It appears therefore that 'home movies' is a cable channel.
e. **False**; the two products are complementary, shown by the CED **being negative**.

f. **False**; YED $= 1.6$; therefore using the simple elasticity formula (reasonably accurate for small changes) the *change in demand will be* **1.6×5% = 8%**.

g. **False**; change is $1.2 \times 10\% = 12\%$, but this is a *change in quantity demanded*, corresponding to a movement along a demand curve (unlike the previous part of the question, which involves a shift in the demand curve).

h. **False**; current sales are given by
$Q = 9.83(60)^{-1.2} (120)^{2.5} (28)^{1.6} (45)^{-1.4} = \textbf{11,420 units}$.

i. **False**; the demand curve is given by
$Q = 9.83P^{-1.2}(120)^{2.5}(28)^{1.6}(45)^{-1.4}$ or $Q = \textbf{1,554,039P}^{-1.2}$.

j. **True**; the **CED** *is larger in absolute magnitude than the* **PED**. This is an unusual situation but arises because of the nature of cable TV service. The service is only a means to an end, that of receiving certain channels.

k. **False**; since *demand is elastic, an increase in price has an unknown effect on profit*. More information would be required.

SP3.2 Marginal effects and elasticity

PK Corp estimates that its demand function is as follows:

$$Q = 150 - 5.4P + 0.8A + 2.8Y - 1.2P^*$$

where

$Q =$ quantity demanded per month (in 1000s)
$P =$ price of the product (in £)
$A =$ firm's advertising expenditure (in £'000 per month)
$Y =$ per capita disposable income (in £'000)
$P^* =$ price of BJ Corp (in £).

a. During the next five years, per capita disposable income is expected to increase by £2,500. What effect will this have on the firm's sales?

b. If PK wants to raise its price by enough to offset the effect of the increase in income, by how much must it raise its price?

c. If PK raises its price by this amount, will it increase or decrease the PED? Explain.

d. What is the relationship between PK and BJ? Explain your answer.

e. If next year PK intends to charge £15 and spend £10,000 per month on promotion, while it believes per capita income will be £12,000 and BJ's price will be £3, calculate the income elasticity of demand. What does this tell you about the nature of PK's product?

f. What effect would an increase in advertising of £1000 have on profitability, if each additional unit costs £10 to produce?

Solution

a. Use the marginal effect of income on quantity demanded:

$\Delta Q/\Delta Y = 2.8$
$\Delta Y = 2.5$
$\Delta Q/2.5 = 2.8$
$\Delta Q = 2.8 \times 2.5 = 7,$ or **7,000 units**

b. Use the marginal effect of price on quantity demanded:

$\Delta Q/\Delta P = -5.4$
$-7/\Delta P = -5.4$
$\Delta P = -7/-5.4 = $ **£1.30**

c. $PED = \partial Q/\partial P \times P/Q = -5.4P/Q$

As P increases and Q stays constant (because of rising income), PED increases in absolute magnitude, meaning that demand becomes **more elastic**.

d. The two companies make **complementary products** because the marginal effect of the price of BJ on the quantity of PK is negative.

e. $YED = \partial Q/\partial Y \times Y/Q$
$$= 2.8 \times 12/(150 - 5.4 \times 15 + 0.8 \times 10 + 2.8 \times 12 - 1.2 \times 3)$$
$$= 2.8 \times 12/107 = \textbf{0.3140}$$

(staple product)

f. If $\Delta A = 1, \Delta Q = 0.8 = 800$ units, $\Delta R = 800 \times 15 = $ £12,000
$\Delta C = 800 \times 10$ (production) $+ \Delta A$ (£1,000) = £9,000

Thus every additional £1,000 spent on advertising increases profit by £3,000.

This problem tests the ability of the student to distinguish between the concepts of marginal effect and elasticity, and apply each one accordingly. In part (f), in particular, it is important to use marginal effect, not elasticity, since profit is measured in money units. It is also important that the student observes the units in which the variables are measured.

SP3.3 Arc elasticities

LAD Enterprises sells mobile phones, currently charging £80 and earning £9,600 per week. It is considering a price cut of 20 per cent to increase its market share, estimating its PED to be -1.6.

a. Estimate the effect of the price cut on LAD's revenue, stating any assumptions.

b. If a competitor responds to the price cut by also reducing its price by 20 per cent, estimate the effect on LAD's revenue, assuming the CED is 0.8.

c. Compare the profits in (a) and (b) above with the original level of profit.

Solution

a. $Q_1 = 9,600/80 = 120$ $P_1 = 80$ $P_2 = 64$

$$-1.6 = \frac{Q_2-120}{-16} \times \frac{(80+64)}{120+Q_2}$$

$Q_2 = 172$ $R_2 = 172 \times 64 = \mathbf{11,008}$

b. $0.8 = \frac{Q_2-172}{-0.2P'} \times \frac{P'+0.8P'}{172+Q_2}$

$Q_2 = 144$ $R_2 = 144 \times 64 = \mathbf{9,216}$

c. in (a), R rises, C rises, therefore effect on profit uncertain.
in (b), R falls, C rises, therefore profit falls.
This problem illustrates several points:

1 Arc elasticities can be used in a chained sequence where the Q_2 from one calculation becomes the Q_1 for the next calculation.
2 The effect of a competitor's price change can be calculated without knowing the level of price, as long as the percentage change is known.
3 A price war can often result in lower profit.

SP3.4 Point elasticities and power form

Pritti Sprays is a manufacturer of cosmetic products. Its management is currently engaged in an analysis of the lipsticks produced by the firm, examining the future demand for them. Market research indicates that advertising expenditure, price and average income are three major variables affecting the demand for the lipsticks. The advertising elasticity for demand is estimated to be 1.5, the price elasticity -1.2 and the income elasticity 1.8. In addition, the following data are available.

Year	Sales (units)	Advertising expenditure	Price	Income
2001	2,369	£21,000	£6.50	£25,000
2002		£21,000	£6.50	£27,000
2003		£24,000	£6.80	£29,000

a. Estimate sales for 2002 and 2003.

b. A competitor plans on reducing its price from £6.90 to £6.40 in 2003; assuming the CED is 1.5, how much would Pritti have to spend on advertising to achieve the same rate of growth of sales as from 2001 to 2002?

Solution

Since the elasticities are given as constants we can use these to calculate the power demand function:

$Q = aP^{-1.2}A^{1.5}Y^{1.8}$

$2369 = a(6.5)^{-1.2}21^{(1.5)}25^{(1.8)}$ where promotion and income are measured in £'000

$a = 0.7087$

a. Sales in 2002 $= 0.7087(6.5)^{-1.2}(21)^{1.5}(27)^{1.8} = $ **2,721 units**
   Sales in 2003 $= 0.7087(6.8)^{-1.2}(24)^{1.5}(29)^{1.8} = $ **3,581 units**

b. Growth from 2001 to 2002 $= (2,721/2,369) - 1 = 14.86\%$
   Required sales in 2003 $= 3,125$
   $2,721 = a(6.5)^{-1.2}(21)^{1.5}(27)^{1.8}(6.9)^{1.5}$
   $a = 0.0391$
   $3,125 = 0.0391(6.8)^{-1.2}A^{1.5}(29)^{1.8}(6.4)^{1.5}$
   $A^{1.5} = 114.8$
   $A = 23.627$;   advertising $= $ **£23,627**

This problem illustrates how the use of point elasticities in the power form can be used to approach a similar problem to SP3.2 when different independent variables change, assuming that the elasticities are constant. The advantage of the above method is that any number of variables can be changed simultaneously, whereas with the arc method only one variable can be changed at a time, thus lengthening the calculations.

Case study 3.2: The Oresund bridge

A not-so-popular Nordic bridge[31]

It was not quite what the planners had in mind when Sweden and Denmark opened their expensive bridge across the Oresund strait in July. After an early boost from summer tourism, car crossings have fallen sharply, while trains now connecting Copenhagen, the Danish capital, and Malmo, Sweden's third city, are struggling to run on time. Many people think the costs of using the bridge are simply too high. And, from the point of view of Scandinavian solidarity, the traffic is embarrassingly one-sided: far more Swedes are going to Denmark than vice versa. So last week the authorities decided to knock almost 50% off the price of a one-way crossing for the last three months of this year.

The two governments, which paid nearly $2 billion for the 16km (10-mile) state-owned bridge-cum-tunnel, reckoned that, above all, it would strengthen economic ties across the strait and create, within a few years, one of the fastest-growing and richest regions in Europe. But ministers on both sides of the water, especially in Sweden, have been getting edgy about the bridge's teething problems. Last month Leif Pagrotsky, Sweden's trade minister, called for a tariff review: the cost of driving over the bridge, at SKr255 ($26.40) each way, was too high to help integrate the region's two bits.

Businessmen have been complaining too. Novo Nordisk, a Danish drug firm which moved its Scandinavian marketing activities to Malmo to take advantage of 'the bridge effect', has been urging Danish staff to limit their trips to Malmo by working more from home. Ikea, a Swedish furniture chain with headquarters in Denmark, has banned its employees from using the bridge altogether when travelling on company business, and has told them to make their crossings – more cheaply if a lot more slowly – by ferry.

The people managing the bridge consortium say they always expected a dip in car traffic from a summer peak of 20,000 vehicles a day. But they admit that the current daily flow of 6,000 vehicles or so must increase if the bridge is to pay its way in the long run. So they are about to launch a new advertising campaign. And they are still upbeat about the overall trend: commercial traffic is indeed going up. The trains have carried more than 1m passengers since the service began in July.

Certainly, the bridge is having some effect. Many more Swedes are visiting the art galleries and cafés of Copenhagen; more Danes are nipping northwards over the strait. Some 75% more people crossed the strait in the first two months after the bridge's opening than during the same period a year before.

Other links are being forged too. Malmo's *Sydsvenska Dagbladet* and Copenhagen's *Berlingske Tidende* newspapers now produce a joint Oresund supplement every day, while cross-border

ventures in health, education and information technology have begun to bear fruit. Joint cultural ventures are also under way.

And how about linking eastern Denmark more directly with Germany's Baltic Sea coastline, enabling Danes to go by train from their capital to Berlin in, say, three hours? Despite the Danes' *nej* to the euro, it is still a fair bet that this last much-talked-about project will, within ten years or so, be undertaken.

Questions

1 Explain why the demand for the bridge is likely to be price-elastic.
2 If the Swedish government estimates that the price elasticity is −1.4, calculate the effect on traffic using the bridge, stating any assumptions.
3 Why is the calculation above not likely to give an accurate forecast for the long term?

Case study 3.3: The Texas state bird

Southwest Airlines is a major carrier based in Texas, and has made a strategy of cutting fares drastically on certain routes with large effects on air traffic in those markets. For example on the Burbank–Oakland route the entry of Southwest into the market caused average fares to fall by 48 per cent and increased market revenue from $21,327,008 to $47,064,782 annually. On the Kansas City–St Louis route, however, the average fare cut in the market when Southwest entered was 70 per cent and market revenue fell from an annual $66,201,553 to $33,101,514.

Questions

1 Calculate the PEDs for the Burbank–Oakland and Kansas City–St Louis routes.
2 Explain why the above market elasticities might not apply specifically to Southwest.
3 If Southwest does experience a highly elastic demand on the Burbank–Oakland route, what is the profit implication of this?
4 Explain why the fare reduction on the Kansas City–St Louis route may still be a profitable strategy for Southwest.

Case study 3.4: Oil production

OPEC's oil shock[32]

OPEC has surprised the markets with an output cut of 900,000 barrels per day, to take effect at the beginning of November. Observers had expected the oil producers' cartel to hold its quotas steady because production in Iraq has been hit by sabotage.

Before the regular meeting of the Organisation of Petroleum Exporting Countries (OPEC) in Vienna on Wednesday September 24th, most of the drama was

provided by Hugo Chávez, the Venezuelan president, who opined that the Iraq representative should not have been at the get-together because he was an illegitimate stooge of American occupiers. If that is so, Ibrahim Bahr al-Uloum behaved very oddly. His bullish predictions that Iraq could produce at least 3.5m barrels per day (bpd) by 2005 seem to have been among the factors that persuaded the ten members of OPEC's quota system to approve a surprise production cut of 900,000 bpd, to 24.5m bpd.

The effect of the cut was to send oil prices sharply higher. Equities in America retreated on fears that a higher oil price could stymie the incipient economic recovery: the Dow Jones Industrial Average of 30 leading shares fell by 1.57% that day.

In their official communiqué, OPEC's oil ministers pointed to their expectation of a 'contra-seasonal stock build-up' at the end of this year and the beginning of next year. Normally, oil stocks decline over the winter in the northern hemisphere, thanks to heavy use of heating oil. But this year, demand for oil, according to OPEC, will grow merely at its 'normal, seasonal' level, despite an improving world economy. OPEC expects supply to grow faster than demand, thanks to continued increases in production from Iraq and non-OPEC countries (of which Russia, the world's second-biggest oil exporter, is the most important).

OPEC expects this supply–demand mismatch to translate into a stock increase of 600,000 bpd in the final quarter of this year. This contrasts with an estimated stock reduction of 500,000 bpd in the final quarter of 2001, and 1m bpd in the last quarter of 2002. Larry Goldstein, president of the Petroleum Industry Research Foundation, believes OPEC has got its sums wrong. In remarks to the *Wall Street Journal*, he said he thought stocks would be flat over the coming three months.

Although the communiqué did not explicitly say so, OPEC members are keen to keep worldwide oil stocks below their ten-year average. That would give the cartel more power to determine the price. American oil stocks have been creeping up again after hitting 26-year lows earlier this year. America's energy secretary, Spencer Abraham, was clearly disappointed by OPEC's move, saying: 'Sustained global economic growth requires abundant supplies of energy. The US believes oil prices should be set by market forces in order to ensure adequate supplies.' America's opposition Democrats have been even more outspoken. Last month, they publicly rebuked Saudi Arabia, OPEC's (and the world's) leading producer, for reducing exports in August, thus causing an unpopular rise in American petrol prices.

Some observers are also speculating that OPEC may be sneakily trying to shift its price target above the current $22–28 range (per barrel, for a basket of Middle Eastern crudes, which tend to trade a couple of dollars below West Texas crude). After all, the oil price has been well within that range for the past few

months. Why cut production when current supply levels are achieving their aim? In fact, the oil price has stayed higher than many expected: it was widely expected to fall well below $20 per barrel after the end of the Iraq war. However, unrest in Nigeria, a big producer, and the continuing attacks on Iraq's oil facilities put paid to that.

OPEC's fears about non-OPEC production may be well-founded. After decades of communism, the industry in Russia is ramping up output: so far this year, it has been pumping an average of 800,000 bpd more than last year. Oil and gas are the country's biggest exports, earning hard currency that is seen as a key ingredient of economic revival. Moreover, the oil industry is in private hands, so even if the government in Moscow wanted to put a lid on production, it has less influence over its oil companies than OPEC governments have over theirs. The president of OPEC, Abdullah bin Hamad al-Attiyah, told the *Wall Street Journal* that the cartel would not cut production below 24m bpd unless big oil exporters outside OPEC, including Mexico and Norway as well as Russia, were prepared to cut production too.

OPEC's stance on Iraq is very different. Here, the cartel seems to be taking an overly rosy view. Iraq says it is currently producing around 1.8m bpd, well below the 2.5m bpd that it was pumping before the country was invaded in the spring (and even that was well below its potential, owing to years of sanctions). Moreover, exports, which are a crucial source of revenue for reconstruction, are still running at only about 500,000 bpd, compared with 2m bpd before the war. These have been seriously disrupted, and continue to be threatened by sabotage. Currently, oil is being exported mainly through the north: the southern ports on the Gulf coast are operating far below capacity.

For those who take OPEC's optimistic view of Iraqi production at face value, the cartel's move should not have come as a surprise. But the sharp reaction from oil markets and stockmarkets suggests it did. Many speculators had sold oil in the futures market, or 'shorted' it, expecting the price to fall in the short term – they clearly weren't expecting a big cut in output quotas any time soon. According to the Commodity Futures Trading Commission, the American regulator for commodity futures markets, the increase in short positions over September was equivalent to 470,000 barrels of oil. OPEC's decision led to a scramble to 'cover' such positions by buying oil. Whether prices stay higher will depend on two key factors. Will OPEC members stick to their new quotas? (They have a history of cheating.) And will Iraqi militants continue to destroy their own country's wells and pipelines?

Questions

1 OPEC currently produces about 38 per cent of the world output of oil. Assuming the short-term price elasticity of demand is −0.28, estimate the effect of the output cut on the current price, stating any assumptions in your calculations.

2 Describe the factors currently driving the world demand for oil; why has the price not fallen below the $20 level as many expected?

3 Explain the effect of other non-OPEC producers on the cartel's output decisions.

Summary

1 The term 'demand' can be used in many contexts, as in demand schedules, curves, equations, functions and quantity demanded. It is important to distinguish between these different meanings.

2 Graphs and equations can be drawn and written with either price or quantity as the dependent variable.

3 Coefficients in demand equations can have either graphical or economic interpretations.

4 Marginal effects and elasticities are two different ways of describing the effect of a variable on quantity demanded.

5 Indifference curve analysis can be used to determine the inverse relationship between price and quantity demanded.

6 Price changes have two simultaneous effects on quantity demanded: an income effect and a substitution effect. The size and direction of these will determine the PED.

7 Although the basic neoclassical analytical framework and assumptions have certain limitations, the model is very versatile and is capable of being extended to apply to more complex situations.

8 There are a large number of factors which affect demand in reality; it is useful to distinguish between controllable and uncontrollable factors.

9 The concept of elasticity is vital in understanding and analysing demand relationships.

10 Theoretical considerations relating to the sign and size of elasticities must always be tested empirically.

Review questions

1 Explain the problems for government policy if it tries to use supply-oriented policies rather than demand-oriented ones in trying to discourage the consumption of certain products.

2 Explain the significance for economic theory of the relationship between price and perceived quality.

3 Analyse the effects on the demand for cars of the following:

  a. A higher tax on gasoline
  b. A tax on car parking
  c. Increased automation on subways
  d. Government legislation for increased safety in cars, like side impact protection
  e. A 'congestion' tax imposed on cars using certain routes at certain times.

4 Select a company from the FT.com website and analyse the factors affecting its demand according to the categories described in this chapter.

5 Referring to Table 3.4 showing empirical estimates of price elasticities, draw some general conclusions relating to the products involved. Identify any apparent anomalies in the table and give some possible explanations.

6 Referring to Table 3.6 for income elasticities, repeat the procedure in the previous question.

Problems

3.1 BAD Enterprises is considering increasing the price of its harmonicas, currently $20, by 25 per cent. BAD's current revenue is $12,000 a month, and the PED for its harmonicas is estimated to be −1.8.

  a. Calculate the effect of the price change on BAD's revenue.
  b. BAD now considers increasing its advertising budget to restore its sales revenue to its previous level. BAD is currently spending $1,500 a month on advertising and estimates its AED to be 1.5. What will its new budget have to be?
  c. What can you say about what will happen to profit in both (a) and (b) compared with the original level of profit?

3.2 Vik and Fleet produce trainers in the sports-shoe market. For one of their main products they have the following demand curves:

$$\text{Vik} \quad P_V = 175 - 1.2Q_V$$

$$\text{Fleet} \quad P_f = 125 - 0.8Q_f$$

where P is in £ and Q is in pairs per week.
The firms are currently selling 80 and 75 pairs of their products per week respectively.

  a. What are the current price elasticities for the products?
  b. Assume that Vik reduces its price and increases its sales to 90 pairs and that this also causes a fall in Fleet's sales to 70 pairs per week. What is the cross-elasticity between the two products?

c. Is the above price reduction by Vik to be recommended? Explain your answer.

3.3 R and B Railroad decided to reduce their fares to see if it would help their business. They reduced their ticket prices by 25 per cent on average and their revenues increased from $325,000 per month to $332,000 on average.

a. Without doing any calculations, comment on the PED.
b. Calculate the PED.
c. R and B decided that the fare reduction was a failure; why might they have done this?

3.4 Sales of cars declined by 15 per cent in a recent recession. During this period the price of cars rose by 6 per cent, average income fell by 4 per cent and the price of petrol rose by 20 per cent. It has been estimated that the PED for cars is − 0.8 and the YED is 1.25.

a. Estimate the effect of the decline in income on car sales.
b. Estimate the effect of the car price rise on sales.
c. Estimate the CED between petrol and cars; compare your estimate using simple elasticities and additive effects with the estimate obtained using a power form of demand equation.

3.5 MK Corp estimates that its demand function is as follows:

$$Q = 400 - 12.5P + 25A + 14Y + 10P^*$$

where Q is the quantity demanded per month, P is the product's price (in $), A is the firm's advertising expenditure (in $'000 per month), Y is per capita disposable income (in $'000), and P^* is the price of AJ Corp.

a. During the next five years, per capita disposable income is expected to increase by $5,000 and AJ is expected to increase its price by $12. What effect will this have on the firm's sales volume?
b. If MK wants to change its price by enough to offset the above effects, by how much must it do so?
c. Compare the profitability of maintaining sales volume by either changing price or changing advertising spending.
d. If MK's current price is $60 and it spends $10,000 per month on advertising, while per capita income is $25,000 and AJ's price is $70, calculate the price elasticity of demand with the price change.
e. What can be said about the effect of the above price change on profit?
f. What can be said about the relationship between the products of MK and AJ?

Notes

1 A. Marshall, *Principles of Economics*, London: Macmillan, 1890.
2 J. R. Hicks, 'The valuation of social income', *Economica*, n.s., **7** (1940): 105–124.

3 K. Lancaster, 'A new approach to consumer theory', *Journal of Political Economy*, **74** (1966): 132–157.

4 J. A. Howard and J. N. Sheth, *The Theory of Buyer Behaviour*, New York: John Wiley, 1969.

5 P. E. Green and Y. Wind, *Multiattribute Decisions in Marketing: A Measurement Approach*, Hinsdale, Ill.: Dryden Press, 1973.

6 J. H. Myers and M. L. Alpert, 'Determinant buying attitudes: meaning and measurement', *Journal of Marketing*, **32** (October 1968): 13–20.

7 D. Kahneman and A. Tversky, 'Prospect theory: an analysis of decision under risk', *Econometrica*, **47** (1979): 263–291.

8 R. H. Frank, *Passions within Reason*, New York: Norton, 1988.

9 A. Damasio, *Descartes's Error: Emotion, Reason and the Human Brain*, London: Picador, 1995.

10 G. S. Becker, 'Irrational behaviour and economic theory', *Journal of Political Economy*, **70** (1962): 1–13.

11 J. H. Kagel and R. C. Battalio, 'Experimental studies of consumer demand behavior', *Economic Inquiry*, **8** (March 1975): 22–38.

12 V. Smith, Talk to the Human Behavior and Evolution Society meeting, Santa Barbara, June 1995 (posted on the HBES e-mail list).

13 ' Does M&S have a future?' *The Economist*, 28 October 2000.

14 J. M. Cigliano, 'Price and income elasticities for airline travel: the North American market', *Business Economics*, **15** (September 1980): 17–21.

15 L. S. Houthakker and L. D. Taylor, *Consumer Demand in the United States*, 2nd edn, Cambridge, Mass.: Harvard University Press, 1970.

16 D. B. Suits, 'Agriculture', in W. Adams (ed.), *Structure of American Industry*, 7th edn, New York: Macmillan, 1986.

17 D. Heien and G. Pompelli, 'The demand for alcoholic beverages: economic and demographic effects', *Southern Economic Journal*, **56** (January 1989): 759–769.

18 *Annual Report of the National Food Survey Committee*, MAFF, HMSO, 1995.

19 C. J. Huang, J. J. Siegfried and F. Zardoshty, 'The demand for coffee in the United States, 1963–1977', *Quarterly Review of Economics and Business*, **20** (Summer 1980): 36–50.

20 W. G. Manning and C. E. Phelps, 'The demand for dental care', *Bell Journal of Economics*, **10** (Autumn 1979): 503–525.

21 R. D. Stone and D. A. Rowe, 'The durability of consumers' durable goods', *Econometrica*, **28** (1960): 407–416.

22 J. N. Wilkinson, 'Marketing in the health club industry', Ph.D. thesis, City University.

23 A. Deaton, *Models and Projections of Demand in Post-war Britain*, London: Chapman and Hall, 1975.

24 D. Cracknell and M. Knott, 'The measurement of price elasticities – the BT experience', *International Journal of Forecasting* **11** (1995): 321–329.

25 *Annual Report of the National Food Survey Committee*, MAFF, HMSO, 1989.

26 E. A. Roistacher, 'Short-run housing responses to changes in income', *American Economic Review*, **67** (February 1977): 381–386.

27 R. Halvorsen, 'Energy substitution in U.S. manufacturing', *Review of Economics and Statistics*, **59** (November 1977): 381–388.

28 D. M. Heien, 'The structure of food demand: interrelatedness and duality', *American Journal of Agricultural Economics*, **64** (May 1982): 213–221.

29 M. R. Baye, D. W. Jansen and T. W. Lee, 'Advertising in complete demand systems', *Applied Economics*, **24** (1992): 1087–1097.

30 E. T. Fujii *et al.* 'An almost ideal demand system for visitor expenditures', *Journal of Transport Economics and Policy*, **19** (May 1985).

31 'A not-so-popular Nordic bridge', *The Economist*, 7 October 2000.

32 'OPEC's oil shock', *The Economist*, 26 September 2003.

4

Demand estimation

Objectives

1 To explain the meaning of demand estimation.
2 To examine different methods of demand estimation.
3 To explain the nature of empirical studies.
4 To illustrate the principles in drawing graphs of empirical data.
5 To explain the OLS regression model.
6 To explain and interpret measures of goodness of fit.
7 To explain different mathematical forms of the regression model.
8 To describe forecasting methods.
9 To explain the multiple regression model and its advantages compared to simple regression.
10 To examine the implications of empirical studies in terms of economic theory.
11 To enable students to perform empirical studies and test economic theories.
12 To explain a problem-solving approach that enables students to use empirical studies as an aid to managerial decision-making.

4.1 Introduction

In the previous chapter it was generally assumed that the demand function for a firm or market was known; in practice it has to be estimated from empirical data, and that is the subject of this chapter. When we speak of estimation there are a number of stages involved in this process. Some of these stages may be omitted in the simpler methods of estimation, like the first two described in the next section. However, with a statistical study, or **econometric analysis** as it is often called, there are essentially the following seven stages:

1 *Statement of a theory or hypothesis.* This usually comes from a mixture of economic theory and previous empirical studies. An example of such a theory might be that the quantity people buy of a particular product might depend more on the past price than on the current price. This obviously has implications regarding perfect knowledge, information costs, habit formation and 'irrational' behaviour.
2 *Model specification.* This means **determining what variables should be included in the demand model and what mathematical form or forms such a relationship should take**. These issues are again determined on the basis of economic theory and prior empirical studies. Various alternative models may be specified at this stage, since economic theory is often not robust enough to be definitive regarding the details of the form of model. This aspect is discussed in section 4.3.
3 *Data collection.* This stage can only be performed after the demand model has been specified, otherwise it is not known for which variables we have to collect data. However, there may be some interaction between the two stages,

particularly as far as the mathematical form is concerned; as stated above, economic theory alone may be unable to specify this and we may have to refer to graphs of the data or even statistical calculations, as explained in sections 4.3 and 4.7, in order to do this. Therefore the presentation of data will also be considered in this stage. We have to discuss both the type of data to be collected and the sources of data. These issues are considered in section 4.4.

4 *Estimation of parameters.* This means computing the values of the coefficients of the variables in the model, which as we have seen in the previous chapter correspond to the effects of an independent variable on the dependent variable. These effects can be measured in different ways, for example in terms of the marginal effects and elasticities already discussed. We have to have a technique to estimate these values, and the method of **ordinary least squares** (OLS) regression will be used in this context. This stage is examined in sections 4.5, 4.7 and 4.9; the justification of the method is explained in appendix A.

5 *Checking goodness of fit.* Once a model, or maybe several alternative models, have been estimated, it is necessary to examine how well the models fit the data and to determine which model fits best. If the fit is not good it may be necessary to return to step 2 and respecify the model before moving on to the next stage. This aspect is considered in section 4.6.

6 *Hypothesis testing.* Having determined the best model, we want to test the hypothesis stated in the first step; in the example quoted we want to test whether current price or past price has a greater effect on sales. This stage is discussed in appendix A, since it involves inferential statistics of a more advanced nature than the rest of the chapter.

7 *Forecasting.* This is the ultimate focus of most econometric analysis. In this context we are trying to forecast sales, and maybe producing many forecasts in the light of various possible scenarios. Some aspects of this can be considered without covering the previous stage, and these are discussed in section 4.8.

It should be clear from the above process that, as far as managerial decision-making is concerned, the last two stages are the most important. However, it is not possible to test hypotheses or make forecasts reliably without a good understanding of the prior stages.

4.2 Methods

There are a variety of ways that can be used to estimate demand, each of which has certain advantages and disadvantages.

4.2.1 Consumer surveys

Firms can obtain information regarding their demand functions by using interviews and questionnaires, asking questions about buying habits, motives and intentions. These can be quick on-the-street interviews, or in-depth ones. They might ask, for example, how much more petrol respondents would buy if its price were reduced by 15 pence per litre, or which brand of several possibilities they prefer. These methods have certain drawbacks:

1 *Validity*. Consumers often find it difficult to answer hypothetical questions, and sometimes they will deliberately mislead the interviewer to give the answer they think the interviewer wants.
2 *Reliability*. It is difficult to collect precise quantitative data by such means.
3 *Sample bias*. Those responding to questions may not be typical consumers.

In spite of these problems, there are advantages of surveys:

1 They give up-to-date information reflecting the current business environment.
2 Much useful information can be obtained that would be difficult to uncover in other ways; for example, if consumers are ignorant of the relative prices of different brands, it may be concluded that they are not sensitive to price changes. Firms can also establish product characteristics that are important to the buyer, and priorities. Methods such as multidimensional scaling can be used to give rating scores on product characteristics.

4.2.2 Market experiments

As with consumer surveys these can be performed in many ways. Laboratory experiments or consumer clinics seek to test consumer reactions to changes in variables in the demand function in a controlled environment. Consumers are normally given small amounts of money and allowed to choose how to spend this on different goods at prices that are varied by the investigator. However, such experiments have to be set up very carefully to obtain valid and reliable results; the knowledge of being in an artificial environment can affect consumer behaviour.

Other types of market study involve using real markets in different geographic locations and varying the controllable factors affecting demand. This kind of **test marketing** has the advantage that direct observation of consumers' actual spending behaviour is possible rather than just recording answers to hypothetical questions regarding such behaviour. There are still a number of problems with this method, however:

1 There is less control in this case, and greater cost; furthermore, some customers who are lost at this stage may be difficult to recover.
2 The number of variations in the variables is limited because of the limited number of market segments available. Thus only a small number of sample observations is possible.
3 Experiments may have to be long-lasting in order to reveal reliable indications of consumer behaviour. We have seen in the previous chapter that

price elasticity, for example, can be very different in the long run from in the short run because it takes time for consumers to change their habits.

4.2.3 Statistical methods

While the above methods are useful, they often do not provide management with the kind of detailed information necessary to estimate a useful demand function, and thereby test the relevant hypotheses and make forecasts. Statistical techniques, especially regression analysis, provide the most powerful means of estimating demand functions. Regression techniques do have various limitations:

1 They require a lot of data in order to be performed.
2 They necessitate a large amount of computation.
3 They suffer from a number of technical problems, which are discussed in appendix B.

In spite of these limitations, regression techniques have become the most popular method of demand estimation, since the widespread availability of powerful desktop PCs and software packages have made at least the first two problems easy to overcome. They are therefore the main subject of this chapter.

4.3 Model specification

As stated in the introduction, there are two aspects to this stage. In order to understand this we must first distinguish a **statistical relationship** from a **deterministic relationship**. The latter are relationships *known with certainty*, for example the relationship among revenue, price and quantity: $R = P \times Q$; if P and Q are known R can be determined exactly. Statistical relationships are much more common in economics and involve an element of uncertainty. The deterministic relationship is considered first.

4.3.1 Mathematical models

It is assumed to begin with that the relationship is deterministic. With a simple demand curve the relationship would therefore be:

$$Q = f(P) \tag{4.1}$$

If we are also interested in how sales are affected by the past price, the model might in general become:

$$Q_t = f(P_t, P_{t-1}) \tag{4.2}$$

where Q_t represents sales in one month, P_t represents price in the same month and P_{t-1} represents price in the previous month. This last variable, involving

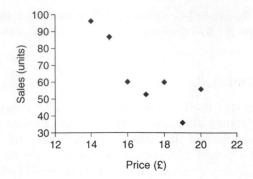

Figure 4.1. Demand Graph.

values in a previous time period, is known as a **lagged variable**. Other variables could also be included on the righthand side if economic theory or previous empirical studies indicated that they might be important.

The decision regarding which variables to include is a difficult one. Theory often tells us that certain variables, like price, promotion and income, should affect sales, but before we collect the data and analyse the results we do not know for certain which variables are relevant; in fact, even after analysing the data we do not know *for certain* which variables are important because we are estimating a relationship from sample data, and therefore we can only make conclusions in probabilistic terms. Therefore there is always a grey area if *a priori* economic theory conflicts with *a posteriori* empirical results. Subjective judgement cannot be avoided in this case.

However, both of the relationships (4.1) and (4.2) are simply stated as functions; the mathematical form of the relationship is not indicated. As mentioned in the introduction, economic theory is often not **robust** enough, meaning sufficiently specific, to be able to do this. We therefore often use scattergraphs, explained in the next section, to help us to specify the mathematical form. These are particularly useful for **bivariate**, or two-variable, relationships, although several graphs can be used for **multivariate** relationships, which involve many variables. For example, in the situation above we might draw graphs of both sales as a function of current price and sales as a function of previous month's price. From these graphs it might be possible to determine whether a linear or power relationship is the more appropriate mathematical form. As seen in the previous chapter, the linear and power forms of sales as a function of current price can be shown as follows:

$$\text{Linear: } Q = a + bP \tag{4.3}$$

$$\text{Power: } Q = aP^b \tag{4.4}$$

Frequently it is not possible to determine the mathematical form from the graphs either; for example, in Figure 4.1 the mathematical form is not obvious. To complicate matters further, there may be additional mathematical forms that we want to consider, as explained in section 4.9. In these cases we have to resort to statistical computations to determine the mathematical form, as explained in section 4.6.

4.3.2 Statistical models

In practice we can very rarely specify an economic relationship exactly. Models by their nature involve simplifications; in the demand situation we cannot hope to include all the relevant variables on the righthand side of the equation, for a number of reasons:

1 We may not know from a theoretical viewpoint what variables are relevant in affecting the demand for a particular product.
2 The information may not be available, or impossible to obtain. An example might be the marketing expenditures of rival firms.
3 It may be too costly to obtain the relevant information. For example, it might be possible to obtain information relating to the income of customers, but it would take too much time (and may not be reliable).

If we simplify the relationship to just two variables, as in expression (4.1), the scattergraph in Figure 4.1 shows that the relationship is far from perfect; in a perfect relationship the points would exactly fit a straight line, or some other 'regular' curve. Regular in this context means corresponding to one of the mathematical forms described in section 4.9.

We therefore have to specify the relationship in statistical terms, using a **residual** term to allow for the influence of omitted variables. This is shown for the linear form as follows:

$$Q_i = a + bP_i + d_i \qquad (4.5)$$

where d_i represents a residual term. Thus, even if P is known, we cannot predict Q with complete accuracy because we do not know for any observation what the size or direction of the residual will be.

4.4 Data collection

Statistical methods place a big demand on data; therefore, the collection of data is crucial in practice. This stage is often ignored in the kinds of problems with which students are frequently faced, where they are already presented with data in a usable form; this stage of the analysis is also usually discussed in more detail in market research courses. Three aspects are discussed here: types of data, sources of data and presentation of data.

4.4.1 Types of data

There are two main types of data that firms can collect.

a. Time-series data

This refers to data on a **single entity** at **different periods of time**. These data can be collected annually, quarterly, monthly or at any regular interval. Thus sales of firm A in the period 1994–99 would involve time series data. Such data may be **quantitative**, meaning that they are measured numerically on an ordinal or cardinal scale (see Chapter 3); examples are sales, prices and income. Alternatively, data may be **qualitative**, meaning that they are **nominal**, or expressed in categories; examples are male/female, married/single/widowed/divorced, east/west. The treatment of such variables, often called **dummy variables**, is considered in section 4.9, under extensions of the model.

b. Cross-section data

This refers to data on **different entities** at a **single period of time**. In managerial economics these entities are normally firms, thus sales of firms A–F in 1999 would involve cross-section data. Sometimes the entities are individuals, industries or areas.

The different types of data have certain advantages and disadvantages to the investigator that will become more apparent in sections 4.8 and 4.9. In practice the investigator may have little choice, because only one type of data may be available or feasible to use. Sometimes the two types of data can be **pooled**, that is combined together. For example, a study of six firms over six time periods would yield thirty-six observations; such data allow more observations, which is an advantage in analysis. However, pooling data has to be done with care to avoid problems of interpretation.

4.4.2 *Sources of data*

In practice we should try to collect data relating to all the variables that we think might affect sales, on either a time-series or cross-section basis, according to how we have specified the model. Later, after the statistical analysis, some of these variables may be omitted, as will be explained in section 4.9. There are many sources of data available, but in general the following are the most important in demand estimation, and indeed in most of managerial economics.

1 *Records of firms*. Sales, marketing and accounting departments keep records of many of the key variables of interest. Such data are normally up to date.
2 *Commercial and private agencies*. These include consulting firms, market research firms and banks. In addition, a firm may want to commission one of these agencies to carry out a particular study, but it would have to consider the cost involved compared with using freely available data.
3 *Official sources*. These include government departments and agencies, and international agencies like the EU, OECD, WTO and the various UN agencies. Such data tend to be more macroeconomic in nature, although there are also many industry studies. The data may also be somewhat out of date, since it

takes time to collect, collate and publish it, sometimes as long as a couple of years.

Much of the above data is now available on the Internet, particularly those from the third source and some of those from the second. It is important to appreciate that the use of any of the above sources, whether published on the Internet or not, involves **abstraction**. This means using *data that have been collected by someone else*; such data are frequently referred to as **secondary data**. Although it is obviously easier and cheaper to use such data, there are limitations of which the investigator has to be aware. The data have been collected for a different purpose from that of the current investigation and the investigator does not know the conditions under which the data were collected. The definitions used may be different from those now desired. For example, the price variable measured and recorded in a firm's records may be the quoted price, not the actual price allowing for any discounts. Clearly it is the second measure that is important in demand estimation, but the investigator may not be aware of the original definition used.

4.4.3 *Presentation of data*

a. Tables

The most basic method of presenting demand data is in the form of a table, as seen in the previous chapter. To begin with, we will take a two-variable study, involving just quantity (sales) and current price, to simplify the analysis. In reality this is only justified if either:

1 no other variables affect sales (highly unlikely), or
2 other variables do affect sales but remain constant (still fairly unlikely).

This assumption is dropped in section 4.9. The main advantage of limiting the study to two variables is that such relationships can easily be shown graphically.

Consider the example in Table 4.1, relating to a cross-section study of seven firms. The reason for recording the price variable in the last column, after

Table 4.1. Demand table

Firm	Y Sales (units)	X Price (£)
A	96	14
B	88	15
C	60	16
D	52	17
E	60	18
F	36	19
G	56	20

sales, will be explained in Section 4.9. In this example the values in the price column show regular increments of one unit; although one is unlikely to find such regularity in practice, it simplifies the numerical analysis and allows easier insights as far as statistical inference is concerned, as is shown in appendix A.

b. Graphs

In order to examine the relationship more closely the next step is to draw a graph. There are two main principles involved here:

1 Sales (Q) should be measured on the vertical axis as the dependent variable; this is contrary to most price–quantity graphs, but the rationale for this was explained in the previous chapter.
2 Scales should be selected so as to have the data spread over the whole graph; this involves looking at both the highest and lowest values in the data. Scales should not therefore automatically start at zero.

The result is a **scattergraph**, as shown in Figure 4.1; no attempt is made to join the points together in any way. We can see several things from this graph:

1 There is generally an inverse relationship between the variables.
2 The relationship is not a perfect one; the points do not lie exactly on a straight line or hyperbola. This is because of the omission of other variables affecting sales, meaning that the assumption made earlier regarding these variables (that they did not affect sales or remained constant) was not completely justified.
3 The relationship is approximately linear, although a hyperbola may also fit well.

For simplicity we will assume, to begin with, that the relationship is linear. If we want to describe the relationship using an equation, we need to draw a line of best fit. There are three basic criteria for the method of doing this. It should be:

1 objective
2 mathematically sound
3 easy to compute.

Although the second and third criteria are somewhat vague, they provide a simple justification for using the method of OLS (ordinary least squares) regression, which satisfies all the above criteria. In addition, and ultimately more important, OLS is justified on two, more technical criteria: the Gauss–Markov theorem and maximum likelihood estimation (MLE). Unfortunately these involve much more complex concepts; therefore a discussion of the first is relegated to appendix A, while a discussion of MLE is outside the scope of this text.

4.5 Simple regression

4.5.1 *The OLS method*

Simple regression means two-variable regression. The method of **least squares** means finding **the line that minimizes the sum of the squares of the differences between the observed values of the dependent variable and the fitted values from the line**. This is easier to follow in terms of mathematical symbols combined with a graph.

We have to find the line $\hat{Y} = a + bX$ which minimizes $\sum (Y_i - \hat{Y}_i)^2$ where $\hat{Y}_i = a$ fitted value from the regression line. This is shown in Figure 4.2 for the general situation.

In terms of the graph we could also say that we are trying to estimate the values of a and b, the parameters of the equation, which minimize $\sum d_i^2$. The deviation, or d_i, is often referred to as a *residual*, as mentioned in section 4.3. The technique for solving for the values of a and b is to use partial differentiation with respect to both a and b, set both expressions equal to zero to minimize them, and solve them simultaneously. This mathematical process is omitted here, but is explained in many texts on statistics or econometrics.[1] The resulting solutions are given here, although they can be expressed in other ways:

$$b = \frac{n\, \Sigma XY - \Sigma X\, \Sigma Y}{n\, \Sigma X^2 - (\Sigma X)^2} \tag{4.6}$$

$$a = \frac{\Sigma Y}{n} - \frac{b\Sigma X}{n} \tag{4.7}$$

4.5.2 *Application of OLS*

The OLS procedure is normally performed on a computer using a software package like SPSS, SAS or Minitab. In the case of simple regression many

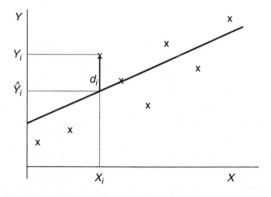

Figure 4.2. Method of least squares (OLS).

calculators are programmed to do the necessary calculations; the data are entered, the relevant commands are given and the values of a and b are then displayed. For the data set in Table 4.1 this can be achieved in a matter of a few seconds. However, this is of no help in performing statistical inference, as seen in the next section. Therefore, it is preferable initially to perform the calculations manually, especially since this will aid insight into the procedures.

There is, however, one procedure which can be performed to simplify the calculations, at least in the example in Table 4.1. This is to transform the X variable by taking deviations from the mean; this involves using a new variable x that is given by $(X - \overline{X})$. The advantage of this procedure is that it ensures that $\Sigma x = 0$, by definition. Graphically this is equivalent to shifting the Y-axis to the right so that it now intersects the X-axis at the mean of X. The new vertical intercept is now called a' in order to distinguish it from a. This in turn means that the expressions for a and b in expressions (4.6) and (4.7) can be simplified and transformed as follows:

$$b = \frac{n \sum xY - \sum x \sum Y}{n \sum x^2 - (\sum x)^2} = \frac{n \sum xY}{n \sum x^2} = \frac{\sum xY}{\sum x^2} \tag{4.8}$$

$$a' = \frac{\sum Y}{n} - \frac{b \sum x}{n} = \frac{\sum Y}{n} = \overline{Y} \tag{4.9}$$

where the regression line is given by:

$$Y = a' + bx$$

The initial calculations towards obtaining the values of a' and b are shown in Table 4.2. The results are then used as follows:

$$\sum Y = 488 \quad \sum X = 119 \quad \sum x = 0 \quad \sum xY = -224 \quad \sum x^2 = 28$$

$$\overline{Y} = 448/7 = 64 \quad \overline{X} = 17$$

$$a' = 64$$

$$b = \frac{\sum xY}{\sum x^2} = \frac{-224}{28} = -8$$

$$b = -8$$

Table 4.2. Simple regression calculations

Y Sales (units)	X Price (£)	x	xY	x^2
96	14	−3	−288	9
88	15	−2	−176	4
60	16	−1	−60	1
52	17	0	0	0
60	18	1	60	1
36	19	2	72	4
56	20	3	168	9

Thus $Y = 64 - 8x$ or $Y = 64 - 8(X - 17) = 64 - 8X + 136 = 200 - 8X$
Therefore we can write the regression line as:

$$Y = 200 - 8X$$

We can now express the demand equation in terms of sales and price as:

$$Q = 200 - 8P \qquad (4.10)$$

The value of b is particularly important in the equation; as seen in the previous chapter it represents the marginal effect of price on quantity. Thus the demand equation can be interpreted as saying that for every £1 the price rises the quantity sold will fall by eight units.

4.6 Goodness of fit

Whereas **regression** analysis examines the *type* of relationship between variables, **correlation** analysis examines the *strength* of the relationship, or goodness of fit. This refers to how closely the points fit the line, taking into consideration the units of measurement. Some idea of this can be obtained from a visual inspection of the graph, but it is better to use a quantitative measure.

4.6.1 Correlation

More specifically the **correlation coefficient (r)** measures the degree of linear association between variables. It should be noted that correlation says nothing about causation. The causation between the variables could be reversed in direction, or it could act in both directions in a circular manner. For example, high sales could lead to economies of scale in production, enabling firms to reduce their price. An alternative explanation of correlation between variables is that there may be no causation at all between two variables; they may both be influenced by a third variable. A notorious example is that empirical studies show that there is a strong relationship between the number of teachers in a country and alcohol consumption. This does not mean that teachers are heavy drinkers, or that people who are heavy drinkers become teachers! It is more likely that both the number of teachers and the level of alcohol consumption are influenced by the level of income in the country. If one substitutes purchases of TV sets or mobile phones for alcohol the same relationship would still hold good, since all these consumer goods are much influenced by income.

It should also be stressed that correlation only applies directly to linear relationships, meaning that weak correlation does not necessarily imply a weak relationship; there might be a strong non-linear relationship. Thus drawing a graph of the data is important, since this can give an insight into this possibility.

The formula for calculating the correlation coefficient can be expressed in a number of ways, but probably the most common is:

$$r = \frac{n\Sigma XY - X\Sigma Y}{\sqrt{[n\Sigma X^2 - (\Sigma X)^2][n\Sigma Y^2 - (\Sigma Y)^2]}} \qquad (4.11)$$

Thus we obtain for the data in Table 4.1:

$$r = \frac{7(7392) - 119 \times 448}{\sqrt{(196)(18{,}368)}} = \frac{-1568}{1897.4} = \mathbf{-0.8264}$$

4.6.2 The coefficient of determination

The problem with the correlation coefficient is that it does not have a precise quantitative interpretation. A better measure of goodness of fit is the **coefficient of determination**, which is given by the square of the correlation coefficient, and is usually denoted as $\mathbf{R^2}$. This does have a precise quantitative interpretation and it measures **the proportion of the total variation in the dependent variable that is explained by the relationship with the independent variable**.

In order to understand this measure more fully it is necessary to examine the statistical concept of **variation** and the components of **explained** and **unexplained variation**. This is best done with the aid of a graph (Figure 4.3).

In statistical terms, variation refers to the sum of squared deviations. Thus the total variation in Y is the sum of squared deviations from the mean of Y, or Σy^2. In terms of Figure 4.3 we can think of this as ΣTD^2. This is also referred to as the total sum of squares, or TSS. However, each deviation, or TD, can be partitioned into two components, explained deviation (ED) and unexplained deviation (UD). The first component is explained by the regression line, in other words the relationship with X. Thus:

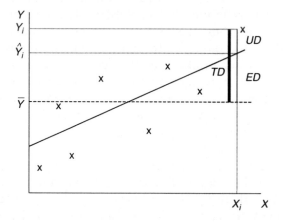

Figure 4.3. Explained and unexplained variation.

Table 4.3. ANOVA table

Source of variation	Sum of squares (SS)	Degrees of freedom (d.f.)	Mean sum of squares (MSS)	F
Regression (explained)	$ESS = 1792$	1	1792	10.77
Residual (unexplained)	$RSS =\ 832$	5	166.4	
Total	$TSS = 2624$	6		

$$TD = ED + UD \tag{4.12}$$

It can also be shown that:

$$\Sigma TD^2 = \Sigma ED^2 + \Sigma UD^2 \tag{4.13}$$

Expression (4.13) can also be written:

Total sum of squares = explained sum of squares + unexplained sum of squares or:

$$TSS = ESS + RSS \tag{4.14}$$

where RSS is the residual sum of squares and is unexplained by the regression line. These relationships are frequently illustrated in an analysis of variance, or ANOVA, table. For the data in Table 4.1 this is shown in Table 4.3. Variance, or mean sum of squares, is given by variation (SS) divided by degrees of freedom. The values in the second column are calculated in Table 4.13 in Appendix A.3. The last three columns will be explained in more detail in section 4.9.

The definition of the coefficient of determination at the beginning of this subsection indicates that it is given by:

$$R^2 = ESS/TSS \tag{4.15}$$

For the data set above, $R^2 = 1792/2624 = \mathbf{0.6829}$

This means that **68.29 per cent of the variation in sales is explained by the linear relationship with price**. The corollary of this is that 31.71 per cent of the variation in sales is unexplained by the relationship, and therefore it must be explained by other omitted variables. Thus when R^2 is low it means that other variables play an important part in affecting the dependent variable and should preferably be taken explicitly into account (if they can be identified and measured) in a **multiple regression** analysis, as described in section 4.9.

4.7 Power regression

It was assumed in the above analysis that the relationship between the variables was linear. Demand relationships are usually considered to be in linear or power form as seen in the last chapter. Rarely do we have a strong *a priori* belief regarding which mathematical form is correct from the point of view of economic theory; therefore, we tend to see which form fits the data best in practice and use that one. We now need to see how to estimate the power form of equation.

4.7.1 Nature of the model

The power form, $Q = aP^b$, cannot be estimated directly using the OLS technique because it is a linear method, meaning that the estimators a and b are linear combinations of the values in the data. However, the power equation can be transformed into a linear one by taking the logarithms of both sides to obtain:

$$\log(Q) = \log(a) + b\log(P) \qquad (4.16)$$

This ignores the error term for the sake of simplicity of expression. The logarithms used may be to the base of ten or, more commonly, to the base of the mathematical constant e, for reasons explained in section 4.9. The relationship is now linear in logarithms and therefore OLS can be applied. Sometimes the estimated equation is expressed in the form above and sometimes it is transformed back into the power form.

4.7.2 Application of the model

Many calculators now will perform regression analysis on many different mathematical forms, as long as they involve linear transformations. This is explained in more detail in section 4.9, where extensions of the regression model are considered. This means that the power model can be estimated without using logarithms on the calculator. When the data set in Table 4.1 is analysed, the resulting power regression equation is:

$$Q = 22,421P^{-2.089} \qquad (4.17)$$

This can also be expressed in logarithmic form:

$$\ln Q = 10.02 - 2.089\ln P \qquad (4.18)$$

where $\ln Q$ and $\ln P$ represent the natural logarithms (using the base of e) of Q and P.

A comparison of the linear model in (4.10) and power model in (4.17) is shown in Figure 4.4. The main application of the power model is to estimate elasticities. We can now see that the *price elasticity of demand for the product is − 2.089*.

In order to see if this power equation fits better than the linear equation estimated earlier in (4.10) we have to examine the R^2. In this case it is 0.6618, which is lower than the 0.6829 that was found for the linear relationship. This tells us that the power relationship does not explain as much of the variation in sales; in other words it does not fit as well as the linear relationship. For the data set in Table 4.1 it is therefore the linear relationship that would normally be used for drawing the regression line and for making forecasts. This forecasting aspect is now considered.

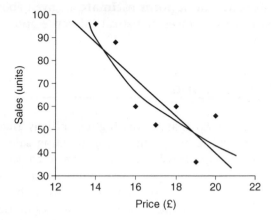

Figure 4.4. Comparison of linear and power models.

4.8 Forecasting

4.8.1 Nature

Forecasting means **estimating a specific value of a variable**, as opposed to estimating a whole relationship. Again there are various methods involved, both qualitative and quantitative, but generally the most reliable, based on the discussion in this chapter, is regression analysis. In this case a value (or values) of the independent variable(s) is given, or estimated in turn, and these values are substituted into the appropriate demand equation.

4.8.2 Application

a. The appropriate demand equation

As seen in section 4.6 we can think of this as the one that fits best. For the data set in Table 4.1 the relevant equation was given by expression (4.10):

$$Q = 200 - 8P$$

If we want a forecast for a firm charging a price of £18 we obtain a sales value of 56 units.

b. Assumptions

It is always assumed in forecasting that other things remain equal, meaning that there is no change in the variables excluded from the equation. In addition, if forecasts are being made outside the range of the data, for example a price of £22, it is also assumed that the estimated relationship is still valid. The mathematical model used may only fit well for a limited range of data.

Forecasts are always subject to an element of error because of the fact that the relationship is not a perfect one and that the regression line has to be estimated from sample data. The better the fit of the data, in other words the higher the R^2, the more accurate forecasts will be. In practice it may be helpful to managers to have not just a **point estimate** as given above, but also an **interval estimate**. This involves statistical inference and is therefore discussed in appendix A.

4.9 Multiple regression

It was stated in section 4.3 that it was highly unlikely that in a demand relationship there would only be one factor affecting sales, or that other factors would remain constant. We therefore have to consider the multiple regression model in order to analyse more complex but more realistic situations. This section will focus on the differences between the multiple regression (MR) and simple regression (SR) models as far as assumptions, estimation and hypothesis testing are concerned. Since the MR model is unlimited in terms of the number of independent or explanatory variables that it can include, we must also consider how to determine which variables to include in the model in any particular situation.

4.9.1 Nature of the model

It has already been stated that if a simple regression model produces a low R^2 this is an indication that other factors should be explicitly included in the analysis, thereby involving a multiple regression model. The population regression function therefore assumes the linear form:

$$Q_i = \alpha + \beta_1 P_i + \beta_2 A_i + \beta_3 Y_i + \beta_4 P'_i + \ldots + e_i \qquad (4.19)$$

where $\beta_1, \beta_2 \ldots$ are regression coefficients representing the marginal effects of different independent variables, and e represents the error term.

This population regression function has to be estimated from sample data, using a sample regression function:

$$Q_i = a + b_1 P_i + b_2 A_i + b_3 Y_i + b_4 P'_i + \ldots + d_i \qquad (4.20)$$

The assumptions regarding the error term in the MR model are similar to the five assumptions described for the SR model in appendix A, but with one addition:

There is no exact multicollinearity between any of the explanatory variables.

Multicollinearity is said to exist if there is a *linear relationship between two or more of the explanatory variables*; this would be the case, for example, if P and Y in the model in (4.20) were perfectly correlated. The consequences of this, or near multicollinearity, are examined in Appendix B.

Before moving on to consider the advantages of the MR model we can give an example of a situation where such a model is appropriate; this can be done by referring back to the introduction to this chapter, where we were

Table 4.4. Demand data for multiple regression analysis

Y	X_1	X_2
Sales (units)	Current Price (£)	Past Price (£)
96	14	13
88	15	15
60	16	17
52	17	18
60	18	16
36	19	20
56	20	16

considering the hypothesis that sales might depend more on past price than on current price. Assuming that no other variables were regarded as affecting sales, or that they remained constant, the mathematical model (for a sample) would be specified in linear form as:

$$Q_t = a + b_1 P_t + b_2 P_{t-1} \qquad (4.21)$$

In view of this we might obtain the sample data shown in Table 4.4. This is simply an extension of Table 4.1 to include data for past price.

4.9.2 Advantages of multiple regression

The multiple regression model has three main advantages compared with simple regression:

1 The effects of several explanatory variables on a dependent variable can be estimated.
2 Even if we are only interested in the effect of a single variable it is still better to use multiple regression to avoid a biased estimation of the regression coefficient.
3 Because of the better fit to the data, shown in the higher R^2, standard errors of coefficients are reduced, thus producing more reliable estimates of coefficients and forecasts; confidence intervals for these are reduced.

All three of the advantages above can be seen by estimating the MR model from the data in Table 4.4. The calculations involved are tedious to perform manually, so the results described below were obtained using the SPSS software package. A more detailed display and interpretation of the results is given later in this section.

The regression equation is:

$$Q_t = 235.2 - 3.890 P_t - 6.394 P_{t-1} \qquad (4.22)$$

Thus we can see the effects of both current price and past price. The interpretation is that for every £1 the current price rises, sales will fall by 3.89 units, assuming no change in the past price. Also it can be seen that for every £1 increase in past price (obviously this is no longer a controllable factor), current sales will be 6.394 units lower, assuming current price stays the same.

We can also see that our original estimate of the effect of current price, using the SR model, was biased. The marginal effect in (4.10) of -8 was exaggerated because it also included the effect of past price, the two variables being positively correlated. The marginal effect in (4.22) of -3.890 is a more accurate estimate because it isolates the effect of the current price from the effect of past price.

The fit of the model is much improved, with the R^2 increasing from 0.6829 to 0.9656. This is a **multiple R^2**, meaning that current price and past price together explain 96.56 per cent of the variation in sales. This better fit in turn means that the estimates of the regression coefficients are more reliable (meaning that they have smaller standard errors, and therefore larger t-ratios), and that forecasts will also be more reliable.

Having covered the basic features of the multiple regression model we can now move on to consider some of its more advanced aspects; a better understanding of these can be achieved only after an examination of the material in appendix A on statistical inference.

4.9.3 Dummy variables*

It is frequently desired to use qualitative rather than quantitative data in regression analysis. As mentioned in section 4.4 this considerably broadens the scope of analysis. For example, we might want to estimate the effect of an individual's sex on their demand for chocolate. Sex comes in two categories (although some geneticists are now suggesting that there should be five); therefore it is convenient to represent this characteristic by using a dummy, or $0 - 1$, variable. Thus males may be given a **0** value and females a **1** value. The choice of which value to attach to each category is entirely arbitrary; as long as one is consistent in the interpretation of results it does not matter, as will be shown.

Some characteristics require several categories, for example an individual's nationality. Another common use of dummy variables where several categories may be required is in the analysis of seasonal data; this might be classified into four quarters. In this case, three dummy variables would be required. In general, if there are m categories, $m - 1$ dummy variables are needed. Dummy variables are a very useful tool in analysing a wide variety of different problems, and are involved in both the case studies at the end of the chapter. An example of the recording of dummy variables is shown in Table 4.5, which relates to individuals of four different nationalities. The dummy variables for nationality are recorded as follows:

$N_1 = 1$ if person is British, 0 if not.
$N_2 = 1$ if person is French, 0 if not.
$N_3 = 1$ if person is German, 0 if not.

Thus an American will have a 0 value recorded in all three columns for nationality.

Table 4.5. Recording of dummy variables

Individual	S	N_1	N_2	N_3
Anne (German)	1	0	0	1
Barry (American)	0	0	0	0
Charles (British)	0	1	0	0
David (British)	0	1	0	0
Emily (French)	1	0	1	0
Florence (German)	1	0	0	1
...	...	...	...	...

Obviously other explanatory variables may be relevant in the relationship and therefore the regression model may involve a mixture of quantitative and qualitative data. Consider the following example:

$$Q = 455 - 6.52P + 1.56Y + 2.61S - 1.57N_1 - 3.83N_2 - 2.49N_3 + \cdots \quad (4.23)$$

where Q represents number of chocolate bars consumed per week, P is price (in £) and Y is income (in £,000 per year).

The coefficients of the dummy variables are interpreted as follows:

S Females eat 2.61 more chocolate bars per week than males, other things being equal.

N_1 The British eat 1.57 fewer chocolate bars per week than the Americans, other things being equal.

N_2 The French eat 3.83 fewer chocolate bars per week than the Americans, other things being equal.

N_3 The Germans eat 2.49 fewer chocolate bars per week than the Americans, other things being equal.

All the nationality comparisons above are with Americans since that nationality is used as the base of zero for each of the dummy variables. However, it is easy to make other comparisons, by subtracting coefficients; for example the British eat 2.26 more chocolate bars than the French ($-1.57 - -3.83 = +2.26$). If a different nationality were used as a base, the coefficients of the dummy variables would be different, but the same interpretation could be obtained. For example, if being British is used as the base and N_1 has the value of 1 for French and 0 otherwise, then the coefficient of N_1 would be -2.26.

4.9.4 Mathematical forms*

There is a wide variety of mathematical forms that are used in different regression models. Six models are commonly used and are now discussed; the first four of these forms involve transformations to make them linear. Table 4.6 shows these four forms of mathematical model (in just two variables and without the error term for simplicity), along with the relevant transformations and interpretations. The other two common forms involve **inverse** and

Table 4.6. Mathematical forms of the regression model

Model	Form	Transformation	Interpretation
Linear	$Y=a+bX$	none	$X \times 1$ unit $\rightarrow Y \times b$ units constant marginal effect
Power (log–log)	$Y=aX^b$	$\ln Y = a' + b \ln X$	$X \times 1\% \rightarrow Y \times b\%$ constant elasticity
Exponential (log–lin)	$Y=ae^{bX}$	$\ln Y = a' + bX$	$X \times 1 \rightarrow Y \times bX$ 100% constant growth
Logarithmic (lin–log)	$Y=a+b \log X$	$Y=a+b \ln X$	$X \times 1\% \rightarrow Y \times b/100$ units

polynomial functions. These do not have direct interpretations but may be useful in modelling certain situations.

The notation a' represents $\ln a$. It should also be noted that logarithms cannot be applied to dummy variables since one cannot take the logarithm of zero.

1 *Linear Model.* This has already been explained in some detail; it tends to be used most frequently because of its simplicity.

2 *Power Model.* As seen in section 4.7, this involves a logarithmic transformation to convert it into a linear form and make it amenable to regression analysis. It is also frequently used, since it enables the estimation of elasticities.

3 *Exponential Model.* This model is used mainly to estimate growth rates for time-series data; however, it can be used for any demand function.

4 *Logarithmic Model.* This model tends to be used less often than those described above, although for the simple regression data in Table 4.1 it actually fits best, as will be seen in Table 4.10.

5 *Inverse or Reciprocal Model.* This takes the form:

$$Y = a + b(1/X) \tag{4.24}$$

It is very versatile in terms of the shape of curve it can give, depending on the signs of a and b. If a and b are both positive it can give a downward-sloping curve similar to the power curve, and can therefore be a good fit for demand data. The problem, as stated above, is that there is no direct economic interpretation of the coefficients; for this reason it is not used as much as the models in Table 4.6.

6 *Polynomial Model.* This takes the form:

$$Y = a + b_1X + b_2X^2 + b_3X^3 + \dots \tag{4.25}$$

It is also versatile, and is useful for modelling cost functions, as seen in Chapter 7.

4.9.5 *Interpretation of the model results**

When data are entered into a computer using a standard regression program there are a large number of statistics that are usually produced on the screen

Table 4.7. Multiple regression results – model summary

Model	R	R^2	Adjusted R^2	SEE
Linear	.983	.966	.948	4.7521

Table 4.8. Multiple regression results – ANOVA

Model	Sum of squares	d.f.	Mean square	F	Sig.
Regression	2533.669	2	1266.835	56.098	.001
Residual	90.331	4	22.583		
Total	2624.000	6			

Table 4.9. Multiple regression results – coefficients

Model	Unstandardized coefficients		t	Sig.
	b	SE		
Constant	235.165	16.552	14.208	.001
Current price	−3.890	1.149	−3.384	.028
Past price	6.391	1.116	−5.731	.005

and printout. These now need to be interpreted. The data set in Table 4.4 is used to illustrate the situation. When these data are analysed using the SPSS program, the results for the linear form are as given in Tables 4.7–4.9.

The following aspects of the results need to be interpreted:

a. Regression coefficients

The general economic interpretation of these coefficients in different models has already been considered, and the particular coefficients in Table 4.9 were interpreted in subsection 4.9.2.

Let us now consider the interpretation of the coefficients for the other three mathematical forms that were estimated (not shown in Tables 4.7–4.9):

1. Power

$$\ln Q_t = 11.373 - 0.842 \ln P_t - 1.749 \ln P_{t-1} \qquad (4.26)$$

This means that for every 1 per cent the current price increases, the sales will fall by 0.842 per cent, other things being equal, and that for every 1 per cent increase in the past price, sales will be 1.749 per cent lower. Again we can see that the use of simple regression resulted in a large overestimation of the price elasticity: the value of −0.842 is a more accurate measure than the value of −2.089 obtained in (4.17).

2. Exponential

$$\ln Q_t = 6.783 - 0.0511\,P_t - 0.110\,P_{t-1} \tag{4.27}$$

This is interpreted that for every £1 the current price rises, sales will fall by about 5 per cent, other things being equal; similarly, for every increase in £1 of the past price, sales will be 11 per cent lower.

3. Logarithmic

$$Q_t = 533.557 - 64.437\,\ln P_t - 102.987\,\ln P_{t-1} \tag{4.28}$$

The interpretation in this case is that for every 1 per cent increase in the current price, sales will fall by 0.64 units, other things being equal; similarly, for every increase of 1 per cent in the past price, sales will be 1.03 units lower.

b. Standard errors of coefficients

These are useful in showing the margin of error of estimation, and can be used to calculate confidence intervals. They can also be used to calculate t-statistics, as explained below. However, much of the discussion of the following measures involves a more detailed understanding of statistical theory; the reader is therefore recommended to refer to appendix A before continuing further with this section.

c. t-statistics

A t-statistic or t-ratio is given by the relevant coefficient divided by its standard error (b/σ_b). Thus the t-statistic for the current price variable is $-3.890/1.149 = -3.384$. The t-statistics are used to test the significance of individual independent variables. Usually the null hypothesis that the regression coefficient is 0 is used; if the t-statistic exceeds a certain critical value (which depends on the significance level chosen, whether the test is one-or two-tail, and the number of degrees of freedom), the null hypothesis is rejected. This means that there is evidence of a relationship between the dependent and independent variable, because the probability of such a large t-statistic occurring if there were no relationship is very small, typically less than 0.05 (the 5 per cent level of significance is normally used).

Applying this to our data set we would expect both current and past price to have a negative effect on sales, therefore resulting in one-tail tests. There are four degrees of freedom; this is given by $n - k - 1$, where k is the number of regressors or explanatory variables. At the 5 per cent level of significance the critical value of t is 2.132. Since both t-statistics exceed this in absolute magnitude, we would reject the null hypothesis that either β_1 or $\beta_2 = 0$ in favour of the alternative hypothesis that both β_1 and $\beta_2 > 0$. There is thus evidence that both current price and past price negatively affect sales.

d. Significance values

These are sometimes called prob-values or *p*-values because they indicate the probability of a calculated *t*-statistic occurring if there is no relationship between the dependent and independent variable. Thus if the *t* statistic exceeds the critical value at the 5 per cent level of significance the *p*-value must be less than 0.05 (assuming a two-tail test).

In Table 4.9 the *t*-statistic for current price is -3.384 and the significance value is 0.028. This means that the result would be significant at the 2.8 per cent level if we were performing a two-tail test. Since we would in this case perform a one-tail test the result is significant at the 1.4 per cent level. Likewise the past price significantly affects sales at the 0.25 per cent level.

e. Standard error of the estimate (SEE)

This refers to the standard deviation of the dependent variable *Y* after controlling for the effects of all the *X* variables; in symbols it is represented as:

$$s = \sqrt{(Y - \hat{Y})^2/n - k - 1} \qquad (4.29)$$

where *k* refers to the number of regressors.

It is a very useful measure of $\hat{Y}$ the accuracy, or goodness of fit, of a regression model; its value would be 0 if the relationship were perfect. It is thus inversely related to R^2.

In Table 4.7 the SEE is given as 4.7521. This compares with the SEE from the simple regression model of 12.90. Thus the fit of the relationship has been substantially improved.

f. Coefficient of determination (R^2)

This measure has already been interpreted in section 4.6 for the simple regression model, and has been extended to the multiple regression model in explaining the advantages of using multiple regression. We have seen that by including the past price in the regression model we have increased the proportion of the variation in sales explained by the model from 68.29 per cent to 96.56 per cent.

g. Adjusted coefficient of determination (adj. R^2)

There is a problem in using the R^2 as a measure of goodness of fit; as more variables are included in the regression equation, the R^2 will increase even if the additional variables are not related to the dependent variable. To compensate for this, and to enable the investigator to select the model with the best fit, a corrected or adjusted R^2 can be used; this adjusts for the number of degrees of freedom, so that the R^2 does not automatically increase as more variables are included. The formula for calculating the adjusted R^2 is:

$$adj.R^2 = 1 - (1 - R^2)(n - k)/(n - k - 1) \qquad (4.30)$$

Unfortunately there is no direct interpretation of the adjusted R^2 value. Its use is discussed further in the next subsection.

h. F-statistic

Although both the above measures provide an indication of the strength of the relationship between the dependent and independent variables, they do not indicate whether the relationship is significant. The F-statistic is a measure of the statistical significance of the relationship between the dependent variable and the independent variables taken as a group. It is the ratio of explained variance to unexplained variance (variance is variation divided by degrees of freedom). If there is just one independent variable the F-statistic gives the same result as the t-statistic.

In Table 4.8 the F-statistic is given as 56.098. This is obtained by dividing the mean square of the regression (which is the explained variance) of 1266.835 by the mean square of the residual (which is the unexplained variance) of 22.583. The significance of this value is indicated in the next column of the ANOVA table; in this case it shows that the relationship is significant at the 0.1 per cent level. It is therefore highly unlikely that such sample data would be observed if there were no relationship between the variables involved.

4.9.6 Selecting the best model*

We have so far specified the model in various forms; now we have to decide which of these forms is the best one to use. Most of the results analysed in the previous subsection related to the linear model. However, as already explained, economic theory alone cannot determine the mathematical form of the model in demand situations. Therefore, although theoretical considerations should always come first in specifying the model, in this case we have to let the empirical results determine the best form to use. There are two issues here:

1 *Which variables should we include in the model?* This means considering whether we should use current price only, past price only, or both, in the model.
2 *Which mathematical form should we use?* This means comparing the four different forms considered in order to see which fits best.

We therefore need to compare the values of the adjusted R^2 for the different models. This is the measure that must be used to compare models with different numbers of variables. The results are shown in Table 4.10.

Table 4.10. Comparing goodness of fit for different models

Model	Current price	Past price	Current and past price
Linear	.620	.840	.948
Power	.594	n/a	.929
Exponential	.563	n/a	.956
Logarithmic	.659	n/a	.949

The relevant statistics for the relationship with past price only have not been computed since it is apparent from the values already computed that the best model should include both explanatory variables. There is little to choose between the different mathematical forms, but the exponential form fits marginally better than any of the others. It will always be the case that the SEE statistic and the adjusted R^2 are inversely related; thus, selecting the model with the highest adjusted R^2 will always result in obtaining the model with the lowest SEE. Strictly speaking the R^2 or adjusted R^2 values of mathematical forms with different dependent variables are not directly comparable,[2] but we will overlook this here for simplicity. Therefore the best form of the model is the one in (4.27):

$$\ln Q_t = 6.783 - 0.0511\ P_t - 0.110\ P_{t-1}$$

This is generally the model we should use, especially for forecasting purposes. We can test our original hypothesis using this model: changes in past price have about twice the effect of changes in current price, and the t-statistic is much more significant for past price.

The procedure described above for finding the model with the highest adjusted R^2 can be tedious if there are a large number of possible explanatory variables and we are not sure from a theoretical viewpoint which ones to include. Fortunately, there is a rule to aid this decision. It can be shown that the adjusted R^2 will increase if the absolute value of t for a coefficient is greater than 1, assuming the null hypothesis was that the population coefficient was 0 (meaning that the variable had no effect on the dependent variable). Thus, if there is no prior or

---

Case study 4.1: The demand for coffee

An empirical study by Huang, Siegfried and Zardoshty[3] estimated a demand function for coffee in the United States between 1961 and 1977, using quarterly time-series data. The results were:

$$\ln Q_t = 1.2789 - 0.1647\ \ln P_t + 0.5115\ \ln Y_t$$
$$\quad\quad\quad\quad (-2.14)\quad\quad\quad (1.23)$$
$$\quad + 0.1483\ \ln P'_t - 0.0089\ T - 0.0961\ D_1$$
$$\quad\quad (0.55)\quad\quad\quad (-3.326)\quad (-3.74)$$
$$\quad - 0.1570\ D_2 - 0.0097\ D_3$$
$$\quad\quad (-6.03)\quad\quad (-0.37)$$
$$R^2 = 0.80$$

where

Q = pounds of coffee consumed per head
P = the relative price of coffee per pound at 1967 prices
Y = per capita personal disposable income (in \$,000 at 1967 prices)
P' = the relative price of tea per quarter pound at 1967 prices

T = the trend factor, with $T = 1$ for 1961-I to $T = 66$ for 1977-II
$D_1 = 1$ for the first quarter
$D_2 = 1$ for the second quarter
$D_3 = 1$ for the third quarter

Questions

1 Interpret the PED for coffee; does price significantly affect consumption?
2 Interpret the YED for coffee; does income significantly affect consumption?
3 Interpret the CED between tea and coffee; does the price of tea significantly affect the consumption of coffee?
4 Why do you think that advertising expenditure is omitted from the equation?
5 Interpret the trend factor.
6 Interpret the seasonal pattern in coffee consumption in the USA.
7 How well does the model fit the data?

theoretical reason for including a particular explanatory variable, we should exclude it from the model if the absolute value of its t-statistic is less than 1.

4.10 Implications of empirical studies

Over the last few decades, thousands of empirical studies have been performed examining demand relationships. The purpose here is to summarize three of the most important findings in terms of the implications for economic theory.

4.10.1 The price–quality relationship

Many studies show that consumers tend to use price as an indicator of quality, particularly in the absence of other quality cues. Consider the following two examples.

1 *Buying a personal computer*. In this situation there are many quality indicators: brand name, type and speed of processor, amount of RAM, DVD availability, size of hard disk, size of monitor and so on. In this case consumers are less likely to use price as an indicator of quality.
2 *Buying a bottle of wine*. There may be quality indicators here too, such as country and region of origin and vintage, but a consumer who is not familiar with these cues may simply assume that 'you get what you pay for'.

Obviously much depends on the knowledge of the individual consumer, but the assumption of consumers, in the second situation above, results in the price variable having two separate effects on sales: apart from the normal inverse relationship there is a positive relationship with perceived quality which in turn has a positive relationship with sales. It is possible that the indirect positive effects working through perceived quality may outweigh the normal inverse relationship, resulting in the demand curve appearing to be upward-sloping. Strictly speaking this is not a true demand curve since it invalidates the *ceteris paribus* assumption in the price–quantity relationship, but this technicality is not what concerns managers. Managers are concerned with the possibility that they can raise the price of a product and simultaneously increase sales if they are successful in persuading consumers that the quality of the product has improved. This has important marketing implications in terms of promotion and packaging, which can be used to reinforce this change in attitudes.

4.10.2 Lack of importance of price

Economists sometimes assume that price is the most important variable in the marketing mix because of its role in allocating resources, as discussed in Chapter 1. Empirical studies often contradict this; in Houthakker and Taylor's landmark study of consumer demand in the United States,[4] it was found that in their analysis of eighty-three products, price significantly affected sales in only forty-five cases. One reason for this is the phenomenon referred to above where a change in price may be associated with a change in quality. In other cases, studies have shown that consumers are ignorant of prices, or that they may know the current price of the products they buy but not the past price, and therefore cannot detect a price change. This research indicates the importance of habit formation and brand loyalty.

4.10.3 *Dynamic relationships*

These are relationships that include lagged variables, meaning that consumer decisions involve data from past periods. In the study above, Houthakker and Taylor found that a dynamic demand relationship fitted best for seventy-two of the eighty-three products. There were three main variations in the nature of the dynamic relationship, with sometimes all of them appearing in the same equation, as, for example, in the demand for radio and television receivers, records and musical instruments:

$$Q_t = .6599Q_{t-1} + .0167\Delta C_t + .0060C_{t-1} - .0946\Delta P_t - .0340P_{t-1} \qquad (4.31)$$

where:

Q_t = quantity demanded in quarter t
Q_{t-1} = quantity demanded in quarter $t-1$
ΔC_t = change in total consumer expenditure between quarter t and quarter $t-1$
C_{t-1} = total consumer expenditure in quarter $t-1$
ΔP_t = change in relative price between quarter t and quarter $t-1$
P_{t-1} = relative price in quarter $t-1$

This shows the relevance of:

1 *Lagged endogenous variables*, where the amount of a product bought depended on the amount bought in the previous time period, again indicating the existence of habit formation.
2 *Lagged exogenous variables*, such as total expenditure and income.
3 *Changes in variables*, showing consumers may react to changes in prices or incomes.

4.11 A problem-solving approach

Essentially there are seven main stages in estimating demand, as described in the introduction to this chapter:

1 *Statement of a theory or hypothesis.* This must relate in some way to a demand relationship.
2 *Model specification.* This involves identifying variables that may be relevant in the demand relationship, determining how to measure them and considering functional form and time lags.

3 *Data collection.* This involves determining whether to use time-series or cross-section data, and sample selection. Practical considerations here may relate to decisions in the previous stages.

4 *Estimation of parameters.* This stage is largely mechanical, involving calculators and computers with the relevant programs.

5 *Checking goodness of fit.* This is necessary to examine how well a particular model fits and find the model that fits best.

6 *Hypothesis testing.* This combines with statistical inference, and is explained in section 4.9 and appendix A.

7 *Forecasting.* This was explained in section 4.8.

With most problems that students face the first three aspects are not relevant, because they are given a data set to work with. The third stage is relatively straightforward, so the main difficulties occur with interpretation. A lack of understanding of the theoretical underpinnings of the regression model is often the fundamental problem. The model is easy to use mechanically, but aspects of statistical inference are much more complex. These are best approached with **visual aids of graphs and diagrams**, for example to explain bias and efficiency of estimators; although these visual aids relate mainly to simple regression, if this model is understood it can easily be extended to the multiple regression model.

However, in practice the first three stages of the process may pose considerable problems to investigators. Therefore, two case studies are presented in this section that illustrate the problems in these stages. Furthermore, the last of the review questions involves a consideration of the third stage as well as the first two.

Three solved problems are now presented.

SP4.1 Revenue relationships

KA Products has just carried out a survey of the demand for their guidebooks to spoken English. They have found the following results over the last six months.

Sales revenue ($,000)	356	398	372	360	365	350
Price ($)	4.5	4.0	4.2	4.5	4.3	4.8

a. Estimate an appropriate demand relationship.
b. Draw a graph of the data and the above relationship.
c. Make a forecast of sales revenue for a price of $5, stating any assumptions.
d. Estimate the price elasticity of demand for the data as a whole.
e. If price is raised 10 per cent in general terms, what will happen to revenue?

Solution

a. $Q=985.1P^{-1.67}$ $r^2=97.79$ per cent
b. Power relationship
c. $335,000 assuming other things apart from price stay the same and that the estimated relationship is still valid outside the price range.
d. −1.67, elastic
e. Revenue falls 6.7 per cent; this result can be obtained from computing the revenue function $R=PQ=985.1P^{-0.67}$

SP4.2 Lagged relationships

MC Corp. makes alarm clocks and has observed the following pattern of sales over the last 8 months:

	Jul.	Aug.	Sep.	Oct.	Nov.	Dec.	Jan.	Feb.
Sales (units)	380	430	410	420	450	440	480	500
Income ($,000)	26	25	27	29	28	31	32	32

a. Is it appropriate to use a lagged relationship in the above situation? Give your reasons.
b. Estimate an appropriate relationship.
c. Draw a graph of the data and appropriate relationship.
d. Estimate sales in March, stating any relevant assumptions.
e. How much of the variation in sales is explained by the relationship with income?

Solution

a. It may be appropriate in theory to lag the relationship because income is often received at the end of the month. To check whether it is actually appropriate in this case we have to estimate the relationship with a lag and see if it fits better than the unlagged relationship. The lagged relationship does in fact fit better, with a coefficient of determination (COD) of 94.33% compared with the unlagged relationship with a COD of 60.79%.

b. Unlagged linear: $Q=121.9+11.02Y$ COD$=60.79\%$
   Unlagged power: $Q=41.31Y^{0.7033}$ COD$=58.35\%$
   Lagged linear: $Q=98.70+12.32Y_{t-1}$ COD$=94.33\%$
   Lagged power: $Q=34.32Y_{t-1}^{0.7682}$ COD$=93.61\%$

   Therefore the appropriate relationship is the lagged linear.
c. Sales should be on vertical axis; scales should be such as to give a spread of the data points; the lagged data should be used resulting in

seven points on the scattergraph; and the regression line should be drawn accurately.

d. 493 units, assuming that all other factors that affect sales remain the same.

e. 94.33%

SP4.3 Interpretation of regression model

The following regression is based on a random sample of 200 persons:

$$\text{LOGIN} = 0.12\text{LOGFIN} + 0.05\text{EDUC} - 0.15\text{FEMALE}$$

(t ratios)	(3.28)	(2.50)	(3.05)
(p values)	(.001)	(.006)	(.001)

$R^2 = 0.82$

where:

LOGIN = natural log of the person's income
LOGFIN = natural log of the father's income
EDUC = number of years in education
FEMALE = 1 if female; 0 if male.

a. Interpret the regression coefficients.
b. Interpret the p-values for the t-statistics.
c. John and Jim are alike in all respects except income and their father's income. John's father earns £60,000 and John himself earns £40,000. If Jim's father earns £54,000, estimate Jim's income.
d. Jane is John's sister but has had three more years in education; estimate her income.
e. Interpret the R^2.

Solution

a. 1% increase in father's income increases son's income by 0.12%.
   one year more education increases income by 5%.
   Females earn 15% less than males.
   All the above assume other things remain equal.
b. All three independent variables significantly affect income, particularly the first and last.
c. 1.2% less than £40,000 = £39,520
d. £40,000

e. 82% of the variation in income is explained by the relationship with the independent variables.

Case study 4.2: Determinants of car prices

See *What CAR?* data, which is accessible as an Excel spreadsheet at http://www.cambridge.org/ 0521526256.

Questions

1 Investigate how car prices are affected by size, power and degree of luxury, using the sample data.
2 Are there any significant differences in pricing practices among the different makes?

Case study 4.3: The Sports Connection[*5]

The Sports Connection is a chain of health clubs operating in Los Angeles. They have been interested in evaluating the effects of various elements of their marketing strategy; in particular, this strategy involved changing the terms of their offer to consumers at regular intervals, normally every month. These offer terms include a number of variables: current price, amount of time free on top of one year's membership, and guaranteed renewal price. The firm would also sometimes offer a referral programme, which would reward new members for bringing in other new members within their first month of membership.

In some months the firm would change the offer twice, rather than once; they observed that this seemed to bring in more new members because of

Table 4.11. Sales at Sports Connection clubs, 1986–87

Sales (new members)	Santa Monica	South Bay	Beverly Hills	Encino	Long Beach
Dec. 1987	447	336	274	202	201
Nov.	501	339	237	171	176
Oct.	358	286	239	161	165
Sep.	386	220	221	171	219
Aug.	418	273	215	201	170
Jul.	388	272	219	178	161
Jun.	325	210	213	233	183
May	350	282	360	264	268
Apr.	340	270	331	289	225
Mar.	455	203	331	321	255
Feb.	392	201	277	204	233
Jan.	498	302	439	204	241
Dec. 1986	408	271	295	214	187
Nov.	358	278	310	210	205
Oct.	363	280	285	212	136
Sep.	389	329	389	208	221
Aug.	280	313	334	219	228
Jul.	291	268	346	300	267
Jun.	311	283	284	234	228
May	332	350	291	240	212
Apr.	409	336	375	229	275
Mar.	480	292	307	247	285
Feb.	419	289	297	229	246
Jan.	487	365	348	235	311

Table 4.12. Sales parameters for Sports Connection clubs, 1986–87

	Price ($)	Timefree (months)	Referral programme	Renewal price ($)	Number of offer changes	Income ($ billion)
Dec. 1987	381	3.6	No	149	1	2,745.1
Nov.	399	5.4	No	151	1	2,710.5
Oct.	433	7.2	No	150	1	2,731.0
Sep.	400	7.2	No	195	1	2,683.3
Aug.	404	7.2	No	190	1	2,686.3
Jul.	412	7.2	No	185	1	2,682.2
Jun.	387	7.2	No	180	1	2,662.8
May	369	3.6	No	171	2	2,676.8
Apr.	361	3.6	No	166	2	2,603.6
Mar.	388	7.2	No	180	1	2,680.3
Feb.	424	9.6	No	166	1	2,687.2
Jan.	414	9.6	No	147	1	2,656.3
Dec. 1986	377	3.6	No	180	1	2,661.9
Nov.	386	5.6	No	180	1	2,655.5
Oct.	386	8.4	No	180	1	2,652.6
Sep.	353	3.6	Yes	221	2	2,652.2
Aug.	331	3.6	Yes	213	1	2,653.4
Jul.	329	3.6	No	204	1	2,654.1
Jun.	364	3.6	No	168	1	2,649.4
May	375	8.4	No	168	1	2,628.0
Apr.	374	3.6	Yes	168	2	2,640.9
Mar.	371	2.4	No	168	1	2,602.6
Feb.	392	9.6	No	168	1	2,583.0
Jan.	380	3.6	No	168	1	2,558.1

Price= Average price for the month, taking into account different types of membership sold ($)
Time free= Average amount of free time offered during the month (in months).
Renewal price= Average annual renewal price offered ($).
Income= National disposable personal income at annual rate ($ billion at 1982 prices).

the 'deadline effect'. Whenever customers made membership enquiries they were told that the existing offer would be ending soon, and that the new offer would in some way be less favourable; either the price would go up, the amount of time free would be less, or the renewal price would go up. By using many variables in the offer terms the firm was continuously able to have some 'special' on offer, either a low price, more time free or a low renewal price, and to rotate these terms. As the deadline for the end of any offer drew near, the number of buyers increased. Thus it seemed that having two 'close-outs' in some months was a desirable strategy.

Table 4.11 shows sales for the five different Sports Connection clubs in 1986–87. In Table 4.12 the values of different variables are shown for the time series data; the values are the same for all five clubs.

Questions

1 Is there evidence that having two close-outs in a month has a beneficial effect on sales?
2 The company is concerned that having two close-outs in a month simply results in people joining sooner than they would otherwise join, with no overall benefit in terms of new membership sales. Is there evidence of a dip in sales in months following a month with two close-outs?
3 Examine the effect of the level of price on new membership sales; compare this effect with the effect of having two close-outs in a month.
4 Examine the effects of offering time free, the referral program and the renewal price.
5 Is there evidence of a trend effect?
6 Is there evidence of a 'New Year's resolution' effect?
7 What conclusions can you draw from your analysis regarding the marketing strategy of the Sports Connection?

Appendix A. Statistical inference*

This section is more difficult because it assumes that the student already has some knowledge of inferential statistics, in terms of hypothesis testing and the *t*-distribution.

A.1 Nature of inference in the OLS model

The term **inference** here means drawing conclusions from a sample of observations about a whole population. It is important to recognize that in practice we are almost always limited to collecting data relating to just a sample; in the demand situation considered so far the observations represent just some of the possible quantities sold for the prices charged. If more observations, relating to other firms producing the same product or the same firms at different time periods, were made at the same prices, then different sales quantities would be observed. This concept is easier to visualize in terms of a graph; Figure 4.5 represents some additional observations, involving a total of five samples (although still not the whole population).

Therefore, although we can mechanically compute a **sample regression line** for a set of sample data, as in section 4.5, we cannot be sure that this sample regression line or function is representative of the whole population. Each sample regression line will be somewhat different, meaning that each will have different values of the intercept and slope coefficients *a* and *b*. The true **population parameters** for the intercept and slope, often referred to as α and β, are unknown and, in practice, have to be estimated from a single sample. The situation is illustrated in Figures 4.6 and 4.7. In order to draw conclusions about these population parameters we must make certain assumptions about the nature of the population.

A.2 Assumptions

Using the symbols defined above we can express the **population regression function** as:

$$Y_i = \alpha + \beta X_i + e_i \tag{4.32}$$

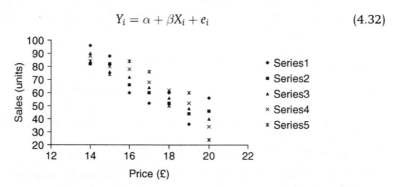

Figure 4.5. Demand graph of population.

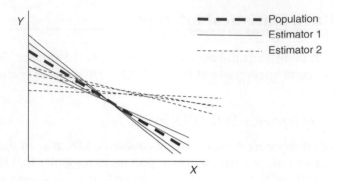

Figure 4.6. Biased and unbiased estimators.

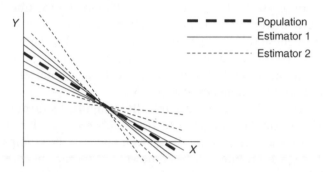

Figure 4.7. Efficient estimators.

Where e represents an **error term** that is unknown in practice, because α and β are unknown. It is important to note the difference between the error term and the residual; they both arise for the same reason, the omission of other variables, but the residuals can be computed from the sample regression line, while the error terms cannot be calculated since they come from the unknown population regression line.

There are five main assumptions relating to this population regression function, and these are only outlined here; a more thorough explanation is outside the scope of this book, but is covered in most texts on econometrics, for example that of Gujarati.[6]

1 The independent variable is uncorrelated with the error term e.   (4.33)

This will always be true if the X variable is **deterministic**, meaning that it takes on fixed values, as assumed in the above example. This will not necessarily happen if it is **stochastic**, meaning that it takes on random values.

2 The expected value or mean of the error term is zero, or $E(e_i) = 0$.   (4.34)

3 The variance of the error term is constant, or **homoscedastic**.

$$\text{This can be written: var}(e_i) = \sigma^2 \qquad (4.35)$$

Table 4.13. Calculations for inference

Y Sales (units)	X Price(£)	x	xY	x²	Ŷ	Y-Ŷ	(Y-Ŷ)²	y	y²	Ŷ-Ȳ	(Ŷ-Ȳ)²
96	14	-3	-288	9	88	8	64	32	1,024	24	576
88	15	-2	-176	4	80	8	64	24	576	16	256
60	16	-1	-60	1	72	-12	144	-4	16	8	64
52	17	0	0	0	64	-12	144	-12	144	0	0
60	18	1	60	1	56	4	16	-4	16	-8	64
36	19	2	72	4	48	-12	144	-28	784	-16	256
56	20	3	168	9	40	16	256	-8	64	-24	576
Σ			-224				832		2,624		1,792

4 The error terms are independent of each other; this means that there is *no* **autocorrelation**. This can be written : $\text{cov}(e_i, e_j) = 0$ (4.36)

5 The error terms are normally distributed. (4.37)

The third and fourth assumptions will be examined in more detail in appendix B, in terms of their nature and of the consequences when the assumptions are not valid.

A.3 *Calculations for statistical inference*

As stated in section 4.5, there is one procedure which can be performed to simplify the calculations involved in statistical inference, at least in the example in Table 4.13 . This is to transform the X variable by taking deviations from the mean; this involves using a new variable x that is given by $(X - \bar{X})$. The advantage of this procedure is that it ensures that $\Sigma x = 0$, by definition. Graphically this is equivalent to shifting the Y-axis to the right so that it now intersects the X-axis at the mean of X. The new vertical intercept is now called a' in order to distinguish this value from a. This in turn means that the expressions for a and b in (4.6) and (4.7) can be simplified and transformed as follows:

$$b = \frac{n\Sigma xY - \Sigma x \Sigma Y}{n\Sigma x^2 - (\Sigma x)^2} = \frac{n\Sigma xY}{n\Sigma x^2} = \frac{\Sigma xY}{\Sigma x^2}$$ (4.38)

$$a' = \frac{\Sigma Y}{n} - \frac{b\Sigma x}{n} = \frac{\Sigma Y}{n} = \bar{Y}$$ (4.39)

where the regression line is given by:

$$Y = a' + bx$$

The above transformation is shown graphically in Figure 4.8 and the relevant calculations to obtain the values of a' and b are shown in Table 4.13 . Without such a transformation the calculations necessary for statistical inference become very tedious without the use of an appropriate computer program.

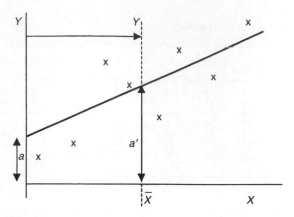

Figure 4.8. Transformation of X

The last four columns in Table 4.13 are necessary for the calculations related to R^2 and analysis of variance, explained in section 4.6.

$$\Sigma Y = 448 \qquad \Sigma X = 119 \quad \Sigma x = 0 \qquad \Sigma xY = -224 \quad \Sigma x^2 = 28$$
$$\overline{Y} = 448/7 = 64 \quad \overline{X} = 17$$
$$a\prime = 64$$
$$b = \frac{\Sigma xY}{\Sigma x^2} = \frac{-224}{28} = -8$$

Thus $Y = 64 - 8x$ or $Y = 64 - 8(X - 17) = 64 - 8X + 136 = 200 - 8X$

Therefore we can write the regression line as:

$$Y = 200 - 8X$$

We can now express the demand equation in terms of sales and price as:

$$Q = 200 - 8P$$

as in (4.10).

Using the above transformation of X into x, and a similar transformation of Y into y, the formula for calculating the correlation coefficient becomes:

$$r = \frac{\Sigma xY}{\sqrt{(\Sigma x^2 \Sigma y^2)}}$$
$$= \frac{-224}{\sqrt{(28)(2624)}} = \frac{-224}{271.1} = -0.8264 \qquad (4.40)$$

A.4 Consequences of assumptions

There are three main conclusions that we can form from the above assumptions. These relate to the standard errors of estimators, the Gauss–Markov theorem and usefulness of the assumptions in inference.

a. Standard errors of estimators

First of all, the first four assumptions (the last one is not necessary for this), enable us to estimate the standard errors of the OLS **estimators**, a and b. An estimator refers to a ***method of estimating a population parameter***; it is not to be confused with an **estimate**, which is a ***particular value of an estimator*** from a given sample. For example, the value of -8 is the OLS estimate of β from the sample in the previous subsection. The standard error of b, the more important statistic, is given by:

$$\sigma_b = \frac{\sigma}{\sqrt{\sum x^2}} \tag{4.41}$$

where σ represents the standard error of the error term. Because σ is again a population parameter which is unknown, it has to be estimated from sample data. The estimator of σ is often called s, which is referred to as the **standard error of the estimate** (SEE) or the **residual standard error**. It measures *the standard deviation of the Y values about the sample regression line* and is given by:

$$s = \sqrt{\{\Sigma(Y - \hat{Y})^2/n - 2\}} \tag{4.42}$$

Now we can use the values in Table 4.13 to calculate the value of s:

$$s = \sqrt{(832/5)} = 12.90 \tag{4.43}$$

and

$$\sigma_b = 12.90/\sqrt{28} = 2.438 \tag{4.44}$$

b. The Gauss–Markov theorem

The assumptions justify the use of the OLS method. Again on the basis of the first four assumptions, the **Gauss–Markov theorem** states that the OLS estimators are the **best linear unbiased estimators** (BLUE).
These terms now need to be briefly explained:

1 *Linear*. This means that the estimators are linear combinations of the variables X and Y.
2 *Unbiased*. This means that the estimator is generally 'on target'; given that the target is the population parameter, this can be written more formally as:

$$E(a) = \alpha \quad \text{and} \quad E(b) = \beta$$

This situation is illustrated in Figure 4.6. For each estimator four sample lines are shown: estimator 1 is unbiased while estimator 2 is biased since $E(b) < \beta$.
3 *Best*. The best estimator will not only be unbiased but will also have minimum variance. This is illustrated in Figure 4.7 where two unbiased estimators are

compared. Estimator 1 is better because it has less variance and therefore an estimate from a single sample is more likely to be 'on target'. Such an estimator is said to be more **efficient**.

c. Usefulness in inference

Having explained why the OLS method is a good method of estimating relationships, we can now move on to consider how it can be used for statistical inference. There are two main branches of statistical inference: estimation and hypothesis testing. Both of these involve using the distributions of the sample statistics a and b. The fact that a and b have distributions is again illustrated by Figures 4.6 and 4.7, but to make useful conclusions regarding the characteristics of these distributions involves using the final assumption (4.37). With this assumption it can be shown that both a and b are random variables that will tend to be normally distributed as sample size increases. With smaller sample sizes they follow the t-distribution.

A.5 Estimation

We have already seen in the earlier subsection how to estimate values of a and b using the OLS method. However, the estimates that were obtained were **point estimates**, i.e. single values; for example, from Table 4.2 the values of a and b were 200 and -8. It is also useful to have **interval estimates**. These involve giving a confidence interval, usually 95 per cent for the estimate. If b is normally distributed the 95 per cent confidence interval is given by:

$$b \pm 1.96\sigma_b \qquad (4.45)$$

Since we are often using small samples, this becomes:

$$b \pm t_{.025}\sigma_b \qquad (4.46)$$

Therefore from Table 4.13 we can calculate a 95 per cent confidence interval for b as follows: $-8 \pm 2.571(2.438) = -8 \pm 6.27$ or from $-\mathbf{1.73}$ **to** $-\mathbf{14.27}$.

This should not be interpreted as meaning that we can be 95 per cent sure that the true value of β will be included in this interval. It means that *if we construct similar intervals repeatedly, 95 per cent of the time they will include the true value of β*

A.6 Hypothesis testing

We frequently want to test whether the sample estimate of b is significantly different from some hypothesized value of β; this hypothesized value is 0 in the case where we are testing to see if some independent variable, for example price, has an effect on the dependent variable, in this case sales. Thus the **null hypothesis** in this situation is that $\beta = 0$. It should be noted that this does not mean that we lean towards believing that the hypothesized value is correct, that is that we believe that price has no effect on sales. The null hypothesis is established merely for convenience of testing. The **alternative hypothesis** depends on our prior belief, as determined by theory; in this case we would perform a **one-tail test**, since the alternative hypothesis is that $\beta < 0$. This means that we believe that price has a negative effect on sales. We then compute the **t-statistic** as:

$$t = b/\sigma_b \qquad (4.47)$$

Thus $t = -8/2.438 = -3.282$.

This is then compared (in absolute magnitude) with the critical value of t; this value depends on the **level of significance** used, whether one is performing a one-tail or a two-tail test, and the number of **degrees of freedom**. In simple regression there are $n - 2$ degrees of freedom, since it takes more than two points to give an indication of the error involved (we can always draw a straight line that goes exactly through two points).

The critical value of t using a 5 per cent level of significance (the most commonly used level) is 2.015. Since the computed t-statistic is more than the critical value, we reject the null hypothesis in favour of the alternative hypothesis. ***Thus we conclude that price does have a significant negative effect on sales.*** If we perform a two-tail test and reject the null hypothesis, the relevant conclusion in general terms is that the explanatory variable has a significant effect on the dependent variable. We can perform similar hypothesis tests on the intercept value, a, but generally we are more interested in the value of b, since this shows the effect of one variable on another.

A.7 Confidence intervals for forecasts

There are two kinds of forecast that we may want to make: (a) mean values of Y; (b) individual values of Y.

a. Mean values of Y

We may, for example, want to forecast a 95 per cent confidence interval for the mean sales of all firms charging the price of £18. The standard error of such a forecast is given by:

$$SE = s\sqrt{(1/n + x_0^2/\Sigma x^2)} \qquad (4.48)$$

Where x_0 represents the deviation of the value of X that we are forecasting for (£18) from the mean of X (£17).

Thus the 95 per cent confidence interval is given by:

$$\hat{Y_0} \pm t_{.025}\, s\sqrt{(1/n + x_0^2/\Sigma x^2)} \qquad (4.49)$$

where $\hat{Y}_0$ is the point forecast.

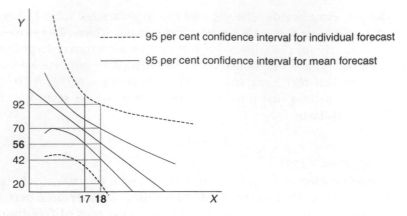

Figure 4.9. 95 per cent confidence bands for forecasts.

In our example this gives:

$$56 \pm 2.571 \times 12.90\sqrt{(1/7 + 1^2/28 + 1)} \qquad \text{or} \qquad \mathbf{56 \pm 14.02 \ units}$$

This equates to the interval from 42 to 70 units.

b. Individual Values of Y

We may, for example, want to forecast a 95 per cent confidence interval for the sales of a single firm charging the price of £18. This interval is wider because we have to allow for the variability in the sales of a single firm. The standard error in this case is given by:

$$SE = s\sqrt{(1/n + x_0^2/\Sigma x^2 + 1)} \tag{4.50}$$

Thus the 95 per cent confidence interval is given by:

$$\hat{Y}_0 \pm t_{.025} \, s\sqrt{(1/n + x_0^2/\Sigma x^2 + 1)} \tag{4.51}$$

In our example this gives:

$$56 \pm 2.571 \times 12.90\sqrt{(1/7 + 1^2/28 + 1)} \qquad \text{or} \qquad \mathbf{56 \pm 36.01 \ units}$$

This equates to the interval from 20 to 92 units.

It should be noted that both types of confidence interval will increase as we make forecasts that are further away from the mean of X. The implication here is that we have to be careful when we make forecasts using an X value that is a long way from the sample mean of X. This situation is illustrated in Figure 4.9.

Computer software packages will usually produce both types of confidence interval for forecasts.

Appendix B: Problems of the OLS model*

Although regression analysis is a powerful tool for investigating demand and other economic relationships there are various limitations and problems associated with using it. Some of these problems have already been touched on.

First, it has to be repeated that statistical techniques cannot replace economic theory; they are merely an aid to developing and testing economic theories. Judgement still has to be used in determining the type of model to use and *a priori* theoretical considerations will always be relevant.

Another problem relates to the lack of availability of current data. This is often a practical problem which investigators face; cross-section data may be impossible to obtain from different firms and time-series data may no longer be valid if demand relationships are volatile.

A further problem related to the availability of data is **hidden extrapolation**. Estimated relationships are only valid within the data range to which they apply. In simple regression it is easy to see if extrapolation is involved, but in multiple regression it is much more difficult since as we move within the range of one variable we may move outside the range of another; thus any extrapolation is hidden.

We will now concentrate on certain technical problems of the OLS model.

B.1 Specification error

We have already seen that if the model is misspecified, by omitting variables, the resulting regression coefficients will be biased. In the case of the data in Table 4.4 we will considerably exaggerate the effect of current price on sales if we omit the variable for past price. It is therefore important to include all variables in the model that we think might affect sales, even if we are not explicitly interested in the individual effects of these variables.

B.2 The identification problem

Economic relationships often involve a system of equations rather than a single equation. This applies to the demand relationship, which exists in a simultaneous relationship with supply. In this case there are two equations, each involving Q and P, but with other non-price variables included as well in each case; in the demand relationship promotion, income and the price of related products may be included, while in the supply case we may want to include the level of wages, prices of raw materials and indirect taxes. Consider the graph in Figure 4.10:

Observations of price and quantity are made at points A, B and C, so it appears to the observer that the demand curve is upward-sloping; in reality it

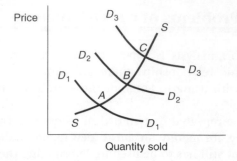

Figure 4.10. The identification problem.

is the supply curve that has been estimated, not the demand curve. This would happen if the demand were continually changing owing to exogenous factors while supply was stable.

In general it can be shown that **an equation can be identified if the number of exogenous variables excluded from the equation at least equals the number of endogenous variables included on the righthand side of the equation**. Consider the following two situations:

1 Demand: $Q = a + bP$
  Supply: $Q = c + dP + eR$ $R =$ rainfall
  Demand is identified but not supply.

2 Demand: $Q = a + bP + cY$
  Supply: $Q = d + eP + fR$
  Both equations are identified.

It is important to note that it is not possible to reliably estimate equations statistically unless they are identified, no matter how much data is available. The identification issue is therefore a separate issue from the issue of estimation (making inferences about a population based on a sample).

The estimates of coefficients obtained using OLS will be biased: this is often referred to as **simultaneous-equations bias**. It is possible to overcome this problem, provided that the demand equation can be identified, by using more advanced methods like Indirect Least Squares (ILS) and Two-Stage Least Squares (2SLS); the discussion of these methods is outside the scope of this text.[7]

B.3 Violation of assumptions regarding the error term

The regression model relies on various assumptions in order to test hypotheses; if these are violated the consequences are often that the estimated coefficients are no longer BLUE and that statistical inference cannot be performed. The main problems are **heteroscedasticity** (changing variance) and **autocorrelation** (serial correlation between error terms). These problems are now discussed in turn.

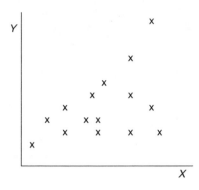

Figure 4.11. Heteroscedasticity.

a. Heteroscedasticity

In this situation ***the variance of the error term is changing across observations***. In many cases this variance will increase as the size of an explanatory variable increases. For example, when sales are related to income, there may be more variability in sales at higher levels of income. In this case the OLS estimators, while still unbiased, no longer have minimum variance. As a result the usual confidence intervals and hypothesis tests are unreliable. The initial detection of this problem is often from a graphical examination of the residuals. The result is shown in Figure 4.11 . It can be seen that as X increases the variance of Y, seen from the range of Y values for a given X-value, also increases.

Heteroscedasticity can also be detected by certain tests, such as the Glejser test and the Park test. If such tests do indicate the presence of heteroscedasticity, one remedy is to use a variation of OLS, involving a transformation; this is called Weighted Least Squares, or WLS.[8]

b. Autocorrelation

This means that ***the error term of one observation is related to or affected by the error term of another observation***; in other words it is correlated to it. This often happens in time-series data, when consecutive error terms are positively correlated. This tends to happen when a variable has some 'momentum' related to it, often connected with some kind of feedback loop. For example, consumer spending is affected by confidence in the economy, which in turn is affected by spending. However, autocorrelation can also happen with cross-section data, particularly when a model is misspecified. Consider the demand graph in Figure 4.12. If the relationship is misspecified as being linear the residuals will have the pattern shown in the bottom part of the graph, exhibiting autocorrelation. It can now be seen that there are a number of similar features between autocorrelation and heteroscedasticity. Not only are they often initially detected by a graphical examination of the residuals, but their consequences are similar: again the OLS estimators, while still unbiased, no

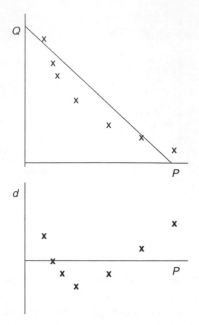

Figure 4.12. Autocorrelation.

longer have minimum variance. As a result the usual confidence intervals and hypothesis tests are unreliable.

A more advanced test for detection is the Durbin–Watson test, although the results of this may be inconclusive. One possible remedy is another variation on the OLS method, taking first differences; again the discussion of this technique is outside the scope of this text.

B.4 Multicollinearity

This refers to the situation where **two or more of the independent variables are highly correlated with each other**. This might happen, for example, if the demand for a group of goods was treated as a function of the overall level of prices (measured by a price index) and the level of money income. The latter variable is also a function of the price level. The consequence of multicollinearity is that, although the OLS estimators are still BLUE and the model may fit well with a high R^2, the standard errors of the coefficients are large because it is difficult to disentangle the effects of each variable. With perfect multicollinearity this is impossible, no matter how much data is available. In the above example it is easy to solve the problem by using real income instead of money income as a regressor. In the example in Table 4.4 we should check to see if there is a strong correlation between current and past price; in this case there is not, the R^2 between these variables being only 39 per cent. Therefore, multicollinearity is not a problem in this situation.

In other cases, variables may have to be omitted from the equation. Many computer programs automatically alert the user to the presence of multicollinearity, but the investigator must still determine the best way of dealing with the problem.

Summary

1 There are several stages involved in demand estimation: stating a hypothesis, model specification, data collection, estimating parameters, checking goodness of fit, hypothesis testing and forecasting.
2 Statistical models are stochastic in nature while mathematical models are deterministic.
3 Statistical inference means drawing conclusions from a sample about a whole population; in practice we are almost always limited to using sample data.
4 In order to make inferences we need to make assumptions about the nature of the population regression function.
5 On the basis of these assumptions we can conclude that the OLS estimators are BLUE.
6 We can also make conclusions regarding the distributions of the sample regression coefficients, which in turn enable us to compute confidence intervals and test hypotheses.
7 The coefficient of determination, or R^2, is a very useful measure of goodness of fit.
8 Power regression is used to estimate elasticities.
9 Multiple regression is a superior technique to simple regression in most situations, having a number of advantages.
10 Regression analysis involves certain technical problems, but the wary investigator can usually detect and overcome these.

Review questions

1 Explain the advantages of using multiple regression compared with simple regression.
2 Explain the nature of the identification problem, and how it relates to demand relationships.
3 Explain the nature of dummy variables and their use in regression analysis.
4 Explain the importance of correct model specification.
5 Explain the difference between demand estimation and demand forecasting.
6 What is meant by the price–quality relationship? What are its implications?
7 Explain why lagged variables are useful in analysis.
8 Explain how you would perform an empirical study to investigate the factors affecting house prices in Kensington, London, using the www.findaproperty.com site.

Problems

4.1 AIKON Inc. has recently carried out a survey of the demand for their mobile phones. They observed the following over the last fifteen months:

Sales ('000 units)	56	60	68	68	61	70	67	75	72	70	75	78	80	70	76
Price (£)	48	54	48	42	54	40	46	44	42	50	38	42	40	44	46
Advertising (£'000)	90	100	110	90	100	90	100	110	100	110	90	100	110	90	110

a. Estimate three appropriate demand curves.
b. Why is it necessary to estimate three different demand curves?
c. Estimate sales when the price is £50 and advertising is £100,000, stating any assumptions that you need to make.
d. If the firm charges £50 but increases advertising to £110,000, what conclusions can you derive in terms of revenues and profits?

4.2 The following data show how sales of a product increased over a six-year period:

Year	1994	1995	1996	1997	1998	1999
Sales (units)	32	47	74	109	163	242

a. Estimate the average rate of growth of sales over the period.
b. How well does the trend pattern fit?
c. Draw a graph of the data and appropriate relationship.
d. Forecast sales in 2000 and 2001, stating any assumptions.

4.3 The following data relate to the sales of a product over an eight-month period:

Month	Jan.	Feb.	Mar.	Apr.	May	Jun.	Jul.	Aug.
Sales (units)	56	72	70	65	68	75	66	67
Price (£)	75	65	59	69	69	49	59	59

a. Investigate whether sales are affected more by the level of price or by the change in price of the product.
b. Interpret the regression coefficient of the explanatory variable.
c. Draw an appropriate graph of the data and relationship.
d. Forecast sales in September if price is £65.

4.4 KAD has estimated the following demand relationship for its product over the last four years, using monthly observations:

$$\ln Q_t = 4.932 - 1.238 \ln P_t + 1.524 \ln Y_{t-1} + 0.4865 \ln Q_{t-1}$$
$$(2.54) \quad (1.38) \qquad\qquad (3.65) \qquad\qquad\qquad (2.87)$$

$$R^2 = 0.8738$$

where Q = sales in units, P = price in £, Y is income in £,000, and the numbers in brackets are t-statistics.

a. Interpret the above model.
b. Make a sales forecast if price is £9, income last month was £25,000 and sales last month were 2,981 units.
c. Make a sales forecast for the following month if there is no change in price or income.
d. If price is increased by 5 per cent in general terms, estimate the effect on sales, stating any assumptions.

Notes

1 D. N. Gujarati, *Essentials of Econometrics*, 2nd edn, New York: McGraw-Hill, 1999, pp. 150–151.
2 D. N. Gujarati, *Basic Econometrics*, 3rd edn, New York: McGraw-Hill, 1995, pp. 209–210.
3 H. C. Huang, J. J. Siegfried and F. Zardoshty, 'The demand for coffee in the United States, 1963–1977', *Quarterly Review of Economics and Business*, **20** (Summer 1980: 36–50.
4 H. S. Houthakker and L. D. Taylor, *Consumer Demand in the United States*, 2nd edn, Cambridge, Mass.: Harvard University Press.
5 J. N. Wilkinson, 'Marketing in the health club industry', unpublished Ph.D. thesis, City University, 1996.
6 Gujarati, *Essentials of Econometrics*, pp. 484–492.
7 Ibid., pp. 359–360.
8 Ibid., pp. 393–394.

PART III
PRODUCTION AND COST ANALYSIS

Part III (Chapters 5-7) is concerned with the analysis of production and cost relationships. A knowledge of these is fundamental to capacity planning in the long run, as well as scheduling and purchasing in the short run. Managers can then operate the firm efficiently, manipulating the use of inputs appropriately. Chapter 5 is concerned with the nature of production relationships between inputs and outputs, which in turn determine cost relationships with outputs. The latter are examined in detail in Chapter 6, with a particular emphasis on the use of cost-volume-profit analysis. Chapter 7 is concerned with the estimation of cost relationships, and again makes use of the statistical methods explained in Chapter 4, while describing the particular problems associated with measuring cost relationships. The results of empirical studies are also discussed.

5

Production theory

Contents

Objectives

1 To introduce the concept of production and explain its relevance to managerial decision-making.
2 To explain the meaning and significance of different time frames.
3 To describe the different factors of production and explain the concept of the production function.
4 To explain the different concepts of efficiency.
5 To explain the concept of an input-output table and its applications to different time frames and to isoquants.
6 To explain isoquant analysis and its applications in both short-run and long-run situations.
7 To explain how an optimal combination of inputs can be determined in both short-run and long-run situations.
8 To explain the parallels between production theory and consumer theory.
9 To describe different forms of production function and their implications.
10 To explain the concept of returns to scale and its relationship to production functions and empirical studies.
11 To describe and explain relationships between total, average and marginal product, and the different stages of production.
12 To enable students to apply the relevant concepts to solving managerial problems.

5.1 Introduction

In the previous chapters we have seen how firms are usually profit-oriented in terms of their objectives and we have focused on the revenue side of the profit equation by examining demand. We now need to examine the other side of the profit equation by considering costs. However, just as we had to examine consumer theory in order to understand demand, we must now examine production theory before we can understand costs and cost relationships. In doing this we shall see that there are a number of close parallels between consumer theory and production theory; there is a kind of symmetry between them. At the end of the chapter we will consider the importance of production theory for managerial decision-making, the focus of this text.

What is production theory? Essentially it examines the *physical relationships between inputs and outputs*. By physical relationships we mean relationships in terms of the variables in which inputs and outputs are measured: number of workers, tons of steel, barrels of oil, megawatts of electricity, hectares of land, number of drilling machines, number of automobiles produced and so on. Managers are concerned with these relationships because they want to optimize the production process, in terms of efficiency. Certain important factors are taken as given here: we are not considering what type of product we should be producing, or the determination of how much of it we should be producing. The first question relates to the demand side of the firm's strategy, while the second involves a consideration of both demand and cost, which is examined in pricing. What we are considering is how to produce the product in terms of the implications of using different input combinations at different levels of output. For example, we can produce shoes in factories that make extensive use of automatic machinery and skilled labour in terms of machine operators, or we can produce them in factories employing more labour-intensive methods and unskilled labour. We cannot say that one method or technology is better or more efficient than the other unless we have more information regarding the relationships and costs of the inputs involved.

5.2 Basic terms and definitions

We cannot proceed any further in analysis without defining and explaining some basic terms that will be used extensively throughout the next three chapters. One example has already emerged from the discussion in the previous paragraph, and indeed in previous chapters: the term **efficiency**. As we shall see, there are different ways of defining this concept. However, before moving on to efficiency, there are a number of other terms that need to be considered.

5.2.1 *Factors of production*

This term refers to *inputs* or *resources*; these terms are used interchangeably in this text. They refer to *anything used in the production and distribution of goods and services*. When economists use the term **factors of production** they usually classify them into three, or sometimes four, categories: land, labour and capital. Entrepreneurship is sometimes added as a fourth factor. These terms are not self-explanatory so each is now discussed in turn.

a. Land

Land is really a combination of two different factors. First, there is the area of land that is needed to produce the good. This may be agricultural land, factory area, shop space, warehouse space or office space. Second, land relates to all **natural resources**, that is anything that comes from the surface of the land, underneath it or on top of it. Thus we include minerals, crops, wood, and even water and air, though it may seem strange to refer to these as land.

b. Labour

Labour is the easiest of the factors to understand, the input of labour being measured in number of workers, or more precisely, in number of hours worked. Of course, labour is not homogeneous and manual labour is often divided into unskilled, semi-skilled and skilled categories. Labour also includes administrative and managerial workers, though some empirical studies have omitted this important input.[1] In practice we may wish to distinguish between these different categories of labour, especially if we want to evaluate their different contributions to output, as will be seen.

c. Capital

This term can again be confusing to students. It does not refer to money, or to capital market instruments; rather it refers to capital goods, that is **plant and machinery**. Like labour, this is a highly heterogeneous category, and in practice we might want to distinguish between different types of capital, again especially if we want to evaluate their different contributions to output. For example, we may want to classify personal computers, photocopying machines, printers, fax machines and coffee machines separately.

d. Entrepreneurship

Entrepreneurship refers to the **ability to identify and exploit market opportunities**. It therefore includes two separate functions. This input is often not considered in economic analysis; it is really more relevant in long-run situations, and it is notoriously difficult to measure. For one thing it is difficult to separate entrepreneurship from management; top management should be concerned with both the functions of entrepreneurship, if they are truly representing the interests of shareholders.

5.2.2 Production functions

These represent the relationships between inputs and outputs in symbolic or mathematical form. In general terms we can say that any production function can be expressed as:

$$Q = f(X_1, X_2, X_3, \ldots)$$

where Q represents output of a product and $X_1, X_2, X_3, \ldots$ represent the various inputs. This function is often expressed as:

$$Q = f(L, K) \tag{5.1}$$

where L represents the labour input and K represents the capital input. This is obviously a considerable oversimplification since not only can there be more inputs but there can also be more outputs, with a complex relationship between them. A company like Daimler-Chrysler, for example, uses a huge variety of different inputs and produces many outputs, some of which are also inputs. Components like fuel injection units, headlight units, brake discs and so on are both inputs into the final product of automobiles and, at the same time, outputs that are sold separately.

The production function in (5.1) does not imply any particular mathematical form. The significance and implications of mathematical form will be considered in more detail later, but at this stage we can consider some of the basic variations, assuming the general form in (5.1) with two inputs:

1 $Q = aL + bK$	Linear		(5.2)
2 $Q = aL + bK + c$	Linear plus constant		(5.3)
3 $Q = aL + bK + cLK$	Linear plus interaction term		(5.4)
4 $Q = aL^2 + bK^2 + cLK$	Quadratic		(5.5)
5 $Q = aLK + bL^2K + cLK^2 + dL^3K + eLK^3$	Cubic		(5.6)
6 $Q = aL^bK^c$	Power		(5.7)

5.2.3 Fixed factors

These are the factors of production that **cannot be changed in the short run**. This does not mean that they cannot be changed at all; they can be changed in the long run. In practice these factors tend to involve that aspect of land that relates to area of land, and capital equipment. The nature of these factors will vary from firm to firm and industry to industry. It also may be physically possible to change these factors in the short run, for example close down a factory, but it is not economically feasible because of the high costs involved (redundancy payments and so on).

5.2.4 Variable factors

These are the converse of the fixed factors, meaning that they are **inputs that can be varied in both short and long run**. In practice this applies mainly to that part of land that relates to raw materials and to labour. Not all labour may be easily varied however, since salaried staff may have long-term contracts, making it difficult to reduce this input. It may be easier to increase it, but even here job searches can take time, especially for top positions.

5.2.5 The short run

This is again a term that has a different interpretation in economics from other aspects of business, including finance. In finance the short run or short term refers to a period of a year or less. In economics this is not such a useful definition because it does not permit so many generalizations, bearing in mind the large differences between firms in terms of their business environments. It is therefore more useful to define the short run as being **the period during which at least one factor input is fixed while other inputs are variable**. In practice this will vary from firm to firm and industry to industry according to the circumstances. It also means that a firm might have several short-run time frames as more and more factors become variable. This tends to be ignored in analysis since the same general principles apply to any short-run situation, as long as at least one factor is fixed. Sometimes economists refer to the 'very short run', defined as being the period during which all factors are fixed. Although output cannot be varied under such circumstances, different amounts can be supplied onto the market depending on inventory levels.

5.2.6 The long run

This is the converse of the short run, meaning that it is **the period during which all factors are variable**. One can now see that all the last four definitions are interdependent. It may seem initially that this circularity is a problem and is not getting us anywhere, but we will see that these definitions permit some very useful analysis. Some economists also refer to the 'very long run', which they define as being the period during which technology can also change. However, this is not a frequently used term, perhaps because technology is changing more quickly now; most economists assume that technology is changeable in the long run but not in the short run.

5.2.7 Scale

This term refers to scale of production or organization. It relates to **the amount of fixed factors that a firm has**. It follows therefore that a firm cannot change its scale in the short run. A firm's scale determines its **capacity**; this can be defined in various ways, but the simplest is that it refers to the **maximum output that a firm can produce in the short run**. It is also sometimes defined as the output where a firm's level of average cost starts to rise. This may be easier to measure, since in practice it is very rare for a firm to produce at maximum capacity. Producing at maximum capacity is not usually desirable either, although it might initially seem so, because it is not normally efficient. This brings us to the next definition.

5.2.8 Efficiency

It was mentioned at the beginning of this section that efficiency may also be defined in various ways. The two types that concern us here are **technical efficiency** and **economic efficiency**.

a. Technical efficiency

This means that a firm is producing the ***maximum output from given quantities of inputs***. Any production function assumes that a firm is operating at technical efficiency. It follows from this that a given output may be produced in many ways, each one of which may be technically efficient; in other words, that output is the maximum output that can be produced from each different combination of inputs.

b. Economic efficiency

This involves ***producing a given output at least cost***. This usually involves a unique combination of inputs, the levels of these inputs depending on their substitutability and complementarity, and also on their prices. While this aspect is discussed to some extent in this chapter, it is dealt with in more detail in Chapter 6.

5.2.9 Input-output tables

The relationships between inputs and outputs can be represented in an input-output or production table. Table 5.1 shows such a table for a cubic function relating to Viking Shoes, a company that makes trainers. The outputs, measured in pairs of shoes produced per week, are rounded to the nearest unit. The specific form of the function used is as follows:

$$Q = 4LK + 0.1L^2K + 0.2LK^2 - 0.04L^3K - 0.02LK^3 \qquad (5.8)$$

The shaded column relates to the short-run situation where capital input is held constant at three machines. This is examined in more detail in the next

Table 5.1. Viking Shoes: input-output table for cubic function

		Capital input (machines), K							
		1	2	3	4	5	6	7	8
	1	4	9	13	18	23	27	31	35
	2	8	17	27	36	45	54	62	70
	3	12	26	39	53	67	80[B]	92	102
Labour input (workers), L	4	16	33	50	68	85	102	117	131
	5	18	38	59	80[C]	100[A]	119	137	153
	6	20	42	64	87	110	131	150	167
	7	20	43	66	90	113	135	155	171
	8	19	41	64	87	110	131	149	164

section. In the long run, any combination of inputs is feasible, and it is again assumed in the production function (and the table derived from it) that technical efficiency is achieved.

5.3 The short run

In the short run we have seen that at least one factor is fixed. The following analysis assumes a two-factor situation, involving labour and capital, where one factor, capital, is fixed. It is relatively easy to generalize the analysis to apply to situations where there is more than one of either type of factor.

5.3.1 Production functions and marginal product

In the previous section it was stated that the production function may take various mathematical forms. As we have seen in Chapter 3 the mathematical form of a function is important because it indicates the way in which the explanatory variables affect the dependent variable; these effects can be seen in particular in terms of the marginal effect and the elasticity. We can now examine these effects as they relate to the various forms of production function described in (5.2) to (5.7). First we need to explain more precisely the economic interpretation of marginal effects in the context of production theory.

A marginal effect is given mathematically by a derivative, or, more precisely in the case of the two-input production function, a partial derivative (obtained by differentiating the production function with respect to one variable, while keeping other variables constant). The economic interpretation of this is a **marginal product**. The marginal product of labour is the *additional output resulting from using one more unit of labour, while holding the capital input constant*. Likewise the marginal product of capital is the *additional output resulting from using one more unit of capital, while holding the labour input constant*. These marginal products can thus be expressed mathematically in terms of the following partial derivatives:

$$MP_L = \partial Q / \partial L \text{ and } MP_K = \partial Q / \partial K$$

Expressions for marginal product can now be derived for each of the mathematical forms (5.2) to (5.7). These are shown in Table 5.2, in terms of the

Table 5.2. Production functions and marginal product

Production function	Marginal product (of labour)
$Q = aL + bK$	a
$Q = aL + bK + c$	a
$Q = aL + bK + cLK$	$a + cK$
$Q = aL^2 + bK^2 + cLK$	$2aL + cK$
$Q = aLK + bL^2K + cLK^2 + dL^3K + eLK^3$	$aK + 2bLK + cK^2 + 3dL^2K + eK^3$
$Q = aL^bK^c$	$abL^{b-1}K^c$

marginal product of labour. The marginal product of capital will have the same general form because of the symmetry of the functions.

The linear production function has constant marginal product, meaning that the marginal product is not affected by the level of either the labour or the capital input. This is not normally a realistic situation and such functions, in spite of their simplicity, are not frequently used. The linear form with an interaction term is more realistic, since the marginal product depends on the level of capital input, but the quadratic function is normally preferable to any linear function since it shows marginal product as depending on the level of both labour and capital inputs. The value of a would normally be negative (and c positive), meaning that marginal product is declining (linearly) as the labour input increases, because of the law of diminishing returns, which is explained later in this section.

However, the last two production functions are the ones most commonly used in practice as being the most realistic. In both cases, marginal product depends on the level of both labour and capital inputs. The cubic function involves marginal product increasing at first and then declining (a quadratic function, with b positive and d negative). The power function, often referred to as the **Cobb–Douglas function**, has declining marginal product at all levels of input (assuming b is less than 1), but the decline is increasing as the input increases. This is generally more realistic than the linear decline associated with the quadratic model.

The main advantage of this last model, the Cobb–Douglas function, is that it involves constant elasticities. The elasticities in this case represent **output elasticities**; the coefficient b refers to the elasticity of output with respect to labour. It means that *every 1 per cent increase in labour input will increase output by b per cent, assuming that the capital input is held constant*. A similar interpretation applies to the coefficient c.

Apart from marginal effects and elasticities, one other important economic interpretation can be derived from the mathematical form of the production function. This relates to the concept of returns to scale. The interpretation of this aspect will be considered in the next section, since it relates to the long run.

5.3.2 Derivation of the short-run input-output table

In the long-run situation considered in the previous section the production function that was used to generate the input-output table in Table 5.1 was a cubic. Let us assume that Viking's capital input is fixed at three machines. We can now compute the short-run production function by substituting the value of $K=3$ into the cubic function given by expression (5.8):

$$Q = 4LK + 0.1L^2K + 0.2LK^2 - 0.04L^3K - 0.02LK^3$$

This gives the following cubic form for the short-run production function:

$$Q = 13.26L + 0.3L^2 - 0.12L^3 \tag{5.9}$$

Table 5.3. Viking Shoes: effects on output of adding more variable input

Labour input, L	Total output, Q	Marginal product, MP	Average product, AP
0	0		—
		13	
1	13		13
		14	
2	27		13.5
		12	
3	39		13
		11	
4	50		12.5
		9	
5	59		11.8
		5	
6	64		10.7
		2	
7	66		9.4
		−2	
8	64		8

This can then be used to compute the input-output table for the short run, which is given by the shaded column in Table 5.1. As before, these outputs are rounded to the nearest unit. This table can now be augmented with further information; as well as measuring total output or product we can also record marginal product (*MP*) and average product (*AP*). These can either be computed from the output column or by deriving their mathematical functions, as follows:

$$MP = \partial Q/L = 13.26 + 0.6L - 0.36L^2 \qquad (5.10)$$

$$AP = Q/L = 13.26 + 0.3L - 0.12L^2 \qquad (5.11)$$

In Table 5.3 the values of *MP* and *AP* are computed from the output column for ease of comparison. Two things should be noted regarding this table:

1 The values of *MP* should correspond to mid-values of *L*. This is because the marginal product is associated with the increase in labour input. Thus when labour is increased from two to three workers, for example, the resulting *MP* of 12 units corresponds to $L = 2.5$. This is important for computing the correct values of *MP* from function (5.10). In this case:

$$MP = 13.26 + 0.6(2.5) - 0.36(2.5)^2 = 12.51$$

The same principle also applies to graphing *MP*, as seen in Figure 5.1.

2 The values of *MP* are given to the nearest unit since they are computed from the total output column. They may therefore not correspond exactly to the values obtained by using function (5.10) because of rounding errors. This does not apply to *AP*, where fractions are given.

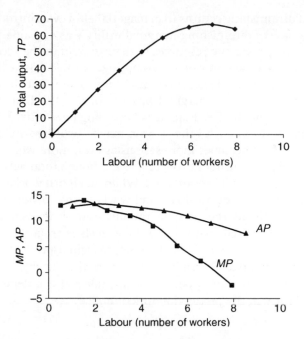

Figure 5.1. Viking Shoes: total, marginal and average product.

5.3.3 Increasing and diminishing returns

It can be seen from Table 5.3 that marginal product increases for up to two workers, but when more than two workers are used in combination with the fixed capital input of three machines the marginal product starts to fall. This now needs to be explained.

a. Increasing returns

When the variable input is very low the fixed input, in this case capital, is **underutilized**; thus one worker cannot use the three machines very efficiently, because he has to do everything himself. When another worker is employed they are able to use the principle of the **division of labour** and specialize in performing different jobs. This increases productivity. As more workers are employed the scope for this increased specialization is reduced, the advantages depending on the amount of capital input and the technology used.

b. Diminishing returns

The **law of diminishing returns** is one of the most important foundations of neoclassical economic theory. It states that **when additional units of a variable factor are combined with a fixed amount of another factor(s) the additions to total output, in other words the marginal product, will eventually decline.** We have already come across two different applications of this principle: in Chapter 2 the concept of diminishing returns to managerial effort was introduced, and in Chapter 3 the law of diminishing marginal utility was explained. In the first case the fixed factor was the resources of the firm and in the second case the fixed factor was the time frame for consumption. In Table 5.3 the fixed factor is the amount of capital available, three machines. Given that fixed input, and the technology in use, the marginal product of the third worker starts to decline. At this point the fixed factor is becoming **overutilized**; the workers are beginning to get in each other's way, maybe waiting to use one of the machines. This effect becomes more serious as even more workers are added and marginal output continues to decline, even though total output continues to increase until seven workers are used. When an eighth worker is added the fixed factor becomes so overutilized and workers so crowded together that total output starts to fall; the marginal product now becomes negative.

It must be emphasized that the word *eventually* is important. The law of diminishing returns does not indicate when marginal product will begin to decline. If more of the fixed factor is used, more of the variable factor may also be used in combination with it before the law takes effect, depending on the mathematical form of the production function.

5.3.4 *Relationships between total, marginal and average product*

Some aspects of these relationships have already been examined in the previous section, but at this point a graphical illustration is helpful. This is given in Figures 5.1 and 5.2. Figure 5.1 is based on the values in Table 5.3 and thus shows the specific pattern for total output, marginal product and average product for Viking Shoes, using the cubic production function in (5.8) and (5.9). Figure 5.2 is more general. It again relates to a cubic form, but not to any specific values; it is shown in order to illustrate various relationships between variable input and total product, marginal product and average product. Figure 5.2 also shows the three stages of the production function, which now need to be explained.

a. Cubic production functions

Three points on the production function or total product (*TP*) curve in Figure 5.2 need to be examined: *A*, *B* and *C*.

Point A.   It can be seen in Figure 5.2 that the *TP* curve is convex (to the horizontal axis) from the origin to point *A*. As more of the variable input is used the curve now becomes concave, meaning that the slope is decreasing. The slope of the *TP* curve is given by $\partial Q / \partial L$, and this represents the marginal product (*MP*). Thus the *MP* is at a maximum at point *A*, corresponding to the level of input L_1.

Point B.   The slope of the line, or ray, from the origin to the *TP* curve is given by Q/L and this represents the average product (*AP*). This slope is at a maximum when the line from the origin is tangential to the *TP* curve, at point *B*. This corresponds to the level of input L_2. It can also be seen that this occurs when *AP*

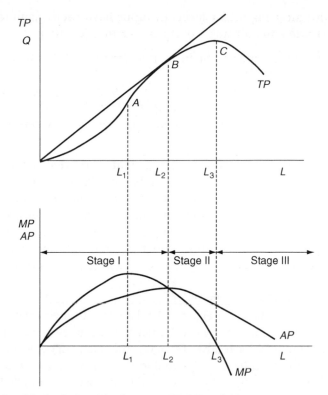

Figure 5.2. Graphical relationships between *TP*, *MP* and *AP*.

and *MP* are equal. This relationship between *AP* and *MP* is important and is paralleled in cost relationships, as we shall see in the next chapter; it therefore needs some explanation. This is most easily done with an analogy to which students can readily relate.

Many students receive a succession of grades or marks on a particular course, assuming continuous assessment is used. It does not matter whether these grades or marks are alphabetical or numerical; they still represent a score. As the course continues, students can compute their average score up to that point. If they wish to improve their average score, their next score, which we can think of as their marginal score, must exceed their existing average. Thus when *MP* is above *AP*, *AP* must be rising (up to input level L_2). If the student's marginal score is less than their average this will pull their average down. Thus when *MP* is below *AP*, *AP* must be falling (above input level L_2). If the marginal score is the same as their average, the average will remain unchanged. Thus when *AP* and *MP* are equal, *AP* remains unchanged and must therefore be a maximum (it is no longer rising and is about to fall).

Point C. The *TP* curve reaches a peak or maximum at point *C*; this means that the slope is 0 and therefore *MP* is 0. This corresponds to the level of input L_3. Above this level of input *TP* declines and *MP* becomes negative.

Now that the most important levels of input have been examined we can explain the three different stages of the production function:

- *Stage I.* This corresponds to the input range between zero and L_2, where AP reaches a maximum.
- *Stage II.* This corresponds to the input range between L_2 and L_3, where AP is falling but TP is still rising, meaning that MP is still positive.
- *Stage III.* This corresponds to the input range beyond L_3, where TP is falling, meaning that MP is negative.

The significance of these different stages is that a firm that is operating with economic efficiency will never produce in the stage III region. This is because it is possible to produce the same total output with less of the variable input and therefore less cost. It will be shown in Chapter 8 that, if it is operating in a perfectly competitive environment, the firm should produce in the stage II region in order to maximize profit. Under different demand conditions it is possible for the profit-maximizing output to be in the stage I region.

b. Cobb–Douglas production functions

The shapes of curve shown in Figure 5.2 relate specifically to cubic functions, since these are often found in practice, for reasons explained in the subsection on increasing and diminishing returns. However, the shapes of curve for TP, MP and AP are different for the Cobb–Douglas production function, another function that is found in empirical studies. This function has the form given by (5.7), that is:

$$Q = aL^b K^c$$

Since the output elasticities with respect to labour and capital are both positive the TP curve is a continually increasing function.

It was seen in Table 5.2 that the MP for this function is given by:

$$MP = abL^{b-1}K^c \tag{5.12}$$

and:

$$AP = Q/L = aL^{b-1}K^c \tag{5.13}$$

If it is assumed that the output elasticity with respect to labour (b) is less than 1, it can be seen from these expressions that both MP and AP are continually decreasing functions, and that MP will be below AP. The relevant curves in this case are shown in Figure 5.3.

5.3.5 *Determining the optimal use of the variable input*

Assuming that the capital input, or indeed any input in general terms, is fixed, a firm can determine the optimal amount of the variable input to employ if it uses information relating to product prices and factor costs. This involves an explanation of the concepts of **marginal revenue product** (MRP) and **marginal factor cost** (MFC).

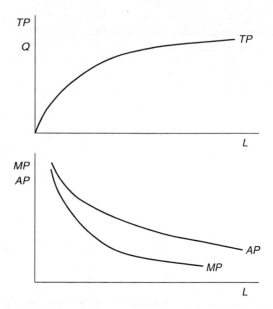

Figure 5.3. Graphical relationships for Cobb–Douglas production functions.

a. Marginal revenue product

This is defined as **the addition to total revenue from using an additional unit of the variable factor**, or:

$$MRP_L = \Delta R/\Delta L \text{ or } \partial R/\partial L \qquad (5.14)$$

assuming that labour is the variable input. This change in total revenue will equal the marginal product of labour times the marginal revenue from selling the additional units of output:

$$MRP_L = (MP_L)(MR_Q) \qquad (5.15)$$

The marginal revenue from additional units will be constant if the firm is operating under the conditions of perfect competition, examined in detail in Chapter 8. Let us assume that the selling price for Viking shoes is £75. We can now incorporate this information in Table 5.4 in computing MRP_L.

b. Marginal factor cost

This is defined as **the addition to total cost from using an additional unit of the variable factor**, or:

$$MFC_L = \Delta C/\Delta L \text{ or } \partial C/\partial L \qquad (5.16)$$

Let us assume that the cost of labour is £400 per week. It is also assumed that the firm is operating in a perfectly competitive labour market, meaning that it can employ as many workers as it wants at this going market price. Thus the MFC_L is constant at all input, and therefore output, levels.

Table 5.4. Viking shoes: marginal revenue product and marginal factor cost

Labour input, L (number of workers)	Total output, Q (pairs of shoes)	Marginal product, MP_L (shoes per worker)	Total revenue, $TR = P \times Q$ (£)	Total labour cost, $TLC = L \times MFC_L$ (£)	Total profit, $\Pi = TR - TC$ (£)	MRP_L (£)	MFC_L (£)
0	0		0	0	−1500		
		13				975	400
1	13		975	400	−925		
		14				1,050	400
2	27		2,025	800	−275		
		12				900	400
3	39		2,925	1,200	225		
		11				825	400
4	50		3,750	1,600	650		
		9				675	400
5	**59**		**4,425**	**2,000**	**925**		
		5				375	400
6	64		4,800	2,400	900		
		2				150	400
7	66		4,950	2,800	650		
		−2				−150	400
8	64		4,800	3,200	100		

c. Profit maximization

We can now combine the information relating to marginal revenue product and marginal factor cost to determine the profit-maximizing level of use of the variable factor. This will be achieved by expanding the operation as long as the marginal benefits exceed the marginal costs; thus the optimal level of input use is given by the condition:

$$MRP_L = MFC_L \tag{5.17}$$

It can be seen from Table 5.4 that this occurs when the labour input is five workers. Up to this level $MRP_L > MFC_L$, meaning that the additional workers are adding more to revenue than to costs. If more workers are added beyond this level $MRP_L < MFC_L$, the marginal revenue product of the sixth worker is only £375 whereas the marginal factor cost is £400. Thus profit is reduced from £925 to £900. It should be noted that the profit is calculated by subtracting the total cost from total revenue, where the total cost equals the total labour cost plus the cost of using the capital input, assumed in this case to be £1,500 (three machines at £500 each). The profit function can also be expressed mathematically:

$$\Pi = R - C = PQ - C = 75(13.26L + 0.3L^2 - 0.12L^3) - (1500 + 400L)$$
$$\Pi = -1500 + 594.5L + 22.5L^2 - 9L^3$$

$$\tag{5.18}$$

The situation is illustrated graphically in Figure 5.4. If the mathematical approach is used, the optimal value of L can be calculated by differentiating the profit function with respect to L and setting the derivative equal to zero.

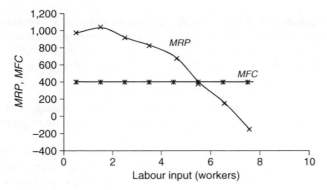

Figure 5.4. Viking Shoes: marginal revenue product and marginal factor cost.

$$\frac{d\Pi}{dL} = 594.5 + 45L - 27L^2 = 0$$

This expression requires solving a quadratic equation. The reader may recall that for the general equation $ax^2 + bx + c = 0$, the solutions for x are given by:

$$x = \frac{-b \pm \sqrt{(b^2 - 4ac)}}{2a}$$

Thus $L = -45 \pm \frac{\sqrt{[45^2 - 4(-27)(594.5)]}}{2(-27)} = 5.60$ (the other solution is negative).

Now that the relevant principles have been discussed as far as the short run is concerned we can turn our attention to a couple of case studies that examine the relevance and application of the law of diminishing returns in real-life situations.

Case study 5.1: Microsoft – increasing or diminishing returns?

In some industries, securing the adoption of an industry standard that is favourable to one's own product is an enormous advantage. It can involve marketing efforts that grow more productive the larger the product's market share. Microsoft's Windows is an excellent example.[2] The more customers adopt Windows, the more applications are introduced by independent software developers, and the more applications that are introduced the greater the chance for further adoptions. With other products the market can quickly exhibit diminishing returns to promotional expenditure, as it becomes saturated. However, with the adoption of new industry standards, or a new technology, increasing returns can persist.[3] Microsoft is therefore willing to spend huge amounts on promotion and marketing to gain this advantage and dominate the industry. Many would claim that this is a restrictive practice, and that this has justified the recent anti-trust suit against the company. The competitive aspects of this situation will be examined in Chapter 12, but at this point there is another side to the situation regarding returns that should be considered.

Microsoft introduced Office 2000, a program that includes Word, Excel, PowerPoint and Access, to general retail customers in December 1999. It represented a considerable advance over the previous package, Office 97, by allowing much more interaction with the Internet. It also allows easier collaborative work for firms using an intranet. Thus many larger firms have been willing to buy upgrades and pay the price of around $230.

However, there is limited scope for users to take advantage of these improvements. Office 97 was already so full of features that most customers could not begin to exhaust its possibilities. It has been estimated that with Word 97 even adventurous users were unlikely to use more than a quarter of all its capabilities. In this respect Microsoft is a victim of the law of diminishing returns.[4] Smaller businesses and home users may not be too impressed with the further capabilities of Office 2000. Given the enormous costs of developing upgrades to the package, the question is where does Microsoft go from here. It is speculated that the next version, Office 2003, may incorporate a speech-recognition program, making keyboard and mouse redundant. At the moment such programs require a considerable investment in time and effort from the user to train the computer to interpret their commands accurately, as well as the considerable investment by the software producer in developing the package.

Questions

1 Is it possible for a firm to experience both increasing and diminishing returns at the same time?
2 What other firms, in other industries, might be in similar situations to Microsoft, and in what respects?
3 What is the nature of the fixed factor that is causing the law of diminishing returns in Microsoft's case?
4 Are there any ways in which Microsoft can reduce the undesirable effects of the law of diminishing returns?

Case study 5.2: State spending

A particularly controversial example of the law of diminishing returns is in the area of state, or public, spending. Some recent studies indicate that diminishing returns have been very much in evidence in developed countries in recent decades, with returns even being negative in some cases. An example is the IMF paper by Tanzi and Schuknecht,[5] which examined the growth in public spending in industrial economies over the past 125 years and assessed its social and economic benefits.

At the beginning of this period, 1870, governments confined themselves to a limited number of activities, such as defence and law and order. Public spending was only an average of 8% of GDP in these countries at this time. The higher taxes that were introduced to pay for the First World War allowed governments to maintain higher spending afterwards. Public spending rose to an average of 15% of GDP by 1920. This spending increased again in the years after 1932 in the surge of welfare spending to combat the Great Depression. By 1937 the average for industrial countries had reached nearly 21% of GDP.

The three decades after the Second World War witnessed the largest increase in public spending, mainly reflecting the expansion of the welfare state. By 1980 the proportion of GDP accounted for by state spending was 43% in industrial countries, and by 1994 this had risen to 47%. By this time there were large variations between countries: the EU average was 52%, in the UK it was 43%, in the USA 33%. In the newly industrializing countries (NICs) the average was only 18%. These variations over time and area allow some interesting comparisons regarding the benefits of additional spending.

Tanzi and Schuknecht found that before 1960 increased public spending was associated with considerable improvements in social welfare, such as in infant-mortality rates, life expectancy, equality and schooling. However, since then, further increases in public spending have delivered much smaller social gains, and those countries where spending has risen most have not performed any better in social or economic terms than those whose spending has increased least. In the higher-spending countries there is much evidence of 'revenue churning': this means that money taken from people in taxes is often returned to the same people in terms of benefits. Thus middle-income families may find their taxes returned to them in child benefits. Furthermore, in many of those countries with the lowest increase in public spending since 1960, efficiency and innovation appear to be greater; they have lower unemployment and a higher level of registered patents.

Another study found a similar pattern in Canada specifically.[6] In the 1960s public spending, at modest levels, helped the development of Atlantic Canada. Most of the money went into genuinely needed roads, education and other infrastructure. Later large increases in spending not only had a smaller effect, but in general had a negative effect. For example, generous unemployment insurance reduced the supply of labour and impeded private investment. Subsidized industries, like coal, steel and fishing, involved using labour that could have been employed in more productive areas, as well as in the last case decimating the cod stocks. Even the roads eventually deteriorated, as local politicians had little incentive to spend public funds wisely, and voters felt unable to discipline them.

Questions

1 In what areas of public spending do there appear to be increasing returns?
2 In what areas of public spending do there appear to be diminishing or negative returns?
3 Explain the difference between diminishing and negative returns in the context of public spending, giving examples.
4 Explain what is meant by 'revenue churning', giving examples.
5 Why do local politicians have little incentive to spend public money wisely?
6 Is it possible to talk about an optimal level of public spending? How might this level be determined?

5.4 The long run

The analysis so far has assumed that at least one factor is fixed, and in the example of Viking Shoes this factor has been capital, being fixed at three machines. We now need to consider the situation where the firm can vary both of its inputs. This means that we need to examine the input-output data in Table 5.1 in more general terms, with both factors being considered as variable. The data in Table 5.1 can also be represented in a three-dimensional graph, but these are generally not very useful for analytical purposes. In order to proceed with any analysis it is necessary to introduce the concept of **isoquants**.

5.4.1 Isoquants

An isoquant is a curve that shows *various input combinations that yield the same total quantity of output*. It is assumed that the output involved is the maximum that can be produced from those combinations of inputs. Thus the position or equation of an isoquant can be derived from the production function. It corresponds to the concept of an indifference curve in consumer theory, and has analogous properties. For example we can talk of an **isoquant map**, where each curve represents a greater quantity of output as one moves further away from the origin.

The three main properties that isoquants have in common with indifference curves are:

1 *Negative slope.* This is because the inputs are usually assumed to be substitutable for each other; if a firm uses more of one input it needs less of another.
2 *Convexity.* This means that their slope is decreasing from left to right; the reason for this relates to the properties of the **marginal rate of technical substitution**, explained shortly.

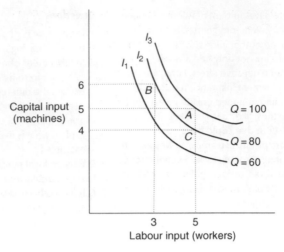

Figure 5.5. Viking Shoes: isoquant map.

3 *Non-intersection.* It is technically possible for isoquants to intersect, as will be seen in the next section, but this will not occur in the economically feasible range of output. If curves intersect it means that a certain output is being produced using more of both inputs, and this is obviously not efficient in economic terms.

Figure 5.5 shows an isoquant map, based on the data in Table 5.1. Points *A*, *B* and *C* correspond to the values indicated in the table. Thus it can be seen that the output of 80 units can be achieved by using either six machines and three workers (point *B*) or four machines and five workers (point *C*). On the other hand, in order to produce 100 units of output it is necessary to use five machines and five workers (point *A*), though other combinations (involving fractions of inputs) can also produce the same output. It should be noted that the isoquant for the output of 100 units starts to curve upwards as more than seven workers are used; this is because it is not possible to produce 100 units with less than five machines. The maximum output from using only four machines is 90 units, no matter how much labour is used.

5.4.2 *The marginal rate of technical substitution*

The marginal rate of technical substitution (*MRTS*) is a measure of the degree of substitutability between two inputs. More specifically, **the MRTS of X for Y corresponds to the rate at which one input (X) can be substituted for another (Y), while maintaining total output constant.** It is shown by the absolute value of the slope of the isoquant; thus in moving from point *B* to point *C* the MRTS is 1, meaning that if two more workers are used we can give up two machines and still produce 80 units of output. The slope of the isoquant is decreasing in absolute magnitude from left to right. This means that as more and more labour is used to produce a given output, the less easily the capital input can be substituted for it. The reason for this is the occurrence of the **law of diminishing returns**, explained in the previous section. Thus as more labour is used and less capital, the marginal product of additional labour falls and the marginal product of the capital lost increases. Relating this to Viking Shoes, it means that as less and less machinery is used it becomes harder to produce a given output with increasing amounts of labour.

At this stage another parallel with consumer theory can be seen: in that case the slope of the indifference curve was shown by the marginal rate of substitution (*MRS*). This was also decreasing in absolute magnitude from left to right, because of the law of diminishing marginal utility.

It was also seen that the *MRS* was given by the ratio of the marginal utilities of the two products. It should not be too difficult for the reader to draw another parallel at this point: the *MRTS* is given by the ratio of the marginal products of the two inputs. The mathematical proof of this is analogous to the one relating to the *MRS*.

When the firm moves from point B to point C it gains output from using more labour, given by $\Delta L \times MP_L$, and it loses output from using less capital, given by $\Delta K \times MP_K$. Since the points are on the same isoquant and therefore must involve the same total output, the gains must equal the losses, thus:

$$\Delta L \times MP_L = \Delta K \times MP_K$$

Since the slope of the isoquant is given by $\Delta K / \Delta L$, we can now express the absolute magnitude of the slope as:

$$\Delta K / \Delta L = MP_L / MP_K \tag{5.19}$$

There are two extreme cases of input substitutability. **Zero substitutability** occurs when the inputs are used in fixed proportions, for example when a machine requires two workers to operate it and cannot be operated with more or less than this number of workers. Isoquants in this case are L-shaped, meaning that the *MRTS* is either zero or infinity. **Perfect substitutability** is the opposite extreme, resulting in linear isoquants; this means that the *MRTS* is constant. It also implies that output can be produced using entirely one input or the other. These extremes are shown in Figure 5.6.

5.4.3 *Returns to scale*

We frequently want to analyse the effects on output of an increase in the scale of production. An increase in scale involves a **proportionate increase in all the inputs** of the firm. The resulting proportionate increase in output determines the **physical returns to scale** for the firm. Two points need to be explained before moving on to the description and measurement of returns to scale:

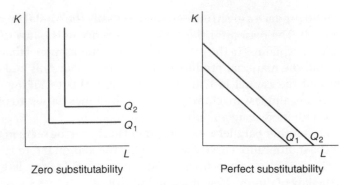

Figure 5.6. Extreme cases of input substitutability.

1 *Proportionate increase in all the inputs*. It is always assumed in referring to returns to scale that all inputs increase by the same proportion. This is not necessarily optimal for the firm in terms of economic efficiency. If inputs increase by different proportions we have to talk about **returns to outlay** (measured in money terms).

2 *Physical returns to scale*. Returns to scale can be described in physical terms or in money terms, as will become clear in the next chapter. The two meanings do not necessarily coincide; for example, it is possible for a firm to experience constant physical returns to scale yet have increasing returns to scale in money terms (better known as economies of scale).

a. Types of returns to scale

Returns to scale, in physical or money terms, can be of three types. The following are the three types of physical return:

1 *Constant returns to scale (CRTS)*. This refers to the situation where **an increase in inputs results in an exactly proportional increase in output**.

2 *Increasing returns to scale (IRTS)*. This refers to the situation where **an increase in inputs results in a more-than-proportional increase in output**.

3 *Decreasing returns to scale (DRTS)*. This refers to the situation where **an increase in inputs results in a less-than-proportional increase in output**.

The reasons for these different returns to scale will be considered in the next chapter, when they are compared with the monetary aspects of returns to scale. We can, however, use Table 5.1 to examine these different possibilities from the standpoint of quantitative measurement. The easiest way to do this is by examining the numbers in the leading diagonal. When inputs are increased from one worker/one machine to two workers/two machines this represents a doubling of inputs; however, output increases from 4 to 17 units, an increase of more than fourfold. Thus this situation involves, IRTS. If inputs increase from two of each factor to three of each factor this is an increase of 50 per cent; output increases from 17 to 39 units, over 100 per cent. Thus there are still

IRTS. This situation continues until seven units of each input are used; when each input is increased to eight units this represents an increase of about 14 per cent, while output increases from 155 to 164 units, an increase of less than 6 per cent. Thus there are now DRTS.

Generalizing from this we can conclude that with a cubic production function the returns to scale are not the same at all levels of scale or output. The type or pattern of returns to scale will obviously depend on the nature of the mathematical form of the production function. In order to understand this more clearly we need to consider the concept of a **homogeneous production function**.

b. Homogeneous production functions*

These functions are useful for modelling production situations because of their mathematical properties. If the inputs in a function are multiplied by any constant λ and if this constant can then be factored out of the function then the production function is said to be homogeneous. This can be explained more precisely in mathematical terms by stating that a production function is said to be homogeneous of degree n if:

$$f(\lambda L, \ \lambda K) = \lambda^n f(L, K) \tag{5.20}$$

If the degree of homogeneity is equal to 1 then the production function is said to be **linearly homogeneous**. The degree of homogeneity indicates the type of returns to scale:

if $n = 1$ there are CRTS

if $n > 1$ there are IRTS

if $n < 1$ there are DRTS.

These concepts now need to be applied to particular forms of production function. Let us take the simple **linear** form in (5.2) first:

$$Q = aL + bK$$

When each input is multiplied by λ, output is given by:

$$a(\lambda L) + b(\lambda K) = \lambda(aL + bK)$$

Thus λ can be factored out of the function and the function is linearly homogeneous. This means that linear production functions like (5.2) feature constant returns to scale at all levels of output. This is not true for the linear function with a constant term in (5.3); this is not a homogeneous function. Nor is the linear function with an interaction term in (5.4).

Now let us consider the **quadratic** function in (5.5):

$$Q = aL^2 + bK^2 + cLK$$

When inputs are multiplied by λ, output is given by:

$$a(\lambda L)^2 + b(\lambda K)^2 + c(\lambda L)(\lambda K) = \lambda^2(aL^2 + bK^2 + cLK)$$

The quadratic function is also homogeneous, but of the second degree; therefore, there are increasing returns to scale in this case.

Let us now consider the **cubic** function in (5.6):

$$Q = aLK + bL^2K + cLK^2 + dL^3K + eLK^3$$

This function is not homogeneous since the first term will be multiplied by λ^2, the next two terms will be multiplied by λ^3 and the last two terms will be multiplied by λ^4. Since the first three terms are generally positive while the last two are negative we cannot say anything about the type of returns to scale in general. As we have already seen with the cubic function in (5.8), there are increasing returns to scale to begin with and then decreasing returns.

c. Cobb–Douglas production functions

Finally let us consider the Cobb–Douglas production function in (5.7):

$$Q = aL^bK^c$$

When inputs are both increased by λ, the resulting output is given by:

$$a(\lambda L)^b(\lambda K)^c = \lambda^{b+c}(aL^bK^c)$$

Thus this type of production function featuring constant output elasticities is homogeneous of order $(b+c)$. This in turn tells us about the type of returns to scale that will occur; *any increase in inputs of 1 per cent will increase output by (b + c) per cent:*

1 If $b+c = 1$ there are CRTS: a 1 per cent increase in inputs will increase output by 1 per cent.
2 If $b+c > 1$ there are IRTS: a 1 per cent increase in inputs will increase output by $>$ 1 per cent.
3 If $b+c < 1$ there are DRTS: a 1 per cent increase in inputs will increase output by $<$ 1 per cent.

Cobb–Douglas production functions are very useful in practice because of the information they reveal regarding the type of returns to scale in a firm or industry. Empirical findings relating to this aspect will be discussed in Chapter 7, because of their implications regarding costs.

5.4.4 Determining the optimal combination of inputs

The isoquants that were considered in the previous analysis all assume that the firm is producing with technical efficiency, which, as we have seen, means that the outputs involved are assumed to be the maximum that could be produced from the combinations of inputs employed. However, for each iso-quant there is only one combination of inputs that is economically efficient, meaning minimizing cost, given a set of input prices. The determination of this input combination requires information regarding both the production function, determining the relevant isoquant, and the prices of the inputs employed. This involves moving into aspects of cost analysis, the subject of the next chapter, but there is a difference of perspective. At this point it is assumed that there is a target level of output that is given. The next chapter focuses more on relationships between costs and output where output is treated as a variable.

a. Isocost lines

The prices of the inputs can be used to compute an **isocost** line. This line shows the *different combinations of inputs that can be employed given a certain level of cost outlay*. We can now see that an isocost line corresponds to the concept of a budget line in consumer theory. Thus the slope of the isocost line is given by the ratio of the input prices, P_L/P_K. Likewise we can derive the firm's optimal position in the same way that we derived the consumer's optimal position.

Let us at this point review the concept of the consumer's optimal position or equilibrium, since it will shed light on the similarities of, and differences between, the optimization procedures involved. In consumer theory the objective was to maximize total utility subject to a budget constraint. The objective that we are now considering in production theory is to minimize cost subject to an output constraint, meaning that we have to produce a certain output. This is called the **dual** of the problem in consumer theory; this corresponds to a kind of mirror image. The differences are as follows:

1 The objective is one of minimization rather than maximization.
2 The isoquants represent maximum outputs that are constraints in production theory, whereas indifference curves represent utilities that are to be maximized in consumer theory.
3 Isocost lines represent costs that are to be minimized in production theory, whereas budget lines represent budgets that are constraints in consumer theory.

In spite of dealing with the 'mirror image' of the problem in consumer theory we can essentially use the same technique of analysis. This can be seen in the graph in Figure 5.7. The optimal point is where the isoquant is tangential to the lowest isocost curve. This is the 'mirror image' of the optimal point in consumer theory, where the budget line is tangential to the highest indifference curve.

It is assumed in the example of Viking Shoes that labour costs £400 per worker per week and capital costs £500 per machine per week. The isocost line C_1 represents a total cost of £3,000 per week, C_2 represents £4,000 per week and C_3 represents £5,000 per week. It can be seen from the graph that the

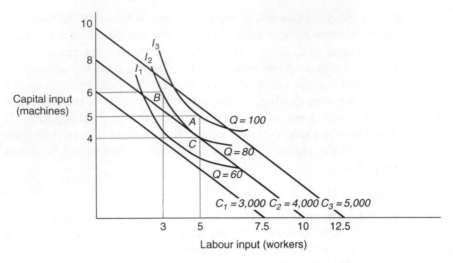

Figure 5.7. Viking Shoes: determining the optimal combination of inputs.

minimum cost to produce an output of 80 units is £4,000, shown by point C, and that the input combination required is five workers and four machines. Other combinations of inputs required to produce the same output would cost more than £4,000; for example, the combination at point B, three workers and six machines, costs £4,200.

b. Conditions for cost minimization

The cost minimization problem can be examined in more general terms. We have just seen that the condition for optimality is that the isoquant is tangential to the lowest isocost curve. Thus we can equate the slopes of the two curves. The slope of the isoquant is given by the marginal rate of technical substitution, which we have also seen to be given by the ratios of the marginal products, MP_L/MP_k. The isocost line has the equation:

$$C = P_L L + P_K K \tag{5.21}$$

where P_L and P_K represent the prices of labour and capital. The slope of this line, in absolute terms, is given by the ratio of the input prices, P_L / P_K. Thus:

$$MP_L/MP_K = P_L/P_K, \text{ or } MP_L/P_L = MP_K/P_K \tag{5.22}$$

This means that *a firm should produce using the combination of inputs such that the ratio of the marginal product of each input to its own price is equal across the last units employed of all inputs*. This principle can be generalized to apply to any number of inputs. It is analogous to the principle in consumer theory that a consumer should spend so that the marginal utility of the last unit of money spent on each product is the same. This was expressed mathematically in (3.14) as:

$$MU_X/P_X = MU_Y/P_Y$$

c. Dual nature of the optimization problem

It has already been indicated that the optimization problem in production theory is in many ways the mirror image of the optimization problem in consumer theory. However, in saying this we are assuming that the nature of the firm's situation is that it has a given target output which it is trying to produce at minimum cost. This is not always the situation. For example, in the public sector the budget may be the given factor and the objective may be to produce the highest output with that given level of budget. This is an output-maximization problem rather than a cost-minimization problem and it exactly parallels the situation of utility maximization in consumer theory. The optimal combination of inputs is again given by the point where the isocost line (in this case a fixed single line) is tangential to the highest isoquant (in this case a variable line). Thus the condition expressed in (5.21) still applies.

d. Changes in input prices

The levels of input prices determine the position and slope of the isocost curves. If the relative prices of the inputs change this will affect the slope of the curves, which we have seen is given by P_L/P_K. If, for example, labour becomes more expensive relative to capital the slope of the isocost curves will become steeper. This will result in the point of tangency moving along the relevant isoquant, upwards and to the left, and a higher level of cost, assuming a given target output. Not surprisingly, less of the more expensive input is used than before, and more of the input that is now relatively cheaper. The situation is illustrated in Figure 5.8. In this example it is assumed that the labour input increases in price from £400 to £500 per week. The isocost curve $C' = 4,000$ shows the effect of the price increase and the fact that the output of 80 units can no longer be achieved at the cost of £4,000. To attain this output, assuming economic efficiency, now involves a cost outlay of about £4,400.

There are again obvious parallels in consumer theory, corresponding to the situation where product prices change. In that case it was seen that rational consumers should respond to the situation by buying less of the more expensive product. The main difference is that, because of the dual nature of the situation, consumers are assumed to have a fixed budget line; therefore when a product price rises they are forced onto a lower indifference curve.

e. Expansion paths

Another application of this type of analysis is to consider what happens when the firm's target output increases, or to express the situation in terms of its dual, when the firm's budget increases. As the firm attains higher and higher

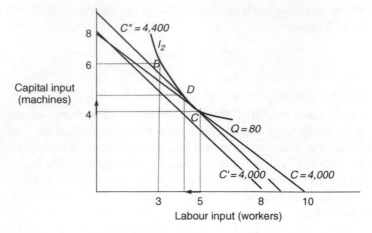

Figure 5.8. Viking Shoes: effects of changes in input prices.

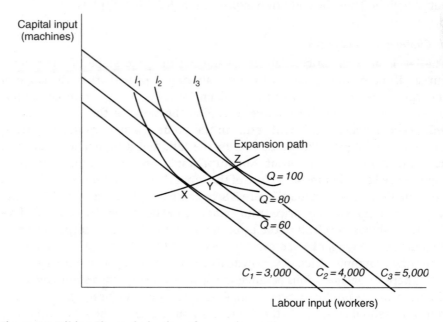

Figure 5.9. Viking Shoes: derivation of expansion path.

output levels the optimal combinations of inputs involved will trace an **expansion path**. This is illustrated in Figure 5.9. The expansion path goes through all the points of tangency, X, Y and Z. This path can be used to determine the long-run relationships between costs and output that are examined in the next chapter. However, the graph in Figure 5.9 assumes that the prices of the inputs remain constant, or at least that their ratio remains constant, which as we shall see is not very realistic.

5.5 A problem-solving approach

It is possible to identify three main management principles that emerge from the preceding discussion of production theory. These are all key points in terms of decision-making.

5.5.1 Planning

It can be seen from Table 5.3 that in the short run the range of output for Viking Shoes associated with stage II of the production function is from 27 to 66 units per week. Under most circumstances Viking's optimal operating output should be in this range. If we make the additional assumptions regarding the price of output and the prices of inputs in subsection 5.3.6 we can conclude that optimal output is 59 units; however, it must be remembered that this output is only optimal given the choice of scale by the firm. The implication as far as planning is concerned is that the firm must ensure that it is using the best scale in order to maximize profit. For example, it may be that at the price charged customers might want to buy less than 27 units or more than 66 units, forcing the firm to operate in stage I or stage III. In this situation the firm's scale would be too large or too small respectively. This aspect of planning, **capacity planning**, means that the firm must be able to have accurate forecasts of demand, and communicate the relevant information to its marketing and production departments. These two departments need to communicate with each other, so that sales forecasts by marketing people can be met by the relevant production capacity. Likewise, information relating to production constraints needs to be communicated to the marketing department, so they do not 'oversell' the product.

5.5.2 Marginal analysis

This is particularly relevant to optimization problems in neoclassical economic theory. We have now seen various applications of it, in Chapters 2 and 3 and now here in production theory. It will again be important in Chapters 6, 8, 9 and 10. The essential principles are the same in each case. Marginal benefits (profits, utility, product or revenue) tend to be large at low levels of operation (operation can be measured in terms of input, output or expenditure). The operation should be increased until these benefits become equal to the marginal costs. Further expansion is wasteful or non-optimal. The following solved problem will illustrate the application of marginal analysis to production theory.

SP 5.1 Short-run production function

A firm has the following short-run production function:

$$Q = 150L + 18L^2 - 1.5L^3$$

where Q = quantity of output per week
L = number of workers employed.

a. When does the law of diminishing returns take effect?
b. Calculate the range of values for labour over which stages I, II and III occur.
c. Assume that each worker is paid £15 per hour for a 40-hour week, and that the output is priced at £5. How many workers should the firm employ?

Solution

a. $$MP = dQ / dL = 150 + 36L - 4.5L^2$$
   MP is at a maximum when diminishing returns occur, therefore we have to differentiate the expression for MP to find the relevant value of L. This is the first-order necessary condition for a maximum.

$$d(MP)/dL = 36 - 9L = 0$$

$$L = 4$$

In order to confirm that this gives a maximum value of MP rather than a minimum we have to consider the second-order condition. This means examining the sign of the second derivative; since this is negative we do indeed have a maximum value of MP when $L = 4$.

b. Stage II begins where AP is at a maximum.

$$AP = 150 + 18L - 1.5L^2$$
$$d(AP)/dL = 18 - 3L = 0$$
$$L = 6$$

Again we can confirm from the second derivative that this gives a maximum.

Stage III begins where $MP = 150 + 36L - 4.5L^2 = 0$

$$L = \frac{-36 \pm \sqrt{\{36^2 - 4(-4.5)(150)\}}}{2(-4.5)} = \frac{-36 \pm 63.21}{-9}$$

$$L = 11.02 \text{ or } 11$$

c. $MRP = MP \times P = (150 + 36L - 4.5L^2)5$ in £ per week

$MFC = 15 \times 40 = 600$

Setting $MRP = MFC$:

$$750 + 180L - 22.5L^2 = 600$$

$$22.5L^2 - 180L - 150 = 0$$

$$L = \frac{180 \pm \sqrt{\{180^2 - 4(22.5)(-150)\}}}{45} = 8.76 \text{ or } 9$$

5.5.3 Evaluating trade-offs

We have seen right from the beginning of this book that the concept of opportunity cost is of paramount importance in all areas of economics. In production theory the concept applies to trade-offs between inputs. The most obvious example is the trade-off between capital and labour, as has been seen in the example of Viking Shoes. In this situation the trade-off only applies in long-run time frames. However, many other trade-offs can exist, some of them in the short run.

1 *Labour–labour*. There are different types of labour, with different skills, and these can often be substituted for each other. In a marketing department, for example, salespeople are substitutes for administrative workers to some extent. The managerial problem is to determine the optimal mix of different personnel.
2 *Labour–raw materials*. A good example of this trade-off is in the restaurant business.[7] Many customers may notice that generous portions of condiments and sauces are offered, which may seem wasteful. However, if smaller portions were served, customers would make greater demands of waiters, and the additional labour-time involved might easily offset the savings in terms of raw material costs.
3 *Materials–materials*. Many materials are substitutes for each other. In many cases, substitution of one material for another may affect the quality of the final product, but even if there is no significant difference here, there may well be implications in production. For example, more cars these days are being made out of composite materials. This does affect quality of output in terms of durability, weight and other characteristics; however, there are other implications of substituting composites for metal. Amounts of materials needed and prices are different; the relevant processing of these materials is also different, e.g. moulds are used instead of panel-pressing machinery.
4 *Capital–capital*. Many machines can be substituted for each other, even if their functions are quite different. A manager may have to allocate the

departmental capital budget between photocopy machines, PCs, fax machines and even coffee machines. All contribute directly or indirectly to the total output of the department so again the optimal mix between them must be found.

Many of these trade-offs are relevant in Case Study 5.3 on the National Health Service. The following solved problem also illustrates the situation.

SP 5.2 Optimal combination of inputs

A bottling plant employs three different types of labour: unskilled manual workers, technicians and supervisors. It has estimated that the marginal product of the last manual worker is 200 units per week, the marginal product of the last technician is 275 units per week and the marginal product of the last supervisor is 300 units per week. The workers earn £300, £400 and £500 per week respectively.

a. Is the firm using the optimal combination of inputs?
b. If not, advise the firm on how to reallocate its resources.

Solution

a. The optimal combination is achieved when the marginal product of each type of worker as a ratio of the price of labour is equal, i.e.:

$$\frac{MP_m}{P_m} = \frac{MP_t}{P_t} = \frac{MP_s}{P_s} \qquad (5.23)$$

$$\frac{MP_m}{P_m} = 200/300 = 0.67$$

$$\frac{MP_t}{P_t} = 275/400 = 0.6875$$

$$\frac{MP_s}{P_s} = 300/500 = 0.6$$

This combination of inputs is therefore not optimal.
b. It is better to use more of the most productive input, i.e. technicians, and less of the least productive input, i.e. supervisors. By reallocating resources in this way the firm will cause the MP of the most productive input to fall and the MP of the least productive input to rise, until an optimal point is reached where condition (5.22) is satisfied.

Case study 5.3: Factor substitution in the National Health Service

The National Health Service (NHS) in the UK was founded in 1948 and was the first state-run free health service in the world. It originated at a time of national euphoria following victory in World War II, which generated a sense of confidence and solidarity among politicians and public. In particular it was felt that class distinctions were finally disappearing. The extensive rationing of products, both during and after the war, played a big part. Not only did this result in queuing for goods by rich and poor alike, but it gave the government a sense that state control of distribution was not only possible but in many cases desirable. The basic objective was to provide all people with free medical, dental and nursing care.

It was a highly ambitious scheme that rested on various premises that have since proved flawed. These were:

1 The demand for health care was finite; it was assumed that some given amount of expenditure would satisfy all of the nation's health wants.
2 Health care provision could be made independent of market forces; in particular doctors were not supposed to consider costs in deciding how to treat individual patients.
3 Access to health care could be made equal to all; this means that there would be no preferential treatment according to type of customer, in particular according to their location.

The flaws became more obvious as time went by, and were aggravated by the fact that the system was based on the old pre-war infrastructure in terms of facilities. This meant that the provision was highly fragmented, with a large number of small hospitals and other medical centres. The first flaw became apparent very quickly: in its first nine months of operation the NHS overshot its budget by nearly 40 per cent as patients flocked to see their doctors for treatment. Initially it was believed that this high demand was just a backlog that would soon be cleared, but events proved otherwise. Webster,[8] the official historian of the NHS, argues that the government must have had little idea of the 'momentous scale of the financial commitments' which they had made. Since its foundation, spending on the NHS has increased more than fivefold, yet it has still not kept pace with the increase in demand. This increase in demand has occurred because of new technology, an ageing population and rising

expectations. At present it is difficult to see a limit on spending; total spending, public and private, on healthcare in the USA is three times as much per person as in the UK.

However, when it comes to performance compared with other countries the UK does not fare that badly. In spite of far larger spending in the USA, some of the basic measures of a country's health, such as life expectancy and infant mortality, are broadly similar in the two countries. The United States performs better in certain specific areas, for example in survival rates in intensive-care units and after cancer diagnosis, but even these statistics are questionable. It may merely be that cancer is diagnosed at an earlier stage of the disease in the USA rather than that people live longer with the disease.

Performance can also be measured subjectively by examining surveys of public satisfaction with the country's health service. A 1996 OECD study of public opinion across the European Union found that the more of its income that a country spends per person on health, the more content they are about the health service. This showed that, although the British are less satisfied with their health service than citizens of other countries are with theirs, after allowing for the amount of spending per head the British are actually more satisfied than the norm.[9] Italy, for example, spends more per head, yet the public satisfaction rating is far lower.

There are a number of issues that currently face the NHS. The most basic one concerns the location of decision-making. This is an aspect of government policy which is discussed in Chapter 12, and largely relates to normative aspects, though there are some important economic implications in terms of resource allocation. The other issues again have both positive and normative aspects. The use of private-sector providers and charges for services are important issues, again examined in Chapter 12. In terms of spending, once it is recognized that resources are limited, there is the macro decision regarding how much the state should be spending on healthcare in total. Then there is the micro question of where and how this money should be spent, and this issue essentially concerns factor substitution and opportunity cost. A number of trade-offs are relevant here, and some examples are discussed in the following paragraphs.

1. Beds versus equipment. Treatments are much more capital-intensive than they used to be in past decades, owing to improved technology. This has the effect of reducing hospital-stay times, and 60 per cent of patients are now in and out of hospital in less than a day[10] compared with weeks or months previously. This can reduce the need for beds compared with equipment.

2. Drugs versus hospitals. Health authorities may be under pressure to provide expensive drugs, for example beta interferon for the treatment of multiple sclerosis. This forces unpleasant choices. Morgan, chief executive of the East and North Devon Health Authority, has stated 'It will be interferon or keeping a community hospital, I can't reconcile the two.'[11]

3. Administrators versus medical staff. In recent years the NHS has employed more and more administrators, whilst there has been a chronic shortage of doctors and nurses. This was partly related to the aim of the Conservatives when they were in office to establish an internal market (discussed in more detail in Chapter 12). The health secretary, Milburn, was trying to reverse this trend; in a 'top-to-toe revolution' Milburn appeared to want a new modernization board of doctors and nurses to replace the existing board of civil servants. The NHS's chief executive, Langlands, resigned. In the hospitals also there were more administrators, and these took over much of the decision-making previously done by doctors regarding types of treatment. This became necessary because of the clash between scientific advance, increasing costs and budgetary constraints. It became increasingly obvious that rationing had to take place. Related to this issue, nurses were also having to do a lot more administrative work which could be performed by clerical workers. This happened for the same basic reason as before: more information needed to be collected from patients in order to determine the type of treatment.

4. Hospital versus hospital. Because of the piecemeal structure that the NHS inherited it has tended to provide healthcare in an inefficient way. Hospitals and other facilities are not only old and in need of repair, but in many cases small, separated geographically, and duplicating facilities. Division of labour is often non-optimal. In Birmingham, for example, there is an accident and emergency unit at Selly Oak Hospital, whereas the brain and heart specialists who might need to perform urgent operations on those involved in car crashes or suffering heart attacks are at the neighbouring Queen Elizabeth Hospital. Thus the issue often arises whether it is preferable to concentrate facilities and staff by building a new and larger hospital to replace a number of older facilities.

5. Area versus area. At present there is much variation in the services provided by different local health authorities. For example, some restrict, or do not provide, procedures such as *in vitro* fertilization, cosmetic surgery and renal dialysis. This has led to the description 'postcode prescribing'. Much of this has to do with the differences in budgets relative to demand in different areas, and is another example of the greater visibility of rationing.

Questions

1 Illustrate the trade-off between administrators and medical staff using an isoquant/isocost graph. Explain the economic principles involved in obtaining an optimal situation. How would this situation be affected by an increase in the pay of doctors and nurses?

2 What problems might be encountered in determining this solution in practical terms?

3 Illustrate the hospital-versus-hospital trade-off using an isoquant/isocost graph and explaining the economic principles involved in obtaining an optimal situation. In what important respects does this issue differ from the issue in the previous question?

Summary

1 A production function shows the maximum amounts of output that can be produced from a set of inputs.

2 All points on a production function involve technical efficiency, but only one represents economic efficiency, given prices for the inputs.

3 The functional form of a production function is important because it gives information about the marginal products of the inputs, output elasticities and returns to scale.

4 An isoquant shows different combinations of inputs that can produce the same technically efficient level of output.

5 The marginal rate of technical substitution (*MRTS*) of *X* for *Y* shows the amount of one input *Y* that must be substituted for another *X* in order to produce the same output. It is given by the ratio MP_X / MP_Y and graphically by the slope of the isoquant.

6 Returns to scale describe how a proportionate increase in all inputs affects output; they can be increasing, constant or decreasing.

7 The optimal combination of inputs in the long run is achieved when the marginal product of each input as a ratio of its price is equal.

8 In the short run, production is subject to increasing and then diminishing returns.

9 The optimal level of use of the variable factor in the short run is given by the condition $MRP = MFC$.

10 There are three main applications of production theory in terms of managerial decision-making: capacity planning, marginal analysis and evaluation of trade-offs.

Review questions

1 Give examples of daily activities where the law of diminishing returns applies.

2 Explain the difference between technical and economic efficiency.

3 What is meant by the three stages of production in the short run?

4 Explain the shapes of the total product, marginal product and average product curves for a Cobb–Douglas production function in the short run.

5 Figure 5.10 shows an isoquant and an isocost curve.
  Show the effects of the following changes:

  a. The price of *L* rises.
  b. The prices of *L* and *K* rise by the same proportion.

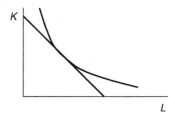

Figure 5.10. Isoquant and isocost curves.

c. The firm's budget increases.

d. Improved technology makes K more productive.

e. Improved technology makes both L and K more productive by the same proportion.

Problems

5.1 CD Inc. has estimated that it has the following production function:

$$Q = 80L^{0.4}K^{0.6}$$

a. Draw up an input-output table for this function up to the input of eight units of capital and labour.

b. Comment on returns to scale from the function; how can you check this from your table in (a)?

c. If capital is fixed at four units, draw a graph of total, marginal and average product.

d. Explain why marginal and average product are continuously declining.

5.2 A restaurant owner has the following short-run production function:

$$Q = 30L - 2L^2$$

where Q = number of meals served per day, and L = number of workers.

a. Draw up a table showing total, marginal and average product up to an input of ten workers, and plot these on a graph.

b. Show the range of labour where stages I, II and III of production occur.

c. If workers can be hired for £40 per day and the average meal is £6, how many workers should be hired?

5.3 LM Corp. has estimated that it has the following production function:

$$Q = 1.5LK - 0.3L^2 - 0.15K^2$$

Labour costs £60 and capital costs £75. LM wants to maximize output subject to the cost constraint of £1,500.

a. What amounts of labour and capital should be used?

b. What is the total output from the above combination?

5.4 The following are different types of production function. Determine whether each one has constant, increasing or decreasing returns to scale.

a. $Q = 20L + 20K + 50$

b. $Q = 30L^2 + 25K^2$

c. $Q = 40L + 20K + 10LK$

d. $Q = 25L^{0.4}K^{0.8}$

e. $Q = 20L^{0.3}K^{0.6}M^{0.2}$

Notes

1 C. W. Cobb and P. H. Douglas, 'A theory of production', *American Economic Review*, **16** (1928): 139–165.
2 'The theory that made Microsoft: increasing returns', *Fortune*, **29** (April 1996): 65–68.
3 J. R. McGuigan, R. C. Moyer and F. H. deB Harris, *Managerial Economics: Applications, Strategy, and Tactics*, 8th edn, Cincinatti: South-Western College, 1999, p. 273.
4 'Like Topsy', *The Economist*, 6 December 1999.
5 V. Tanzi and L. Schuknecht, 'The growth of government and the reform of the state in industrial countries', *IMF Working Paper* no. 95/130, December 1995.
6 F. McMahon, *Retreat from Growth*, Halifax, Nova Scotia: Atlantic Institute for Market Studies, 2000.
7 P. Keat and P. K. Y. Young, *Managerial Economics*, New York: Macmillan, 1992, p. 278.
8 C. Webster, *The National Health Service: A Political History*, Oxford University Press, 1998.
9 'Bevan's baby hits middle age', *The Economist*, 2 July 1998.
10 'Battle of the bedpans', *The Economist*, 10 December 1999.
11 'Milburn's balancing act', *The Economist*, 24 February 2000.

6

Cost theory

Outline

Objectives

1 To explain the meaning and use of different concepts of cost.
2 To show how different concepts of cost are relevant for managerial decision-making.
3 To explain how production relationships underlie cost relationships.
4 To explain cost behaviour in the short run.
5 To explain cost behaviour in the long run.
6 To explain how cost relationships can be derived in mathematical terms.
7 To explain the purpose and principles of cost–volume–profit analysis.
8 To describe a problem-solving approach for applying cost–volume–profit analysis.

6.1 Introduction

6.1.1 *Importance of costs for decision-making*

Demand analysis is fundamentally concerned with the revenue side of an organization's operation; cost analysis is also vital in managerial economics, and managers must have a good understanding of cost relationships if they are to maximize the value of the firm. Many costs are more controllable than are factors affecting revenue. While a firm can estimate what effect an increase in advertising expenditure will have on sales revenue, this effect is generally more uncertain than a decision to switch suppliers, or invest in new machinery, or close a plant.

Just as with production theory, the distinction between short run and long run is an important one. In the short run, managers are concerned with determining the optimal level of output to produce from a given plant size (or plant sizes, for a multiplant firm), and then planning production accordingly, in terms of the optimal input of the variable factor, scheduling and so on. In the long run, all inputs are variable so the most fundamental decision the firm has to make is the scale at which to operate. The optimal scale is the one that is the most efficient, in economic terms, for producing a given output.

Cost analysis is made complex because there are many different definitions and concepts of cost, and it is not always straightforward to determine which costs to use and how to measure them in a particular situation. The focus here is on the **relevant costs for decision-making**. In order to clarify this aspect the following four distinctions are important.

6.1.2 Explicit and implicit costs

Explicit costs can be considered as *expenses* or out-of-pocket costs (rent, raw materials, fuel, wages); they are normally recorded in a firm's accounts. However, the economic cost of using a resource is its **opportunity cost**, which is *the cost of forgoing the next most profitable use of the resource, or the benefit that could be obtained from the next-best use*. This involves both explicit and implicit costs. Let us take the example of a student considering undertaking an MBA; the relevant costs can be classified as either explicit costs or implicit costs.

Explicit costs include fees, books, accommodation, food, transportation, recreation and entertainment and so on. Not all of these may be directly related to doing an MBA, the last category for example, so they can be regarded as incidental costs. Money still has to be made available to pay these costs.

Implicit costs are non-cash costs, like the salary that could have been earned, leisure time forgone (if work required on the MBA exceeds the hours of salaried work), and interest forgone on assets which have to be used to pay MBA expenses.

Opportunity costs would include elements of both, but are not simply the sum of the two; for example, accommodation is not an opportunity cost if the student would be in the same accommodation whether they were doing the MBA or not. Opportunity costs should be used for decision-making purposes, meaning making the fundamental decision whether to do the MBA or not. These costs then have to be compared with the expected benefits, monetary and non-monetary, of undertaking an MBA programme. This does not mean that the other costs are unimportant; they are still relevant in cash planning.

6.1.3 Historical and current costs

Historical costs represent **actual cash outlay** and this is what accountants record and measure. This means measuring costs in historical terms, at the time they were incurred. Although this is relevant for tax purposes it may not reflect the **current costs**.

Current costs refer to **the amount that would be paid for an item under present market conditions**. Often current costs exceed historical costs, particularly with inflation. In some situations, for example IT equipment, current costs tend to be below historical costs because of rapid improvements in technology. In this case the item being costed may no longer be available, and the appropriate cost is the **replacement cost**. This is the cost of duplicating the productive capability of the item using current technology. Replacement cost is the relevant cost for decision-making. The following example illustrates this principle.

Assume that Clearglass Conservatories is offered a contract to build a conservatory at a property, at a price of £60,000. The labour costs are £40,000 and the materials necessary to complete the job are already in inventory, valued at the historical cost of £15,000. If the job is accepted, Clearglass, as an ongoing concern, will have to replace the materials, but the price of these has risen, so the current cost is £22,000. If Clearglass uses historical cost to cost the job they will accept it, expecting to make a profit of £5,000. They should, however, reject it since they will really make a loss of £2,000. This can be seen more clearly if we consider what happens if they accept the job and then restore their inventory to the previous level. They will end up receiving £60,000 and paying out £62,000 (£40,000 for labour and £22,000 for materials), thus losing £2,000.

6.1.4 Sunk and incremental costs

Sunk costs are **costs that do not vary according to different decisions**. An example was given earlier in the case of the MBA student's accommodation; the accommodation cost was the same whether or not the student did the MBA. Often these costs refer to outlays that have already occurred at the time of decision-making, like the cost of market research conducted before deciding whether to launch a new product.

Incremental costs refer to **changes in costs caused by a particular decision**. Using the same example, if the student would have to pay £4,000 for yearly accommodation doing a salaried job and £6,000 for accommodation to do the MBA, the incremental cost associated with the decision to do the MBA would be £2,000 (assuming simplistically that there are no other costs or benefits related to the differences in accommodation). Incremental costs are the relevant costs for decision-making.

6.1.5 Private and social costs

Private costs refer to costs that accrue directly to the individuals performing a particular activity, in other words they are **internal costs**. For private firms these are the only costs that are relevant, unless there are ethical considerations (see Chapter 12).

Social costs also include **external** costs that are passed on to other parties, and are often difficult to value. For example, motorists cause pollution and congestion which affect many other people (this is the economic justification for fuel duties, which are an attempt to internalize these externalities, as seen in Chapter 12). Therefore when a resource like oil or petrol is used there are both internal and external costs. The social costs are the sum of the two, meaning the total cost to society of using a resource (being careful not to double-count any duties). Social costs are relevant for public policy decision-making. In this situation the technique of **cost-benefit analysis** is often used. However, since we are largely concerned with managerial decision-making, social costs and cost-benefit analysis will not be examined here.

6.1.6 Relevant costs for decision-making

For private firms it has been shown above that it is the opportunity costs, the replacement costs and the incremental costs that are relevant. These concepts are all illustrated in the following case study.

Case study 6.1: Brewster Roofing

Mr Brewster operates a roofing company in London and has been asked by the local government authority of Merton to repair the roofs of several of their properties damaged in a recent storm. The job must be completed during the next four weeks (twenty working days), and Merton has offered £16,000 for the job. Mr Brewster has estimated that the job requires seventy-five work days, but he can only use his regular three workers for the job because it is a very busy period for the industry as a whole. Fortunately, Mr Brewster's son, Will, can take time off from his regular job (paying £80 per day) to help complete the work. Mr Brewster has estimated that, for his regular employees, the cost per work day is £150. This consists of a wage of £100 (which is only paid if the employee is working) and £50 in contributions to the government (which are paid annually regardless of how many days the employees work).

Brewster Roofing has all the equipment necessary for the job and has some of the materials available in inventory. The materials cost £5,000 originally, but these costs have since increased by an average of 5 per cent. Additional materials costing £3,000 are also required.

Mr Brewster has costed the job as follows:

Revenue	£16,000
Costs	
Labour	£9,000
Materials	£8,000
Total costs	£17,000
Profit	(£1,000)

On the basis of the above analysis Mr Brewster rejects the job.

Questions

1 Prepare a revised cost estimate for the job, taking into account opportunity costs, replacement costs and incremental costs. Assume that Mr Brewster considers the job from the viewpoint of a family business, including himself and his son together.
2 Advise Mr Brewster regarding whether he should accept the job, stating any assumptions involved in your analysis.

6.1.7 Summary of cost concepts

Several points emerge from the above discussion of costs:

1 There is not always a right and a wrong way to use cost concepts. The right costs for decision-making are not the right costs for estimating tax liability and vice versa.

2 Managers must be very careful in using cost information prepared by accountants, since it has been collected and categorized for different purposes.
3 The determination of costs is not always purely objective; this is particularly true of implicit costs, where a considerable degree of judgement is often required.

6.2 Short-run cost behaviour

Managers want to know the nature of the cost functions pertaining to their firm for the following reasons:

1 To make pricing decisions – this aspect is considered in Chapters 8 and 10.
2 To determine the appropriate levels of other factors in the marketing mix – this is considered in Chapters 9 and 10.
3 To forecast and plan for the costs and input levels associated with a given level of output.

6.2.1 Classification of costs

It was seen in Chapter 5 that the short run in economic terms is defined as the period during which at least one factor of production is fixed and others are variable. This leads to a further classification of costs, into fixed costs and variable costs.

Fixed costs are **related to the fixed factors and do not vary with output in the short run**. Examples are rent, insurance, interest payments, and depreciation (if estimated on a time basis). These costs may vary in the short run, for example if the interest rate rises, but not because of a change in output. Fixed costs have to be paid even if output is zero for any period, for example when there is a strike.

Variable costs are **related to the variable factors and vary directly with output**. This was assumed in some of the analysis in Chapter 3, for example in Table 3.4 relating price changes to profit. Examples of variable costs are raw materials, wages, depreciation related to the use of equipment, and some fuel costs.

In practice a clear distinction between fixed and variable costs is not always possible; some costs, like fuel above, may have fixed and variable elements. Other costs, like administrative salaries, may be fixed over a certain output range, but if output exceeds the range an increase in staff may be required, thus increasing costs.

6.2.2 Types of unit cost

Managers are often more interested in units costs than in total costs, for the following reasons:

1 Unit costs provide a better measure of the performance of the firm in terms of efficiency. This means that comparisons on a time-series or cross-section basis are easier to make.
2 Unit costs can be compared directly with price, and conclusions drawn regarding profit. This is explained in section 6.5 on CVP analysis.
3 It is easier to understand cost relationships with output in terms of unit costs.

There are four main types of unit cost in the short run:

1 *Marginal cost (MC)*. This can be defined as **the additional cost of producing an additional unit of output**. Thus we can write:

$$MC = \text{change in total costs/change in output} = \Delta C/\Delta Q \quad (6.1)$$

In the limiting case where the change in output is infinitely small we can write:

$$MC = dC/dQ \quad (6.2)$$

2 *Average variable cost (AVC)*. This refers to the total variable costs divided by output; thus we can write:

$$AVC = VC/Q \quad (6.3)$$

3 *Average fixed cost (AFC)*. This refers to total fixed costs divided by output; we can write:

$$AFC = FC/Q \quad (6.4)$$

4 *Average total cost (ATC)*. This refers to total costs divided by output; we can write:

$$ATC = TC/Q \quad (6.5)$$

or

$$ATC = (FC + VC)/Q = FC/Q + VC/Q = AFC + AVC \quad (6.6)$$

All of the above types of unit cost can be derived from the production table in Table 5.3, provided that we know the prices of the inputs, labour and capital.

6.2.3 *Derivation of cost functions from production functions*

In the example relating to Viking Shoes in Chapter 5 it was assumed that the price of labour was £400 per worker per week and the price of machines was £500 per week. We can now compute the various costs and unit costs related to the inputs and outputs in Table 5.3; these values are shown in Table 6.1. Note that once again the marginal values, in this case *MC*, have to be plotted corresponding to the mid-values of outputs. This is also important in plotting the values on the graph in Figure 6.1. The final row of Table 5.3 is omitted since the use of eight workers with three machines is not technically efficient.

Table 6.1. Viking shoes: short-run cost functions

Output, Q (units)	Capital, K (machines)	Labour, L (workers)	Fixed cost, FC	Variable cost, VC	Total cost, TC	$AFC = FC/Q$	$AVC = VC/Q$	$ATC = TC/Q$	$MC = \Delta C/\Delta Q$
0	3	0	1,500	0	1,500	–	–	–	
13	3	1	1,500	400	1,900	115	31	146	31
27	3	2	1,500	800	2,300	56	30	85	29
39	3	3	1,500	1,200	2,700	38	31	69	33
50	3	4	1,500	1,500	3,100	30	32	62	36
59	3	5	1,500	2,000	3,500	25	34	59	44
64	3	6	1,500	2,400	3,900	23	37	61	80
66	3	7	1,500	2,800	4,300	23	42	65	200

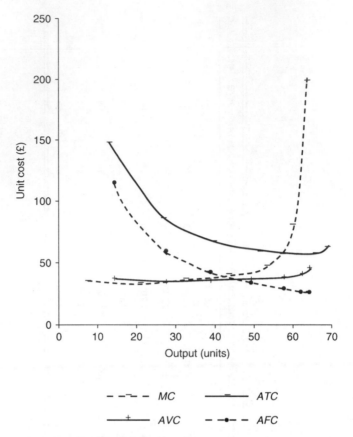

Figure 6.1. Viking shoes: unit cost functions.

The four unit cost functions in the last four columns of Table 6.1 can be illustrated in a graph. They are shown in Figure 6.1. The relationships between unit costs and output are now explained, with the aid of Figure 6.2. This shows the unit cost relationships in general terms, and their correspondence to production relationships and total cost relationships.

6.2.4 Factors determining relationships with output

It is helpful to begin the explanation of unit cost behaviour with marginal cost since this determines the shape of both the *AVC* and *ATC* curves.

a. Marginal cost
There are two features of the *MC* curve that need to be explained.

1. The MC curve is U-shaped.   *MC* falls to begin with as output rises, because of increasing returns, and then, after reaching output Q_1, it begins to rise because of diminishing returns. This is best explained by considering the following relationship:

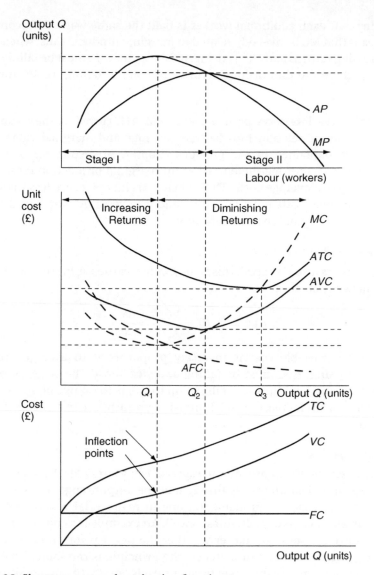

Figure 6.2. Short-run cost and production functions.

$$MC = \Delta C/\Delta Q = \frac{\Delta C/\Delta L}{\Delta Q/\Delta L}$$

where $\Delta C/\Delta L$ = the additional cost of hiring one more worker, in other words the price of labour, P_L, and $\Delta Q/\Delta L$ = the marginal product of labour MP_L.

Thus we can write:

$$MC = \frac{P_L}{MP_L} \qquad (6.7)$$

Assuming that each additional worker is paid the same wage, P_L is constant. This means that MC is inversely related to marginal product. Thus, when there are increasing returns and MP_L is rising, it follows that MC must be falling; after output Q_1 there are diminishing returns and MP_L is falling, so MC must be rising.

2. The MC curve intersects both the AVC and ATC curves at their minimum points. The basic relationships between average and marginal values have already been explained in the previous chapter, in section 5.3. A similar relationship exists for marginal costs as for marginal product, in terms of its relationship with average costs. Thus when marginal costs are less than average costs, average costs must be falling and vice versa. Average fixed cost is unaffected by marginal cost, by definition.

b. Average variable cost

The AVC curve is also U-shaped; this is for similar reasons as for the MC curve. It can be shown that:

$$AVC = VC/Q = \frac{VC/L}{Q/L} = \frac{P_L}{AP_L} \tag{6.8}$$

Thus average variable cost is inversely proportional to average product; when AP is rising, AVC must be falling and vice versa. The range of output when AP is rising, and thus AVC falling (up to Q_2), is the range of operation of stage I. Once again increasing and diminishing returns are responsible for this behaviour.

c. Average fixed cost

As output rises the fixed costs become spread over a larger level of output, thus causing AFC to fall continuously throughout the output range. The concept of spreading fixed cost is a fundamental one in managerial economics and is relevant in many everyday activities as well. An example is a consumer buying a season ticket; it does not matter whether the ticket is for public transportation or going to see football matches, the principle is the same. Unless the consumer is going to use the ticket frequently it is not worth buying, since they will not be able to spread the fixed cost of the ticket over a sufficiently large output, meaning trips or matches.

d. Average total Cost

This is also U-shaped because it is the sum of AVC and AFC. These are summed vertically on the graph. At low levels of output, ATC falls because both AVC and AFC are falling. Beyond the level of output Q_2, AVC starts to rise while AFC continues to fall. Beyond output Q_3, AVC rises faster than AFC falls; this means that the effect of diminishing returns more than offsets the spreading of fixed costs, causing ATC to rise. The significance of output Q_3 in terms of efficiency is explained in the next subsection.

6.2.5 Efficiency

As was seen in the last chapter, there are various different concepts of efficiency in economics. Since it was assumed that all the output values in the production functions shown in Tables 5.1 and 5.3 involved technical efficiency, it follows that all the outputs in Figure 5.1 also involve technical efficiency since they are based on the same production function. It is also true that all these outputs involve economic efficiency, in that they all involve a least-cost combination of inputs in the short run, *assuming a given output*. However, only one of these outputs results in the unit cost (average total cost) being minimized if we no longer assume a given output, and that is output Q_3. It can therefore be said that Q_3 is the most efficient level of output in the short run for a firm of given plant size(s). Unfortunately, in many microeconomics texts this output is referred to as the 'maximum capacity' rather than maximum efficiency; this terminology is confusing. It is more accurate to apply the term 'maximum capacity' to the maximum output for the firm in the short run. This does not imply that the most efficient output is an optimal output as far as the firm is concerned, because only costs are considered, not revenue; therefore it tells us nothing about profit.

This type of efficiency in the short run can be viewed as **a compromise between spreading fixed costs and getting diminishing returns**. If more output than Q_3 is produced, less is gained from the further spreading of fixed costs than is lost from getting diminishing returns; therefore ATC rises beyond this level of output.

6.2.6 Changes in input prices

Since it has been assumed that the firm is operating at technical and economic efficiency, it cannot reduce the controllable elements of its cost structure. However, some of its costs are uncontrollable and may rise or fall in the short run. For example, the interest rate on the firm's borrowing may rise, and this will have an immediate effect on the unit cost curves. Since it has been assumed that capital is a fixed factor, the increased interest cost represents an increase in fixed cost. This will shift the AFC and ATC curves upwards, while AVC and MC remain unchanged.

Likewise, if the price of raw materials rises, this represents an increase in a variable cost and will therefore shift the MC, AVC and ATC curves upwards. A decrease in price will similarly shift the same curves downwards.

6.2.7 Different forms of cost function

In most economic analysis, the form of short-run cost function that is most frequently used is the cubic total cost function. This is the form that gives rise to the shapes of function shown in Figures 6.1 and 6.2.

a. Cubic cost functions

These are related to the cubic production functions examined in the previous chapter. The relationship between the two types of function can be seen most easily in the relationships between marginal product and marginal cost. Both of these are quadratic functions that are inversely related, as shown in (6.7), and this is illustrated graphically in Figure 6.2.

Two other forms of total cost function are also sometimes used in economic analysis; these are the **quadratic** form and the **linear** form. These forms and their implications in terms of unit costs and graphical shapes are now considered.

b. Quadratic cost functions*

These have the general form:

$$C = a + bQ + cQ^2 \tag{6.9}$$

In this case the marginal cost is given by:

$$MC = b + 2cQ \tag{6.10}$$

This is a linear function, as shown in Figure 6.3. The economic implication of this is that the law of diminishing returns takes effect as soon as the firm starts to produce.

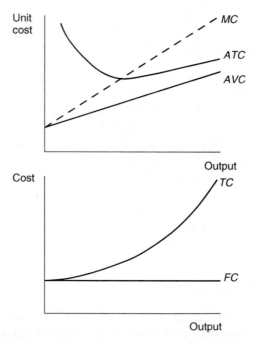

Figure 6.3. The quadratic cost function.

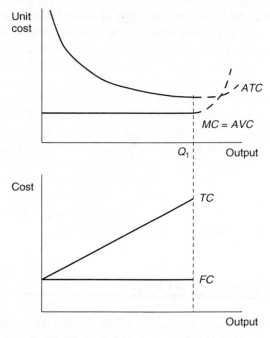

Figure 6.4. The linear cost function.

It can also be shown that a quadratic cost function will occur if the production function is of the Cobb–Douglas type with the output elasticity of labour equal to 0.5:

$$Q = aL^{0.5}K^c \tag{6.11}$$

From this an expression for L can be derived as follows:

$$L = (aK^c)^{-2}Q^2$$

Since $C = P_L L + P_K K$, we can now express C as the following quadratic function:

$$C = P_K K + P_L(aK^c)^{-2}Q^2 \tag{6.12}$$

In more general terms, with any Cobb–Douglas production function $Q = aL^bK^c$, the short-run cost function will be a polynomial of degree b^{-1}.

c. Linear cost functions

These have the general form:

$$C = a + bQ \tag{6.13}$$

In this case the marginal cost is given by:

$$MC = b \tag{6.14}$$

This is obviously the simplest form of cost function from a mathematical viewpoint, but it is also important empirically. As seen in more detail in

Chapter 7, many firms do observe this type of cost relationship with output in the short run; this is the reason why this form of function is most frequently used in cost–volume–profit analysis, the subject of section 6.5.

What are the economic implications of this type of function? Since marginal cost is constant it means that the firm does not encounter either increasing or diminishing returns, *at least over its normal output range*. It is this last condition that gives this mathematical form its empirical validity. As seen in Figure 6.4, the *MC* curve is horizontal, but this does not mean that the curve would remain horizontal over all outputs. The firm's normal output range may extend up to Q_1; beyond this level of output it is possible for diminishing returns to occur as the firm approaches full capacity. This possibility is illustrated by extending the unit cost curves using dashed lines. A further implication of this type of cost function is that *AVC* is also given by the constant *b*. Thus *MC* and *AVC* are both equal to each other and constant.

6.3 Long-run cost behaviour

In the long run the firm can change all its inputs; therefore all costs are variable. In this context the main decision that managers must make is the determination of the optimal plant size or scale of the firm, given a certain target level of output. Once the optimal combination of inputs is selected, some of these inputs, like plant and equipment, become fixed in the short run.

6.3.1 *Derivation of cost functions from production functions**

This analysis has already been considered for short-run functions. In the long run the situation is more complicated mathematically, since all the inputs are variable. However, for the commonly considered cubic function in Table 5.1, it was seen that there were increasing returns to scale to begin with but that at higher levels of output there were decreasing returns to scale. In more general terms the type of cost function can be derived from the firm's expansion path, as shown in Figure 5.9; this shows various least-cost combinations of inputs for producing given outputs in the long run.

With the Cobb–Douglas production function it can be shown that the long-run cost function is a power function. More precisely, with any Cobb–Douglas production function $Q = aL^bK^c$, the mathematical form of the cost function is as follows:

$$C = a'Q^{1/(b+c)} \tag{6.15}$$

The proof of this derivation is beyond the scope of this text,[1] and involves Lagrangian multiplier analysis. However, the economic implications are important. It has already been seen that the powers in the Cobb–Douglas production function represent output elasticities, which, when summed together, indicate the type of returns to scale. For example, if the output elasticities sum to one, there are constant returns to scale: a 1 per cent increase in all inputs will cause output to increase by 1 per cent. From (6.15) it can be seen that in this case the power of Q will also be equal to 1; this value represents the cost elasticity with respect to output and again is an indicator of returns to scale, assuming that input prices remain constant. If the output elasticities sum to more than 1 it follows that the cost elasticity will be less than 1; this is again an indicator of returns to scale, in this case increasing returns to scale. Likewise, if the output elasticities sum to less than 1, it follows that the cost elasticity is more than 1 and there are decreasing returns to scale. Unlike the cubic cost function the returns to scale are the same at all levels of output.

However, an assumption in all of the above analysis is that input prices remain constant. In the long run the cost elasticity will depend not only on physical returns to scale but on monetary aspects as well: unit costs may rise or fall depending on the scale of the firm independently of the physical returns to scale. Both of these aspects, physical and monetary, now need to be examined in detail.

6.3.2 Economies of scale

Economies of scale (EOS) can be defined as *aspects of increasing scale that lead to falling long-run unit costs*. They can be classified in various ways, as discussed in the following three paragraphs.

1. *Internal/external.* Internal economies *arise from the growth of the firm itself*; in this sense they are controllable and under the influence of management decision-making. External economies *arise from the growth of the industry*, and are independent of the size of the firm. They are therefore further removed from managerial decision-making, though not entirely so; location decisions in particular may depend on these economies. External economies are sometimes called **economies of concentration** because they tend to arise when firms in the same industry are located close together. Further discussion of external economies and diseconomies is given in Chapter 8. Internal economies of scale are usually more important in terms of their effects on unit costs. Therefore, in view of these factors and the aspects of management control, it is the internal economies that we will concentrate on here.

2. *Physical/monetary.* This distinction has already been mentioned above, but will become clearer with the examples explained shortly. Physical economies cause increasing returns to scale; monetary economies reduce input prices.

3. *Level: product, plant and firm.* Again the distinction between these different levels at which economies occur will become clearer with the examples below. In general some of the cost advantages arise from producing more of one product, some from producing with a larger plant size, and some from producing with a larger firm.

There are four main categories of internal economies of scale:[2]

a. Technical economies

These arise mainly from *increased specialization* and *indivisibilities*. Larger firms can make use of more specialized equipment and labour in the production process, for example by using assembly lines. Virtually every product that is produced for the mass market, from jeans to CDs, computer chips to bottled soft drinks, is produced on some kind of assembly line. This has the advantage of increasing both labour and capital productivity. Such processes need a large initial investment, because they cannot perform the relevant functions on a small scale; thus indivisibilities are involved. A good example of this is car production; assembly lines for producing cars have to be very large in order to perform all the necessary tasks. Low-volume car producers, like the British companies Morgan and TVR, cannot afford to use assembly-line methods because they would not be able to spread the high level of fixed cost. These economies are physical and occur at the level of the product.

Indivisibilities also occur in other forms: larger firms are able to use more expensive but often more effective advertising media, like television, and they can afford to undertake research and development activities that small firms could not afford. Such economies are at the level of the firm as a whole.

Other technical economies relate to *increased dimensions*: as size increases, volume increases more rapidly than surface area. Since volume often determines output while surface area determines cost, unit costs fall as size increases. This is particularly important in the transportation and storage industries, and explains the development of jumbo (now super-jumbo) jets and supertankers. Another example is the trucks used to transport rocks and other materials in mining; in the 1950s the average capacity of these vehicles in the United States was 20 tons, by the 1970s it was 150 tons, and it is now about 300 tons. These economies occur mainly at the level of the plant.

A final technical economy relates to *massed resources*: larger firms find it easier to combine equipment or facilities with different capacities more efficiently, with less idle capacity. For example, a car manufacturer needs to use an engine-block casting facility, a panel-pressing facility, a paint shop and various machining and assembly facilities; these all tend to be of different sizes for technical reasons. Similarly, larger firms have a proportionately lower need for reserves of spare parts and maintenance workers. These economies are sometimes called *multiplant* economies, as opposed to *intraplant* economies, because they occur at the level of the firm rather than the individual plant.

These technical economies tend to be the most important source of economies of scale for most firms. They occur particularly in mass manufacturing, public utilities and mass transportation.

b. Managerial economies

Large firms find it easier to attract and use more specialized managers, who are more skilled and productive at performing specific managerial functions. Thus a small firm may employ a general manager for all managerial functions; a mid-sized firm may employ separate managers for the main managerial functions of production, marketing, finance and human resources; a large firm may employ various managers within the marketing department, for example in purchasing, advertising, sales, public relations and market research. Like the technical economies these are physical in nature; they also occur mainly at the level of the whole firm.

c. Marketing economies

These relate mainly to obtaining bulk discounts; by buying in bulk larger firms can often enable their suppliers to obtain the technical economies of scale above. These discounts relate not just to buying raw materials and components but also to buying advertising. For example, if a firm buys twice as much advertising space or time, the total cost will usually less than double, thus unit costs will fall (assuming the firm sells twice as much). This type of economy of scale is obviously of a monetary nature.

d. Financial economies

The most obvious factor here is that large firms can often borrow at a lower interest rate, because they have a better credit rating, representing a lower default premium. In addition they have more sources of finance; they can use the capital markets, for example by issuing commercial paper, bonds and shares. These forms of raising finance often involve a lower cost of capital. Finally, a larger firm can enable its supplier of funds, normally a bank, to gain economies of scale of an administrative nature. Again these economies are clearly monetary and at the level of the whole firm.

The above economies of scale all represent cost advantages that larger firms can gain. There may be additional advantages in terms of the learning curve, described in a later section, and in terms of gaining monopoly power in the market. This last advantage is a demand rather than a cost advantage, and is discussed in Chapter 8.

6.3.3 Diseconomies of scale

Diseconomies of scale (DOS) are *aspects of increasing scale that lead to rising long-run unit costs*. Again they can be internal or external, physical or monetary, and can arise at the level of product, plant or firm. There are again four main sources of diseconomies of scale, though these do not correspond exactly to the four categories of economies of scale described above.

a. Technical diseconomies

Increased specialization can lead to problems as well as benefits. Workers doing repetitive jobs can suffer from low motivation, which reduces productivity and increases the chance of industrial unrest. The number of days lost through strikes tends to be higher in industries that feature such processes, for example car manufacturing, mining, engineering and transportation and communications.[3] Furthermore, a stoppage in such industries, whether caused by industrial unrest or by some other event like a machine breakdown, can cause the whole production process to come to a halt because of the interdependence of operations.

b. Managerial diseconomies

Large firms are more difficult to manage because communications tend to break down, both vertically and horizontally. This creates inefficiencies as co-operation and co-ordination within the firm suffer. Firms may try to combat this tendency by employing more administrative workers, but this is also going to increase unit costs. This communications problem is a major reason why many large firms are trying to contract services out to other firms and create flatter organizational structures, for example IBM and GM.

c. Marketing diseconomies

Although larger firms can often gain discounts in buying raw materials in bulk, there may be offsetting disadvantages of buying inputs in large quantities. If the firm is relying on local sources that are in limited supply, the high demand may drive up the price of such inputs; for example, the firm may have to offer higher wages to attract the desired quantity of workers.

d. Transportation diseconomies

Larger firms, particularly if they only use one plant, may face additional transportation costs as they try to increase the size of their market; the average transportation distance of goods to customers will increase. Again the above diseconomies relate only to cost disadvantages of large firms, or conversely the cost advantages of small firms. Larger firms may have other disadvantages, in terms of having less flexibility, a slower speed of response to environmental changes and the reduced ability to offer personal service to their customers.

6.3.4 Economies of scope

Whereas economies of scale relate to cost reductions caused by increasing scale, **economies of scope** occur when *changing the mix of operations has cost benefits*. For example, producing 100,000 units of product X may involve a unit cost of £100 if X is produced by itself; but if 100,000 units of X are produced along with a quantity of product Y, then the unit cost of producing X may fall. The same may happen to the unit cost of Y compared with producing it by itself. There are two main causes of this:

1 The products may use common processing facilities; for example, different car models being produced at the same plant.
2 There may be cost complementarity, especially when there are joint products or by-products, for example petrochemicals.

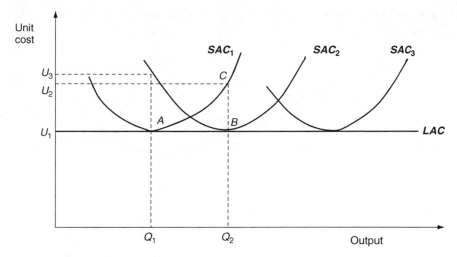

Figure 6.5. Short-run and long-run average cost functions in the absence of EOS and DOS.

It is also possible for a firm to experience diseconomies of scope if it sells products that 'clash' with each other in some way. An example would be EMI Records in the late 1970s when they signed the punk rock band the Sex Pistols, who openly advocated the use of violence. Since EMI was also marketing hospital equipment at the time, it faced considerable criticism and decided to drop the recording contract, at considerable cost.

The extent of economies of scope can be measured by estimating the percentage cost reduction caused by joint production, as follows:

$$S = \frac{C(Q_1) + C(Q_2) - C(Q_1 + Q_2)}{C(Q_1 + Q_2)} \qquad (6.16)$$

where $C(Q_1)$ and $C(Q_2)$ represent the costs of producing outputs Q_1 and Q_2 independently, and $C(Q_1 + Q_2)$ represents the cost of producing outputs Q_1 and Q_2 jointly. If economies of scope exist, the joint cost is less than the sum of the individual costs, thus S is positive. The larger the value of S, the greater the economies of scope; if S is zero there are no economies of scope. Other measures of economies of scope are described in the next chapter.

6.3.5 Relationships between short- and long-run cost curves

In the long run the firm is able to use the least-cost combination of inputs to produce any given output, meaning that it can select the scale appropriate to its level of operation. This means that its long-run (*LAC*) curve is an envelope of its short-run average cost (*SAC*) curves. This is illustrated in Figures 6.5 and 6.6.

a. Optimal scale

In Figure 6.5 there are no economies or diseconomies of scale, thus unit costs are constant in the long run and the *LAC* curve is horizontal. Thus if the firm

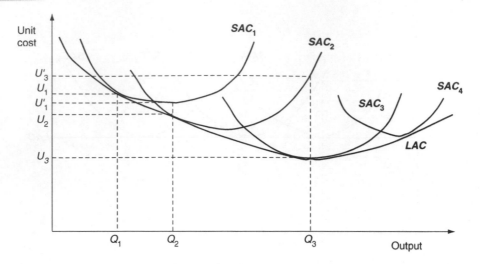

Figure 6.6. Short-run and long-run average cost functions with EOS and DOS.

wants to increase output from Q_1 to Q_2 in the long run it can move from point A to point B, and unit costs will remain constant at U_1. On the other hand, if the firm wants to increase output from Q_1 to Q_2 in the short run it has to move from point A to point C on SAC_1, with its unit costs rising to U_2 because it will be getting diminishing returns. We can say that for producing output Q_2 the scale or plant size associated with SAC_2 is the **optimal scale**; this means that this scale will result in the *minimum average cost*. However, for producing output Q_1 the scale associated with SAC_1 is preferable; the scale of SAC_2 is too large for this output, and the firm will be unable to spread its fixed costs sufficiently, unit costs being U_3.

When there are economies or diseconomies of scale the situation is made more complicated. In Figure 6.6 there are economies of scale in the lower output range up to Q_3, and diseconomies of scale in the output range above Q_3. The optimal scale for producing output Q_1 is the scale associated with SAC_1, since this is the scale that will produce Q_1 at the minimum unit cost (U_1). However, it should be noted that the reverse is not true: output Q_1 is not the optimal output for the scale of SAC_1; the optimal output for this scale is output Q_2, since that is the most efficient output for this scale, at the minimum point of the SAC_1 curve, where unit costs are U'_1.

The student may well ask at this point: what is going on here? Well, to be fair, even the economist Jacob Viner, who originally drew these graphs, did not know to begin with. The story goes that he asked his draughtsman to draw a long-run average cost curve as a U-shaped envelope going through all the minimum points of the short-run cost curves. The draughtsman then pointed out that this could not be done, but Viner insisted that the curve be drawn in this way. There was a sequel to this episode, which has become part of the legend relating to John Maynard Keynes. Viner also expressed his lack of admiration for Keynes's work in the 1930s, and when Keynes was asked

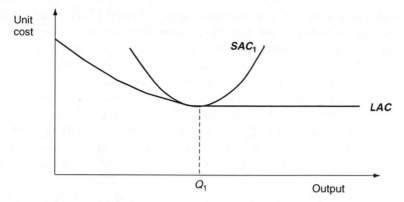

Figure 6.7. Minimum efficient scale.

whom he regarded as the greatest living economist, he replied that modesty forbade him from naming the greatest, but surely the second greatest was Jacob Viner's draughtsman!

It can be seen that only if the *LAC* curve is horizontal as in Figure 6.5 will it pass through all the minimum points of the *SAC* curves. If there are economies of scale it means that it is more efficient to use a larger scale at less than maximum efficiency than use a smaller scale at maximum efficiency, because more is gained from economies of scale than is lost from a failure to spread fixed cost. Thus in order to produce Q_2 it is better to use the scale of SAC_2, resulting in unit cost U_2, than to use the scale of SAC_1, resulting in the higher unit cost U'_1.

We have to be careful therefore in using the concept of optimal scale or plant size; a scale can only be optimal for a given output. It is true that the most efficient scale in general is the one associated with SAC_3, since this is the scale where unit costs are minimized in the long run. However, this scale would not be optimal for producing output Q_1 or Q_2 because it is too large and the firm would be unable to spread its fixed cost sufficiently. It may well happen that the size of the market is not sufficient to justify the use of a larger scale, even if such a scale is capable of reducing unit cost at a larger level of output.

b. Minimum efficient scale

The minimum efficient scale (MES) is defined as **the smallest scale at which long-run average cost is minimized**. In Figure 6.6 this is the scale of SAC_3. However, as will be seen in the next chapter, not all *LAC* curves in practice turn out to be U-shaped; in some industries the *LAC* curve may take an L-shape; in this case the minimum efficient scale is where the curve flattens out, shown by output Q_1 in Figure 6.7.

c. Multiplant production

In the analysis to this point we have tended to use the terms 'scale' and 'plant size' interchangeably, although it has been pointed out that economies and diseconomies of scale can occur at three different levels: product, plant and firm. For firms that operate just one plant the optimal plant size and optimal scale are synonymous. However, many firms operate more than one production facility. Sometimes these facilities involve the same stage in the production process, in which case the firm is said to be **horizontally integrated**. If the facilities operate at different stages of the production process, for example with a car manufacturer using different plants for pressing body panels, paint spraying and assembly, the firm is said to be **vertically integrated**. The analysis of optimal plant size is more complicated in this situation. It may be, for example, that the *LAC* curve is U-shaped if a firm operates a single plant, because as the plant size increases beyond a certain size, diseconomies at the plant level occur. The firm may be able to avoid these by using two or more smaller plants at minimum efficient scale; in effect this makes the *LAC* curve L-shaped and enables the firm to produce at lower unit cost.

6.3.6 *Strategy implications*

Managers must make decisions regarding optimal plant size and scale of operation in a dynamic environment. Demand may change unexpectedly, given the large range of uncontrollable factors affecting it discussed in Chapter 3. In this situation, managers must be prepared for the eventuality that there may be a mismatch between the quantity that the firm produces and the quantity that it sells.

If the *LAC* curve is U-shaped or L-shaped a firm might find that a change in demand might cause a problem in the short run, in that to meet the change in demand might require producing at above the minimum level of long-run average cost in the short run, in other words above the *LAC* curve. For example, referring to Figure 6.6, a firm may plan for output Q_2 and therefore operate at the scale of SAC_2; demand may then increase so that the quantity of Q_3 is demanded at the existing price. There are now various strategy options for the firm, each of which has certain advantages and disadvantages.

1. *Produce Q_3 with the existing scale.* Unit costs will rise in this case, from U_2 to U'_3. The firm may therefore plan to increase its scale in the future, but only if it regards the increase in demand as being likely to continue.

2. *Continue to produce Q_2, and use inventories to meet the excess demand.* In this case the firm is using inventories as a buffer to meet changes in demand, so that in the case of an unexpected shortfall in demand, inventory levels would be allowed to rise. This allows the firm some time to assess whether the change in demand is likely to be a lasting one. However, there is a cost: additional inventory levels involve additional holding cost.

3. *Continue to produce Q_2, and use order backlogs to meet the excess demand.* This again is only appropriate if the increase in demand is seen as temporary. Otherwise the firm's order books will continue to increase in length, as will the waiting time for

customers to receive the product. The cost of this strategy is that increased customer waiting time will result in a loss of customers, so the firm will have to assess how sensitive its customers are to increases in waiting time.

4. *Increase the price to a level where only Q_2 will be demanded*. This may be regarded as a temporary measure if the increase in demand is seen as temporary; it may also be a temporary measure if the increase in demand is seen as a lasting one, while the firm takes the necessary time to increase its scale. The cost in this case is that the increase in price, even if temporary, may result in a loss of customers, who may not return later even if the price is reduced to its former level. The firm may lose some goodwill if it is seen as exploiting customers in the event of a shortage.

A more detailed discussion of the implications of the different strategies would require more information and the analysis introduced in Chapter 8.

6.4 The learning curve

There are many situations, not just in business but also in everyday life, where we learn better ways of doing something over time. Examples are playing tennis, using a keyboard, driving a car, or solving problems in managerial economics. In the workplace the factors that are involved are increased familiarization with the tasks involved, improvements in production methods, more efficient use of raw materials and machinery and fewer costly mistakes. These factors are obviously interdependent. The improvement in performance can be measured in a number of ways, depending on the situation, but the most common are in terms of unit cost or unit time to produce a product. This improvement is a function of experience, although when the concept was originally used in the 1930s in the analysis of aircraft production, the reason proposed for the learning curve effect was the learning by production workers, resulting in direct labour costs being reduced. It was only later that additional benefits in terms of production methods and indirect labour and other costs were considered. Hence, although the term **experience curve** is often used interchangeably with learning curve, some economists claim that there is some difference between the two concepts.[4] Experience is normally measured in terms of cumulative output, that is the total output since production of a product began. Thus we can express the learning curve relationship as:

$$U = f(T) \tag{6.17}$$

where U is some measure of unit cost and T represents cumulative output.

It is important to note that this function is fundamentally different from the normal cost functions analysed so far, because of the nature of cumulative output. This means that the learning curve is neither a short-run nor a long-run cost function but can apply to any time horizon. Its effect is to cause the cost functions considered so far to shift downwards over time.

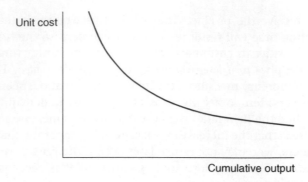

Figure 6.8. The learning curve.

We expect the relationship to be an inverse one if we learn from experience, but everyday experience of the experience curve(!) tells us that we tend to learn relatively quickly to begin with, and then our rate of learning slows down because of the familiar law of diminishing returns. Thus we would normally expect the situation that is shown in Figure 6.8.

This indicates that the appropriate mathematical form of the relationship is a power function:

$$U = aT^b \qquad (6.18)$$

where U is normally measured as the marginal cost of a unit. The parameter b has a negative value, indicating an inverse relationship between marginal cost and cumulative output.

Learning curves are often described in terms of how a doubling of cumulative output affects marginal cost; if such a doubling results in a 20 per cent reduction in marginal cost it is said that the **learning rate** is 80 per cent. This learning rate is given by 2^b. The mathematical proof of this is as follows: let the initial cumulative output $= T_1$ and the initial marginal cost $= U_1$; then the marginal cost of double the output $= a(2T_1)^b = 2^b(aT^b_1) = 2^b(U_1)$.

This means that *every time cumulative output doubles the marginal cost becomes 2^b times what it was previously*. Other aspects of interpretation of the learning curve, its estimation and use in forecasting, and the results of empirical studies, are discussed in the next chapter, along with a numerical example.

6.5 Cost–volume–profit analysis

6.5.1 *Purpose and assumptions*

Cost–volume–profit (CVP) **analysis** *examines relationships between costs, revenues and profit on the one hand and volume of output on the other*. It is applied mainly to short-run situations. It is also sometimes referred to as

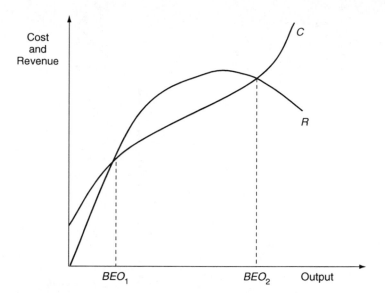

Figure 6.9. CVP graph: non-linear cost and revenue functions.

break-even analysis, but this term is somewhat narrow in scope; a firm's break-even output is specifically *the output where the firm makes zero profit*. CVP analysis covers a broader range of situations. The easiest approach is graphical.

On the basis of the analysis in the previous sections and assuming normal demand conditions (a downward-sloping demand curve), the graph shown in Figure 6.9 may result. In this situation the total cost curve is a cubic and the revenue curve is a quadratic. There will be two break-even outputs, and between them there will be a profit-maximizing output (not shown yet).

Although such situations can be analysed using CVP methods, it is more common to make the following assumptions:

1 MC is constant at all levels of output. This implies that the total cost function is linear, and the justification of this was given in subsection 6.2.7.
2 Firms are price-takers, meaning that they are operating under conditions of perfect competition.

The advantage of the above assumptions is that they result in linear total cost and revenue functions, thus simplifying the analysis mathematically. This situation is shown in Figure 6.10.

In this case there is only one break-even output; if the firm produces less than this it makes a loss (L_2 at output Q_2) and if it produces more it will make a profit (Π_1 at output Q_1). The more the firm produces the more profit it makes under the above assumptions.

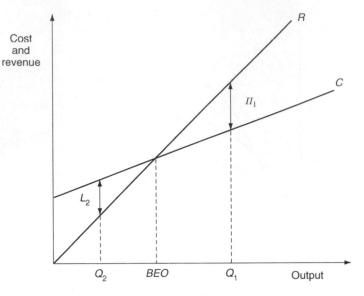

Figure 6.10. CVP graph: linear cost and revenue functions.

6.5.2 Break-even output

This can be derived mathematically, using linear cost and revenue functions. The revenue function, $R = PQ$, is set equal to the cost function, $C = a + bQ$, and we then solve for Q:

$$PQ = a + bQ$$

$$Q(P - b) = a$$

This gives the following expression for the break-even output:

$$BEO = a/(P - b) \tag{6.19}$$

where $a =$ fixed cost, $b =$ average variable cost, $P =$ price. The denominator in this expression, $(P - b)$, is often referred to as the profit contribution.

6.5.3 Profit contribution

This is defined as **the money amount that each unit sold contributes to fixed costs and profit**. It is best explained with an example. A firm may have fixed costs of £10,000 per month and variable costs of £12 per unit; the market price may be £20.

$$\text{Profit contribution}(\Pi_C) = 20 - 12 = £8$$

To interpret this it is necessary to find the break-even output:

$$BEO = 10,000/8 = 1,250 \text{ units per month.}$$

If the firm produces 1,251 units, $\Pi = £8$; if it produces 1,252 units, $\Pi = £16$. Thus the firm is **contributing £8 to profit for every unit it produces above break-even output**.

If the firm produces no output it makes a loss of £10,000 (its fixed costs); if it produces 1 unit it makes a loss of £9,992. Thus the firm is **contributing £8 to fixed costs for every unit it produces below break-even output**.

6.5.4 Operating leverage*

The **degree of operating leverage** (DOL) refers to the **percentage change in profit resulting from a 1 per cent change in units sold**. This can be expressed mathematically as:

$$DOL = \frac{\%\Delta\Pi}{\%\Delta Q} \tag{6.20}$$

Thus it can be interpreted as an **elasticity of profits with respect to output** and can be measured in a similar way to the demand elasticities in Chapter 3:

$$DOL = \frac{d\Pi/\Pi}{dQ/Q} = d\Pi/dQ \times Q/\Pi \tag{6.21}$$

With linear cost and revenue functions the profit function must also be linear, therefore the *DOL* will vary with output. It will always be largest close to the break-even output. In the above example, if the firm is producing 1,500 units per month, the *DOL* is calculated as follows:

$$C = 10,000 + 12Q$$
$$R = 20Q$$
$$\Pi = 8Q - 10,000 = £2,000 \text{ at output of 1,500 units}$$
$$DOL = 8 \times 1,500/2,000 = 6$$

The interpretation of this result is that **a 1 per cent increase in output will increase profit by 6 per cent**.

6.5.5 Limitations of CVP analysis

CVP analysis can be a very useful aid to managerial decision-making, as illustrated in the following solved problems and case studies. There are, however, some important limitations of the technique. The main one is the set of restrictive assumptions on which it is often based. Profit does not usually increase linearly with output; many firms will have to reduce price in order to increase sales because they are not price-takers. Furthermore, as output increases they are likely to face diminishing returns as they approach capacity in the short term; inefficiencies and the payment of overtime wages may increase unit variable costs.

In the long run a number of factors may invalidate the simplified analysis above. The firm may change its capacity, thereby changing fixed costs. It may also change the quality of its products and its product mix. Therefore, as with other decision tools, CVP analysis must be used with care.

6.6 A problem-solving approach

This approach is designed as an aid to solving CVP problems. As with problems in demand theory students may 'know' the principles but sometimes do not know how to apply them to practical problems. Assuming linear cost and revenue functions, all CVP analysis is based on the following five equations:

1 Cost $\qquad\qquad C = a + bQ \qquad\qquad$ (6.22)

2 Revenue $\qquad\qquad R = PQ \qquad\qquad$ (6.23)

3 Profit $\qquad\qquad \Pi = R - C \qquad\qquad$ (6.24)

4 Break-even $\qquad\qquad BEO = a/(P - b) \qquad\qquad$ (6.25)

5 Profit contribution $\qquad\qquad \Pi_C = P - b \qquad\qquad$ (6.26)

At this point it is necessary to review some basic algebraic principles. The equations often have to be **used in a sequence**. The key to success is using the equations in the **correct sequence**, starting off with values that are known and working towards the required unknown. If the equations are used in the wrong sequence there will be too many unknowns to solve the equation. However, in more complex problems, like SP6.2 below and the Nissan study (Case study 6.3), the existence of an equation with two or more unknowns does not necessarily create an impasse; it may be necessary to treat the problem as a **system of equations that need to be solved simultaneously**. In the case where there is an equation with two unknowns we have to find another equation in the same unknowns. If we have two equations in four unknowns then we need another two equations in the same unknowns to solve the system. The mathematical rule is that **we always need the same number of equations as unknowns in order to solve for the unknowns**. This does not guarantee a solution in general terms; it is a necessary condition, but not a sufficient one. However, in linear CVP problems the rule is a useful one.

There is one other useful aid to solving these more complex problems: it is often helpful to tabulate the data in a T-table with two columns, one relating to each entity, before processing it, as illustrated in SP6.2. This step can help to identify which equation or equations to use in order to begin the analysis. These principles are now applied in the following two problems.

SP6.1 CVP analysis

Last month Susie Q sold 24,000 litres of ice-cream. The variable costs were £2.70 per litre and each litre contributed 25 per cent of its revenue to fixed costs and profits. It has just discovered a new supplier which will enable it both to reduce its cost by £0.40 per litre and to improve its quality. However, it estimates that it will have to spend another £3,000 on advertising per month to inform customers of the improvement. Profits last month were £10,000.

a. What is the previous month's cost function?
b. What is the new cost function with the new supplier?
c. How many litres will Susie Q have to sell to increase profit by 20 per cent, assuming it keeps its price the same?
d. If Susie Q can raise its price by 10 per cent, what difference will this make to the sales in (c) above?

Solution

a. $Q = 24,000$, $AVC = £2.70$, $\Pi_C = 0.25R/Q = 0.25P$, $\Pi = £10,000$

We want $C = a + bQ$.
We know $b = 2.7$, so have to find a.
Cannot use equation (4) because BEO also unknown.
So we have to find C from (3), but this means finding R first from (2); in turn this means finding P from (5).
Thus the correct sequence of using the equations is (5), (2), (3), (1).

$\quad$ (5) $\Pi_C = P - b$
$\quad\quad 0.25P = P - 2.7$
$\quad\quad 0.75P = 2.7$
$\quad\quad\quad P = 3.6$

$\quad$ (2) $R = PQ$
$\quad\quad R = 3.6 \times 24,000 = 86,400$

$\quad$ (3) $\Pi = R - C$
$\quad\quad 10,000 = 86,400 - C$
$\quad\quad\quad C = 76,400$

$\quad$ (1) $76,400 = a + 2.7 \times 24,000$
$\quad\quad 76,400 = a + 64,800$
$\quad\quad\quad\quad a = 11,600$
$\quad\quad\quad\quad C = 11,600 + 2.7Q$

b. $\quad\quad\quad C = 14,600 + 2.3Q$

c. From (3), $12,000 = 3.6Q - (14,600 + 2.3Q)$
$\quad\quad\quad 26,600 = 1.3Q$
$\quad\quad\quad\quad\quad Q = 20,462$ litres

d. $12,000 = 3.96Q - (14,600 + 2.3Q)$
    $26,600 = 1.66Q$
        $Q = \textbf{16,024 litres}$

SP6.2 CVP analysis

Lite and Brite produce lamps which they sell for £40. Lite has fixed costs of £8,000 less than Brite and average variable costs of £33, which is 10 per cent more than Brite. Lite has a break-even output which is 15 per cent less than Brite, and produces 25 per cent less revenue than Brite. Lite also makes £12,000 less profit than Brite.

a. Calculate the cost functions of both firms.
b. Calculate the outputs of both firms.
c. Calculate the profits of both firms.

Solution

This type of problem, which we can call a 'two-firm' problem, is sometimes approached more easily by setting out the data in tabular form, as shown in Table 6.2; this helps us to see the relevant relationships more easily, thereby providing a handle to start the analysis. No calculations are performed at this stage.

a. $33 = 1.1(AVC_B)$
              $AVC_B = 30$
              $BEO_L = FC_L/(40 - 33)$ (1) $7BEO_L = FC_L$
              $BEO_B = FC_B/(40 - 30)$ (2) $10BEO_B = FC_B$

We have two equations in four unknowns, so we need two more equations in the same unknowns:

                (3) $FC_L = FC_B - 8,000$

Table 6.2. CVP data For two-firm problem

	Lite	Brite
Price	£40	£40
FC	−£8,000	
AVC	£33	
AVC	+10 %	
BEO	−15 %	
R and Q	−25 %	
Profit		+£ 12,000

(4) $BEO_L = 0.85BEO_B$

We need to reduce these four equations to one equation in one unknown, e.g. BEO_B.

$$7BEO_L = FC_B - 8,000$$

$$7(0.85BEO_B) = FC_B - 8,000$$

$$5.95BEO_B = 10BEO_B - 8,000$$

$$4.05BEO_B = 8,000$$

$$BEO_B = 1,975$$

$$FC_B = 19,753$$

$$C_L = 11,753 + 33Q_L \qquad C_B = 19,753 + 30Q_B$$

b. (1) $\Pi_L = 7Q_L - 11,753$ (2) $\Pi_B = 10Q_B - 19,753$
Again we have two equations in four unknowns, so we need two more in the same unknowns:
(3) $\Pi_L = \Pi_B - 12,000$ $R_L = 0.75R_B$, but $P_L = P_B$

(4) $Q_L = 0.75 Q_B$
$7Q_L - 11,753 - 10Q_B - 19,753 - 12,000$
$20,000 = 10Q_B - 7Q_L = 10Q_B - 7(0.75Q_B) - 10Q_B - 5.25Q_B = 4.75Q_B$
$Q_B = 4,211$
$Q_L = 3,158$
c. $\Pi_L = £10,353$ $\Pi_B = £22,353$

SP6.3 Mathematical analysis of cost relationships*

XTC Ltd has total costs of £45,000 and it is currently producing 5,000 units. It has examined its cost structure and has found that, of its variable costs, half vary in a linear relationship with output; the other variable costs increase by £1 for every 1,000-unit increase in output. Fixed costs are £10,000, and these determine the capacity of 6,000 units. The market price is £10.

a. Determine the MC, AVC and ATC functions for the firm.
b. Determine the current profit of the company.
c. Determine the degree of operating leverage at current output.

Solution

a. $TVC = 45{,}000 - 10{,}000 = 35{,}000$

VC_1 has a linear relationship with output, so $AVC_1 = MC_1 = $ constant.

$MC_1 = 17{,}500/5{,}000 = 3.5$

$MC_2 = a + 0.001Q$ where a is a constant

$$VC_2 = 17{,}500 \int (a + 0.001Q) = 17{,}500$$

$$[aQ + 0.0005Q^2] = 17{,}500$$

$$5{,}000a + 0.0005(5{,}000)^2 = 17{,}500$$

$$5{,}000a = 5{,}000$$

$$a = 1$$

$$MC_2 = 1 + 0.001Q$$

$$\mathbf{MC = 4.5 + 0.001Q}$$

$$TC = 10{,}000 + 4.5Q + 0.0005Q^2$$

$$\mathbf{AVC = 4.5 + 0.0005Q}$$

$$\mathbf{ATC = 10{,}000/Q + 4.5 + 0.0005Q}$$

b. $TC = 10{,}000 + 4.5(5{,}000) + 0.0005(5{,}000)^2$

$$TC = 45{,}000; \; TR = 10 \times 5{,}000 = 50{,}000$$

$$\mathbf{\Pi = \pounds 5{,}000}$$

c. $DOL = d\Pi/dQ \times \mathbf{Q}/\Pi$

$$\Pi = 10Q - (10{,}000 + 4.5Q + 0.0005Q^2)$$

$$d\Pi/dQ = 5.5 - 0.001Q = 5.5 - 0.001(5{,}000) = 0.5$$

$$DOL = 0.5 \times 5{,}000/5{,}000$$

$$\mathbf{DOL = 0.5}$$

Case study 6.2: Converting to LPG – is it worth it?

Green fuel runs out of gas[5]

The cost of converting a car to run on liquefied petroleum gas (LPG) is about £1,500 in the UK, towards which a government grant would contribute about £700. From September 1 2004, LPG will on average cost 40.7p per litre, compared with 79.1p for ordinary unleaded petrol. However, LPG cars usually have slightly worse fuel consumption, losing about 13% in terms of miles per gallon.

Questions

Fast-Trak company owns a fleet of 20 cars, which are bought new and are used for 30,000 miles over two years before being sold off. The cars average 30 miles to the gallon (imperial) on petrol. The conversion to LPG does not affect the price in the secondhand market.

1 Calculate the profit contribution per hundred miles of LPG compared with unleaded petrol, for one of Fast-Trak's cars.
2 Calculate the break-even mileage for the cars with the LPG conversion.
3 Calculate the effect on the profit of Fast-Trak of converting to LPG.
4 The government wants to encourage the use of LPG to protect the environment by reducing the break-even mileage to 10,000 miles; how large a grant should it offer for the LPG conversion?

Case study 6.3: Rescuing Nissan

On the rocky road to marriage[6]

A year ago it looked like mission impossible: rescuing Nissan after Renault had bought a controlling stake. Now Carlos Ghosn's recovery plan may be working, putting a full merger on the cards

Since last July, Mr Ghosn's job has been to rescue Japan's ailing car manufacturer; he is chief operating officer, but collects the title of president after this summer's general meeting. With the title goes a heavy responsibility. Nissan's plight is awful: losses in seven out of eight years, a domestic market share that drifted to an all-time low of 19% last year, and a pile of debt, totalling ¥1.4 trillion, plus ¥1.2 trillion in its financing division. 'It looked like mission impossible,' he admits, but we are on track to make profits in fiscal year 2000, ending next March. If we don't do that, we won't be credible.' [In 1999, Nissan's revenue was ¥6.3 trillion, and it made a loss of ¥30 billion.]

You do not have to be a rocket scientist to realise that a car maker able to make 2.4m vehicles a year in Japan, but producing fewer than 1.3m, is running its plants at a disastrously low level. To reach 75% utilisation, at which point most car firms break even, capacity needs to shrink by at least 30%. Under Mr Ghosn's plan, Nissan's domestic capacity is to drop to a more realistic 1.65m units a year by 2002, maybe raising utilisation to 82%. First to go, by March 2001, will be the assembly plants at Murayama near Tokyo, the Nissan Shatai factory in Kyoto and the Aichi Kikai Minato plant in Nagoya. Next will be the Kurihama engine plant in Kanagawa and the Kyushu engine shop in Fukuoka.

Buttressed by his Renault experience, Mr Ghosn is likewise ignoring internal opposition to his changes at Nissan. His view is that the situation had become so desperate under the old regime that it had lost all credibility, so he has carte blanche to sort things out. But he is no autocrat. When he arrived last July, he formed nine cross-functional teams (CFTs) of middle managers to come up with plans to transform the company. According to Kiyoaki Sawada, a senior finance manager leading one team, these are not like ordinary project teams. 'We had those before, but everybody just represented their department's interest,' he says. The new teams are different.

The CFTs were a device that Mr Ghosn first used in America to bring about the merger of Michelin and another tyre company, Uniroyal Goodrich. He also installed them in Renault four years ago. He is hooked on the cross-functional approach, for several reasons. It works in a crisis, he says, because people can understand the need for rapid action. It makes people act outside their specific areas. 'In most companies people make a specific contribution to the company in their function,' he says. 'But it is not expressed in terms of profit, only in terms of performing their function better.' Instead Mr Ghosn, who meets all the teams monthly, gets them to focus on profit creation, which he reckons lies in the interstices of different company functions. 'Profit is the most global aspect of a business, and it is cross-functional.'

The first product of the teams helped to form the basis of the Nissan revival plan unveiled last October. In the land of lifetime employment (at least for many workers in big companies), Mr Ghosn shocked Japan by announcing the closure of five factories employing over 16,000 people in Japan alone, cutting capacity by 30% to bring it more into line with sales and boosting utilisation rates to around the 80% rate.

Already machinery is being moved out of the doomed plants into those that will survive, and some workers have been transferred. Strong demand in the American market (and to a lesser extent in Europe) means that production is actually running about 10% higher than last year, so extra labour is needed in some other Japanese factories. Mr Ghosn hopes to avoid actually sacking workers, which is expensive in Japan. The second phase of his plan – to rationalise the Nissan and Renault distribution and dealer networks in Europe – has just been announced, and

aims to produce savings of about $1 billion. Mr Ghosn hopes to cut costs at Nissan's British plant, already Europe's most efficient, by 30%, but thinks more pain is inevitable.

Questions

Assume:

a. The second phase of the Ghosn plan does not come into effect until after the year 2000.
b. The target operating profit for 2000 is 100 billion yen.
c. Nissan earns 70 per cent of its revenues from vehicle sales and that other operations break even and will do the same in 2000.
d. Average prices of vehicles sold are kept at the same level as 1999.
e. Taxes are not included in the figures given.

1 Calculate the average price of vehicles sold.
2 Calculate average variable costs for 1999 and the target for 2000.
3 Calculate the size of the overall Japanese vehicle market in 1999.
4 If Nissan can reduce its variable costs in vehicle production by 5 per cent in 2000 compared with its target, estimate the effect on profit and return on sales.

Explain any assumptions in the above analysis.

Case study 6.4: Earls Court Gym

The management at Easyloan Bank is interested in offering a corporate fitness programme for its employees. It has decided to offer a 50 per cent subsidy to all who participate. The gym has agreed to offer the bank a 20 per cent discount on all fees for its employees, provided that they all have the same terms of membership. The bank's management observe from the membership information (Table 6.3) that there are various membership options. From a survey of its employees it establishes that they would use the

gym only. Of their visits, 75 per cent would be during weekdays and 25 per cent at weekends. Half their weekday visits would be before 12 noon and the other half would be after 5 p.m.

Questions

1 Identify the feasible membership options and express these as cost functions for the bank.
2 Draw a graph showing the above options and explain how the bank's management should select the optimal one.

Table 6.3. Earls Court Gym: membership information

Earls Court Gym P.O. Box 755 254 Earls Court Road London SW5 9AD Tel: 020–7370 1402

Membership Rates

Membership type	Period	Unrestricted access (i.e. anytime during opening hours)		Restricted access (i.e. Mon. to Fri. 9 a.m. to 5 p.m. & anytime at weekends)	
		New member	Renewal	New member	Renewal
Gym & Aerobics					
Full use of gym and all exercise classes, plus shower, sauna and changing facilities	12 months	£450	£416	£292	£270
	9 months	£399	£368	£261	£241
	6 months	£283	£260	£182	£167
	5 months	£268		£172	
	4 months	£243		£158	
	3 months	£199		£129	
	2 months	£153		£99	
	1 month	£85		£54	
	3 weeks	£66		£44	
	2 weeks	£46		£30	
	1 week	£27		£20	
	1 day	£10	£7 (Sat. & Sun.: £10)		
Gym only					
Unlimited use of gym and shower, sauna and changing facilities	12 months	£362	£335	£232	£216
	9 months	£318	£294	£210	£195
	6 months	£227	£211	£145	£134
	5 months	£214		£139	
	4 months	£195		£127	
	3 months	£160		£103	
	2 months	£123		£81	
	1 month	£67		£44	
	3 weeks	£53		£35	
	2 weeks	£38		£24	
	1 week	£21		£16	
	1 day	£3.50 (9 a.m. to 12 noon Mon. to Fri.) £5.00 (12 noon to 5 p.m. Mon. to Fri.) £7.50 (After 5 p.m. Mon. to Fri. and anytime Sat. and Sun.)			

Table 6.3. (cont.)

Earls Court Gym P.O. Box 755 254 Earls Court Road London SW5 9AD Tel: 020–7370 1402

Membership Rates

Membership type	Period	Unrestricted access (i.e. anytime during opening hours)	Restricted access (i.e. Mon. to Fri. 9 a.m. to 5 p.m. & anytime at weekends)
Aerobics only			
Access to all exercise classes and shower, sauna and changing facilities	Membership Charge:	And:	
	12 months	£50	
	6 months	£34	£2.50 per morning or evening class, Mon. to Fri.
	3 months	£24	£3.50* per evening or weekend class
	1 month	£17	

The daily rate for non-members is £3 per morning or afternoon class (Mon. to Fri.) & £5* per evening or weekend class.
*An additional charge will be made for classes of more than 1 hour

Social membership
A special class of membership for the infrequent visitor, giving access to the gym or classes and sauna, etc.

Annual fee of £100
and:
£3.00 per visit before 5 p.m. on Mon. to Fri.
£4.50 per visit after 5 p.m. on Mon. to Fri. and at weekends

Sunbeds
Per session   £6.50
Block of 5 sessions £28.50
Block of 10 sessions £55.00

Opening times

	Membership with unrestricted access		Membership with restricted access
		Gym closes	
Mon. to Fri.	9 a.m. to 10 p.m.	9.40 p.m.	9 a.m. to 5 p.m.
Sat.	10 a.m. to 7 p.m.	6.40 p.m.	Anytime
Sun.	11 a.m. to 5 p.m.	4.40 p.m.	Anytime

Lockers
Lockers are provided in the changing rooms free of charge. A key may be picked up at Reception on production of a current membership card.

Towels
Towels are available for hire at Reception at 75p each.

Food supplements & sportswear
A range of sportswear and food supplements is available for sale at Reception.

Gym assessments
Bookings may be made at Reception or by ringing 020–7370 1402.

Memberships
Each member will be provided with a membership card which must be produced and surrendered to Reception on each visit.

Memberships are not transferable and no refunds will be made.
Membership (new and renewals) is at the discretion of the Management.

Summary

1 The relevant costs for decision-making involve opportunity costs, replacement costs and incremental costs.
2 The nature of a firm's production function determines the nature of its cost functions, both in the short run and in the long run.
3 Managers want to know the type of cost function their firm has in order to make pricing and other marketing mix decisions, and to forecast and plan for the level of costs and inputs for producing a given level of output.
4 In the short run the law of diminishing returns causes marginal cost, average variable cost and average total cost to rise beyond a certain level of output.
5 The most efficient level of output in the short run for a given plant size involves a trade-off between spreading fixed costs and getting diminishing returns.
6 Short-run cost functions can take several mathematical forms: linear, quadratic and cubic.
7 Managers want to know the nature of their firm's long-run cost function in order to determine the appropriate plant size.
8 In the long run, unit costs are affected by economies and diseconomies of scale, which often cause the long-run average cost curve to be U-shaped.
9 Economies of scale are aspects of increasing scale that lead to falling long-run average costs; diseconomies of scale are the opposite. They can thus be regarded as the cost advantages and cost disadvantages for a firm or plant in growing larger.
10 Economies and diseconomies can arise at the level of the product, the plant and the firm as a whole.
11 Because of uncertainties regarding demand levels there may be a mismatch between the level of output produced by the firm and its sales; there are a number of different strategies that firms can use in this situation.
12 Economies of scope arise when there are cost complementarities of producing products together.
13 The learning curve describes the situation where unit costs are reduced as cumulative output increases, because of learning better ways of performing a task or tasks.
14 CVP analysis analyses relationships between output levels and costs, revenues and profits. It is normally based on the assumption that both total cost and total revenue functions are linear.

Review questions

1 Explain the difference between the explicit cost of buying a textbook on economics and the opportunity cost, stating any assumptions. How are these costs relevant for the decision to buy the book?

2 Explain the relationship between a firm's short-run production function and its short-run cost function.

3 Explain whether the following statements are true or false:

   a. In the long run a firm might choose to operate a larger plant at less than maximum efficiency rather than a smaller plant at maximum efficiency.

   b. Maximum efficiency is achieved when *AVC* and *MC* are equal.

   c. An improvement in technology will shift the *LAC* curve upwards.

   d. If *AVC* and price stay the same when there is an increase in fixed costs the *BEO* will decrease.

   e. A firm can have diminishing returns and increasing returns at the same time but not economies and diseconomies of scale.

4 Explain how the linearity assumption in CVP analysis compares with conventional economic theory.

5 Explain how a firm might gain economies of scope without gaining economies of scale.

6 Explain why it is important to distinguish between economies of scale and the learning curve if they both cause unit costs to decrease.

Problems

6.1 Quikpak sells returnable containers to major food processors. The price received for the containers is £2 per unit. Of this amount £1.25 is profit contribution. Quikpak is considering an attempt to differentiate its product through quality improvement at a cost of 5p. per unit. Current profits are £40,000 on sales of 100,000 units.

   a. Assuming that average variable costs are constant at all output levels, find Quikpak's total cost function before the proposed change.

   b. Calculate the total cost function if the quality improvement is implemented.

   c. Calculate Quikpak's break-even output before and after the change, assuming it cannot increase its price.

   d. Calculate the increase in sales that would be necessary with the quality improvement to increase profits to £45,000.

6.2 Two business students are considering opening a business selling hamburgers next summer. The students view this as an alternative to taking summer employment with a local firm where they would each earn £3,000 during the three-month summer period. It would cost £2,000 to obtain a licence to operate their stand, £1,000 per month to rent the stand with the necessary equipment and £100 per month for insurance. Petrol costs are estimated at £10 per day. Hamburger meat can be bought for £4.00 per kilo and buns cost £1.20 per dozen. The burgers would sell in 125 gram patties for £1.50 each.

a. Find the accounting cost function for the proposed business.
b. Find the economic cost function for the proposed business.
c. Calculate the level of output where the business would make normal profit.
d. Cheese slices for the burgers can be bought for £2.40 for twenty slices and it is estimated that 30 per cent of customers would ask for the cheeseburgers, with these selling for £1.95. Calculate the effect of this on the output necessary to make normal profit.
e. If the students can sell 150 burgers a day, 30 per cent with cheese, estimate the economic profit they would make. Advise them whether they should enter the business.

6.3 Blunt Corporation manufactures calculators, involving a product line of two models. The current price charged for its B1 model is £8, and profit contribution is 25 per cent. Sales have been disappointing for this model, so Blunt is considering a quality improvement at a cost of 50p. per calculator. Advertising would be increased by £40,000 to promote the improvement. Current profit is £60,000 on sales of 80,000 items per month. There is a relationship between sales of B1 and B2 models, such that for every four extra sales of a B1 model there is one less sale of a B2 model, as some consumers switch from one model to the other. The B2 models sell for £6 and have an average variable cost of £5.

a. Determine the cost function for the B1 model with the changes that Blunt is considering.
b. Calculate the increase in sales of B1 models necessary with the quality improvement in order to earn increased profits of £40,000, ignoring the effect on sales of B2 models.
c. Calculate the increase in sales of B1 models necessary with the quality improvement in order to earn increased profits of £40,000, taking into account the effect on sales of B2 models.

6.4 Haedoo is presently struggling to survive in the motor car industry. Competition is increasing and the company is plagued by overcapacity. Its capacity is 2 million units per year, but it is currently operating at only 70 per cent of this level, and this is resulting in an annual loss of $480 million. Its profit contribution per unit is 25 per cent. Haedoo has now set targets for its performance in two years' time: it aims to reduce its capacity to 1.5 million units and operate at 80 per cent of this level; it aims to have a profit of $800 million; and in order to achieve its target output and sell it, it aims to keep its prices the same, while reducing its level of unit variable costs to 90 per cent of their current level by rationalizing its supply procedures and standardizing components.

a. Calculate the target average level of price for Haedoo.
b. Calculate the target level of unit variable costs.
c. Calculate the target level of break-even output.

6.5 Two firms, PRO and CON, produce a homogeneous product, which they sell at the going market price. PRO has fixed costs that are 40 per cent more than CON and average variable costs of $21, which is 20 per cent lower than CON's. PRO has a profit contribution of 30 per cent of revenue and a break-even output 4,000 units less than CON's; it produces 10 per cent more revenue than CON and makes 660 per cent more profit than CON.

   a. Calculate the market price.
   b. Calculate the cost functions of both firms.
   c. Calculate the outputs of both firms.
   d. Calculate the profits of both firms.

6.6 Fyrwood is a firm of mortgage brokers which operates an office in London. An analysis of its monthly operating costs indicates that it has average variable costs given by:

$$AVC = 952 - 0.048Q$$

where **AVC** is in £ and **Q** is the number of mortgages sold. Fixed costs are estimated at £36,000 per month. Fyrwood charges a fee of £800 for each mortgage arranged, and 20 per cent of this is paid to its sales consultants.

   a. Calculate the volume of mortgages that have to be sold in order to make a profit of £60,000 per month.
   b. Calculate the degree of operating leverage at the above output and interpret your result.

Notes

1 See, for example, J. R. McGuigan, R. C. Moyer and F. H. deB. Harris, *Managerial Economics: Applications, Strategy, and Tactics*, 8th edn, Cincinatti: South-Western College, 1999, p. 348.
2 F. M Scherer, and D. Ross, *Industrial Market Structure and Economic Performance*, 3rd edn, Boston: Houghton Mifflin, 1990, chap. 4.
3 'Large industrial stoppages in Great Britain', *Employment Gazette*, 86 (January 1980).
4 See, 'for example', B. D. Henderson, 'The application and misapplication of the experience curve', *Journal of Business Strategy*, 4 (Winter 1984): 3–9.
5 'Green fuel runs out of gas', *The Sunday Times*, 28 March 2004.
6 'On the rocky road to marriage', *The Economist*, 20 May 2000.

Outline

Objectives

Objectives

1 To explain the importance of cost estimation for managerial decision-making.
2 To explain the different methods of cost estimation and their relative advantages and disadvantages.
3 To describe the different types of empirical study which are used in cost estimation.
4 To explain the types of problem which are encountered in statistical cost estimation.
5 To explain how these problems apply in different ways to short-run and long-run situations.
6 To explain how these problems can be overcome.
7 To describe and interpret the different types of cost function in mathematical terms.
8 To explain the specification and estimation of the learning curve.
9 To examine and interpret the findings of various empirical studies.

7.1 Introduction

After discussing the theory of demand in Chapter 3 we proceeded to examine the estimation of demand functions in the following chapter. Now that we have discussed the theoretical aspects of production and cost we need to examine the estimation of cost functions.

7.1.1 *Importance of cost estimation for decision-making*

We have already seen in the previous chapter why managers need to understand the nature and application of cost functions in various aspects of decision-making. Since these functions are not self-evident, they have to be estimated using an appropriate method. Managers cannot apply their knowledge of the firm's cost functions unless these have been estimated in the first place. Therefore, cost estimation is important for the same reasons as an understanding of cost theory, that is:

1 To determine the pricing of the firm's products.
2 To determine the other components of the marketing mix.

3 To determine the optimal output of the firm in the short run and the relevant input mix.
4 To determine the optimal scale of operation of the firm in the long run.
5 To determine whether to accept or refuse an order from a potential customer at a particular price.
6 To determine the impact of potential mergers and acquisitions on unit costs.

7.1.2 Types of cost scenario

The word **scenario** is used here to indicate a distinction between a cost function's time period and a cost function's mathematical form. Scenario in this context refers to time period, although we shall see that there is some relationship between time period and mathematical form.

It is vital for an investigator to determine which type of cost scenario is desired before collecting the data which are necessary to estimate the relevant cost function. This is because different scenarios require different types of data in order to estimate them. Essentially there are three possible main scenarios involved in cost estimation:

1 The short run – discussed in section 7.2.
2 The long run – discussed in section 7.3.
3 The learning curve – discussed in section 7.4.

The differences between these scenarios have already been explained in the previous two chapters, but the implications in terms of estimation have still to be discussed.

7.1.3 Methodology

As with demand estimation, there are different methods of estimation that can be used. However, once again we find that statistical analysis tends to be the preferred method, with its advantages being essentially the same as for demand analysis. Most of the remainder of this chapter will examine various aspects of statistical cost estimation, but before we move on to this it is helpful to consider two alternative methods of estimation: *engineering analysis* and the *survivor method*.

a. Engineering analysis

This is mainly concerned with **estimating physical relationships between inputs and outputs in order to estimate a production function**. This in turn can be used to obtain the cost function of the firm, once we know the prices of the inputs, and assuming that the firm produces with economic efficiency. In the short run the production process will often determine how the inputs are combined. Technical factors frequently determine, for example, how many workers can use a particular machine, how many hours a machine can operate in a day, how much raw material and what components are required to manufacture a finished product, how much fuel and power is required, and so on. Often relationships here may be linear, so that, for example, producing twice as much output requires twice as much material; sometimes, however, as with fuel requirements, the relationship may be non-linear; a machine operating twice as fast may require more than twice as much fuel.

Having established production relationships, the next step is to price these inputs. This may involve some of the problems mentioned in the previous chapter, in that accounting data may be historical rather than current. Also the data may be aggregated in such a way as to make it difficult to estimate prices for particular types of labour or materials. The final step with this approach is to derive the cost function on the basis that optimal production methods are used. This may also present problems, since there may be some flexibility in terms of input substitution; for example, taking the variable factors in the short run, one material might be substituted for another, such as steel for aluminium in car production. Thus the firm has to determine the least-cost cost function, in other words the cost function that involves producing each output at minimum cost. This is the familiar mathematical problem that we have seen in Chapter 5, where the objective is to minimize total cost subject to a series of output constraints (shown as shifting isoquants). The only difference is that in this case both inputs are variable in the short run.

There are three main shortcomings of engineering analysis.

1. Some production processes are highly complex, involving a large number of inputs. This makes it difficult to determine the mathematical model of the relationships between these inputs and output. The problem is even more difficult if there is more than one output and there are interdependencies between these outputs, for example if a plant is producing different models in a product line.

2. No consideration is given to indirect costs. Thus management, administrative and distribution inputs and costs are ignored in the analysis. Since these are also related to output in practice, they can have a considerable impact on the firm's cost function.

3. There is often no consideration of optimization of the input-output relationships. Existing combinations of inputs and outputs are often used in the analysis, with no regard as to whether these are optimal. In order to determine the optimal combinations the aspect of flexibility of input substitution discussed above must be examined; this can make the analysis considerably more difficult, and may require some costly, and risky, experimentation by the firm in terms of varying its production processes.

b. Survivor method

This method was originally developed by Stigler,[1] and only applies to long-run cost estimation. The method does not rely on the use of accounting data, and therefore avoids the problems arising from the unreliability of such data. The method simply involves categorizing the firms in an industry according to size, observing the industry over a relatively long time period, and *recording the growth or decline of the different size categories*. Some conclusion is then formed regarding the most efficient size of firms in the industry according to which size categories are growing fastest. Stigler applied this technique to the steel industry in the United States, using data from 1930 to 1951, and observed that the medium-size firms (between 2.5 per cent and 25 per cent of industry capacity) had gained most in terms of total market share. He concluded that these firms must be the most efficient and that therefore the industry featured a U-shaped *LAC* curve. Apart from its avoidance of unreliable accounting data, the other advantage of the survivor method is its simplicity. It does however suffer from three serious problems.

1. It does not estimate costs or unit costs at any level of output, and therefore is not very useful for most aspects of managerial decision-making. One exception may be the consideration of mergers and acquisitions.

2. It assumes that the industry is highly competitive, so that firms that are performing below maximum efficiency will not survive. It thus ignores market power and barriers to entry, discussed in the next chapter.

3. It ignores changing technology and its impact on optimal size. In the steel industry for example it has become easier in recent decades for smaller firms to compete by using smaller plant size with new technology, resulting in unit costs comparable to larger firms. The survivor method may not reveal such a reduction in minimum efficient scale if it has only occurred in the more recent years of the long period under consideration.

c. Statistical analysis

In view of the problems described above, statistical methods are often used to estimate cost functions. These overcome some of the problems, but are not without problems of their own, as we shall see. Much of the pioneering work in this area was carried out by Dean,[2] who also wrote the first textbook on managerial economics. He conducted some of the empirical studies that are discussed later in the chapter. Johnston reviewed and extended this work,[3] and much of the material in this chapter is based on their work.

The procedure for statistical cost estimation is essentially the same as for demand estimation. The same seven steps are involved:

1 *Statement of a hypothesis*. An example here might be that a firm's short-run total cost function is linear.

2 *Model specification*. This means determining what variables should be included in the cost function and what mathematical form or forms such a relationship should take. These issues are again determined on the basis of economic theory and prior empirical studies; obviously output is the most important explanatory variable. Various alternative models may be specified at this stage, since economic theory is often not robust enough to be definitive regarding the details of the form of model.

3 *Data collection.* This stage can only be performed after the cost function has been specified, otherwise it is not known for which variables we have to collect data.

4 *Estimation of parameters.* This means computing the values of the coefficients of the variables in the model. These effects can be measured in different ways, for example in terms of the marginal effects and elasticities already discussed. Clearly we must use some technique to estimate these values and the method of OLS regression will again be used in this context.

5 *Selecting the best model.* Once several alternative models have been estimated, it is necessary to examine how well each model fits the data and which model fits best. The situation is somewhat different here from the demand situation. In the latter case, as we have seen, economic theory is not usually robust enough for us to specify a mathematical form. However, in cost situations, theoretical considerations may be dominant in selecting suitable forms, as will be seen in the remainder of this chapter. If the fit is not good it may be necessary to return to step 2 and respecify the model before moving on to the next stage.

6 *Testing a hypothesis.* In the example above this is determined by comparing the goodness of fit, as described in the previous stage.

7 *Forecasting.* Once the appropriate cost function has been estimated cost forecasts for different outputs can be computed.

7.2 Short-run cost estimation

Short-run cost functions assume, as we have seen, that at least one factor is fixed. Thus changes in cost are caused mainly by changes in the level(s) of the variable factor inputs. This has important implications regarding the type of empirical study used. Different measures of cost are sometimes used as the dependent variable, depending on the availability of data; thus the cost function may be specified as:

$$VC = f(Q) \tag{7.1}$$

$$TC = a + f(Q) \tag{7.2}$$

$$AVC = f(Q)/Q \tag{7.3}$$

$$ATC = [a + f(Q)]/Q \tag{7.4}$$

$$MC = f'(Q) \tag{7.5}$$

In each case it is assumed that there is only one explanatory variable, output. Once one particular form of cost function has been estimated, other forms can be obtained mathematically from that form.

7.2.1 Types of empirical study

Various approaches are possible here. In some cases, experiments can be specifically designed for the purposes of cost estimation, or panel data may be used, as discussed in the chapter on demand estimation. However, as with demand studies, there are two main types of study that can be performed: time-series and cross-section. Each involves different constraints and problems. These are explained briefly here and then expanded in the next subsection.

a. Time-series studies

In this case the researcher needs data relating to a specific plant or firm over a period of time. However, it is important that the time period involved be relatively short, since in order to qualify as a short-run analysis neither the size of the plant, the scale of the firm nor the technology in use should change. There must be sufficient time periods, and there must also be some variation in production levels from one period to another, for the analysis to be reliable. Otherwise the estimated coefficients of the variables in the equation will have large standard errors. To obtain sufficient observations in the short time period such observations may have to be made at monthly intervals, or even more frequently. This may pose problems, which are discussed later.

b. Cross-section studies

A researcher can estimate a short-run cost function for an industry by examining different firms of the same scale. However, a firm can only use a cross-section study to estimate its particular cost function if it has several plants. Since managers are usually concerned with the analysis of firm-specific data, this places a constraint on the use of cross-section studies. If the firm does operate several plants, these plants must be of the same size, and use the same technology, in order for the study to qualify as a short-run analysis. Furthermore, these plants must all be producing the same product, and involve the same stage of the production process, in other words the firm must be horizontally integrated. Again, for the results to be reliable, there must be some variation between the outputs of the different plants. Given the constraints described above, time-series studies are more commonly used for short-run cost estimation.

7.2.2 Problems in short-run cost estimation

In Chapter 4 on demand estimation it was seen that there were a number of problems related to the estimation process. There are again problems with cost estimation, but they tend to be of a different nature. The main problematic area is in data collection and measurement, as explained below.

a. Dynamic environment

If time-series analysis is used it must be recognized that the cost function is really a dynamic relationship that is changing over time. Thus there is an

identification problem similar to the situation discussed under demand estimation. This means that each observation could relate to a different cost
function if care is not taken to keep other factors equal; if other factors cannot
be kept equal then certain adjustments must be made to the values of the
variables recorded. One of the most important factors that needs to be kept
equal is the product quality; this is more difficult to achieve with a time-series
study, as quality improvements may be being made unknown to the
researcher. This problem of a dynamic environment is explained in more
detail in conjunction with the next problem.

b. Use of accounting data

Researchers are inevitably constrained to using data collected and recorded
by the firm's accountants. As already seen in the last chapter, this information has been collected and recorded for different purposes from those of the
researcher: to conform to legal requirements and externally imposed
accounting standards, and for other external uses like providing shareholder
information. Managers who want to use the data for internal purposes, therefore, are faced with a number of problems. The principles involved are the
same as those discussed in the previous chapter: the relevant costs for
decision-making purposes are economic costs rather than accounting costs,
current costs rather than historical costs, and incremental rather than sunk
costs. The application of these principles to cost estimation involves the
following specific aspects.

1. Adjustment for changes in prices.   Prices of labour, materials and other
inputs must be adjusted so that current prices are used. The best way of
doing this is to use a specific cost index for the relevant input. Say, for example,
that labour costs were recorded as being £10,000 for a particular time period,
and that wage rates had increased by 12 per cent since then; these labour costs
should be recorded at the estimated current costs of £11,200. If a specific cost
index is not available, a general price index like the wholesale price index can
be used (this is preferable to the retail price index, as being more relevant to
input prices).

2. Measurement of depreciation.   Accountants often measure depreciation on
an essentially arbitrary basis from an economist's viewpoint, for example to
perform easier calculations (straight-line method), or to reduce tax liability.
This means that depreciation is often calculated on a time-related basis,
whereas economists are interested in the usage-related aspect of depreciation.
Furthermore, accountants calculate depreciation based on historical cost,
whereas economic depreciation should be based on replacement value.

c. Multiproduct firms

We have assumed up to this point that the firm is producing a single product. If
a firm produces different products from different plants cost estimation may

not be too difficult; different cost functions can be estimated for each product from each plant. There is still a problem of overhead allocation, discussed below, but the situation is still more simple than if more than one product is produced from a single plant, as is often the case with a product line. There are two possible approaches to this problem.

1. Combination of products into a single output variable. This is most easily explained by means of an example. Say that a firm produces two models of car, model A and model B. In a particular time period a plant may produce 2,000 of A and 3,000 of B. Since the models may have different prices according to the different production costs involved, it may be preferable to take these prices into account in measuring total output, rather than just adding the crude output figures together. Thus if A is priced at £8,000 and B is priced at £12,000, the total value of output is £52 million for the period. This can then be divided by an average price of £10,000 to obtain a proxy or combined measure of output of 5,200 units. This figure can then be compared with outputs from other periods, provided that once again allowance is made for any changes in prices, this time of the outputs.

2. Estimating separate cost functions for different products. The main problem here is the allocation of fixed overhead costs. Accountants again tend to allocate these on an arbitrary basis, sometimes on the basis of the **net realizable value** of the different products. Net realizable value is usually defined as *revenues minus direct costs*. This basis for allocating overheads causes problems for the estimation of cost functions because it treats a cost category as being variable when it is really fixed. The result is that this method can result in nonsensical cost functions with negative average variable costs, as shown by Dobbs.[4] The problem of estimating cost functions becomes even more serious when there are cost interdependencies among the different products.

d. Timing of costs

It has already been stated that in a time-series approach to short-run cost estimation the total time period for the study must be of relatively short duration, and this can necessitate the use of short time intervals, such as a month or less, for observations in order to obtain sufficient observations. The lower time limit for these intervals is set by the accounting periods for the firm. Costs, or at least some costs, may not be recorded on a weekly basis.

However, there is another problem related to short observation intervals, and this concerns **spillover effects**. There is a danger of *recording costs in the wrong time period*; for example, billing dates may not match production and usage. Some costs may appear before or after the period to which they relate. In addition to this, some costs can be scheduled according to convenience rather than production; this applies particularly to maintenance, which is often scheduled for quiet periods when production is low. In reality this maintenance cost is related to previous periods when production levels were higher. Only when researchers are very knowledgeable regarding production activity and the accounting practices of the firm are they likely to be able to avoid these pitfalls.

In addition to the problems described above, it should also be noted that the function being estimated is based on actual costs that have been incurred by the firm(s) in the study; if the firm or firms have not been operating efficiently the cost function estimated will not be an optimal cost function. It will tend to overstate the 'true' values of the cost parameters.

7.2.3 Different forms of cost function, interpretation and selection

a. Forms

We saw in the previous chapter that cost functions can take a variety of forms in the short run. The polynomial form is the most common form, consisting of linear, quadratic and cubic functions. In each case the relationships between total cost, average cost and marginal cost were examined. Therefore, as stated earlier in this chapter, it does not matter which of these is specified in the cost model, since the other measures can be calculated mathematically from the measure specified. This is briefly reviewed below.

The marginal cost and average variable cost relationships have been seen to have a U shape in many situations, because of increasing and then diminishing returns. This translates mathematically into a quadratic unit cost function of the general form:

$$MC = b + cQ + dQ^2 \tag{7.6}$$

We can then obtain the *TC* function by integration, producing the following cubic:

$$TC = a + bQ + (c/2)Q^2 + (d/3)Q^3 \tag{7.7}$$

In this case $FC = a$ and $VC = bQ + (c/2)Q^2 + (d/3)Q^3$

Thus

$$AFC = a/Q \quad \text{and} \quad AVC = b + (c/2)Q + (d/3)Q^2 \tag{7.8}$$

and

$$ATC = a/Q + b + (c/2)Q + (d/3)Q^2 \tag{7.9}$$

Alternatively, a particular form of *TC* function may be specified; in this case the *MC* function can be derived by differentiation. It can be easily seen that if the *TC* function is the quadratic:

$$TC = a + bQ + cQ^2 \tag{7.10}$$

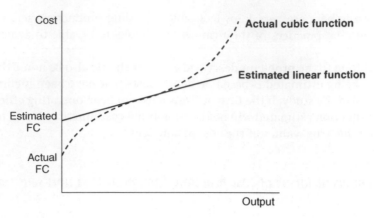

Figure 7.1. Error from mis-specifying the cost function.

then the MC function is linear:

$$MC = b + 2cQ \tag{7.11}$$

and AVC is also linear, but with half the slope:

$$AVC = b + cQ \tag{7.12}$$

An example involving this type of analysis was given as solved problem SP6.3. The simplest type of cost function is the linear form:

$$C = a + bQ \tag{7.13}$$

where FC is given by a, and MC and AVC are both given by b.

b. Interpretation

Although regression analysis can estimate the values of these coefficients, care must be taken in their interpretation, particularly of the value of a. This is because the function estimated is only valid over the output range of the data; this is unlikely to include zero output. Thus the interpretation of the value of a as being the level of fixed costs often involves a huge extrapolation. If the function estimated is not valid over other parts of the output range the result could be a large error in the estimation of fixed costs. In essence this is a mis-specification error. This is illustrated in Figure 7.1, where a cubic function is mis-specified as linear.

c. Selection

Since the researcher cannot normally be confident regarding which mathematical form is the best one to use from a theoretical viewpoint, the procedure for selecting the best model is essentially the same as for estimating demand functions: different mathematical forms are estimated, usually linear, quadratic and cubic, and the one which fits best (on the basis of adjusted R^2) is selected.

7.2.4 *Implications of empirical studies*

Many empirical studies of short-run cost functions have been conducted, both at the level of the individual firm and at industry level, since the 1930s. The landmark studies, which are frequently quoted at length in textbooks, are those by Dean[5] in 1941 (hosiery) and Johnston in 1960[6] (road passenger transport). Both these researchers also estimated cost functions in other industries, as have other researchers, and there are now extensive studies of the furniture, food processing, steel, electricity, coal, cement and other manufacturing industries. It is not necessary to consider any of these in detail here, since they come to largely the same conclusions. Walters[7] has summarized many of the earlier findings, concluding that they generally do not support the hypothesis of the U-shaped average cost curve. More recent studies also tend to indicate that total cost functions are frequently linear, with constant marginal costs, at least in the normal range of output of firms. For example, in a study of a firm producing plastic containers,[8] it was found that for all ten products manufactured by the plant the linear cost function provided the best fit.

Economists have come to some different conclusions based on these findings, in order to reconcile them with the U-shaped average cost curve of economic theory:

1 The data used have related only to a limited range of output, the normal output range of the firms studied. As already explained in the previous chapter, it may well be that the law of diminishing returns only starts to take effect as firms approach full capacity, perhaps at around 95 per cent of maximum output. Firms do not normally operate at this level, and indeed managers try to avoid such operation because of the rising unit costs.
2 The studies have actually been long-run rather than short-run, because capital inputs have varied, allowing the ratio of labour to capital to remain constant.

Therefore, it is not necessary to re-evaluate the premises of economic theory in view of the empirical findings. Furthermore, there is one other finding in practice that tends to confirm that, ultimately, marginal cost curves must be rising at higher levels of output. This is the fact that an increase in demand for a product results in an increase in both the quantity supplied and the price of the product in the short run. It will be seen in the next chapter that an upward-sloping supply curve is dependent on an upward-sloping marginal cost curve.

7.3 Long-run cost estimation

Many of the basic aspects of cost estimation in the long run are similar to those for the short run, thus the structure of this section is the same as for the previous one. However, we shall see that there are some different types of constraints and problems associated with the long run, that different mathematical forms are often used, and that the implications of empirical studies are of a different nature.

7.3.1 Types of empirical study

As with short-run studies, empirical studies can be classified into time-series and cross-section categories. These are now discussed separately, in terms of the constraints and procedures involved.

a. Time-series studies

In this case it is necessary to use a time period that allows the firm or plant to experience several changes in capacity; this is because the aim of such a study is to estimate the effect on costs of these changes in capacity in terms of economies and diseconomies of scale. We shall see that this creates some serious problems for this type of study.

b. Cross-section studies

These involve collecting data from firms or plants of different sizes or scales. If a firm-specific function is desired then this is only possible if the firm has several plants, each producing the same product, involving the same stage of the production process and using the same technology, but with the plants being of different sizes. This constraint may make such a study impracticable, since it may be that the long-run average cost curve is U-shaped, resulting in only a certain plant size being efficient. In this situation it would not be sensible for a firm to operate different plants with different capacities. However, if a cross-section study is possible, it is generally preferable to a time-series study, because the problems involved tend to be less serious. These problems are now examined.

7.3.2 Problems in long-run cost estimation

Since the nature of these problems is different according to whether the study is time-series or cross-sectional, it is again best to discuss these problems separately.

a. Time-series studies

The main problem here is that, in order to allow the firm sufficient time to change its capacity several times, such a long time period is involved that technology also changes. It then becomes difficult to separate the effects of increased scale from the effects of improved technology. The problem can sometimes be overcome by the use of a dummy variable (or more than one such variable) in the cost function to represent different levels of technology.

Another problem is that the firm may not be operating at maximum efficiency with each plant size. It is always assumed in drawing the long-run average cost curve as an envelope to the short-run curves that maximum

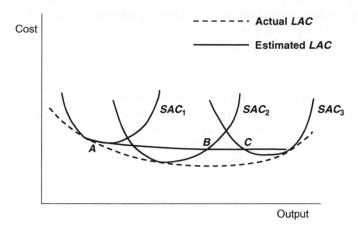

Figure 7.2. Estimation error arising from sub-optimal operation of plants.

efficiency is achieved from each scale of operation. This problem may cause the *LAC* curve to be estimated wrongly, as shown in Figure 7.2. In this case the firm moves from point *A* to point *B* to point *C* and it appears that the *LAC* curve shows no economies or diseconomies of scale.

Other problems discussed in short-run cost estimation are also often present, for example allowing for changes in input prices, the correct measurement of depreciation and overhead costs, and the measurement of output for multiproduct firms. The problem of changes in input prices becomes greater in the long run than in the short run. This is because a greater variation is often present and the longer time period allows managers to adjust input combinations to these different prices. If prices are all adjusted to a particular base, this ignores these managerial adjustments and prevents an accurate analysis of the cost–output relationship. On the other hand, the problem of the timing of costs and the matching of costs to production periods is usually less serious, since the intervals between observations tend to be longer.

b. Cross-section studies

These studies often avoid some of the more difficult problems above. For example, the problem of changing technology may not occur if observations are all made at the same time period. The problem of allowing for changes in input prices may also not be relevant for the same reason. However, these problems may not be altogether avoided, for the following reasons:

1 Different plants may use different technologies, especially if they have been built at different times. As with time-series studies, it may be possible to allow for this by using dummy variables.
2 Different plants may face different input costs, especially if they are located in different geographical areas. Labour, raw materials or power and fuel prices may vary from area to area; transportation costs may also be different. It may be possible to allow for these variations by some adjustment to a

constant base, but this creates the further problem of ignoring managerial adjustments, described above.

3 Plants may not operate at maximum efficiency, leading to the same problem as that outlined for time-series studies above, and illustrated in Figure 7.2.

4 Different firms may record accounting data differently, if an industry study is being conducted. This applies especially to the measurement of depreciation, the valuation of inventory and the allocation of overhead expenses. Different firms may pay their labour differently also; this applies particularly to managers, and most recently to managers in high-tech companies who are often paid largely in terms of stock in the company.

7.3.3 Different forms of cost function

Whereas polynomial functions tend to be the favoured form for short-run cost functions, it has been seen in the previous chapter that, in the long run, power functions are the favoured form. These can be expressed as follows (assuming a single product firm):

$$C = aQ^b \qquad (7.14)$$

In this case we are using the symbol C for total costs, since in the long run there is no distinction between total costs and variable costs; all costs are variable. Alternatively, the cost function can be written in log-linear form:

$$\ln C = a' + b \ln Q \qquad (7.15)$$

If a dummy variable is required to indicate a different level of technology this equation can be expanded to:

$$\ln C = a' + b \ln Q + cT \qquad (7.16)$$

where $T = 0$ for the base technology and $T = 1$ for a newer technology. Obviously additional dummy variables are necessary if there are more than two different levels of technology.

The advantage of this power form, as we have again seen in the previous chapter, is that it allows us to estimate cost elasticities, which in turn are an indicator of the existence of economies or diseconomies of scale. The solved problem SP7.2 involves this type of analysis, including the problem of allowing for different technologies.

7.3.4 Implications of empirical studies

Again, much of the early empirical work involving long-run studies was conducted by Dean and Johnston. Both researchers found U-shaped average cost curves, in the shoe retailing[9] and building society[10] industries respectively, although in the first case the rising average costs were not interpreted as due to

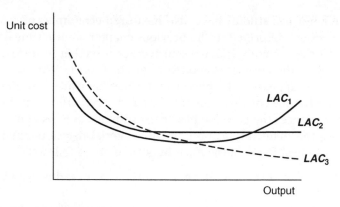

Figure 7.3. Different shapes of *LAC* curve.

diseconomies of scale. In other studies by Johnston, of electricity, road passenger transport and life assurance, he found declining average costs.

More recent empirical work has examined cost structures in a wide variety of manufacturing industries, and there have also been studies relating to service industries such as banking and information technology. Industries can generally be categorized into three classes:

1 Those with U-shaped *LAC* curves – specialized retailing and many services.
2 Those with L-shaped *LAC* curves – general and chain retailers; most manufacturing.
3 Those with continuously falling *LAC* curves – mass manufacturing and public utilities.

These different situations are shown graphically in Figure 7.3.

The extent of economies of scale in a firm or industry is often measured in terms of the **cost gradient**. This measures *the increase in unit cost as a result of a firm or industry operating at a specified percentage of the optimal size, usually 50 per cent*. An extensive summary of studies concerning economies of scale in manufacturing in the UK, the USA and Germany has been carried out by Pratten.[11] This showed cost gradients at 50 per cent of minimum efficient scale varying from 1 per cent (in footwear) to 36 per cent (in book printing).

Another method of measuring the extent of economies of scale is to compute the minimum efficient scale (MES) as a percentage of total output in a national or international market. Certain industries had a higher MES than the size of the UK market, for example dyes, aircraft and diesel engines. In addition, many firms featured economies of scale of a non-technical type at the level of the firm rather than at the level of the plant, with these economies continuing to occur at much higher levels of output. Pharmaceuticals and cars are good examples. In the latter case the optimal scale from a technical viewpoint has been found to be up to 2 million cars per year,[12] but non-technical economies relating to finance and research and development increase this optimal output to 5 million cars per year.

Various empirical studies have also measured economies of scope. Apart from the measure described in the previous chapter, another measure sometimes used is the percentage increase in average costs that results from producing only half of the number of models or product forms. With motor vehicle production this appears to be higher than other industries, at around 8 per cent; with pharmaceuticals, electrical machinery, office machinery and domestic appliances the increase has been estimated at 5 per cent.[13]

What are the main implications for managerial decision-making arising from these studies? Some of the most important are as follows:

1 The optimal size of the firm depends on the type of industry in which it is operating.

2 In some industries like pharmaceuticals and car manufacturing, where the LAC curve resembles LAC_3 in Figure 7.3, bigger is better from the point of view of cost efficiency. This encourages mergers and acquisitions, and also joint ventures. These are often on an international scale; in silicon chip manufacturing, for example, Siemens and IBM, Toshiba and Motorola, NEC and AT&T, all have some kind of agreement between them. In car manufacturing there have been various international mergers, such as Daimler-Chrysler and Renault-Nissan; joint venture agreements are also becoming more common, as firms like Mitsubishi and Chrysler have co-operated on research and using common platforms.

3 In those industries where the **MES** is greater than the size of the national market it is most efficient for production to be undertaken by a multinational firm, in order to gain the full benefit from the economies of scale available.

There now follow three case studies involving banking, airlines and electricity generation, all of which have been studied extensively in empirical terms. These will allow the reader to see how different cost considerations apply in different types of industry.

Case study 7.1: Banking

There are various theoretical reasons why economies of scale should occur in the banking industry:

1 Specialization of labour. There is considerable scope for this as cashiers, loan officers, account managers, foreign exchange managers, investment analysts and programmers can all increase their productivity with increased volume of output.

2 Indivisibilities. Banks make use of much computer and telecommunications technology. Larger institutions are able to use better equipment and spread fixed costs more easily.

3 Marketing. Much of this involves fixed costs, in terms of reaching a given size of market; large institutions can again spread these costs more easily.

4 Financial. Banks have to raise finance, mainly from depositors. Larger banks can do this more easily and at lower cost, meaning that they can afford to offer their depositors lower interest rates.

There are also reasons why banks should gain from economies of scope; many of their products are related and banks have increasingly tried to cross-sell them. Examples are different types of customer account, accounts and credit cards, accounts and mortgages or consumer loans, and even banking services and insurance.

There has also been a spate of bank mergers and acquisitions in recent years, often involving related institutions like building societies, investment banks and insurance companies. Many of these institutions have been very large in size, with assets in excess of $100 billion. Examples are Citibank and Travellers Insurance (now Citigroup), Bank of America and NationsBank, Chase Manhattan and J. P. Morgan, HSBC and Midland; both NatWest Bank and Abbey National Bank in the UK have been the object of recent takeover bids. This would tend to support the hypothesis that 'bigger is better'.

The empirical evidence, however, is not supportive of the 'bigger is better' policy that many banks seem to be following. A number of empirical studies have been carried out regarding commercial banking and related activities, in both Europe and the United States. Some US studies in the early 1980s found diseconomies for banks larger than $25 million[14] or $50 million[15] in assets, a very small size compared with the current norm (the largest banks now have assets in excess of $500 billion). More recently a greater availability of data has enabled research to be carried out on much bigger banks, as deregulation in 1980 led to interstate banking in the United States.

Shaffer and David[16] examined economies of scale in 'superscale' banks, that is banks with assets ranging from $2.5 billion to $120 billion in 1984. They estimated that the minimum efficient scale of these banks was between $15 billion and $37 billion in assets, and that these larger banks enjoyed lower average costs than smaller banks.

Many of the studies have been summarized by Clark in the USA.[17] In particular, Clark's conclusions were that there are only significant economies of scale at low levels of output (less than $100 million in deposits). Furthermore, it appeared that economies of scope were limited to certain specific product categories, for example consumer loans and mortgages, rather than being generally applicable.

Questions

1 What shape of long-run average cost curve appears to be appropriate for the commercial banking industry?
2 What mathematical form of cost function would be most appropriate to use to test the existence of economies of scale in banking?
3 What factors might cause the *LAC* curve to flatten out at high levels of output?
4 In view of the empirical evidence, what factors do you think might be responsible for the current trends of increasing size and mergers?

7.4 The learning curve

The concept of the learning curve was introduced in the previous chapter; it was seen that there are various factors involved which cause individuals and firms to learn better ways of doing something with experience. We now need to consider how to estimate a learning curve in practice.

7.4.1 Types of specification

The general model of the learning curve has been expressed as a power function:

$$U = aT^b \qquad (7.17)$$

which is a repetition of (6.18). However, within this general model, there are a number of variations in terms of how the variables can be defined and measured. The T variable almost always represents cumulative output, although sometimes it is defined as a time variable, showing how unit costs change over time. There are many possible ways of defining U. It most often relates to a

Case study 7.2: Airlines

The airline industry has very marked differences in structure between the United States and Europe. US airlines were deregulated in 1978, leading to intense competition on many routes, bankruptcies and mergers. In Europe the airlines have remained highly regulated, with governments protecting their own largely state-owned airlines. The deregulation in the US has led to much lower fares per passenger-mile and has caused some radical changes in structuring and therefore unit costs.

Economies of scale arise if airlines can make use of a single type of plane. For example, Southwest Airlines only flies the Boeing 737, while the struggling US Airways uses a number of different aircraft. This was largely because US Airways came into existence as a result of a series of mergers. Southwest can therefore reduce its maintenance costs, crew training and scheduling costs compared with US Airways. This was reflected in the fact that in 1993 its costs were only 7 cents per available seat mile, compared with over 11 cents for US Airways.

Economies of scope are also very important in the airline industry. Clearly it is cheaper for an airline to carry passengers and freight in the same aircraft than carry them in separate aircraft. However, the most important economy of scope arose from a change in routing: instead of having a large number of point-to-point services between different cities, airlines like Southwest and Continental switched to using a 'hub and spoke' system. This meant that customers flew from one city to a central hub, and then from there to their final destination, as shown in Figure 7.4. This gave these

airlines a number of advantages. They could fly a much larger number of routes, in terms of joining city-pairs, with a given number of aircraft and miles flown. This would attract more passengers. Since these passengers all landed at the hub, before being transferred to their final destination, it allowed the airlines to fill the flights more comprehensively. It also became possible to combine passengers with different characteristics more effectively; thus routes that largely carried business passengers could now attract vacation customers.[18]

The above economies of scale and scope have not prevented many airlines from getting into serious financial difficulties recently. Although the events of 11 September 2001 did not help the industry, there were already many problems brewing in terms of overcapacity and industrial relations. Many airlines now appear likely to go out of business unless they receive government subsidies, a controversial issue discussed in more detail in Chapter 12.

Questions

1 Explain how you would conduct an empirical study to investigate the availability of economies of scale in the airline industry.
2 What implications are there regarding mergers of different airlines?
3 What disadvantages might be incurred with the hub and spoke system compared with the point-to-point system?
4 Explain why the hub and spoke system relates to economies of scope rather than economies of scale.

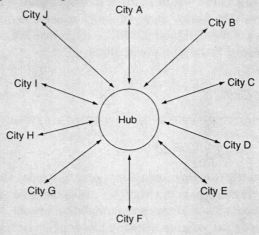

Figure 7.4. Hub and spoke airline connections.

Case study 7.3: Electricity generation

This industry has been the subject of many empirical studies in different countries, going back to the 1950s. These studies have been facilitated by three factors:

1 Output is easy to measure (electricity produced, usually in billions of kilowatt-hours).
2 Different companies, or state utilities, have plants of different sizes.
3 Large amounts of data are available, since producers often have to record this for regulatory purposes.

Johnston[19] estimated long-run cost functions using both time-series and cross-sectional data, for the period 1928–47 and for twenty-three firms. Although a cubic total cost function was specified, he found that the cubic term was not statistically significant in any of the regression equations; the quadratic term was found to be significant in only six of the equations, and was positive in three cases and negative in the other three cases. In general, the linear total cost model tended to fit best.

Two major studies were conducted in the United States in the 1970s. Christensen and Greene[20] used a cross-sectional study involving 1970 data for 114 firms, specifying a power model to test for the presence of economies and diseconomies of scale. They found significant economies of scale below about 20 billion kwh in output, relating to 85 per cent of the firms and nearly 49 per cent of total output. Between this output and 67 billion kwh they observed no significant economies of scale; this related to another 14 per cent of the firms and 45 per cent of output. Above this output they found that diseconomies of scale occurred for the one remaining firm, producing about 7 per cent of total output. This pattern of average costs is shown in Figure 7.5.

Another study by Huettner and Landon[21] examined seventy-four utility firms, using 1971 data, and specifying a cubic model. Their conclusions were broadly the same as for the previous study: the *LAC* curve was U-shaped.

Since the 1970s there have been great changes in the electricity generation industry. Alternative sources of power have become more important, owing to a combination of market forces, environmental concern and improvements in technology. The fossil fuels, coal and oil, have declined in importance, while natural gas, a much cleaner fuel, has gained in importance. Unfortunately, for many utility companies who have had to buy electricity recently from gas-powered sources, demand has far outstripped supply, and prices of gas have soared, in turn causing electricity prices on the wholesale market to soar. In northern

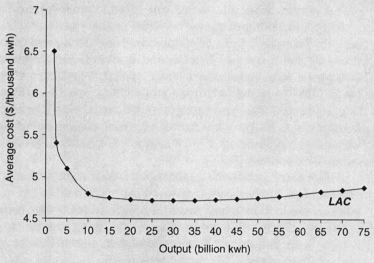

Figure 7.5. *LAC* curve for electricity generation.

California, for example, electricity prices are now ten times their level at the beginning of 2000. Hydroelectric power, from dams, has also become more popular on a global basis, though this too has caused environmental and political problems.

When the electricity utility firms were deregulated in the United States from the 1980s, deregulation posed problems for many of them. The traditional means of producing electricity, whether coal- or oil-fired power stations or hydroelectric plant, involved very high fixed costs. Being sunk costs, these costs then became 'stranded' after deregulation, since electricity buyers could then buy from out-of-state suppliers; this practice is known as 'freewheeling'. Many utility firms lost customers to these competitive suppliers, which forced them to move to the left and upwards along their *LAC* curves, thereby increasing unit costs; this in turn made them even less competitive. These and other aspects of deregulation will be considered in another case study in Chapter 12.

Improvements in technology have led to cleaner methods of producing electrical power in recent years. Although still insignificant in terms of global market share, wind power is becoming more important, particularly in countries like Denmark and Germany. The cost structure of this technology is also different, and many of the indivisibilities of the older methods of production are avoided. A large 1.65 megawatt turbine now costs less than £1 million to build; although this is 20 times that of the 1980s version, it produces 120 times as much energy. Given the problems with other sources of energy, in terms of environmental pollution or volatile costs, wind power may prove to be a major source of energy in the future, along with other new-technology sources like hydrogen power.

Questions

1 Interpret the results obtained by Johnston in terms of the quadratic terms of three equations being positive and the quadratic terms of the other three being negative.

2 Explain the relative advantages and disadvantages of using power or cubic cost functions to estimate *LAC* curves for electricity production.

3 Explain the meaning of 'stranded costs'; why are they a problem?

4 What is happening to unit costs for producing wind power?

unit cost measure, although sometimes this is only one element of cost, like labour cost. U can also be defined as the level of input involved in producing a unit of output, or the amount of time taken to produce a unit of output.

Further variations of the model relate to how these variables are measured: cost, for example, is most often measured as the marginal cost of the last unit produced, but it can also be measured as average cost for the current production period, or as cumulative average cost since production began. The example in Table 7.1 relates to Nuprod plc and illustrates the different possibilities. In practice it is often easier to specify the model with U being the cumulative average cost *(CAC)*, since this makes it easier to compute other values and make various types of forecasts. *(CAC)* is computed as cumulative total cost divided by cumulative output *(CTC/CQ)*.

Before moving on to the application of the learning curve, it is necessary to consider one further aspect of specification. Sometimes it is desired to test whether a reduction in unit cost over time is caused by the learning curve or by economies of scale; this can be done by specifying a model that includes both factors. If we call output Q and cumulative output X, with average cost or marginal cost being U, the model becomes:

$$U = aQ^b X^c \tag{7.18}$$

Table 7.1. Nuprod plc: learning curve estimation

Time period	Output, Q (units)	Total costs, TC(£)	Cumulative total costs, CTC(£)	Cumulative output, CQ (= X)(units)	Cumulative average, costs CAC (= Y)(£)
January	23	184	184	23	8.00
February	28	122	306	51	6.00
March	29	126	432	80	5.40
April	35	128	560	115	4.87
May	30	115	667	145	4.60
June	45	107	798	190	4.20

Alternatively the model can be specified in logarithmic form. In either case it separates the learning effect from the effect of economies of scale.

7.4.2 Application of the learning curve

We shall use the solved problem of Nuprod plc to illustrate the application of the learning curve. There is obviously only a small sample of observations in this example, with a greater chance of sampling error occurring, but the simplicity of the situation aids presentation. The main application of the learning curve, as with other aspects of estimation, is to make forecasts.

SP7.1 Learning curve estimation

Nuprod plc first started producing a particular product in January. It records output and costs over the next six months as shown in the accompanying table. Nuprod's management are planning to produce fifty units in July.

Time period	Output, Q(units)	Total costs, T(€)
January	23	184
February	28	122
March	29	126
April	35	128
May	30	115
June	45	107

a. Estimate a learning curve for the data.
b. How well do the data fit a learning curve?
c. Estimate the cumulative average costs for July.
d. Estimate the cumulative total costs for July.
e. Estimate the total costs for July.
f. Estimate the average costs for July.
g. Estimate the marginal cost for the last unit produced in July.

Solution

The first step is to transform the original data relating to output and costs into a form that can be used to estimate the relationship. We can now compute the learning curve equation from the last two columns, using regression analysis of a power form:

a. $$Y = 19.91X^{-0.2970} \qquad (7.19)$$

where Y is the cumulative average cost in £, and X represents cumulative output in units.

b. It is now necessary to check the goodness of fit by examining the R^2. In this case this is over 99 per cent, showing very strong evidence of a learning curve. As seen in the previous chapter, the **learning rate** can be calculated as 2^b. In this case the learning rate is 81 per cent. The interpretation of this is that *every time cumulative output doubles, the cumulative average cost becomes 81 per cent of what it was previously*.

c. *CAC* for July: $CQ = 190 + 50 = 240$
   $CAC = 19.91(240)^{-0.2970} = £3.91$

d. *CTC* for July: $CTC = 3.91 \times 240 = £938$

e. *TC* for July: $TC = 938 - 798 = £140$

f. *AC* for July: $AC = 140/50 = £2.80$

g. *MC* for last unit in July:
   $\frac{d(CTC)}{d(CQ)} = a(b+1)X^b = 19.91(0.2970+1)240^{-0.2970} = £2.75$

7.4.3 Implications of empirical studies

As stated in the last chapter, the learning curve was first applied empirically in the 1930s to aircraft production. Since then it has been applied in many industries, with the fastest learning rates being found in the production of electrical components and microcomputing. In both cases the learning rate was estimated at 70 per cent. For various other industries, for example ball-bearings, plastics, equipment maintenance and life assurance, the learning rate has been estimated at below 80 per cent,[22] meaning that cumulative average costs are reduced by more than 20 per cent with a doubling of cumulative output. In oil refining on the other hand the learning rate has been estimated at only 90 per cent.

In general the learning rate appears to be faster under the following conditions:

1 Intensive use of skilled labour.
2 A high degree of capital intensity and research and development intensity.[23]
3 Fast market growth; this compresses the time involved under which learning takes place.

4 Supply and demand are highly interdependent, creating a virtuous circle; thus the learning effect reduces costs and price, and this in turn leads to a higher quantity demanded, more output and more learning.

7.5 A problem-solving approach

There are many similarities here between cost estimation and demand estimation in terms of general procedure. Essentially the main stages are the same as in estimating demand:

1 *Stating a theory or hypothesis*. This must relate in some way to a cost relationship. An example of this is that there are economies of scale in a firm or industry.
2 *Model specification*. This involves identifying variables that may be relevant in the cost relationship, determining the relevant definitions, and considering the functional form. This will depend to some extent on whether the study is of a short-run, long-run or learning curve type.
3 *Data collection*. This involves determining whether to use time-series or cross-sectional data, and dealing with problems of definition, measurement and timing.
4 *Data processing*. This stage involves estimating the parameters of the model(s) and is largely mechanical, involving calculators and computers with the relevant programs.
5 *Interpretation of results*. This combines checking goodness of fit with statistical inference.
6 *Forecasting*. This involves substituting relevant values into the estimated equation, and clarifying any assumptions that are involved.

With most problems that students encounter, the first and third aspects are not relevant, because they are given a data set to work with, although sometimes some processing of these data is necessary before estimating the relevant relationship. This is particularly important with the learning curve. The most fundamental problem is model specification. With most problems that students face, a linear or polynomial function is used for short-run situations and a power function is used for long-run situations. As with demand estimation, a lack of understanding of the theoretical underpinnings of the regression model can also cause problems; this is particularly relevant in interpreting the significance of the regression coefficients.

In practice the third stage of the process, data collection, may pose considerable problems to researchers, and these problems have been discussed in some detail in the chapter to try to give students some flavour of this aspect.

The following solved problems are intended to acquaint the student with how to perform the various stages outlined above. Since there are three main cost scenarios, short-run, long-run and learning curve, and an example has already been given of the application of the learning curve, only two further solved problems need to be presented.

SP7.2 Short-run cost estimation

A study is carried out for DP Corp. regarding its costs and output over a period of eight months, during which time its capacity has remained constant. The results are:

Output ('00)	50	64	60	64	70	60	68	76
Total costs (£ '000)	23	29	27	30	35	26	34	42

a. Draw a graph of the average cost curve.
b. Estimate an appropriate total cost function for the firm.
c. Estimate total costs if the firm produces 8,000 units.
d. What can be said about returns to scale in the industry? Give your reasoning.
e. Estimate average costs at 8,000 units.
f. Estimate the marginal cost of the 8,000th unit.

Solution

a. Graph showing rising average costs.
b. The linear total cost function is $C = -16.95 + 0.7453Q$; $R^2 = 92$ per cent
   The quadratic cost function is $C = 69.16 - 2.027Q + 0.022Q^2$
   The **quadratic form** is more appropriate since it can be seen from the graph that average cost is increasing with output. A cubic function could also be fitted, if a computer were used to perform the necessary

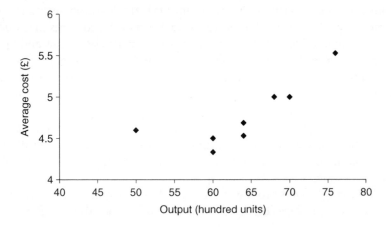

calculations. This could then be compared with the quadratic function by examining the adjusted R^2.

c. $TC = £48,000$

d. Nothing; the scale is not changing

e. $AC = £47,860/8,000 = £5.98$

f. $MC = -2.027 + 2(0.022)(80) = £1.49$

SP7.3 Long-run cost estimation

A survey is carried out regarding the costs and outputs for eight firms in an industry that have different plant sizes. Some of the firms use a newer Hiflow (H) technology, whereas the others use the older Loflow (L) technology. The results are:

Firm	A	B	C	D	E	F	G	H
Technology	L	L	L	H	L	H	H	H
Output ('00)	60	134	90	178	84	200	152	108
Total costs (£ '000)	28	56	40	51	38	52	45	35

a. Estimate an appropriate cost function in the industry.

b. Does the newer technology significantly affect costs? If so, by how much?

c. What can be said about returns to scale in the industry? Give your reasoning.

d. Estimate costs for a firm using the newer technology that produces 12,000 units.

e. Estimate the marginal cost of the 12,000th unit for the firm above.

Solution

a. Specify power function for long run, and estimate two models: one ignoring technology; the other incorporating the differences in technology using a dummy variable ($T = 1$ for Hiflow).

 1 $C = 3.995^{0.4946}$ or $\ln C = 1.385 + 0.4946\ln Q$; adj. $R^2 = 71.9$ per cent
 2 $\ln C = 0.147 + 0.787\ln Q - 0.305T$; adj. $R^2 = 97.6$ per cent

b. **Yes**, t-statistic $= -8.006$, $p = 0.000$.
 Cost is reduced by 30.5 per cent, other things being equal.

c. **Economies of scale**, since coefficient of $\ln Q < 1$ every 1 per cent increase in output only increases total costs by 0.787 per cent.

d. $\ln C = 0.147 + 0.787 \ln (120) - 0.305 = 3.610$
 $C = £37,000$

e. $MC = 0.4946 (3.995) (120)^{(0.4946 - 1)} \times 1000/100 = £1.76$

Summary

1 Cost estimation is important for managerial decision-making for many reasons: determining the optimal marketing mix, determining the optimal output and scale of the firm, and various types of forecast which can be used for determining whether to accept contract offers or engage in mergers and acquisitions.

2 There are three main cost scenarios: the short run, the long run and the learning curve.

3 Statistical methods are the most sophisticated and popular methods for estimating costs.

4 Statistical methods involve essentially the same procedural steps as with demand studies.

5 Time-series studies are generally used more in short-run situations while cross-sectional studies are more common for long-run situations.

6 Many of the problems in the statistical estimation of cost functions are concerned with definition and measurement relating to the use of accounting data.

7 Polynomial cost functions are used more to specify short-run functions while power functions are used more to specify long-run ones. However, the quadratic form can be used for long-run average cost functions if there are economies of scale and diseconomies of scale in different ranges of output.

8 Empirical studies indicate that short-run total cost functions are often linear, with constant marginal costs; most economists interpret this as meaning that these firms are operating at substantially less than full capacity and are therefore not suffering from the law of diminishing returns.

9 Empirical studies indicate that the type of long-run cost function depends on the industry in which the firm is operating. Some industries, particularly those involved in mass production, have a greater incidence of technical economies of scale.

10 The learning curve is also more relevant in industries where mass production is used, where there is a significant amount of skilled labour, and where there are substantial interdependencies between supply and demand.

Review questions

1 Explain the relative advantages and disadvantages of time-series and cross-section studies for estimating cost functions in the short run.

2 Explain the relative advantages and disadvantages of time-series and cross-section studies for estimating cost functions in the long run.

3 Explain the relative advantages and disadvantages of using a polynomial cost function compared with a power function for a long-run analysis.

4 If a polynomial cost function is used for short-run analysis, how should one determine what degree of polynomial to use?
5 What would it mean if cumulative average cost were increasing over time?
6 What does an 80 per cent learning rate mean? If the learning rate is 70 per cent, is the firm (or individual) learning faster or slower?

Problems

7.1 Data are collected from eight firms regarding their costs in the last year, each firm having the same level of fixed assets:

a. Estimate an appropriate cost relationship.
b. A firm of the same type is aiming to produce 48,000 units next year; estimate its total costs, stating any assumptions that you need to make.

Total costs ($ million)	245	260	272	265	248	282	295	288
Output ('000)	31	35	38	36	32	40	44	42

c. Estimate average costs for the firm next year.
d. What can be said about returns to scale for the firms in this industry?
e. Estimate the marginal cost of the last unit produced by the firm next year.
f. If the firm is currently charging $8,000, estimate the break-even level of output for the firm.
g. Estimate the effect on costs for each firm in the industry of an increase in output of 5,000 units.

7.2 A survey of costs and output is carried out for eight firms in an industry that have different plant sizes. The results are:

Output (x100)	50	134	90	178	84	200	152	108
Costs ($'000)	23	56	42	75	38	84	64	48

a. Estimate an appropriate cost function in the industry.
b. Estimate costs for a firm producing 12,000 units.
c. What can be said about returns to scale in the industry? Give your reasoning.
d. Estimate average costs at 12,000 units.
e. Estimate the marginal cost of the 12,000th unit.
f. If the going price in the industry is $4.60, calculate the break-even output.

7.3 The following cost models are estimated for a firm, based on short-run data:

$$
\begin{array}{ll}
 & \underline{\text{adj.}R^2} \\
C = -3,376.0 + 11.81Q & .886 \\
\quad\quad\quad\quad (9.320) & \\
C = 2,493 - 27.17Q + 0.126Q^2 & .987 \\
\quad\quad\quad (-6.115)\quad\quad (8.815) & \\
C = 1,595 - 8.461Q + 0.0003Q^3 & .989 \\
\quad\quad\quad (-3.920)\quad\quad\quad (9.556) &
\end{array}
$$

a. Which is the best model to use? Explain your answer.
b. Interpret the coefficients in the model in terms of what they indicate.
c. What are the implications of your model in part (a) as far as break-even output is concerned?

7.4 MJ, a management consultant, is processing 500 questionnaires that the firm has received from respondents. MJ starts work on Monday at 9 a.m., takes an hour for lunch at 1p.m. and finishes at 5 p.m. The following progress is noted:

Time	Total questionnaires processed since 9 a.m.
9.30	3
10.00	8
10.30	15
11.00	24

a. Is there evidence of a learning curve? Give your reasons.
b. Estimate and interpret the learning rate.
c. How long did the first questionnaire take to process?
d. Estimate the day and time when MJ will finish processing all the questionnaires.
e. How long will the last questionnaire take to process?
f. How many questionnaires will be processed by the end of Tuesday?

Notes

1 G. Stigler, 'The economies of scale', *Journal of Law and Economics*, **1**(1958): 54–81.
2 J. Dean, *Statistical Cost Estimation*, Bloomington: Indiana University Press, 1976, pp. 3–35.
3 J. Johnston, *Statistical Cost Analysis*, New York: McGraw-Hill, 1960.
4 I. M. Dobbs, *Managerial Economics*, Oxford: Oxford University Press, 2000, p. 190.

5 J. Dean, *Statistical Cost Functions of a Hosiery Mill*, Studies in Business Administration, **11** (4), Chicago: University of Chicago Press, 1941.

6 Johnston, *Statistical Cost Analysis*, pp. 74–86.

7 A. A. Walters, 'Production and cost functions: an econometric survey', *Econometrica*, **31** (January–April 1963): 1–66.

8 R. S. Coot and D. A. Walker, 'Short-run cost functions of a multi-product firm', *Journal of Industrial Economics*, **18** (April 1970): 118–128.

9 J. Dean and R. W. James, *The Long-Run Behavior of Costs in a Chain of Shoe Stores: A Statistical Analysis*, Studies in Business Administration, **13** (3), Chicago: University of Chicago Press, 1942.

10 Johnston, *Statistical Cost Analysis*, pp. 103–105.

11 C. Pratten, 'A survey of the economies of scale', report prepared for the European Commission, 1987.

12 G. Rhys, 'Competition in the car industry', in *Developments in Economics*, vol. IX, Ormskirk: Causeway Press, 1993.

13 'The economics of 1992', *European Economy*, March 1988.

14 G. Benston, G. A. Hanweck and B. Humphrey, 'Scale economies in banking: a restructuring and reassessment', *Journal of Money, Credit and Banking*, **14** (1982): 435–456.

15 T. Gilligan, M. Smirlock and W. Marshall, 'Scale and scope economies in the multiproduct banking firm', *Journal of Monetary Economics*, **13** (1984): 393–405.

16 S. Shaffer and E. David, 'Economies of superscale in commercial banking', *Applied Economics*, **23** (1991): 283–293.

17 J. A. Clark, 'Economies of scale and scope at depository financial institutions: a review of the literature', *Economic Review* (Federal Reserve Bank of Kansas City), **73** (September–October 1998): 16–33.

18 F. McGowan and P. Seabright 'Deregulating European airlines', *Economic Policy* **2**, (October 1987).

19 J. Johnston, *Statistical Cost Analysis*, pp. 44–63.

20 L. R. Christenson and W. H. Greene, 'Economies of scale in U.S. electric power generation' *Journal of Political Economy*, **84** (August 1976).

21 D. A. Huettner and J. A. Landon, 'Electric utilities: scale economies and diseconomies', *Southern Economic Journal*, **45** (April 1978): 883–912.

22 'The economics of 1992.'

23 M. B. Lieberman, 'Learning curves in the chemical processing industry', *Rand Journal*, **15** (1984): 213–228.

PART IV
STRATEGY ANALYSIS

Part IV (Chapters 8–12) examines the nature of
strategic behaviour and various decision-making
tools that managers can use in determining strategy. Chapter 8 considers market structure, which
forms the environmental framework within
which strategic behaviour takes place. Chapter 9
examines game theory in some detail, and discusses its implications in terms of decision-making.
It is stressed that many of its conclusions are
counter-intuitive, but are the only way of explaining many aspects of firms' behaviour that are
empirically observed. Chapters 10 and 11 consider
the detailed aspects of pricing and investment
strategies respectively. Finally, Chapter 12 examines government policy insofar as it impacts on
managerial decision-making.

Market structure and pricing

Objectives

1 To define and explain the meaning of markets.
2 To explain the concept of market structure and its significance.
3 To describe the characteristics of the different types of market.
4 To examine the relationships between structure, conduct and performance.
5 To explain the equilibrium conditions for different types of market in terms of price and output, both in graphical and algebraic terms.
6 To explain the types and significance of entry and exit barriers.
7 To give examples of different industries where different market conditions exist, explaining their prevalence.
8 To examine some welfare implications regarding different forms of market.
9 To emphasize the importance of oligopolistic markets, and examine the particular problems relating to their analysis.

8.1 Introduction

In order to maximize profits or shareholder wealth, managers must use the information that they have relating to demand and costs in order to determine strategy regarding price and output, and other variables. However, managers must also be aware of the type of market structure in which they operate, since this has important implications for strategy; this applies both to short-run decision-making and to long-run decisions on changing capacity or entering new markets.

It is useful to start by explaining the characteristics of markets and different types of market structure, with a general examination of the relationships between structure, conduct and performance. The four main types of market structure are then discussed and analysed in terms of their strategic implications.

8.1.1 *Characteristics of markets*

A **market** can be defined as *a group of economic agents, usually firms and individuals, who interact with each other in a buyer–seller relationship*. This is fine as a general definition but it lacks practical applicability in defining a specific market. How for example can we define the market for Coca-Cola? We can refer to a cola market, a carbonated drinks market, a soft drinks market, or a beverage market; all of these have different boundaries in terms of the number and types of product involved. Of course, Coca-Cola operates in all of these markets, but which definition is relevant? One might respond to this problem that this is purely a matter of semantics and is not a significant issue. This, however, is not the case. In 1986 the Federal Trade Commission (FTC) in the United States tried to block the merger between Coca-Cola and Dr Pepper, and the judgement in this case, as in many anti-trust cases, hinged on the definition of the relevant market.[1] In another case, in 1984, the FTC had to determine whether General Foods' Maxwell House brand of coffee had engaged in unfair competition with Proctor and Gamble's Folgers brand in certain US cities.[2] Again the FTC had to determine what constituted the relevant coffee market, this time in terms of geographical boundaries.

It can be seen from these examples that markets can be defined in terms of both product characteristics and geographical characteristics. In the first case the cross-elasticity of demand is an important measure in terms of indicating the degree of substitution between products. Thus in the Coca-Cola case it was determined that the relevant market was carbonated soft drinks. In the second case it was determined that the relevant market involved the whole of the United States, not just certain local areas, since the two companies competed nationwide. Of course, this raises an issue regarding global markets; many firms compete internationally, in which case the relevant market extends across national boundaries, even though this may pose problems for anti-trust authorities.

8.1.2 *Types of market structure*

Economists usually classify market structures into four main types: **perfect competition**, **monopoly**, **monopolistic competition** and **oligopoly**. These types of market structure are different according to the following characteristics: number of sellers, type of product, barriers to entry, power to affect

Table 8.1. Characteristics of different markets

Market structure	Number of sellers	Type of product	Barriers to entry	Power to affect price	Non-price competition
Perfect competition	Many	Standardized	None	None	None
Monopolistic competition	Many	Differentiated	Low	Low	Advertising and product differentiation
Oligopoly	Few	Standardized or differentiated	High	Medium	Heavy advertising and product differentiation
Monopoly	One	Single product	Very high	High	Advertising

price and the extent and type of non-price competition. Perfect competition (PC) is invariably used as a benchmark for comparison, in terms of price, output, profit and efficiency (of different types). It is therefore discussed before the other types of market, not because it is the norm in practice, but because it represents an ideal in certain respects. The conditions for PC are explained in more detail in the next section, but essentially it involves many buyers and sellers of a stan͠ d product. An example would be farmers producing wheat (tho· ͡eaking there are different varieties of wheat). This ·s one extreme of the competition spectrum (max-·monopoly represents the other, where a single seller ͡ is rare in practice, but does tend to occur in public ·ctricity supply, particularly on a local basis. ·opoly are intermediate cases, and are more ·rmer involves many sellers of a differen-·ants, whilst the latter involves a few sellers ·xample the car industry. The most important ·fferent markets are summarized in Table 8.1; in this competition decreases from one row to the next.

8.1.3 Relationᵤ ᵤs between structure, conduct and performance

Economists tend to relate **conduct** and **performance** in different markets to market structure. In this context, conduct refers to strategic behaviour, in particular in terms of price and output determination, but also in terms of advertising, product differentiation and practices regarding entry and exit barriers. This chapter focuses mainly on the aspects of price and output determination, while Chapters 9 and 11 examine other aspects of strategic behaviour. Performance refers to aspects of profit and efficiency. Traditionally the relationships between structure, conduct and performance have been viewed in terms of a one-way causation sequence: structure determines conduct which in turn determines performance. Structure itself has been seen as largely determined by technical factors, mainly the type of technology, but with government policy, infrastructure and geographical factors all being relevant. Currently the relationships between the different aspects are seen as being more complex, with various feedback mechanisms between them.

These will be seen as the chapter progresses and each type of market structure is examined in detail. The involvement of the government in terms of these relationships is examined in Chapter 12.

8.1.4 Methodology

For each type of market structure the necessary conditions for its existence are first explained. A static, partial equilibrium analysis then follows, usually assuming certainty or perfect information. This analysis is initially graphical, following the lines of introductory microeconomics texts with which the student may be familiar. The analysis then moves on to an algebraic approach involving optimization techniques. A knowledge of basic calculus is assumed at this point. Some of the limitations of these methods are then discussed, but the implications of these limitations are not developed until Chapter 9, when strategic behaviour in a dynamic environment under conditions of uncertainty is examined in more detail.

8.2 Perfect competition

It should be understood that this form of market structure is not necessarily 'perfect' in an economic sense, i.e. resulting in an optimal allocation of resources, although this may happen. It simply represents a situation where competition is at a maximum; it is therefore sometimes referred to as pure competition or atomistic competition.

8.2.1 Conditions

There are five main conditions for perfect competition to exist:

1 *Many buyers and sellers.* Each of these must buy or sell such a small proportion of the total market output that none is able to have any influence over the market price.
2 *Homogeneous product.* Each firm must be producing an identical product, for example premium unleaded petrol or skimmed milk.
3 *Free entry and exit from the market.* This means that there are no barriers to entry or exit that give incumbent firms an advantage over potential competitors who are considering entering the industry. These barriers, which can represent either demand or cost advantages, are explained in more detail in the next section.
4 *Perfect knowledge.* Both firms and consumers must possess all relevant market information regarding production and prices.
5 *Zero transportation costs.* This means that it does not cost anything for firms to bring products to the market or for consumers to go to the market.

Under the above conditions, firms in the market will be **price-takers**; there will be one, and only one, market price, meaning that the product will sell at the same price in all locations. Most treatments of perfect competition concentrate on the first four conditions, but the last one is relevant, as will be seen in the following example. It is not uncommon for motorists driving along a busy road to see two or three petrol stations close to each other, at a major crossroads for example, with these firms selling petrol at somewhat different prices. There are many buyers and sellers of petrol, the different prices can be for the same homogeneous product like premium unleaded petrol, barriers to entry are not relevant in the short run and consumers can see the different prices being charged by the different petrol stations. Yet these price differentials may persist because motorists may not be willing to cross the road to obtain a cheaper price and then cross the road again to continue in their intended direction. This is quite rational if the opportunity cost of the time taken to cross and recross the road exceeds the savings on the cost of the petrol. Thus, in practice, transportation costs can be important in explaining price differentials which could not be explained in terms of the first four conditions.

It is clear that these conditions are rarely achieved in reality; however, this does not negate the usefulness of the analysis of perfect competition. Once again it is necessary to remember that a theory should be judged not on the basis of the realism of its assumptions but on its ability to explain and predict. The conditions are approximately approached in some markets, for example agricultural products and stock markets. Furthermore, the analysis and conclusions in terms of conduct and performance provide a useful benchmark for comparing other forms of market structure.

8.2.2 Demand and supply

In order to perform either a graphical or algebraic analysis we must consider the determination of demand and supply functions. It is important to distinguish between the individual firm and the industry as a whole; we will discuss the individual firm first.

a. The firm's demand function

We have just seen that under the conditions of PC the firm will be a price-taker. This means that each firm faces a perfectly elastic (horizontal) demand curve, at the level of the prevailing market price. The economic interpretation of this is that if the firm charges above the market price it will lose all its customers, who will then buy elsewhere, and that there is no point in charging below the market price, because the firm can sell all it wants, or can produce, at the existing price. The level of the prevailing market price is determined by demand and supply in the industry as a whole, as shown in Figure 8.1(i). The demand curve in this case represents both average revenue (AR) and marginal revenue (MR), since both of these are equal to the market price.

b. The firm's supply function

This refers to the quantities of a product that a firm is willing to put onto the market in a given time period at different prices. It can be seen that this

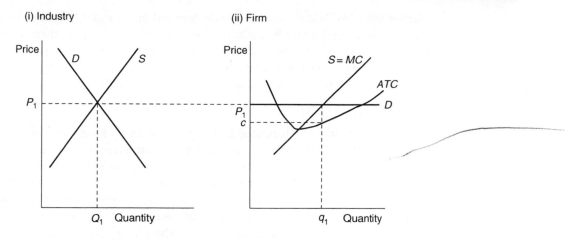

Figure 8.1. Short-run equilibrium in perfect competition.

definition corresponds in terms of its parameters to the definition of demand given in Chapter 3. In order to derive the firm's supply curve we must make the assumption that the firm wishes to maximize profit. In order to do this it must produce the output where marginal revenue equals marginal cost, as with any firm. Since the firm is a price-taker the marginal revenue is given by the price; thus the firm maximizes profit by producing the output where price equals marginal cost. It was seen in Chapter 6 that this curve was generally upward-sloping in the short run. Therefore, the firm will tend to produce more output as the market price increases, and its supply curve will be its marginal cost curve, as shown in Figure 8.1(ii). More precisely, the firm's short-run supply curve will be that part of its marginal cost curve that lies above the average variable cost (*AVC*) curve; if the price falls below the minimum level of *AVC* the firm will shut down production, since it will not be able to cover its variable costs let alone make any contribution to fixed costs.

c. The industry's demand function

As explained in Chapter 3, this can be viewed as the sum of all the individual consumers' demand functions; graphically, these are summed horizontally.

d. The industry's supply function

This is obtained by summing the supply functions of all the individual firms in the industry; this is again a horizontal sum when represented graphically. However, this is actually an oversimplification, since when the behaviour of firms is aggregated this has an effect on input prices, bidding them up.

8.2.3 Graphical analysis of equilibrium

We can now show the equilibrium situation for a firm and industry in perfect competition. This is represented as a static short-run equilibrium. The equilibrium market price, P_1, is determined by the demand and supply functions in the industry as a whole. The firms in the industry, as price-takers, then have to determine what output they will supply at that price. This output, q_1, is where $P_1 = MC$, since this will maximize profit. It is important to distinguish between short-run and long-run equilibrium, as will be explained.

a. Short-run equilibrium

Whether the situation illustrated in Figure 8.1 is also a long-run equilibrium depends on the profit that is made. Since it is assumed that opportunity costs are included in the measurement of unit costs, as explained in Chapter 6, it can be deduced that if the market price is equal to average total cost (ATC), the firm will just make **normal profit**. This is defined as *the profit that a firm must make in order for it to remain in its current business*. If a firm cannot cover all its opportunity costs, meaning that $P < ATC$, then it should leave the industry in the long run since the owners of the business can use the resources more profitably elsewhere. If $P < AVC$ then the firm should shut down in the short run since it cannot even cover its variable costs, let alone make any contribution to fixed costs.

However, if $P > ATC$, the firm is making **abnormal** or **supernormal** profit. In Figure 8.1(ii) this is given by $(P_1 - c)q_1$. This means that the industry is more profitable than average and this will in turn attract new firms into the industry in the long run, since it is assumed that there are no entry or exit barriers. This long-run situation can now be considered.

b. Long-run equilibrium

It is possible in the long run for firms to enter or leave the industry; it should be recalled that this is not feasible in the short run, since it involves a change in the level of fixed factors employed. Existing firms can also change their scale and will maximize profit by producing where price equals long-run marginal cost ($P = LMC$). The presence of abnormal profit will always serve to attract new entrants into the industry, and this factor, combined with firms increasing their scale, will shift the industry supply curve to the right, in turn causing the market price to fall. The industry supply curve will shift from S_1 to S_2 in Figure 8.2(i), and the market price will fall from P_1 to P_2. It is assumed here that there is no change in demand. Such changes are examined in a later section.

In order to aid the visual presentation, two separate diagrams are shown for the firm's situation. Figure 8.2(ii) shows the comparison of the two short-run equilibria, while Figure 8.2(iii) compares the new short-run equilibrium with the long-run equilibrium.

At the new equilibrium the price and long-run average cost (LAC) of the firm are equal, and the firm is now producing at the minimum level of both its new SAC curve (SAC_2) and its LAC curve at the output q_2. This is shown in Figure 8.2(iii). At this point all the abnormal profit has been 'competed away'. There is, therefore, no further incentive for firms to enter the industry and the firm

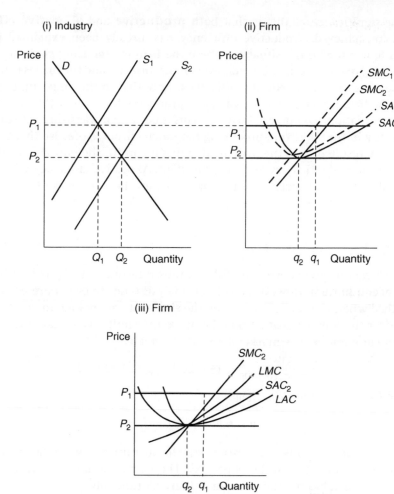

Figure 8.2. Long-run equilibrium in perfect competition.

and industry are in long-run equilibrium. If there were an excessive entry of new firms this would shift the industry supply curve even further to the right, the price would fall below P_2, and firms would not even be able to make normal profit. Some firms would therefore leave the industry until the price rose back to P_2.

It is helpful to remember in this graphical analysis that essentially a two-step procedure is involved:

1 *Determining the* **profit-maximizing output.** This means examining P and **MC**.
2 *Determining the* **size of the profit.** This means examining P and **ATC**.

In this long-run equilibrium the following conditions hold:

$$P = SMC = LMC = SAC = LAC = MR = AR \qquad (8.1)$$

The significance of this is that both **productive** and **allocative efficiency** are achieved. Productive efficiency has already been explained in Chapter 6; it refers to the situation where the firm is *producing at the minimum level of average cost*. This is achieved in the long run and the firm is using the optimal scale with maximum efficiency. Note that in the long run, even though the firm is using a larger scale, it is producing less output than in the short-run situation, q_2 compared with q_1. This is because it was using the scale inefficiently in the short run, producing too much output. Note also that this inefficiency resulted from the firm maximizing its profit, showing that profit maximization and efficiency are not equivalent. Allocative efficiency will be explained in the next section on monopoly, when the two types of market structure are compared.

8.2.4 Algebraic analysis of equilibrium

The graphical analysis above is useful and illustrates many insights into the nature of equilibrium. However, algebraic analysis tends to be a more powerful method when it comes to modelling the situation and making forecasts.

Consider the following situation. The market for milk in a certain town is perfectly competitive. The market demand is given by:

$$Q = 16 - 20P$$

Alternatively this can be written as:

$$P = 0.8 - 0.05Q \tag{8.2}$$

where P is the price of milk in £/litre and Q is the quantity of milk in the market in hundreds of thousands of litres per day. There are a hundred firms in the industry and each has the following marginal cost function:

$$P = 0.44 + 4q \tag{8.3}$$

where q is the quantity produced by each firm.

Firms also have fixed costs of £80 per day. We can now derive both the short- and long-term equilibria in this market; it will be assumed for simplicity that the firm is currently operating at its most efficient scale (with the equivalent of the marginal cost curve SMC_2 in Figure 8.2).

First we must obtain the market supply curve by summing all the firms' supply curves. Each firm's supply curve is given by its marginal cost curve. The equation for this curve can be turned around to give:

$$q = -0.11 + 0.25P$$

Therefore the industry supply curve is given by $Q = 100q = -11 + 25P$

This can be turned around to give:

$$P = 0.44 + 0.04Q \tag{8.4}$$

The equations (8.2) and (8.4) can be solved simultaneously to give:

$$0.36 = 0.09Q \text{ so } \mathbf{Q} = \mathbf{4}, \ \mathbf{P} = \mathbf{0.6}$$

Thus the short-run equilibrium price in the market is **£0.60/litre** and the quantity produced is **400,000 litres per day**.

Each firm will sell **4,000 litres per day** ($q = 0.04$), and its average cost is calculated by substituting this value into its *ATC* function. This function can be obtained by considering the firms' *TC* function. The *TC* function is obtained by integrating the *MC* function. This gives:

$$TC = a + 0.44q + 2q^2$$

where a represents the fixed costs of the firm.

Since *TC* is measured in hundreds of thousands of pounds (because of the units of q and Q), this gives:

$$TC = 0.0008 + 0.44q + 2q^2 \tag{8.5}$$

and

$$ATC = 0.0008/q + 0.44 + 2q \tag{8.6}$$

Therefore

$$ATC = 0.02 + 0.44 + 0.08 = 0.54$$

This means that each firm will make an economic profit given by $(0.6 - 0.54)0.04 = 0.0024 = \mathbf{£240\ per\ day}$. In the long run this will attract new firms into the industry and drive the price down to the minimum level of long-run average cost. Since it has been assumed that the firm is already operating at the most efficient scale, we have to find the minimum level of average cost for this scale and this will also be the minimum level of long-run average cost. We therefore have to differentiate the *ATC* function and set the derivative equal to 0:

$$\frac{d(ATC)}{dq} = -0.0008q^{-2} + 2 = 0$$

This gives $q = 0.02$(2,000 litres per day) and

$$ATC = 0.04 + 0.44 + 0.04 = 0.52.$$

Therefore the long-run equilibrium price is **£0.52 per litre** and the market output is given by the demand function (8.3):

$$0.52 = 0.8 - 0.05Q; Q = 5.6 \ or \ \mathbf{560,000} \text{ litres per day.}$$

8.2.5 Adjustment to changes in demand

Now that we have examined the short- and long-run equilibria for a perfectly competitive market we can consider how such a market adjusts to changes in

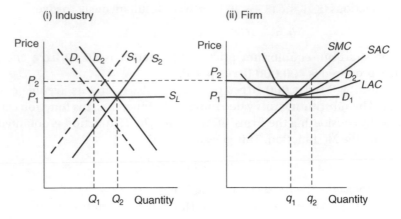

Figure 8.3. Adjustment under constant costs.

demand. The nature of the adjustment depends on the cost conditions under which the industry is operating. In this context the cost conditions refer to the existence of external economies and diseconomies of scale, which were defined in Chapter 6. Under **constant cost conditions** the firm experiences *no external economies or diseconomies* when the industry grows in size. Under **increasing cost conditions** the firm experiences *external diseconomies of scale*; these can be caused by the prices of inputs being driven up by the increased demand for them. Thus firms may have to pay higher raw material costs and wages as the industry expands, particularly if the industry has already reached a mature phase. This means that the firms will find both short- and long-run unit cost functions shifting upwards. Under **decreasing cost conditions** the firm experiences *external economies of scale*; in this case input prices are falling as the industry expands. This is most likely to happen in the initial growth phase of the industry, as the presence of other firms, particularly in the same locality, helps to provide an infrastructure of complementary firms, services and skilled labour. This has the effect of shifting the unit costs downwards. These different cost conditions are now examined graphically.

a. Constant costs

The effects of an increase in demand are shown in Figure 8.3. In the short run the increase in demand causes an increase in price (from P_1 to P_2), since firms face increasing marginal costs in producing more output (q_2 instead of q_1) and no new firms can enter the industry in this time frame. In the long run the supply curve shifts to S_2 as more firms enter the industry, the price falls back to P_1 at the minimum point of *LAC*, and the firms' demand curve falls from D_2 back to D_1. Each firm in the industry ends up selling the same amount as originally (q_1), but with more firms the total industry output increases from Q_1 to Q_2. The long-run supply curve in the industry is therefore horizontal, as shown by S_L.

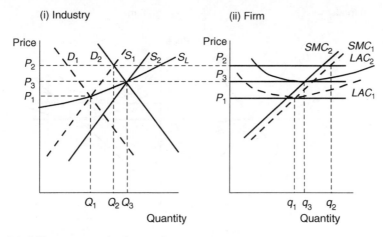

Figure 8.4. Adjustment under increasing costs.

b. Increasing costs

The effects of an increase in demand in this situation are shown in Figure 8.4. In the short run the increase in demand causes an increase in price (from P_1 to P_2), since firms have to move along their SMC_1 curve in producing more output (q_2 instead of q_1) and no new firms can enter the industry in this time frame. In the long run the supply curve shifts to S_2 as more firms enter the industry, and the price falls back to P_3. This is higher than the original price because as more firms enter the industry the firms' cost curves shift upwards, so that the firms end up producing at the minimum point of LAC_2. Each firm in the industry ends up selling the amount q_3, which is more than their original output (q_1), but less than immediately after the change in demand (q_2). With more firms the total industry output increases from Q_1 to Q_3. The long-run supply curve in the industry is therefore upward-sloping, as shown by S_L.

c. Decreasing costs

The effects of an increase in demand in this situation are shown in Figure 8.5. In the short run the increase in demand causes an increase in price (from P_1 to P_2), since firms again have to move along their SMC_1 curve in producing more output (q_2 instead of q_1) and no new firms can enter the industry in this time frame. In the long run the supply curve shifts to S_2 as more firms enter the industry, and the price falls back to P_3. This is lower than the original price because as more firms enter the industry the firms' cost curves shift downwards, so that the firms end up producing at the minimum point of LAC_2. Each firm in the industry ends up selling the amount q_3, which is more than their original output (q_1), but less than immediately after the change in demand (q_2). With more firms the total industry output increases from Q_1 to Q_3. The long-run supply curve in the industry is therefore downward-sloping, as shown by S_L.

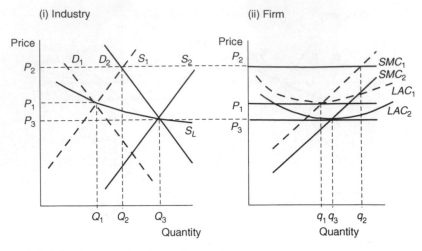

Figure 8.5. Adjustment under decreasing costs.

8.3 Monopoly

After an analysis of perfect competition it is usual to consider monopoly next. Again, this is not because this is a frequently found type of market structure, but because as an extreme form it provides a benchmark for comparison. As we shall see, it can also be claimed that many firms are in effect limited monopolies.

8.3.1 Conditions

Economists have defined monopoly in many different ways. Literally, it means a *single seller* in an industry. However, it is preferable to define a monopoly as being *a firm that has the power to earn supernormal profit in the long run*. This ability depends on two conditions:

1 *There must be a* **lack of substitutes** *for the product*. This means that any existing products are not very close in terms of their perceived functions and characteristics. Electricity is a good example.
2 *There must be* **barriers to entry or exit**. These are important in the long run in order to prevent firms entering the industry and competing away the supernormal profit. We now need to examine them in detail.

8.3.2 Barriers to entry and exit

These can be defined as factors that allow incumbent firms to earn super-normal profits in the long run by making it unprofitable for new firms to enter the industry. It is useful to distinguish between **structural** and **strategic** barriers. Structural barriers, often referred to as natural barriers, occur because of *factors outside the firm's control*, mainly when an incumbent firm has natural cost or marketing advantages, or is aided by government regulations. Strategic barriers occur when an incumbent firm **deliberately deters entry**, using various restrictive practices, some of which may be illegal.

a. Structural barriers

There are six main types of structural barrier.

1. Control of essential resources. This often occurs for geographical reasons, because of the concentration of such resources in certain areas. For example, oil, gas and diamonds are only found in limited supplies and locations; certain areas are very advantageous for the production of quality wines. These resources may also include the expertise of resource owners, who may be skilled surgeons or scientists. Patent ownership is relevant here, although this also relates to the sixth barrier described later.

2. Economies of scale and scope. If these are significant it means that the minimum efficient scale (MES) will be large in the industry, as seen in Chapter 6. In order for new firms to compete in terms of cost they will have to enter on a large scale and this may be a problem if the MES is large compared to market demand. The problem is that the entry of another large firm in the industry would cause a substantial reduction in the market price, thus reducing profitability. Of course the industry would no longer be a monopoly in this situation, but the problem remains that market demand may not be sufficient to support two firms in the industry if the MES is large and the cost structure is high. This situation applies in particular to public utilities, like gas, water and electricity supply; such industries are, therefore, sometimes referred to as natural monopolies.

3. Marketing advantages of incumbents. Brand awareness and image are very important in many industries, with consumers being unwilling to buy unknown brands. This applies more to oligopolistic industries, like electrical and electronic appliances, banking and other financial services, but may also relate to industries like telecommunications. Such brand awareness can take time and a heavy cost to develop.

4. Financial barriers. New firms without a track record find it more difficult and more costly to raise money, because of the greater risk they impose on the lender. This disadvantage does not apply to the same extent to existing firms who are entering a new industry, although even here there are usually additional risks.

5. Information costs. In order for a new firm to enter an industry, or an existing firm to enter a new industry, much market research needs to be carried out to investigate the potential profitability of such entry. This again imposes a cost.

6. Government regulations.   Patent laws have already been mentioned as a reason for blocking the entry of new firms. They are particularly important in an industry like the pharmaceutical industry, where it takes a long time to get approval to use a product after it has originally been developed. Many governments also deliberately create monopolies through a licensing system. Thus public utilities and postal services in many countries operate as legally protected monopolies, with only one firm being allowed to supply the market.

Some of the above barriers also serve as **barriers to exit**; such barriers are in the form of sunk costs. From Chapter 6 it should be remembered that these are costs that are not affected by a particular decision; this means that once the decision to enter an industry has been made, these *costs cannot be recovered by the entrant* should it leave the industry. These costs include advertising costs to create brand awareness, market research costs, loss on the resale of assets, redundancy payments that have to be paid to workers, and so on. The existence of such costs increases the risk of entering a new industry.

b. Strategic barriers

It may be profitable for monopolists to employ strategies that deter entry if such strategies change the expectations of the potential entrants regarding the nature of the market after they have entered. The following strategies to deter entry may be used.

1. Limit pricing.   This refers to the practice where an incumbent tries to discourage entry by *charging a low price before any new firm enters*. However, it has been shown using game theory that this strategy should only work if the potential entrant does not know the cost structure of the incumbent. Otherwise the firm will enter anyway, believing that any price reduction by the incumbent is only temporary; this is because it is rational for the incumbent to raise price after entry, since this would maximize its profit. On the other hand, if the potential entrant does not know the incumbent's cost structure, a low price may fool it into believing that the incumbent has low costs and can profitably maintain the low price[3]. In this case it would not be profitable to enter. The behaviour of incumbent and potential entrant may change over time as the latter may gain more accurate knowledge of the incumbent's cost structure and therefore may be more inclined to enter. Airlines, in particular Continental, have practised limit pricing to discourage competitors on particular routes. Note that the monopoly is limited in this case to that route.

2. Predatory pricing.   This refers to the practice where an incumbent tries to encourage exit, meaning drive firms out of the industry, by *charging a low price after any new firms enter*. Again it has been shown that this strategy should only work if the new entrant does not know the cost structure of the incumbent. The reasoning is basically the same as with limit pricing, and has been illustrated by what is known as 'the chain-store paradox'.[4] In the United States and some other countries predatory pricing is prohibited by law.

3. Excess capacity.   Most firms typically operate at about 80 per cent of full capacity. Firms may have extra capacity for a number of reasons, either deliberate or accidental, but excess capacity can serve as a credible threat to potential entrants. This is because it is easy for incumbents to expand output with little extra cost, thus forcing down the market price and post-entry profits; if these profits are less than the sunk costs of entry, the entrant will be deterred from entering the market. This would apply even if the potential entrant had full knowledge of the incumbent's cost structure.

4. Heavy advertising.   This forces the potential entrant to respond by itself spending more on advertising, which has the effect of increasing its fixed costs, thus increasing the minimum efficient scale in the industry. It also adds to the marketing advantages of the incumbent, as discussed earlier.

These practices will not be possible if the market is **contestable**. The concept of contestable markets was developed by Baumol, Panzar and Willig[5] and is examined in more detail in the next chapter. The following conditions are necessary for a market to be contestable:

1 There are an unlimited number of potential firms that can produce a homogeneous product, with identical technology.
2 Consumers respond quickly to price changes.
3 Incumbent firms cannot respond quickly to entry by reducing price.
4 Entry into the market does not involve any sunk costs.

Under such conditions a monopolist cannot raise price above the level of a perfectly competitive market. The result would be that a firm could enter on a hit-and-run basis, by undercutting the incumbent, and exiting quickly if the incumbent retaliates. Railway operating companies and airlines are generally quoted as examples of industries where such conditions may apply, since firms are supposed to be able to sell the necessary rolling stock or aircraft on secondary markets with no loss.

Unfortunately for the theory there appears to be little empirical evidence supporting it, at least in terms of the airline industry,[6] where it was supposed to apply. This appears to be because it takes longer for firms to enter or leave the industry than it takes to adjust prices. Empirical evidence suggests that entry and exit barriers are often high, causing considerable differences in profitability, both between firms in the same industry and between different industries. Although entry is frequent, both by new firms and by existing firms in other markets, exit is also frequent, and entry does not appear to be that responsive to differences in profitability, or to affect profitability significantly.[7] The most that can be claimed regarding contestability is that some

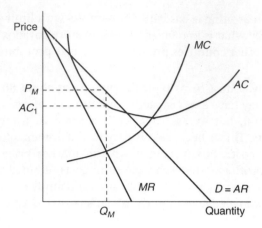

Figure 8.6. Equilibrium in monopoly.

markets are partially contestable, in that monopolists may reduce prices some-what under the threat of potential competition.

This completes the discussion of entry barriers for the moment. Further aspects of this topic will be covered in the next chapter, particularly those relating to game theory and making credible threats, for example threats to enter a market or reduce price.

8.3.3 Graphical analysis of equilibrium

In the case of monopoly the firm and the industry are one and the same thing, and therefore only one graph needs to be drawn. The graph in Figure 8.6 shows a short-run equilibrium situation, but the same will apply in the long run since barriers to entry will prevent new firms from entering. The only difference is that the relevant cost curves would be long-run, as opposed to short-run, cost curves (*LMC* and *LAC* instead of *SMC* and *SAC*). It should be noted that there is no supply curve in this case. This is because a supply curve shows the quantities that producers will put onto the market at different prices, thus assuming that firms are price-takers. A monopoly on the other hand is a price-maker.

This also has implications on the demand side. In perfect competition, price, average revenue and marginal revenue are identical. Thus if the price is £0.52 per litre this will also be the average revenue and marginal revenue for the firm. This is not the case in monopoly, or indeed in any situation where the demand curve is less than perfectly elastic, in other words is downward-sloping. This is because in order to sell more of the product the firm must reduce its price not just on the additional products sold but also on all the other units (unless it is able to practise price discrimination, explained in Chapter 10). This means that marginal revenue will always be less than average revenue. It was shown in Chapter 3 that for a linear demand curve the marginal revenue curve will have twice its slope, and this was illustrated in Figure 3.9. The same principles apply to the situation shown in Figure 8.6.

The profit-maximizing output is given by Q_M, where $MC = MR$. If the monopolist produces less than this output it can increase profit by producing more because it will be adding more to revenue than to costs. Similarly, if the monopolist produces more than Q_M it will be reducing its profit, since it will be adding more to costs than to revenue. The price that this output will fetch on the market is determined by the demand curve; this is the price P_M. Readers should check that they understand the nature of this profit-maximizing position, since it is of fundamental importance in much optimization behaviour.

The profit of the monopolist can also be seen from the graph; the profit per unit is given by $P_M - AC_1$, therefore total profit is given by the area of the rectangle $(P_M - AC_1)Q_M$. Again, as with perfect competition, it should be noted that there is a two-stage procedure involved in the analysis, the first stage examining profit maximization and MC and MR, with the second stage examining the size of the profit and AC and AR.

8.3.4 Algebraic analysis of equilibrium

Let us now assume that the milk market described and analysed in subsection 8.2.4 is supplied by a monopoly rather than a perfectly competitive market. In this case the marginal cost curve will be linear rather than quadratic as portrayed in the previous section, but otherwise the analysis is similar. We therefore have the following functions describing the market:

$$\text{Demand: } Q = 16 - 20P \tag{8.7}$$

$$\text{Marginal cost: } MC = 0.44 + 0.04Q \tag{8.8}$$

$$\text{Total cost: } TC = 0.08 + 0.44Q + 0.02Q^2 \tag{8.9}$$

We are assuming that the fixed costs of the monopolist are the sum of the fixed costs of all the competitive firms. The units are the same as previously. We can now determine the equilibrium of the monopolist by deriving the MR function and setting it equal to the MC function in order to solve for Q. This value can then be substituted into the demand equation to solve for P. To obtain MR we first need to obtain a revenue function in terms of output by multiplying P (given by the demand function) by Q. These steps are now shown in the appropriate sequence:

1 $P = 0.8 - 0.05Q$
2 $R = PQ = (0.8 - 0.05Q)Q = 0.8Q - 0.05Q^2$
3 $MR = 0.8 - 0.1Q$
4 $MC = MR$
  $0.44 + 0.04Q = 0.8 - 0.1Q$
  $0.14Q = 0.36$

$Q = 2.57143$ or **257,143** litres per day

5   $P = 0.8 - 0.05(2.571) = £0.67$

The price is higher and the output lower than in perfect competition and this comparison will be developed further in subsection 8.3.6. Profit can also be calculated by computing the total costs and revenues. Total revenue is £172,286, total cost is £134,244, and this gives a total profit of £37,942 per day. This compares with total profit in the industry of £24,000 per day under perfect competition (in the short run).

8.3.5 Pricing and price elasticity of demand

There are some important relationships between the optimal price (assuming a profit-maximizing objective) and price elasticity of demand (PED). These relationships do not just relate to monopolists but to any firm that has some element of control over price, or in other words faces a downward-sloping demand curve. The simplest of these relationships involves profit margin.

a. Profit margin

Profit margin is defined as **the difference between the price and the marginal cost, expressed as a percentage of the price**. It can thus be written as:

$$M = \frac{P - MC}{P} \times 100 \tag{8.10}$$

The optimal margin will be obtained by setting MC equal to MR. We can now obtain MR in terms of the PED, as follows:

$$MR = \frac{dR}{dQ} = \frac{d(PQ)}{dQ} = P\frac{dQ}{dQ} + Q\frac{dP}{dQ} = P + Q\frac{dP}{dQ} = P + P\frac{Q}{P} \times \frac{dP}{dQ}$$

$$= P\left(1 + \frac{Q}{P} \times \frac{dP}{dQ}\right) \tag{8.11}$$

$$MR = P(1 + 1/\varepsilon)$$

where ε represents the PED. Thus, assuming profit maximization, we can also write:

$$MC = P(1 + 1/\varepsilon) \tag{8.12}$$

We can now obtain the optimal profit margin in terms of the PED:

$$M = \frac{P - P(1 + 1/\varepsilon)}{P} = 1 - (1 + 1/\varepsilon) = -1/\varepsilon \tag{8.13}$$

This shows that products with more elastic demand should have a lower profit margin. Obviously, in perfect competition, when PED is infinite, there is no profit margin because $P = MC$.

Table 8.2. PED and mark-up

PED	Mark-up (%)
− 10	11
− 5	25
− 4	33
− 3	50
− 2	100
− 1.5	200
− 1	∞

b. Mark-up

Many students confuse margin with mark-up. Mark-up is defined as **the differ-ence between the price and the marginal cost, expressed as a percentage of the marginal cost**. It can thus be written as:

$$U = \frac{P - MC}{MC} \times 100 \qquad (8.14)$$

We have seen in (8.12) that at profit maximization $MC = P(1 + 1/\varepsilon)$. Therefore

$$P - \frac{MC}{1 + 1/\varepsilon} \qquad (8.15)$$

We can also write:

$$P = MC(1 + U) \qquad (8.16)$$

Therefore

$$MC(1 + U) = \frac{MC}{1 + 1/\varepsilon}$$

$$1 + U = \frac{1}{1 + 1/\varepsilon}; \quad 1 + U = \frac{1}{\frac{\varepsilon + 1}{\varepsilon}} = \frac{\varepsilon}{\varepsilon + 1}$$

$$U = \frac{\varepsilon}{\varepsilon + 1} - 1 = \frac{\varepsilon - (\varepsilon + 1)}{\varepsilon + 1} = \frac{-1}{\varepsilon + 1} \qquad (8.17)$$

Again we can see that products with more elastic demand should have a lower mark-up. The relationship between PED and mark-up is shown in Table 8.2.

It does not follow that firms or industries with higher margins and mark-ups are more profitable. For one thing, when managers refer to mark-ups they often do not use the same measure of cost that economists use. Some of these problems of cost measurement were discussed in Chapter 6. Managers, for example, often use some measure of average variable cost or average total cost, and do not take into account opportunity costs. This tends to result in mark-ups that are greater than true economic mark-ups. However, even

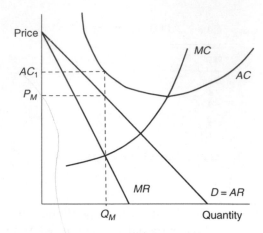

Figure 8.7. Loss-making monopoly.

when mark-up is measured in economic terms, a high mark-up does not necessarily indicate high profit, because it does not take into account the level of fixed costs. In some industries, fixed costs and mark-ups are very high. For example, in the airline industry capital costs are very high; in the breakfast cereal industry a very high proportion of revenue is spent on advertising and promotion (35 per cent); in the pharmaceutical industry huge amounts are spent on R&D. This leads us on to two common misconceptions regarding monopoly:

1 Monopolies always make large profits.
2 Monopolies have inelastic demand.

The first misconception can easily be seen to be incorrect by examining the performance of the state-run monopolies in the UK and elsewhere in Europe before privatization programmes began in the 1980s. These industries invariably made considerable losses, an issue examined in more detail in Chapter 12. A more theoretical approach is used in Figure 8.7. This graph is essentially the same as in Figure 8.6, but with the average cost curve shifted upwards. The equilibrium price and output are the same as before, but in this case a loss is made, given by $(AC_1 - P_M)Q_M$. This loss is unavoidable because the AC curve always lies above the demand curve; there is no output where the monopoly can cover its costs. Unless such a firm is state-subsidized it will not stay in business in the long run.

The second misconception, regarding monopolies having inelastic demand can be seen as false by recalling an important conclusion from Chapter 3: a firm will always maximize profit by charging a price where demand is elastic. We can also use Table 8.2 to see this; as demand approaches unit elasticity the optimal mark-up approaches infinity. There is therefore no reason for a firm to charge a price where demand has less than unit elasticity, in other words where demand is inelastic.

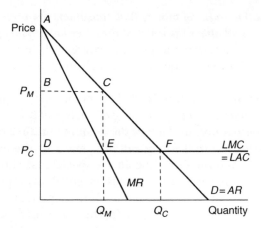

Figure 8.8. Comparison of perfect competition and monopoly.

8.3.6 *Comparison of monopoly with perfect competition*

There are four factors that can be compared here: price, output, profit and efficiency. It is helpful for analysis if both forms of market structure are shown on the same graph, as in Figure 8.8. This gives a long-run perspective. For the sake of simplicity it is assumed that long-run marginal costs are constant. This indicates that there are constant returns to scale, so that LMC and LAC are equal. P_M and Q_M represent the price and output of the monopolist and P_C and Q_C represent the price and total output of the industry in perfect competition (PC).

The factors listed above can now be examined in turn.

a. *Price.* In monopoly the price is higher than in PC.
b. *Output.* In monopoly the output is lower than in PC.
c. *Profit.* There is an element of supernormal profit in monopoly, given by the area of the rectangle BCED, although as we have just seen this is not always the case in monopoly. In perfect competition the price and long-run average cost are equal, resulting in only normal profit being made.

The fourth factor listed was *efficiency.* We now need to explain the difference between productive and allocative efficiency, the other type of efficiency mentioned earlier in the section on perfect competition.

1. *Productive efficiency.* In Figure 8.8 both the monopolist and the firm in PC are achieving productive efficiency, since they both have a constant level of LAC. However, if the monopolist has a rising LMC curve as in Figure 8.6, it will not be producing at the minimum point of its LAC curve, but at a point to the left of this. It will therefore not be achieving productive efficiency. The monopolist will be using too small a scale, and using it at less than optimal capacity.

2. *Allocative efficiency.* This refers to **the optimal allocation of resources in the economy as a whole**. In order to consider this aspect we need to introduce the concepts of consumer surplus and producer surplus. **Consumer surplus**

represents *the total amount of money that consumers are prepared to pay for a certain output over and above the amount that they have to pay for this output*. It is given by the area between the demand curve and the price line. Thus in perfect competition the consumer surplus is given by the area of triangle AFD in Figure 8.8.

Producer surplus, sometimes called economic rent, represents *the total amount of money that producers, meaning all factors of production, receive for selling a certain output over and above the amount that they need to receive to stay in their existing use in the long run*. It is given by the area between the marginal cost curve and the price line. In the special case shown in Figure 8.8 where *MC* is constant, producer surplus is equal to supernormal profit. However, if the *MC* curve is rising and there is perfect competition, the producer surplus will not be realized in the form of supernormal profit, since this will be competed away. The surplus will instead be distributed to the other factors of production, such as labour.

In order to examine and compare the allocative efficiency of the two types of market structure we need to consider the effects on total economic welfare of a change from perfect competition to monopoly. In perfect competition, total welfare is maximized because output is such that price equals marginal cost. This condition for allocative efficiency means that total welfare cannot be increased by any reallocation of resources; any gain for producers will be more than offset by a greater loss for consumers. In monopoly, output is such that price exceeds marginal cost, meaning that consumers would value any additional output more than it would cost the monopolist to produce it. However, it would not profit the monopolist to produce the additional output because their marginal revenue would fall below marginal cost. The total welfare loss can be seen in Figure 8.8. Although producers gain a surplus of BCED, as already mentioned, the size of the consumer surplus is reduced from AFD to ACB. This means that there is an *overall loss of welfare*, sometimes called a **deadweight loss**, of CFE.

One might ask at this point what relevance the total economic welfare aspects have for managerial decision-making; after all, managers are only concerned with the welfare of the firm. The reason for their relevance is that they affect government policy. As will be seen in more detail in Chapter 12, most governments monitor monopolistic industries and take an active role in discouraging restrictive practices. The impact of such policies on firms' strategies and profits can be considerable.

So far the picture painted of monopoly is an unfavourable one. However, to present a more balanced picture, it is necessary to stress that the analysis to this point has made some important and restrictive assumptions. For one thing, economies of scale have been ignored. In some industries, as seen in Chapter 6, these are of very great importance. Therefore, in industries like public utilities a monopoly may be able to produce more output more cheaply than firms in perfect competition, since firms can avoid the wasteful duplication of infrastructure like pipelines, railway tracks and cable lines.

Another factor ignored up to this point concerns the dynamic aspects of monopoly. Dynamic aspects relate to all the factors that influence economic change and growth over time. Most economists believe that such factors, such as R&D and innovation, are much more important than efficiency as far as long-run growth in productivity and living standards is concerned. In the comparative static analysis used above it is not possible to estimate the incentive effects that monopoly may have on R&D and innovation. Since a monopoly has the ability to profit from these over the long run, it may have a greater incentive to conduct R&D and develop new products than a firm in PC, which knows that any profit from such activities will rapidly be competed away. Empirical evidence regarding these aspects is somewhat inconclusive at present.

There now follows a case study on electricity generation, which explores in particular the relationships between cost structure and market structure, along with the impact of new technology.

Case study 8.1: Electricity generation

Here and now[8]

Distributed power generation will end the long-distance tyranny of the grid.

For decades, control over energy has been deemed too important to be left to the markets. Politicians and officials have been dazzled by the economies of scale promised by ever bigger power plants, constructed a long way from consumers. They have put up with the low efficiency of those plants, and the environmental harm they do, because they have accepted that the generation, transmission and distribution of power must be controlled by the government or another monopoly.

Yet in the beginning things were very different. When Thomas Edison set up his first heat-and-power co-generation plant near Wall Street more than 100 years ago, he thought the best way to meet customers' needs would be to set up networks of decentralised power plants in or near homes and offices. Now, after a century that saw power stations getting ever bigger, transmission grids spreading ever wider and central planners growing ever stronger, the wheel has come full circle. The bright new hope is micropower, a word coined by Seth Dunn of the WorldWatch Institute in an excellent report.* Energy prices are increasingly dictated by markets, not monopolies, and power is increasingly generated close to the end-user rather than at distant stations. Edison's dream is being revived.

The new power plants of choice the world over are using either natural gas or renewable energy, and are smaller, nimbler, cleaner and closer to the end-user than the giants of yesteryear. That means power no longer depends on the vagaries of the grid, and is more responsive to the needs of the consumer. This is a compelling advantage in rich countries, where the digital revolution is fuelling the thirst for high-quality, reliable power that the antiquated grid seems unable to deliver. California provides the best evidence: although the utilities have not built a single power plant over the past decade, individuals and companies have added a whopping 6gW of non-utility micropower over that period, roughly the equivalent of the state's installed nuclear capacity. The argument in favour of micropower is even more persuasive in developing countries, where the grid has largely failed the poor.

This is not to say that the existing dinosaurs of power generation are about to disappear. Because the existing capital stock is often already paid for, the marginal cost of running existing power plants can be very low. That is why America's coal-fired plants, which produce over half the country's power today, will go on until the end of their useful lives, perhaps decades from now – unless governments withdraw the concessions allowing them to exceed current emissions standards.

While nobody is rushing to build new nuclear plants, old ones may have quite a lot of life left in them if they are properly run, as the success of the Three Mile Island nuclear power plant in Pennsylvania attests. After the near-catastrophic accident in 1979 that destroyed one of the plant's two reactors, the remaining one now boasts an impressive safety and financial record. Safety and financial success are intimately linked, says Corbin McNeill, chairman of Exelon and the current owner of the revived plant. He professes to be an environmentalist, and accepts that nuclear power is unlikely to be the energy of choice in the longer term: 'A hundred years from now, I have no doubt that we will get our energy using hydrogen.' But he sees nuclear energy as an essential bridge to that future, far greener than fossil fuels because it emits no carbon dioxide.

GOOD OLD GRID

The rise of micropower does not mean that grid power is dead. On the contrary, argues CERA, a robust grid may be an important part of a micropower future. In poor countries, the grid is often so shoddy and inadequate that distributed energy could well supplant it; that would make it a truly disruptive technology. However, in rich countries, where nearly everyone has access to power, micropower is much more likely to grow alongside the grid. Not only can the owners of distributed generators tap into the grid for back-up power, but utilities can install micropower plants close to consumers to avoid grid bottlenecks.

However, a lot of work needs to be done before any of this can happen. Walt Patterson of the Royal Institute of International Affairs, a British think-tank, was one of the first to spot the trend toward micropower. He argues that advances in software and electronics hold the key to micropower, as they offer new and more flexible ways to link parts of electricity systems together. First, today's antiquated grid, designed when power flowed from big plants to distant consumers, must be upgraded to handle tomorrow's complex, multi-directional flows. Yet in many deregulated markets, including America's, grid operators have not been given adequate financial incentives to make these investments. To work effectively, micropower also needs modern command and communications software.

Another precondition is the spread of real-time electricity meters to all consumers. Consumers who prefer stable prices will be able to choose hedged contracts; others can buy and sell power, much as day traders bet on shares today. More likely, their smart micropower plants, in cahoots with hundreds of others, will automatically do it for them.

In the end, though, it will not be the technology that determines the success of distributed generation, but a change in the way that people think about electricity. CERA concludes that for distributed energy, that will mean the transition from an equipment business to a service business. Already, companies that used to do nothing but sell equipment are considering rental and leasing to make life easier for the user.

Forward-looking firms such as ABB, a Swiss-Swedish equipment supplier, are now making the shift from building centralised power plants to nurturing micropower. ABB is already working on developing 'microgrids' that can electronically link together dozens of micropower units, be they fuel cells or wind turbines.

Kurt Yeager of the Electric Power Research Institute speaks for many in the business when he sums up the prospects: 'Today's technological revolution in power is the most dramatic we have seen since Edison's day, given the spread of distributed generation, transportation using electric drives, and the convergence of electricity with gas and even telecoms. Ultimately, this century will be truly the century of electricity, with the microchip as the ultimate customer.'

* 'Micropower: the next electrical era', by Seth Dunn. WorldWatch Institute, 2000.

Questions

1 Explain why power generation has traditionally been a monopoly in all developed countries.
2 What is meant by a transmission grid? How is this feature related to a monopolistic market structure?
3 What is meant by micropower? What are its implications for grid systems?
4 What are the implications of micropower for the environment?
5 How do you think changes in technology will affect the market structure of the power generation industry?

8.4 Monopolistic competition

Although economics textbooks tend to concentrate more on discussing perfect competition and monopoly, monopolistic competition and oligopoly are more prevalent in practice. The theory of monopolistic competition, as an intermediate form of market structure between perfect competition and monopoly, was originally developed by Chamberlin[9] in 1933. Its characteristics were summarized in Table 8.1 and we can now examine the conditions for monopolistic competition in more detail.

8.4.1 Conditions

There are five main conditions for monopolistic competition to exist:

1 There are many buyers and sellers in the industry.
2 Each firm produces a slightly differentiated product.
3 There are minimal barriers to entry or exit.
4 All firms have identical cost and demand functions.
5 Firms do not take into account competitors' behaviour in determining price and output.

As far as the first condition is concerned, there may be a few large dominant firms with a large fringe of smaller firms, or there may be no very large firms but just a large number of small firms. Grocery retailing is an example of the first situation, while the car repair industry is an example of the second. In both cases there is product differentiation, and the significance of this is that firms are not price-takers, but, rather, have some control over market price. However, this control is not as great as that of the monopolist for two reasons. First the firms' products have closer substitutes than the product of a monopolist, making demand more elastic. The second reason is related to the third condition above: the low barriers to entry mean that any supernormal profit is competed away in the long run. This also involves the fourth condition, that firms have identical cost curves. We can now examine this situation graphically.

8.4.2 Graphical analysis of equilibrium

In the short run the equilibrium of the firm in monopolistic competition is very similar to that of the monopolist. Profit is again maximized by producing the output where $MC = MR$. Supernormal profit can be made, depending on the position of the AC curve, because the number of firms in the industry is fixed. The only real difference between the two situations is that in Figure 8.9, relating to monopolistic competition, the demand curve (and hence the MR curve) is flatter than the demand curve in Figure 8.6 relating to monopoly. This is because of the greater availability of substitutes.

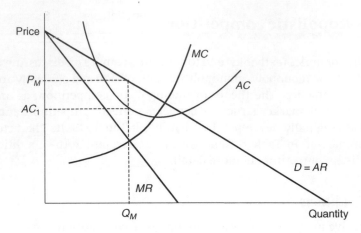

Figure 8.9. Short-run equilibrium for firms in monopolistic competition.

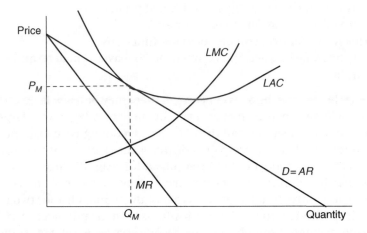

Figure 8.10. Long-run equilibrium for firms in monopolistic competition.

In the long run, new firms will enter the industry, attracted by the supernormal profit. This will have the effect of shifting the demand curve downwards for existing firms. The downward shift will continue until the demand curve becomes tangential to the AC curve (LAC in this case), at which point all supernormal profit will have been competed away. This situation is illustrated in Figure 8.10.

8.4.3 Algebraic analysis of equilibrium

Let us take a market where firms have the following demand and cost functions:

$$\text{Demand}: P = 140 - 4Q$$
$$\text{Cost}: TC = 120Q - 12Q^2 + 2Q^3$$

where P is in £, TC is in £ and Q is in thousand units.

In this case the total cost function is a cubic function, with no fixed costs (for the sake of simplicity).

$$MR = 140 - 8Q$$

$$MC = 120 - 24Q + 6Q^2$$

$$140 - 8Q = 120 - 24Q + 6Q^2$$

$$6Q^2 - 16Q - 20 = 0$$

$$Q = \frac{16 \pm \sqrt{[16^2 - (4)(6)(-20)]}}{12} = 3.594 = \textbf{3,594 units}$$

$$P = \textbf{£125.60}$$

$$\text{Profit} = (P - AC)Q$$

$$AC = 120 - 12(3.594) - 2(3.594)^2 = £102.70$$

$$\text{Profit} = (125.6 - 102.7)3.594 = 82.30 = £82,300$$

This profit will attract new entrants into the industry in the long run, causing the demand curve for existing firms to shift downwards. We will assume that this is a parallel shift, with no change in slope; in other words, there is no change in the marginal effect of price on sales. We will also assume for simplicity that the long-run cost curves are identical to the short-run curves. The new demand curve faced by firms is given by:

$P = a - 4Q$ where a is a constant to be determined

$$MR = a - 8Q$$

$$MC = 120 - 24Q + 6Q^2 = a - 8Q$$

$$a = 120 - 16Q + 6Q^2$$

In long-run equilibrium, $P = AC$, as all supernormal profit is competed away.

$$a - 4Q = 120 - 12Q + 2Q^2$$

$$a = 120 - 8Q + 2Q^2$$

Thus:

$$120 - 16Q + 6Q^2 = 120 - 8Q + 2Q^2$$

$$4Q^2 = 8Q$$

$$Q = 2 = \textbf{2,000 units}$$

$$a = 120 - 16(2) + 6(2)^2 = 112$$

New demand curve is:

$P = 112 - 4Q$

$P = 112 - 4(2) = £104$

8.4.4 Comparison with perfect competition and monopoly

There are four areas where comparison can be made:

a. *Price*. This tends to be higher than in perfect competition (PC), being above the minimum level of average cost, in both the short run and the long run (similar to monopoly).

b. *Output*. This tends to be lower than in PC, since firms are using a less than optimal scale, at less than optimal capacity (similar to monopoly).

c. *Productive efficiency*. This is lower than in PC, for the reason stated previously.

d. *Allocative efficiency*. There is still a net welfare loss, because $P > MC$.

It is to be noted that even though no supernormal profit is made in the long run, neither productive nor allocative efficiency is achieved. This has led a number of people to criticize the marketing function of firms. This activity creates product differentiation and is thus claimed to cause inefficiency. In order to evaluate this argument one would also have to assess the benefits of the marketing function in terms of increasing customer awareness and knowledge, and reducing transaction costs.

Some of the assumptions involved in the above analysis should be examined at this stage. The last three conditions in subsection 8.4.1 are all questionable in terms of their realism. Entry and exit barriers may be low rather than non-existent, and some firms may be more efficient than others. Thus the relaxation of the third and fourth assumptions may result in some firms being able to make supernormal profit in the long run. Only the marginal firm, meaning the least efficient firm, may in fact just be making normal profit, while all other firms make some amount of supernormal profit, depending on their efficiency and the level of entry and exit barriers.

8.4.5 Comparison with oligopoly

It is the last assumption, regarding the independence of firms' decision-making that has attracted the most attention from economists. Many economists claim for example that monopolistic competition is not really a distinct form of market structure.[10,11] This claim is based on the observation that firms are typically faced with competition from a limited number of neighbouring firms, with markets being segmented spatially. Segmentation may also be in terms of product characteristics.

An example will illustrate this situation. The restaurant industry is not a single market. An individual restaurant does not compete with all other restaurants in the country, or even in the same town. It may compete with other restaurants within a one-mile radius; furthermore, it may not compete strongly with some of these restaurants because they are not seen as being close substitutes. Thus an Indian restaurant may not compete with Italian, French, Greek or Mexican restaurants to any great degree. This degree of competition can be examined empirically by measuring the cross elasticity of demand. Of course, it can be argued that if there are few competitors then the product is not *slightly* differentiated, as required in monopolistic competition, but highly differentiated. However, regardless of how the assumptions of monopolistic competition are violated, it seems that in view of these factors it is often preferable to consider firms in many situations as being involved in a system of intersecting oligopolies, with low entry and exit barriers.

It is to oligopoly that we must now turn our attention. However, before doing this, it is useful to consider a situation that has received much attention in the media lately, since it relates to price-fixing and cartels. The situation is examined in more detail in Chapter 12, when competition policy is discussed, but it is appropriate to consider certain aspects in the current context.

Case study 8.2: Price cuts for medicines

Chemists at risk as prices are slashed[12]

BY NIGEL HAWKES, HEALTH EDITOR

Big price cuts on a wide range of medicines and vitamins were promised by the supermarket chains yesterday as 30 years of price-fixing were swept aside.

Many popular products, including painkillers, cough medicines, indigestion tablets and nutritional supplements are being halved in price from last night, with reductions of between 20 and 40 per cent on many others.

The Office of Fair Trading called it excellent news for consumers but the body representing small pharmacies said that many would close, threatening community services.

The big supermarkets trumpeted 'millions of pounds-worth of savings' as they competed to offer the biggest reductions. At Asda, a packet of 16 regular Anadin will be 87p, instead of £1.75, and Nurofen tablets will cost £1.14 for 16, rather than £2.29.

Reductions at Tesco included a 40 per cent cut in Anadin Extra, to £1.29 for 16, while Sainsbury's matched the Asda price for Nurofen, and reduced Seven Seas Evening Primrose Oil from £5.59 for a 60-pack to £2.79.

The cuts came after the Community Pharmacy Action Group, representing small retailers, withdrew its opposition to a High Court action brought by the Office of Fair Trading. The OFT had sought the abolition of resale price maintenance in the industry, exempted 30 years ago from general price-fixing rules to try to ensure the survival of small pharmacies. There are 13,500 pharmacies in Britain, of which 9,000 are small shops serving local high streets and rural communities.

The action group backed out after Mr Justice Buckley said that he believed there was insufficient proof that a large number of independent pharmacies would close, or that the range of products would be reduced. But the group's chairman, David Sharpe, said that the outcome would be a devastating blow. 'Many pharmacists will simply not be able to survive given the buying power and aggressive pricing of the supermarkets' he said. 'It's a sad day for Britain. The potential losers are the elderly, disabled and young mothers who rely on the free advice and range of services offered by the local pharmacist. We'll fight on and hope the public will remain loyal.'

The changes will cover about 2,500 products sold without requiring a doctor's prescription, and will have no effect on prescription drugs or on cosmetics sold by pharmacists.

Prices are likely to fall even lower as competition grows. In the United States, where prices are unregulated, comparable products are markedly cheaper.

Richard Hyman, chairman of the Verdict retail research consultancy, said: 'This is a market made for supermarkets. Medicines are small, they fit on shelves and supermarkets are going to make a lot of noise about the great prices that they will be offering. Soon medicines will become like any other product and be part of the weekly shop.'

John Vickers, Director-General of Fair Trading, said: 'This is excellent news for consumers, who will now benefit from lower and more competitive prices for common household medicines. Consumers will save many millions of pounds a year.'

The Proprietary Association of Great Britain, which represents medicine and food supplement manufacturers, said it was disappointed.

Questions

1 What kind of market structure is involved for the sale of medicines and vitamins?
2 What can be said about barriers to entry in this market?
3 Might there be a change in market structure after the change in the law?
4 Explain the disadvantages of the abolition of resale price maintenance (RPM) for this market.
5 When RPM was abolished for book sales in 1995, the same concerns as those expressed in the above case were voiced. Since then, 10 per cent of bookshops have gone out of business. What conclusions might this help you to draw regarding the future of small pharmacies?
6 How does the rise of the Internet affect this situation?

8.5 Oligopoly

An oligopolistic market structure describes the situation where a few firms dominate the industry. The product may be standardized or differentiated; examples of the first type are steel, chemicals and paper, while examples of the second type are cars, electronics products and breakfast cereals. The most important feature of such markets that distinguishes them from all other types of market structure is that firms are interdependent. Strategic decisions made by one firm affect other firms, who react to them in ways that affect the original firm. Thus firms have to consider these reactions in determining their own strategies. Such markets are extremely common for both consumer and industrial products, both in individual countries and on a global basis. However, there is a considerable amount of heterogeneity within such markets. Some feature one dominant firm, like Intel in computer chips; some feature two dominant firms, like Coca-Cola and Pepsi in soft drinks; some feature half a dozen or so major firms, like airlines, mobile phones or athletic footwear; and others feature a dozen or more firms with no really dominant firm, like car manufacturers, petroleum retailers, and investment banks. Of course, in each case the number of major firms depends on how the market is defined, spatially and in terms of product characteristics.

8.5.1 Conditions

The main conditions for oligopoly to exist are therefore as follows:

1 A relatively small number of firms account for the majority of the market.
2 There are significant barriers to entry and exit.
3 There is an interdependence in decision-making.

As far as the first condition is concerned there are a number of measures that are used to indicate the degree of **market concentration** in an industry. The easiest to interpret are the four-firm or eight-firm **concentration ratios**. These indicate *the proportion of the total market sales accounted for by the largest four or eight firms in the industry*. A more detailed measure, though more difficult to interpret, is the **Herfindahl index**. This index is computed by taking *the sum of the squares of the market shares of all the firms in the industry*. For example, if two firms account for the whole market on a 50:50 basis, the Herfindahl index (H) would be $(0.5)^2 + (0.5)^2 = 0.5$. In general terms, the index is given by:

$$H = \Sigma S^2 \qquad (8.18)$$

where $S =$ the proportion of the total market sales accounted for by each firm in the industry. A value of this index above 0.2 normally indicates that the market structure is oligopolistic. Another measure, related to the Herfindahl index but easier to interpret, is the **numbers-equivalent of firms** (NEF); this is given by *the reciprocal of the H value*. It corresponds to the number of firms that would exist in the industry, given a certain value of H, assuming that all firms had an equal market share. We can see in the example of two firms above that the NEF $= 1/0.5 = 2$. Thus an industry with an H-value of 0.2 corresponds to a situation where the market is shared by five firms equally.

In order for oligopolies to evolve and maintain their market structure there must be significant barriers to entry and exit. These barriers have been discussed in the section on monopoly, but economies of scale, sunk costs and brand recognition are all important. Such barriers prevent or discourage the entry of new firms and allow existing firms to make supernormal profit, even in the long run. The strategic use of these barriers is discussed in the next chapter.

The third condition above, interdependence in decision-making, is also discussed in the next chapter. This is because the kind of analysis involved is different from that so far discussed, and is heavily dependent on a branch of decision theory known as game theory. This requires a fairly lengthy exposition in order to convey the important principles, and some of the material is advanced in nature. Therefore, it is important to stress that this chapter will present only a brief overview of the essential aspects of oligopolistic market structures. This means that the only model introduced at this stage is a highly simplified and in many ways incomplete model. The more complex and realistic models are developed in the next chapter.

8.5.2 The kinked demand curve model

This model was originally developed by Sweezy[13] and has been commonly used to explain **price rigidities** in oligopolistic markets. A price rigidity refers to a situation where *firms tend to maintain their prices at the same level in spite*

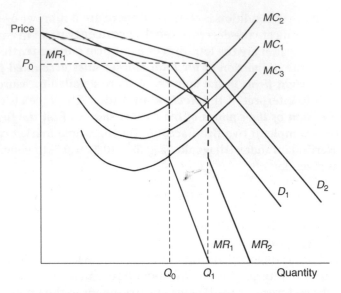

Figure 8.11. The kinked demand curve and price rigidity.

of changes in demand or cost conditions. The model assumes that if an oligopolist cuts its prices, competitors will quickly react to this by cutting their own prices in order to prevent losing market share. On the other hand, if one firm raises its price, it is assumed that competitors do not match the price rise, in order to gain market share at the expense of the first firm. In this case the demand curve facing a firm would be much more elastic for price increases than for price reductions. This results in the kinked demand curve shown in Figure 8.11. It should be noted that this is not a 'true' demand curve as defined in Chapter 3, since it no longer assumes that other things remain equal, apart from the price charged by the firm. If the price charged falls below P_0, it is assumed that other firms react to this and reduce their own prices. We might call it an 'effective' demand curve.

The kink in the demand curve causes a discontinuity or break in the MR curve. The consequence of this is that if the marginal cost function shifts from the original function MC_1 upwards or downwards within the range from MC_2 to MC_3, then the profit-maximizing output will remain at Q_0 and the price will remain at P_0, since the MC curve passes through the MR curve in the vertical break. Similarly, if the demand curve shifts from D_1 to D_2, the MR curve will shift to the right to MR_2, but the original MC curve will still pass through the vertical break. This means that the profit-maximizing output will increase from Q_0 to Q_1, but the price will remain the same at P_0. The reason for this is that the vertical break occurs below the kink in the demand curve, which is at the prevailing price P_0.

The above model can be criticized on three main grounds:

1 It takes the prevailing price as given; there is no attempt to explain how this prevailing price is determined in the first place.

2 It makes unrealistic assumptions regarding firms' behaviour in terms of following price increases. It will be seen in the next chapter that there may be good reasons for following a price increase as well as following a decrease.

3 Empirical evidence does not generally support the model.[14] As mentioned above, in reality firms tend to follow price increases just as much as they follow price reductions.

In spite of the above shortcomings the kinked demand curve model remains a popular approach to analysing oligopolistic behaviour. For one thing, it suggests that firms are likely to co-operate on the monopoly price, and this fact is easily observed in practice. We now need to turn our attention to such co-operation.

8.5.3 Collusion and cartels

Collusion is the term frequently used to refer to **co-operative behaviour** between firms in an oligopolistic market. Such collusion may be explicit or tacit; this chapter discusses the first type of collusion, whereas the next chapter discusses the second type. Explicit collusion often involves the firms forming a **cartel**. This is **an agreement among firms, of a formal or informal nature, to determine prices, total industry output, market shares or the distribution of profits**. Most such agreements are illegal in developed countries, though they are still widely practised on an informal basis because their existence is difficult to prove. In some cases, cartels are actually encouraged and protected by governments, for example the various agricultural marketing boards in the UK and in other countries. There are also producers' associations, for example representing taxi drivers, which may have the legal right to restrict entry into the industry, at least on a local scale. On an international basis the best-known cartel is OPEC, the Organization of Petroleum Exporting Countries, which has existed for decades with a mixed record of success for its members. The most important issues to discuss regarding cartels are first the incentives to form them, and second the factors determining their likely success.

a. Incentives

Firms in an oligopolistic market structure can increase profit by forming a cartel. This is most easily explained by considering a simple example. Let us take an industry producing a standardized product, with just two firms; the market demand curve is $P = 400 - 2Q$, with each firm having a constant marginal cost of £40 and no fixed costs. This situation is shown in Figure 8.12. Essentially the situation is similar to that in Figure 8.8, comparing perfect competition and monopoly. If the two firms compete in price (so-called Bertrand competition), the price will be forced down to the level of marginal cost. This is because each firm can grab 100 per cent of the market share by undercutting the competitor, so this undercutting will continue until all

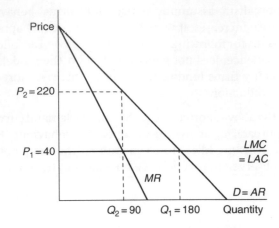

Figure 8.12. Effects of a cartel.

supernormal profit is competed away. Obviously the price will be £40 in this case, and the total market output will be 180 units (from the demand equation).

If the firms form a cartel they can charge the monopoly price. In order to determine this we have to determine the output where $MC = MR$. This is done as follows:

$P = 400 - 2Q$

$R = 400 - 2Q^2$

$MR = 400 - 4Q$

$MC = 40$

$400 - 4Q = 40$

$4Q = 360, \ \mathbf{Q} = 90$

$\mathbf{P} = 400 - 2(90) = \mathbf{£220}$

In this case the industry will make a profit given by

$$(P - AC)Q = (220 - 40)90 = \mathbf{£16,200}.$$

Thus, assuming that the profits are shared equally, each firm can make a profit of £8,100. This is clearly preferable to the competitive situation. At this stage we are ignoring the more complicated situation where the firms compete in terms of output by considering what output the other firm will put on the market. This is called Cournot competition, and both Cournot and Bertrand competition are discussed in the next chapter.

Although both firms can make supernormal profit by forming a cartel, this profit can only be sustained if the firms agree to restrict total output. This usually involves setting output quotas for each firm; in the above example the quotas would be 45 units each. The enforcement of output quotas creates a problem for cartels; each member firm can usually profit at the expense of the others by 'cheating' and producing more than its output quota, thus making the cartel unstable. We now need to consider the factors that affect the likelihood of success of a cartel.

b. Factors affecting success of a cartel

There are a number of factors that are relevant, and the most important ones are examined here.

1. Number of sellers. As the number of sellers increases it is more likely that individual firms will ignore the effects of their pricing and output on other firms, since these will be smaller. A big increase in one firm's output will not have as much effect on the industry price when there are a dozen firms in the industry than when there are just two firms. Furthermore, firms are more likely to have disagreements regarding price and output strategies if there are more firms, and therefore they are again more likely to act independently. This has been a problem for OPEC because of the relatively large number of members. OPEC's problems are increased because, having once controlled 55 per cent of world oil output, it currently only controls less than 30 per cent.

2. Product differentiation. Co-operation is easier for firms if they are producing a homogeneous or standardized product, because in this case the firms can only compete in terms of price. With differentiated products competition can occur over a whole array of product characteristics. Even with a product like crude oil there is not complete homogeneity; there are different grades according to country of origin, and sellers can also vary payment terms as a form of competition.

3. Cost structures. As with differences in product, differences in cost structures can make co-operation more difficult. Co-operation is also more difficult in capital-intensive industries where fixed costs are a high proportion of total costs. This is because if firms are operating at less than full capacity it is possible to increase profits considerably by increasing output and cutting prices.

4. Transparency. If the market is transparent it will not be possible for a firm to undercut its competitors secretly. Cartels may therefore take steps to publicize information regarding the transactions of members in order to prevent them from conducting secret negotiations. However, it may still be possible to hide certain details of transactions, such as payment terms, which in effect can amount to a price reduction.

Because many of the above characteristics have not been favourable, many cartels have proved to be unstable in practice, and have been short-lived. Again, the stability of cartels is examined in the next chapter, since the behaviour of the members tends to conform to a repeated game. Some cartels in Europe that have in the past enjoyed government protection, for example the coal and steel industries, are now also in trouble; recent pressures related to competition in the so-called single market have undone much of this valued protection. However, recent protectionist measures by the US administration involving these industries and others may change this picture to some extent. These aspects of government policy will be examined in more detail in Chapter 12.

8.5.4 Price leadership

A commonly observed pattern of behaviour in oligopolistic industries is the situation where one firm sets a price or initiates price changes, and other firms follow the leader with a short time lag, usually just a few days. There are various ways in which such behaviour can occur, depending on two main factors.

1. *Product differentiation.* For homogeneous products the followers normally adjust their prices to the same level as the leader. In the more common case of differentiated products the price followers generally conform to some structure of recognized price differentials in relation to the leader. Thus Ford may adjust the prices of various models so that they are given percentages lower or higher than some benchmark GM model.

2. *Type of leadership.* There are two main possibilities here. **Dominant** price leadership refers to the situation where the price leader is usually the largest firm in the industry. In this case the leader is fairly certain of how other firms will react to its price changes, in terms of their conforming to some general price structure, as described above. This certainty may be increased by the implicit threat of retaliation if a competitor does not follow the leader. The other main type of price leadership is called **barometric**. This time the price leader is not necessarily the largest firm, and leaders may frequently change. There is more uncertainty in this case regarding competitive reactions, but the leader is normally reacting to changes in market demand or cost conditions, and suggesting to other firms that it is in their interests to follow the changes.

When prices and outputs are determined under a price leadership situation there is no explicit collusion among firms, even though the almost simultaneous price changes may cause consumers and regulatory authorities to be suspicious. In the next chapter we shall see what makes firms conform to such changes so quickly. The following case studies examine the factors which can affect the success of collusion in two industries that have been exposed to the media spotlight.

Case study 8.3: Mobile phone networks

Predatory roaming[15]

They were in the bank, toting guns, as lots of money happened to go from the vault. That was the essence of last week's claim by Mario Monti, the European Union's competition commissioner, that mobile-phone operators have gouged customers by colluding to raise rates for roaming – ie, when you use your mobile phone abroad. Mr Monti's case is circumstantial, but he says the network operators will have to answer it.

In December Mr Monti's office issued a report on the market for roaming. Most countries in the European Economic Area (EEA), the report found, have a roaming market that is ripe for collusion. The product is undifferentiated, and the number of sellers small. Pricing in the wholesale market is transparent, making it easy for a market leader to raise prices, and for other operators to take the hint and follow suit. The costs of running mobile networks do not vary that much. As a result, says the report, sellers' pricing structures tend to run in parallel, at 'high and rigid' levels. Mr Monti cites 'an almost complete absence of competition', and says that 'prices appear to be converging', towards €1 (89 cents) a minute.

To be fair, the conditions for collusion, apart from the small number of sellers cited above, could also be present in a perfectly competitive market. And retail prices in Europe are not quite as similar as Mr Monti's comments suggest. For a call from Belgium to Britain today, using a British mobile phone, rates range from 51p (73 cents) to 99p a minute. Rates for receiving calls also vary widely. On One2One, a monthly charge of only £2.50 can lower the receiving rate from 76p to 16p. That is an indication of just how low the marginal cost of roaming calls might be.

Looking closely at wholesale rates, the commission found that the cheapest in Europe were about €0.46 a minute. In Belgium, Britain, the Netherlands and Norway, some operators had rates at least twice as high as the average of the five cheapest. Yet even the lowest wholesale rates in Europe may be gouging consumers. Just look at what is on offer in North America. MicroCellnet, a Canadian operator that has 1m customers, recently launched a flat-rate American roaming service: for customers on a standard monthly service agreement, the retail price of calls made anywhere to Canada or within the United States is 20 cents a minute – less than half even the lowest wholesale rates in Europe.

Perhaps Europe's costs are so different from North America's that they justify BT Cellnet's roaming rate of 99p a minute? It seems unlikely. Chris Doyle, an economist at Charles River Associates, points out that roaming generates up to 35% of European operators' revenues, although it accounts for a much smaller share of the time customers spend on the telephone. Asked exactly what costs and market forces determine its roaming rates, BT Cellnet says the question is 'too commercially sensitive to answer'.

Market concentration also points to a lack of competition. In each of 11 EEA countries, a single operator had a market share of at least 50%. Still, the biggest obstacle to a competitive market for roaming may be the ease with which the operators can exploit consumers. They have little incentive to compete over roaming rates – to quit the cartel, Mr Monti might say – since mobile users do not usually use rates abroad as a basis for choosing a provider. Few customers know how much they are paying for roaming. Even fewer actively choose which local network to roam on.

The commission's report recommends making choice easier for consumers. In the best of worlds, roamers would be able to get rate information piped through to their telephones from various providers, before choosing which service to use. Mr Doyle believes that call-back services, which allow roamers to replace higher calling fees with lower receiving fees, will put pressure on operators to cut rates. If the commission wants to see rates fall swiftly, however, it will have to take action itself.

Questions

1 Why is the roaming market in the EEA 'ripe for collusion'?
2 What is the nature of the barriers to entry in the market?
3 Why is it easy for the operators to exploit consumers in this case?
4 If the commission does not take action, do you think it is likely that rates will fall much in the future?

Case study 8.4: Private school fees

Private schools in row over fee-fixing[16]

Some of Britain's top private schools stand accused of price-fixing after meeting to plan steep increases in fees, which lawyers say could breach competition laws.

Eton, Westminster and Marlborough are among the schools that appear to have colluded on the fees they charge. The Office of Fair Trading is now considering launching an investigation as parents face record hikes in fees averaging 10%, four times the rate of inflation. In the past decade fees have risen by 56%.

Across the country, local and national groups of schools have 'cartel-style' private meetings where they share sensitive financial information. The result is near-identical increases in fees.

One bursar admitted last week that he had shared pricing information with other schools and compiled a dossier of his rivals' future fees that would be presented to his governing body before finalising his own.

David Chaundler, bursar at Westminster school, said he acquired details of rivals' fee proposals and costs from meetings of the Eton Group of 12 top private schools. At one meeting in February each bursar announced their school's proposals for increasing fees.

'We do compare school fees,' Chaundler said. 'If I went to my governors with a rise substantially above the others they might tell me to rethink. We do ensure we are pretty well in line.'

Competition lawyers believe the relationship could constitute a cartel. Jonathan Tatten, a partner at Denton Wilde Sapte, said the schools, which have charitable status and are non-profit-making, were not exempt from competition laws: 'Showing confidential pricing information to competitors is a very serious breach of competition rules. You know where you can safely pitch your own fees and it's a way of fixing the market.'

The maximum punishment if a cartel is found is a five-year prison term, he added. In America, a price-fixing inquiry into Ivy League colleges ended without any principals going to jail but led to new rules banning discussion of fees with each other.

Westminster and the other schools say they still make independent decisions on the precise level of fees, and claim the prices are close because many schools have similar cost bases.

This year private schools face a financial crunch from higher salaries and pension payments for teachers, plus Gordon Brown's rise in National Insurance contributions. Fearing a backlash from parents against big fee rises, this spring schools were particularly keen to present a united front. Top boarding schools are set to cross the £20,000-a-year fees watershed for the first time.

On February 7 the Eton Group, including Westminster, Marlborough, King's College school (London), Sherborne, Tonbridge and Bryanston, met at Dulwich College, south London. Each of the bursars outlined the fees they proposed to charge for the next year.

Andrew Wynn, of Eton, admitted: 'We do meet and talk about fees to get some idea of what other schools are thinking. We are a co-operative bunch, and we are not out to slit each other's throats.'

Although their academic results vary, the group's six provincial boarding schools are already closely aligned on fees of £6,300 to £6,445 a term. Its two major London boarding schools, Westminster and Dulwich, charge fees of more than £6,000 and are just £138 apart. Day school members Highgate and nearby University College school have charged exactly the same for the past two years.

A similar meeting held by a rival network, the Rugby Group, whose members include Winchester, Radley, Harrow, Clifton College and Shrewsbury, is also understood to have discussed plans for the first £20,000 annual fees.

William Organ, bursar of Winchester, said: 'Sometimes schools feel they are too far ahead in fees and row back a bit, or the other way round. They look at their competitors in the area and say: Gosh, we're slipping behind in the fees league we'd better catch up.'

A network of six leading private day schools in Manchester, known as the Consortium, holds similar meetings. The schools including Manchester Grammar, William Hulme's Grammar and Stockport Grammar, last year charged about £1,900 a term, with a difference of £131 between them.

Elizabeth Fritchley, William Hulme's bursar, said the group met every term and phoned each other in March: 'We decide what our increase is to be and then phone the other schools. If we are thinking of putting the fees up by, say, 15% and the rest were proposing far less, then it would make us rethink our strategy.'

Yesterday Mike Sant, general secretary of the Independent Schools' Bursars Association, denied any cartels were operating: 'Schools will decide where they want to be in the market and will be watching their competition and move fees accordingly. All the schools are so different they are just not in competition. They do exchange information, but just to get a feel for what others are doing.'

Questions

1 If a group of schools simultaneously raises their fees by a similar amount, is this evidence of collusion? What other explanation might be possible?

2 If fees have risen much faster than the rate of inflation, 56 per cent over a decade, is this evidence of collusion, or are other explanations possible?

3 Describe the factors that are favourable to the formation of a successful cartel, and those that are unfavourable, for the elite private schools mentioned in the article. Use the statements in quotations as evidence.

8.6 A problem-solving approach

The essential problem in the issue of market structure is the determination of price and output, given the different market conditions involved. Conclusions relating to profit and efficiency follow from this. The starting point is always the **demand and cost functions**. In some situations that the student may face these will not be given in equation form, as for example in Problem 8.1. The first step in that case is to derive the demand and cost functions from the information given. Once this is done there is a straightforward **five-step procedure** to solving the problem. There are no additional solved problems in this chapter because examples of these have already been given in the text, under each form of market structure. The student should be able to see from these examples that in each case the following general steps are involved:

1 Derive demand function in the form $P = f(Q)$.
2 Derive revenue function in the form $R = f(Q)$.
3 Derive marginal revenue function in the form $MR = \dfrac{dR}{dQ} = f(Q)$.
4 Derive marginal cost function in the form $MC = \dfrac{dC}{dQ} = f(Q)$.
5 Set $MC = MR$ and solve for Q.

Once the value of Q is obtained the value of P can be obtained from the demand equation. Profit can be calculated either by taking revenue minus costs, or by using the equation:

$$\text{Profit} = (P - AC)Q$$

The above procedure is very robust and can be used with any mathematical form of demand and cost function. The algebra may vary, as seen for example in the case of monopolistic competition, where a cubic cost function is used, but in each problem the general procedure is identical.

It should be noted at this stage that the above procedure is not the only approach that can be used for solving problems. Another approach is to **derive the profit function** for the firm, in terms of either price or output. This function can then be differentiated and set equal to zero to obtain a maximum. The second-order conditions should also be examined in this case to verify that the profit is indeed maximized, rather than minimized. This approach can be used in Problem 8.1 in particular, since that question specifically requires a profit function to be obtained. The profit function approach is also used in Chapter 10 to deal with more complex demand functions involving other elements in the marketing mix.

Summary

1 Market structure describes the different conditions in markets that affect the way in which prices and outputs are determined.
2 The four main types of market structure are perfect competition, monopoly, monopolistic competition and oligopoly.
3 Market structure, conduct, performance and technology are all interdependent.
4 The determination of price and output can be examined graphically or algebraically.
5 In any type of market the profit-maximizing output is always given by the condition $MC = MR$.
6 Firms can only make supernormal profit in the long run if there are barriers to entry and exit.
7 Barriers can be either structural or strategic.
8 When comparing the performance of markets the key variables to examine are price, output, profits and efficiency (both productive and allocative).
9 Allocative efficiency is concerned with the optimality of resource allocation from the point of view of the economy as a whole, considering the effects on both consumer and producer. This has important implications for government policy.
10 Oligopoly is the most complicated type of market structure to analyse, since the strategic decisions of firms are interdependent.
11 Oligopoly is in practice the most important type of market structure, since the majority of most countries' output is produced in this type of market structure. This is especially true if we consider that many markets that appear to feature monopolistic competition are, in reality, limited intersecting oligopolies that are differentiated in terms of product and spatial characteristics. Restaurants are a good example.

Review questions

1 Why is perfect competition normally regarded as being 'better' than monopoly?
2 In what ways may perfect competition not be 'perfect'?
3 Explain the meaning and significance of limited intersecting oligopolies.
4 What is meant by monopoly power? What factors determine the extent of this power?
5 Explain why OPEC has been one of the most successful cartels in recent decades. What factors have limited this success?

6 Explain what is meant by the kinked demand curve. What shortcomings does this approach have in the analysis of oligopoly?

Problems

8.1 An apartment block has seventy units of accommodation. It is estimated that it is possible to let them all if the rent is $2,000 per month, and for each $100 per month the rent is increased there would be one unit vacant. LG, the manager of the block, finds that a vacant unit costs $100 per month to maintain whereas an occupied one costs $300.

   a. If profit from the lettings is measured as revenue minus maintenance costs, find an expression for profit in terms of the number of units let.
   b. What rent should LG charge to maximize profit?
   c. KA, a contractor, offers to be responsible for the maintenance of the entire block at a rate of $150 per unit, whether the units are occupied or not. Would it be more profitable for LG to employ KA?

8.2 XL Corp has estimated its demand and cost functions to be as follows:

$$P = 60 - 0.2Q$$
$$C = 200 + 4Q + 1.2Q^2$$

where Q is in units, P is in $ and C is in $.

   a. Calculate the profit-maximizing price and output.
   b. Calculate the size of the profit.
   c. Calculate the price elasticity of demand at the above price.
   d. If there is a $14 tax placed on the good, so that the producer has to pay the government $14 for every unit sold, calculate the new profit-maximizing price and output.
   e. What would happen to profit if the firm tried to pass on all the tax to the consumer in the form of a higher price?
   f. If fixed costs rise by $200 how would this affect the firm's situation?

8.3 Lizzie's Lingerie started selling robes for $36, adding a 50 per cent mark-up on cost. Costs were estimated at $24 each: the $10 purchase price of each robe, plus $6 in allocated variable overhead costs, plus an allocated fixed overhead charge of $8. Customer response was such that when Lizzie's raised prices from $36 to $39 per robe, sales fell from 54 to 46 robes per week.

   a. Estimate the optimal (profit-maximizing) pricing strategy assuming a linear demand curve.
   b. Estimate the optimal pricing strategy assuming a power demand curve.
   c. Explain why there is a difference between the above two strategies.
   d. Estimate the size of the profit at both prices, assuming a power demand curve.

e. Estimate the optimal price if the cost of buying the robes rises from $10 to $11, assuming a power demand curve.

8.4 Crystal Ball Corp. has estimated its demand and cost functions as follows:

$$Q = 80 - 5P$$
$$C = 30 + 2Q + 0.5Q^2$$

where P is in $, Q is in thousands of units and C is in $,000.

a. Calculate the profit-maximizing price and output.
b. Calculate the size of the above profit.
c. Calculate the price elasticity of demand at the above output; is demand elastic or inelastic here? What should it be?
d. Calculate the marginal cost at the above output.
e. If unit costs rise by $2 at all levels of output and the firm raises its price by the same amount, what profit is made?
f. What is the profit-maximizing strategy given the above rise in costs?
g. How much profit is the firm forgoing by raising its price $2?

Notes

1 D. Besanko, D. Dranove and M. Shanley, *Economics of Strategy*, 2nd ed., New York: Wiley, 2000, p. 233.
2 J. Hilke and P. Nelson, 'Strategic behavior and attempted monopolization: the coffee (General Foods) case', in J. Kwoka and L. J. White (eds.), *The Antitrust Revolution*, Glenview, Ill.: Scott Foresman, 1989, pp. 208–240.
3 P. Milgrom and J. Roberts, 'Limit pricing and entry under incomplete information', *Econometrica*, **50** (1982): 443–460.
4 G. Saloner, 'Dynamic limit pricing in an uncertain environment', mimeo, Graduate School of Business, Stanford University.
5 W. J. Baumol, J. C. Panzar and R. D. Willig, *Contestable Markets and the Theory of Market Structure*, New York: Harcourt Brace Jovanovich, 1982.
6 S. Borenstein, 'Hubs and high fares: dominance and market power in the U.S. Airline Industry', *RAND Journal of Economics*, **20** (1989): 344–365.
7 P. Geroski, 'What do we know about entry?', *International Journal of Industrial Organization*, **13** (1995): 421–440.
8 'Here and now', *The Economist*, 2 August 2001.
9 E. Chamberlin, *The Theory of Monopolistic Competition*, Cambridge, Mass.: Harvard University Press, 1993.
10 D. M. Kreps, *A Course on Microeconomic Theory*, London: Harvester-Wheatsheaf, 1990.
11 J. Tirole, *The Theory of Industrial Organization*, Cambridge, Mass.: MIT Press, 1993.
12 'Chemists at risk as prices are slashed', *The Times*, 16 May 2001.
13 P. M. Sweezy, 'Demand under conditions of oligopoly', *Journal of Political Economy*, **47** (1939): 568–573.
14 G. Stigler, 'The kinked oligopoly demand curve and rigid prices', *Journal of Political Economy*, **55** (1947): 442–444.
15 'Predatory roaming', *The Economist*, 3 May 2001.
16 'Private schools in row over fee-fixing', *The Sunday Times*, 27 April 2003.

9

Game theory

Outline

Objectives

1 To define and explain the significance of strategic behaviour.
2 To explain the characteristics of different types of games and show how differences in these characteristics affect the behaviour of firms.
3 To examine the various concepts of equilibrium in terms of strategies.
4 To examine the concepts of Cournot and Bertrand competition.
5 To explain the relationships between static and dynamic games.
6 To explain the solution of dynamic games using the backward induction method.
7 To explain the importance of strategic moves and commitment.
8 To discuss the concept of credibility and the factors which determine it.
9 To examine games with uncertain outcomes and explain different approaches to their solution.
10 To examine repeated games and how their nature leads to different solutions from one-shot games.
11 To examine a variety of different applications, in order to relate game theory concepts to much of the other material in the book.
12 To demonstrate how game theory explains much firm behaviour that cannot be explained by traditional analysis.
13 To stress that many of the conclusions of game theory are counter-intuitive.

9.1 Introduction

In the previous chapter we have indicated that oligopoly is in practice the most common form of market structure. Most of the products that people consume, from cars to consumer electronics, cigarettes to cereals, domestic appliances to detergents, and national newspapers to athletic shoes, are supplied in oligopolistic markets. This also applies to many services, like supermarket retailing, travel agencies and, at least in the UK, commercial banking. When we take into account that many markets are separated in terms of product and spatial characteristics, we can also include markets like restaurants and car repair, as seen in the last chapter. However, up to this point our analysis of such situations has made some important but unrealistic assumptions. Since one main accusation frequently levelled at the subject of managerial economics is that it takes too narrow a view of the firm's behaviour, it is important to address this criticism. The purpose of this chapter is, therefore, to relax these assumptions and introduce a broader and more realistic perspective, not just to the analysis of competition theory, but also to managerial economics in general. Unfortunately, as happens so often with economic analysis, it also means that we have to introduce more advanced and complex methods.

Nature and scope of game theory

The essential nature of game theory is that it involves **strategic behaviour, which means interdependent decision-making**. We have at this point seen quite a few examples of situations where such decision-making is involved, particularly in the areas of the theory of the firm and competition theory. Some examples which will be analysed in more detail concern the tragedy of the commons, contracting between firms, contracting between an employer and employee, and oligopolistic situations in terms of determining price and output, and limiting entry.

The essence of these interdependent decision-making situations is that when A makes a decision (for example regarding price, entry into a market, whether to take a job), it will consider the reactions of other persons or firms to its different strategies, usually assuming that they act rationally, and how these reactions will affect their own utility or profit. It must also take into account that the other parties (from now on called players), in selecting their reactive strategies, will consider how A will react to their reactions. This can continue in a virtually infinite progression. In this situation there is often a considerable amount of uncertainty regarding the results of any decision.

These kinds of situation occur in all areas of economics, not just in managerial economics. They are common in macroeconomic policy, labour economics, financial economics and international economics. Game theory situations also occur in politics, sociology, warfare, 'games' and sports, and biology, which make the area a unifying theme in much analysis. Game theorists, therefore, have come from many different walks of life, although the main pioneers were von Neumann and Morgenstern,[1] and Nash,[2] who were essentially mathematicians.

Elements of a game

The concept of a game, as we are now using it, embraces a large variety of situations that we do not normally refer to as games. Yes, chess, poker and rock–paper–scissors are games in the conventional sense, as are tennis and football (either American football or soccer); but games also include activities like going for a job interview, a firm bargaining with a labour union, someone applying for life insurance, a firm deciding to enter a new market, a politician

Table 9.1. Prisoner's Dilemma

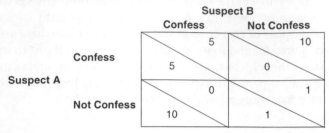

		Suspect B	
		Confess	Not Confess
Suspect A	Confess	5 / 5	10 / 0
	Not Confess	0 / 10	1 / 1

announcing a new education/transport/health policy, or a country declaring war. What do these diverse activities have in common?

The following are the key elements of any game:

1 *Players*. These are the relevant decision-making identities, whose utilities are interdependent. They may be individuals, firms, teams, social organizations, political parties or governments.
2 *Strategies*. These are **complete plans of action for playing the game**. Although strategies may simply involve choosing a single action, it is important to understand that in some games there may be many actions involved. A complete plan means that every possible contingency must be allowed for.
3 *Payoffs*. These represent changes in welfare or utility at the end of the game, and are determined by the choices of strategy of *each* player. It is normally assumed that players are rational and have the objective of maximizing these utilities or expected utilities. Notice that the word *each* is important; what distinguishes game theory from decision theory is that, in the latter, outcomes only depend on the decisions of a single decision-maker, as seen in Chapter 11 on investment analysis.

The **normal-form representation** of a game specifies the above three elements.

Now that we have stated the key elements in games, an example of a game can be presented, which will aid the ensuing discussion. The example is the well-known **Prisoner's Dilemma (PD)**. The reasons for presenting this situation here are twofold. First, although it does not directly involve a business predicament, the situation can easily be changed to a business predicament, and this is done shortly. Second, the conclusions regarding strategy appear paradoxical; this is a common finding in game theory, many conclusions being counter-intuitive. The classic PD situation involves two prisoners who are held in separate police cells, accused of committing a crime. They cannot communicate with each other, so each does not know how the other is acting. If neither confesses, the prosecutor can get them convicted only on other minor offences, each prisoner receiving a one-year sentence. If one confesses while the other does not, the one confessing will be freed while the other one receives a ten-year sentence. If both confess they will each receive a five-year sentence. This game is represented in normal form in Table 9.1.

Table 9.2. Prisoner's Dilemma for Coke and Pepsi

		Pepsi	
		Maintain Price	**Discount**
Coke	**Maintain Price**	50 / 50	70 / −10
	Discount	−10 / 70	10 / 10

The values in the table represent payoffs, in terms of jail sentences; the payoffs for Suspect A are below the diagonal, while the payoffs for Suspect B are above the diagonal. The objective for each suspect in this case is obviously to minimize the payoff in terms of jail time. The problem that they have in this case is that the best combination payoff for the pair of them is for them both not to confess, in other words to '**co-operate**' with each other. However, as we shall see shortly, this is not an equilibrium strategy. The equilibrium strategy is for both suspects to confess, or to '**defect**'. This equilibrium situation represents a paradox, since they will both end up serving a longer time in jail than if they had co-operated. The equilibrium still applies even if the suspects had agreed to co-operate beforehand; they will still tend to defect once they are separated and do not know how the other is acting.

The reader may wonder at this stage what the type of situation described above has to do with business strategy. To illustrate this, let us consider the situation of Coke and Pepsi. At any given time period each firm has to decide whether to maintain their existing price or to offer a discount to the retailers who buy from them. Table 9.2 shows the payoff matrix for this situation, with the payoffs referring to profits, measured in millions of dollars per month. The payoffs for Pepsi are shown above the diagonal and the payoffs for Coke are shown below it. The objective in this situation is to maximize, rather than minimize, the payoffs.

The reader may notice an important difference between the situation described in the original Prisoner's Dilemma (PD) in Table 9.1 and that involving Coke and Pepsi in Table 9.2. The first situation is a 'one-off' whereas the second is likely to be repeated regularly. As we shall see, this makes a big difference in determining optimal strategy.

In this game, maintaining price represents co-operating, while offering a discount represents defecting. As with the original Prisoner's Dilemma in Table 9.1, there is a specific ordering of payoffs, as shown in Table 9.3. Just as in the Prisoner's Dilemma, the best combined payoff, or profit, is if both firms co-operate and maintain price. Note that co-operation here does not mean explicit collusion, rather it refers to tacit co-operation. Again, this is not an equilibrium situation; the equilibrium (explained shortly) is for both firms to discount.

Table 9.3. Structure of payoffs in Prisoner's Dilemma

Strategy pair (self/other)	Name of payoff
Defect/co-operate	Temptation (70)
Co-operate/co-operate	Reward (50)
Defect/defect	Punishment (10)
Co-operate/defect	Sucker's payoff (−10)

Before we move on to an analysis of this situation and explain the conclusions above, it is helpful to broaden the perspective by considering the different types of game that can occur in business situations.

9.1.3 Types of game

There are many different types of game theory situation, and different methods of analysis are appropriate in different cases. It is therefore useful to classify games according to certain important characteristics.

a. Co-operative and non-cooperative games

In co-operative games the players can communicate with each other and collude. They can also enter into third-party enforceable binding contracts. Much of this type of activity is expressly prohibited by law in developed countries, so most of the games that are of interest in economic situations are of the non-cooperative kind. This type of game involves forming self-enforcing reliance relationships, which determine an equilibrium situation. The nature of such equilibria is discussed in the next section.

b. Two-player and multi-player games

Both versions of the PD situation above are two-player games. However, both games are capable of being extended to include more than two parties. This tends to increase the likelihood of defection, particularly in the 'one-off' situation. Such a situation is sometimes referred to as 'the tragedy of the commons'. The reasoning is that with more players it is important to defect before others do; only if defectors are easily detected and punished will this be prevented. Again this has important implications for oligopoly, as seen in the last chapter. It is also relevant in international relations. The depletion of fish stocks in the North Sea due to overfishing, and the resulting conflicts, are an example of the tragedy of the commons. Property rights theory is obviously relevant in this area. With multi-player games there is also the opportunity for some of the players to form coalitions against others, to try and impose strategies that would otherwise be unsustainable.

c. Zero-sum and non-zero-sum games

With zero-sum games the gain of one player(s) is automatically the loss of another player(s). This can apply for example in derivatives markets, where certain transactions occur between two speculators. However, most business situations involve non-zero-sum games, as can be seen in the Coke/Pepsi situation earlier. The combined profit of the two firms varies according to the strategies of both players.

d. Perfect and imperfect information

In both versions of the PD presented earlier it was assumed that all the players knew for certain what all the payoffs were for each pair of strategies. In practice this is often not the case, and this can also affect strategy. In some cases a player may be uncertain regarding their own payoffs; in other cases they may know their own payoffs but be uncertain regarding the payoffs of the other player(s). For example, an insurance company may not know all the relevant details regarding the person applying for insurance, a situation leading to adverse selection, as we have seen in chapter 2. Likewise, bidders at an auction may not know the valuations that other parties place on the auctioned item. Games with imperfect information are, unsurprisingly, more difficult to analyse.

e. Static and dynamic games

Static games involve **simultaneous moves**; the PD game is a simultaneous game, meaning that the players make their moves simultaneously, without knowing the move of the other player. In terms of analysis the moves do not have to be simultaneous in chronological terms, as long as each player is ignorant of the moves of the other player(s). Many business scenarios involve **dynamic games**; these involve **sequential moves**, where one player moves first and the other player moves afterwards, knowing the move of the first player. Investing in building a new plant is an example of this situation. As we shall see, the order of play can make a big difference to the outcome in such situations.

f. Discrete and continuous strategies

Discrete strategies involve situations where each action can be chosen from a limited number of alternatives. In the PD game there are only two choices for each player, to confess or not confess; thus this is a discrete strategy situation. In contrast, a firm in oligopoly may have a virtually limitless number of prices that it can charge; this is an example of a continuous strategy situation. As a result the analytical approach is somewhat different, as will be seen in the subsection on oligopoly.

g. 'One-off' and repetitive games

The distinction between these two types of situation has already been illustrated by the two different versions of the PD in Tables 9.1 and 9.2. Most short-run decision scenarios in business, such as pricing and advertising, are of the repetitive type, in that there is a continuous interaction between competitors, who can change their decision variables at regular intervals. Some of these games may involve a finite number of plays, where an end of the game can be foreseen, while others may seem infinite. Long-run decisions, such as invest-ment decisions, may resemble the 'one-off' situation; although the situation may be repeated in the future, the time interval between decisions may be several years, and the next decision scenario may involve quite different payoffs.

9.2 Static games

As stated above, these games involve simultaneous moves, as in the PD game. We shall concern ourselves at this stage only with games involving perfect information, and with 'one-off' situations; all the players know with certainty all the possible payoffs, and the game is not repeated. The nature of this type of game raises the following questions:

1 How does a firm determine strategy in this type of situation?
2 What do we mean by an equilibrium strategy?
3 Is there anything that firms can do to change the equilibrium to a more favourable one, meaning to ensure co-operation?

These issues are addressed in the following subsections.

Equilibrium

In order to determine strategy or an equilibrium situation, we must first assume that the players are rational utility maximizers. We can now consider three types of equilibrium and appropriate strategies in situations involving different payoffs. These are dominant strategy equilibrium, iterated dominant strategy equilibrium, and Nash equilibrium. It is important to consider these equilibria in this order, as will be seen.

a. Dominant strategy equilibrium

A strategy S_1 is said to strictly dominate another strategy S_2 if, given any collection of strategies that could be played by the other players, playing S_1 results in a strictly higher payoff for that player than does playing S_2. Thus we can say that if player A has a **strictly dominant strategy** in a situation, *it will always give at least as high a payoff as any other strategy, whatever player B does*. A rational player will always adopt a dominant strategy if one is available. Therefore, in any static game involving discrete strategies, we should always start by looking for a dominant strategy. This is easiest in a two-strategy situation; when there are many possible strategies, dominant strategies have to be found by a process of eliminating dominated strategies, as shown in the subsection on Nash bargaining. To start with, let us take the PD situation in Table 9.2, involving Coke and Pepsi. The reader may have wondered why we said earlier that the equilibrium in the PD situation was for both players to 'defect', with the result being that their combined payoff was less than the optimal combined payoff; both players end up worse than they could be if they 'co-operated'.

Table 9.4. Iterated dominant strategy equilibrium

	Pepsi	
	Maintain Price	**Discount**
Coke **Maintain Price**	50 / 80	70 / −10
Coke **Discount**	−10 / 70	10 / 10

Consider the situation from Coke's viewpoint. If Pepsi maintains a high price, Coke is better off discounting, getting a payoff of 70 compared with 50. Similarly, if Pepsi discounts, Coke is still better off discounting, getting a payoff of 10 compared with −10. Thus discounting is a dominant strategy for Coke. By the same line of reasoning, discounting is also the dominant strategy for Pepsi. We could also say that maintaining price is in this case a **dominated strategy** for both firms; this means that *it will always give a lower or equal payoff, whatever the other player does*.

Therefore, given the payoffs in Table 9.1, it is obvious that there is a **dominant strategy equilibrium**, meaning that *the strategies pursued by all players are dominant*. In the situation in Table 9.2 both firms will discount, regardless of the fact that they will both be worse off than if they had maintained prices. By individually pursuing their self-interest each firm is imposing a cost on the other firm that they are not taking into account. It can therefore be said that in the PD situation the dominant strategy outcome is **Pareto dominated**. This means that *there is some other outcome where at least one of the players is better off while no other player is worse off*. However, Pareto domination considers total or social welfare; this is not relevant to the choice of strategy by each firm.

b. Iterated dominant strategy equilibrium

What would happen if one firm did not have a dominant strategy? This is illustrated in Table 9.4, which is similar to Table 9.2 but with one payoff changed. Coke now gets a payoff of 80 instead of 50 if both firms maintain price. Although Pepsi's dominant strategy is unchanged, Coke no longer has a dominant strategy. If Pepsi maintains price it is better off maintaining price, but if Pepsi discounts, Coke is better off also discounting.

In this case, Coke can rule out Pepsi maintaining price (that is a dominated strategy), and conclude that Pepsi will discount; Coke can therefore **iterate** to a dominant strategy, which is to discount. Thus the equilibrium is the same as before.

c. Nash equilibrium

The situation becomes more complicated when neither player has a dominant strategy. This is illustrated in Table 9.5. Note that this is no longer a Prisoner's Dilemma, since the structure of the payoffs has changed.

Table 9.5. Game with no dominant strategy

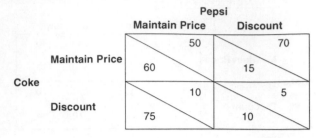

In this situation, Coke is better off discounting if Pepsi maintains price, but is better off maintaining price if Pepsi discounts. The same is true for Pepsi. There is no single equilibrium here. Instead we have to use the concept of a **Nash equilibrium**. This represents *an outcome where each player is pursuing their best strategy in response to the best-reply strategy of the other player*. This is a more general concept of equilibrium than the two equilibrium concepts described earlier; while it includes dominant strategy equilibrium and iterated dominant strategy equilibrium, it also relates to situations where the first two concepts do not apply. There are two such equilibria in Table 9.5, as already seen:

1 If Coke maintains price, Pepsi will discount; and, given this best response, Coke's best reply is to maintain price.
2 If Coke discounts, Pepsi will maintain price; and, given this best response, Coke's best reply is to discount.

The same equilibria could also be expressed from Pepsi's point of view:

1 If Pepsi discounts, Coke will maintain price; and, given this best response, Pepsi's best reply is to discount.
2 If Pepsi maintains price, Coke will discount; and, given this best response, Pepsi's best reply is to maintain price.

Coke will prefer the second strategy, while Pepsi will prefer the first. However, there is no further analysis that we can perform to see which of the two equilibria will prevail. This presents a problem for strategy selection if the game is repeated, as will be seen later.

The concept of a Nash equilibrium is an extremely important one in game theory, since situations frequently arise where there is no dominant strategy equilibrium or iterated dominant strategy equilibrium.

9.2.2 Oligopoly models

There are various static models of oligopoly that have been proposed. One of these, the Sweezy model, was discussed in the previous chapter. However, we saw that there were a number of shortcomings of the model; in particular it assumed an initial price, and that firms would match price cuts but not price rises. This means that it is not a truly interactive model in terms of considering all the implications of strategic interaction. Therefore it will not be considered further here. The models that will be considered at this point are the Cournot model, the Bertrand model and the contestable markets model.

Although the Cournot and Bertrand models were developed independently, are based on different assumptions, and lead to different conclusions, there are some common features of the models that can be discussed at this stage before each is examined in detail. These features are easier to discuss in a two-firm framework, meaning a duopoly. Both models consider the situation where each firm considers the other firm's strategy in determining its own demand function. The other firm's strategy is considered to relate to either the output or price variable. Thus these demand functions can be expressed as reaction or response curves which show one firm's strategy, given the other firm's strategy. The equilibrium point is where the two response curves intersect, meaning that the two firms' strategies coincide. To understand what all this is about we now have to consider each model separately.

a. The Cournot model

This model, originally developed in 1835,[3] initially considered a market in which there were only two firms, A and B. In more general terms we can say that the Cournot model is based on the following assumptions:

1 There are few firms in the market and many buyers.
2 The firms produce homogeneous products; therefore each firm has to charge the same market price (the model can be extended to cover differentiated products).
3 Competition is in the form of output, meaning that each firm determines its level of output based on its estimate of the level of output of the other firm. Each firm believes that its own output strategy does not affect the strategy of its rival(s).
4 Barriers to entry exist.
5 Each firm aims to maximize profit, and assumes that the other firms do the same.

An essential difference between this situation and the ones considered until now is that strategies are continuous in the Cournot model. This allows a more mathematical approach to analysis.

The situation can be illustrated by using the example relating to the cartel in the previous chapter. In that case the market demand was given by $P = 400 - 2Q$ and each firm had constant marginal costs of £40 and no fixed costs. We saw that the monopoly price and output were £220 and 90 units, while price and output in perfect competition were £40 and 180 units. The analytical procedure can be viewed as involving the following steps.

Step 1. Transform the market demand into a demand function that relates to the outputs of each of the two firms. Thus we have:

$$P = 400 - 2(Q_A + Q_B)$$
$$P = 400 - 2Q_A - 2Q_B \tag{9.1}$$

Step 2. Derive the profit functions for each firm, which are functions of the outputs of both firms. Bearing in mind that there are no fixed costs and therefore marginal cost and average cost are equal, the profit function for firm A is as follows:

$$\Pi_A = (400 - 2Q_A - 2Q_B)Q_A - 40Q_A = 400Q_A - 2Q_A^2 - 2Q_BQ_A - 40Q_A$$
$$= 360Q_A - 2Q_A^2 - 2Q_BQ_A \tag{9.2}$$

Step 3. Derive the optimal output for firm A as a function of the output of firm B, by differentiating the profit function with respect to Q_A and setting the partial derivative equal to zero:

$$\frac{\partial \Pi_A}{\partial Q_A} = 360 - 4Q_A - 2Q_B = 0$$
$$4Q_A = 360 - 2Q_B \tag{9.3}$$
$$\boldsymbol{Q_A = 90 - 0.5Q_B}$$

Strictly speaking, the value of Q_B in this equation is not known with certainty by firm A, but is an estimate. Equation 9.3 is known as the **best-response function** or **response curve** of firm A. It shows *how much firm A will put on the market for any amount that it estimates firm B will put on the market.*

The second and third steps above can then be repeated for firm B, to derive firm B's response curve. Because of the symmetry involved, it can be easily seen that the profit function for firm B is given by:

$$\Pi_B = 360Q_B - 2Q_B^2 - 2Q_BQ_A \tag{9.4}$$

And the response curve for firm B is given by:

$$\boldsymbol{Q_B = 90 - 0.5Q_A} \tag{9.5}$$

This shows how much firm B will put on the market for any amount that it estimates firm A will put on the market. The situation can be represented graphically, as shown in Figure 9.1.

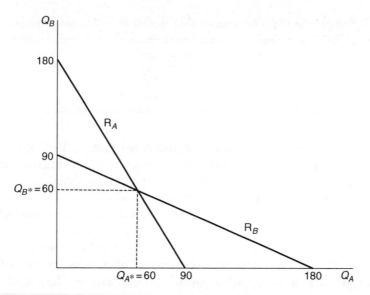

Figure 9.1. Cournot response curves.

Step 4. Solve the equations for the best-response functions simultaneously to derive the **Cournot equilibrium**. The properties of this equilibrium will be discussed shortly.

$$Q_A = 90 - 0.5Q_B$$
$$Q_B = 90 - 0.5Q_A$$
$$Q_A = 90 - 0.5\,(90 - 0.5Q_A)$$
$$Q_A = 90 - 45 + 0.25Q_A$$
$$0.75Q_A = 45$$
$$\mathbf{Q_A = 60}$$
$$\mathbf{Q_B} = 90 - 0.5(60) = \mathbf{60}$$

The market price can now be determined:

$$P = 400 - 2(60 + 60)$$
$$\mathbf{P = \pounds160}$$

We can now compare this situation with the ones discussed in the previous chapter relating to perfect competition, monopoly and cartels. This is shown in Table 9.6.

A Cournot duopoly clearly does not make as much profit as a cartel involving the two producers; by colluding, the two firms could restrict output to increase profit. The reason for this is that, when one firm increases output, the price for the market as a whole is reduced. However, the firm does not consider

Table 9.6. Comparison of perfect competition, monopoly and Cournot duopoly

Market structure	Price (£)	Output in the industry	Profit in the industry (£)
Perfect competition	40	180	0
Monopoly (or cartel)	220	90	16,200
Cournot duopoly	160	120	14,400

the effect of the reduced revenue of the other firm, called the **revenue destruction effect**, since it is only concerned with maximizing its own profit. Thus it expands its output more aggressively than a cartel would, since a cartel is concerned with the profit of the industry as a whole.

This Cournot equilibrium is also called the **Cournot–Nash equilibrium** (CNE), since it satisfies the conditions stated in the last subsection regarding the nature of a Nash equilibrium. The CNE represents *the situation where the strategies of the two firms 'match', and there will be no tendency for the firms to change their outputs*; at any other pair of outputs there will be a tendency for the firms to change them, since the other firm is not producing what they estimated. The Cournot equilibrium is therefore a comparative static equilibrium. This can be illustrated in the following example of the adjustment process.

Let us assume that both firms start by producing 80 units. Neither firm will be happy with their output, since they are producing more than they want, given the other firm's actual output. Say that firm A is the first to adjust its output. It will now produce $90 - 0.5(80) = 50$ units. Firm B will react to this by producing 65 units; firm A will then produce 57.5 units; firm B will then produce 61.25 units and so on, with the outputs converging on 60 units for each firm.

It should be noted that the Cournot–Nash equilibrium has stronger properties than other Nash equilibria. If strictly dominated strategies are eliminated, as shown in the above example, only one strategy profile remains for rational players, the **Cournot–Nash equilibrium**. It can therefore be concluded that this represents a *unique iterated strictly dominant strategy equilibrium of the Cournot game*.

All the preceding analysis has been based on a two-firm industry. As the number of firms in the industry increases, the market price is reduced and market output increases. The reason for this is related to the revenue destruction effect described earlier. With more firms in the industry, any increase in output by one firm has a smaller effect on the market price, and on its own profit, but the effect on the combined revenues of all the other firms increases in comparison to the effect on its own profit.

The Bertrand model

This model dates back to 1883.[4] The assumptions involved in the model are as follows:

1 There are few firms in the market and many buyers.
2 The firms produce homogeneous or differentiated products; therefore each firm has to charge the same market price in the case of homogeneous products, but there is some scope for charging different prices for differentiated products.
3 Competition is in the form of price, meaning that each firm determines its level of price based on its estimate of the level of price of the other firm. Each firm believes that its own pricing strategy does not affect the strategy of its rival(s).
4 Barriers to entry exist.
5 Each firm has sufficient capacity to supply the whole market.
6 Each firm aims to maximize profit, and assumes that the other firms do the same.

It can be seen that the first, fourth and fifth assumptions are the same as for the Cournot model but that competition is in the form of price rather than output. We can begin by taking the Cournot equilibrium analysed above, where each firm charges £160 and sells 60 units. If a firm in Bertrand competition believes that its rival will charge £160 it can undercut its rival slightly, by charging say £159, and capture the whole market, since we have assumed that the product is homogeneous, and that firms have sufficient capacity to do this. This action would considerably increase its profit. However, any rival will then react by undercutting price again, to say £158, and again capture the whole market. Thus, no matter how many or how few firms there are in the market, price reductions will continue until the price has been forced down to the level of marginal cost. The conclusion, therefore, is that, with homogeneous products, the Bertrand equilibrium is identical with that in perfect competition, with no firm making any economic or supernormal profit. The more important situation in practical terms, where the products are differentiated, is discussed shortly.

Why is there such a big difference between the Cournot and Bertrand models in terms of their conclusions regarding prices, outputs and profits? The assumptions underlying the models are fundamentally different. In the Cournot model, firms make production decisions that tend to involve long-run capacity decisions; once these decisions have been made, firms tend to sell their output at whatever price it will fetch, thus avoiding price competition. In the Bertrand model, price competition is much more intense, and each firm believes that it can steal a rival's market by cutting its price just slightly. Production is very flexible under these assumptions, so that a firm can increase output considerably in order to supply a large number of new customers.

When products are differentiated, as they are in most oligopolistic markets, the analysis of Bertrand competition becomes more complex, and resembles the Cournot model in some respects. First of all, a firm will not lose its whole market if a rival undercuts its price, it will lose only some of its customers, depending on the cross-elasticity of demand. Assuming a two-firm situation again for simplicity, the model is based on each firm having a demand function related both to its own price and to that of its competitor. This corresponds to the Cournot situation where each firm has a demand function related both to its own price and to the *output* of the competitor. Again similarly to the Cournot analysis, profit functions for each firm are derived (assuming that each firm's cost function is known) and these functions are maximized by differentiating them and setting the derivatives equal to zero. The resulting equations yield the best-response functions of the firms, which can then be solved simultaneously to derive the equilibrium prices. Thus the analysis is essentially similar to the four-step procedure described in the Cournot situation.

It is useful at this stage to illustrate the procedure by using an example.

Step 1. Let us take two firms, A and B, with the following demand functions:

$$Q_A = 60 - 4P_A + 2.5P_B$$
$$Q_B = 50 - 5P_B + 2P_A$$

where Q is in units and P is in £. In this case the individual demand functions are given; market demand would be the sum of the two functions. Firm A has marginal costs of £5 and Firm B has marginal costs of £4. Note that these marginal costs can be different because the product is differentiated, unlike the Cournot case. It is assumed for simplicity that there are no fixed costs.

Step 2. Derive profit functions for each firm (profit = $(P - AC)Q$):

$$\Pi_A = (P_A - 5)(60 - 4P_A + 2.5P_B)$$
$$= 60P_A - 4P_A^2 + 2.5P_AP_B - 300 + 20P_A - 12.5P_A \qquad (9.6)$$
$$= 80P_A - 4P_A^2 + 2.5P_AP_B - 300 - 12.5P_A$$

$$\Pi_B = (P_B - 4)(50 - 5P_B + 2P_A)$$
$$= 50P_B - 5P_B^2 + 2P_BP_A - 200 + 20P_B - 8P_A \qquad (9.7)$$
$$= 70P_B - 5P_B^2 + 2P_BP_A - 200 + 8P_A$$

Step 3. Differentiate the profit functions and set equal to zero in order to derive best-response functions:

$$\frac{\partial \Pi_A}{\partial P_A} = 80 - 8P_A + 2.5P_B = 0$$
$$\mathbf{P_A = 10 + 0.3125P_B} \qquad (9.8)$$

$$\frac{\partial \Pi_B}{\partial P_B} = 70 - 10P_B + 2P_A = 0$$
$$\mathbf{P_B = 7 + 0.2P_A} \qquad (9.9)$$

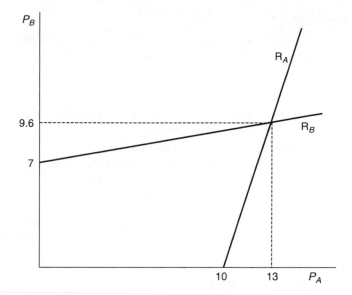

Figure 9.2. Bertrand response curves.

Step 4. Solve best-response functions simultaneously to derive the equilibrium price:

$$P_A = 10 + 0.3125(7 + 0.2)P_A$$
$$P_A = 12.1875 + 0.0625P_A$$
$$0.9375P_A = 12.1875$$
$$\mathbf{P_A = \pounds 13}$$
$$P_B = 7 + 0.2(13)$$
$$\mathbf{P_B = \pounds 9.60}$$

This last step can also be illustrated by drawing a graph of the response curves. This is shown in Figure 9.2.

Note that the response curves are positive sloping in this case. This means that the higher the price that one firm thinks the other firm will charge, the higher the price it will itself charge.

Some readers might think at this point that the kind of analysis above is too theoretical and abstract to be of much use in practice. This is not true. In an empirical study of the cola market in the United States from 1968 to 1986,[5] precisely the methodology above was used to estimate the prices that Coca-Cola and Pepsi should charge. It was concluded that Coca-Cola's price should be $12.72 and Pepsi's price should be $8.11. When one compares these estimates with the actual average prices over the period of $12.96 and $8.16, one can see that the Bertrand model is capable of forecasting actual pricing behaviour with remarkable accuracy.

c. Contestable markets

This concept, originally developed by Baumol, Panzar and Willig,[6] was discussed in the previous chapter; we can now conduct a game theory analysis and see that such a situation leads to Nash equilibrium. We first restate the assumptions in game theory terms:

1 There are an unlimited number of potential firms that can produce a homogeneous product, with identical technology.
2 Consumers respond quickly to price changes.
3 Incumbent firms cannot respond quickly to entry by reducing price.
4 Entry into the market does not involve any sunk costs.
5 Firms are price-setting Bertrand competitors.

Let us take the example of two firms providing train services, Fast-trak and Pro-rail, which compete to provide service on a given route. The cost function for each firm is given by:

$$C = 40 + 80Q \quad \text{for } Q > 0$$
$$C = 0 \text{ when } Q = 0 \text{ (because there are no sunk costs)}$$

where C is total costs (in £'000 per month) and Q is number of passengers (in thousands per month).

The market demand is given by:

$$P = 125 - 5Q$$

where P is the ticket price (£). Consumers will buy at the lowest price, the product being homogeneous, and if both firms charge the same price it is assumed that customers will choose randomly between them. The firms have two elements in their strategies, the ticket price and the number of tickets they sell; they simultaneously announce their ticket prices and also the maximum number of tickets that they will sell. This is therefore a modified Bertrand price-setting game, which can be shown to have two Nash equilibria.

First we need to calculate the quantity and price where all profits are competed away. If we set revenue equal to costs we find that P is £85 and Q is 8,000 passengers per month. It follows that in both equilibria the ticket price is £85. In one equilibrium, Fast-trak's strategy is to sell no tickets if Pro-rail also announces a price of £85, but otherwise to sell to all customers; Pro-rail's strategy is to sell to all customers whatever price Fast-trak charges. The second equilibrium is simply the reverse of this situation.

In order to see why these are equilibria, consider the first situation from Fast-trak's viewpoint. Given that Pro-rail charges £85, if they charge above £85 they will sell no tickets and make zero profit. If they charge £85 they will sell half the total number of tickets sold, that is 4,000; they will make a loss at this output, so it is better to sell no tickets in this case. If they charge less than £85 they will make a loss, and therefore it is better to sell no tickets. Thus there is no price that Fast-trak can charge and make a profit, and it is better to stay out of the market. Now considering Pro-rail's position, given that Fast-trak stays out of the market, their best strategy is to charge £85. The other equilibrium can be viewed in a similar way, giving the reverse result.

9.2.3 Property rights*

We saw in Chapter 2 that the Coase theorem states that, if property rights are well defined and there are no bargaining costs, people can negotiate to a Pareto-optimal outcome, regardless of the disposition of property rights. On the other hand, if bargaining is not efficient, the allocation of property rights may affect behaviour and resource allocation.

There are three models that can be analysed using game theory, based on the Coase theorem, relating to the following situations:

1 Property rights are not well defined; this is a 'tragedy of the commons' situation.
2 Property rights are defined, and bargaining is costless.
3 Property rights are defined, but bargaining is costly.

For reasons of brevity we shall limit our analysis to the first situation, that involving undefined property rights.

An example of this situation, concerning fishing rights, was mentioned earlier. We shall now develop a formal example to show the social inefficiency or waste that results when resources are jointly owned. First, we need to consider a model of the resource itself. The growth in the population or stock of fish in any area depends on the size of the existing population. If this is small it is difficult for fish to find mates and therefore the growth of the population is slow. As the population increases in size, it tends to grow more quickly, as it becomes easier to find a mate, up to the point where competition for food supplies starts to increase the death rate. As the population grows further still the death rate will continue to increase. The overall rate of growth is given by the rate of births minus the rate of deaths; there is said to be a **steady-state equilibrium** (SSE) when *the birth and death rates are equal, and the population is static*. This situation can be represented by the following equation:

$$G = P(1 - P) \qquad\qquad (9.10)$$

where G represents the overall or net growth rate and P represents the population of fish, both measured in millions of fish. In SSE the value of G is zero; thus there are two SSEs in this situation: when the population is zero and when it is 1 million.

When the resource is fished, the resulting catch affects the equilibrium. The SSE will become the point where the growth rate (G) is equal to the catch rate (C). In order to catch the fish the fishermen must put in effort (E); this involves buying and maintaining boats and other equipment, hiring crew, spending time fishing and so on. The resulting catch depends on two factors: the amount of effort expended and the size of the fish population. This can be expressed as follows:

$$C = P.E \qquad (9.11)$$

In equilibrium the growth rate and catch rate are equal $(G = C)$, therefore it follows that:

$$P(1 - P) = P.E \qquad (9.12)$$

We can then see that the equilibrium population is given by:

$$P = 1 - E \qquad (9.13)$$

This expression can be used to express the catch output in terms of effort, by combining it with (9.11):

$$C = E(1 - E) \qquad (9.14)$$

Let us now assume for simplicity that there are just two fishing firms, called Adam and Bonnie (A and B). We shall also assume that both are rational, long-term profit maximizers. By long-term we mean that they know that their current fishing efforts affect the size of the fish population in the future, and hence future profits. Therefore, they want to maximize their **steady-state profits**, meaning the *profits that result from steady-state equilibrium*. Both firms know that if the catch is too high the population of fish will continue to fall, along with profits, until each become zero.

We have seen that the size of the catch depends on the total amount of effort expended by both A and B. We also assume that each firm is equally efficient at catching fish, meaning that their proportions of the total catch are equal to their proportions of total effort. We can now write:

$$E_T = E_A + E_B \qquad (9.15)$$

where E_T is total effort, E_A is effort by A and E_B is effort by B and

$$C_A = (E_A/E_T)C_T = (E_A/E_T)E_T(1 - E_T) = (E_A/E_T)E_T[1 - (E_A + E_B)] \qquad (9.16)$$

$$C_A = E_A - E_A^2 - E_A E_B$$

Similarly

$$C_B = E_B - E_B^2 - E_A E_B \qquad (9.17)$$

These last expressions represent production functions for each firm, showing that their fish output depends not only on their own effort, but also on the effort of competitors, in an inverse relationship.

In order to measure profits we assume for simplicity that the price of fish is £1 per fish and that fishing effort costs £0.10 per unit. The profit function of A is given by:

$$\Pi_A = E_A - E_A^2 - E_A E_B - 0.1 E_A = 0.9 E_A - E_A^2 - E_A E_B \qquad (9.18)$$

And the profit function of B is given by:

$$\Pi_B = E_B - E_B^2 - E_A E_B - 0.1 E_B = 0.9 E_B - E_B^2 - E_A E_B \qquad (9.19)$$

where profit is measured in millions of pounds. We now have the familiar problem of calculating the best-response functions of both firms. It can be seen that:

$$E_A = 0.45 - 0.5 E_B \qquad (9.20)$$

and

$$E_B = 0.45 - 0.5 E_A \qquad (9.21)$$

Thus

$$E_A = E_B = 0.3 \qquad (9.22)$$

This means that total effort is 0.6 effort units and the resulting total catch is given by:

$$C_T = 0.6(1 - 0.6) = 0.24 \text{ or } 240,000 \text{ fish} \qquad (9.23)$$

The reason why this is wasteful is that the same total catch could be achieved if $E = 0.4$. Thus 50 per cent more effort is spent catching fish than is necessary. It should be noted that the amount of this wasted effort depends on the cost of fishing. This issue is addressed in Problem 9.3.

9.2.4 Nash bargaining

There is one final application of the theory of static games that will be considered, consisting of a simple bargaining game. Bargaining games can take many forms, and some other forms will be considered later in the chapter, but the situation examined now is one where a sum of money is available to be shared between management and a labour union. The example is presented, first, to illustrate the application of game theory to the theory of the firm, and, second, to illustrate the primary importance of dominant and dominated strategies compared with Nash equilibrium.

The situation assumed here is that management and the union are negotiating on the basis of a one-shot bid. Let us take an amount of £1,000; to simplify the example we will also assume that there are only three possible discrete strategies, with each player simultaneously bidding either 0, £500 or the full £1,000. If the sum of the amounts bid does not exceed £1,000 then the players receive what they bid; if the sum of the bids exceeds £1,000 then negotiations

Table 9.7. Nash bargaining

		Union		
Strategy		0	500	1000
	0	0, 0	0, 500	0, 1000
Management	500	500, 0	500, 500	0, 0
	1000	1000, 0	0, 0	0, 0

break down and both players receive nothing. The normal form of this game is shown in Table 9.7. The management payoffs are shown first, followed by the payoffs for the union.

The problem is to determine the appropriate strategies for each player in terms of how much they should bid, assuming that they want to receive the maximum payoff, and do not care about the payoff of the other player. It might be thought that, since there appears to be no dominant strategy, we have to look for any Nash equilibria. There are then seen to be three of these, (1000, 0), (500, 500) and (0, 1000). There appears to be no definite conclusion on what each player should do, since any bid will have some other complementary bid associated with it in a Nash equilibrium.

This conclusion is false; it ignores the principle that we should eliminate dominated strategies before searching for an equilibrium. Bidding 0 is a dominated strategy for both players; both management and the union can do at least as well by bidding 500. This reduces the game to a two-strategy game. We can then see that the strategy of bidding 500 is dominant compared with the strategy of bidding 1000. Thus there is indeed a dominant strategy equilibrium

Case study 9.1: Experiments testing the Cournot equilibrium

An experiment was conducted in 1990 regarding the behaviour of people in a Cournot-type situation. Participants were put into groups of eight players and each player was given ten tokens. Each token could be redeemed for 5 cents or it could be sold on a market. When tokens were sold on the market the price was determined by how many tokens were offered by all eight players, in the following equation:

$$P = 23 - 0.25Q_T$$

where Q_T is the total number of tokens put up for sale by all eight players. Players could choose how many of their tokens to put up for sale and how many to redeem for the fixed price of 5 cents. At the end of each trial the total surplus was calculated, being measured as the excess value received by all the players over the 5 cents per token redeemable value. For example, if a total of sixty tokens are sold, the market price is 8 cents and the total surplus is 180 cents.

Questions

1 If the players collude, what will be the market price and the total surplus gained?

2 If the players act as in a Cournot oligopoly, what will be the market price and the total surplus gained?

3 In eighteen trials of the experiment the average surplus gained was 36 per cent of the maximum possible from collusion. Does this evidence support the existence of Cournot–Nash behaviour?

in this situation, with each player bidding 500. Some writers have called this a **'focal point' equilibrium**, because it *involves a 50–50 split between the players, generally perceived to be fair*. However, we should be wary of such intuitive analyis; many results of game theory are counter-intuitive. We shall indeed see at the end of the chapter that empirical studies confirm that the 'fairness' principle has some validity, but the reasons for this are more complex than they might seem at first sight.

9.3 Dynamic games

Many business scenarios tend to involve sequential moves rather than simultaneous moves. An example is the decision to invest in new plant. Sometimes firms can change a simultaneous game into a sequential game, whereas in other situations the game is naturally of a sequential type, for example when a management makes a wage offer to a labour union. Consider a situation of the first type, where there are two firms competing in an oligopolistic industry. Both firms are considering an expansion of their capacity in order to increase market share and profit. The resulting profits (in millions of pounds) are shown in Table 9.8.

It is assumed for simplicity that only two strategies are available to each firm, whereas, in reality, different scales of expansion would probably be possible; thus we are making the game into one of discrete rather than continuous strategies. This simplification does not affect the nature of the situation.

Equilibrium

In a simultaneous game Firm A has the dominant strategy of making no change, and Firm B iterates to the strategy of expanding. Thus Firm A will get a payoff of 70 and B will get its maximum payoff of 40. Firm A is not happy with this situation since it is better off if Firm B makes no change, but how can it persuade Firm B to do this? By moving first and taking the strategy of expanding. This transforms the game into a sequential one.

Dynamic games are best examined by drawing a **game tree**. The relevant game tree for Table 9.8 is shown in Figure 9.3. Such a game tree represents the game in extensive form. An **extensive-form game** not only *specifies the players, possible strategies, and payoffs, as in the normal-form game, but also specifies when players can move, and what information they have at the time of each move*.

In order to analyse this game tree we must derive the **subgame perfect Nash equilibrium** (SPNE). This is the situation where *each player selects an optimal action at each stage of the game that it might reach, believing the other player(s) will act in the same way*.

Decision nodes for each firm are shown by rectangles, and payoffs are shown with Firm A first in each pair.

Table 9.8. Transforming a simultaneous game into a sequential game

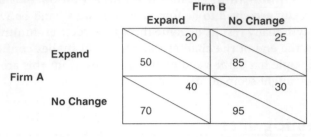

| | Firm B | |
	Expand	No Change
Firm A **Expand**	20 / 50	25 / 85
No Change	40 / 70	30 / 95

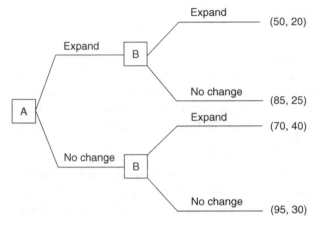

Figure 9.3. Game tree for capacity expansion game.

The SPNE is obtained by using the **'fold-back'** or **backwards induction** method.[7] This means that we proceed by *working backwards from the end of the tree, at each stage finding the optimal decision for the firm at that decision node*. Thus, if Firm A expands, the best decision for Firm B is to make no change (payoff of 25, compared with 20 for expanding). If Firm A makes no change the best decision for Firm B is to expand, with a payoff of 40 compared with 30 for making no change. Knowing this, Firm A can now make its original decision. If it expands, Firm B will make no change, and Firm A will get a payoff of 85; if it makes no change, Firm B will expand and Firm A will get a payoff of 70. Therefore, Firm A, acting first, will make the decision to expand. This yields an improvement of 15 compared with the original payoff of 70. Thus the apparently strange strategy of expansion by Firm A makes sense.

The game tree shown in Figure 9.3 applies to the situation where strategies are discrete. If strategies are continuous, game trees are less useful, since in this case strategies are generally represented as best-response functions, as we have already seen in the Cournot and Bertrand cases. However, game trees can still be an aid to clarifying the order of actions taken, and therefore the order of analysis.

9.3.2 *Strategic moves and commitment*

The move by Firm A is an example of a **strategic move**. This is an action *'designed to alter the beliefs and actions of others in a direction favourable to yourself'*.[8] The decision by Firm A to expand may seem strange, for two reasons:

1 Firm A's profit from making no change is greater than its profit from expanding, regardless of what strategy Firm B takes.
2 Moving first and investing in expansion limits Firm A's options and creates inflexibility.

This limitation of one's own options, combined with the credible commitment to do so, is the key feature of strategic moves. It has been called the **paradox of power**.[9] Let us consider a few realistic examples from various walks of life. Examples of making commitments are: protesters handcuffing themselves to railings, and 'doomsday' nuclear devices designed to automatically strike the enemy if attacked. An archetypal example of commitment is the burning of one's boats, as when Cortēs landed in Mexico to conquer the Aztec empire. This caused his soldiers to fight harder than otherwise, since they knew that they had no alternative.

The situation described in Figure 9.3 is an example of commitment. It illustrates the important point that strategies that may initially appear strange can in fact make sense. The inflexibility factor can cause other players to behave in ways in which they otherwise would not, and which favour the player making the commitment.

For a commitment to be successful in causing other players to change their behaviour it must be visible, understandable and credible. The first two characteristics are fairly self-explanatory, but the aspect of **credibility** needs to be examined in some detail. For a strategic move to be credible *it must be more in the player's interest to carry out the move than not to carry it out*. A key factor here is **irreversibility**. Consider the situation in Table 9.8. If Firm A merely announces in the media its intention to expand, this action has little credibility because it is easy to reverse. However, if Firm A actually starts building operations, then this action is much more costly to abandon. This is particularly true if the investment activity involves considerable sunk costs. Thus although it was stated in Chapter 6 that sunk costs are not important in decision-making, in this context sunk costs *are* an important factor. They create the kind of inflexibility that is necessary for a commitment to be credible. There are a number of factors that can create such irreversibility.

1. *Writing contracts.* These legal agreements can make it difficult and costly for a player to change its actions later. Thus, although we have seen that contracts are important in order to prevent the other party from opportunistic behaviour, by limiting their actions, they can also be useful in making credible commitments by limiting one's own actions.

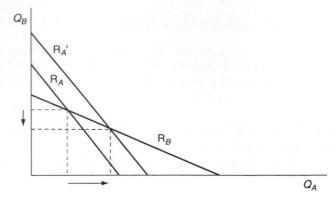

Figure 9.4. The effect of commitment on Cournot response curves.

2. *Reputation effects*. The threat of losing one's reputation can serve as a credible commitment. For example, when one firm offers to provide a service to another firm, and moral hazard is involved because the performance of the service cannot be immediately observed, the firm offering the service can claim that it cannot afford to provide a bad service because it would lose its reputation.

3. *Burning one's bridges*. The example of Cortēs in Mexico shows the effect of this type of action. However, the action does not have to be as drastic as this. For a politician, a publicized policy statement may be sufficient, although politicians have been known to do 'U-turns'.

4. *Breaking off communications*. This again prevents the player from changing their actions at a later date. However, such a move can also create other problems in terms of discovering the effectiveness of one's strategy in relation to the other player(s).

a. Cournot commitment

The kind of commitment related to the situation described in Table 9.8 can also be illustrated using the analysis of Cournot competition. This is competition in terms of output, and a credible commitment to expand will shift Firm A's response curve to the right. For any given output of Firm B, Firm A will now produce more than before, as shown in Figure 9.4. This in turn causes a change in the equilibrium situation, with Firm A producing more output and Firm B producing less output than before the commitment, just as we saw using the game tree analysis.

b. Bertrand commitment

The commitment to expand is only one type of commitment. Let us return to the pricing competition in Figure 9.4. This was originally a simultaneous game involving a Prisoner's Dilemma; the dominant strategy for Pepsi (Firm B) was to discount, thus leading Coke also to discount. The situation is reproduced in general terms in the game matrix of Table 9.9.

Table 9.9. Prisoner's Dilemma in price competition

		Firm B	
		Maintain Price	**Discount**
Firm A	**Maintain Price**	50 / 80	70 / −10
	Discount	−10 / 70	10 / 10

As we have already seen, both players end up worse off in this situation than they would be if they both maintained price. How can a firm credibly commit to a strategy of maintaining price? Merely announcing an intention to maintain price is not sufficient, since this has no credibility, given the dominant strategies of both firms. An ingenious solution to this problem has been commonly implemented by many firms in oligopolistic situations. This involves a firm using a '**most favoured customer clause**' (MFCC). Essentially what this involves is *a guarantee to customers that the firm will not charge a lower price to other customers for some period in the future*; if it does, it will pay a rebate to existing customers for the amount of the price reduction, or sometimes double this amount. This is particularly important in consumer durable markets. The reason why this strategy is ingenious is that it serves a dual purpose.

1. *Ostensibly, it creates good customer relations.* Many customers are concerned when they are considering buying a new consumer durable that the firm will reduce the price of the product later on. This applies particularly when there are rapid changes in technology and products are phased out over relatively short periods, for example computers and other electronics products.

2. *The MFCC creates a price commitment.* It would be expensive for the firm to reduce price at a later stage, since it would have to pay rebates to all its previous customers. Thus other firms are convinced that the firm will maintain its price, and this causes prices to be higher than they would be without such commitment, as is seen below.

A commitment by Firm A to maintain price in this situation will not achieve the desired effect; Firm B will discount, and Firm A will end up worse than before. However, there is scope for Firm B to make such a commitment; in this case it would be in Firm A's best interest also to maintain price, obtaining a payoff of 80, compared with 70 if it discounts. Thus Firm B will end up better off than originally without such a commitment, obtaining a payoff of 50, compared with 10. Ironically, contrary to what customers might have expected, the MFCC by Firm B causes prices to be higher than they otherwise would have been.

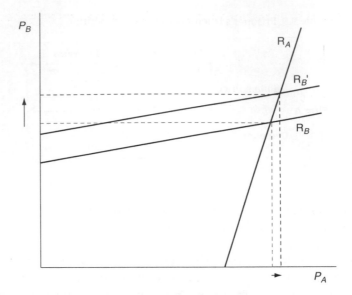

Figure 9.5. The effect of commitment on Bertrand response curves.

The situation here can again be represented graphically, this time in terms of Bertrand competition. The commitment by Firm B to maintain price has the effect of shifting its reaction curve upwards, meaning that for any given price charged by Firm A, it will charge a higher price than before. The effect is to change the equilibrium, with both firms charging a higher price than before the commitment. This is illustrated in Figure 9.5.

We have now considered two kinds of commitment, one in terms of output and one in terms of price. Another type of output commitment is the investment in excess capacity, which serves as a deterrent to entry. Potential entrants recognize the ability of an existing firm to increase output substantially, at low marginal cost; thus driving down the market price. The incumbent firm can afford to do this because of its low marginal cost; thus the threat to potential entrants is credible. Other types of commitment can also be considered, as well as other methods of achieving credibility. For example, commitments can also be made in terms of product quality and advertising expenditure.

9.3.3 Stackelberg oligopoly

We have now examined various models of oligopoly using static games. We have also considered some dynamic models involving discrete strategies. There is one other oligopoly situation that needs to be considered in this context; this is a dynamic oligopoly game, involving continuous strategies. This is commonly called the Stackelberg model;[10] although it was originally developed in non-game theory terms, we will apply a game theory analysis to the situation. The basic assumptions underlying the **Stackelberg model** are as follows:

1 *There are few firms and many buyers.*
2 *The firms produce either homogeneous or differentiated products.*
3 *A single firm, the leader, chooses an output before all other firms choose their outputs.*
4 *All other firms, as followers, take the output of the leader as given.*
5 *Barriers to entry exist.*
6 *All firms aim to maximize profit, and assume that the other firms do the same.*

We shall now refer to the same situation, in terms of demand and cost functions, as that assumed earlier for the Cournot duopoly and examine how equilibrium is determined. We shall then draw certain conclusions regarding the differences in outcomes.

Market demand was given by:

$$P = 400 - 2Q$$

Each firm has a cost function given by:

$$C_i = 40Q_i$$

Thus we can write the market demand as:

$$P = 400 - 2(Q_L + Q_F)$$
$$P = 400 - 2Q_L - 2Q_F \tag{9.24}$$

where Q_L is the output of the leader and Q_F is the output of the follower.

We need to analyse the situation by first considering the situation for the follower, in keeping with the 'foldback' method discussed earlier. It is essentially acting in the same way as a Cournot duopolist. Thus its profit function is given by:

$$\Pi_F = (400 - 2Q_L - 2Q_F)Q_F - 40Q_F = 400Q_F - 2Q_F^2 - 2Q_LQ_F - 40Q_F$$
$$\Pi_F = 360Q_F - 2Q_F^2 - 2Q_LQ_F \tag{9.25}$$

The next step is to obtain the response function for the follower, by deriving the optimal output for the follower as a function of the output of the leader; thus we differentiate the profit function with respect to Q_F and set the partial derivative equal to zero:

$$\frac{\partial \Pi_F}{\partial Q_F} = 360 - 4Q_F - 2Q_L = 0$$

$$4Q_F = 360 - 2Q_L$$
$$\mathbf{Q_F = 90 - 0.5Q_L} \tag{9.26}$$

It should be noted that this is the same as the Cournot result as far as the follower is concerned. However, the leader can now use this information regarding the follower's response function when choosing the output that maximizes its own profit. Thus it will have the demand function given by:

$$P_L = 400 - 2Q_L - 2(90 - 0.5Q_L) \tag{9.27}$$

Or

$$P_L = 220 - Q_L \tag{9.28}$$

The leader's profit function is given by:

$$\Pi_L = (220 - Q_L)Q_L - 40Q_L \tag{9.29}$$

$$\frac{\partial \Pi_L}{\partial Q_L} = 220 - 2Q_L - 40 = 0$$

$$\mathbf{Q_L = 90} \tag{9.30}$$

We can now obtain the output of the follower by using the response function in (9.26), giving us $\mathbf{Q_F = 45}$.

These outputs allow us to obtain the market price:

$$\mathbf{P = 400 - 2(90 + 45) = £130} \tag{9.31}$$

We can now obtain the profits for each firm:

$$\Pi_L = (130 - 40)90 = £8,100$$

and

$$\Pi_F = (130 - 40)45 = £4,050$$

Total profit for the industry is **£12,150**.

These results can be compared with the Cournot situation (CS), yielding the following conclusions:

1 Price is not as high as in the CS (£130 compared with £160).
2 Output of the leader is higher and output of the follower lower than in the CS.
3 Profit of the leader is higher and profit of the follower lower than in the CS.
4 Total profit in the industry is lower than in the CS (£12,150 compared with £14,400).

Thus we can see that in the Stackelberg situation there is an advantage to being the first mover, just as there was in the market entry situation. However, we should not think that there is always an advantage to being first mover, as we shall see in the next section.

A case study is now presented involving the concepts of equilibrium discussed in this section. Ostensibly the main application of the case concerns the use of monetary policy, a macroeconomic issue. However, at a deeper and more general level, the situation is important in terms of organization theory, since conflicts between strong-willed senior executives, board members and major shareholders may well involve similar payoffs and strategies.

Case study 9.2: Monetary policy in Thailand

The games people play[11]

Let's have fun with game theory, which can shed some light on the outcome of the monetary policy dispute between Prime Minister Thaksin Shinawatra and former Bank of Thailand governor MR Chatu Mongol Sonakul.

Many might be perplexed by Chatu Mongol's abrupt dismissal after he refused to cave in to the government's demand to raise interest rates. But by applying game theory to analyse the jostling between the two, one may find a surprising answer and become more aware of the usefulness of the tool. We know that Thaksin and Chatu Mongol took polar positions on the issue and are by nature rather proud and stubborn. So let us begin by constructing what the payoff matrix for the interest rate policy would have been before Chatu Mongol was sacrificed.

Faced with Thaksin's command to 'review' the central bank's longstanding low interest rate policy, Chatu Mongol could do one of two things – concede to Thaksin, or not give way. Similarly, Thaksin had two options in dealing with the obstinate governor – either fire him or keep him. In order to keep the game simple, we rank the preferences for the possible outcomes from worst to best, and assign the respective payoffs the numbers 1 through to 4. Chatu Mongol had made it perfectly clear that he had no intention of changing the low interest rate policy. Therefore, the worst outcome for Chatu Mongol was to concede but then get fired, so that outcome would have a payoff of 1 for him.

The second worst outcome was to concede and not be fired, but that would leave Chatu Mongol with his integrity bruised and the central bank with its independence impaired.

The third worst outcome was not to concede, and get fired. Though he might lose his job, he could still maintain his integrity and time could prove his stance correct.

Chatu Mongol's strongest preference was not to concede, but still keep his job. This outcome would have a payoff of 4 for him. This would mean he had beaten Thaksin in their two-way gamesmanship. Meanwhile, the worst outcome for Thaksin would be for Chatu Mongol to defy his demand, but to keep the maverick as central bank governor.

The second worst option was for Chatu Mongol to make a concession, but for the PM to have to fire the governor anyway to avoid future trouble. The next worst scenario was for Thaksin to fire Chatu Mongol for his defiance. Thaksin's highest preference was for Chatu Mongol to fully agree with his demand so that he would not have to get rid of him as governor.

Questions

1. Describe the type of game that is involved in the above situation.
2. Draw a game tree of the situation, with the appropriate payoffs.
3. Using the backward induction method, analyse the game tree and explain the result observed.

9.4 Games with uncertain outcomes*

All the games considered up to this point have been **deterministic**; this means that *the outcome of any strategy profile, or pair of strategies corresponding to a cell in the normal form, is known with certainty*. In practice there may be a number of causes of uncertainty concerning the effects of any action. For example, when a firm enters a market it is not sure what profit it will make, even given the strategy of a rival firm. We will start by considering situations where the uncertainty relates to the choice of the other player's strategy.

In some games there are no Nash equilibria at all, at least in the sense discussed so far. A familiar example of a game of this type is the 'paper–rock–scissors' game. In this game there are two players, who simultaneously raise

Table 9.10. Paper–rock–scissors game

Strategy		Player B	
	Paper	Rock	Scissors
Paper	0, 0	1, −1	−1, 1
Rock	−1, 1	0, 0	1, −1
Scissors	1, −1	−1, 1	0, 0

Player A labels the rows: Paper, Rock, Scissors.

their hands to indicate any one of three possible strategies: paper, rock or scissors. The rule for determining the winner is that paper beats (wraps) rock, rock beats (blunts) scissors, while scissors beats (cuts) paper. This game is shown in normal form in Table 9.10. In order to see why there is no Nash equilibrium here, consider what happens when player A plays paper; player B is then best off playing scissors, but then player A is better off playing rock. A similar situation occurs with any choice of strategy.

9.4.1 *Mixed strategies*

Many 'games' have the same essential characteristic of the 'paper–rock–scissors' game, in terms of having no ordinary Nash equilibrium. For example poker and tennis are in this category, as are many business situations, like monitoring employees at work. Before examining these in more detail, we need to contrast two types of strategy, pure strategies and mixed strategies. All the strategies considered so far in this chapter have been **pure strategies**. These are strategies where *the same action is always taken*; for example a discounting strategy means discounting all the time. **Mixed strategies** involve the player *randomizing over two or more available actions, in order to prevent rivals from being able to predict one's action*. This is particularly important in the repeated game context discussed in the next section. Poker players, for example, do not always want to bet heavily when they have a good hand and bet lightly or fold when they have a bad hand. This would enable other players to predict the strength of their hands, so that a heavy bet would cause other players to fold early and prevent a big win. Bluffing becomes a vital part of the game in this context; this means that players will sometimes bet heavily on a bad hand, not just to try and win that hand, but to prevent rivals from being able to tell when they have a good hand. Similarly, if a tennis player always serves to his opponent's backhand, the other player will come to anticipate this and better prepare to return the serve; if the server mixes the serve, in direction, speed and spin, this is likely to unsettle the opponent. However, for the mixed strategy to be effective it must be randomized; if the other player detects a pattern, for example that the server alternates serving to backhand and forehand, then this defeats the purpose, since once again the action becomes predictable.

Table 9.11. Game with no pure strategy equilibrium

		Worker	
	Strategy	Work	Shirk
Manager	Monitor	− 1, 1	1, − 1
	Do not monitor	1, − 1	− 1, 1

It can be shown that in cases where there is no Nash equilibrium in pure strategies, there will always be a Nash equilibrium in mixed strategies. The proof of this theorem is beyond the scope of this text. The problem then becomes: how does one randomize the strategies effectively? In order to explain this we will consider a different situation, a common one in business. This concerns the monitoring of employees. In a simplified situation the manager can either monitor or not monitor the worker, while the worker can choose either to work or to shirk. Both players are assumed to choose their strategies simultaneously. If the manager monitors while the worker works, then the manager loses since it costs the manager to monitor, while there is in this case no gain. If the manager monitors and the worker shirks, then the worker loses, since they are caught and may lose their job. If the manager does not monitor and the worker works, then the worker loses, since they could have taken things easy. If the manager does not monitor and the worker shirks then the manager loses, since the firm ends up paying for work that is not performed. A simple example of the normal form of this game is shown in Table 9.11.

a. Symmetrical payoffs

In the initial situation shown in Table 9.11 the payoffs are arbitrary in terms of units, and are chosen on the basis of simplicity and symmetry.

Just as with the paper–rock–scissors game it can be seen that there is no equilibrium in pure strategies. For example, if the manager monitors, it is best for the worker to work; but if the worker works, it is best for the manager not to monitor. Note how important it is that the choice of strategies is simultaneous. If one player moves first the other player will automatically use a strategy to defeat the first player, again as with the paper–rock–scissors game. We can now see that in such games the first mover would be at a disadvantage, unlike the games considered earlier. In terms of randomizing strategy, in this case the manager should monitor on a fifty–fifty chance basis. This choice can be determined by tossing a coin. It may seem strange that business managers should determine strategy in this way, but the essence of randomization is not the method chosen by the randomizing player but how the player's strategy choice is perceived by the other player. As long as the worker thinks that there is a fifty–fifty chance of the manager monitoring, this will achieve the desired objective. The same considerations apply to

Table 9.12. Game with no pure strategy equilibrium and asymmetric payoffs

		Worker	
	Strategy	Work	Shirk
Manager	Monitor	10, 8	5, 0
	Do not monitor	15, 10	2, 15

randomizing the worker's strategy. Both players need to appear to be unpredictable to the other player.

Asymmetric payoffs

The situation becomes more complicated if the payoffs are not symmetrical as they are in Table 9.11. For example, it may cost the worker a lot more if they are caught shirking and lose their job than it costs the manager if the manager needlessly monitors them when they are working. The result may be a payoff matrix like the one in Table 9.12.

There is still no Nash equilibrium in this situation, so again we have to consider a mixed strategy equilibrium. How then do the players randomize, given the nature of the payoffs?

In order to find this solution we need to consider the probabilities of each player taking each action. Let us call the probability of the manager monitoring p_m, and the probability of the worker working p_w. Therefore the probability of the manager not monitoring is given by $(1 - p_m)$ and the probability of the worker shirking is given by $(1 - p_w)$. Since we are assuming that the players randomize independently we can now say that the probability of the manager monitoring and the worker working is given by $p_m p_w$, while the probability of the manager monitoring and the worker shirking is given by $p_m(1 - p_w)$, and so on. This enables us to compute the expected payoffs to each player as follows:

$$EV_m(p_m, p_w) = 10p_m p_w + 5p_m(1 - p_w) + 15(1 - p_m)p_w + 2(1 - p_m)(1 - p_w)$$

This shows that this expected payoff to the manager is a function of both the probability of monitoring and the probability of working. This value simplifies to:

$$EV_m(p_m, p_w) = 13(2/13 + p_w) + 8p_m(3/8 - p_w) \tag{9.32}$$

Likewise the expected payoff to the worker can be computed as follows:

$$EV_w(p_m, p_w) = 8p_m p_w + 0p_m(1 - p_w) + 10(1 - p_m)p_w + 15(1 - p_m)(1 - p_w)$$

Thus

$$EV_w(p_m, p_w) = 15(1 - p_m) + 13p_w(p_m - 5/13) \tag{9.33}$$

Table 9.13. Probabilities of outcomes in mixed strategy equilibrium

		Worker	
	Strategy	Work ($p = 3/8$)	Shirk ($p = 5/8$)
Manager	Monitor ($p = 5/13$)	$15/104 = 0.144$	$25/104 = 0.240$
	Do not monitor ($p = 8/13$)	$24/104 = 0.231$	$40/104 = 0.385$

The mixed strategy combination of probabilities is a Nash equilibrium if and only if the four following conditions hold:

1. $0 < p_m^* < 1$
2. $0 < p_w^* < 1$
3. p_m^* maximizes the function $EV_m(p_m, p_w^*)$
4. p_w^* maximizes the function $EV_w(p_m^*, p_w)$

where p_m^* denotes the optimal value of p_m, given p_w^*, and p_w^* denotes the optimal value of p_w, given p_m^*.

Examining (9.32) we can see that it is a strictly increasing function of p_m when $p_w < 3/8$, is strictly decreasing when $p_w > 3/8$, and is constant when $p_w = 3/8$. Therefore $\boldsymbol{p_w^* = 3/8}$. This means that when the probability of the worker working is 3/8 the manager is indifferent between monitoring and not monitoring; this creates the desired unpredictability. Likewise, examining (9.33) we can see that $\boldsymbol{p_m^* = 5/13}$. From these probabilities we can now compute the probabilities of outcomes when the mixed strategy equilibrium exists. This situation is shown in Table 9.13.

Finally, it should be noted that in the above case the mixed strategy equilibrium is the only equilibrium; this does not imply that when there is a pure strategy equilibrium a mixed strategy equilibrium is not possible. There are situations where both pure and mixed strategy equilibria exist.

9.4.2 Moral hazard and pay incentives

The design of appropriate pay incentives is an important aspect of the organization of the firm. Let us consider the situation of a firm wanting to hire research scientists. If these researchers make a breakthrough, the rewards to the firm will be large, but such rewards are uncertain since the research output, measured in terms of breakthroughs, is not guaranteed. The nature of such a game is that the firm moves first, offering a pay package, the employee accepts or rejects, and then decides how much effort to put in. There is moral hazard because the effort cannot be directly observed, only the eventual output. The objective of the firm, as principal, is to align the interests of the worker, as agent, with its own. We shall assume for simplicity that the workers are risk-neutral, as is the firm. We shall also assume that the workers' strategies are discrete: they can make either a low effort or a high

Table 9.14. Pay and incentives[12]

Strategy	Probability of success	Average revenue ($,000)	Salary payments ($,000)	Average profit = revenue − salary ($,000)
Low effort	0.6	300	125	175
High effort	0.8	400	175	225

effort. A concrete example of this situation is shown in Table 9.14. The profit from a breakthrough is valued at $500,000; scientists can be hired for $125,000, but will only give a low effort for this sum. To obtain a high effort from the scientists the salary must be $175,000.

The firm is obviously better off getting a high effort from the scientists; the problem is how to design a system of pay incentives that will motivate the scientists to deliver the high effort.

Clearly, paying them $175,000 will not achieve this, since their effort is unobservable. Some kind of bonus is necessary, based on the achievement of a breakthrough. There are two stages involved in determining the appropriate pay system: first, determination of the size of the bonus; and, second, determination of the payments for success and failure.

1. *Determination of the size of the bonus.* The bonus is the pay differential between achieving success (a breakthrough) and suffering failure. We can write this as:

$$B = x_s - x_f \tag{9.34}$$

where B is the size of the bonus and x_s and x_f are the payments made to the scientists for success and failure.

The principle involved in determining the size of the bonus is that it should be just large enough to make it in the employee's interest to supply high effort. It should therefore equal the ratio of the salary differential to the probability differential for success; this can be expressed as follows:

$$B = \frac{\Delta S}{\Delta P_S} \tag{9.35}$$

Therefore, in this case, $B = \frac{175-125}{0.8-0.6} = \frac{50}{0.2} = 250$, or **$250,000**

2. *Determination of the payments for success and failure.* The principle involved here is that the expected pay for success should equal the high-effort salary. This can be expressed as follows:

$$p_s x_s + p_f x_f = S_h \tag{9.36}$$

where p_s is the probability of success, p_f is the probability of failure, and S_h is the high-effort salary.

Thus

$$0.8x_s + 0.2x_f = 175$$

We can now substitute (9.34) into (9.36) and solve simultaneously:

$$B = x_s - x_f = 250$$

giving

$$x_s = 225, \text{ or } \textbf{\$225,000}$$

and

$$x_f = -25, \text{ or } -\textbf{\$25,000}$$

Of course it may not be possible in practice to use such a payment scheme, particularly since it involves a penalty paid by the worker for not achieving success. There may be legal restrictions. We have also ignored the wealth effects discussed in Chapter 2, and different attitudes to risk by the firm and the workers.

9.4.3 *Moral hazard and efficiency wages*

In the second chapter of this text there was much discussion of agency theory, moral hazard and its effects. We are now in a position to examine these effects in a more detailed manner. We will consider a dynamic multistage game as follows. A firm is hiring workers, and has to make two strategy choices: what wage it should pay the workers (W) and how many workers it should hire (L). Workers then have to decide whether to accept the wage or not. If they do not accept they have a reservation utility (M), based on the wage that they could obtain elsewhere. If a worker accepts the wage they then have to decide how much effort to exert (E). This measures the fraction of the time the worker actually spends working, and is treated as a continuous variable having a value between 0 (no work) and 1 (no shirking). This is a hidden action, but can sometimes be detected by the firm; the probability of being caught shirking is inversely related to the amount of effort exerted. Workers caught shirking are fired, and revert to their reservation utility; it is assumed that the firm can replace such workers costlessly. It is also assumed here that monitoring workers is costless.

We will assume the following functions:

1 Revenue for firm(a function of L and E) $= \ln(1 + LE)$ (9.37)

   This mathematical form corresponds to the situation where revenue is zero when L and E are zero, and is a decreasing function of both variables. The graphical relationship between revenue and number of workers is shown in Figure 9.6.

2 The utility function for the workers is given by:

$$U(W, E) = W(1 - 0.5E) \qquad (9.38)$$

   This means that the utility from working is a function of both the wage and the work effort.

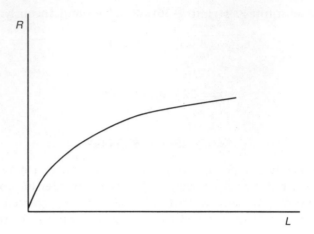

Figure 9.6. Relationship between revenue and number of workers.

3 The probability of being caught shirking is given by:

$$P_s = 1 - E \tag{9.39}$$

We can now obtain the profit function for the firm:

$$\Pi(W, L, E) = \ln(1 + LE) - WL \tag{9.40}$$

The extensive-form game is now shown in Figure 9.7 in order to aid analysis. The payoffs are omitted for the sake of clarity.

We can now proceed to use backward induction to determine the optimal wage (W^*), the optimal number of workers to hire (L^*) and the optimal work effort for the workers to exert (E^*). The first decision to consider is the work effort by the workers. First we have to estimate their expected utility, given that there is a chance of being caught shirking (this is where the uncertainty element lies).

$$\begin{aligned} \text{Exp}.U(W,E) &= (1 - E)M + EW(1 - 0.5E) \\ &= M + (W - M)E - 0.5WE^2 \end{aligned} \tag{9.41}$$

To find the optimal effort that maximizes the workers' utility we have to differentiate the expected utility function with respect to effort and set the result equal to zero:

$$\frac{\partial U}{\partial E} = W - M - WE^* = 0$$
$$E^* = (W - M)/W \tag{9.42}$$

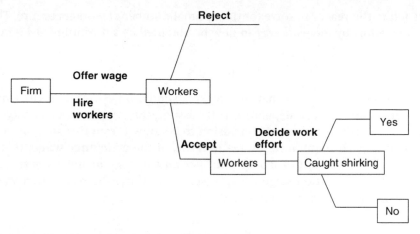

Figure 9.7. Moral hazard in the labour market.

This expression can now be substituted into the profit function for the firm to obtain:

$$\Pi(W,\ L,\ E) = \ln[1 + L(W - M)/W] - WL \qquad (9.43)$$

We can now obtain the profit-maximizing levels of wages and workers by differentiating (9.41) with respect to both W and L. It is necessary to recall that to differentiate a logarithmic function we have to use the rule that if $y = \ln(u)$ where $u = f(x)$, then

$$\frac{dy}{dx} = \frac{1}{u}\frac{du}{dx}$$

Therefore

$$\frac{\partial \Pi}{\partial W} = \frac{LM/W^2}{1 + L(W - M)/W} - L = 0$$

and

$$\frac{\partial \Pi}{\partial L} = \frac{(W - M)/W}{1 + L(W - M)/W} - W = 0$$

We now need to solve these equations simultaneously in order to solve for W^* and L^*.

$$L = \frac{M - W^2}{(W - M)/W} \qquad (9.44)$$

This expression can now be substituted in order to obtain W^*:

$$W^* = 2M \qquad (9.45)$$

It is left to the reader to solve for the optimal number of workers to hire. The optimal effort by the workers can now be obtained by substituting (9.45) into (9.42):

$$E^* = 0.5 \tag{9.46}$$

This conclusion indicates that the workers should only work half the time! Obviously this fraction depends on the assumptions made in our analysis. There is one more important conclusion to be drawn from this analysis, and this concerns the equilibrium wage in terms of the **efficiency wage**; this is defined as the ***amount of money paid per unit of time actually worked***. At present the reservation wage is expressed as a utility; the reservation wage can be obtained by turning around (9.38):

$$W_r = \frac{M}{1 - 0.5E} \tag{9.47}$$

Assuming that effort is 50 per cent, the reservation wage is **4/3(M)**.

This reservation wage is the market-clearing wage, meaning the wage where the quantity of labour demanded equals the quantity supplied. However, in this case it is not an equilibrium wage. The firm is prepared to pay a higher wage, 50 per cent higher, in order to deter workers from shirking. At the higher wage, workers have more to lose through being caught shirking and reverting to the reservation wage; therefore, they are encouraged to work harder.

9.5 Repeated games*

Many games in business situations involve repeated plays, often with imperfect information. This is obvious in the pricing situation. Firms have the opportunity to change their prices monthly or weekly, or in some cases even more frequently. This adds a whole new dimension to the consideration of strategy, especially in the Prisoner's Dilemma situation. Returning to the original Coke and Pepsi game matrix in Table 9.2, we have seen that in the one-shot situation it is an optimal strategy for both firms to 'defect' and discount. When the game is repeated this conclusion is not necessarily justified, as it is possible for co-operation to become in the interests of both players. In order to develop the analysis further we must draw a distinction between infinitely repeated games and finitely repeated games.

Infinitely repeated games

These are games where ***the same game is played over and over again forever, with players receiving payoffs after each round***. Given this situation we have to consider the time value of money in order to calculate the present value of payoffs. More specifically, in order to determine the optimal strategy in this situation, we have to compare the present values of two different strategies: co-operate at start and defect at start. These strategies involve situations where making a decision to defect in any one time period may be met with a retaliatory decision to defect by the other firm in the next time period. Thus the gain from defecting has to be offset by any expected loss in the future arising from such an action. This loss depends on the strategy of the other player(s).

a. Strategies and payoffs

The strategies involved are now explained and the resulting payoffs are computed, based on the one-shot payoffs in Table 9.2.

1 *Co-operate at start.* In the Coke–Pepsi case this means maintaining price; we then need to calculate the discounted payoffs in the two situations where the rival also maintains price forever and when it discounts forever.
2 *Defect at start.* This means discounting forever; again we need to calculate the payoffs from the two possible rival strategies being considered.

These payoffs are now calculated as follows, assuming an interest rate of 20 per cent (for the time being):

1 *Co-operate at start*

a. If the rival also co-operates and maintains price the stream of payoffs will be:

$$PV = 50 + \frac{50}{(1+i)} + \frac{50}{(1+i)^2} + \ldots = \frac{50(1+i)}{i} = 50(1.2/0.2) = \mathbf{300}$$

b. If the rival defects, it is assumed that the player reverts to discounting after the first round, and continues to discount forever.

$$PV = -10 + \frac{10}{(1+i)} + \frac{10}{(1+i)^2} + \ldots = -10 + \frac{10}{i} = -10 + 50 = \mathbf{40}$$

2 *Defect at start*

a. If the rival starts by co-operating the player gets a big payoff at the start, but then it is assumed that the rival switches to discounting and continues to do so.

$$PV = 70 + \frac{10}{(1+i)} + \frac{10}{(1+i)^2} + \ldots = 70 + \frac{10}{i} = 70 + 50 = \mathbf{120}$$

b. If the rival also defects from the start, all the payoffs are identical.

$$PV = 10 + \frac{10}{(1+i)} + \frac{10}{(1+i)^2} + \ldots = \frac{10(1+i)}{i} = 10(1.2/0.2) = \mathbf{60}$$

Table 9.15. Infinitely repeated Prisoner's Dilemma

	Pepsi	
	Maintain price	**Discount**
Coke **Maintain price**	300 / 300	120 / 40
Discount	40 / 120	60 / 60

We can now compile the normal form for this infinitely repeated game, based on the assumptions made, and this is shown in Table 9.15.

In this repeated situation there is no longer any dominant strategy; rather there are two Nash equilibria where the players either both co-operate or both defect. Clearly the co-operation equilibrium is mutually much more desirable in this case; to some extent this is caused by the relative sizes of the payoffs, but the result is also sensitive to changes in the interest rate used for discounting. It can be shown in the above example that the co-operation strategy leads to higher mutual payoffs as long as the discount rate is less than 200 per cent. It might seem that this is a convincing case for co-operation, but there is no guarantee that it will occur. This uncertainty in the result is caused by the **trigger strategy** that we have assumed. In general, a trigger strategy involves *taking actions that are contingent on the past play of the game*. Different actions by the rival will trigger different responses, not necessarily just to the last round of the game, but maybe to previous rounds as well.

b. Trigger strategies

The trigger strategy we have assumed so far is called a '**grim trigger strategy**' (GTS). This means that any decision to defect by a rival is met with a permanent retaliatory defection in all following time periods. The main feature of such a strategy is that it has a strong deterrent effect on defection. The GTS, if credible, can ensure co-operation, provided that rivals can first of all detect any defection easily, and second, if they can, change prices fairly quickly. However, there is a significant weakness associated with the GTS: it is highly vulnerable to '**misreads**'. A misread means that either a firm mistakes the real price that a rival is charging, or it misinterprets the reasons for the pricing decision. Such misreads can easily occur in practice. For example, one firm may adopt the habit of offering regular rebates off the actual price, and advertise the price with the rebate deducted; another firm may not allow for such rebates in assessing the rival's price and underestimate it. Thus a GTS can initiate a perpetual price war, which ultimately harms all the participating firms.

An attempt to improve on this strategy is a '**trembling hand trigger strategy**' (THTS), which allows one mistake by the other player before defecting continually. However, this strategy is subject to exploitation by clever opponents if it is understood. A more forgiving strategy than GTS or THTS is '**tit-for-tat**' (TFT). This simple rule involves repeating the rival's previous move. Defection is punished in the next round of play, but if the rival reverts to co-operating, then the game will revert to mutual co-operation in the following round. Thus TFT is less vulnerable to misreads than GTS. It has therefore been argued that TFT is a preferable strategy in situations where misreads are likely.[13] An even more forgiving strategy is '**tit-for-two-tats**' (TFTT); this allows two consecutive defections before retaliation. However, if such a strategy is read by the opponent, they can take advantage and continually defect for a single time period without incurring punishment.

One might wonder at this point how it would be possible to test different strategies in such repetitive games in order to measure their success against each other. The mathematics of such situations rapidly becomes intractable, given a multitude of players and strategies. Therefore such tests have to be carried out by computer simulation. Axelrod[14] was the first researcher to explore these possibilities. He investigated the issue of optimal strategy in repeated PD by having 151 strategies competing against each other 1,000 times. His conclusions were that successful strategies had the following characteristics:

1 *Simplicity.* They are easy to understand by opponents, making misreads less likely.
2 *Niceness.* They initiate co-operation.
3 *Provocability.* They have credible commitments to some punishment rule.
4 *Forgiveness.* This is necessary in order for the game to recover from mistakes by either player.

It was found that TFT won against all other strategies in the tournament through its combination of the above characteristics.

After Axelrod's work was published, a number of criticisms were made, particularly regarding the conclusion that TFT was generally a superior strategy. Martinez-Coll and Hirshleifer[15] commented that it was easy to design conditions for a tournament in which TFT would not triumph. Binmore[16] pointed out that TFT was incapable of winning single games against more aggressive strategies. As computer simulations became more realistic, with different strategies battling against each other for survival, some of the weaknesses of TFT became more evident. In particular, it is too vulnerable to mistakes; as soon as one partner defects, a continuous debilitating stream of defections by each player occurs, as in a prolonged price war.

In order to find more stable winning strategies, other researchers have since introduced more realistic elements into their computer-simulated tournaments. Nowak *et al.*[17] introduced a stochastic model rather than using the previous deterministic one; strategies made random mistakes with certain probabilities, or switched tactics in some probabilistic manner. Players could also learn from experience and shift strategies accordingly. Nowak *et al.* found that a new strategy, called '**generous tit-for-tat**' (GTFT), came to dominate over TFT. GTFT occasionally forgives single defections, on a random basis so as not to be exploited. This 'nicer' strategy is therefore less vulnerable to mistakes and the consequent endless rounds of retaliation.

However, although GTFT proved superior to TFT, it was still vulnerable to other strategies. Because of its generosity it allowed '**always co-operate**' (AC) to spread. This strategy is easily overcome by '**always defect**' (AD), the 'nastiest' strategy of all. Thus, although AD could not survive against GTFT, the fact that GTFT led to AC encouraged the spread of AD. Again, the model had no stable winning strategy. Then Nowak *et al.* introduced a new strategy (actually an old strategy, originally examined by Rapaport),[18] called '**Pavlov**' (P), that came to dominate against all others. This is essentially a 'win–stay, lose–change' strategy, meaning that if either of the best two payoffs is obtained the same strategy is used as in the last play, whereas if either of the worst two payoffs is obtained the strategy is changed.

Further additions to these models, increasing their realism, have been made by Frean and Kitcher.[19] Frean's contribution was to make the PD game sequential rather than simultaneous. A strategy that defeated Pavlov evolved, called '**firm-but-fair**' (FBF). This was slightly more generous, continuing to co-operate after being defected on in the previous turn. This is intuitive, in the sense that if one has to make a move before the other player, one is more likely to be 'nice'.

Kitcher's contribution was to transform the PD from a two-person to a multi-person game. This is not only more applicable to real-life situations in general, but is more applicable to oligopolistic markets in particular. Admittedly, in Kitcher's model the players had the option of refusing to play certain other players, which is not usually possible in oligopoly, except for potential entrants, but his conclusions still have value. Previous researchers had doubted the ability of co-operation to evolve in multi-person games,[20] because of the problems of increasing probability of defection, detecting defection, and enforcing punishment. Kitcher showed that mechanisms involving coalitions and exclusion could be powerful in eliciting co-operation, thus supporting the earlier conclusions of Axelrod. The experiments by these more recent researchers point to four main conditions that are necessary for co-operation to evolve in these more realistic scenarios:

1 Repeated encounters between players
2 Mutual recognition
3 The capacity to remember past outcomes
4 The capacity to communicate a promise.

The first three of these are self-explanatory in business situations. The fourth condition involves some of the strategic practices discussed earlier, such as price leadership, announcements of future price changes, and most-favoured-customer clauses. These practices therefore are strong indicators of collusion, which has regulatory implications, as examined in Chapter 12. It should be noted at this point that such practices are widespread, and this has resulted in frequent action by regulatory authorities in recent years, notably in the vitamin supplement industry.

Finitely repeated games

In some cases these games will have a known end period, while in others the end period will be uncertain. For example, in the pricing game described above, it might be more accurate to call this a finite game with an uncertain end period. This is because at some point in the future the product will be phased out or substantially modified, and either the game will end or a new modified game will take its place. However, as long as the end period is uncertain, it can be shown that this has no substantial effect on the result in terms of equilibrium strategies. The uncertainty has a similar effect to the interest rate used for discounting in the infinitely repeated case.

However, this result does not hold if the game continues for a certain number of time periods. It has been shown that if the number of time periods of the game is certain, the game will unravel, since at each stage from the end of the game backwards it pays any player to defect. Thus if the game ends with the thirtieth play, it pays to defect on that play; however, if it pays to defect on the last play and end the game, it will also pay to defect on the twenty-ninth play, and so on right back to the first play. This unravelling effect is known as the **chainstore paradox**.

9.6 Limitations of game theory

As game theory applications have become more widespread throughout economics and the other social and natural sciences, certain criticisms have arisen regarding the validity of its conclusions. There have been various empirical studies where the findings have been contrary to game theory predictions. A well-known example of this is Frank's ultimatum bargaining game. This is a dynamic game where a sum of money, say £100, is to be divided between two players. The first player makes a bid regarding how the money should be split, and the second player can either accept or reject the amount offered. If the second player rejects the offer neither player receives anything. According to conventional game theory, the first player should only offer a nominal amount, say £1, since it would be irrational to refuse even this small amount; £1 is better than nothing. The majority of studies show that when players are dealing face to face this result does not occur; not only do people generally refuse offers of less than half the total amount, but the first player generally does not make such low offers.

How do we explain this result? First of all we should realize that the result is not in any way a refutation of game theory. It is a reminder that we should always check our assumptions before drawing conclusions.

Case study 9.3: Credible commitments[21]

John Lott's book *Are Predatory Commitments Credible? Who Should the Courts Believe?* (1999) is an attempt to test one of the implied assumptions of game-theoretic models.

The key questions for NIO (new industrial organization) models developed by game theorists are: 'Are CEOs hawks or doves, and how can an entrant tell the difference?' Predatory pricing in the NIO arises when a dominant firm can credibly signal that it will price below cost if anyone enters the market. If the signal is credible, the entrant will not enter. The Chicago School had shown that predatory pricing would be costly to the dominant firm and argued that therefore it would be unlikely to be practiced. Proponents of the NIO agree that predatory pricing is costly, but they argue that to keep an entrant out, no firm need actually practice predatory pricing if the threat to do so is credible.

A 'hawk' is a firm that will actually cut prices to drive out an entrant. A 'dove' is a firm that will acquiesce to entry because it cannot bear the short-term losses entailed by engagement in predatory pricing. Of course, doves threaten predatory pricing just as hawks do. How can the entrant discover who is a hawk and who a dove?

Lott's answer is that a hawk-CEO must have high job security. As the entrant enters, the hawk-CEO goes to war against the entrant by driving down prices and thereby greatly reducing profits. If the CEO must answer to stockholders for declines in the price of stock, or if his own pay is tied to the stock price through options or other means, then he will be unwilling to prosecute the war. The signal required to make a predatory commitment credible is a system of corporate governance that allows the CEO more control over the corporation than stockholders would otherwise give him. In short, to signal credibly, the CEO must be a dictator rather than an elected representative. Dictatorship, of course, has its costs, in nations or in firms, so not every firm will want to be a hawk.

Lott proposes that this difference in corporate governance presents an opportunity to test the NIO theory of credible commitments. He examines twenty-eight firms accused of predatory pricing between 1963 and 1982. Is the corporate governance of these firms more hawklike than that of other firms? It is not. Lott finds few differences in CEO turnover, incorporation in a state with antitakeover provisions, stock ownership, or CEO pay sensitivity between the firms accused of predatory pricing and a control group. One of the key assumptions of the NIO is therefore wrong. The question remains, 'Why would firms that had no better commitment strategy than a control group have been accused of predatory pricing?' Although this question lies beyond the scope of Lott's book, one can only conjecture that those firms were accused of predatory pricing not because they actually practiced it but because their competitors wanted to stop competition (see Fred S. McChesney and William F. Shughart II, *The Causes and Consequences of Antitrust: The Public Choice Perspective*, Chicago: University of Chicago Press, 1995).

If firms accused of predatory pricing do not seem to differ systematically from the control group, is any firm capable of following a predatory-pricing strategy? In effect, could any organization commit to not maximizing profits, if only for a limited period of time? Lott's answer is that one group of firms can make such a commitment: publicly owned firms. The basic idea comes from Niskanen's model (William Niskanen, *Bureaucracy and Representative Government*, Chicago: Aldine Atherton, 1971): publicly owned firms maximize size rather than profit. Lott gives several examples, but none hits closer to home than the public university, which must maintain enrollment in order to maintain the size of the faculty and therefore sets prices considerably below costs.

Lott's second type of evidence that publicly owned firms practice price predation is the fact that dumping cases – the international version of predatory-pricing complaints – have been filed under the General Agreement on Tariffs and Trade more frequently against firms from communist countries than against firms from noncommunist countries. Lott shows, therefore, that the NIO theory of predatory pricing makes sound predictions (hawks practice predatory pricing more than doves), but it has limited application to the private-enterprise system, to which its advocates intended it to apply.

Lott's third argument supplements the theory of predatory pricing. He extends Jack Hirshleifer's observation that inventors of public goods can internalize at least some of the value of their invention by taking long or short positions in assets whose price will change after the discovery is made public (see Jack Hirshleifer, 'The private and social value of information and the reward to inventive activity', *American Economic Review*, **61** (1971): 561–574). Lott extends this idea by arguing that an entrant facing an incumbent with a reputation for toughness should take a short position in the incumbent's stock, enter, and reap trading profits. In effect, the incumbent firm with a reputation for toughness finances the entry of its own competitors. The entrant can also make profits by exiting. If the entrant enters and finds that it cannot withstand the attack of the hawk, it can take a long position in the incumbent's stock, exit, and collect the trading profits. Either way, trading profits increase the incentive to enter because whether or not entry ultimately succeeds, trading profits allow the entrant to make a profit. As Lott puts it, 'the more successfully a predator deters entry, the greater the return that trading profits create toward producing new entry. Creating a reputation to predate can thus be self-defeating' (p. 115).

Lott provides several anecdotes about the use of trading profits, but he admits he can find few recent examples. The problem, of course, is that a firm holding a short position in a competitor's stock would not want to advertise that fact to the market. Therefore, we would expect such evidence to be thin. The trading-profits idea does suggest that the threat to practice predatory pricing would be more successful when the incumbent firm was closely held, and therefore entrants could not easily buy shares of it. This relationship might make predatory pricing more likely in developing countries that are dominated by family-run firms and that lack well-developed equity markets.

One of the basic insights of economics is that well-established markets threaten rents. Lott's simple application of this wisdom ought to change the way economists think about antitrust cases and the way they are litigated both as private and as public cases. The notion that trading profits can mitigate or eliminate the private damage from predatory pricing should certainly give antitrust experts cause to worry about the efficiency of treble damages. I await the day when the defendant in an antitrust case will respond, 'If my actions were predatory, why didn't the plaintiff just buy my stock short and use the profits to stay in the market.'

Questions

1 What is meant by a hawk-CEO?
2 Why should hawk-CEOs need high job security?
3 Contrast the NIO and Chicago School theories of predatory pricing.
4 What is Lott's conclusion relating to empirical evidence for the NIO?
5 Explain Lott's theory of trading profits and how it relates to predatory pricing; how does the theory support his conclusion that 'Creating a reputation to predate can thus be self-defeating'?

There are two main points here. First, the ultimatum bargaining game can be modelled as either a one-off or a repeated game. Obviously, in a repeated game there is an advantage in gaining co-operation, as we have seen. However, this does not explain all the findings, since the prevailing fifty–fifty split tends to occur even in one-off situations.

The second point is that game theory generally assumes people act rationally in their self-interest. Some writers comment rather lamely that this assumption is inadequate and does not take into account our innate sense of fairness. This answer just begs the question of how such a sense of fairness originated or evolved. This is not the place to expand on this issue in detail, but the factors involved were touched on in the second chapter, in the section on motivation. Rational self-interest is sometimes taken in too narrow a context in terms of being a guide to behaviour. Frank's model of the emotions serving as commitment is often a better model.[22] In the ultimatum bargaining game context, people who are too ready to let others take advantage of them are not as likely to survive in a competitive environment. People with a sense of 'justice' or fairness are less likely to get cheated, because if they are, they get angry and are likely to retaliate. Thus people with such tendencies tend to pass on the relevant characteristics or genes to their children, and people with a sense of fairness tend to prosper.

9.7 A problem-solving approach

Because of the variety of situations examined in this chapter there is no universal approach to problem-solving. It is true that certain types of problem lend themselves to certain specific approaches; we have seen this for example in examining the Cournot and Bertrand models. Although it is not possible, as in other chapters, to describe an all-embracing approach, two main points emerge from this chapter, which are sometimes ignored in the decision-making process:

1 *The effect of one's decisions on the actions of competitors should always be considered.* Competitors' responses are particularly important in oligopolistic markets, where interdependence is more relevant and significant.
2 *In game theory situations there is a hierarchical process to finding equilibrium solutions.* One should always look for dominant strategies before looking for other Nash equilibria. The search for dominant strategies should start by eliminating dominated strategies. If no Nash equilibrium is found in pure strategies, then a mixed strategy solution should be sought.

Summary

1 Strategic behaviour considers the interdependence between firms, in terms of one firm's decisions affecting another, causing a response affecting the initial firm.
2 Game theory provides some very useful insights into how firms, and other parties, behave in situations where interdependence is important.
3 There are many parameters in game situations: static/dynamic games, co-operative/non-cooperative games, one-shot/repeated games, perfect/ imperfect information, two players/many players, discrete/continuous strategies, zero-sum/non-zero-sum games.
4 Game theory has particularly useful applications in the areas of the theory of the firm and competition theory.
5 Cournot and Bertrand models are helpful in gaining a better understanding of how firms behave in oligopolistic markets when static situations are considered.
6 The Stackelberg model is appropriate for dynamic models of oligopoly when there is a price leader.
7 In some cases there is an advantage to being first mover, while in other situations it is a disadvantage.

8 Static games are best represented in normal form, while dynamic games are best represented in extensive form.

9 In practice many games are repeated; conclusions regarding the players' behaviour depend on whether the end of the game can be foreseen or not.

10 In particular, game theory indicates that co-operation or collusion between firms is likely when a small number of firms are involved in repeated, interdependent decision-making situations.

Review questions

1 Explain the differences between the Cournot and Bertrand models of competition; why are these models not true models of interdependent behaviour?

2 Explain the following terms:

a. Dominant strategy
b. Nash equilibrium
c. Most favoured customer clause
d. Mixed strategies.

3 Explain the relationship between strategic moves, commitment and credibility.

4 Explain how you would formulate a strategy for playing the paper–rock–scissors game on a repeated basis.

5 Explain why it makes a difference in a repeated game if the end of the game can be foreseen.

6 Explain why in ultimatum bargaining games the result is often a fifty–fifty split between the players. Does this contradict the predictions of game theory?

Problems

9.1 The cement-making industry is a duopoly, with two firms, Hardfast and Quikrok, operating under conditions of Cournot competition. The demand curve for the industry is $P = 200 - Q$, where Q is total industry output in thousands of tons per day. Both firms have a marginal cost of £50 per ton and no fixed costs. Calculate the equilibrium price, outputs and profits of each firm.

9.2 A market consists of two firms, Hex and Oct, which produce a differentiated product. The firms' demand functions are given by:

$$Q_H = 100 - 2P_H + P_O$$
$$Q_O = 80 - 2.5P_O + P_H$$

Hex has a marginal cost of £20, while Oct has a marginal cost of £15. Calculate the Bertrand equilibrium prices in this market.

9.3 Examine the problem on property rights and fishing; how is the situation affected if the cost of catching fish increases from £0.10 to £0.20 per fish?

9.4 Two banks are operating in a duopolistic market, and each is considering whether to cut their interest rates or leave them the same. They have the following payoff matrix:

		Bank B	
		Maintain rate	Cut rate
Bank A	Maintain rate	(50, 50)	(20, 70)
	Cut rate	(70, 20)	(30, 30)

a. Does either bank have a dominant strategy?

b. Does the above game represent a Prisoner's Dilemma? Explain.

c. Is there any way in which the two banks can achieve co-operation?

9.5 Assuming a linear market demand function and linear cost functions with no fixed costs, show the differences in output, price and profits between the Cournot and Stackelberg oligopoly models.

Notes

1 J. von Neumann and O. Morgenstern, *Theory of Games and Economic Behavior*, Princeton University Press, 1944.

2 J. Nash, 'Non-cooperative games', *Annals of Mathematics*, **51** (1951): 286–295.

3 A. Cournot, 'On the competition of producers', in *Research into the Mathematical Principles of the Theory of Wealth*, trans. N. T. Bacon, New York: Macmillan, 1897.

4 J. Bertrand, 'Book review of *Recherche sur les principes mathématiques de la théorie des richesses*', *Journal des Savants*, **67** (1883): 499–508.

5 F. Gasini, J. J. Laffont and Q. Vuong, 'Econometric analysis of collusive behavior in a soft-drink market', *Journal of Economics and Management Strategy*, **1** (Summer 1992): 277–311.

6 W. J. Baumol, J. C. Panzar and R. D. Willig, *Contestable Markets and the Theory of Market Structure*, New York: Harcourt Brace Jovanovich, 1982.

7 J. Harsanyi and R. Selten, *A General Theory of Equilibrium Selection in Games*, Cambridge, Mass.: MIT Press, 1988.

8 A. Dixit and B. Nalebuff, *Thinking Strategically: The Competitive Edge in Business, Politics, and Everyday Life*, New York: Norton, 1991.

9 J. Hirshleifer, *The Dark Side of the Force*, Cambridge University Press, 2001.

10 H. von Stackelberg, *Marktform und Gleichgewicht*, Vienna: Julius Springer, 1934.

11 W. Chaitrong, 'The games people play', *Nation*, 8 June 2001.

12 Adapted from Dixit and Nalebuff, *Thinking Strategically*.

13 Gasini, Laffont and Vuong, 'Econometric analysis of collusive behavior in a soft-drink market'.

14 R. Axelrod, *The Evolution of Cooperation*, New York: Basic Books, 1984.

15 J. C. Martinez-Coll and J. Hirshleifer, 'The limits of reciprocity', *Rationality and Society*, **3** (1991): 35–64.

16 K. Binmore, *Game Theory and the Social Contract*, Vol. I: *Playing Fair*, Cambridge, Mass.: MIT Press, 1994.

17 M. A. Nowak, R. M. May and K. Sigmund, 'The arithmetics of mutual help', *Scientific American*, **272** (1995): 50–55.

18 A. Rapaport, *The Origins of Violence*, New York: Paragon House, 1989.

19 P. Kitcher, 'The evolution of human altruism', *Journal of Philosophy*, **90** (1993): 497–516.

20 R. Boyd, 'The evolution of reciprocity when conditions vary', in A. H. Harcourt and F. B. M. de Waal, eds., *Coalitions and Alliances in Humans and Other Animals*, Oxford University Press, 1992.

21 Adapted from book review by E. A. Helland, 'Are predatory commitments credible?', *Independent Review*, **5** (2001), 449–452.

22 R. H. Frank, *Passions within Reason: The Strategic Role of the Emotions*, New York: Norton, 1988.

10

Pricing strategy

Objectives

1 To explain the significance of pricing, both in the economic system as a whole and from a management perspective.
2 To explain the context in which pricing decisions are and should be made.
3 To relate the concepts and analysis of the previous chapters to more complex and detailed pricing situations.
4 To explain the importance of the concept of competitive advantage.

5 To explain the concept of value creation and to show its significance in a purchasing model.

6 To explain the meaning of market positioning and its strategic implications.

7 To discuss market segmentation and targeting strategies.

8 To explain the meaning and uses of price discrimination.

9 To analyse pricing decisions for firms producing multiple products.

10 To analyse pricing decisions for firms producing joint products.

11 To explain the concept of transfer pricing and the issues involved.

12 To examine the dynamic aspects of pricing, by discussing pricing over the product life-cycle.

13 To consider other pricing strategies that firms tend to use in practice.

10.1 Introduction

Pricing is often treated as being the core of managerial economics. There is certainly a fair element of truth in this, since pricing brings together the theories of demand and costs that traditionally represent the main topics within the overall subject area. However, as indicated in various parts of this text, this can lead to an over-narrow view of what managerial economics is about. This chapter will continue to examine pricing in a broader context, but first it is helpful to consider the role of pricing in the economic system.

Price determination is the core of microeconomics; this whole subject area examines how individual components in the economic system interact in markets of various kinds, and how the price system allocates scarce resources in the system. It is a well-established body of theory, with its main elements dating back over a hundred years to the Neoclassical School. Economists may well disagree about how well the market economy works in practice, and this aspect is discussed in the last chapter, but the general framework of analysis regarding the price system is not in serious dispute. Microeconomists tend to focus on pricing at the level of the industry, and on the welfare aspects in terms of resource allocation. As stated in Chapter 2, this perspective on price is what lies behind the assumption that price is the most important variable in the marketing mix. However, although this perspective is important for government policy, it is not the perspective that managers have, or should have, if their objective is profit or shareholder-wealth maximization, or indeed any of the other objectives discussed in Chapter 2.

As far as managers are concerned, price is just one of many decision variables that they have to determine. The majority of managers do not consider it to be the most important of these decision variables, but they do tend to realize the interdependence involved in the decision-making process. Therefore it makes sense at this point to discuss the context of the pricing decision, before focusing on the more detailed analysis of pricing situations. The starting point for this discussion is the concept of competitive advantage.

10.2 Competitive advantage

The concept of competitive advantage was introduced by Porter[1] in 1980, and has been utilized and further developed by many writers on business strategy since then. It provides a very useful means of analysing a firm's success or lack of it in any market. A discussion of competitive advantage is therefore necessary in order to understand the nature of many of the decision variables that are involved in a firm's business strategy, and to put these into a broad perspective. As mentioned in the introduction to the chapter, this involves examining non-price decisions, and explaining the context within which price decisions are or should be made.

10.2.1 Nature of competitive advantage

In order to place the concept in context we initially need to recognize that a firm's profitability depends in general on two factors: market conditions and competitive advantage.

1. *Market conditions*. These relate to external factors, not just for the firm, but also for the industry as a whole. Industries vary considerably in terms of their profitability; thus throughout the 1990s, computer software firms, biotech firms and banks achieved higher than average profitability, while steel firms, coal producers and railways did badly. It is clear that these industry trends can vary from country to country, according to differences in external factors. These external factors are sometimes discussed in terms of another of Porter's concepts, **five-forces** analysis (internal rivalry, entry, substitutes and complements, supplier power and buyer power), or in terms of the **value net** concept of Brandenburger and Nalebuff.[2] These forces essentially are the ones that were discussed in Chapter 3 as being uncontrollable factors affecting demand, although we should also now be considering the effects on costs. A 1997 study by McGahan and Porter[3] concluded that these factors explained about 19 per cent of the variation in profit between firms.

2. *Competitive advantage*. This relates to internal factors, specifically those that determine *a firm's ability to create more value than its competitors*. The study above concluded that these factors explained about 32 per cent of the variation in profit between firms. The concept of **value creation** now needs to be discussed.

10.2.2 Value creation

The value created by a firm can be expressed in the following way:

Value created = perceived benefit to customer − cost of inputs

$$V = B - C \tag{10.1}$$

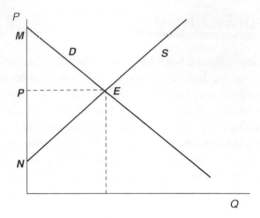

Figure 10.1. Value, consumer surplus and producer surplus.

where V, B and C are expressed in monetary terms per unit. These concepts and their relationships to other important measures can be examined in terms of the graph in Figure 10.1. The demand curve shows the value that consumers place on buying an additional unit of a product, thus indicating perceived benefit in terms of marginal utility, as seen in Chapter 3. The supply curve indicates the marginal cost to firms of producing an additional unit, as seen in Chapter 6. Thus value per unit is measured as the vertical distance between the demand and supply curves, and total value created is measured by the area MEN. The equilibrium price, P, at the intersection of the demand and supply curves can be seen to divide this value into two parts, **consumer surplus** (CS) and **producer surplus** (PS). Consumer surplus is given by $B - P$ in general terms, which, as we have already seen in the last chapter, represents the amount that a consumer is prepared to pay over and above that which they have to pay. Producer surplus is given by $P - C$, which represents supernormal or economic profit. Thus we can write:

$$CS = B - P \qquad (10.2)$$

$$PS = P - C \qquad (10.3)$$

$$V = CS + PS = (B - P) + (P - C) = B - C \qquad (10.4)$$

For the first unit of consumption consumer surplus is given by $M - P$ and producer surplus is given by $P - N$. At the equilibrium point no further value can be created by the firm by producing more output.

In order to make the situation less abstract, consider the following example. A particular consumer may pay £200 for a VCR; they may be prepared to pay £250 for that particular model, even though the marginal cost of production is only £130. In this case the value created by that product item is £120, of which £50 is consumer surplus and £70 is producer surplus.

In order to relate the above analysis to competitive advantage we need to introduce the concept of **consumer surplus parity**. We will assume to start with that consumers have identical tastes, though we will relax this assumption later. When comparing different products and making a purchase decision, rational consumers will try to maximize their total consumer surplus. Firms can be considered as making bids for consumers by offering them more surplus than competitors; a market will be in equilibrium when *each product is offering the same surplus as its rivals*. Thus in the athletic shoe market a particular model of Nike shoe may sell for £10 more than a competitor's product, but if consumers perceive the benefit to be £10 greater, they will obtain the same surplus from consuming each product and therefore be indifferent between the two products. This equilibrium will mean that each product would maintain its market share relative to other products.

If a firm (or product) has a competitive advantage, it is in a position to make more profit than competitors. Firms are able to do this essentially in two different ways: pursuing a **cost advantage** or pursuing a **benefit advantage**. These concepts are examined in more detail shortly but can be briefly summarized here:

1 *Cost advantage.* In this case the greater value created $(B - C)$ depends on the firm being able to achieve a **lower level of costs than competitors, while maintaining a similar perceived benefit**.
2 *Benefit advantage.* In this case the greater value created depends on the firm being able to achieve a **higher perceived benefit than competitors, while maintaining a similar level of costs**.

In order to discuss these issues further we must now consider the assumptions that were made earlier, in Chapter 8 on market structure, regarding the nature of the pricing decision. These included, in particular:

1 The firm produces for a single market.
2 The firm charges a single price for the product throughout the whole market.
3 The firm produces a single product rather than a product line.
4 The firm produces a single product rather than a product mix.
5 The firm is considered as a single entity, rather than as consisting of different divisions, sometimes in different countries.
6 Price is the only instrument in the marketing mix.
7 Pricing is considered from a static, single-period viewpoint.

These assumptions are relaxed in the following sections, taking each in turn. The following case study applies the concept of competitive advantage to a very high-profile firm in the telecommunications industry.

Case study 10.1: Mobile phones – Nokia

Emergency Calls[4]

As bad news flows thick and fast, it has become clear that a vicious shake-out is under way in the global telecoms industry, led by the mobile operations on which dozens of companies have staked their futures. Many will want to forget April 24th, a black Tuesday that saw a string of announcements typifying the problems faced by operators and manufacturers alike:

1 In Japan, NTT DoCoMo, the wireless arm of NTT, postponed the commercial launch of its third-generation (3G) mobile network from next month until October. It said the system needed further tests before it would be robust enough. The blow is to DoCoMo's prestige rather than its profits, as the firm is still reckoned to be a leader in 3G technology. But the news worried heavily indebted rivals that have looked to DoCoMo to show that 3G can be made to work.

2 Germany's Deutsche Telekom announced a first-quarter net loss of €400m ($369m), and said that it had shifted its focus away from acquiring new mobile customers towards making more money from existing ones. T-Mobile, its wireless arm, made pre-tax profits of €590m, almost 70% more than in the same period last year, and has just won approval to merge with VoiceStream, an American mobile firm. But Telekom remains in trouble. It is shackled with €57 billion of debt and would like to float T-Mobile, but market conditions are too awful.

3 Motorola, an American mobile handset and equipment manufacturer, said it was closing its biggest factory in Britain, with the loss of more than 3,000 jobs. It blamed a sudden collapse in demand for mobile telephones and may have to hand back almost £17m ($25m) in state aid. Other equipment makers are having a torrid time, too. JDS Uniphase, a market leader in fibre optics for high-speed telephony, announced a $1.3 billion loss for its third quarter and said it would cut its workforce by a fifth.

4 Lastly, Ericsson of Sweden, the world's third-biggest maker of mobile handsets, announced a joint mobile-phone venture with Sony. The new business, which will be launched in October, aims to develop new mobile consumer brands and to become a long-term global competitor.

In normal times, Ericsson's deal might have looked like the only piece of good news on an otherwise miserable day. But it came almost immediately after the company had announced a big retrenchment and 12,000 job losses. In the first quarter of this year, it made a SKr4.9 billion ($502m) pre-tax loss, and it admitted that its mobile handset business is looking shaky. Its shares are worth around 70% less than they were a year ago, and have fallen by more than one-third since the beginning of March.

So it is hardly surprising that Kurt Hellstrom, Ericsson's chief executive, looked subdued at the press conference to announce the tie-up with Sony. He is paying a heavy price for having missed the strategic shift as mobile phones became trendy consumer goods rather than purely functional items. Ericsson underinvested in design and has been eclipsed by niftier rivals, notably Nokia of Finland.

Thus, the deal with Sony is better seen as a measure of how quickly Ericsson has fallen from grace. It has conceded 50% of the venture to the Japanese, even though it is far bigger, selling 43m phones last year against Sony's 7.5m. In an industry that moves quickly, the new venture will produce its first products only some time next year. Mr Hellstrom might no longer be the boss by then.

All over the industry there are clear signs that the telecoms boom has ended. Dramatic retrenchment by top-notch competitors may look panicky, but the truth is that most have little alternative. As the mobile sector has matured, its growth has inevitably begun to slow, leading investors to question the prospects of traditional operators that have placed huge bets on mobile technologies. Not only have capital markets become choosier about telecoms-related financings, but weak equity markets have made it almost impossible to float off mobile ventures and pay back debt. The knock-on effect for mobile-handset manufacturers has become all too evident – not least because they have had to provide billions of dollars in 'vendor financing' so that mobile-network operators can continue to buy their products.

A rare bright spot has been Nokia, the world's biggest mobile maker. Total sales in 2000 increased by 54% over the previous year, to around €30 billion. Net profit also increased by 53%. Even in the turbulent first quarter of 2001 total sales increased 22%, while operating profit rose 8%. These first-quarter results were better than expected and its share of the global handset market is edging up towards 40% as Ericsson's falls. So are its shares doing well? Relatively, yes: at the end of April they were a mere 40% below their level of a year before.

Nokia succumbs[5]

Then on June 12th there was proof, if proof were still needed, that no technology company is bulletproof. Nokia, the world's leading manufacturer of mobile telephones, gave warning that its second-quarter profits would be lower than expected, and that annual sales growth, previously forecast at 20%, would in fact be less than 10%. Nokia's shares fell by 23%, though they later recovered slightly. Other telecoms firms' share prices suffered too, with the exception of BT, whose shares rose after news of a 3G network-sharing deal with Deutsche Telekom.

Nokia's announcement was portrayed by Jorma Ollila, the firm's boss, as an indication that the slowdown in the American economy is having knock-on effects in Europe. But this explanation is a red herring, says Mark Davies Jones, an analyst at Schroder Salomon Smith Barney. Although Nokia has been slightly affected by falling consumer demand in America, the real cause of its problems is that the market for handsets, which account for nearly three-quarters of its sales, is saturated.

The problem is that people are neither buying new phones, nor upgrading their old ones, as often as they used to. In part this is because network operators, most of which are struggling with huge debts, feel less inclined to subsidise handsets. But it is also because there is no compelling reason to upgrade your phone once it is small and sexy enough. The days of double-digit growth in handset sales are over: the number of handsets sold worldwide – 400m last year, of which 32% were Nokia's – is not expected to rise this year. Any sales growth at Nokia this year will come from increasing its market share. In the UK

there are now over 40 million mobile phone subscribers, and the market penetration rate is around 70%, one of the highest in the world.

What now? The industry has a plan, which is to introduce new mobile-data services. Operators will benefit by being able to charge for these services (since revenues from voice traffic have stopped growing) and handset manufacturers will be able to sell everybody new phones. The problem is that the first incarnation of mobile data, Wireless Application Protocol (WAP) services, was a flop. So the industry's hopes are now pinned on a new technology, General Packet Radio System (GPRS), which is faster than WAP and offers 'always on' connections.

Nokia has extensive 3G contracts in the UK, including three-year agreements with Orange to deliver the radio-access network from their 3G network, and a three-year agreement with Hutchison to deliver a complete range of 3G mobile network infrastructure worth around €500 million.

On June 13th, the GSM Association, an industry standards-setting body, announced a scheme called the 'M-Services Initiative', which defines a standard way to offer graphics and other multimedia content on GPRS phones. The idea is that these new features will encourage users to upgrade their handsets, and thus plug the gap before the arrival of 3G phones in a couple of years' time. The big operators and manufacturers, including Nokia, are backing the scheme, and the first handsets sporting graphics should be in the shops by Christmas. One way or another, this week could prove to be a turning point for the industry.

Questions

1 How would you describe Nokia's competitive advantage?
2 Explain the implications of the saturation of the handset market for Nokia's competitive advantage, making strategy recommendations.

10.3 Market positioning, segmentation and targeting

Positioning in the market is the most fundamental aspect of a firm's marketing strategy; it precedes any consideration of the marketing mix discussed in Chapter 3. A firm must begin by examining its resources and capabilities relative to the business that it is in, or any business that it could be in. These resources and capabilities include things like management know-how, technical expertise, reputation and image, patents and trademarks, organizational culture, ownership of specialist resources, relationships with customers and suppliers and location. It should be noted that these factors tend to be ingrained within the organization, meaning that they are not dependent on the presence of certain individuals. Another important characteristic is that they are not easily duplicated. If there is a close match between these firm-specific factors and the key success factors in the industry then the firm may be able to obtain a competitive advantage in either cost or benefit terms.

10.3.1 Cost advantage

In basic terms this means achieving a lower level of C while maintaining a level of B that is comparable to competitors. Examples of firms that have pursued this strategy are Woolworth, Wal-Mart, Asda (now owned by Wal-Mart) and McDonald's. In some cases the firm claims to have the same quality as competitors at a lower cost, while in other cases the firm's perceived quality may be lower, but the cost and price substantially lower. In this situation we no longer need to assume that consumers have identical tastes; the firm can provide at least as much consumer surplus to some customers as competitors, while maintaining at least the same profit. The determination of how the value created should be divided into consumer surplus and producer surplus involves pricing strategy, and this is considered in subsection 10.3.3.

Cost advantage can be achieved in a number of ways: economies of scale and scope, the learning curve, production efficiency, control over inputs, transaction efficiencies and favourable government policies may all play a part. We will take the car industry as an overall example. In the case study on Nissan in Chapter 6, it was seen that transactional efficiencies in terms of dealing with suppliers formed an important component of a cost reduction strategy, as did increasing capacity utilization. When BMW took over Rover in the UK they were hoping, among other things, to obtain favourable government treatment in terms of grants and subsidies. Other car firms are concentrating on producing a smaller number of basic platforms for their different models in order to gain more economies of scale. Korean car manufacturers, like Hyundai and Daewoo, have concentrated on producing no-frills cars of lower perceived quality, but at a much lower price than other cars. The British sports car manufacturer TVR produces high-performance cars at a lower price than cars of similar performance levels produced by other manufacturers; this is achieved by simplifying the production process, using components from other cars, omitting some high-tech gadgetry and cutting back on marketing overheads.

10.3.2 Benefit advantage

A strategy aimed at achieving a benefit advantage involves offering a product with a higher level of B than competitors while maintaining a similar level of C.

Examples of firms in the car industry that have pursued this type of strategy are Honda, BMW (particularly in the 3 series) and Toyota with its Lexus model, although with this Toyota originally pursued both ends of the spectrum by producing a car at a lower price than the luxurious Mercedes and BMW saloons, but which used and provided more in the way of new technology. Other companies aiming at a benefit advantage may price their products somewhat higher than competitors but boast a significantly greater quality. Porsche is an example. Some companies, like Aston Martin and Ferrari, take this to the extreme; they charge very high prices, but promise the very best in quality.

Just as with cost advantage, benefit advantage can be achieved in a number of ways, even in a given industry. Reputation or marque counts for a large amount in the luxury car market. The Japanese manufacturers in general have tried to make up for a lack of this characteristic by using and providing more advanced technology, such as ABS, traction control, variable valve timing, four-wheel steering, climate control, satellite navigation and other gadgets. Aston Martin emphasizes build quality and customer service. BMW stresses 'German' engineering and reliability. It should be emphasized however that firms pursuing a benefit advantage do not have to be producing a luxury product; the quality of the product does not have to be high in general, it simply has to be perceived as being higher than competitors in that particular market segment. For example, the Japanese manufacturers mentioned earlier have mostly been producing cars in the medium or low price range. Again, as with cost advantage, the firm must determine how the value created should be divided into consumer and producer surplus. This means determining a pricing strategy. The general considerations regarding this are discussed in the next subsection.

10.3.3 *Competitive advantage, price elasticity and pricing strategy*

We now need to apply the concept of price elasticity of demand (PED), examined in Chapter 3, to the concept of competitive advantage in order to see how firms should generally price their products. The more detailed and quantitative aspects of pricing strategy will be considered in later sections of the chapter.

a. Cost advantage

There are two possible strategies for firms with a cost advantage:

1 The greater value that it creates can be given over to customers in the form of consumer surplus by charging a lower price, with the firm maintaining the same profit margin as competitors; in this case the firm should increase its market share and thus make more total profit.
2 The greater value created can be translated into producer surplus, meaning a greater profit margin, by charging the same price as competitors and providing the same perceived quality.

Table 10.1. Price elasticity and competitive advantage

	High PED	Low PED
Cost advantage	Cut price Gain market share	Maintain price Gain profit margin
Benefit advantage	Maintain price Gain market share	Increase price Gain profit margin

Choice of the appropriate strategy depends on the PED of the product. If PED is high, a lower price will allow the firm to capture significant market share from competitors. On the other hand, if PED is low, large price cuts will not increase market share much; in this case it is better to keep price at the same level as competitors and increase profit margin; see Table 10.1.

b. Benefit advantage

Again there are two possible strategies:

1 The greater value created can be given over to customers in the form of a larger consumer surplus by charging the same price as competitors and translating the greater consumer surplus offered into greater market share.
2 The greater value created can be translated into producer surplus by charging a higher price than competitors, while still maintaining the same consumer surplus. This will increase profit margin.

In this situation of benefit advantage, if PED is high it is better to maintain price at the same level as competitors and gain market share. If PED is low then it is better to increase price, since this will not affect market share much, and concentrate on increasing profit margin; again see Table 10.1.

10.3.4 Segmentation and targeting

These two aspects of strategy are closely related to competitive advantage and positioning. A **market segment** refers to *a group of consumers in a wider market who are homogeneous in some respect related to their buying behaviour*. Markets can be segmented in many ways according to different characteristics: demographic factors (income, age, ethnicity and sex, for example), location, frequency of purchase or use, lifestyle and newspaper readership are all common means of segmentation.

Why is it useful for firms to segment markets? Different segments have different tastes and therefore respond differently to the various marketing mix variables. A high-income segment, for example, may have a lower PED for a product than a lower income segment, meaning that they may be less price-sensitive; on the other hand, they may be more quality-sensitive. A firm may therefore want to select target markets according to its competitive advantage.

However, strategy selection does not always occur in this order. For example, a firm may observe that a certain market segment is not currently being adequately catered for in the market; it may therefore pursue a competitive advantage in producing some product or range of products that appeal to that segment. In the first case we could say that the firm is **supply-driven**, while in the second case the firm is **demand-driven**.

Targeting strategies are often classified into two main categories: **broad coverage** strategies and **focus** strategies.

a. Broad coverage strategies

These strategies aim to *provide for the needs of all or most of the segments in the market*. This can be achieved either by providing a general product line of a 'one-size-fits-all' type, or by providing a product line consisting of a variety of related products that are more-or-less customized for each segment. An example of the first approach is the strategy used by most commercial banks for attracting bank depositors, at least until recently. Little distinction was made according to age, income, occupation or frequency of cheque-writing. The main attraction of this approach is that it allows more standardization, and therefore leads to greater economies of scale.

However, most firms try to appeal to different segments by producing different products in a product line. For example, Nike produces athletic shoes in a huge variety, according to type of usage, frequency of usage, weight and build of user, sex of user, aesthetic preference of user and so on; prices therefore vary considerably, from about £20 a pair to over £100. Mercedes has recently reinvented itself in this direction; having originally specialized in producing luxury saloons, it is now selling sports cars, the economy 'A' class, and SUVs, with a price range from £15,000 to over £100,000. With this type of strategy economies of scale are less important, while economies of scope may be more important. This is not to say that cost advantage is always relevant here; benefit advantage may be more important, at least in certain market segments.

b. Focus strategies

These involve a firm either *offering a single product, or serving a single market segment, or both*. The first strategy may apply in markets where there is a lot of product homogeneity, like steel production, or it may apply to small specialist firms, particularly in industrial markets. More commonly a firm will specialize in providing for a single market segment; TVR specializes in producing high-performance sports cars, as do Lotus and Marcos. Bose specializes in producing high-quality speaker systems. Tag Heuer specializes in producing high-quality watches, particularly for sporting people. However, the focus does not have to be on high quality, associated with benefit advantage. Firms like Asda, K-mart, McDonald's and Woolworth have specialized in providing goods of 'adequate' quality at a low price. In this case, economies of scale and other cost reduction factors are of vital importance in yielding a cost advantage.

10.3.5 Role of pricing in managerial decision-making

We can now see that pricing is best considered as one of many interdependent decisions that firms have to make, and often is not the most fundamental. Firms need to start from their objectives in general terms, and then consider their competitive advantage in terms of their resources and capabilities, in conjunction with the external conditions of the market in terms of customers and competitors. Normally (with exceptions examined later in this chapter) this means starting with a positioning decision, leading to a product decision, and then considering the other elements of the marketing mix. Pricing is considered in this context, and affects the buying decisions of consumers through determining the amount of consumer surplus created.

Firms can pursue either a cost advantage or a benefit advantage. In either case the firm has to create more value $(B - C)$ than competitors. A firm then must determine a pricing policy to divide this value between consumer surplus and producer surplus. If a firm wants to increase market share, it has to create more consumer surplus $(B - P)$ than its competitors. An alternative strategy is for the firm to increase profit margin by creating more producer surplus $(P - C)$.

It can be seen, therefore, that the main priority of management is to identify and determine products where value creation is possible. Only then is the division of such value into consumer and producer surplus considered. Thus pricing is usually seen as being a secondary consideration.

Some of the more complex methods of increasing consumer surplus through pricing strategy are considered at the end of the chapter in section 10.7. First of all, the main techniques of pricing must be considered, based on the methodology in Chapter 8, but relaxing the other assumptions listed earlier.

However, before moving on to techniques of pricing, the concepts of positioning, segmentation and targeting are examined in the context of the handheld computer industry.

Case study 10.2: Handheld Computers – Palm

One Palm flapping[6]

Carl Yankowski is having a hard time turning Palm's promise into profits

By rights, it should not have been this hard. Carl Yankowski, chief executive of Palm, the leading maker of handheld computers, is a former president of Sony's American operations. He is a big, dressed-in-black 'gadget guy' with just the right combination of consumer-marketing experience and technology savvy to straddle the gap between computing and consumer electronics. From its start in 1996, Palm single-handedly generated the personal digital assistant (PDA) craze, succeeding where many had failed before, and it is now leading a drive into the new wireless world. Computing meets telecoms meets consumer electronics – the palmtop becomes the new desktop. And here, or so it might seem, in the right place at the right time, is Mr Yankowski.

Yet he is struggling. For all Palm's success in defining and leading a booming new industry – its operating system runs more than three-quarters of the world's PDAs, giving it an almost Microsoft-like monopoly – the company itself is in a very un-Microsoft-like financial mess. Recently, it issued a warning that its losses in the current quarter would be twice what had been expected – as much as $190m. Its sinking fortunes also scuttled a planned merger with Extended Systems, a deal that was meant to take it to new heights in the corporate market. Palm's shares have fallen by 90% over the past six months.

The company's difficulties do not all lie at the feet of Mr Yankowski – he took over only a year and a half ago, as Palm was freeing itself from 3Com, its former corporate parent and the source of its risk-averse corporate culture. But, like it or not, they are now his to solve.

The biggest problem is that Palm is having a hard time finding the right strategy. At the moment, it follows a combination of Microsoft's with Apple's that ends up weaker than either. Like Apple, it makes its own hardware and software: a line of PDAs and the famed Palm operating system (OS) that is the secret of its success. Like Microsoft, it also licenses its OS to other companies, ranging from Handspring, which was started by Palm's original founders, to Sony and several mobile-phone makers.

The downside to this is that Palm's licensees have proved all too good at making hardware. Today, a mere two years after it released its first PDA, Handspring is beating Palm in sales. And both Sony and Handspring have pushed their hardware further than Palm, introducing innovations such as expansion slots and add-on devices from phones to music players. The result is that the PDA business is quickly taking on the savage character of the PC industry, with commodity products, falling margins and cut-throat competition.

Mr Yankowski inherited most of this, and it had too much momentum for him to change it quickly or easily. If Palm stops licensing its operating system, it risks losing out to OS competitors such as Microsoft and Psion. If it stops making hardware entirely, it would take the best-known brand of PDA out of circulation.

The enthusiasm over Mr Yankowski's arrival in late 1999 was based largely on his background, which suggested that there might be a third way for the company. Aside from his Sony experience, which placed him at the heart of the best consumer-electronics firm just as it was embracing digital technology, his career has been a virtual tour of great marketing firms: Reebok, General Electric, Pepsi, Memorex and Procter & Gamble. Starting it all was an engineering degree from MIT.

The hope was that Mr Yankowski could combine Sony's design and marketing skills with Palm's technology. His type of consumer-marketing experience can make the difference between a niche gadget and a Walkman-like hit. Which is why it is so puzzling that Palm has changed so little since his arrival.

CORPORATE PRIORITY

Many expected him to push the company faster into the consumer market, with brightly-coloured PDAs and extra consumer features such as MP3 and video. Instead, he has made his main priority the staid corporate market. At present, most Palms make it into the office thanks to somebody's personal expense account. Mr Yankowski's aim is to encourage IT managers to purchase them directly for employees, much as they buy PCs.

This is not a bad strategy – the corporate PDA market is about the same size as the consumer market, and both have lots of potential – but it may be a waste of Mr Yankowski's special talents. While he tries to sell his firm's strait-laced productivity tools, in black and grey, to corporate purchasing managers, his old company, Sony, is generating enviable buzz with a cool purple PDA that plays videos and has a headphone jack. Worse, the corporate market is the one in which Palm faces its toughest competition, in the form of Research in Motion's Blackberry interactive pagers, which have generated Sony-like excitement among the suits.

Palm's recent results have at last provoked Mr Yankowski into thinking more broadly. He is now in management retreats with his staff and is expected to announce a new strategy soon. But his options get more limited by the day. Palm's finances are too rocky to get into a consumer-marketing race with Sony. Nor does it have the products to justify that. The first Palms designed on Mr Yankowski's watch are now out. They do little more than add an expansion slot like the one Handspring has had for two years.

Meanwhile, the collapse of the planned merger with Extended Systems, which has had success selling to IT managers, limits the push into the corporate sector. And abandoning hardware entirely would reduce Palm to a software and services firm – hardly the place for a consumer-marketing guru. Mr Yankowski does not have much more time to find the right answer.

Questions

1 Describe Palm's positioning in the market, in terms of resources, capabilities, cost and benefit advantage.
2 What criteria can Palm use to segment its market?
3 Evaluate Palm's targeting strategy.

10.4 Price discrimination

10.4.1 Definition and conditions

a. Definition

Price discrimination has been defined in a number of different ways. The simplest definition relates to the situation where a firm sells the same product at different prices to different customers. However, the most useful definition involves a firm **selling the same or similar products at different prices in different markets, where such price differentials are not based on differences in marginal cost**. This latter definition covers a broader range of situations and leads to a greater understanding regarding the nature of price discrimination. Using this definition we can consider the following common practices as price discrimination:

- Airlines that charge different fares for the same journey at different seasons of the year.
- Universities that charge higher fees to overseas students than to home students.
- Restaurants that offer 'early bird' dinners.
- Professional people, like doctors, accountants and consultants, who charge richer clients higher fees than poorer clients for the same service.
- Exporters who charge lower prices abroad than they charge domestically.
- Prestige outlets that charge higher prices than high street or discount stores for the same products.
- Health clubs that sell off-peak memberships.
- Supermarkets that offer points or reward schemes to regular shoppers.
- Happy hour.

We can now consider the conditions that are necessary for price discrimination to be possible.

b. Conditions

There are two fundamental conditions:

1 There must be different market segments with different demand elasticities.
2 The market segments must be separated so that there is no possibility of resale from one segment to another.

In order to illustrate the importance and application of these conditions let us consider the example of a butcher. Instead of advertising his meat prices he may wait until the customer comes into the shop and charge prices according to an assessment of the individual customer's ability and willingness to pay. Such a strategy may be successful in the case of customers who are ignorant of the prices being charged to other customers; however, once they become aware of this situation, and assuming that other butchers are following the same practice, high-paying consumers will find ways to avoid paying higher prices by buying their meat from other customers, in other words **arbitrage** will occur. Arbitrage refers to the practice of *buying at a lower price and selling at a higher price to make a riskless profit*. Thus in this instance a butcher cannot successfully practise price discrimination. On the other hand, a dentist is in a position to do so; patients cannot ask other patients to have their teeth capped for them. Thus price discrimination is generally easier in the markets for services, especially personal and professional services.

At this point one might ask why a firm would want to practise price discrimination. Essentially it is a method of reducing the amount of consumer surplus and transferring it to the producer in terms of additional profit. This aspect is most easily seen by considering different types of price discrimination.

10.4.2 Types of price discrimination

There are different ways of classifying these types of discrimination. We will discuss the degree of price discrimination first, since it leads to a better understanding of the resulting impact on profit; then bases for price discrimination will be considered, in terms of different ways of segmenting markets.

a. Degree of price discrimination

Economists tend to classify price discrimination into three main categories, according to the extent to which consumer surplus is transferred to the producer.

1. First-degree price discrimination. This is sometimes referred to as perfect price discrimination, since all the consumer surplus is transferred to the producer. For this to be possible the producer must have complete knowledge of its demand curve, in terms of knowing the highest price that each customer is prepared to pay for each unit, and be able to sell the product accordingly. This situation is extremely rare, but an example is an auction market, like the Treasury Bill market. Figure 10.2 illustrates the situation. It is assumed in this case that marginal costs are constant, for simplicity. The whole consumer surplus, GCP_3, becomes revenue and profit for the producer.

2. Second-degree price discrimination. In this situation a firm may charge different prices for different levels of consumption. The first Q_1 units may be sold at the high price of P_1; the next block of units, $Q_2 - Q_1$, may be sold at the price P_2, and the last block of units, $Q_3 - Q_2$, may be sold at the price of P_3. This situation is also shown in Figure 10.2 and the size of the consumer surplus is given by the three triangles, GAP_1, ABE and BCF. This type of strategy may be used in the selling of a product like electricity.

   In other situations a reverse type of strategy is sometimes used, where early buyers pay a lower price and later buyers have to pay more. Examples are the

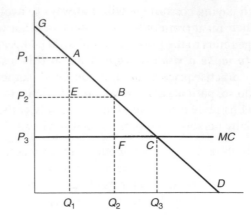

Figure 10.2. Degrees of price discrimination.

selling of tickets to certain events, like concerts, and the selling of certain types of club membership. Usually buying early involves more inconvenience or inflexibility for the buyer, thus segmenting the market.

Second-degree price discrimination often features a two-part tariff or pricing system. There is some lump sum charge and then a user charge. Examples are cellular phone and cable television providers, car rentals, and various types of club membership. In the first two cases the lump sum is minimal and the user fees relatively large; with cable for example, the boxes are heavily subsidized by the provider and are often supplied free of charge, but if a second box is required, the buyer has to pay around £300. This also explains the apparent anomaly that replacement blades for many razors cost more to buy than whole disposable razors. On the other hand, with many club memberships the lump sum charge, or entry fee, is relatively large, while user fees are nominal.

3. Third-degree price discrimination.   This is, in practice, the most common form, where a firm divides its market into segments and charges different prices accordingly. Markets can be segmented in various ways for this purpose, and this aspect is now discussed.

b. Segmentation for price discrimination

Firms can segment markets on different bases; the following are the most common.

1. Time.   Many products that have seasonal demand have different prices at different time periods; airlines, hotels, restaurants, cinemas, power providers and many other industries have this feature. Demand is less elastic at peak season, so prices are higher then.

2. Location.   In some cases the price of a product may be higher in one location than another because of a higher transportation or other cost. This is not price discrimination. However, when the price in one location is higher than is justified by a difference in marginal cost, because of demand being less elastic, then this does involve discrimination. It should also be mentioned that sometimes a kind of reverse price discrimination occurs. Instead of charging different prices when marginal cost is the same, some firms will charge the same price even when marginal costs are different. This occurs, for example, when there are differences in transportation costs between different markets, but a universal price is charged. Again this could be justified by differences in demand elasticities between different markets, if demand is more elastic in those areas with higher transportation costs.

3. Product form. Many firms offer a product line where the top-of-the-line model is considerably more expensive than the other products in the line. This may be true even when there is little difference in the cost of production of the different products. In this case there may be some consumers who are determined to have the best (stereo, television, car, mountain bike, tennis racquet), and therefore, again, their demand is less elastic in the normal price range.

4. Customer. This is the most controversial type of price discrimination because of concerns regarding fairness. Recalling the discussion in Chapter 1, fairness is a normative issue and is not relevant to the present analysis. Unfortunately the term 'discrimination' is an emotive word and tends to be associated with normative issues, but it is not our purpose to discuss these here. It is simply necessary to point out that firms can increase their profit by charging higher prices to customers whose demand is less elastic, provided that there is no possibility of resale between market segments, as explained earlier. This explains the discrimination carried out by many providers of professional services, including universities. It also explains the price discrimination practised by many exporters, charging higher prices in the domestic market in spite of lower costs; it is worth noting that in this case there are limited opportunities for arbitrage, which is why many UK residents are now buying expensive consumer durables like cars in mainland Europe and shipping them back to the UK. This aspect is discussed in more general terms in the next subsection.

10.4.3 Price discrimination in the European Union

The recent introduction of the single currency in the euro zone has had very important implications for the practice of price discrimination in the EU. This has always existed on the basis of both customer and location, but the practice has been obscured in the past by the fact that prices were quoted in different currencies. Now that the euro is in circulation such discrimination is much more transparent, as prices in different countries are directly comparable. *L'Expansion*, a French magazine, conducted a survey of the euro zone in early 2001 and found that huge discrepancies existed for many products. For example, a kilo of beef cost €9.90 in Madrid, €15 in Paris, and €21 in Amsterdam; a 5-kilo pack of detergent cost €9.80 in Brussels but €24.30 in Helsinki; a packet of proprietary aspirin cost €3.70 in Athens but €12.90 in Rome and Berlin.

The introduction of the euro has therefore caused many multinational firms to re-evaluate their pricing strategies. Some firms, like *The Economist* magazine, have taken to charging a universal single price in all countries, €4.35, which is approximately the average of its previous prices. It has adopted this strategy on the basis that 'it was better to send a consistent price signal to customers than to price by market'.[7] While this may be true, it could also be claimed that, in a situation of price transparency, the possibility of resale from one market segment to another meant that the second condition for price discrimination to operate successfully was not applicable, and therefore *The Economist* really had no choice. **Parallel importing**, the practice of ***buying more cheaply in one country and selling at a higher price in another country***, is a form of arbitrage and has become very profitable within the European Union. It is particularly common in the pharmaceutical industry, where price differentials are very large; it has been estimated that parallel imports of drugs are worth £700 million annually in the UK alone.

Other firms are not necessarily in the same situation as *The Economist*, since they often sell differentiated products in different markets. For example Mandarina Duck is an Italian company that makes fashionable handbags and accessories. In the past it has practised price discrimination based on different standard mark-ups for fashion accessories in different countries; in Italy retailers operate on mark-ups of about 2.15 times the wholesale price, while in France the multiple is 2.29, and in Germany the multiple is 2.5. Although its prices in different countries have converged with the introduction of the euro, the firm now concentrates on tailoring its products to suit particular markets, selling more expensive items in the wealthier markets and cheaper ranges in the less wealthy areas.

However, even with the increased transparency brought about by the single currency, it will still be difficult to compare the true prices charged by manufacturers and retailers. This is because of the varied systems of incentives that are often offered by suppliers, involving rebates based on annual sales volumes and subsidized credit terms. A. T. Kearney, a management consultancy firm, recently found 216 different pricing structures in contractual terms between buyers and suppliers in Europe's main consumer-goods markets. Given this situation it is likely that a considerable amount of price discrimination will persist even after the introduction of the single currency.

Having discussed the different degrees of price discrimination, bases for segmenting markets, and some practical examples, we can now move on to a more detailed quantitative analysis of the situation.

10.4.4 *Analysis*

Consider the following situation:

SP10.1 Price discrimination

Valair is an airline flying a particular route that has seasonal demand. The firm's total demand is given by:

$$Q = 600 - 4P \qquad (10.5)$$

where Q is the number of passengers per year, in thousands, and P is the fare (in £). In the peak season the demand is given by:

$$Q_H = 320 - 1.5P_H \qquad (10.6)$$

and in the off-season the demand is given by:

$$Q_L = 280 - 2.5P_L \qquad (10.7)$$

assume that fixed costs are £6 million per year and that marginal costs are constant at £60 per passenger. Thus the cost function is given by:

$$C = 6000 + 60Q \qquad (10.8)$$

where C is total costs (in £'000).

a. Calculate the profit-maximizing price and output without price discrimination, and the size of the profit.
b. Calculate the profit-maximizing price and output with price discrimination, and the size of the profit.
c. Calculate the demand elasticities of the two segments at their profit-maximizing prices.

Solution

a. *Without price discrimination*
   Reviewing the procedure described in Chapter 8:

   1 $P = (600 - Q)/4$
      $R = (600Q - Q^2)/4$

   2 $MR = (600 - 2Q)/4$

   3 $MR = MC$
      $(600 - 2Q)/4 = 60$
      $600 - 2Q = 240; 2Q = 360$
      $Q = 180$, or **180,000 passengers per year**

4 $P = (600 - 180)/4 = $ **£105**

The profit is given by $R - C$:

$$= 105(180,000) - [6,000 + 60(180)]1,000$$
$$= 18,900,000 - 16,800,000$$
$$= \textbf{£2,100,000}$$

b. *With price discrimination*
We now examine each segment in turn:
Peak segment (H)

1    $P = (320-Q)/1.5$
$R = (320Q - Q^2)/1.5$

2    $MR = (320 - 2Q)/1.5$

3    $MR = MC$
$(320 - 2Q)/1.5 = 60$
$320 - 2Q = 90$
$2Q = 230$
$Q = 115$, or **115,000 passengers per year**

4    $P = (320 - 115)/1.5 = $ **£136.67**

Off-peak segment (L)

1    $P = (280-Q)/2.5$
$R = (280Q - Q^2)/2.5$

2    $MR = (280 - 2Q)/2.5$

3    $MR = MC$
$(280 - 2Q)/2.5 = 60$
$280 - 2Q = 150$
$Q = 65$, or **65,000 passengers per year**

4    $P = (280 - 65)/2.5 = $ **£86**

In order to obtain the size of the profit it is necessary to calculate total revenue and subtract total costs. Note that it is incorrect to compute the profits in each segment separately and then add them together. This would double-count the fixed costs.

Total revenue $= R_H + R_L = 136.67(115{,}000) + 86(65{,}000) = £21{,}307{,}050$
Total costs $= [6{,}000 + 60(115 + 60)]1{,}000 = £16{,}800{,}000$
Profit $= £4{,}507{,}050$

c. The demand elasticities in each segment can also be obtained using the point elasticity formula:

$$\text{Peak: PED} = -1.5(136.67/115) = -1.783$$
$$\text{Off-peak: PED} = -2.5(86/65) = -3.308$$

At this point a number of general conclusions can be drawn from comparing the situation with price discrimination and the situation without price discrimination:

1 Total output is the same in both situations (note that this is not true if the cost function is non-linear).
2 The prices with discrimination 'straddle' the price without discrimination, meaning that one is higher and the other is lower. If there are more than two market segments one or more prices will always be higher and one or more prices will always be lower.
3 The segment with the higher price will have less elastic demand and vice versa.
4 Profit is always higher under price discrimination. This is because some of the consumer surplus is transferred to producer surplus, as seen earlier.

The following case study examines price discrimination in the airline industry, concentrating on bases for discrimination and the importance of differences in price elasticity of demand.

Case study 10.3: Airlines

Britain takes to the air[8]

Low-cost carriers are transforming not just the travel business in Britain, but also the way people live

The air of gloom surrounding much of European business made Ryanair's results, announced on June 25th, particularly impressive. The low-cost airline reported a 37% year-on-year increase in pre-tax profits, and its chief executive, Michael O'Leary, said he expects business to grow by 25% over the next year.

Thanks to Ryanair and its sort, Britons are beginning to hop on and off planes the way Americans do.

Air travel in and around Britain has grown by nearly 40% in the past five years, but the really spectacular growth has come from the low-fare airlines, which have carried around 20m passengers in the past year. By spotting and satisfying the untapped demand for travel from and between the regions, they have fuelled the growth of Britain's smaller airports and undermined Heathrow's dominance.

EasyJet, the first of the low-cost carriers, was set up in 1995 at Luton. Eastwards around the M25 at Stansted are Ryanair, Go, the low-cost offshoot of British Airways (BA) sold to a management buy-out earlier this year, and Buzz, the British arm of KLM, which uses the airline partly to feed its international hub at Amsterdam. While Heathrow has seen the number of passengers rise by about 19% over that period, traffic at Luton and Stansted has more than trebled. Traffic at Liverpool's airport nearly quadrupled.

Demand for air travel is highly elastic. Bring down the price and sales rise sharply. The low-fare carriers are often cheaper not just than the mainstream operators but also than the railways. While low-fare airlines keep their fixed costs to a minimum, the railways are burdened by the need to maintain and improve their crumbling network. Last year was a disaster for them. A crash blamed on a cracked rail led to mass disruption as managers tried to locate and mend other dodgy rails. Delays drove passengers onto the airlines.

Low-cost airlines fill their planes differently from mainstream carriers. BA, British Midland, Air France and Lufthansa aim to make their money out of business travellers who pay over the odds to enjoy meals and loads of drinks in the air and on the ground in exclusive lounges. The economy seats are sold off, discounted as need be, some in advance and some at the last minute. Cheap seats are made available through downmarket travel agencies which publicise their deals through newspapers' classified columns.

The low-cost carriers see their aircraft as a series of buckets. The first set of buckets are the lowest-priced seats, with the eye-catching prices. Once these are all sold, demand flows into the next, slightly more expensive, bucket of seats. As the flight's departure approaches, seats get progressively more expensive. On a typical low-cost flight there could be up to ten different price buckets, with one-way fares ranging from £30 ($42) to £210. But even the most expensive tickets tend to be cheaper than for the mainstream airlines.

Early assumptions that the low-cost carriers would struggle to make headway in the business market, because businessmen do not care how much their companies pay for their tickets, have turned out to be wrong. Stelios Haji-Ioannou, EasyJet's founder, says that one of the things he first noticed when the airline launched was how many business passengers he

seemed to be carrying. Not that business travellers are set apart, since everybody piles into the same no-frills cabin, with free-for-all seating and pay-for-all drinks and sandwiches; but business travellers tend to book late (and so more expensively) and travel mid-week. It turns out that businessmen are more price-sensitive than had been assumed. Some, presumably, are running their own businesses, so have an interest in keeping costs down; others are responding to cost-cutting memos from above.

WIRED FOR TAKE-OFF

The Internet has also helped the low-cost airlines. Airline tickets rival pornography as the hottest-selling commodity on the Internet, with sales estimated at more than $5 billion worldwide. Mainstream airlines sell around 5% of tickets over the web. EasyJet decided to focus on Internet sales, so it offers discounts for online booking and has built a site that is easy to use. These days, some 90% of EasyJet bookings are made online. Ray Webster, EasyJet's chief executive, reckons that older or techno-illiterate people get a younger or more wired friend to do it for them.

Some 65% of Ryanair's bookings are made online. Even this figure is twice as high as the highest e-booking airline in America, Southwest, the original low-fare, no-frills carrier which was the model for the British low-cost operators.

The low-cost airlines have not just brought down the price of flying. They have changed the way British people travel, and also where they live, holiday and work. Air travel no longer involves the crowded hell of scheduled flights at Heathrow or charter flight delays at Gatwick. Cheap fares and European second homes have almost replaced house prices and school fees as a topic for dinner party chat.

At four o'clock on a summer afternoon at Luton airport, a queue is forming for the 5.40 to Edinburgh. A holidaying couple are returning to Edinburgh from Spain. The EasyJet flight was so cheap that it was worth their while taking an Airtours package from Luton, rather than flying from Scotland. Behind them is a management consultant who uses EasyJet from Luton because he lives just three exits up the M1 and it is quicker than hacking round the M25 to Heathrow. A technology transfer specialist at the Medical Research Council in Edinburgh says EasyJet is a way of coming down to London once a month for a fraction of the fare on British Airways or British

Midland. 'It seems ... ... e
dealing with publi ... ..., she ... ...
   Businessmen fr ... ... like
are hopping onto ... ...
shipping and trav ... ...
Marine, a Liverpoo ... ...
company, reckons he is saving £50,000 a year by
using budget airlines. Half of his company's regular
30 trips a month from Liverpool to Amsterdam are by
EasyJet, at £120 each, instead of the £350 he would
spend on a scheduled airline. Travelling to Spain, he
saves around £500 a trip. And, he says, the low-cost
airlines make it easier to change passenger names if
one employee has to substitute for another at a
meeting. According to airport managers at Liverpool,
since Ryanair and EasyJet have built up their flights
from the city, the number of executive-type cars
parked at the airport has shot up.
   Leisure travel is changing too. Until recently, most
people flew once or twice a year, to Florida or the
south of Spain. These days, people increasingly hop
on planes several times a year. It's no big deal any
more. A salesman in a London electronics shop says
his parents have a holiday house in the south of
France, which he had stopped visiting after they
stopped paying for his holidays. Recently, however,
he has discovered that if he books ahead on the

Internet, he can fly EasyJet to Nice and back for
under £50, making a monthly visit an affordable
treat.
   Perhaps the most astounding change is the
number of long-distance commuters using the new
airlines. Hang around long enough at Luton and you
will meet a businessman or woman, usually middle-
aged owners of companies in the south-east, who
spend half their week as lotus eaters in Provence,
nipping back for the other half to oversee their
business being handled day-to-day by their staff.
Most incredible of all, there is a resident of the Luton
area who commutes to bustling Glasgow every
morning, only to return to lovely Luton in the evening.
That could be called some sort of progress.

Questions

1 What conditions make price discrimination
   possible in the airline industry, and what types of
   price discrimination are possible? Explain how
   different demand elasticities are relevant.
2 Explain the differences in pricing strategy between
   the mainstream airlines and the low-cost airlines,
   in terms of the different types of price
   discrimination used.
3 Explain the role of the Internet in the pricing
   strategies above.

10.5 Multiproduct Pricing

10.5.1 Context

In all the analysis of pricing so far it has been assumed that the firm is
producing a single product. However, it was explained in Chapter 3 that this
common assumption is not at all realistic; indeed it is difficult to think of many
firms that do only produce a single product, while it is easy to think of firms
that produce or sell thousands of different products. The reasons for making
this assumption were also outlined in Chapter 3, and relate to the simplification of the analysis involved. It is true that there are some firms that produce or
sell a wide diversity of products that are not related to each other in any way,
either in terms of demand or production; in this situation the firm's pricing
and output decisions can be examined using the same analytical framework as
the single-product firm. However, this is a relatively rare situation. More often
than not, firms producing multiple products face both demand and production
interrelationships. It is now necessary to consider these relationships in more
detail.

10.5.2 Demand interrelationships

Multiproduct firms frequently produce a product line or range of product lines, and many examples of this have already been discussed in previous chapters: cars, domestic appliances, athletic shoes, consumer electronics, and also services like banking, accounting and insurance. In some cases the products or models are substitutes for each other to some degree, which is usually the case within product lines, but in other cases the products are complementary, for example when Gillette produces shavers, blades and aftershave.

The consequence of such interrelationships is that a change in the price of one product affects the demand for others of the firm's products. If we consider a firm producing two products, X and Y, then the total revenue of the firm is given by:

$$TR = TR_X + TR_Y \qquad (10.9)$$

where TR_X is the total revenue from product X, and TR_Y is the total revenue from product Y. The marginal revenues of each product are given by:

$$MR_X = \frac{\partial TR}{\partial Q_X} = \frac{\partial TR_X}{\partial Q_X} + \frac{\partial TR_Y}{\partial Q_X} \qquad (10.10)$$

and

$$MR_Y = \frac{\partial TR}{\partial Q_Y} = \frac{\partial TR_X}{\partial Q_Y} + \frac{\partial TR_Y}{\partial Q_Y} \qquad (10.11)$$

These equations show that when the quantity of one product sold by the firm changes, it not only affects the revenue obtained from the sale of that product, but it also affects the revenue obtained from the sale of other products of the firm. This is shown in the interaction term at the end of each expression; this term can be either positive or negative, depending on the nature of the relationship with the other product. If X and Y are in the same product line, and are therefore substitutes, the interaction term is negative, while if the products are complementary, as in the Gillette example, the interaction term is positive.

What are the implications of this interaction term? If firms ignore demand interdependencies they can make serious errors in decision-making. Take a firm like GM, with its various divisions. If the Chevrolet division cuts the price of its Camaro model, this will undoubtedly increase its sales and possibly revenues, if demand is elastic. The management of the Chevy division may regard this as a profitable exercise, if the increase in revenues exceeds any increase in costs. However, the corporate management at GM may take a different view if they look over at the Pontiac division, specifically the Pontiac Firebird, essentially a sister-car to the Camaro and a close substitute, and see its sales and revenues fall.

An opposite error can occur in the case of the Gillette example. A price cut in its shavers may not increase the revenue or profit from those shavers involved, and therefore such a price cut may be rejected as unprofitable. However, if the resulting increased sales in complementary products like blades and after-shave are considered, the price cut may be a profitable strategy for the firm as a whole.

10.5.3 Production interrelationships

When firms produce many products, and sometimes when they produce a single product, other products tend automatically to be generated at the same time because of the nature of the production process. These other products are often referred to as **by-products** or **joint products**. A good example is the production of petrol, which automatically involves the production of diesel oil and heating oil, among other products. Sometimes the resulting by-products are not desired; for example the production of many chemicals involves the creation of toxic substances and pollution. Since this often does not affect the firm's profit directly, this raises a public policy issue, which will be discussed in Chapter 12.

In many cases there are production interrelationships which are not inevitable but which are desirable. In Chapter 6 the concept of economies of scope was discussed; this referred to situations where it is less costly to produce two (or more) products together than to produce them separately. Such economies of scope are common in car production, the production of machinery and domestic appliances. Thus car manufacturing firms find it less costly to produce many different models, because they can share platforms and many production facilities. Better utilization of plant capacity becomes possible. The different models are not strictly joint products, but any pricing decision relating to one product must consider the effect on other products. For example, if Ford cuts the price of the Fiesta, the resulting increased sales may help to reduce unit costs of the Ford Focus, thus increasing profit through the **cost complementarity** between the two products.

10.5.4 Joint products

With joint products the production interrelationship is inevitable; when product X is produced, product Y will also be produced, whether this is desired or not. It is useful to classify such joint products into two main categories: those that are produced in fixed proportions and those that are produced in variable proportions.

a. Joint products produced in fixed proportions
This situation is easier to analyse because the products cannot be effectively separated from a production or cost standpoint, and therefore such products are not really multiple products at all, but are really product bundles.

Consider the following example:

SP10.2 Pricing of joint products

Procon PLC produces two products, pros and cons, in fixed proportions on a one-to-one basis, so that for every one pro produced one con is produced. The firm has the following total cost function:

$$C = 150 + 50Q + 2.5Q^2 \qquad (10.12)$$

where Q is the number of product bundles produced, consisting of one pro and one con each. The demand functions for the two products are:

$$P_P = 200 - 2Q_P \qquad (10.13)$$

$$P_C = 120 - 3Q_C \qquad (10.14)$$

Where P_P and Q_P are the price (in £) and output of pros and P_C and Q_C are the price and output of cons.

Determine the optimal price and output for each product.

Solution

The above situation can be examined graphically or algebraically.

1. Graphical analysis. This is shown in Figure 10.3. This graph looks confusing at first, because it shows a lot of information. The two demand curves are labelled D_p and D_c, and the individual marginal revenue curves are shown as dashed lines and labelled MR_p and MR_c. The total or combined marginal revenue, MR, is kinked at the output of twenty units, since at that output, marginal revenue of cons becomes zero. Therefore beyond the output of twenty bundles the combined marginal revenue curve is the same as the MR curve for pros. The profit-maximizing equilibrium output is where $MR = MC$, and the corresponding prices for pros and cons can be obtained from the respective demand curves.

2. Algebraic analysis. Again this is based on the procedure in Chapter 8.

1   Total revenue $= R$

$= (200 - 2Q_P)Q_P + (120 - 3Q_C)Q_C$

$= 200Q_P - 2Q_P^2 + 120Q_C - 3Q_C^2$

Now $Q = Q_P = Q_C$ since product bundles contain one pro and one con

$R = 320Q - 5Q^2$

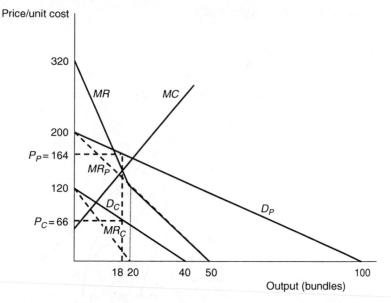

Figure 10.3. Optimal pricing for joint products produced in fixed proportions.

2 $MR = 320 - 10Q$

3 $MR = MC$
   $320 - 10Q = 50 + 5Q$
   $-15Q = -270$
   $Q = 18 \text{ units}$

4 $P_P = 200 - 2(18) = £164$
   $P_C = 120 - 3(18) = £66$

The situation is made a little more complicated when the combined *MR* curve intersects the *MC* curve at an output larger than the level where the *MR* of cons becomes zero, which in the case of Figure 10.3 is twenty units. In this case the quantity of pros to be sold is still determined in the same way as before, but the quantity of cons sold will not exceed twenty. Any excess output must be thrown away, since releasing it onto the market will depress the price so much that profit will fall.

b. Joint products produced in variable proportions

This is again a more complicated situation, but, as usual, a more realistic one. An exact fixity of proportions is usually only observed in chemical reactions, when compounds are transformed into other substances in particular

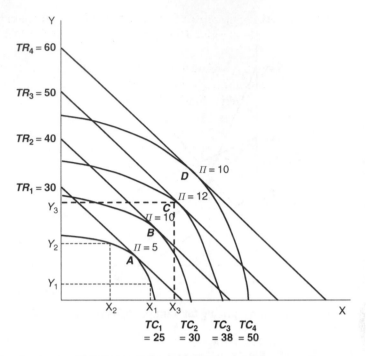

Figure 10.4. Optimal outputs of joints products produced in variable proportions.

quantities according to the laws of physics. Otherwise there is some flexibility in the processes involved that can increase or decrease the proportions according to profitability. The most common method of analysing this situation is to use a graphical approach, involving isocost and isorevenue curves. This is illustrated in Figure 10.4.

The concave (to the origin) curves on the graph are **isocost curves**: these curves represent **combinations of outputs which can be produced at the same total cost**. For example, TC_1 represents a total cost of 25 units; given this cost it is possible to produce X_1 units of X along with Y_1 units of Y, or X_2 units of X along with Y_2 units of Y, or any other combination of X and Y on the same curve. The isocost curves are shown as being concave to the origin, because it is assumed that there are diminishing returns in producing more of one product.

The sloping straight lines on the graph are **isorevenue curves**: these curves represent **combinations of outputs which result in the same total revenue**. These curves are shown as linear, which implicitly involves the assumption that the firm is a price-taker in each of the product markets. Points of tangency between isocost and isorevenue curves represent profit-maximization positions for any given cost or revenue. Thus point A on TC_1 and TR_1 yields more profit than any other point on TC_1 or TR_1; any other point on TC_1 will produce less revenue and therefore less profit, while any other point on TR_1 will involve more cost and therefore less profit. In order to find the overall profit-maximizing combination of outputs we have to find the point of tangency with the highest profit; this occurs at point C, where combined profit from selling X and Y is 12 units. The optimal outputs of X and Y are therefore X_3 and Y_3.

The reader may have observed that, while Figure 10.3 was concerned with the determination of optimal prices of joint products, Figure 10.4 was concerned with the determination of optimal outputs. The reason for this difference lies in the assumptions involved. There were a number of simplifying assumptions made in the model in Figure 10.4, for example only two products were involved. Most important in this context though is the assumption that the firm was a price-taker; thus the only relevant managerial decision was regarding the quantities of output. However, the price-taking assumption, which caused the total revenue curves to be linear, can easily be relaxed without affecting the analysis in any fundamental way. The profit-maximizing positions will still involve points of tangency between the total cost and total revenue curves. Once optimal outputs are determined, the prices of these outputs can be derived from the appropriate demand curves.

10.6 Transfer pricing

10.6.1 Context

As firms become larger there is a tendency for them to adapt a structure involving various divisions that in many cases are semi-autonomous. These divisions may be organized in various ways: they may perform parallel activities within the same areas, as is the case with GM; they may perform parallel activities in different areas or countries, as is the case with many multinationals; or they may perform vertically integrated activities in either the same or different areas. It is the last situation where transfer pricing is largely relevant. A transfer price represents **an internal price within a firm, which is charged by one division to another for some intermediate product**. There are two main functions of charging such an internal price:

1 To foster greater efficiency within the firm as a whole, so that the whole firm will maximize profit.
2 To evaluate the performance of the various divisions of the firm, as profit centres in their own right.

As will be seen, these two functions can conflict with each other. Before considering an example it should be explained that transfer pricing can occur under three different conditions as far as the product is concerned: when there is no external market, when there is a perfectly competitive external market, and when there is an imperfectly competitive external market. These situations are now discussed in turn in conjunction with an example.

10.6.2 *Products with no external market*

Consider the following situation:

SP10.3 Transfer pricing

Due to the expansion of business in Gogoland in recent years, SR Products has set up a marketing division there responsible for selling a new product. The head office and manufacturing plant remain in the United States. The company has estimated that the total cost of manufacturing in the USA and the cost of transportation of the product is given by the function:

$$C = Q^2 + 20Q + 40 \qquad (10.15)$$

where C = total cost per week in \$ and Q = units sold. This cost appears in the accounts of the manufacturing division.

The total cost for the marketing division in Gogoland is given by:

$$C = Q^2 + 140Q + 200 \qquad (10.16)$$

This includes the \$100 per unit which is the transfer price paid by the marketing division to the manufacturing division. This total cost appears in the accounts of the marketing division. The revenue function for the marketing division is estimated as:

$$R = 500Q - 8Q^2 \qquad (10.17)$$

where R = total revenue per week in \$.

a. Calculate the optimal policy for the company as a whole, showing the price, output and overall profits of the firm.
b. Calculate the optimal policies for the marketing division and the manufacturing divisions, assuming a transfer price of \$100, showing the overall profit of the firm in each case.
c. Calculate the optimal transfer price in order to make the optimal policies for both divisions the same as that for the company as a whole.
d. What does the above situation imply regarding managerial strategy?

As with all pricing problems discussed so far, the problem can be analysed either graphically or algebraically. In this case an algebraic approach will be used.

Solution

a. Let us consider the firm as a whole to begin with. We can obtain the profit-maximizing position by finding the *MC* and *MR* for the firm as a whole and equating them. First we can obtain the total cost to the firm by adding the costs of the manufacturing (N) and marketing (K) divisions:

$$TC = (Q^2 + 20Q + 40) + (Q^2 + 40Q + 200) = 2Q^2 + 60Q + 240 \quad (10.18)$$

Note that 100Q has been deducted from the costs of the marketing division, since this cost related to paying the transfer price to the manufacturing division, and was not a cost to the firm as a whole. Thus:

$$MC = 4Q + 60 \quad\quad\quad\quad\quad\quad (10.19)$$

Total revenue is given by $500Q - 8Q^2$; thus:

$$MR = 500 - 16Q \quad\quad\quad\quad\quad (10.20)$$

Equating MC and MR:

$$4Q + 60 = 500 - 16Q$$
$$20Q = 440$$
$$Q = \textbf{22 units}$$

Price can be derived by substituting the value of Q into the demand equation; price is the same as average revenue, thus the demand equation is given by:

$$P = 500 - 8Q$$
$$P = 500 - 8(22) = \textbf{\$324}$$

This is the external price charged by the firm's marketing division.

The total profit of the firm can be obtained from its profit function:

$$\text{Profit} = R - C = (500Q - 8Q^2) - (2Q^2 + 60Q + 240)$$
$$= -10Q^2 + 440Q - 240 \quad\quad\quad (10.21)$$
$$= \$4600$$

The above prices, output and profit are optimal for the firm as a whole.

b. However, the above result will not be achieved with the current strategy of charging a transfer price of $100. Consider the manufacturing division: profit_N is maximized where $MR_N = MC_N$

$$MR_N = 100 \text{ (the current transfer price)}$$
$$MC_N = 20 + 2Q$$
$$\text{Equating: } 100 = 20 + 2Q$$
$$2Q = 80$$
$$Q = \textbf{40 units}$$

Given the firm's demand curve $P = 500 - 8Q$, this means that the firm will be able to sell this output at the price of **\$180**.

Total profit of the firm is obtained by substituting $Q = 40$ into the profit function in (10.21), giving a profit of **$1,360**.

Now considering the marketing division:

$Profit_K$ is maximized where $MR_K = MC_K$

$$MR_K = MR - MC_K = 500 - 16Q - (2Q + 40) = 460 - 18Q$$
$$MC_K = 100$$

Equating: $460 - 18Q = 100$
$$18Q = 360$$
$$Q = \textbf{20 units}$$

Substituting this value of Q into the demand equation $P = 500 - 8Q$, the firm will charge the price of **$340**.

Total profit of the firm is obtained by substituting $Q = 20$ into the profit function, giving a value of **$4,560**.

c. In order to obtain the transfer price we need to consider the transferring division's marginal cost, that is MC_N. With no external market this represents the firm's optimal transfer price. The reason for this is that the firm wants to produce the profit-maximizing output for the firm as a whole, and the way to motivate the manufacturing (transferring) division to produce this output is to ensure that the division maximizes its profit at this output. Setting the transfer price, which is the manufacturing division's MR, equal to its MC at the overall profit-maximizing output ensures this. This condition can be seen more plainly by using the following analysis, which represents an alternative method of obtaining the optimal output for the firm, but which also shows how to compute the transfer price.

Profit maximization occurs when $MR = MC$

$$MR_K = MR - MC_K$$
$$MC_N = MC - MC_K$$

Therefore profit maximization occurs when

$$MR_K = MC_N \tag{10.22}$$

In the above example

$$MR_K = 500 - 16Q - (2Q + 40) = 460 - 18Q \tag{10.23}$$

and $MC_N = 20 + 2Q$

Equating: $460 - 18Q = 20 + 2Q$
$$-20Q = -440$$
$$Q = 22 \text{ units (as before)}$$

The optimal transfer price (P_T) is therefore given by:

$$P_T = 20 + 2(22) = \textbf{\$64}$$

Table 10.2. Implications of different transfer pricing strategies

	Transfer price	Market price	Output	Total profit	Profit of manufacturing division	Profit of marketing division
Firm	64	324	22	4,600	1,236	3,364
Manufacturing division	100	180	40	1,360	1,560	(200)
Marketing division	100	340	20	4,560	1,160	3,400

d. The results of the different transfer pricing strategies are shown in Table 10.2.

The situation above shows the importance to management of setting an optimal transfer price in order to maximize the profit of the firm as a whole. If the transfer price is too high, as here, the manufacturing (or transferring) division will produce too much, depressing the selling price and reducing overall profit. The marketing division would not want to buy as much as the optimal quantity, and again overall profit suffers.

10.6.3 Products with perfectly competitive external markets

Having considered the situation where there is no external market, it is now time to examine the situation where there is a perfectly competitive external market. In this situation the intermediate product can either be sold by the manufacturing division to another firm, or bought by the marketing division from another firm, at a fixed price. The optimal transfer price is the same as the external market price. If the transfer price were lower than this, it would be more profitable for the manufacturing division to sell the product externally, while if the transfer price were higher than this, it would be more profitable for the marketing division to buy the product externally.

One major difference between this situation and the one where there is no external market is that there may well be a mismatch between the amount that the manufacturing division wants to sell and the amount that the marketing division wants to buy. If the former exceeds the latter, then the excess can be sold on the open market, while if the latter exceeds the former, the excess can be purchased on the open market.

10.6.4 Products with imperfectly competitive external markets

This case is somewhat more complex than when external markets are perfectly competitive. The optimal transfer price this time equates the marginal cost of the manufacturing (transferring) division to the marginal revenue derived from the combined internal and external markets. The resulting optimal output is divided between internal transfers and external sales. The amount that is transferred internally is determined by equating the marginal cost of the manufacturing division with the net marginal revenue from final product sales:

$$MC_N = MR_F - MC_K \qquad (10.24)$$

The amount of the intermediate product that is sold in the external market is determined by equating the marginal cost of the manufacturing division with the marginal revenue from sales in the external market:

$$MC_N = MR_E \qquad (10.25)$$

10.7 Pricing and the marketing mix*

So far we have ignored the other elements of the marketing mix in discussing pricing. Intuitively this would not appear to be sensible; if product quality is high, we would expect the price to be high, and a higher price might necessitate more spending on advertising and distribution. Thus we would generally expect there to be some interaction between the marketing mix variables. This interaction now needs to be examined.

10.7.1 An approach to marketing mix optimization

Let us assume that a firm has a marketing mix demand function of the following general form:

$$Q = f(P, L, A, D) \qquad (10.26)$$

This is essentially (3.15) repeated. The firm's cost function can be expressed as follows:

$$C = g(Q, L)Q + A + D + F \qquad (10.27)$$

where unit production cost $c = g(Q, L)$, meaning that unit cost is a function of output and product quality; A and D are discretionary costs of advertising (or promotion) and distribution, and F is a non-discretionary fixed cost. The profit function can now be expressed as follows:

$$\Pi = R - C = P f(P, L, A, D) - [g(Q, L)Q + A + D + F] \qquad (10.28)$$

$$\Pi = P f(P, L, A, D) - g[(f(P, L, A, D), L] f(P, L, A, D) - A - D - F \qquad (10.29)$$

This clumsy-looking expression shows how much profit depends on all the different aspects of the marketing mix; both revenues and costs are affected by the levels of the marketing mix variables.

The necessary condition for finding the levels of these variables which optimize the marketing mix is obtained by partially differentiating the profit function with respect to each of the variables and setting the partial derivatives equal to zero:

$$\frac{\partial \Pi}{\partial P} = \frac{\partial \Pi}{\partial L} = \frac{\partial \Pi}{\partial A} = \frac{\partial \Pi}{\partial D} = 0 \tag{10.30}$$

The mathematics involved in solving these equations is omitted for the sake of brevity, but can be found in an advanced marketing text, such as that by Kotler.[9] The resulting conditions for optimization can be expressed in terms of the different elasticities, as follows:

$$\varepsilon_P = \frac{(PQ)}{A}\,\varepsilon_A = \frac{(PQ)}{D}\,\varepsilon_D = \frac{P}{c}\varepsilon_L \tag{10.31}$$

This is one form of the Dorfman–Steiner theorem,[10] and it shows the relationships in optimality between the elasticities of the various marketing mix instruments. However, because the functions are only stated in general terms, the theorem does not directly give the optimal values of the variables. In order to see this more clearly we must be more specific regarding the form of the demand and cost functions, and this is the subject of the next subsection. We will then be able to see how an optimal ratio of advertising to sales revenue can be derived in terms of the ratio of the price and advertising elasticities (10.39).

In the following models, only three marketing mix instruments are considered: price, advertising and distribution. Product quality is omitted because its measurement is more complex, and in practice it is often estimated as a function of unit cost, as discussed in Chapter 3. Thus the concept ε_L in (10.31) relating to product quality elasticity can be understood as referring to the percentage change in demand caused by a 1 per cent change in quality, as measured in terms of unit cost.

10.7.2 The constant elasticity model

a. Nature of the model

It was seen in Chapter 3 that the constant elasticity demand function was in the power form:

$$Q = aP^b A^c D^d \tag{10.32}$$

whereas the linear model, featuring constant marginal effects, was in the form:

$$Q = a + bP + cA + dD \tag{10.33}$$

In these models, only three marketing mix instruments are considered: price, advertising and distribution. It was also explained in Chapter 3 that the power model is more realistic than the simpler linear model for two reasons:

1 *It involves non-constant marginal effects*. This allows for the existence of diminishing returns to marketing effort.

2 *It involves interactions between the elements in the marketing mix.* This means that marginal effects depend not only on the level of the variable itself but also on the values of the other marketing mix variables.

Thus in the linear model the marginal effect of advertising is given by:

$$\frac{\partial Q}{\partial A} = c$$

whereas in the power model the marginal effect is given by:

$$\frac{\partial Q}{\partial A} = caP^b A^{c-1} D^d = cQ/A \tag{10.34}$$

Since the value of Q is affected by the values of the other elements in the marketing mix, it can be seen that the marginal effect depends on the levels of these other elements.

We can now assume a linear cost function of the form:

$$C = uQ + A + D + F \tag{10.35}$$

where u represents a constant level of unit production cost. We can now apply the technique of partial differentiation of the profit function to obtain expressions for the optimal levels of price, advertising and distribution.

$$\Pi = R - C = (P - u)Q - A - D - F$$

$$\frac{\partial \Pi}{\partial P} = (P - u)\frac{\partial Q}{\partial P} + Q = 0$$

$$\frac{\partial Q}{\partial P} = bQ/P \text{ similar to } (10.34)$$

Therefore

$$\frac{\partial \Pi}{\partial P} = (P - u)bQ/P + Q = Q(b - bu/P + 1) = 0$$

$$b - bu/P + 1 = 0$$

$$bu/P = b + 1$$

$$\boldsymbol{P^* = bu(b + 1)} \tag{10.36}$$

This expression is basically a rearrangement of expression (8.15) which was obtained in finding the optimal price and mark-up in terms of the price elasticity. However, we are now also in a position to find the optimal level of advertising and distribution in a similar manner:

$$\frac{\partial \Pi}{\partial A} = (P - u)\frac{\partial Q}{\partial A} - 1 = 0$$

Substituting (10.34):

$$\frac{\partial \Pi}{\partial A} = (P - u)\frac{cQ}{A} - 1 = 0$$

$$A^* = cQ(P - u) \qquad (10.37)$$

$$\frac{\partial \Pi}{\partial D} = (P - u)\frac{\partial Q}{\partial D} - 1 = 0$$

Since

$$\frac{\partial Q}{\partial D} = dQ/D$$

similarly to (10.34):

$$\frac{\partial \Pi}{\partial D} = (P - u)\frac{dQ}{D} - 1 = 0$$

$$D^* = dQ(P - u) \qquad (10.38)$$

It should be noted that the second-order conditions for optimality are not considered here, for reasons of brevity.

The question now is: how can these optimal levels of the marketing mix instruments be interpreted?

b. Interpretation of the model

Several interesting and not entirely intuitive conclusions arise from the above analysis. Assuming no interactions between firms, as discussed in the previous chapter, the following conclusions are the most important.

1. The optimal level of price is independent of the levels of the other marketing mix variables. This is in particular a surprising result, coming from expression (10.36). The explanation is that the other marketing mix variables, advertising and distribution, are essentially treated as sunk costs. However, it is possible that these other variables may be relevant in affecting the optimal price if they influence the price elasticity. This possibility is considered in the next subsection.

2. The optimal price appears to be independent of uncontrollable factors affecting demand. These include, for example, seasonal factors and the marketing mix of competitors. However, as in the above case, these other variables may affect the optimal price through their influence on price elasticity.

3. The optimal ratio of advertising to sales revenue can be calculated. This is performed by combining equation (10.36) and (10.37); the resulting ratio is given by:

$$\frac{A^*}{P^*Q} = -c/b = AED/PED \text{ in absolute terms} \qquad (10.39)$$

This means that advertising and price should be set so that the resulting advertising-to-sales ratio is equal to the ratio of the advertising elasticity to the price elasticity. The implication here is that firms should not simply use an arbitrary fixed ratio in order to determine advertising budgets; furthermore, the ratio should be adjusted if the firm suspects that either the advertising or price elasticities have changed.

4. The optimal ratio of advertising to distribution expenditure is equal to the ratios of their respective elasticities. This result is obtained by dividing (10.37) by (10.38), as shown below:

$$\frac{A^*}{D^*} = \frac{cQ(P-u)}{dQ(P-u)} = \frac{c}{d} \tag{10.40}$$

This means that if, for example, a firm's promotional elasticity is twice the level of its distributional elasticity, it should spend twice as much on promotion as on distribution. Again this is not entirely intuitive; some firms have reacted to having a higher elasticity by spending less on the relevant instrument, because they regard it as being unnecessary to spend so much in order to have the same effect.

10.7.3 Complex marketing mix interactions

The constant elasticity model is a very useful general model for representing the effects of the different elements of the marketing mix on sales and profit. However, managerial analysts may want to incorporate certain specific interactions into their demand models. A couple of examples will illustrate the situation.

1 It may be considered that the marginal effect of advertising is a function of distribution, because a greater number of retail outlets will increase the effects of a given advertising expenditure. A linear relationship may be involved as follows:

$$\frac{\partial Q}{\partial A} = eD \text{ where } e \text{ is a constant} \tag{10.41}$$

2 It may be considered that a greater level of advertising reduces price elasticity, by increasing brand loyalty. This may be modelled as follows:

$$PED = f/A \text{ where } f \text{ is a constant} \tag{10.42}$$

These relationships then have to be incorporated into the demand equation, according to its mathematical form. For example, if (10.42) is substituted into a constant elasticity demand function, we obtain:

$$Q = aP^{f/A}A^cD^d \tag{10.43}$$

The above examples just give an idea of the kind of interactions that can be incorporated into the marketing mix demand model. Obviously the equations become harder to work with mathematically, and may cause problems in regression analysis, but they may lead to more reliable and useful results, both in terms of testing economic theories, and in terms of making better managerial decisions.

10.8 Dynamic aspects of pricing

10.8.1 *Significance of the product life-cycle*

This refers to the concept that a firm will tend to adopt different pricing practices for a product at different stages of its product life-cycle. This area of pricing strategy has been somewhat neglected in many economics and marketing texts, and indeed in research.[11] However, it is apparent when we consider many products that their prices have changed significantly since the date they were originally introduced in the market. In some cases prices have risen considerably, while in other cases they have dropped significantly. The reasons for these changes and differences need to be examined.

It was stated at the beginning of the chapter that the pricing decision was generally not the most fundamental one that management has to take. The positioning and product decisions tend to be paramount, but, as will be seen in the next chapter, these are long-run decisions and require a long-run frame of analysis. They also involve an interdependence of marketing mix instruments, in particular the interdependence between product characteristics and price. Therefore, any discussion of pricing strategy should take into consideration both this interdependence and the fact that a product's price should normally change during the course of the product life-cycle. The interdependence aspects are discussed more fully in the next section; this section is concerned with the relationships between pricing strategy and the product life-cycle.

The long-run decisions regarding whether to produce a particular product or not involve a discussion of investment analysis, which is the topic of the next chapter. Without anticipating this discussion in detail, it involves an examination of profits or cash flows over the whole lifetime of a project. This in turn means that future prices of the product have to be estimated. Since demand and cost factors change over a product's life-cycle it follows that the product's price is likely to change during the course of the cycle. It is of great importance to management to be able to estimate these changes as accurately as possible before launching the product in order to make the initial fundamental decision on whether to produce the product.

10.8.2 *Early stages of the product life-cycle*

The evidence available,[12-14] tends to suggest that price elasticity can be expected to decrease for the first three phases of the cycle: introduction, growth and maturity. At the introduction stage there is normally much expenditure on promotion to gain recognition and awareness; discounting, coupons and free samples are common. This means that a **market penetration** strategy is often advantageous, because demand is highly elastic. As the product gains in image and brand loyalty, and product differentiation increases, demand becomes less elastic, and prices are generally raised.

Of course, it is easy to think of products where the opposite has occurred. This applies in particular to high-technology consumer durables, like VCRs, microwaves and mobile phones. Consumer behaviour in this situation involves innovators and early adopters being willing to pay high prices to own a product that has some prestige value in terms of being novel and exclusive. Thus demand tends to be less elastic and a **market skimming** strategy is advantageous. In this case the price can fall considerably as the product passes through the introduction and growth stages. Competition springs up, often with better or more advanced products, and unit costs fall on account of economies of scale and learning curve effects.

10.8.3 Later stages of the product life-cycle

Once a product has reached maturity there is usually a considerable amount of competition in the market. Emphasis tends to switch from product innovation to process innovation; products become more standardized and cost minimization becomes an important factor. At this point, evidence suggests that demand elasticity increases again, as the product moves into the decline phase. Curry and Riesz[15] have found that the mean price of all brands within a product form tends to decline over time (net of inflation), and that the price variance within a designated product form also tends to decline over time. This is again what one would expect with an increase in competition and the availability of close substitutes. Curry and Riesz suggested that 'Price, which previously may have been a real or fictitious surrogate for product quality, gradually loses its flexibility as both a strategic and functional marketing variable.' This conclusion appears to ignore the promotional potential in pricing. This aspect and the relationship between price and product quality are considered in the next section.

10.9 Other pricing strategies

This section is rather miscellaneous in nature; it discusses a number of other pricing strategies that are found in practice, but which are more difficult to model in economic terms. This does not mean that these strategies do not help the firm to maximize profit in the short or long run, but that they tend to relate to more complex aspects of consumer behaviour that are not generally taken into consideration in the neoclassical model. It is more appropriate to refer to these models as **behavioural models**.

These models generally try to identify the key factors that determine consumer buyer behaviour. Zeithaml's means–end model is a good example;[16] this examines perceived quality, perceived price, the price–quality relationship and perceived value. These factors are now considered in turn, along with various pricing strategies that are based on them.

10.9.1 Perceived quality

This concept is a subjective assessment, similar to an attitude, not an objective factor relating to intrinsic physical attributes, although obviously the latter serve as cues from which consumers often infer quality. Thus perceived quality represents an abstract concept of a global nature, and judgements made regarding it are made in a comparative context. Other non-physical cues are extrinsic; these include brand image,[17] store image,[18] advertising level,[19] warranty, and of course price, which is examined in more detail shortly. These cues tend to be more important in purchase situations when intrinsic cues are not available and when there is more perceived risk,[20] for example many services, and when quality is difficult to evaluate, as with experience goods, i.e. goods which have to be experienced before the consumer can evaluate the quality.

10.9.2 Perceived price

The main point here is that the perceived price may be different from the actual price for a number of reasons, some of which have been mentioned in previous chapters. For example, consumers consider search, time and psychic costs as being part of the perceived price.[21] This means that when they encode price information, they include these additional costs.

Evidence suggests that for certain goods, price information is not encoded at all by a substantial proportion of consumers. Dickson and Sawyer[22] reported that for four types of product, margarine, cereal, toothpaste and coffee, 40 per cent or more of consumers did not check price. Most of these consumers said that price was just not important in the purchase decision. Clearly the products mentioned are all fast-moving consumer goods (FMCG) and one might expect that in this situation price would not be an important decision factor; in the purchase of a stereo or holiday one might expect different behaviour.

10.9.3 The price–quality relationship

This aspect of consumer behaviour has been very well researched. However, the findings are difficult to summarize in any brief manner, since there is a considerable amount of conflicting evidence. It appears that there are various other quality cues that are more important, like brand name and store image;[23] also studies show that price is only weakly correlated with objective quality.[24, 25] However, there do appear to be some situations where price is used as an indicator of quality: when other cues are absent, and when there is much price or product quality variation within a product class.

There is certainly evidence that a high price can give prestige to a product, by making it exclusive, even if the evidence of greater objective quality is dubious. This leads to the strategy sometimes referred to as '**prestige pricing**'; German luxury saloon and sports cars, like Mercedes, BMW and Porsche, enjoy this cachet. This is not to imply that such cars are lacking in objective quality! However, other firms may try to employ the same strategy without necessarily ensuring a higher-quality product.

Some researchers have found evidence that consumers have a range of acceptable prices for a product, with too high a price being seen as too expensive, and too low a price indicating inferior quality. [26, 27] This can help to explain the phenomenon of '**odd pricing**', a universally observed pricing strategy. An odd price usually ends in a '9', for example £399. This would be acceptable for a consumer whose price range was £300 to less than £400, which is a common way of defining a price range. Research shows that consumers perceive a much greater price difference between £399 and £400 than between £398 and £399.

Another strategy based on this same concept of acceptable price ranges is '**price lining**'. Instead of starting with a positioning and product concept, a firm starts with a concept of a particular price range which appears to represent a gap in the market, in terms of there being consumer demand in this range but a lack of products currently available in the relevant range. A product is then identified with characteristics that would cause it to be priced accordingly. Japanese consumer electronics firms have used this strategy successfully. Profit maximization can still be the objective, but the normal order of decision-making is reversed.

10.9.4 Perceived value

Consumers can interpret this concept in different ways. To some consumers it simply means a low price. However, in the majority of cases perceived value is a function of the ratio of perceived quality to perceived price, and this concept has been incorporated into Keon's bargain value model.[28] Some empirical evidence supports this model as being a good indicator of probability of purchase.[29]

Many **price promotion** strategies are based on aspects of perceived value. These strategies all involve some kind of discounting. Evidence suggests that these discounts tend to be more effective when **reference prices** are used, [30, 31] for example 'normal price £599, now only £499'. The reference price can be used to persuade consumers that quality is high relative to the current price being charged, implying that they are being offered good value.

Summary

1 Pricing is only one component of the marketing mix and pricing decisions should be interdependent with other marketing mix and positioning decisions.

2 Competitive advantage refers to the situation where a firm creates more value than its competitors, where value is measured in terms of perceived benefit minus input cost.

3 The value created by a firm can be divided into consumer surplus and producer surplus; the former represents the excess of perceived benefit over the price paid, while the latter represents the excess of the price charged over the input cost.

4 Market positioning essentially involves aiming for a cost advantage or a benefit advantage.

5 Positioning depends both on the nature of a firm's competitive advantage, in terms of its resources and capabilities, and on environmental forces in the market, particularly those relating to customers and competition.

6 Price elasticity is important in guiding a firm's general pricing strategy, in terms of aiming for increasing market share or increasing profit margin.

7 Segmentation involves dividing a market into component parts according to relevant characteristics related to buyer behaviour.

8 Segmentation and targeting are important because different strategies are appropriate for different segments.

9 Targeting involves determining whether a broad coverage strategy is appropriate, or whether a focus strategy is better. In the latter case the appropriate product or segment must be selected, again according to competitive advantage.

10 Price discrimination means charging different prices for the same or similar products, where any price differentials are not based on differences in marginal cost.

11 Price discrimination always increases the profit of the seller because it enables the seller to capture some of the consumer surplus.

12 Price discrimination can only occur if market segments have different demand elasticities and they can be separated from each other.

13 Firms producing many products in a product line or product mix face more complex pricing decisions because of demand and cost interdependencies.

14 Transfer pricing occurs when one part of a firm charges an internal price to another part of the same firm, a common practice in large firms.

15 Charging the right transfer price is important to the firm, not just in maximizing overall profit, but also in evaluating the performance of different divisions.

16 Pricing is only one element in the marketing mix, and pricing decisions need to be made in conjunction with other marketing mix decisions.

17 Interactions between different components of the marketing mix need to be carefully considered by managers when constructing the demand models necessary for making pricing and other marketing mix decisions.

18 Firms generally charge different prices for a product during different stages of the product life-cycle, even if there are no changes in quality. These changes have to do with changes in demand elasticity, and also often with unit cost changes.

19 Behavioural models are important in that they can enable managers to understand consumer behaviour and reactions to the firm's marketing strategies. Pricing strategies therefore need to take these models into consideration, even though they are more complex than the traditional neoclassical economic model of consumer behaviour.

Review questions

1 Explain why it is important for managers to know the principles of price discrimination.
2 Explain the relationship between a product line and joint products.
3 Assuming that there is no external market for the product, how should a firm determine the optimal transfer price for an intermediate product?
4 Explain how the price elasticity for a product is likely to change during the product life-cycle.
5 Explain the meaning and significance of the concept of perceived value. How is it related to the strategy of prestige pricing?
6 Why is it not sufficient for a firm to create value in order for it to have a competitive advantage?
7 How does branding relate to competitive advantage? Why do all firms not brand their goods, if this enables them to raise their price?
8 Explain why providers of mobile phone services should segment their markets. What criteria are relevant for segmentation in this situation?
9 Would you expect an airline flying a transatlantic route to pursue a broad coverage or a focus strategy? What factors would affect this decision?

Problems

10.1 GMG, a cinema complex, is considering charging a different price for the afternoon showings of its films compared with the evening ticket price for the same films. It has estimated its afternoon and evening demand functions to be:

$$P_A = 8.5 - 0.25Q_A$$
$$P_E = 12.5 - 0.4Q_E$$

where P_A and P_E are ticket prices (in £) and Q_A and Q_E are number of customers per week (in hundreds). GMG has estimated that its fixed costs are £2,000 per week, and that its variable costs are 50 pence per customer.

a. Calculate the price that GMG should charge if it does not use price discrimination, assuming its objective is to maximize profit.
b. Calculate the prices that GMG should charge if it does use price discrimination.

c. Calculate the price elasticities of demand in the case of price discrimination.

d. How much difference does price discrimination make to profit?

10.2 TT Products produces two items, bibs and bobs, in a process that makes them joint products. For every bib produced two bobs are produced. The demand functions for the two products are:

$$\text{Bibs: } P = 40 - 4Q$$
$$\text{Bobs: } P = 60 - 3Q$$

where P is price in £ and Q is units of each product. The total cost function is:

$$C = 80 + 20Q + 4Q^2$$

where Q represents a product bundle consisting of one bib and two bobs.

a. Calculate the prices and outputs of bibs and bobs that maximizes profit.

b. Calculate the size of the above profit.

10.3 DPC is a firm that has separate manufacturing and marketing divisions. The cost functions of these divisions are as follows:
Manufacturing:

$$C = 2Q^2 + 5Q + 1.5$$

Marketing:

$$C = Q^2 + 3Q + 0.5$$

where C is total cost (in £ million) and Q is output (in millions of units per year). The firm's demand function for its final product has been estimated as:

$$P = 20 - 5Q$$

where P is the price of the final product (in £).

a. Calculate the profit-maximizing price and output of the final product.

b. Calculate the optimal transfer price.

c. Calculate the effect on profit if the transfer price is £6.

d. Calculate the effect on profit if the transfer price is £10.

10.4 Gungho Products has estimated the demand function for its new soft drink to be:

$$Q = 320P^{-1.5}A^{0.4}D^{0.2}$$

where Q is measured in cans sold per month, P is the price in £, A is advertising expenditures in £ per month and D is distribution expenditures in £ per month. Unit production costs are estimated at £0.25 per can and are constant over the firm's output range. The firm has fixed costs of £30,000 per month.

a. Determine the firm's optimal price.
b. Determine the firm's optimal advertising and distribution expenditures.
c. Comment on the relationship between these two expenditures.
d. Determine the optimal advertising-to-sales ratio for the firm.
e. Determine the firm's level of profit.

Notes

1 M. E. Porter, *Competitive Advantage: Techniques for Analysing Industries and Competitors*, New York: Free Press, 1980.
2 A. M. Brandenburger and B. J. Nalebuff, *Co-opetition*, New York: Doubleday, 1996.
3 A. M. McGahan and M. E. Porter, 'How much does industry matter really?' *Strategic Management Journal*, **18** (Summer 1997): 15–30.
4 'Emergency calls', *The Economist*, 26 April 2001.
5 'Nokia succumbs', *The Economist*, 14 June 2001.
6 'One Palm flapping', *The Economist*, 31 May 2001.
7 Survey on European business and the euro, *The Economist*, 1 December 2001.
8 'Britain takes to the air', *The Economist*, 28 June 2001.
9 P. Kotler, *Marketing Decision Making: A Model Building Approach*, New York: Holt, Rinehart and Winston, 1971, pp. 56–73.
10 R. Dorfman and P. O. Steiner, 'Optimal advertising and optimal quality', *American Economic Review*, **44** (December 1954): 826–836.
11 V. R. Rao, 'Pricing research in marketing: the state of the art', *Journal of Business*, **57** (January 1984): 39–60.
12 Kotler, *Marketing Decision Making*.
13 T. Levitt, 'Exploit the product life cycle', *Harvard Business Review*, **43** (November–December): 81–94.
14 H. Simon, 'Dynamics of price elasticity and brand life cycles: an empirical study', *Journal of Marketing Research*, **16** (November 1979): 439–452.
15 D. J. Curry and C. Riesz, 'Prices and price/quality relationships: a longitudinal analysis', *Journal of Marketing*, **52** (January 1988): 36–51.
16 V. A. Zeithaml, 'Consumer perceptions of price, quality and value: a means–end model and synthesis of evidence', *Journal of Marketing*, **52** (July 1988): 2–22.
17 P. Mazursky and J. Jacoby, 'Forming impressions of merchandise and service quality', in J. Jacoby and J. Olson, eds., *Perceived Quality*, Lexington, MA: Lexington Books, 1985, pp. 139–154.
18 J. J. Wheatley and J. S. Chiu, 'The effects of price, store image and product and respondent characteristics on perceptions of quality', *Journal of Marketing Research*, **14** (May 1977): 181–186.
19 P. Milgrom and J. Roberts, 'Price and advertising signals of product quality', *Journal of Political Economy*, **94** (1986): 796–821.
20 R. A. Peterson and W. R. Wilson, 'Perceived risk and price-reliance schema and price-perceived-quality mediators', in Jacoby and Olson, eds., *Perceived Quality*, pp. 247–268.
21 V. A. Zeithaml and L. Berry, 'The time consciousness of supermarket shoppers', Working Paper, Texas A and M University, 1987.
22 P. Dickson and A. Sawyer, 'Point of purchase behaviour and price perceptions of supermarket shoppers', Marketing Science Institute Working Paper Series, Cambridge, Mass, 1986.

23 R. C. Stokes, 'The effect of price, product design, and brand familiarity on perceived quality', in Jacoby and Olson, eds., *Perceived Quality*, pp. 233–246.

24 P. Riesz, 'Price versus quality in the marketplace, 1961–1975', *Journal of Retailing*, **54** (4)(1978):15–28.

25 E. Gerstner, 'Do higher prices signal higher quality?' *Journal of Marketing Research*, **22** (May 1985): 209–215.

26 A. Gabor and C. W. J. Granger, 'Price as an indicator of quality: report of an inquiry', *Economica*, **46** (February 1966): 43–70.

27 K. A. Monroe, 'Some findings on estimating buyers' response functions for acceptable price thresholds', in American Institute for Decision Sciences, *Northeast Conference*, 1972, pp. 9–18.

28 J. N. Keon, 'The bargain value model and a comparison of managerial implications with the linear learning model', *Management Science*, 26 (November 1980), 1117–1130.

29 R. W. Shoemaker, 'An analysis of consumer reactions to product promotions', in Marketing Educator's Proceedings (American Marketing Association), August 1979.

30 E. A. Blair and L. Landon, 'The effect of reference prices in retail advertisements', *Journal of Marketing*, **45** (Spring 1981): 61–69.

31 N. Berkowitz and R. Walton, 'Contextual influences on consumer price responses: an experimental analysis', *Journal of Marketing Research*, **17** (August 1980): 349–358.

11

Investment analysis

Outline

Objectives

1 To explain the nature and significance of capital budgeting.
2 To describe and distinguish between different types of investment or capital expenditure.
3 To explain the process and principles of cash flow analysis.
4 To explain the different methods of evaluating investment projects.
5 To explain the concept and measurement of the cost of capital.
6 To explain the nature and significance of risk and uncertainty in investment appraisal.
7 To examine the measurement of risk.
8 To explain the different ways of incorporating risk into managerial decision-making in terms of investment analysis.
9 To explain the concept of the optimal capital budget and how it can be determined.

11.1 Introduction

11.1.1 *The nature and significance of capital budgeting*

So far in the analysis of the previous chapters we have concentrated largely on the aspects of managerial decision-making that relate to making the most efficient use of existing resources. It is true that some aspects of decision-making in the long run have been considered, for example determining the most appropriate scale for producing a given output (Chapter 6), and the decision to expand capacity in a duopolistic market (Chapter 9), but many factors were taken as given in these situations. This chapter examines these long-run decisions in more detail, and explains the various factors that need to be considered in determining whether to replace or expand a firm's resources. As has been the case throughout the book, it will normally be assumed that the firm's objective is to maximize shareholder wealth, but certain aspects of public sector decision-making will also be considered, and these will be examined in further detail in the final chapter.

First of all, what do we mean by **capital budgeting**? Textbooks on both economics and finance tend to use the terms capital budgeting and investment analysis interchangeably. They both refer to **capital expenditure** by the firm, as opposed to current expenditure. Capital expenditure is *expenditure that is expected to generate cash flows or benefits lasting longer than one year*, whereas current expenditure yields benefits that accrue within a one-year time period. Capital budgeting and investment analysis refer to the process of planning and evaluating capital expenditures.

Why is capital budgeting important? Unlike many other management decisions, capital budgeting decisions involve some commitment by the firm over a period of years, and as seen in Chapter 9, the nature of such decisions is that they are difficult or costly to reverse. Bad decisions can therefore be very costly to the firm. If a firm overinvests, there are resulting financial losses due to low revenues relative to high depreciation charges, and therefore there is a poor return to shareholders' capital. However, if a firm underinvests, the firm is often left with obsolete equipment and low productivity, with the additional problem that it may not be able to satisfy demand in peak periods, thus losing customers to competitors. Both of these problems are examined in more detail in Case Studies 11.2 and 11.3.

11.1.2 Types of capital expenditure

There are a number of different reasons for a firm to invest, and these can be classified in different ways. In each case the considerations, depth of analysis, and level of decision-making are different. The following seven-category classification is useful:

a. *Replacement*. This is the simplest type of investment decision because it involves replacing existing equipment with identical goods. Some decisions are as basic as changing a light bulb, while others, like replacing a photocopier, involve rather more expenditure. These investments must be made if the firm is to continue to operate efficiently with its current products in its current markets. Often such investments do not require a detailed analysis, and do not involve top management.

b. *Expansion*. This refers to expansion involving existing products and markets, thus increasing the scale or capacity of the firm. This is normally in response to an increase in demand, or in anticipation of an increase in demand. Such investments usually involve considerable expense and more uncertainty relating to the future; therefore, a more detailed analysis is generally required, and a higher level of management involved.

c. *New technology*. This type of investment may also involve the replacement of existing equipment, but, in this case, with newer, more productive equipment. The spur to this may be either cost reduction or demand expansion. The latter is relevant if the use of the new technology is seen as being important in attracting new customers. The new technology may therefore be used to produce existing products more cheaply, or to produce new products that are superior in some aspect of quality. There is a wide variation within this category in terms of cost, and therefore in depth of analysis and level of management involvement. The decision by car manufacturers to develop electric cars is obviously at the top end of the cost scale.

d. *Diversification*. This again involves expansion, but into new products or markets. This can change the whole nature of the firm's business, and involve very long-term and large expenditures. In many cases, mergers and acquisitions are involved. Therefore, very thorough and detailed analysis is required, and such decisions generally involve top management.

e. *Research*. This type of investment is sometimes ignored, or included in other categories, but it does have certain distinct features that merit a separate category. The most important of these is that such investment gives the firm options in the future, in terms of possible further investment opportunities. This is best explained by means of an example. If a firm conducts market research into the development of a new product, such research involves certain costs, but unlike any of the previously mentioned categories of investment it is not directly associated with any revenues. Only if the research indicates a favourable consumer response will the firm undertake the further investment necessary to produce and market the new product.

f. *Legal requirement*. Governments often make and change laws relating to such issues as the environment and working conditions. Thus firms may have to change either processes of production or the nature of the products they are selling if they are to continue in business. For example, the introduction of the EU Working Time Directive regarding a maximum working week in the UK has led companies to invest in more equipment of various types, both in order to maintain output levels, and to monitor the working schedules of employees. Even changes in tax conditions can result in such decisions; the high tax on petrol in the UK, including diesel fuel, may lead some firms to invest in converting their vehicles to operating on natural gas.

g. *Ancillaries*. These refer to investment projects that are not directly related to the core activities of the firm. They may include car parks for employees, cafeteria facilities, sporting facilities and suchlike. In many cases there are no direct increases in revenues in terms of cash flow, but there are measurable benefits to the firm that have to be evaluated. In the absence of such benefits there would be no reason for a firm to invest in such facilities. This aspect is examined in some detail in Case Study 11.1.

11.1.3 A simple model of the capital budgeting process

There are a number of steps involved in the capital budgeting process, which parallel those that are used in valuing securities like stocks and bonds. For each potential investment project that is identified by management the following steps need to be taken:

1 The initial cost of the investment must be determined.
2 The expected cash flows from the investment must be estimated, including the value of the investment asset at the end of its expected life.
3 The riskiness of the investment must be assessed.
4 The appropriate cost of capital for discounting the cash flows must be determined.
5 Some criterion must be applied in order to evaluate whether the investment should be undertaken or not. This involves calculating the **net present value** (NPV) and/or **internal rate of return** (IRR) and making the appropriate comparisons.

In practice the last three steps are interdependent, as will be seen, but it is convenient to discuss them in the above order. This is, therefore, the subject matter for the next four sections. Subsequently, the issue of the optimal capital budget for the firm is discussed, before finishing with the usual problem-solving approach.

11.2 Cash flow analysis

This aspect is the most fundamental, and also the most difficult, of all the processes involved in capital budgeting. It relates to both of the first two steps mentioned above, determining the initial cost outlay of the investment project, and estimating the annual cash inflows and outflows associated with it once operation begins. Various departments within the firm are usually involved: the initial cost outlay is often estimated by engineering, design and product development managers; operating costs are estimated by accountants and production, personnel and purchasing managers; revenues are estimated by sales and marketing managers.

A large amount of uncertainty is inevitable in such estimation, even concerning initial cost outlay. Many large-scale projects, for example the Montreal Olympics in 1976 and the Channel Tunnel, have been notorious in coming in at around five times the initial budget estimate. Some projects have exceeded even this. The uncertainty and inaccuracy becomes even greater with estimates of future operational cash flows. This aspect is dealt with in the next section. At this stage we are concerned with the principles of identification and measurement of cash flows.

11.2.1 Identification of cash flows

There are two main points that need to be clarified here.

a. *Cash flows not accounting income and expenses.* The income and expenses that appear in accounting records of profit and loss do not necessarily correspond to cash flows. For example, sales on credit are recorded as an income, but do not result in a cash flow in the corresponding period. Similarly, capital costs are cash flows, but are not recorded as expenses; depreciation on the other hand is recorded as an expense, but is not a cash flow. This creates some complications in terms of measuring cash flows, since the amount of a firm's tax liability is based on profit, not cash flow, yet tax does represent a cash flow. This complication is discussed in the next subsection on measurement. It is vital that cash flows, not income and expenses, are used in order to make the correct investment decision; the reason for this will be seen more clearly in Section 11.5 when evaluation criteria are explained.

b. *Incremental flows not actual cash flows.* The correct cash flows to consider are the differences between the cash flows if the investment project is undertaken and the cash flows if the project is not undertaken:

$$CF_t = CF_t \text{ with project} - CF_t \text{ without project} \qquad (11.1)$$

Only in this way can the effect of the project on the firm be properly seen and the correct investment decision made. The principle will be seen more clearly in the example in the next subsection.

11.2.2 Measurement of cash flows

Again there are a number of factors that have to be taken into consideration here. One, taxes, has just been mentioned, and some of the others have been discussed in Chapter 6, in the context of the relevant costs for decision-making. These factors are best explained in terms of a practical example, so a solved problem is now presented for this purpose, and this is further developed in later sections.

SP11.1 Cash flow estimation

Maxsport produces nutritional supplements for athletes and sports participants. They have developed a new bottled soft drink called Slimfuel, which claims both to provide nutrition and energy and to act as an aid to losing bodyfat. The marketing department has estimated sales to be 30 million bottles a year at a price of £2 per bottle. Research and development costs have already amounted to £500,000. The new product can be produced from the existing plants, but new machinery is required costing £4 million in each of five plants in the year 2002. Production and sales would begin in 2003. Advertising and promotion costs in the first year are estimated at 30 per cent of sales revenues, going down to 20 per cent in later years, with the product having a life of four years. Variable production costs are estimated at 40 per cent of sales revenues, with fixed overhead costs being £5 million per year, excluding depreciation.

Estimate the cash flows from the operation in order to evaluate the investment project, stating any necessary assumptions.

Solution

We can now consider the relevant factors in estimating the cash flows.

a. *Timing*. The timing of cash flows is important because of the **time value of money**. This concept is explained in more detail in section 11.5, but at this point it is sufficient to appeal to intuition that to receive £100 today has more value than receiving £100 in one year's time, which in turn has more value than receiving £100 in two years' time. Strictly speaking, cash flows should be analysed on a daily basis, but in practice some simplification is in order; in evaluating projects most firms assume that cash flows occur on a yearly basis, usually at the end of each year, or in some cases quarterly or monthly. The present example is typical in the sense that there is a considerable outlay at the start of the project, in 2002. Cash inflows begin in 2003 and continue until 2006.

b. *Sunk costs*. As already explained in Chapter 6, sunk costs are not incremental costs and therefore should not be included in the analysis. In this case the R & D costs of £500,000 have no bearing on the decision of whether to undertake the project or not, and should not be included as a cash flow.

c. *Opportunity costs*. These were also considered in Chapter 6, and were seen as being relevant to the decision-making process. Thus in the above situation the firm has spare capacity if it is capable of producing the new product with the same plant. This spare capacity may have other uses that could earn a profit for the firm; if this is the case then any net cash flows forgone by the decision to invest in the Slimfuel project can be regarded as opportunity costs and should be deducted from the cash flows directly generated by the project. We will assume for simplicity that there is no alternative use of the spare capacity, but we will need to return to this point in section 11.5, in the discussion regarding the evaluation of mutually exclusive and independent projects.

d. *Externalities*. This refers to any **effects that the project may have on other operations of the firm**. For example, the production of Slimfuel may boost the sales of other products that are perceived as complementary, or it may detract from sales of existing products that are perceived as substitutes. Maxsport may be currently producing a similar product, Trimfuel, and net cash inflows from this product may be reduced by £2.5 million for the first two years of the project (not allowing for inflation).

e. *Net working capital*. It is often the case that investment projects require an increase in inventories, and sometimes in accounts receivable or debtors. Firms therefore have to consider not only the initial cost outlay in terms of fixed assets, but also any increase in current assets associated with the project. Maxsport may have to have inventories on hand of 10 per cent of the estimated cost of sales at the beginning of 2003. Therefore the initial cost outlay in 2002 will be:

$C_0 = (£4 \text{ million} \times 5) + (10\% \times 40\% \times £60 \text{ million})$

$C_0 = £22.4 \text{ million}$

This is assuming that the cash outflows associated with the inventory are related only to production costs, with no overheads, and that inventory levels are still at the 10% level at the end of the first year of operation.

f. *Taxes.* As mentioned under the identification of cash flows, the existence of taxes creates a complication because they are based on profit after allowing for depreciation. Since this measure of profit is not a cash flow, while taxes are a cash flow, the cash flows from a project have to be measured as follows:

$$CF_t = (R_t - C_t - D_t)(1 - T) + D_t \qquad (11.2)$$

where CF_t represents incremental cash flows in a given time period, R_t represents incremental revenues, C_t represents incremental operating costs, D_t represents incremental depreciation, and T represents the firm's marginal tax rate. Thus in expression (11.2) the term $(R_t - C_t - D_t)$ represents profit before tax and the term $(R_t - C_t - D_t)(1 - T)$ represents profit after tax. Since depreciation does not represent a cash outflow, it then has to be added back to profit after tax in order to estimate the incremental cash flow. We can now apply this procedure to the first year of operation, 2003.

Year 1 (2003)

$R_1 = (£2 \times 30 \text{ million}) - £2.5 \text{ million} = £57.5 \text{ million}$

$C_1 = 40\% \times £60 \text{ million} + 30\% \times £60 \text{ million} + £5 \text{ million} = £47 \text{ million}$

$D_1 = £20 \text{ million} \times 25\% = £5 \text{ million}$ (assuming a straight-line method of depreciation with no salvage value)

Profit before tax = £5.5 million

Profit after tax = £3.3 million (assuming a marginal tax rate of 40%)

$CF_1 = £3.3 \text{ million} + £5 \text{ million}$

$CF_1 = £8.3 \text{ million}$

The cash flows in the later years of operation are estimated after the discussion regarding adjustment for inflation.

g. *Inflation* Most countries experience inflation, meaning a continuing increase in the price level, to some degree. There are certain exceptions, Japan being the most notable in recent times, but even in cases of deflation or disinflation it is necessary to make allowances for changing prices in order to make correct capital budgeting decisions. As will be seen in section

11.4, the cost of capital is normally calculated on a market-determined basis, meaning allowing for inflation. Since we shall also see, in section 11.5, that cash flows are often discounted by this cost of capital in order to evaluate the investment project, it is also necessary to adjust the estimated cash flows to allow for inflation.[1] In reality this can be quite complicated, since not all cash flows are affected in the same way. For example, wage costs may increase more than material costs, and final prices may increase by a still different rate. Depreciation is normally not affected at all. We shall assume in SP11.1 that variable costs, overheads and prices all increase by 3 per cent per year. Therefore in the second and third years of operation the incremental cash flows are estimated as follows:

Year 2 (2004)

R_2 = £2.06 × 30 million) − £ 2.575 million = £59.225 million
C_2 = 40% × £61.8 million + 20% × £61.8 million + £5.15 million = £42.23 million
D_2 = £20 million × 25% = £5 million (assuming a straight-line method of depreciation with no salvage value)
Profit before tax = £11.995 million
Profit after tax = £7.197 million (assuming a marginal tax rate of 40%)
CF_2 = £7.197 million + £5 million
CF_2 = £12.197 million

Year 3 (2005)

R_3 = (£ 2.12 × 30 million) = £ 63.6 million
C_3 = 40% × £63.6 million + 20% × £63.6 million + £5.3045 million = £43.4645 million
D_3 = £20 million × 25% = £5 million (assuming a straight-line method of depreciation with no salvage value)
Profit before tax = £15.1355 million
Profit after tax = £9.0813 million (assuming a marginal tax rate of 40%)
CF_3 = £9.0813 million + £5 million
CF_3 = £14.0813 million

In year 4 of operation it is only necessary to produce 90 per cent of total sales because of starting inventories of 10 per cent of sales. Thus we have:

Year 4 (2006)

R_4 = (£2.18 × 30 million) = £65.4 million
C_4 = 40% × 90% × £65.4 million + 20% × £65.4 million + £5.4636 million = £42.0876 million
D_4 = £20 million × 25% = £5 million (assuming a straight-line method of depreciation with no salvage value)
Profit before tax = £18.3124 million
Profit after tax = £10.9874 million (assuming a marginal tax rate of 40%)
CF_4 = £10.9874 million + £5 million
CF_4 = £15.9874 million

Now that all the incremental cash flows have been estimated, the next stage of the capital budgeting process can be performed. Before this is examined, it is useful to consider a case study involving a situation where the nature of the benefits and cash flows is somewhat different.

Case study 11.1: Investing in a corporate fitness programme

Procal Co. is considering establishing a corporate fitness programme for its employees. The firm currently employs 500 workers, mainly managerial and administrative, in a number of offices in one local area. The type of programme being considered involves subsidizing employees by paying 50 per cent of any membership fees to a specific fitness centre. This subsidy represents the cost of operating the programme, while the main benefits expected are in terms of increased productivity, reduced sickness and absenteeism, and reduced staff turnover costs. The average salary paid to employees is £50,000 per year, and employees work a forty-hour week for fifty weeks in the year. The firm has researched the extent of these costs and benefits and discovered the following information:

1 10 per cent of employees can be expected to participate in the programme.
2 The membership fees are £400 per individual on a group scheme.
3 Workers who do not participate in any fitness programme suffer a drop in productivity of 50 per cent in their last two hours of work each day.

4 The normal sickness/absenteeism rate of eight days lost per year is reduced by 50 per cent for those workers on a fitness programme.
5 Staff turnover should be reduced from 20 per cent a year to 10 per cent.
6 Each new employee involves a total of twelve hours of hiring time.
7 Each new employee takes five days to train, and training is carried out in teams of five new employees at a time.
8 Each new employee has a productivity that is 25 per cent lower than average for their first six weeks at work.

Questions

1 Estimate the costs of operating the programme described above.
2 Estimate the benefits in terms of increased productivity.
3 Estimate the benefits from reduced sickness and absenteeism.
4 Estimate the benefits from reduced staff turnover.
5 What conclusion can you come to regarding the operation of the programme?

11.3 Risk analysis

In all the analysis so far it has been assumed that the cash flows are known with certainty. This is clearly an oversimplification; the existence of risk and uncertainty in the decision-making process was initially discussed in the context of the theory of the firm in Chapter 2, but we now need to discuss its implications in terms of investment analysis. The starting point of this discussion is an explanation of the nature of risk in the capital budgeting situation.

11.3.1 Nature of risk in capital budgeting

Previously we have discussed risk and uncertainty largely as if they related to the same situation, but it was mentioned in Chapter 2 that there was a technical difference between them. We can now consider these different types of scenario in more detail, and stress that it is important at this stage to differentiate between them.[2]

1 **Risk** refers to a decision-making situation where there are *different possible outcomes and the probabilities of these outcomes can be measured in some way*.

2 **Uncertainty** refers to a decision-making situation where there are *different possible outcomes and the probabilities of these outcomes cannot be meaningfully measured, sometimes because all possible outcomes cannot be foreseen or specified*.

As we shall see, different decision-making techniques have to be applied in each case.

It is also necessary to distinguish between different concepts of risk in terms of how they apply to the decision-making situation. There are three types of risk that relate to investment projects:[3] stand-alone risk, within-firm (or corporate) risk, and market risk.

a. *Stand-alone risk*. This examines the *risk of a project in isolation*. It is not usually important in itself, but rather as it affects within-firm and market risk. However, in the presence of agency problems, managerial decisions may be influenced by stand-alone risk; it may affect the position of individual managers, even though it does not necessarily affect the position of shareholders. Stand-alone risk is therefore the starting point for the consideration of risk in a broader context. The measurement and application of this aspect of risk is discussed in subsections 11.3.2 and 11.3.3.

b. *Within-firm risk*. This considers the *risk of a project in the context of a firm's portfolio of investment projects*. Thus the impact of the project on the variability of the firm's total cash flows is examined. It is possible that a project with high stand-alone risk may not have much effect on within-firm risk, or indeed may actually reduce the firm's within-firm risk if the project's cash flows are negatively correlated with the other cash flows of the firm. This issue will be discussed in more detail later.

c. *Market Risk*. This considers *a project's risk from the viewpoint of the shareholders of the firm, assuming that they have diversified shareholding portfolios*. It is sometimes referred to as *systematic risk*, as it relates to factors that affect the market as a whole. This is the most relevant concept of risk when considering the effect of a project on a firm's share price. Again it is possible that a project with high stand-alone risk may not represent high market risk to shareholders.

11.3.2 *Measurement of risk*

It was stated above that the concept of risk involves the measurement of probability. It is assumed that students already have an acquaintance with this topic, but it is worthwhile reviewing it here. Essentially, there are three approaches to measuring probability.

1. *Theoretical.* These probabilities are sometimes referred to as *ex-ante* probabilities, because they *can be estimated from a purely theoretical point of view, with no need for observation.* Such probabilities can therefore be calculated before any experiments or trials are conducted. Tossing a coin or throwing a die are classic examples. The probability of success, for example getting a head or a six, is given by the following expression:

$$P(\text{success}) = \frac{\text{total number of favourable outcomes}}{\text{total number of possible outcomes}} \qquad (11.3)$$

It is assumed here that the coin or die is unbiased, that is all possible outcomes are equally probable. Unfortunately, such situations rarely arise in business management, unless we are considering the management of gambling casinos.

2. *Empirical.* These are sometimes referred to as *ex-post* probabilities, because they *can only be estimated from historical experience.* This is something that actuaries and insurance companies do; by amassing large amounts of data relating to car accidents for example, it is possible to estimate the probability of someone having an accident in any given year. These probabilities can then be revised according to age group, location of residence, occupation, type of car and so on. The probabilities are still calculated according to expression (11.3), but the outcomes can only be determined from empirical observation. It should be noted that the term 'favourable' does not imply any state of desirability, it merely refers to the fulfilment of a specified condition. In the example just quoted possible outcomes refer to the total number of motorists, while 'favourable' outcomes refer to the number of motorists having accidents, paradoxical though that may seem.

3. *Subjective.* In practice, managers often have to resort to estimating probabilities subjectively, for the simple reason that they are *dealing with circumstances that have never occurred exactly before.* They usually have some background of relevant past experience to help them make such estimates, but they cannot rely on the purely objective empirical approach. It is important to realize in later analysis in this chapter that the probabilities discussed are therefore somewhat imprecise because of the subjectivity involved.

Now that the measurement of probability has been discussed we can move on to the measurement of risk, and in particular the risk involved in investment situations.

a. Stand-alone risk

The measurement of risk can first be considered from the point of view of an individual project. There are various sources of risk and uncertainty in this context:

1 The initial capital cost of the project; in practice this may be spread over several years, increasing uncertainty.

2 The demand for the output from the project.

3 The ongoing operational costs of the project.

4 The cost of capital.

These sources can be illustrated by considering the situation in SP11.1.Often the most important variable where there is variability in terms of outcomes is the demand for the output, as shown by projected sales figure of 30 million bottles per year, and also by the projected price. As we have seen in the chapter on demand estimation, such forecasts are often associated with a considerable margin of error. This sales figure can really be regarded as an **expected value** (EV). Since it is assumed that students have a familiarity with this concept and with the topic of probability in general, only a brief review is given here. The definition of an expected value is *the sum of the products of the values of the different outcomes multiplied by their respective probabilities*:

$$EV = \sum p_i X_i \qquad (11.4)$$

Let us assume that there are considered to be three possible sales values, 20 million, 30 million and 40 million, and that the probabilities of each outcome are estimated (subjectively in this case) to be 0.25, 0.5 and 0.25 respectively. Therefore the expected value of sales is given by:

$$EV = (0.25 \times 20m) + (0.5 \times 30m) + (0.25 \times 40m)$$
$$= 5m + 15m + 10m$$
$$= 30m$$

This is a simplified case since it is assumed that the probability distribution of outcomes is discrete. A more realistic scenario is when the distribution is continuous, with a theoretically limitless number of possible outcomes. However, the expected value concept is still applicable to such a distribution, and this situation is represented in Figure 11.1.

The distribution in Figure 11.1 is assumed to be symmetrical but this need not be the case. Once the distribution of outcomes is estimated, not only can the expected value of the distribution be calculated, as above, but also measures of its variability. The standard deviation is the most common measure used here, and the higher the standard deviation of sales the greater the risk of the project in stand-alone terms. The general formula for calculating the standard deviation is given by:

$$\sigma_x = \sqrt{\left(\sum p_i X_i^2\right)} \qquad (11.5)$$

In the above example the standard deviation is given by:

$$\sigma_x = \sqrt{[(0.25 \times 10^2) + (0.5 \times 0^2) + (0.25 \times 10^2)]} = 7.071 \text{ million}$$

So far we have concentrated on the uncertainty related to demand. In some projects, especially those where major capital expenditure is involved, there may be much uncertainty regarding this initial cost. In projects like the

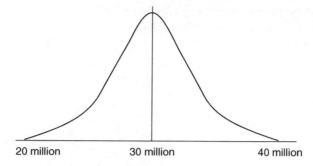

20 million   30 million   40 million

Figure 11.1. Continuous distribution of sales outcomes.

Channel Tunnel it has not been unknown for the eventual cost to be as much as five times the original estimate.

b. Within-firm risk

When a project is considered in the context of corporate risk it is important to consider the correlation between the project's cash flows and those of the firm as a whole. In practice this is often done subjectively: if the project is in the same line of business as the firm's other projects, then there will be high positive correlation and high stand-alone risk will also involve high corporate risk. On the other hand, if the project is in a different line of business then the correlation may be low and the firm's corporate risk may not be much affected. It is even possible, as mentioned earlier, that if the project is in a business area whose prospects are opposite to those of the firm's main line of business, that correlation may be negative and high stand-alone risk may actually reduce corporate risk. This situation is rare however.

c. Market risk

The relationship between stand-alone risk and market risk now needs to be discussed. Market risk is the most relevant type of risk as far as shareholders are concerned. It is also possible to measure this type of risk using an objective, though not necessarily accurate, method. This involves using one of the most important models in financial analysis, the **capital asset pricing model** (CAPM). The CAPM *describes the risk–return relationship for securities, assuming that these securities are held in well-diversified portfolios*. There are a number of other assumptions involved in the model, but for the sake of simplicity these will be largely ignored in this text. Essentially the model shows that the higher the risk to the investor the higher the return required to compensate for that risk. Some government securities (depending on the government) are regarded as risk-free, and pay the risk-free rate k_{RF}. This then represents the minimum rate of return on investors' funds, and rates of return on other investments are correspondingly higher according to the amount of risk associated with holding that firm's securities. The general relationship is shown by the **security market line** (SML), which is depicted in Figure 11.2.

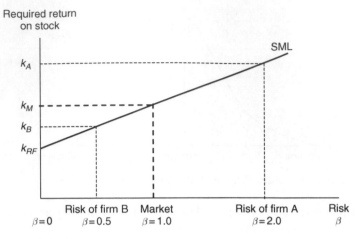

Figure 11.2. The security market line (SML).

Empirically the SML appears to be approximately linear. The problem with which we are now faced is: how can the risk of a security be objectively measured? This involves the concept of a **beta coefficient**. As seen in Chapter 4, a beta coefficient refers to the slope of a regression line. In the current financial context involving the SML, the beta coefficient represents *the slope of the regression line between the returns on an individual security and the returns on the market as a whole*. This line is called the **characteristic line**. An example is given in Figure 11.3, for a firm with a beta coefficient of 2.0. In this case, observations are taken over a five-year period. In year 1 the return on the stock was about 12%, while the average return on the market was about 4%. In year 2, on the other hand, the stock gave a negative return of 4%, and the market also gave a negative return of 4%. From this illustration it can be seen that the greater the variability, or volatility, of the security the steeper the characteristic line and the greater the beta coefficient. The value of beta thus measures the relative volatility of the security compared with an average stock; a security with a beta of 1 has the same volatility as the market as a whole, securities with a beta more than 1, as in Figure 11.3, are more volatile than the market as a whole, while securities with a beta less than 1 are less volatile than the market as a whole. More specifically, a security with a beta coefficient of 2.0 has generally twice the volatility of the average stock; if the market returns rise by 1%, then such a security should find its return rising by 2%. Likewise, if market returns fall by 1%, the return on the security should fall by 2%.

The concept of the beta coefficient can now be applied to the CAPM. It can be seen from Figure 11.2 that the return on the market as a whole is given by k_M. The equation of the SML can also be seen. The intercept is given by the risk-free rate, k_{RF}, and the slope is given by $(k_M - k_{RF})$, by comparing the return with no risk with the return on the market. Thus the equation of the SML is:

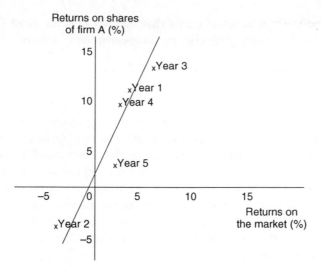

Figure 11.3. Calculation of beta coefficients.

$$k_i = k_{RF} + (k_M - k_{RF})\beta i \tag{11.6}$$

where k_i represents the rate of return on any individual security. We shall see that the CAPM model is also useful in considering the cost of capital in the next section. Finally, in Section 11.5, the aspects involving the application of the measurement of risk to decision-making will be examined.

11.4 Cost of capital

The cost of capital is an important concept for the firm, not just for evaluating investment projects but also for maximizing shareholder value in general. It was seen in Chapter 3 that a firm should discount its expected cash flows by its cost of capital in order to compute the value of the firm. We now need to consider this concept of the cost of capital in more detail.

11.4.1 Nature and components

There are essentially two ways of considering the cost of capital. From the point of view of the firm, representing the demand side, the cost of capital is what the firm has to pay for its sources of funds. These funds, which are liabilities on the balance sheet, are then used to finance new investments, which represent assets on the balance sheet. From a supply point of view, the cost of capital represents the return that investors, who provide the firm with funds, require in order to lend the firm money or buy its shares.

Strictly speaking the capital involved represents all the firm's liabilities, including short-term debt and other aspects of working capital. In practice, however, the main sources of funds that are relevant for most firms when considering investment projects are long-term debt (mainly bonds) and common equity.

11.4.2 Cost of debt

It is helpful, as usual, to make some simplifying assumptions in order to calculate this cost. We shall assume that only one form of debt is used, twenty-year bonds, that the interest rate on these bonds is fixed rather than floating, and that the payment schedule for this debt is known in advance of the issue. Most new bonds are sold at par value, meaning face value, and therefore the coupon interest rate is set at the rate of return required by investors. If we take a normal bond with a par value of £1,000 and a coupon rate of 8 per cent, the cost of debt capital can be obtained using a variation of the present-value formula in Chapter 2:

$$V_0 = \sum \frac{I_t}{(1 + k_d)^t} + \frac{P}{(1 + k_d)^n} \tag{11.7}$$

where V_0 is the current market value of the bond, P is the par value, k_d is the cost of debt, and I_t represents the annual interest payment in period t (the formula has to be slightly modified if interest payments are semi-annual). In the above example we obtain the following:

$$1{,}000 = \frac{80}{(1 + k_d)} + \frac{80}{(1 + k_d)^2} + \frac{80}{(1 + k_d)^3} + \cdots + \frac{1{,}000}{(1 + k_d)^{20}}$$

The value of k_d cannot be solved directly from this equation, and can only be estimated iteratively, but it can be shown on a calculator programmed to perform this kind of calculation that the cost of debt is 8 per cent, the same as the coupon rate of interest.

Two further complications can now be introduced. The most fundamental one concerns tax. The cost of debt shown above is a pre-tax cost; however, interest payments are deductible from the firm's taxable income. Therefore the firm's after-tax cost of debt is given by multiplying the pre-tax cost by 1 minus the firm's marginal tax rate:

$$k_a = k_d(1 - t) \tag{11.8}$$

Assuming as before a marginal tax rate of 40 per cent:

$$k_a = 8(1 - 0.4) = 4.8 \text{ per cent}$$

The final complication that should be mentioned concerns flotation costs. The issuing institution, normally an investment bank, charges a fee for its services to the firm. If this is 1 per cent of the issue, this cost needs to be deducted from the proceeds of the sale of the bonds in order to calculate the cost of debt. In this case the firm would only receive £990 for each bond sold, so the value of V_0 in (11.7) would now be 990.

11.4.3 *Cost of equity*

In a similar way to the cost of debt the cost of equity represents the equilibrium or minimum rate of return required by the firm's common shareholders. These funds can be obtained in two ways: internally, from retained earnings, and externally, from issuing new stock. These two sources are now discussed.

a. Internal sources

The cost of retained earnings represents an opportunity cost to investors. These earnings could be paid out in the form of dividends to investors, who could then reinvest the funds in other shares, bonds or property. Unless the retained earnings can earn at least the same return within the firm as they can outside the firm, assuming the same degree of risk, it is not profitable to use them as a source of funds.

There is no simple way to calculate this internal cost; there are several alternative approaches, which are not mutually exclusive. Two main approaches will be discussed here: the **capital asset pricing model** (CAPM), and the **dividend valuation model** (DVM).

1. The capital asset pricing model (CAPM). The general nature of this model was discussed in the previous section. It was seen that the variability, or volatility, in returns to an individual security can be divided into two components: that part which is related to the corporate risk of the firm, sometimes called **unsystematic risk**, and that part which affects the market as a whole, the **systematic risk**. Rational investors will diversify their portfolios so as to eliminate unsystematic risk; such risk carries no benefit in terms of additional return, since investors can obtain the same returns through holding a diversified portfolio of securities with similar corporate risk, but with reduced market risk.

The cost of equity, in terms of retained earnings, can now be estimated using the equation of the SML in (11.6). Thus, assuming $k_M = 10$ per cent, $k_{RF} = 6$ per cent and a beta coefficient of 2.0, the cost of equity would be:

$$k_e = 6 + (10 - 6)2 = 14 \text{ per cent}$$

While the CAPM may appear to be an objective and precise method for estimating the cost of capital it is subject to a number of drawbacks, which arise from the nature of the assumptions underlying the model. One of the most important of these is the use of beta coefficients based on historical data. In practice this is the only objective method for estimating such coefficients, but conceptually the cost of capital should be based on a model involving expected beta coefficients for the future. It is beyond the scope of this text to examine these assumptions and drawbacks in more detail, but they are discussed in most texts on financial management.

2. The dividend valuation model (DVM). This model is also known as the DCF model since it involves the now familiar present-value formula from Chapter 2, and is similar to expression (11.7). The value of a shareholder's wealth is the sum of expected future returns, discounted by their required rate of return. These returns come in the form of dividends and an increase in the market value of the firm's shares. Thus the present value of the share is given by:

$$V_0 = \sum \frac{D_t}{(1+k_e)^t} + \frac{V_n}{(1+k_e)^n}$$

(11.9)

where D_t is the dividend paid by the firm in period t. Since the future value of the share, V_n, is in turn determined by the sum of expected future dividends, equation (11.9) can be rewritten as the sum to infinity of all expected future dividends:

$$V_0 = \frac{\sum D_t}{(1+k_e)^n}$$

(11.10)

We now make the assumption that the dividends of the firm grow at a constant rate of g per year. Thus the value of the shares is given by:

$$V_0 = \frac{D_1}{(1+k_e)} + \frac{D_1(1+g)}{(1+k_e)^2} + \frac{D_1(1+g)^2}{(1+k_e)^3} + \cdots$$

(11.11)

where D_1 is the dividend that is expected to be paid in the following period. This is a geometric series which can be summed to infinity as long as the terms become smaller, in other words as long as $g < k$. The sum is given by:

$$V_0 = \frac{\frac{D_1}{(1+k_e)}}{1 - \frac{(1+g)}{(1+k_e)}} = \frac{D_1}{k_e - g}$$

(11.12)

This equation can be rearranged to solve for the cost of equity as follows:

$$k_e = \frac{D_1}{V_0} + g$$

(11.13)

For example, if a firm has a current share price of £20, the dividend next year is expected to be £1.20 and dividends have been growing on average at 4 per cent per year, then the cost of equity is given by:

$$k_e = \frac{1.20}{20} + 0.04 = 0.10, \text{ or 10 per cent}$$

Just as the CAPM has its problems, so does the DVM also have drawbacks. Its main failing is essentially the same as with the CAPM: it looks backwards rather than forwards. While historical data can be used to estimate the average growth rate of dividends over the last ten or twenty years say, such information is not a reliable indicator of future dividend growth rates. Furthermore, current share prices can be highly volatile, and many firms do not pay dividends at all if management believes that the funds can be more profitably reinvested in the firm than returned to shareholders. It can therefore readily be seen that many fast-growing high-tech firms would on this basis have very uncertain estimates of their cost of capital.

b. External sources

It is more expensive for a firm to raise equity externally rather than internally for two reasons:

1 There are flotation costs, as discussed with the cost of debt.
2 New shares have to be sold at a price lower than the current market price, in order to attract buyers. The reason for this is that the current price normally represents an equilibrium between existing demand and supply. A new issue involves an increase in supply, thus reducing the equilibrium price.

The result of these factors is that equation (11.13) has to be modified in order to provide an estimate of the cost of external equity as follows:

$$k_{ne} = \frac{D_1}{V^*} + g \qquad (11.14)$$

where k_{ne} represents the cost of new equity, and V^* is the net proceeds to the firm from the new issue (per share) after deducting flotation costs.

11.4.4 *Weighted average cost of capital*

Now that the two main components of the cost of capital have been examined, the overall cost of capital to the firm can be estimated. Since firms generally rely on both debt and equity to finance new projects, some kind of average cost is involved. However, the financial managers need to consider two factors in calculating this cost:

1 Historical costs of capital are not relevant; it is the marginal cost of capital, meaning the cost of raising new capital, which should be used. As already seen, this involves more uncertainty.
2 The relative proportions of debt and equity to be raised need to be estimated; since again this may not be known with certainty beforehand, it is common practice for managers to use the proportions that have been determined in the firm's long-term capital structure. These proportions need to be estimated in order to provide weights for the costs involved.

Once these two issues have been addressed the firm can estimate its weighted average cost of capital (WACC) as follows:

$$k = \frac{D}{D+E} \times k_a + \frac{E}{D+E} \times k_e \qquad (11.15)$$

where D and E refer to the amounts of new debt and equity involved.

For example, if a firm estimates its costs of debt and equity to be 4.8 per cent and 10 per cent, and that 30 per cent of its new capital will be from long-term debt, its WACC will be:

$$k = 0.3(4.8) + 0.7(10) = 8.44 \text{ per cent}$$

Now that the methods for estimating the cost of capital have been examined, we can consider how the cost of capital is relevant in the capital budgeting process.

11.5 Evaluation criteria

Ultimately, managers must decide whether to invest in new projects or not. Once the preliminary stages of estimating the cash flows, assessing the relevant risks and estimating the cost of capital have been performed, some criterion or decision rule must be applied in making the investment decision. There are two main criteria that can be used here, **net present value** and **internal rate of return**, although firms sometimes also use other criteria, usually on a supplementary basis. These criteria are now discussed, and further consideration is given to risk and uncertainty, in terms of how these affect investment decisions.

11.5.1 Net present value

The concept of net present value (NPV) again takes us back to Chapter 2. In that context it was applied to the valuation of shareholder wealth; expected future profits were discounted and summed in order to find the value of the firm, as shown in equation (2.1). The same concept can be applied to an individual investment project, in this case the net present value of the project being the sum of discounted net cash flows (DNCF), as follows:

$$NPV = \sum \frac{NCF_t}{(1 + k)^t} \tag{11.16}$$

The cost of capital is used to discount the cash flows. It should now be clear that any project that has a positive NPV will automatically increase the value of the firm and therefore should be undertaken. Likewise, any project that has a negative NPV will decrease the value of the firm and should not be undertaken. However, this simple rule only applies to **independent** projects, and we now need to distinguish between two main categories of project:

1 *Independent.* These are projects where *the operation of one project has no bearing on whether the other project(s) should be carried out.*
2 *Mutually exclusive.* These are projects where *the operation of one project automatically eliminates the need for the other one(s).* This situation occurs when there are alternative ways of achieving the same objective, this issue being discussed in more detail in subsection 11.5.5. The rule in this case is that if two or more projects have a positive NPV, managers should select the project with the highest NPV.

We can now develop the example given earlier in section 11.2, involving Maxsport. The cost of capital is assumed to be 8.44 per cent, as estimated in the previous section. Table 11.1 shows the estimated net cash flows and the

Table 11.1. NPV calculations

Year	NCF (£m)	DNCF (£m) ($k = 8.44\%$)
2002	(22.4)	(22.4)
2003	8.3	7.654
2004	12.197	10.372
2005	14.0813	11.043
2006	15.9874	11.562
Total		18.231

expected discounted net cash flows from the investment project, with the sum of the latter giving the NPV of £18.231 million. The conclusion is that the project should be accepted if it is independent, since it is expected to increase shareholder wealth by £18.231 million. It should only be rejected if it is mutually exclusive with another project that has a higher NPV.

11.5.2 *Internal rate of return*

The concept of the internal rate of return (IRR) on an investment project corresponds to the concept of **yield to maturity** (YTM) for investors buying securities. The **IRR** is defined as *the discount rate that equates the present value of project's expected net cash flows to zero*. In mathematical terms it is the interest rate, i, that satisfies the following equation:

$$\sum \frac{NCF_t}{(1+i)^t} = 0 \tag{11.17}$$

Thus the IRR calculation essentially makes use of the same equation (11.16) as the NPV calculation, but instead of taking the value of k as given (the cost of capital) and calculating the value of the NPV, it takes the value of NPV as given (zero) and calculates the discount rate.

The criterion for acceptance in this case is that any project that has an IRR greater than the cost of capital should be accepted, since this will generate a surplus that will increase shareholder wealth. Likewise, any project that has an IRR less than the cost of capital will reduce shareholder wealth. This criterion for independent projects must be slightly modified for mutually exclusive projects; in this situation the project with the highest IRR should be accepted, assuming this IRR is greater than the cost of capital.

The solution of the equation to calculate the IRR is, however, more difficult than finding the NPV. In the case of Maxsport we obtain the following equation:

$$-22.4 + \frac{8.3}{(1+i)} + \frac{12.197}{(1+i)^2} + \frac{14.0813}{(1+i)^3} + \frac{15.9874}{(1+i)^4} = 0 \tag{11.18}$$

This kind of equation is best solved using a financial calculator or computer. When this is done the solution obtained is that $i = 0.3744$, or **37.44** per cent.

11.5.3 Comparison of net present value and internal rate of return

At this stage certain questions may well be asked regarding the two criteria described above:

1 Do both criteria result in the same investment decision in all cases?
2 If not, which criterion is better, or are they both equally valid?

The answer to the first question is that for independent projects the two criteria will always yield the same result. Any project with a positive NPV will automatically have an IRR greater than the cost of capital, and any project with a negative NPV will automatically have an IRR less than the cost of capital. Complications arise, however, with mutually exclusive projects. It is possible for a conflict to arise between the two approaches if the two projects are of different size, meaning that their initial cost outlays are different, or if the timings of the cash flows are different, with one project getting high early returns while another project gets high returns later on. In these situations a project with a higher IRR than another project will not necessarily have a higher NPV if the cost of capital is much less than the IRR. This situation arises because of different assumptions made by the two approaches regarding the opportunity cost of reinvestment of cash inflows. These assumptions are summarized below:

1 The NPV approach assumes that inflows can be reinvested at the cost of capital.
2 The IRR approach assumes that inflows can be reinvested at the same rate as the IRR.

These assumptions are inherent in the mathematical calculations for each measure.

This leads us to the second question. It can be seen that the opportunity cost for reinvestment is in fact the cost of capital, assuming that this remains the same for the future, meaning that any future projects can be financed at this same rate. For example, if the cost of capital is 8 per cent this is the opportunity cost for reinvestment purposes, even if projects arise in the future with IRRs of 20 per cent; these future projects can still be financed at a cost of 8 per cent.

Our conclusion therefore is that *the NPV criterion is superior to the IRR criterion*, and that if a conflict arises between the two approaches for mutually exclusive projects, the NPV approach should be used. Having said this, it should also be stated that managers often prefer the IRR approach, since it indicates profitability in percentage terms rather than in money terms, and this is often a more meaningful indicator when comparing different projects.

11.5.4 Other criteria

The two approaches discussed above are by far the most common in sophisticated capital budgeting analysis. However, there are other approaches that are sometimes used by managers, varying from very simple methods to quite complex ones. Four of these are now described briefly.

   a. *Payback method.* This is by far the simplest criterion. It simply calculates *the length of the period it takes for cash inflows to exceed cash outflows*, and compares this with some basic yardstick, for example four years. If the **payback period** is shorter than the yardstick the project is accepted; if it is longer than the yardstick the project is rejected. In the case of Maxsport the payback period is a little over two years, so the project would be accepted if the yardstick were four years. There are a number of obvious drawbacks with this approach: it fails to take into account the time value of money by discounting, it fails to consider cash flows after the payback period, and the selection of the yardstick is entirely arbitrary. However, because of its simplicity, it is still popular with managers, at least as a supplementary guide to decision-making.

   b. *Discounted payback.* This is essentially similar to the ordinary payback method, the only difference being that the cash flows are discounted at the cost of capital. However, the approach still suffers from the other problems mentioned above.

   c. *Profitability index (PI).* This is sometimes referred to as the benefit–cost ratio. It is calculated as follows:

$$PI = \frac{\text{present value of benefits}}{\text{present value of costs}} \qquad (11.19)$$

where benefits refer to cash inflows and costs refer to cash outflows. The criterion for acceptance is that the PI should be greater than one, meaning that the present value of the benefits exceeds the present value of the costs. In the case of Maxsport, the PI $= 40.631/22.4 = 1.814$. This project would therefore be accepted, if it were an independent project. For mutually exclusive projects the one with the highest PI would be accepted.

   With independent projects the PI approach will always yield the same result as the NPV and IRR methods. For mutually exclusive projects, conflict is again possible when comparing projects of different sizes. A large project may have a higher NPV than a smaller project, but a lower PI. Again the NPV method should take precedence in these cases.

   d. *Modified internal rate of return (MIRR).* This approach is designed to eliminate the problem discussed earlier with the IRR, that it assumes cash inflows can be reinvested at the same rate as the IRR. It is also more complex than the methods discussed so far. The MIRR is the interest rate that equates the present value of the cash outflows with the present value of the **terminal value** of the cash inflows. The terminal value is *the future value of the cash inflows at the end of the project, assuming that the inflows are reinvested at the cost of capital*. Thus the terminal value of the cash inflows for Maxsport is given by:

$$8.3(1 + .0844)^3 + 12.197(1 + .0844)^2 + 14.0813(1 + .0844) + 15.9874 = 56.184$$

We then have to solve the equation:

$$22.4 = \frac{56.184}{(1+i)^4}$$

This gives: $(1+i)^4 = 2.5082, i = 0.2585$, or **25.85 per cent**.

This measure of the MIRR is superior to the ordinary IRR as an indicator of a project's real rate of return, but it can still give results which conflict with those using the NPV criterion when comparing mutually exclusive projects of different sizes. Once again, only the NPV approach should be used in these circumstances, as it is the only measure that gives a direct indicator as to how the value of the firm is affected by the investment project.

11.5.5 Decision-making under risk

In the analysis in this section so far we have ignored the existence of risk. The measurement of risk was discussed in section 11.3, but we have not yet examined how measures of risk can be incorporated into the decision-making process. Four techniques will be examined in this context: sensitivity analysis, scenario analysis, decision tree analysis, and simulation.

a. Sensitivity analysis

In considering the nature and measurement of risk it was seen that a number of variables that determine a project's profitability are not known with certainty, but have some variability which might be expressed in terms of a probability distribution with a measurable standard deviation. Sensitivity analysis examines the responsiveness of a project's NPV and IRR to a given change in a particular input variable. We might want to know the sensitivity in response to a 10 per cent fall in sales below the expected level, or to a 20 per cent increase in operating costs. Sometimes these aspects of responsiveness are shown graphically, where the whole relationship between the input variable and the NPV is shown. Projects may have much greater sensitivity to changes in some input variables than to changes in others; for example, a project may be much more sensitive to changes in sales volume than to changes in the cost of capital. In general, projects showing greater sensitivity demonstrate more risk.

b. Scenario analysis

This is really a development of sensitivity analysis. The development is that the amount of the likely variation in a variable is specified, often in terms of its probability distribution, as well as the effect of this variation. Thus worst- and best-case scenarios are often depicted; for example, a worst-case scenario for sales volume might be 20 million units, with a probability of 25 per cent, and a best-case scenario might be 40 million units, again with a probability of 25 per cent. The most likely outcome of 30 million units may have a probability of 50 per cent. The same scenarios and their probabilities can be estimated for other input variables. Resulting worst-case and best-case NPVs can then be calculated, taking into account all the worst-case input variables and all the best-case input variables. The expected NPV of the project can then be calcu-lated, along with its standard deviation.

Scenario analysis is a widely used technique among managers, but suffers from two main shortcomings:

1 It assumes discrete probability distributions for the input variables, whereas continuous distributions are more realistic. The approach, therefore, usually considers only a small number of possible outcomes; furthermore, it is usually unlikely that all the worst outcomes for the different variables will occur simultaneously, and the same applies to the best outcomes.
2 The probabilities of the different scenarios are usually estimated subject-ively and are therefore prone to considerable error.

c. Decision tree analysis

This approach shares a number of characteristics with scenario analysis. Different **states-of-nature** are described, such as high sales or low sales of a product, with associated probabilities. Expected monetary values (EMV) are then calculated, which correspond to expected NPVs in multiperiod situations, and decisions are made based on maximizing EMV.

The main use of decision tree analysis is in situations where sequential decision points are involved, often over many periods. For example, a firm like Maxsport may face an initial decision regarding whether to conduct a market research survey or not. Depending on the results of such a survey they may choose to test-market the product, launch the product nationally, or drop the project. If they test-market the product, they may then face a choice regarding scale of operation, and so on. The probabilities of different states-of-nature may be conditional on previous events. Thus the probability of high sales may depend on the results of the market survey or of the test-marketing process. The objective of the analysis is to calculate the EMVs at each state-of-nature node, and thus determine the optimal decision-making path. A simple exam-ple of the use of decision tree analysis follows.

SP11.2 Decision tree analysis

Maxsport is now considering whether to test-market its new product, Slimfuel. The results of the test-marketing can then be used to decide whether to launch the product nationally or drop it. Alternatively, the firm can skip the test-marketing stage, which costs £3 million, and go straight to national launch. Maxsport estimates that the probability of good test-marketing results is 0.6 and the probability of bad results is 0.4. If the results are good, management estimates that the probability of high sales is 0.8 and the probability of low sales is 0.2. If the results are bad, management estimates that the probability of high sales is 0.3 and the probability of low sales is 0.7. High sales in the situation where test-marketing is conducted represents an estimated NPV of £20 million and

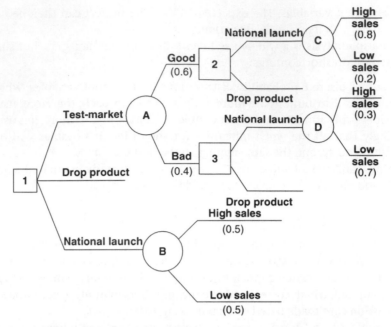

Figure 11.4. Decision tree for Maxsport.

low sales means an estimated NPV of −£10 million. These NPVs do not take into account the cost of test-marketing. If no test-marketing is conducted, there is reckoned to be a fifty-fifty chance of high or low sales, with the NPV of high sales being £23 million and the NPV of low sales being −£7 million. These values are higher than if test-marketing is performed because of the greater advantage gained over competitors. If the product is dropped there is zero NPV from that stage.

Draw a decision tree representing the situation, and determine the optimal decision path.

Solution

There are two types of node in the decision tree (Figure 11.4):

1 *Decision nodes*. These are shown by squares, and are numbered.
2 *State-of-nature nodes*. These are shown by circles, and are lettered; the following states-of-nature have their probabilities shown in brackets.

It is important to realize that **the decision tree is drawn from left to right, but the analysis of it is performed backwards, working from right to left**, meaning from the end of the tree to the beginning. The first stage in the analysis is to calculate the expected NPVs at each state-of-nature node. These NPVs are calculated from the point of view of the start of the project, meaning from decision node 1.

$$\text{At C: NPV} = 0.8(20) + 0.2(-10) - 3 = 11 \text{ million}$$
$$\text{At D: NPV} = 0.3(20) + 0.7(-10) - 3 = -4 \text{ million}$$

We can now start to determine the decision path, bearing in mind that dropping the product after test-marketing results in the NPV of −£3 million.

At 2: if test-marketing results are good, go for national launch.
At 3: if test-marketing results are bad, it is better to drop the product because the negative NPV of £3 million is preferable to the negative NPV of £4 million if the product is launched.

The expected NPVs at A and B can now be calculated.

$$\text{At A: NPV} = 0.6(11) + 0.4(-3) = 5.4 \text{ million}$$
$$\text{At B: NPV} = 0.5(23) + 0.5(-7) = 8 \text{ million}$$

Therefore, at decision node 1 the firm should go straight for a national launch and skip the test-marketing process. This means that the decisions at nodes 2 and 3 will not arise.

d. Simulation

One common feature regarding sensitivity analysis, scenario analysis and decision tree analysis is that they all simplify the decision-making situation by restricting the key decision and state-of-nature variables to certain discrete values. In SP11.2, for example, only a national launch and test-marketing were considered, whereas in practice various scales of investment might be possible, on a multiperiod basis. Likewise, only the states-of-nature of high sales and low sales were considered. A more realistic situation is where such variables can assume any value according to some continuous probability distribution. This situation often makes the mathematical aspects of analysis intractable, but it is still amenable to analysis by computer simulation.

Simulation approaches, sometimes referred to as **Monte Carlo methods** because of their original application to casino gambling, have become widely used in various business situations in recent years, as software packages have become more powerful and prolific. In terms of capital budgeting, the following stages are involved:

1 Specify probability distributions for each variable in the analysis, such as sales volume, price and unit costs; this involves specifying the means and standard deviations of the distributions, and also their shapes.
2 Select random values for each variable, according to their probability distributions. This is performed by the software package.
3 Calculate the resulting net cash flows and NPV for this set of values.

4 Repeat the previous two steps a large number of times, usually 1,000 or so, thus building up a probability distribution for the NPV.

5 The expected value and the standard deviation of the NPV can then be calculated.

Simulation techniques are not without their problems. First of all, it can be difficult to perform the first stage; the characteristics of the relevant probability distributions often have to be estimated subjectively. Second, the distributions may not be independent of each other because some of the variables may be correlated; these correlations can be specified as inputs into the software package in selecting random values for the variables, but it is difficult to estimate the values that should be specified.

To conclude this subsection, we should mention another problem that is common to all the techniques discussed above. Although they show the effect of risk on the NPV, in terms of giving a standard deviation or similar measure, they do not in themselves provide any definitive decision rule. For one thing they only provide a measure of stand-alone risk, and, as we saw in section 11.3, it is the market risk that is the primary concern of well-diversified shareholders. It has also been seen that high stand-alone risk does not necessarily lead to high market risk; the relationship depends on the correlation between the project's returns and the returns on other assets owned by the firm's shareholders. Therefore, in order to fully incorporate risk into the decision-making process, a **risk-adjusted cost of capital** (RACC) should be applied. The RACC *estimates this correlation so that the effect on market risk can in turn be estimated. This can then be reflected in the cost of capital that is used to discount the cash flows and calculate the NPV*. In this whole procedure it is obvious that there are many possible sources of inaccuracy. In practice, firms often use a general rule, such as: for projects with high stand-alone risk add 2 per cent to the cost of capital, while for projects with low stand-alone risk subtract 2 per cent. It is therefore a bold financial manager who can estimate a major investment project's NPV with a high degree of confidence.

11.5.6 Decision-making under uncertainty

Sometimes managers are reluctant to give even subjective estimates of the probabilities of various events or states-of-nature. This tends to be the case when there is very little information to go on regarding the success or failure of a project, because the characteristics of the situation are entirely new and cannot be easily compared with previous projects. Table 11.2 illustrates this situation, where payoffs can be estimated but not their associated probabilities.There are a number of decision rules that can be used in this type of situation, but there is no single best criterion that is widely used. The two main rules are now discussed.

a. *Maximin criterion*. This criterion concentrates entirely on the worst possible outcome, meaning the minimum payoff, from each possible decision, and

Table 11.2. Payoff matrix under uncertainty

		States of nature	
		Success	Failure
Alternative decisions	Invest	80	−60
	Do not invest	0	0

Table 11.3. Regret matrix under uncertainty

		States of nature	
		Success	Failure
Alternative decisions	Invest	0	60
	Do not invest	80	0

selects the decision that maximizes this minimum payoff. Given the situation in Table 11.2, the minimum payoff from investing is −60 and the minimum payoff from not investing is 0. Therefore the maximin criterion would dictate the decision not to invest. It can be seen that this is a very conservative decision rule, and many people would find it inappropriate in most cases. For example, taking an everyday situation, this decision rule would mean that we would never cross a road; taking the decision whether to cross a road or not to cross, crossing would always involve a lower possible payoff (death) than not crossing. Note, however, that this is really an inappropriate situation for using such a criterion; although people do not actually consciously estimate probabilities of success or failure in crossing a road, it is quite possible to do so on the basis of historical experience. This issue is discussed further in the next chapter, in connection with government policy.

b. *Minimax regret criterion.* Regret in this context refers to opportunity cost. The opportunity cost of each decision and each state-of-nature is calculated, and this can be shown in a regret or opportunity cost matrix. The regret matrix corresponding to Table 11.2 is shown in Table 11.3. The decision rule in this case is to select the decision that minimizes the maximum regret or opportunity cost; since the maximum regret from investing is 60 and the maximum regret from not investing is 80, the decision in this case would be to invest. As with the previous criterion, a number of objections can be made to its use.[4]

11.6 The optimal capital budget

We have assumed so far in this chapter that each investment project can be evaluated separately, according to the firm's cost of capital. However, the total capital budget and the cost of capital should be calculated simultaneously, in the same sort of way that price and quantity are determined simultaneously by demand and supply. The resulting cost of capital can then be applied to each individual project. The demand for capital is shown by a firm's **investment opportunity schedule**, and the supply of capital is given by the **marginal cost of capital schedule**. These are now discussed in turn.

11.6.1 The investment opportunity (IO) schedule

This shows the relationship between the internal rates of return on different potential projects and the amount of new capital required. The concept, and the steps involved in deriving it, is best explained by an example. We shall derive an IO schedule for Maxsport, assuming for the sake of simplicity that the different projects considered all involve the same degree of risk. The following steps have to be performed:

1 Identify all the various possible capital projects that the firm can feasibly undertake, specifying which are independent and which are mutually exclusive.
2 Estimate the initial cash outlays, net cash flows and IRRs for each of these potential projects. This is shown in Table 11.4. Note that we do not calculate NPVs at this stage (or MIRRs), since these require a knowledge of the cost of capital, which is what we are trying to estimate.
3 These IRRs are then plotted in descending order against cumulative initial outlay. This is shown for Maxsport in Figure 11.5. Note that there are two IO schedules, since projects B and C are mutually exclusive, and these overlap in places.

11.6.2 The marginal cost of capital (MCC) schedule

The concept of the weighted average cost of capital (WACC) has already been discussed in section 11.4, and it was also stated at that point that it was the cost of new capital, not the historical cost of capital, that was important. However, this cost is not constant; as the firm tries to raise more and more capital it will find that this cost of new capital will rise. There are two main reasons for this:

1 The cost of equity will rise as the firm is forced into issuing new equity rather than relying on retained earnings. As has already been seen, the cost of new equity is greater because of flotation costs.
2 The cost of debt may rise, as higher interest rates are required to attract additional investors to supply funds to the firm.

It is now necessary to estimate the following three measures:

1 The current WACC without issuing new capital.
2 The **retained earnings breakpoint** where it becomes necessary to raise new capital.
3 The WACC of issuing new capital.

Table 11.4. Capital budgeting information for IO Schedule

	Potential investment projects					
	A	B*	C*	D	E	F
Initial outlay (£m)	20	10	15	5	30	10
IRR (%)	15	18	12	10	8	13

Note: Projects B and C are mutually exclusive.

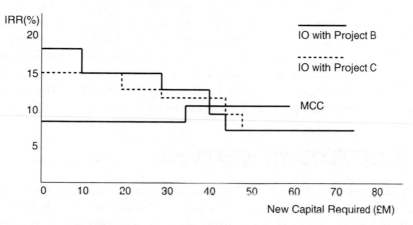

Figure 11.5. IO and MCC schedules for Maxsport.

Let us now assume that the cost of debt is constant at 8%, that 40% of the firm's capital is debt and 60% equity, that the tax rate is 40% and the cost of retained earnings is 11.8%. The current cost of capital is thus:

$$k_a = 0.4(8\%)(0.6) + 0.6(11.8\%) = 9\%$$

In order to estimate the breakpoint we need to estimate the amount of retained earnings that the firm will have, plus any other cash flows, for example from depreciation. Let us assume that Maxsport has estimated retained earnings of £18 million and £5 million in depreciation cash flow during the planning period. We know that the £18 million must be 60% of the total capital raised, with the other 40% being debt; therefore the breakpoint is given by:

$$B = 18m/0.6 + 5m = 35 \text{ million}$$

In order to estimate the WACC of issuing new capital we need to estimate the cost of issuing new equity, taking into account flotation costs. Assuming that this cost is 15%, the new WACC is given by:

$$k_a = 0.4(8\%)(0.6) + 0.6(15\%) = 10.92\%$$

The resulting MCC schedule is shown in Figure 11.5.

11.6.3 *Equilibrium of IO and MCC*

The optimal capital budget and the cost of capital are given by the intersection of the IO and MCC curves. There is an added complication in this case because there are two intersection points, caused by having two different IO curves. In order to obtain the optimal capital budget we can see first of all that the equilibrium marginal cost of capital will be 10.92 per cent. We then have to estimate the total NPV of undertaking projects A, B and F and compare this with the total NPV of projects A, C and F; both strategies involve projects A and F, so we have to compare the NPVs of projects B and C at the cost of capital of 10.92 per cent. The strategy involving the higher NPV is then selected, thus determining the optimal capital budget. If project B has the higher NPV the optimal capital budget is £40 million, while if project C has the higher NPV the optimal capital budget is £45 million.

If the different projects involve different degrees of risk, either from each other or from the firm's existing assets, this complicates the analysis since the MCC has to be adjusted accordingly; this may in turn affect the decision whether to invest in a particular project or not.

11.7 A problem-solving approach

All problems related to the capital budgeting process essentially involve one or more of the five stages described in the first section of this chapter, and examined at length in the remaining sections. The two solved problems, SP11.1 and SP11.2, illustrate particularly important and problematical aspects: cash flow analysis and decision tree analysis. In addition, the three case studies cover similar aspects, concentrating on the following areas:

1 Cash flow analysis when benefits are intangible.
2 Appropriate use of evaluation criteria.
3 Application of risk analysis to high-tech firms.

Case study 11.2: Under-investment in transportation infrastructure

Grinding to a halt[5]

As well as the familiar signs greeting London's Monday morning commuters, such as 'station closed' and 'train cancelled', motorists were confronted by some more unusual sights. Parts of the A40, the main road into London from the west, were under water, as were bits of the M25, London's orbital motorway. Many commuter rail services into London simply stopped, and mainline railway stations emptied. After just one particularly bad night's weather, the transport system of one of the world's biggest and richest cities seemed close to collapse.

Of course, it did not help that Britain's train system was already reeling from the speed limits and track replacements put into place after a deadly rail crash at Hatfield, the previous week. But a consensus is emerging about what is wrong with Britain's transport system. The system is old, and not enough has been spent to keep it up to date.

Population pressure alone is not a sufficient explanation for the travails of the transport system. Take London – 1.1m people travel into Greater London every day, 270,000 to the City of London alone; 394,000 travel in on the Underground. These are similar to the commuting figures for Paris and New York. As Tony Travers of the London School of Economics points out, rather than being uniquely crowded, the London region is very similar in size and population density to New York or the central area of the Netherlands between The Hague and Amsterdam. But London's transport suffers from its age, and from the persistent under-investment in its infrastructure. In this respect, Mr Travers argues that a better comparison with London would be Moscow.

It is probably no coincidence that the most notoriously inefficient of London's underground lines, the Northern, is also the oldest deep-level line in the world. It was first opened in 1890, and has proved hard to modernise. Whereas the number of passengers that the Underground carries has increased in line with the economic boom in the South-East since the mid-1980s, little new track has been laid. In 1982, at the bottom of a recession, there were only 498m passenger journeys a year. The latest figure, for 1998, is 832m passenger journeys. But in the past 30 years, only one new line, the Jubilee, has been built for the Underground.

If history plays its part, so does under-investment. On both the railways and the roads, the disruption that bad weather causes is often the direct result of cutting costs. Take the famous and much derided excuse of the 'wrong kind of snow', trotted out to explain the failure of rail services to run. This was because snow was getting into

electric train motors. The filters that could have prevented the fine snow from getting into the motors were deemed to be too expensive and were not used. Chris Nash, a professor of transport economics at the University of Leeds, also cites the example of the electrification of the east coast line. The cost of the overhead electrical equipment was 'cut to the bone', so the system is not as robust in high winds as it should be.

Since the Beeching Report of 1963, which recommended massive cuts in the network, British railways have been reduced to what has been described as a 'lean system'. Felix Schmid, of the department of mechanical engineering at the University of Sheffield, argues that the system has been 'reduced to the absolute minimum for operating'. This means that it is near full capacity most of the time. In normal times this is efficient. But even quite small disruptions can have serious knock-on effects and the system just 'collapses in a crisis'.

Questions

1 What are the features of a 'lean system'?
2 In terms of the steps described in this chapter, how did the under-investment in transportation infrastructure come about?
3 In what ways is a transportation infrastructure different from other types of investment? How might such differences affect the investment decision?

Case 11.3: Over-investment in fibre optics

Drowning in glass[6]

Can you have too much of a good thing? The history of technology says not, but that was before the fibre-optic bubble.

Dreamy it may seem, but 'build it and they will come' is one of the most fundamental and lasting laws of technology. Each year the labs of Silicon Valley find ways to increase the capacity of everything, from processors to storage space, seemingly beyond all sense and reasonable demand. Yet somehow ways are always found to use it all. In technology, capacity drives demand, rather than the other way round.

The same has been true for communications capacity, which has been growing quickest of all, thanks to fibre optics. But here, the recent stockmarket bubble changed the picture. Investors threw tens of billions of dollars at new telecoms companies that were laying fibre networks in competition with the incumbents. The pace of new fibre laying, already fast, became frenetic: sales growth at leading fibre makers such as Corning hit 50% last year, nearly three times the previous rate. The race to lay new fibre reached such extremes that one company, 360networks, rose to fame not for its network technology but because it invented a railway cable-laying machine that could rise up to let trains pass underneath, saving it from having to waste valuable time scooting off to a siding.

When the stockmarket tumbled, the industry realised that it was looking at an unprecedented overhang of raw fibre. As expensive as it is to lay fibre, it is far more expensive to 'light' it with lasers, amplifiers and other optical equipment, and thus turn potential capacity into usable bandwidth. To light the new fibre that American carriers have already announced they are adding to their networks would cost more than $500 billion over the next three years, more than ten times current spending rates, according to Level 3 Communications, a carrier. Needless to say, that sort of money is no longer available.

Telecoms carriers tend to lay fibre speculatively, but only light it when they have an actual buyer. Now, with the stockmarket in a spin, they do not have as many of those as they were counting on. On March 19th, Corning warned that the growth of its fibre sales this year would be less than half last year's level – and even that will be propped up by a huge backlog of orders from last year, which it will now be able to fill. Over the past six months, concern that the white-hot optics industry was going to slow dramatically has savaged the share prices of its leaders, leaving stars such as JDS Uniphase more than 80% off their peaks.

There is plenty of evidence to support the fear of a fibre glut. Technologies that were expected to consume huge amounts of capacity have been slow to arrive. Fast mobile-data networks using so-called 3G technologies will be delayed for years, a victim of disappointment with the present technologies and a drying-up of the capital markets. Gigabit Ethernet, which allows companies to connect their office networks at blazing speeds, has been held back by slowing corporate technology investment. And Napster, which accounted for an estimated 4% of total Internet traffic at its peak (and much of the demand for home DSL and cable modem connections), now risks being shut down.

Many of the companies that were expected to be the main consumers of new fibre have also been hit by the market downturn. So-called competitive local-exchange carriers, such as ICG, which build fibre networks in cities to compete with big incumbents, are sagging under heavy debt loads; ICG itself is under bankruptcy protection. Most of the upstart firms that planned to offer high-speed DSL

connections to homes and small businesses, such as Covad, are also now on the ropes. All carriers have been hurt by the over-investment of the past few years, which brought more competitors to the market than demand could bear.

One consequence of all this is a gap between the main supply of potential bandwidth capacity (the long-haul networks between cities) and the main sources of new demand (small businesses and homes). From now on, there will be fewer companies connecting these consumers to networks than before, and at slower rates. This "last mile" bottleneck keeps millions of homes and businesses using dial-up modems, consuming trickles of bandwidth when they might want floods, and leaves much of the fibre in long-haul networks unused.

But there is a big difference between a temporary mismatch in supply and demand and a rejection of the 'build it and they will come' rule of technology consumption. The industry clearly overshot in the heady days when money was easy and growth was everything. Yet hardly anybody doubts that almost all the fibre in the ground today will be used eventually. The question is whether the companies that made the investment will be able to stay in business long enough to see the day.

Even in the current slump, Internet and other data traffic continues to more than double each year. Sadly, fibre investments in recent years implied a belief in even higher growth than that. Along with the growth in fibre itself, the optical-equipment industry was developing new gear that could send many more wavelengths down each fibre strand, multiplying the capacity of even existing cables a hundredfold or more. All told, carriers in the United States planned to increase their capacity almost seventyfold over the next three years, according to Level 3. At current rates of growth, demand would have only risen about fourfold over the same period.

But here, price elasticity may help the industry's plight. One of the good things about the fibre glut is that the price of unused fibre, which had remained relatively stable (since it reflects the cost of construction workers more than technology), is now falling quickly. As more companies get in trouble and are forced to dump capacity, the price will fall even faster. The result may be that once the shakeout is over, the survivors will be able to offer unprecedented amounts of bandwidth for unheard-of prices. Companies such as Narad Networks are developing technology that will allow them to offer homes up to 100 megabits of raw bandwidth at less than $100 a month.

With that kind of capacity, applications such as video-on-demand suddenly become economically attractive. If people start watching TV over the Internet, the fibre now in the ground may no longer be enough. And so the cycle will start again, just as it does in Intel's chips and Seagate's hard drives. The only difference is that billions of dollars of investment will have been burned up waiting for that day. Fibre is not so different from other technologies, except for the cost of getting it wrong.

Questions

1 Explain what is meant by the 'last mile' bottleneck; what is its cause, and what effects does it have?

2 In terms of the steps described in this chapter, what has been the main cause of the over-investment in fibre-optic technology?

3 Explain the relevance of price elasticity in the industry's current situation.

4 Explain the nature of the cycle described in the last paragraph. What are the causes of this cycle? Does it happen in all industries?

Summary

1 Capital budgeting is important because it involves long-term decisions and commitment by firms; mistakes can be very costly.

2 There are various types of capital expenditure, whose importance varies considerably in extent; therefore decision-making processes also vary from one type to another.

3 For major decisions there are several steps involved: estimating the initial cost, estimating future cash flows, estimating the degree of risk, estimating the cost of capital, and applying some evaluation criterion.

4 In the identification and measurement of cash flows it is the incremental cash flows that are relevant.

5 There are three types of risk: stand-alone risk, within-firm risk and market risk. The last is the most important in determining the effect of a project on a firm's share price. High stand-alone risk does not necessarily imply high within-firm risk or high market risk.

6 The cost of capital can be considered from both the demand and supply points of view: it represents the cost of raising funds for investment as far as the firm is concerned, and it also represents the rate of return required by the providers of these funds.

7 The two main components of long-term funds for investment are debt and equity; each has a different cost. A firm therefore needs to estimate the weighted average of these costs of capital.

8 There are two main evaluation criteria that are applied to capital budgeting situations: NPV and IRR. The former is the better measure, since any project with a positive NPV is expected to increase shareholder value.

9 However, managers still often prefer the IRR measure since it is expressed as an interest rate and can make for easier comparisons between projects.

10 It is important for managers to estimate the optimal capital budget for the firm. This indicates the total amount that should be spent on capital projects, and can only be estimated simultaneously with the cost of capital when the IO (demand) and MCC (supply) schedules are combined.

Review questions

1 Define and explain the following terms:
   a. Beta coefficient
   b. Stand-alone risk; within-firm risk; market risk
   c. *Ex-ante* and *ex-post* measures
   d. Decision tree analysis
   e. IRR
   f. WACC
   g. SML
   h. IO schedule.
2 Explain the role of simulation in capital budgeting.
3 Explain why the NPV criterion is preferable to the IRR criterion.
4 Explain why the cost of capital can only be accurately estimated when the IO schedule is known.
5 Explain why the stand-alone risk of a project is not of primary concern to shareholders.

Problems

11.1 Blatt Packing Co. is examining the investment in a new air-conditioning system in its factory. The initial cost is £100,000, and it is expected to sell the system for scrap after five years at a salvage value of £20,000. The equipment will be depreciated on a straight-line basis for tax purposes. The tax rate is 40 per cent, with no tax payable on the salvage value. The investment requires an increase in net working capital of £5,000 at the outset. There is no increase in revenues expected, but there is expected to be a saving of £40,000 per year in before-tax operating costs.

   a. Estimate the cash flows involved in the project.
   b. If the firm's cost of capital is 8 per cent, should the firm invest in the system?
   c. How would the decision above be affected if the firm's bond rating was reduced and its cost of capital changed to 10 per cent?

11.2 Moon Systems is considering investing in a new computer system. This has a net cost of £450,000, and is expected to increase pre-tax operating profit (allowing for depreciation) by £300,000 each year. Depreciation has been calculated on a straight-line basis, over three years, with no residual value. Taxes are at 40 per cent. The marginal cost of capital for the firm is 12 per cent. As financial director you are uncertain how long the economic life of the system is likely to be; however, recent indications are that the life may be only two years, or possibly even as little as eighteen months. Estimate the effect of the uncertainty regarding the economic life on the NPV and IRR of the investment project.

11.3 Wilson Products has analysed its investment opportunities for the future as follows:

Project	Cost (£, 000)	IRR (%)
A	100,000	15
B	60,000	12
C	80,000	11
D	50,000	10

The firm expects to achieve retained earnings of £96,000, plus £80,000 in cash flows resulting from depreciation. Its target capital structure involves 25 per cent debt and 75 per cent equity. It can borrow at a rate of 9 per cent. The firm's tax rate is 40 per cent and the current market price of its shares is £40. The last dividend was £2.26 per share, and the firm's expected constant growth rate is 6 per cent. New equity can be sold with a flotation cost of 10 per cent.

a. Calculate the WACC using retained earnings and the WACC issuing new stock.

b. Draw a graph of the IO and MCC schedules.

c. Determine which projects the firm should accept.

11.4 Safetilok is considering producing a new anti-theft device for cars. The initial stage would involve an investment of £20,000 to design the product and apply for approval from the insurance industry. Management believes that there is 75 per cent chance that the design will prove successful and approval will be given. If the product is rejected at this stage the project will be abandoned, with a salvage value of £5,000 after a year. The next step after approval is to produce some prototypes for testing. This would cost £300,000 in one year's time. If the tests are successful the product will go into full production; if not, the prototypes will be sold at scrap value for £50,000 after two years. Management believes that there is an 80 per cent chance of this stage proving successful. If the product goes into production this will cost £2 million after two years. If the market is favourable the net revenues minus operating costs are estimated to be £4 million, occurring after three years. If the market is unfavourable the net revenues minus operating costs are estimated at £1.5 million. Management estimates that there is a fifty-fifty chance of the market being favourable. The firm's marginal cost of capital is 10 per cent.

a. Draw a decision tree for the project.

b. Calculate the expected NPV for the project; should the firm undertake it?

Notes

1 J. C. Van Horne, 'A note on biases in capital budgeting introduced by inflation', *Journal of Financial and Quantitative Analysis*, **6** (January 1971): 653–658.

2 R. D. Luce and H. Raiffa, *Games and Decisions*, New York: Wiley, 1957, p. 13.

3 E. F. Brigham and L. C. Gapenski, *Financial Management: Theory and Practice*, 6th edn, Orlando: Dryden Press, 1991, p. 390.

4 Luce and Raiffa, *Games and Decisions*, p. 281.

5 'Grinding to a halt', *The Economist*, 2 November 2000.

6 'Drowning in glass', *The Economist*, 22 March 2001.

12

Government and managerial policy

Outline

Objectives

1   To explain why government policy is important for managerial decision-making.
2   To discuss the objectives of government policy.
3   To emphasize the distinction between positive and normative aspects of policy.
4   To explain the concept of market failure and its implications for both governments and businesses.
5   To explain the concept of externalities and their relevance to both governments and businesses.
6   To explain the concept of public goods and their relationship with externalities.
7   To discuss the importance of transaction costs and their implications.
8   To discuss certain social and ethical issues which are particularly relevant in business decision-making.
9   To explain why government intervention can be desirable in certain markets.
10 To explain the SCP model and its shortcomings.
11 To discuss the objectives of government policy in the areas of monopoly and competition policy.
12 To point out differences between objectives in the UK, the EU and the USA.
13 To discuss the various policy options in monopoly policy, explaining the relative advantages and disadvantages.
14 To discuss the various policy options in competition policy, explaining the relative advantages and disadvantages.
15 To describe the policies implemented by the UK, the EU and the USA, making comparisons.

12.1 Introduction

12.1.1 Importance of government policy

The first fundamental question here is: why should government policy be important to managers? Government policy affects firms in a multitude of ways and managers need to know what these policy effects are likely to be so that they can anticipate both the policies and their effects. In fact, managers can sometimes do more than just react to these policies; in some cases they can be proactive and influence such policies in a number of ways, particularly if they represent a large firm or an important lobby group. This determines the perspective of this chapter; we will examine government policy not from the point of view of government policy-making *per se*, but from the point of view of managers who have to operate in an environment that is influenced by such policy. However, we need to start by considering the objectives of government policy, since managers must understand these in order to anticipate the measures that a particular government might take.

12.1.2 Objectives of government policy

It might be claimed that it is meaningless to talk about government policy in general, since different governments at different times and in different countries pursue very different policies. However, it is still possible to discuss objectives under certain broad headings, even if specific objectives and policy measures vary greatly. Before any discussion of these objectives it is vital to recall a distinction explained in the first chapter of this text, that between **positive** and **normative** statements. It will become clear that some objectives are concerned with issues related to *efficiency*, a positive issue, while other objectives are related to *equity*, *social justice* or *ethics*, these being normative issues. Some authors fail to make this distinction, and this can lead to inaccurate analysis. The next distinction to make is between microeconomic and macroeconomic objectives; this text has been primarily concerned with microeconomic issues, but nevertheless managers need to be aware of macroeconomic objectives, since the relevant policy measures can have a considerable effect on the firm, for example a drop in interest rates. Both macroeconomic and microeconomic objectives are now outlined.

a. Macroeconomic objectives

In general these fall into four main categories:

1 Full employment
2 Economic growth
3 Price stability
4 Balance of payments stability

All of the above concepts turn out to be difficult to define in practical terms, and different governments will use different guidelines. For example, the European Central Bank (ECB) may define price stability as zero inflation, while the Bank of England may relate it to an inflation rate between 1.5 and 3.5 per cent. Economists generally recognize that, at least in the short term, there is a conflict between the first two objectives and the last two, and this complicates the issue in terms of selecting the appropriate policy instruments.

The traditional instruments are those of **demand management**; these refer to *fiscal and monetary policies*, and tend to be either expansionary or contractionary. The first two objectives tend to require expansionary policies while the last two tend to require contractionary policies. This means that most governments tend to alternate between policy measures according to the priority of their objectives.

How is this relevant to managers in business? They need to identify first of all the important economic indicators, in particular **leading indicators**. These are *variables that indicate where the economy is headed in the future*, rather than where it has been in the past. Such indicators include retail sales, building starts, investment plans and equipment orders, levels of unemployment, the wholesale price index and measures of business and consumer confidence. The government also uses these as a guide to policy. Thus managers can try to anticipate both changes in the economy and changes in government policy. For example, falling sales and rising unemployment levels may indicate a coming recession; the central bank may respond to these by cutting interest rates, depending on current levels and trends of inflation.

The interpretation of these indicators becomes more difficult when different indicators conflict with each other, as many countries have experienced in the period since 2001. For example, in early 2004 the jobs market in the United States was stagnant, with over 2 million net job losses in the previous two years, and inflation was running at only 1 per cent. These indicators pointed to a stumbling economy that could do with a boost. Yet the stock market had risen more in real terms in the previous twelve months than it had for fifty years, and both house prices and household debt had increased faster than for at least twenty years. This makes it very difficult for government policy-makers to determine appropriate action, and also for managers to predict both economic trends and government policy. Again, the decision by the Bank of England in April 2004 to keep interest rates at 4 per cent took many economists and business groups by surprise, in view of the recent rapid increase in personal debt.

Once the manager has some forecast of where the economy is headed, along with the corresponding government policy stance, further more specific forecasts of demand and costs can be generated, as has been seen in Chapters 4 and 7. However, such forecasts also require an analysis of the government's microeconomic policy objectives, and these are now discussed.

b. Microeconomic objectives

There are broadly speaking two main objectives:

1 The correction of market failure
2 The redistribution of income

Sometimes the second objective is included as part of the first, but it is better to separate the two, since market failure is strictly speaking a positive issue whereas the redistribution of income is a normative one. This distinction will be explained in the following section.

We can now consider some of the policy instruments that are used in each case. Regulation and fiscal policy are used to correct market failure, while fiscal policy is also used to redistribute income. These policies are also combined with environmental policy, transportation policy, regional policy, competition and industrial policy, and general social policies, including housing, education and health policies. Since these policies can have a major impact on different firms, the microeconomic objectives now need to be explained in detail.

12.2 Market failure

Capitalist systems rely on the market mechanism to allocate resources in their economies. If markets were perfect there would be no need for government intervention, at least from the point of view of efficiency. Since the existence of market failure is, therefore, the major justification for government intervention in the economy, it is important to have a good understanding of its nature.

12.2.1 Definition and types

Market failure is the situation where *the market mechanism fails to allocate resources efficiently*. This efficiency refers to both productive and allocative efficiency. It should be noted that this only relates to positive issues; there are no normative implications. Some texts[1] have stated that the signals from the market mechanism are not entirely 'operational', which obscures the distinction between positive and normative issues. For example, free markets provide drugs, pornography and prostitution. Whether these are 'good' or 'bad' is a normative issue and not largely a matter of market failure. There are, it should be said, some aspects of market failure involved, related to imperfect knowledge and externalities, but in these respects these products are no different from cigarettes and alcohol (which are drugs in any case), traffic congestion or pollution. Having said this, we can now list the main causes of market failure:

1 Monopolies
2 Externalities
3 Public goods

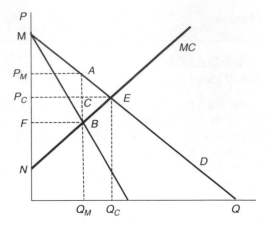

Figure 12.1. Welfare loss under monopoly.

4 Imperfect information
5 Transaction costs

These causes are discussed in the following subsections.

12.2.2 Monopolies

The nature of monopoly was discussed in Chapter 8. It was seen that, although there may not be many recognized monopolies in an economy, there are two factors that make their existence important:

1 Some monopolized industries can be very large and fundamental to the economy, like electricity, gas, water, telecommunications, railways, and coal.
2 Many industries feature limited monopolies, which are smaller firms producing differentiated products.

The economic problem here relates not just to monopoly, but to any form of competition that is less than perfect. It has been seen that in these cases there is a loss of allocative efficiency compared with perfect competition, since the price of the product exceeds the marginal cost of production. This causes a deadweight welfare loss to the economy, as seen in Chapter 8. A short-run illustration of the situation is shown in Figure 12.1.

The total welfare loss, referred to as the deadweight welfare loss, is given by the area ABE. Under perfect competition the total value of consumer surplus and producer surplus is given by the area MEN, as we saw in Chapter 8. Under monopoly, consumer surplus is reduced to the area MAP_M, while producer surplus is given by the area P_MABN. When these areas are added together, making up $MABN$, the difference between this and MEN is the area ABE. At the profit-maximizing output for the monopolist, Q_M, the consumer is prepared to pay more for the last unit of output than it costs the producer to sell it, and this situation applies to all output up to the equilibrium output under perfect competition, Q_C. The implications for government policy and the role of the government in the regulation of monopolies are discussed at length later in the chapter.

12.2.3 Externalities

Economists tend to give somewhat different definitions of **externalities**. A useful definition is that an externality exists when *the action of one agent affects the welfare of other agents, and these effects do not involve a market transaction*. Such effects may be positive or negative. For example, a smoker in a restaurant can impose negative externalities on other restaurant patrons. Likewise, a drug addict who commits a crime (assuming that this is undetected) imposes a negative externality on the victim. A conscientious house-owner who improves the exterior of her property may benefit other house-owners in terms of improving their property values, in this case donating a positive externality. These examples all involve individuals, but the concept of externalities applies equally well to firms, both as producers and consumers. Externalities are discussed in more detail in section 12.4, along with transaction costs, since the two issues are highly related.

12.2.4 Public goods

Public goods are in effect a particular kind of externality. They are *goods which, when provided for one person are automatically provided for others, and where an increase in one person's consumption does not reduce the amount available for others*. This definition, while it may seem clumsy, indicates the two most important features of a public good: **non-excludability** and **non-depletion**. These concepts are best explained in terms of a classic example of a public good, street lighting.

1 *Non-excludability*. Once street lighting is provided for a single person it is impossible, or at least very difficult, to prevent other people from receiving the benefit. The same thing does not necessarily apply to streets themselves, which could have access limited to certain people.
2 *Non-depletion*. Unlike most goods where one person's consumption of the good reduces the amount available for others, the consumption of street lighting by one person does not reduce this amount. Such goods are said to be non-rival in consumption.

The concept of public goods can be reversed to consider public 'bads'; an example would be pollution. In this case the production of pollution to one person may automatically affect many other people, and in doing so the amount of the effect on other people is not reduced.

In practice there are many goods and services that are semi-public goods: libraries, police forces, schools, hospitals, parks, museums and theatres all have the two characteristics described above to some extent. For example, a park can have a charge for access, but if it is provided free it allows any consumer to receive its benefits; however, when the park becomes overcrowded, these benefits start to decline, so the feature of non-depletion or non-rivalry is only partially present. Such goods are sometimes referred to as being **congestible**, in that they are *public goods up to a certain level of consumption, but then they become private goods*.

Why are public goods a cause of market failure? In a pure market system very few of such goods will be provided, because of the **free-rider problem**. Most people (except, maybe, criminals) want services like street lighting, but are reluctant to pay for them because they know that, *provided one person is prepared to pay for the product, they will enjoy its benefits for free*. Thus the argument is that the government needs to provide these essential public services. This issue is discussed further in the next section.

12.2.5 *Imperfect information*

The problem of imperfect information can now be discussed. There are two different aspects to the problem: incomplete information and asymmetric information. The latter was discussed in Chapter 2. Examples of incomplete information are the consumption of drugs or education, where the consumer lacks information relating to the future consequences of buying decisions. Examples of asymmetric information are doctors' prescriptions and unemployment insurance, where either the buyer or seller has more information than the other party in the transaction. These situations are examined in section 12.5.

12.2.6 *Transaction costs*

There are various types of transaction costs that are relevant in the externality situation, all of which present a barrier to conducting negotiations between the relevant parties. As seen in Chapter 2, the most important of these costs are:

1 *Search and information costs*. These involve obtaining the relevant information regarding the size of the costs involved and how they vary according to the amount of the externality caused. Since pollution costs are by their nature difficult to measure, and tend to be greater in the long term than the short term, the costs here can be very significant.
2 *Negotiation costs*. These relate to the time and other costs of having the parties reaching an agreement.
3 *Enforcement costs*. Once an agreement has been reached each party still has to check on an ongoing basis that the other party is abiding by the agreement. This can again be difficult with an externality like pollution, where, for example, chemicals might be dumped in a river by night.

The effect of all of these transaction costs is that, if they exceed the benefits of reaching an agreement, a market solution will not be found; thus the Coase theorem discussed in Chapter 2 will no longer apply. This is particularly likely in multi-party situations, which is frequently the case with pollution; the free-rider problem described earlier also exacerbates the problem. Although the resulting situation may still be Pareto-optimal, this is not really any consolation; it is possible therefore, in the presence of such transaction costs, that some kind of government intervention may improve total welfare. Various government agencies specialize in reducing different types of transaction costs, or help to fund other agencies that do the same. These include citizens' advice bureaux, better business bureaux, consumer watchdog associations, legal aid providers and various professional associations.

The application of the transaction cost problem is seen in section 12.4 concerning externalities.

12.3 Monopoly and competition policy

12.3.1 Basis of government policy

The first issue here is the definition of monopoly. In the UK this is taken to be a situation where a firm or cartel controls at least 25 per cent of any market. The European Commission uses a vaguer definition, but based on a guideline of a minimum market share of 40 per cent. Thus fewer European firms come under the scrutiny of the investigating authorities. In general terms there are four types of policy that can be pursued: public ownership, privatization and regulation, the promotion of competition, and restrictive practices policy. The experiences of the UK, EU and USA are examined, and the advantages and disadvantages of each type of policy are discussed.

It has been seen that, in general, monopoly does not result in economic efficiency, either productive efficiency or allocative efficiency. The short-run situation was illustrated in the previous section, in Figure 12.1. The long-run situation is shown in Figure 12.2, under the assumption that there are constant returns to scale. The situation could also apply in the short run, if there are no fixed costs; we shall return to this point later.

The monopoly price is above the minimum of *LAC*, causing productive inefficiency, and the price is also greater than the marginal cost, causing allocative inefficiency and a deadweight welfare loss to the community, given by the area *CFE*. This loss is the main justification given for government intervention. There are two other arguments that are also sometimes made in favour of intervention.

1. *Rent-seeking behaviour.* It has been argued[2] that the existence of supernormal profits causes people to use resources to obtain and then protect such profit. It is rational to continue to seek such profit as long as the additional profits exceed the additional costs. Thus, for example, firms will incur more legal costs in terms of acquiring patents and policing their exclusivity. In this situation all monopoly profit is actually offset by the rent-seeking costs involved in obtaining and protecting this profit, and therefore the deadweight loss to the community is much larger, given by the area *BCFD*. This argument assumes that

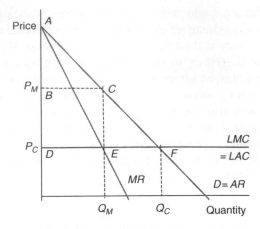

Figure 12.2. Comparison of perfect competition and monopoly.

the market for rent-seeking is perfectly competitive, but even if it is not so, there is still some additional welfare loss compared with the loss of the area *CFE*.

2. *Inequality of income distribution.* To the extent that monopolists tend to earn higher incomes than average, the existence of monopoly in the economy will tend to increase the inequality of income distribution. It should be noted that this is a normative argument, whereas the arguments put forward earlier have been positive, in the sense that they are based on efficiency and involve no value judgement. Of course, it can also be claimed that inequality of income distribution can be corrected so far as is desirable by the use of more general fiscal policies by the government. There is a general principle that is relevant here, in terms of efficiency: that governments should intervene at the closest point in the system to the policy objective in order to maximize overall welfare.

The ultimate objective of any government policy is to improve total welfare, which is clearly a performance-related objective. There may in addition be certain normative objectives related to the distribution of income. Different governments and different countries have emphasized different aspects of monopoly and competition policy, as will be seen, but there are certain general principles that can be outlined at this stage, before moving on to a consideration of policy options.

First of all, it needs to be recognized that any kind of intervention involves costs. This aspect was covered in subsection 12.2.6, but mainly from the point of view of firms. For governments many of the same factors apply: there will be search and information costs, administration costs and enforcement costs. The consequence of this is that a policy of non-intervention may be best if the costs of intervention exceed the benefits. Such costs can be very considerable, particularly in the extreme case of public provision. Regulation of privately owned firms is usually considerably cheaper from the government's viewpoint than public provision, because public ownership requires an initial large expenditure to compensate private shareholders. However, regulation presents a number of problems in the case of natural monopolies, as will be explained shortly.

In summary, a government has to determine what type of intervention is best in each situation. We shall see that different countries have had quite different policy models and experiences. Many of these differences stem from the fundamental philosophical differences between the so-called **Anglo-Saxon model** (ASM) and the **European social model** (ESM). The former, pursued in the United States and to a lesser extent the United Kingdom, favours the operation of free markets, while the latter, followed in the other EU countries, favours more government intervention in order to reduce income inequalities and achieve social justice. It is therefore necessary to discuss policies used in EU countries other than the UK separately from policies used specifically in the UK. While the commonality of EU law has eroded some of these distinctions in recent years, many of them persist. In order to avoid repetition of the clumsy phrase 'EU countries other than the UK' we will now refer to such countries simply as the EU, but the reader must bear in mind that the UK is implicitly excluded from this description in the current context.

The different objectives of the different models lead to certain policy conflicts and this brings us back to the two strands of policy mentioned earlier. The ASM tends to favour less intervention in general, particularly in terms of monopolies; however, because free markets require competition, the ASM can be more interventionist in this area. The two strands of policy are therefore considered in separate subsections, which can be better understood after examining the nature of the structure–conduct–performance model.

12.3.2   The structure–conduct–performance (SCP) model

This model was also referred to in Chapter 8, along with more recent refinements involving feedback loops. The model helps us to see how government intervention is targeted. First, the government has to detect that a monopoly is present or is a potential threat. This is obvious in cases where one firm dominates a whole industry, but in other cases, for example the Coca-Cola case mentioned earlier, this may be questionable. This issue is developed further in the next subsection. Once a monopoly is perceived, the government can pursue policies targeted at structure or at conduct. The choice here depends largely on whether the barriers in the industry are structural or strategic:

1 *Structural.* These might be in the form of economies of scale, for example. Policies here are often better targeted at **conduct**, meaning various types of regulation. It may not be good practice in this case to try to promote a structure of small firms in the industry since this would lead to a loss of productive efficiency.
2 *Strategic.* These might be in the form of predatory pricing practices or exclusive dealing. Government policies in this situation may be targeted at changing the **structure** of the industry, by blocking mergers or even breaking up large firms into smaller units. Once the structure has been changed, the strategic barriers are no longer possible and this saves the government

the administration costs of monitoring the restrictive practices and enforcing the relevant laws.

The different barriers mentioned above, and discussed in detail in Chapter 8, also lead to two different strands of policy in most countries; policies can be aimed at either:

1 *Existing monopolies*. These tend to feature **structural barriers**. Conduct-based policies may therefore be required, or public ownership, which it can be argued is targeted at both structure and conduct, although it is the conduct that is primarily affected by such ownership.

2 *Potential monopolies*. These tend to feature **strategic barriers**, often referred to as restrictive practices. Governments tend to use policies targeted at both structure and conduct in this situation.

The different policies that are used in practice are discussed in the remaining subsections, but first it is necessary to consider the detection of monopolies or potential monopolies.

12.3.3 *Detection of monopoly*

Governments first have to identify situations where monopoly is present. Sometimes this is obvious, as when a single firm dominates an industry. In many situations, however, this is more difficult, especially when considering potential monopolies and restrictive practices. Frequently the government begins by examining the degree of concentration in an industry in order to assess market power. This is in keeping with the SCP paradigm, that structure underlies conduct and performance. In Chapter 8 various measures of concentration were considered, such as four- or eight-firm concentration ratios and the Herfindahl index. Although such measures are useful, a number of problems, discussed in the following paragraphs, still remain.

1. The above measures do not give a complete measure of market power and dominance. For example, an industry could have the four largest firms with market shares of 40%, 10%, 5% and 5%, while another industry could have the four largest firms with 15% each. Both industries have four-firm concentration ratios of 60%, but the first features much more domination by one firm. The Herfindahl index, although it is less often used, gives a better indication of the inequality of distribution in this case.

2. Measures of concentration do not take into account the life-cycle of the industry. In the initial growth stages of an industry there may only be a few firms in the market, but this may only be a temporary situation as new firms take a little time to enter. Also, industries often become more concentrated when they go into decline, heavy manufacturing for example, but this is not necessarily a sign of increased market power. The increased concentration is simply a result of a natural shake-out in the industry and need not be a cause for concern to the government.

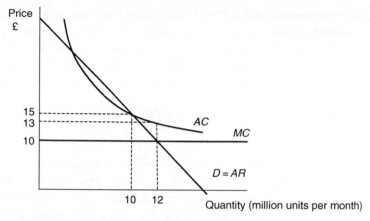

Figure 12.3. Pricing under public ownership.

3. It is often difficult to define the industry or market in the first place; this problem has arisen in a number of cases already mentioned, for example Coca-Cola and Maxwell House. The parameters of definition relate both to product characteristics and to spatial factors.

In view of the above problems, governments in general have tended to take a flexible approach in determining whether there is a monopoly problem, and have dealt with situations on a case-by-case basis, trying to take many factors into account. Different practices are examined in more detail in the following subsections.

12.3.4 Public ownership

This is the most extreme form of government intervention. A firm, or sometimes a whole industry, is nationalized, and then controlled by the state. It is usually argued by its supporters that this is the best way to ensure that the public interest is served and that social welfare is maximized. Once the industry is state-owned then, in theory, price and output can be adjusted to competitive levels, in other words P_C and Q_C in Figure 12.2. This may present problems if there are fixed costs that have to be accounted for, as illustrated in Figure 12.3. Marginal costs are assumed constant in this situation; in later situations, marginal costs are assumed to be rising, so that different types of situation and their implications can be examined. It may also be possible for marginal costs to be falling, when many economies of scale are available.

There are two alternative pricing policies for the government here:

1. *Marginal cost pricing policy.* If the government uses a marginal cost pricing policy, the industry has its price set to equal marginal cost, £10; then it will make a loss and require a subsidy. The loss is £3 per unit sold, giving a total loss of £36 million per month.

2. *Average cost pricing policy.* If the government wishes to avoid giving a subsidy it has to charge the price where demand is equal to the average cost; at this price, £15, the industry can meet the quantity demanded while breaking even. This average cost pricing policy will reduce the quantity demanded by the market to 10 million units. However, there is also allocative inefficiency in this case, with $P > MC$.

We can now consider the advantages and disadvantages of public ownership.

a. Advantages

There is no doubt that public ownership gives greater control to the government, since prices, outputs, investment levels, employment levels, and financing can all be determined directly. Thus it should be easier to maximize social welfare. In practice it is also true that countries with greater public ownership often have a better quality of essential services like transportation, although this was questionable in the UK in the 1970s. Lower income groups, in particular, tend to be favoured by public provision (provided they have a job). Some commentators argue that public provision, especially when accompanied by other aspects of intervention, ensures greater social cohesion by promoting egalitarian effects. The relationships between free markets, wealth inequality and social cohesion are very complex, however, and this issue will always provoke debate.

b. Disadvantages

A number of disadvantages apply to the practical implementation of public provision.

1. Cost.   It is very costly for a government to take over ownership, at least in a democratic country. This applies not just to the initial cost of compensating existing shareholders, but also to the operational and investment costs that are incurred on an ongoing basis. These costs could be justified if the benefits were sufficiently great; however, the benefits may not be as great as expected, because of the following factors.

2. Inefficiency.   When considering the theory of the firm in Chapter 2 it was seen that the objective of profit or shareholder-wealth maximization is a spur to managerial efficiency. Managers tend to lose their jobs if they are not efficient in the private sector. In the public sector, profit maximization is no longer the objective, and performance is more difficult to measure. Thus managers tend not to have the discipline of the market exerted on them; this discipline applies even in monopolistic industries, although not to the same extent as in competitive markets. The result is that in state-owned industries there tends to be **X-inefficiency**, sometimes referred to as organizational slack.

Another kind of inefficiency can arise if the government sets the monopoly price too low. There may be a temptation to do this for social and political

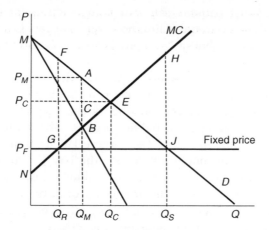

Figure 12.4. Welfare loss under public ownership.

reasons where the monopoly is an essential public service like electricity or railway services. The situation is shown in Figure 12.4.

We have seen in the previous section that the total welfare loss in monopoly compared with perfect competition is given by the area ABE; this is referred to as the deadweight welfare loss. However, if the government fixes the price at P_F, below the perfectly competitive price, this can cause a greater welfare loss than would occur under monopoly. We shall assume that, being in public ownership, the industry supplies the amount that is demanded by the public, Q_S. The situation is different under regulation, and this will be examined in the next subsection. With the price at P_F and the quantity at Q_S, consumer surplus becomes the area MJP_F. However, producers make a loss, given by the area $HJG - P_FGN$; P_FGN is a gain, but the larger area HJG represents loss. Therefore, total welfare with the fixed price is given by $MEGP_F - HJE + P_FGN = MEN - HJE$. The result is that the area HJE represents the welfare loss under public ownership compared with perfect competition, and it can be seen that in Figure 12.4 this loss is greater than the area ABE, the loss under a privately owned monopoly.

3. Lower quality. Although it was previously argued that in general the quality of public services is often better when they are provided by the state, for example transportation, this is not always the case. The quality of British Leyland cars in the late 1970s was notoriously bad, and the quality of the Royal Mail is also dubious; losing a million items a week is not an indicator of good quality. The provision of postal services is the subject of Case Study 12.2.

4. Reduced choice. Some services tend to suffer from reduced choice when they are publicly provided, for example health and education. Having reduced choice would not matter so much to consumers if it were not for the problems of lower quality just described. With a health service like the NHS in the UK it is not so much the quality of in-patient care that is the problem, it is the speed of service, meaning that patients can wait many months, or even years, for treatment. Some people would claim, however, that this is not a problem of public provision as such, but rather a problem of underfunding.

5. Countervailing power. This refers to the situation where the existence of monopoly power on one side of a market can lead to the development of a counteracting monopoly power on the other side of the market.[3] It is noticeable that in the area of public services, labour unions tend to be particularly strong and militant. The largest labour union in the UK is Unison, which represents public employees; the TGWU is also very large and powerful, and again represents many public employees, though some have found themselves transferred to the private sector in recent years because of privatizations. Industrial relations have historically been worse in these areas, and strikes more common, thus reducing productivity.

We can now examine the historical experience of public ownership in different countries. The UK has had very varied approaches to public ownership, in keeping with the different political philosophies of successive governments since the Second World War. Immediately after the war, in a spirit of unified patriotism, the Welfare State was founded and many key industries were nationalized. This trend reached a peak under the Labour government in the 1970s, by which time all the utilities, coal, steel, shipbuilding, airlines, railways and many firms in banking and car manufacturing were under state control. Productivity, particularly in manufacturing, lagged badly behind industrial competitors: by 1980 the average US manufacturing worker was producing two and three-quarters times the average UK worker, and in Germany, France and Japan, productivity was around twice as high. Industrial strife was rampant, and trade unions enjoyed great powers as legislation in their favour was enacted. Strikes and stoppages were frequent, resulting in a three-day week and electricity blackouts. Inflation was also high, reaching over 20 per cent a year, while economic growth lagged behind other OECD countries. These economic problems were not necessarily the result of public ownership of course, and economists still debate the primary causes of the malaise, mainly blaming bad management or excessively strong and recalcitrant trade unions. However, the problems of low productivity and bad industrial relations were a particular feature of the industries that were in public ownership.

When Margaret Thatcher became Prime Minister in 1979, policies were essentially reversed and **Thatcherism** became a philosophy; as stated earlier, this was essentially a free-market model. Most of the industries mentioned above were privatized, and this is discussed further later.

The USA has always been closer to the free-market model than either the UK or the EU. Although it has a long history of anti-trust legislation, relating to monopolies, going back to the Sherman Act of 1890, public ownership has never played a major part in the US economy. This is reflected in the size of its public-sector spending as a proportion of GDP: in the USA this is currently about 32%, while in the UK it is about 42%, and in the EU, about 50%. Government authorities have occasionally taken over or bailed out major firms that were in dire financial trouble, such as Chrysler, Amtrak and Continental Illinois Bank, but these have been very much the exception. After the terrorist attacks in September 2001, government also agreed to bail out the US airline industry, in order to prevent a collapse. This has caused some consternation in the EU, whose airlines have to compete with US airlines on many routes; there is some irony in this, considering the substantial state aid that many EU airlines have received over the last two decades.

Under the ESM most EU countries have experienced considerable state owner-ship in recent decades. The industries involved have generally been the same as for the UK, meaning in economic terms those that are natural monopolies, often because of economies of scale. Some countries, notably France, have tended to promote '**national champions**'; such firms or industries have received large amounts of state aid, for example car-manufacturing firms like Renault, banks like Crédit Lyonnais, airlines like Air France, and computer manufacturers like Honeywell Bull. These firms are often the object of much patriotic pride, in spite of abysmal performance in some cases, and this has resulted in the French government coming into conflict with the EU competition laws. Article 92 of the Treaty of Rome prohibits all state aid to industry. However, the extent of such aid is far and wide and often difficult to assess; it includes not only direct subsidies, but also cheap loans, tax concessions, guaranteed government con-tracts and so on. Some types of state aid are also permitted; this relates to regional policies, social improvement and EU-wide projects.

EU governments have generally favoured public ownership and subsidies in order to promote social objectives. Reducing income inequalities and increas-ing or protecting employment have been important in this respect. Ironically, the measures have often been self-defeating; for the last ten years unemploy-ment in the EU has been about twice as high as in the USA and the UK. Some economists claim that these official figures are misleading because they ignore 'underemployment' and therefore disguise the true numbers of people not working.[4, 5] However, other economists argue that the high level of unemploy-ment is caused by over-regulation of the labour markets in the EU. It is outside the scope of this text to examine this debate or the regulations in detail, but in general many countries in the EU have greater restrictions on firing employ-ees, greater worker protection and benefits, larger employer contributions to health and pension benefits, restrictions on part-time and contract work, lower retirement ages and shorter working hours. Although such provisions may benefit those workers with jobs and provide more security, they have to some extent created a greater pool of unemployment, particularly among young, unskilled workers, and those living in depressed areas.

In consequence it is difficult to assess the advantages and disadvantages of public ownership *per se*, since those countries that favour it tend to feature various other features of the ESM, and it is difficult to isolate the effects of different government policy measures.

12.3.5 Privatization and regulation

To a large extent the policies involved here represent the opposite to public provision. In the United States there has not been much need for privatization since most industries have never featured public ownership, so regulation is the only issue.

Regulation can cover many different aspects of a firm's behaviour. For example, firms can be restricted in terms of the suppliers that they use or the customers they may serve; on the other hand, they may be required to provide services to customers that they would otherwise not wish to serve. However, government authorities are most concerned with the ability of monopolistic firms to earn supernormal profits, and therefore often concentrate on policies that are directly related to such profit. There are essentially three different approaches here.

1. *Profit constraints*. Although profit is measurable and has to be reported regularly by all firms as a legal requirement for tax purposes, there is a fundamental problem related to enforcing a profit constraint on firms. Such a constraint eliminates the incentive to be efficient: managers can increase costs by indulging in perquisites like company cars and expense accounts, knowing that they can maintain profit by raising prices.

2. *Rate of return constraints*. Government policies sometimes focus instead on a firm's rate of return, placing a constraint on this measure of performance. Rate of return is determined by dividing profit by the firm's asset base. This measure is also prone to abuse, since it encourages managers to overinvest in capital assets and have excess capacity, thus enabling them to make more profit while still earning a target rate of return. Again this is not conducive to efficiency.

3. *Price constraints*. In view of the above problems much regulation focuses on the price variable, setting a maximum price, or **price cap**, that a monopolist can charge. This can also cause problems in terms of efficiency, as explained under the heading 'disadvantages' below. Efficiency incentives may also be adversely affected, as seen in the discussion of the experiences of various countries.

a. Advantages

Privatization has often been regarded as one of the key elements of Thatcherism in the UK. This was essentially a political and economic philosophy, and is similar to **Reaganomics** and **supply-side economics** in the USA. All of these doctrines were essentially in favour of the free market. This means that they favoured privatization rather than state ownership, but they did not on the whole favour regulation. As seen later, deregulation was strongly favoured, especially in view of the fact that the UK markets in particular were highly regulated in the 1970s.

It has been argued[6] that privatization in the UK was not, as popularly believed, a political philosophy and essential part of Thatcherism, but rather a practical and opportunist approach to raising money for the government by selling off public assets. More recently this argument has also been proposed regarding other EU countries that have started to go down the same path, including Germany and France. Whatever the merits of this argument, raising funds has certainly been an advantage of such a policy. Others have argued that a further advantage to the government was the reduction in trade union power that followed privatization.

As far as regulation is concerned, it is impossible to discuss the advantages of regulation *per se*; different types of regulation have different advantages and disadvantages, as seen in the case studies. One conclusion does seem to be clear, however, and this is that excessive regulation is harmful, by distorting market forces and incentives for efficiency. This aspect is now examined in more detail.

b. Disadvantages

Those who argue against privatization usually claim that similar benefits in terms of welfare and efficiency can be gained by regulation and promoting competition, without selling off public assets. The gain is mainly in the form of a more equitable distribution of income and wealth, as excessive profits no longer fall into the hands of a few people. However, various problems can arise with regulated prices, as discussed in the following paragraphs.

1. Increased welfare loss. The problems that can arise if the price cap is set too low are illustrated in Figure 12.5 . The situation here is similar to that in Figure 12.4, but in this case it is assumed that, while the government sets the regulated price P_R, the monopolist is free to determine output, which it sets at the profit-maximizing level Q_R. This means that there will be a shortage, with Q_S being demanded and only Q_R supplied. This could entail queues and waiting lists, involving additional costs. Also, the welfare loss compared with perfect competition is given by the area *FEG*, which is greater than the original loss under unregulated monopoly by the area *FABG*.

2. The monopolist may be forced out of business. This may happen if the monopolist is only making normal profit before being regulated. It should be recalled from Chapter 8 that a monopolist is not guaranteed to make a supernormal profit; this depends on the cost structure involved. For example, the situation shown in Figure 12.6 is essentially the same as for a firm in monopolistic competition; the firm is just making normal profit at its profit-maximizing output. If the regulated price is set at the level for perfect competition, where demand and marginal cost are equal, the monopolist will make a loss. There is no output under this situation where the monopolist can cover its costs. The monopolist's marginal revenue curve will now equal the regulated price line and the monopolist will minimize its losses at the output Q_R. In order to keep the monopolist in operation the government would have to pay it a subsidy given by the area $ABCP_R$.

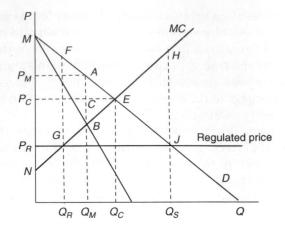

Figure 12.5. Welfare loss under regulation.

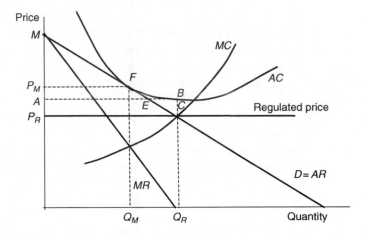

Figure 12.6. Regulation forces monopoly out of business.

In terms of the welfare implications, the original consumer surplus before regulation was MFP_M, and there was no supernormal profit. If the monopolist goes out of business this consumer surplus is eliminated.

In terms of practical experience, privately owned monopolies in the UK are first of all regulated in terms of their operating licences and relevant legislation. Such licences may stipulate that services have to be supplied to certain customers regardless of profitability; this is done to prevent the marginalization of certain rural communities that might otherwise not be provided with basic services. Problems arise with natural monopolies like the utilities, where provision of infrastructure is often divided from the supply or operation of the service. This aspect is explained in the next subsection, since it relates to the promotion of competition.

Each industry has had its own regulator; for example, Ofgem, Ofwat and Ofcom are the regulating authorities for gas and electricity, water and tele-communications/media respectively. These watchdogs are charged with representing consumer interests, and maintaining standards of service. If the standards set are not maintained, financial penalties can be imposed; thus when too many trains did not run on time, the Rail Regulator penalized the train operating companies.

The regulatory bodies have also had the responsibility of setting prices. In the UK this has been done by using the '$RPI - X$' formula; this means that prices are permitted to rise by the rate of inflation minus an allowance for forecast productivity growth in similar industries. The aim here is to allow the monopoly to earn a more-or-less constant rate of return. If the firm performs well and achieves faster productivity growth than expected it will earn a greater-than-average rate of return. The main problem in practice for the regulators has been to forecast productivity growth reliably and then to stick to its formula. Goalposts have been shifted; for example, when BT reported a very large rise in profits in 1991, Oftel, which was then the regulator for telecommunications, responded to consumer pressure by threatening to increase the size of the X-factor. Such shifts have the same effect as the other constraints on profits discussed earlier, in that they reduce managerial incentives to be efficient.

In general the issue of privatization is a controversial one in the UK. Most consumers do not seem to favour it, and associate it with a reckless pursuit of profit regardless of consumer welfare. This has been evident in reactions to the large profits made by some water authorities and in particular to the performance of Railtrack in the light of multiple train crashes. Such media-grabbing headlines have drawn consumers' attention away from the fact that prices for many privatized services have fallen, at least in real terms. The current Labour government is not in general considering renationalization, although recent intervention in the railways industry has certainly come close to it; policies are aimed more at trying to restructure privatization to make it more efficient and accountable.

The problems of the railways provide an interesting case; in some ways these originated in the late nineteenth century when the different private railway companies were regulated in terms of constraints on their rate of return. As explained above, this led to an overinvestment in assets, and for a hundred years the UK has had more kilometres of track per square kilometre than any other major European country. In spite of cutting services on many rural routes during the 1960s this situation continues to the present day: the UK currently has 0.14 km of track per square km of land area compared with figures of 0.10 for Germany and 0.06 for France. The result is that there is much less utilization of capacity in terms of annual passenger-km per km of track: utilization in the UK is only 56 per cent of that in Germany and 50 per cent of that in France.[7] This in turn has led to subsidies for those lines which are less popular, exactly the opposite situation to that which economic theory would recommend; subsidies should go to the commuter routes in order to ease congestion and pollution. Another result is that investment in the maintenance of capital equipment has been thinly spread, resulting in a deterioration of the infrastructure throughout at least the last forty years. Thus, blaming all the problems on the lack of investment since the railways were privatized in 1997 is very wide of the mark.

Currently the government is considering additional privatizations that even Thatcher did not dare to propose, like in the postal services. State education and the hallowed National Health Service are now subjects of private investment initiatives, although there is considerable opposition to this, especially from the trade unions.

In the United States many monopoly suppliers of utilities have been privately owned for many years. They have, however, often been heavily regulated, and only more recently has deregulation been favoured. Much of this regulation and deregulation has recently been in the spotlight, as the electricity industry in California has found itself in increasing problems. These are examined in some detail in Case Study 12.1. It is clear that in this case the problem was not deregulation, because the industry was never truly deregulated. A strict price cap was imposed, so that when wholesale prices rose, suppliers found that they had to pay more for electricity than they were allowed to charge. Furthermore, they were not allowed to hedge their position by buying in the futures markets.

In other US states and in other industries a more satisfactory situation has emerged, but a common feature is the strong influence of lobbying groups. This has sometimes resulted in inefficient solutions that favour one section of the community over others. In the electricity industry it has resulted in a stagnant capacity, as nobody wants power stations built in their local communities.

Regulation in the EU has tended to be heavier than in the UK or the US. Even when monopolies are allowed to be in private ownership they are regulated in many ways in terms of their operating conditions and performance factors. This is becoming more of an issue in the EU now that more firms and industries are becoming privatized. Many of these firms, as in the UK, were loss-makers while in public ownership. This can make them difficult to privatize unless their terms of operation are relaxed to allow them to make a profit.

12.3.6 Promoting competition

It needs to be stressed first of all that this policy is not mutually exclusive with either public provision or privatization and regulation; rather it is an additional approach to both policies. There are a number of methods by which competition can be created or increased.

1. *Liberalization of markets.* This means allowing more firms to supply services; for example, in the airlines industry more firms may be given licences to fly certain routes.

2. *Deregulation.* This has already been discussed in connection with the electricity industry in particular. This has similar effects to liberalization, but applies in particular to privatized industries.

3. *Compulsory Competitive Tendering (CCT).* This relates mainly to local government authorities. Instead of performing operations in-house, like cleaning and catering, these authorities are required to ask for bids from firms on a competitive basis. Sometimes the previous in-house operators establish a firm, make a bid and win the contract.

4. *Creating an internal market.* This means creating a market in a situation where there was none. In the NHS in the UK a Conservative government established an internal market that distinguished buyers (local health authorities) from providers of services (hospitals). This was intended to give choice to buyers and encourage them and the hospitals to be more efficient. The policy was at one point largely abandoned by the subsequent Labour government, in that doctors were no longer given budgets to buy services from hospitals. It is now being reintroduced through Primary Care Trusts which manage three-quarters of the UK's health budget. These organizations will pay hospitals by results. Internal markets have also been created in the public utilities, although this has also proved difficult. It is clearly wasteful to duplicate expensive infrastructure in terms of gas pipelines and the electricity grid, so a distinction has been drawn between suppliers of services and suppliers of infrastructure. While the infrastructure may remain a monopoly, suppliers may compete with each other to use it.

a. Advantages

The promotion of competition has three main advantages.

1. Greater efficiency. This means lower costs and lower prices to the consumer. The example of airlines in the USA compared with those in the EU demonstrates the extent of this advantage.

2. Greater quality. Firms are encouraged not just to compete on price but also in terms of quality. Thus in the UK there has been a huge fall in the proportion of public phone booths that are inoperative; before privatization this proportion was very large. Call-out times for installations and repairs have also been reduced.

3. More choice. Sometimes different providers offer different types of service, for example cable TV operators. Customers are now better able to find the type of service that suits them best.

b. Disadvantages

Two main problems can be discussed here.

1. Practicality. The main problem with promoting competition is that it can be impractical in the case of some natural monopolies. Most people are unable to choose between different water suppliers for example. However, further improvements in technology may reduce this problem.

2. Marginalization of certain communities.   Monopolies can afford to subsidize certain products because of large profits on other products. Thus rail and bus operators can subsidize unprofitable routes, and the postal service can deliver mail to remote areas. Competition reduces the profit on the popular services, thus encouraging operators to cut services in less popular areas. This is even happening in the banking industry, as many banks are reducing their number of branches. The result is that many communities may lack basic services, a particular problem for the elderly and low-income groups who lack mobility.

The promotion of competition by using markets has been more popular with UK Conservative governments than with the Labour government that has been in power since 1997. Labour has always been more suspicious of markets for philosophical reasons, hence the abandoning of the internal market in the National Health Service when Frank Dobson was the minister in charge. However, Labour has by no means turned its back on market mechanisms, and it is perhaps the most important feature of 'New Labour' that it has encouraged market mechanisms in many areas of the economy that were previously anathema to the party, as mentioned earlier. Prime Minister Tony Blair has come under great pressure and criticism, particularly within his own party, over the issues of foundation hospitals and top-up fees for universities, both of which involve market mechanisms. His proposals in both areas have had to be watered down in order to make them more acceptable to the party majority.

US markets have historically been more liberalized and deregulated than those in the UK or EU. Many industries were deregulated in the Reagan years of the 1980s, for example public utilities, railways, road transport and haulage, airlines and shipping. Different states have had different regulations, as mentioned in the case of the Californian electricity utilities. Deregulation of the airlines has resulted in airfares per passenger-km being only half of what they are in the still heavily regulated EU. The industry has also been much more dynamic – or unstable, depending on one's viewpoint – in the sense of firms going out of business and new firms entering.

The ESM is generally more suspicious of market forces than the ASM; therefore liberalization and deregulation have been slow in spreading in the EU, in spite of the fact that it is supposed to be a single market. Therefore, in spite of the Maastricht Treaty of 1992, the Competition Act of 1998 and the Enterprise Act of 2002, there remain significant differences between the approaches of the UK government and EU governments to competition. EU governments have often made considerable efforts to protect their industries from competition, even from other countries in the EU. This has applied in particular to the countries in the southern part of the EU, meaning France, Spain, Portugal, Italy and Greece. Agricultural products enjoy much protection and this has been an ongoing source of conflict with the United States, which has called the World Trade Organization into making rulings on the issue. Germany has also been guilty of substantial protection of certain industries, coal mining for example. Many governments are also unwilling to allow 'national champions' to be taken over by foreign-owned companies. For example, French authorities would not approve a foreign takeover of Crédit Lyonnais, in spite of the firm accumulating losses of over $4 billion over the years, and being a constant drain on public funds. There are also strong restrictions on foreign television and radio programming in France, limiting their market share; the aim in this case is the protection of the French culture.

12.3.7 Restrictive practices

Policies in this area relate to potential monopolies, meaning situations where firms are attempting to use strategic barriers to obtain or increase their monopoly power. In general there are four main types of policy here, relating to mergers, collusion, pricing practices and other restrictive practices. As with the previous subsection these are now discussed in turn, examining the experience of different countries and considering the problems involved in implementation. In general it will be seen that while policies regarding mono-poly have usually been more relaxed in the USA than in the EU, policies regarding restrictive practices have often been more strict. This is because of the conflict mentioned earlier that is inherent in both the ASM and ESM regarding market failure and competition. There is another factor that is relevant here. Prosecution in the United States often involves attorneys who stand to make large profits individually from success; this is not the case in the UK or EU, where prosecution is in the hands of civil servants whose careers are not so much affected by success or failure. Since experiences relating to mergers and collusion vary significantly from one country or area to another, these are discussed separately after a brief general discussion of each of the two issues.

a. Mergers

It is important to realize that mergers can be of different types. In particular it is important to distinguish between mergers that increase **horizontal inte-gration** and those that increase **vertical integration**. Horizontal integration refers to the situation where firms at the same stage of the production process, meaning competitors, are involved. Vertical integration refers to the situation where firms at different stages of the production process are involved, like when a supplier takes over a distributor or vice versa. **Conglomerate inte-gration** refers to the situation where firms operating in different industries are involved. Horizontal mergers are generally seen as being more dangerous in terms of the gaining of market power. Mergers can, however, provide benefits as well as impose costs in the form of reduced competition. These benefits are in the form of reduced costs, from greater economies of scale or from the elimination of wasteful duplication of assets or operating costs, like R&D. These cost savings can be passed on to the consumer in the form of lower prices.

Policies have varied widely regarding mergers, both among different countries and over time. In the UK there are essentially two main regulatory bodies. The **Office of Fair Trading** (OFT) is responsible for monitoring trading practices on an ongoing basis. This office can then refer cases for investigation to the **Competition Commission,** formerly the Monopolies and Mergers Commission. The Competition Commission can only recommend action to block a merger; the action itself can only be taken by the Secretary of State for Trade and Industry. Until the Enterprise Act 2002 the criteria for investigation related to size of market share and size of assets taken over, and the criterion for action was whether a proposed merger was against the public interest. These criteria have been changed by the Act.[8] The assets test has been replaced by a turnover test, relating to any company with UK turnover of more than £70 million. The criterion for action is now whether there is expected to be '**a substantial lessening of competition within any market or markets in the UK**'. The public interest criterion has been replaced by a customer benefits clause, so it is possible that these may outweigh the lessening of competition. In practice only about 1 per cent of all mergers have been judged not to be in the public interest.

An interesting case in 2003, relating to grocery retailing, highlights the current policy of the Competition Commission. In this case the Commission recommended the blocking of the takeover of Safeway by Asda, Sainsbury, Tesco and Morrison's, although the latter firm chose to withdraw its offer.[9] The main reason for blocking the merger was that it was judged that the consequent reduction in competition was likely to have an adverse effect on prices, quality and innovation without any significant offsetting benefit for consumers. The commission judged that, even though some divestment of outlets was likely, 'no reasonable divestment programme would adequately restore a fourth national competitor'. It is interesting that the Commission explicitly recognized the application of game-theoretic considerations in mentioning the interdependence of the operations of the different retailers. It concluded that, even without collusion, the reduction in the number of retailers, combined with high barriers to entry, would have undesirable effects, both on consumers and on suppliers. A complete list of Competition Commission reports can be found at their website.[10]

Merger policy has always been stricter in the USA than in the UK or EU. It opposes mergers of large firms with significant market share on principle, regardless of the public interest. There are again two main regulatory bodies involved: the **Department of Justice** (DoJ) and the **Federal Trade Commission** (FTC). The DoJ can file both civil and criminal cases, while the FTC only has jurisdiction over civil cases. Rulings of the FTC can be appealed in federal courts. Furthermore, unlike the UK and EU, private individuals and companies can file anti-trust cases in the federal courts, and this practice is the most common as far as anti-trust suits are concerned.

Criteria for government action are complex and include a number of fact-ors. Changes in the concentration of the market, based on the Herfindahl index, are relevant, but as already seen this begs a definition of the relevant market. Therefore the issues of product and geographical boundaries are raised. Other issues that are considered are the contestability of the market, the likelihood of failure of the firm to be taken over without the merger, and efficiency gains from the merger.

Another option for the government instead of trying to block the merger is to negotiate a consent decree that allows a merger to occur provided that certain conditions are satisfied. Such conditions generally relate to the anti-competitive effects of the proposed merger.

In the EU the 1990 **Merger Control Regulation** determined that mergers would be referred to the Commission if the combined universal sales of the merged firms were more than 5 billion ECU (European Currency Units), and if the total Community-wide sales of each of at least two of the firms exceeds ECU 250 million. However, if each of the firms involved obtains more than two-thirds of its total sales within any one member state, then such a concentration of market power is to be assessed by that country's own merger policy even if both of the previous two criteria have been satisfied.

This regulation creates two main loopholes for mergers to escape prevent-ive action by the authorities. First, no criterion relating to market share is stipulated, and in practice mergers resulting in 100 per cent of market share have been approved. Second, no attempt is made to define the boundaries of the market in terms of product or geography. The view has seemed to be that even 100 per cent monopoly in a single country may not be harmful, since there may be potential competition from firms in other countries within the EU. Also, such monopolies may represent national champions and on this basis can be encouraged. Thus it is not surprising that a large number of mergers took place in the EU in the 1990s, many involving large firms with significant market share.

One problem that has arisen because of these differences concerns inter-national co-operation. In recent years there have been concerns of a widening gulf between US and European policies regarding merger control. The dispute over the proposed merger between General Electric and Honeywell illustrated the problem: the US Department of Justice (DoJ) approved of the merger, but the European Commission did not. Charles James, Assistant Attorney-General in the DoJ's anti-trust division, said in a recent speech that co-operation between agencies is no longer enough. He warned that the difference between Washington and Brussels 'flowed from an apparent substantive difference, perhaps a fundamental one, between two agencies on the proper scope of anti-trust law enforcement'.[11]

Mr James advocated a new organization to resolve such issues. Such an agency has now been established, the **International Competition Network** (ICN). This brings together anti-trust officials from both the developed world and the developing world, with the aim of fostering consensus on both procedure and policy. This will apply not just to mergers but also to other aspects of competition policy. However, mergers are a top priority, since these are currently a significant problem for multinational companies doing cross-border deals. They have to file a large number of documents in many jurisdictions, each with different and conflicting rules on notification. An initiative called the Merger Streamlining Project has been established, backed by a group of multinational companies and the International Bar Association, in order to simplify this procedure.

b. Collusion

Explicit collusion involves agreements to fix prices, outputs or market shares, supported by legal documents. We have seen in Chapters 8 and 9 the factors that tend to favour the evolution and survival of collusion in oligopolistic markets. Such agreements are illegal in the UK under the Restrictive Practices Acts, in the US under the Sherman Act and in the EU under Article 85 of the Treaty of Rome. They tend therefore not to be important in practice as they are easy to detect. Implicit or tacit collusion is another matter. It is difficult to define, as well as detect. Price leadership, often found in oligopolistic markets, is not generally regarded as collusion. However, the sharing of pricing information by using a jointly owned computerized system has resulted in investigation of the airlines industry in the USA. In certain industries, particularly agriculture, joint price and output fixing is permitted in many countries.

Detection of implicit collusion can be very problematic. In a competitive industry, firms will tend to charge the same price for the same or similar products, and when there are changes in demand or cost conditions, firms will tend to change their prices simultaneously. Thus observation of prices and price changes cannot usually indicate collusion. Only if such changes occur in the absence of demand or cost changes would collusion be suspected, as has happened in the cigarette industry.

The existence of supernormal profit is an additional factor in detection. However, the problem in this case is the existence of asymmetric information. Evidence suggests that firms, being in a better position to know their revenues and costs than any regulators, can manipulate recorded profits to allay suspicions of collusion, particularly if they are aware that they may be under scrutiny.[12]

In conclusion, the detection and consequent prosecution of firms for collusion depends much on the vigilance and efforts of the regulators. In this respect there have again been considerable differences between the experiences of the UK, the US and the EU.

In the UK the Competition Act of 1998, which came into force in 2000, gave the OFT some new powers. It can now levy fines (of up to 10 per cent of turnover) on companies engaged in anti-competitive behaviour. Also, as in the USA, it can offer immunity from prosecution to cartel members who co-operate with the authorities. That puts a premium on speedy disloyalty to the cartel. This clever use of game theory has led to fourteen British companies gaining immunity from civil prosecution.[13] The Enterprise Act 2002 has strengthened the powers of the OFT. Six types of arrangement are specified as illegal: price-fixing, the limiting or preventing of supply, the limiting or preventing of production, market sharing, customer sharing and bid-fixing. However, the prosecution must prove not only that the act was dishonest, but that the defendant knew that they were acting dishonestly.[14] This rather strange provision, seeming to contradict the principle that ignorance of the law is no defence, may be highly relevant in the issue of fee-fixing by public schools, discussed in Case study 8.4. Anyone found guilty is now subject to a jail sentence of up to five years.

However, there has not been the same record of successful prosecution as in the USA or even the EU. In the UK, investigations of the banking industry and credit card issuers have not found evidence of any malpractice in terms of collusion. Even in the business of car retailing, where prices are notoriously high in the UK compared with other countries in the EU, investigation has not resulted in any significant action. The OECD, which praised Britain's competition policy in a report published in October 2002, does not think Britain cartel-free: it says that, in the industries that have been investigated, the presence of cartels keeps prices, on average, 20 per cent higher than they should be.[15]

In the USA, collusion, cartels and price-fixing practices have been pursued more vigorously than elsewhere. There are three factors involved.

1. *Greater resources*. The US authorities have greater resources at their disposal, in particular those of the FBI, than their counterparts in Europe; this is an important factor in the successful prosecution of large international firms, as seen above.

2. *Criminal prosecution of individuals*. Some executives have received prison sentences in the USA for collusion. Taubman, the chairman of the great auction house Sotheby's, served ten months in prison for his involvement in the fixing of commissions between Sotheby's and Christie's in the $4 billion a year auction market.[16]

3. *Whistle-blowing*. The US authorities provide a strong incentive for individuals to come forward with the relevant information, by granting them immunity from all prosecution. This makes clever use of game theory in what is essentially a Prisoner's Dilemma situation. Given the harsher penalties resulting from a successful prosecution in the USA, this whistle-blowing facility plays an important part in the activity of the authorities. It has, for example, been the former CEO of Christie's who has provided information to the DoJ in the investigation into the fixing of commissions. Although Christie's agreed, along with Sotheby's, to pay clients $256 million in 2000, they were exempted from fines; Sotheby's had to pay $45 million to the DoJ and $20 million to the European Commission.

Although in the past the EU authorities have been more relaxed in their activities against collusion, there are various signs now of a stricter stance in this respect. Some car manufacturers have already fallen foul of the competition laws, and there has now been a landmark case against many of the vitamin and food supplement manufacturers. Eight firms, in particular Roche and BASF, have received record fines totalling €855 million for running a price-fixing cartel. The European Commission has imposed fines on nearly twenty cartels, involving nearly a hundred companies, in the past two years. The Commission is also proposing to introduce criminal prosecution and whistle-blowing protection along the lines of the USA and the UK. There may be some problems in ensuring EU uniformity in this respect; the UK welcomes such changes but France does not approve of criminal prosecution in cases of collusion.

c. Pricing practices

Apart from collusion in terms of prices, regulators are also concerned with **predatory pricing**. This is generally defined as the practice of *charging a price lower than average cost in the short run in order to drive competitors out of business, and then raising the price afterwards in order to earn monopoly profit*. This is again illegal in the UK, USA and EU, but once more can be difficult to detect. This applies particularly to multiproduct firms, where a reliable measure of average cost for different products is often not available. This problem was originally touched on in Chapter 2, where the concept of the allocation of joint costs was discussed. Regulators are therefore particularly vigilant regarding situations where price is below average variable cost, but even average variable cost can be difficult to measure accurately for multiproduct firms.

Predatory pricing often involves price discrimination; in the USA, price discrimination is illegal under the Robinson–Patman Act of 1936, and the reasoning is related again to driving competitors out of business. Regulators fear that a low price in one market segment may be used to drive competitors out of that segment, while the losses can be subsidized by monopoly profits from a high price in another segment. The end result may be monopoly in both segments. Detection of price discrimination may be more difficult than it might seem at first sight, however. Firms can often claim a justification for charging different prices in terms of having different cost structures in different segments. Even with price discrimination according to time of usage it can be claimed that costs of supply vary; for example, a cinema may be justified in charging higher prices at peak times because additional ticket-sellers and other staff are necessary, thus possibly increasing average cost per ticket sold.

d. Other restrictive practices

There are a number of other practices that regulators in different countries have found to be in restraint of trade or competition. Two of these are now discussed.

1. Exclusive dealing. This can take a number of forms. Many public houses in the UK are tied houses, meaning that they are restricted to selling the products of a certain brewery. Free houses on the other hand have no such limitations.

Case study 12.1: Electricity

A state of gloom[17]

One of the wealthiest regions in the world is on the brink of an energy crisis of third-world dimensions. How did California come to this?

On January 16th, the Californian state assembly passed a bill giving the state a central role in the local electricity market. This, in effect, turned the clock back on the deregulation of California's power industry begun in 1996 amid grand promises of reduced rates for consumers, more secure supplies for business, and bigger markets for power companies. But in fact the state had few options. On the same day, two of California's largest utilities had their debts reduced to junk by the leading credit agencies after one of them, Southern California Edison (SCE), announced that it would not be paying $596m due to creditors, in order to 'preserve cash'.

That undermined the ability of SCE and of Pacific Gas & Electric (PG&E), the other big utility in the state, to buy power on credit, and pushed them to the brink of bankruptcy. On the same day, a 'stage 3' emergency was declared, the highest level of alert, called only when power reserves fall below 1.5% of demand. On January 17th, one-hour black-outs rolled round the area of northern California served by PG&E. And Governor Gray Davis declared a state of emergency, authorising the state water department to buy power.

This is a dreadful mess for a state that is held up around the world as a model of innovation and dynamic markets, and that was the first in America to pursue deregulation. What on earth has gone wrong?

The short answer is, botched deregulation. The peculiarly bad way in which California's deregulation was organised freed prices for wholesale electricity while putting a freeze on retail rates. As a result, the state's utilities have been forced to buy power on the red-hot spot market (where prices have soared recently) for far more than they are able to recoup from consumers.

Catastrophe has been looming for some time now. The state's residents have already endured a series of annoying and expensive 'brown-outs'. Indeed, power emergencies have become so common that they are announced along with the traffic and weather reports on the morning news.

Only recently, however, have local politicians begun to take action. Earlier this month, the state's legislature approved a temporary rate increase to ease the pain for the utilities. Mindful of the state's noisy consumer lobbies, legislators approved a hike of only about 10%, and then only for three months. And even that is subject to reversal. It came nowhere near the 30% hike that the utilities claim they need to survive.

Mr Davis, the state governor, tried to bully his way out of the crisis during his 'state of the state' speech on January 8th. 'Never again can we allow out-of-state profiteers to hold Californians hostage,' he declared, threatening to seize electricity assets and run them himself if necessary. Needless to say, his speech did not help much. Curtis Hebert, a Republican commissioner on the Federal Energy Regulatory Commission (FERC), the country's top electricity regulator, fumed: 'You've got a governor who cares more about being on a night-time news show than he does about fixing the problem in California.'

BRITISH FOG

If California fails to tackle its power problems swiftly, the knock-on effects could be severe. Morgan Stanley Dean Witter, an investment bank, has just warned that 'California's crisis could magnify the downside for the whole economy. In the end, the state's energy crisis could prove to be an unwanted wild card for the American financial markets and the global economy at large.'

Such fears of contagion explain why the outgoing Clinton administration has been scrambling to organise a series of summits between state and federal officials, the utilities, and their main power suppliers. The legislation passed this week, if it ever becomes law, would allow California's creditworthy Department of Water Resources to buy additional power directly under long-term contracts and to sell it on to the utilities at a fraction of the current spot-market price. But, inevitably, this can serve only as a stop-gap measure; the talks brokered by federal officials, aimed at providing the foundation for a longer-term solution, are due to resume on January 23rd.

To see how California might move forward, look first at how it got itself into such a pickle. Largely inspired by Britain's success in opening up its power sector a decade ago, California led the United States into the brave new world of liberalised electricity markets. After years of haggling among various interest groups – from the big utilities to greens and consumer organisations – the administration of Mr Davis's predecessor, Pete Wilson, put together a compromise deregulation bill with enough bells and whistles to please almost every interest group.

Through the whole process, Britain's power deregulation was the inspiration. Stephen Baum, the boss of Sempra (which owns San Diego Gas & Electric, a utility that is in better financial shape than PG&E and SCE), says that 'California embraced competition as a religion and the English model as our guide.' However, California's zealous reformers forged ahead without taking into account some important differences between California and Britain – for example, in areas such as reserve capacity. In Europe, deregulation has not resulted in reliability problems. But credit for that belongs not to European models of reform, but rather to excess capacity. Europe's top-heavy, state-dominated power sector has tended to 'gold-plate' its assets (through higher tariffs paid by captive customers). California was not in such a happy position.

Another difference between the two models is that Californian officials let pork-barrel politics inhibit the development of the retail market. Rather than allowing prices to fluctuate, politicians decided to freeze electricity rates for a few years – supposedly in the interests of the consumer. But that gave consumers no reason to cut power use even when wholesale prices sky-rocketed – as they have done recently.

Also, under pressure from the big and politically powerful utilities, the state's politicians agreed to compensate the companies generously for 'stranded assets' – such as the big power plants built before deregulation suddenly changed the rules of the game. That sounds fair enough, but California agreed to value those assets much more generously than other states. Worse still, officials decided to burden new entrants to the business with part of the cost of the 'stranded assets' built by the incumbents. Hence newcomers have been severely handicapped in their ability to compete on price.

A number of other states largely avoided making these mistakes. In Texas, for instance, firms are free to enter into long-term contracts in order to hedge against the risk of volatile prices. And Pennsylvania has had great success in spurring competition from newcomers.

California allowed none of this, and the upshot is that hardly any Californians have switched retail suppliers, unlike Pennsylvanians. In Britain, one-quarter of the public has switched. What California dubbed 'deregulation' did very little to unshackle the power sector from the state.

SUPPLY, DEMAND AND POLITICS

Yet even with its half-baked, half-British model, the state might have muddled along for quite some time. The snag is that a bunch of uniquely Californian forces conspired to bring things to a head: fierce opposition to new power supply; a dramatic surge in demand; and, in particular, the politics of pork and populism.

For a start, the state's supply picture has grown ever bleaker. New power plants are rarely popular in any part of the world, but in California the famous 'not in my back yard' (NIMBY) syndrome has reached ridiculous levels, thanks to the state's hyper-democratic balloting process. The state has also long had the toughest environmental laws in America, and these have helped to make power generation unattractive. Thanks to greenery gone mad, neighbourhoods turned selfish and surly, and red tape and regulatory uncertainty run amok, the state's utilities have not built a new power-generation plant in over a decade.

Yet the state's appetite for electricity has shot through the roof. Defying official forecasts made early in the decade, California's power consumption grew by a quarter during the 1990s. The most dramatic factor fuelling the growth in demand has been the digital revolution, spawned in northern California. As computing power has spread to everything from the manufacture of microchips to the frothing of cappuccinos, California has defied eco-pundits and state officials who forecast that the Internet and the 'new economy' would inevitably lead to less consumption of electricity. In San Jose, the heart of Silicon Valley, consumption has been growing at about 8% a year.

The clincher, though, has been the peculiar politics of California. Politicians and regulators have been fiddling with the reform process in ways that are both capricious and counterproductive. Amazed that the free market for wholesale power responded to last summer's supply squeeze by raising prices, panicky officials ordered 'caps' on those prices. Predictably, the caps have failed miserably – as the more recent supply crunch amply demonstrates.

Power prices shot up because supply was scarce, and the right solution would have been to let markets respond – as mid-western states did when they suffered similar price hikes a few summers ago. They did not meddle in the wholesale markets, and generators responded to the price signals by rushing to add supply. Notably, the crises there have not recurred.

The most disturbing failure in California, however, lies with the regulators themselves. Sometimes they trust not at all in market forces: for example, they actually discouraged utilities from hedging their price risks by purchasing derivatives. This lunacy as much as anything explains why the state's utilities are now on the verge of insolvency, compelled to buy power on the spot market.

Yet at other times, the regulators naively expect the market to sort out the problems of transition by itself. When Britain deregulated, for example, its pricing mechanism offered power suppliers an explicit top-up to encourage them to create reserve capacity. Though California deregulated into a much tighter market, its regulators offered no such incentive, relying entirely on the market to secure adequate supplies. This schizophrenia explains why the Californian reforms are a ragbag of muddled half-measures and downright anti-competitive clauses.

Given the imminent collapse of the state's utilities, there is much agitation from all quarters for the state or federal government to do something. But what? James Hoecker, the current head of FERC, says that 'California's market is clearly flawed by design . . . it will be very difficult to reform, but reform it we must, and reform it we can.'

The Clinton administration might have offered some help: Bill Richardson, the departing energy secretary, has long advocated regional price caps. Mr Hoecker saw those caps as too hard to implement, but he too sought a regional solution on the grounds that the Californian crisis is really 'an enormous struggle between sellers of power, mostly in the interior states, and the buyers of power, mostly on the coast'. But both Mr Richardson and Mr Hoecker are leaving office this weekend, and the men chosen by George Bush to replace them will be likely to

oppose anything that calls for heavy-handed federal involvement.

One option for those looking for a way to bring the state out of this mess is to let the utilities go bankrupt. Some market-minded folk argue this case, pointing out that companies in all sorts of industries go bust all the time. Setting aside politics, why not power too? Surely the lights can be kept on, argue such voices, by the bankruptcy court, the state or, ultimately, by the new managers of those assets?

This is a tempting argument, but the reason why bankruptcy is not a solution, argues Tom Higgins of Edison International, the parent of SCE, is that 'this situation is directly the result of government action and inaction; it is not due to management failure'. Any new manager of the utilities' assets would find it impossible to run them under the perverse conditions mandated by California's current regulatory regime.

Another option is for the state to give in to the popular backlash and to re-regulate the power business. That is not such a remote possibility. Carl Wood of the Public Utilities Commission, California's top electricity regulator, wants not only to re-regulate, but to go further and introduce a big state presence in power. Mr Wood says: 'I'm not an economist, so I'm flying by the seat of my pants, but it seems to me that it is orthodox economics that got us into this mess in the first place.' Mr Davis also hinted at a reversal in his recent speech, with its sinister threats of expropriation and criminal action. While such a move cannot be ruled out, it would be sheer folly to let the state's incompetent, bungling politicians and regulators run the power utilities as a reward for having run them into the ground in the first place.

WHAT NEXT?

The sensible way forward is to see any state intervention as a short-term fix that merely buys time to sort out the regulatory mess, and so propels the state towards a market-based long-term solution. Any short-term fix, which must surface soon in view of the parlous state of the utilities' finances, needs to deal with three separate aspects of the current liquidity crunch: paying for yesterday's power; paying for today's power; and paying for tomorrow's power.

Yesterday's power led to the $12 billion or so in debts now owed by the utilities to banks, power producers and other creditors. Any deal will probably include an agreement to allow delayed repayment in return for some sort of guarantee, implicit or explicit, from the state that the creditors will indeed get their money some day. This week's legislation suggests that today's power will probably be purchased by the state. As for tomorrow's power, even the state cannot afford to pay spot prices for long. So some sort of long-term contracts offering prices closer to historical norms are inevitable.

Having bought a few months' respite, which may not last beyond this summer's peak demand, Californian officials must restructure the electricity system to put it on a sounder footing. Mr Baum of Sempra says they must focus on the following: 'What will reduce the demand for power? What will increase power supplies? Unless the basic laws of supply and demand are repealed, those two questions must be answered. Everything else is just a sideshow.'

California needs to reform its laws in order to encourage power generation. This will mean, for example, ensuring that environmental regulations are not needlessly prohibitive. It must also involve paring back red tape. This may not be easy, but surely there is no justification for power-plant approvals taking twice as long in California as elsewhere in America (including places that have similar concerns about air quality).

Officials must also find ways to get around the NIMBY problem. One possibility may be a suggestion by Mr Davis that the state withhold funds from localities that are particularly obstructive, in the way that the federal government withholds highway funds from wayward states. An even better solution would be to remove barriers to entry for distributed generation, and to ensure that the established incumbents do not obstruct new micropower plants.

As important as boosting generation is fixing the consumer market. In the long run, liberalisation and competition will deliver lower electricity prices for companies and households alike. But there is a case for protecting domestic households from price volatility until a genuinely competitive retail market emerges. Unless consumers see fluctuations in prices, however, especially at peak times, they will have no incentive to save power or to shift their use off-peak. This leads to an obscene waste of energy.

To allow retail prices to fluctuate with market conditions requires the installation of sophisticated meters for all the state's consumers. Crucially, proper metering will speed the arrival of such innovations as fixed-price 'energy service' contracts, which promise outcomes such as certain levels of heating, rather than the mere delivery of kilowatts. Price transparency will also allow micropower plants to sell and buy power on the grid as demand dictates, so improving the grid's reliability.

If California's politicians see today's crisis as a chance to fix this deregulation gone awry, then the future may be bright for the state's suffering citizens. Muddling along and hoping for manna from heaven is no longer an option. The state's irresponsible politicians have one last chance to fix the mess that they have created. If they do not, then at best it will be a sweltering summer for Californians this year.

Questions

1 Summarize the mistakes made by the Californian regulators.
2 What external or uncontrollable factors aggravated the situation?
3 Comment on the quote by Carl Wood of the Public Utilities Commission: 'I'm not an economist, so I'm flying by the seat of my pants, but it seems to me that it is orthodox economics that got us into this mess in the first place.'
4 How can California's problems be fixed?

This practice is accepted as not restricting competition. However, the practice of many car manufacturers in the EU of imposing exclusive franchises on their dealers has aroused controversy. Warranties are voided if car owners get their cars serviced by, or buy parts from, non-authorized independent dealers, even if the parts are identical and original. This practice, referred to as a **Selective and Exclusive Distribution** (SED) system, has been tolerated under EU competition laws because the car industry has been given a **block exemption**. In the UK, for example, cars have been as much as 30 per cent more expensive

Case study 12.2: Postal services

Europe's last post[18]

A battle to break the monopolies in Europe's postal industry is about to begin. Can the European Commission create a single market?

When the Council of Ministers met in Lisbon a few weeks ago, Europe's political leaders set out an ambitious goal for this decade: Europe, they proclaimed, should become a dynamic and competitive knowledge-based economy. To speed that, the council called for faster progress on liberalising important economic sectors such as gas, electricity, transport and postal services.

Postal services? Surely the ministers were joking? To date, the European Commission has utterly failed to tackle the powerful state monopolies that dominate the industry. Notably, a directive in 1997 accepted that the lucrative monopoly would persist for letters weighing less than 350 grams (12 ounces). That measure opened to competition a paltry 3% of letter volumes and 5% of incumbent operators' revenues.

Postal services, for all their lack of glamour, represent a surprisingly large sector of the European economy: the annual turnover, of €80 billion ($72 billion), is equivalent to 1.4% of the European Union's GDP, and the public-sector operators employ 1.4m people. They also represent one of the more egregious cases where crude national interests have ridden roughshod over wider European goals. As one senior postal manager puts it, 'If the commission can't deliver a workable regime for the industry, it will be a failure for the entire single-market project.'

It could also, paradoxically, reduce the extent to which Europe benefits from the growth of electronic commerce. The Internet challenges some postal services, such as routine letters. But online retailers need physical delivery, to carry those orders of books and CDs to customers' homes. Inexpensive, efficient postal services are thus an essential adjunct of e-commerce.

However, Europe's postal industry today is at much the same stage as its telecoms industry was a decade ago: dominated by slow-moving, state-owned monopolies. As telecoms were deregulated, Europe's economies enjoyed big benefits because competition spurred incumbents into becoming more efficient. Without competition, postal incumbents may miss opportunities in rapidly developing new markets, such as high-margin services that guarantee delivery at a set time and so-called hybrid mail where the sender of a large business mailing starts the process by sending an e-mail to a specialist printing and mailing firm.

The threat to Europe's post offices is clear from what has happened in the United States. There, too, the market for letters is dominated by a monopoly in the form of the United States Postal Service (USPS), a behemoth with annual revenues in 1999 of $63 billion. After the air-cargo market was deregulated two decades ago, private firms destroyed USPS's grip on the parcels market. Today, seven private firms led by UPS and FedEx control 82% of America's domestic parcels and air freight revenues. The market for express parcels by itself was worth $22.6 billion in 1997.

Today's postal firms face a greater threat than mere deregulation. The way people and companies communicate is changing. Electronic messages are substituting for 'snail mail'. Specialists in logistics are threatening to grab big chunks of the market for moving the goods required by business. As the head of one big European post office admits, in a decade's time, national postal systems may no longer be the basis of Europe's post.

HOW UNIVERSAL?

To bring home these dangers to Europe's politicians will be difficult. In Brussels, the commission is about to try to do so. It has been quietly drafting a revised directive that will determine the next phase of market opening in 2003. Officials say the aim is modernisation, rather than liberalisation. But the idea of an open market appals public-sector giants such as Britain's Post Office and La Poste of France. They argue that they must be protected in order to ensure that they can fulfil an essential public duty: guaranteeing customers a universal standard of service at a single price, regardless of where they live.

In fact, this so-called Universal Service Obligation (USO) is accepted by almost everyone in the industry as a legitimate concern. The disagreements are over how much of a monopoly is required to finance it, and in which areas. In Sweden, which fully opened its postal market to competition in 1994, simple rules protect the USO. Most observers agree that the market has become more efficient since it was liberalised.

A study by the EU found that the costs of the USO vary from 5% to 14% of the state monopolists' revenues. Countries with remote areas such as France, Greece, Britain and Ireland are at the higher end of the range. Suspicious of the commission's figures, the British Post Office and La Poste have recently conducted their own joint study of USO costs. It found that, in a liberalised market, rural consumers might have to pay four times as much as business users. The USO is especially sensitive in France, where La Poste faces pressure to maintain its current branch network and high employment levels. The fact that Sweden Post has shed one-quarter of its workers since liberalisation began in the early 1990s is seen as typical of what happens when state operators have to compete.

Arguably the USO is less important than it appears. Much of the row turns on private letters sent between individuals. In fact, these account for only 8% of total mail volume, and Christmas cards account for half of this. In addition, state operators already use their unique delivery networks as a competitive weapon in the market for bulk business mailings. No commercial operator can rival the reach and distribution of the incumbent post offices, which is therefore just as likely to be a marketing strength to incumbents as an expensive handicap.

FROM PILLAR TO POST

The USO is by far the most politically sensitive issue raised by liberalisation, but it is not the only one. Direct mail (all those irritating advertisements that come by post) is growing strongly, so incumbents would like to keep as much of it as possible. Six European countries have already fully liberalised direct mail. But John Roberts, chief executive of Britain's Post Office, views the prospect as back-door opening of the entire market: 'You can't liberalise one class of mail in isolation,' he argues. A stronger argument comes from the Federation of European Direct Marketing (FEDMA), a trade association which represents the views of companies that use the postal systems. Big mailers such as La Redoute, a French retailer, send millions of pieces of direct mail each year, so it might seem obvious that FEDMA would be in favour of freeing the market as fast as possible.

In fact, FEDMA fears that a speedy market opening would allow strong firms such as Deutsche Post to crush competitors and amass sufficient share to acquire pricing power. FEDMA wants a controlled opening to make sure that public monopolies are not merely replaced with private ones, ultimately forcing users to pay higher charges.

Even if the commission could defuse the USO and direct-mail debates, it would still have difficulty. Opposition to liberalisation runs extraordinarily deep. This became clear after the passing of the first, flawed directive. As usual with European rules, governments were given some time to implement it in national laws. Instead, several countries grabbed the chance to extend the markets reserved for their state postal monopolies.

The EC is currently investigating Italy, France and Spain for these flagrant breaches of competition law. Meanwhile, the commission is caught between governments, postal operators and their privately owned would-be competitors.

Several big European governments, for all their fine words about the future, are implacably opposed to radical liberalisation. Not only do they worry about the social (and electoral) costs. In addition, they tend to see domestic postal operators as national assets, to be protected from the marketplace. If forced to liberalise, they want to coddle their incumbent operators for as long as possible.

Thus Britain, normally pro-liberalisation, is less keen these days. Unpromisingly, Alan Johnson, the minister for competitiveness whose brief includes the Post Office, was himself a postal worker for most of his pre-government life. Under a proposed new postal law, the Post Office will become a company after April 1st next year, although the government will be its only shareholder and it must ask for permission to do any transaction valued at more than £75m ($115m). Although the government would never admit it in public, it wants to give its newly incorporated post office breathing space in which it can learn to operate as a fully commercial entity.

But governments also change their positions. For instance, the German government, once lukewarm about quick liberalisation, is now in favour of it. From being a troubled and overly bureaucratic monolith a few years ago, Deutsche Post has become so efficient that it is on the verge of a flotation. In November, the company plans to sell a stake of at least 25% but perhaps as much as 49%, worth an estimated DM25 billion–50 billion ($11 billion–23 billion), depending on market conditions. This is the prelude to the full liberalisation of Germany's postal market from 2003, something that Deutsche Post keenly advocates.

Most of the other postal operators are more ambivalent. On the surface, they make supportive noises about liberalisation. For instance, Britain's Mr Roberts told a recent conference: 'We know liberalisation is coming and, indeed, we welcome it.' Corrado Passera, managing director since 1998 of Poste Italiane, thinks that the new directive will be 'not a threat, but an opportunity'.

Behind the scenes, however, several of the big operators are furiously campaigning to limit the scope of the forthcoming directive. In the same speech, Mr Roberts was at pains to explain why a continued monopoly below 150 grams was reasonable, even though it would liberate only 4% of mail volumes and 6% of revenues. Twelve of the operators have banded together into PostEurop, a lobbying association which has been picking holes in studies by the commission on the likely effects of different degrees of liberalising the market.

INCUMBENT ADVANTAGE

The position of would-be competitors ought to be more straightforward: frustration at the lack of progress, matched by fear of further costly delays. However, even this picture needs shading. Private firms such as UPS and DHL have concentrated on the parcels and express sectors of the market, which are open to competition. Few, if any, are in a hurry to enter the letters market, except perhaps to cherry-pick in growth areas such as direct mail; business letters are the spoils worth fighting for. Their concern is more about the way the state operators use their letter monopolies to subsidise competing parcels and express operations.

That is a reasonable worry. The past two years have seen a flurry of deals by incumbent operators. The most aggressive acquirers have been Deutsche Post, the British Post Office and TNT Post Groep (TPG) of the Netherlands. The second and third of those businesses have recently formed a joint venture with Singapore's postal operator in international mail. TPG itself is the result of a merger in 1996 between PTT, the original state monopolist in the Netherlands, and TNT, an Australian express and parcels group. Even loss-making Poste Italiane has been an active acquirer.

Deutsche Post's activities are by far the most controversial. It has made acquisitions in all the main European markets and in all the big postal sectors – parcels, express mail and logistics, as well as letters. The firm has spent €5.8 billion on acquisitions in the last two years, €5 billion of that during 1999 alone. Recently, it announced a new joint venture with Lufthansa Cargo. Its international ambitions were clear from its financial results for 1999, published on May 4th, which showed that its international revenues rose to 22% of its €22.4 billion total, a big jump from 2% a year earlier. Deutsche Post has also been investing heavily in e-commerce. For instance, on April 14th it announced that it had bought a 10% stake in GF-X, an online exchange for global air freight in which both Lufthansa Cargo and British Airways have also invested.

The financial results also reveal that almost 90% of its €1.12 billion profit came from the corporate mail division that accounts for only half of its turnover. This is evidence of a problem than overshadows Deutsche Post's partial flotation, despite the company's confident declaration on May 4th that it was 'ready for its IPO'. Deutsche Post is the subject of several legal disputes, the outcome of which may determine whether it can be floated at all.

The most important court case was brought six years ago by UPS, a giant American express and parcels operator, which alleges that Deutsche Post has long benefited from illegal state aid. The central question is whether Deutsche Post is using its lucrative domestic monopoly to deter competition and to subsidise its grand strategic plans. Critics say it must be. They point to the high cost of Germany's post – at DM1.10 for a first-class letter, the basic tariff is twice as expensive as its American equivalent, for instance – as evidence of excessive profits that can be ploughed into other businesses.

The commission is also currently investigating Deutsche Post's parcel-freight business to determine whether, as it suspects, the business has not covered its costs since as far back as 1984. Indeed, losses from the business between 1984 and 1996 are said to amount to DM27.5 billion. If Deutsche Post is found guilty both of receiving illegal state aid and of predatory pricing, critics will have scored a notable victory.

Deutsche Post is confident that the commission will rule in its favour, and that there will be no delay of its flotation. Klaus Zumwinkel, its chairman, says that there are hints that the commission will announce its decision on the state-aid allegation towards the end of June, but he cannot foresee anything that would obstruct the longer-term goal to become a wholly public company.

Perhaps the most vociferous advocate of open competition has been UPS, which raised $5.5 billion in a partial flotation of its own last year. It has consistently battled against incumbent operators from Europe to Canada, taking them to court where it can. Critics say that it uses its own dominant position in the domestic American parcels market to throw its weight around in international markets, although to date UPS has not been sued for any alleged abuse. Not surprisingly, UPS wants full liberalisation of Europe's postal market, but knows it will get something short of this.

A STAKE IN THE GROUND

The question is how far short. The current draft directive, released for consultation within the EU in the first week of May, is surprisingly radical. Frits Bolkestein, the commissioner for the internal market whose cabinet is responsible for the directive, wants to:

1 reduce the letters monopoly to 50 grams
2 liberalise direct mail; and
3 liberalise outbound, but not incoming, cross-border mail.

The cumulative effect, were these measures to be implemented in 2003 as planned, would be to open 27% of incumbent operators' revenues to free competition. By far the biggest impact would come from the reduction of the letter monopoly to 50 grams (16% of revenues), and direct mail (8%).

For comparison, were the letter monopoly to be reduced to 100 grams, the directive would open 20% of incumbents' revenues to competition; at 150 grams, a mere 17%. It is important to grasp that incumbents do not stand to lose 27% of their revenues: rather, they will now have to defend this portion against competitors. Studies suggest that most incumbents should hang on to around 80% of the affected amount.

In addition, the directive spells out how the commission sees the further opening of the postal market. First, it will set up a compensation fund designed to ensure that new entrants contribute to the cost of the USO in each market. Second, Mr Bolkestein is proposing a review period. Once the first step of liberalisation is taken at the start of 2003, there will be at least two years during which the impact on the USO will be assessed.

Depending on the outcome, a further step might take effect in 2007, but it will be left open as to whether this will be to full liberalisation. This is shrewd because a big objection from incumbents has been that the effects of market opening are unknowable and could be disastrous.

Nevertheless, the directive is likely to face howls of complaint. Although it seems reasonable, even unambitious, to outsiders, the proposed 50 gram limit will be politically sensitive. Speaking before the directive's specific proposals were known, Mr Roberts said that the Post Office would vigorously oppose a 50 gram reform on the grounds that it would plunge the operation into loss and put the USO in danger. He calculates that, over a three-year period, the Post Office would lose £100m of its £500m annual profits were the monopoly to be reduced merely to 150 grams: 'So imagine what the effect of 50 grams would be,' he says.

All this suggests that Mr Bolkestein and his cabinet have a tough job on their hands simply to keep what they have drafted. With the support of smaller countries such as Greece and Portugal, Britain and France are likely to try to block the directive or at least to water it down. They might succeed, in which case Europe's postal system will continue on its uncompetitive way. But even if the directive is agreed to by the Council of Ministers and travels unscathed through the European Parliament, it does not go nearly far enough. Mr Zumwinkel of Deutsche Post points out that the liberalisation process still has no end date – a concession to operators defending the USO – and says that, as long as this is the case, there is little incentive for countries to change their ways.

The danger for Europe is that its postal system is left behind as e-commerce grows. Mr Roberts thinks that new entrants, such as online grocers who visit consumers' homes each week to drop off orange juice and toilet paper, could develop more efficient ways to deliver parcels and packages than either the traditional postal firms or the specialist express operators. If Europe's postal system is to flourish in the future, its operators cannot afford to hide behind a lethargic liberalisation. Otherwise, like so many parcels and letters, they will simply get lost.

Questions

1 In what ways has the European Commission been cautious in liberalizing the market in postal services? Why?

2 What are the substitutes or competitors that are involved in this market?

3 What is the relevance of the USO to the issue of liberalizing the market?

4 What, if anything, can be learned from the experience of the USA in the postal services market?

5 Why have the activities of Deutsche Post been controversial?

than similar models on the Continent, although this differential had been reduced by the end of 2001 to 15 per cent. The car manufacturers have justified the practice as being necessary in order to ensure that their products are properly maintained after purchase. However, the European Commission has become tougher with manufacturers who abuse SEDs; it has fined Daimler-Chrysler nearly €72 million, and both Opel (part of GM) and Volkswagen for such practices.

The block exemption expired in September 2002, and the European car industry's trade association, ACEA, has argued in favour of renewing it. The European Commission, however, hired an independent UK consulting firm, Autopolis, to examine the case for renewal. The consultancy concluded strongly that SEDs were against the interests of consumers, and were being used to cross-subsidize car sales with servicing revenues. It therefore seems likely that block exemption will not survive, at least in its present form.

2. Resale price maintenance. This refers to the situation where manufacturers, usually of branded products, insist that distributors charge a minimum price for their products. The Supreme Court in the USA has allowed this practice, in the case of Sharp Electronics. More recently, this practice was also upheld by the European Court as being acceptable, in the case of the Tesco supermarket chain importing Levi's jeans from outside the EU. Part of the justification for this ruling was that certain products involve a quality image. Nevertheless, such judgements seem to run contrary to the spirit of free competition.

This section contains two case studies which highlight the problems of regulation, or more specifically deregulation. Both involve industries which are important in any economy, electricity and postal services, and the issues are universal, although different governments have approached them in different ways.

12.4 Externalities

The definition of externalities has been given in the previous section, along with some examples of both positive and negative effects. The analysis in this section concentrates on the economic aspects of the issue. The nature of the problem here is that there is a '**missing market**'; if a firm produces pollution that harms

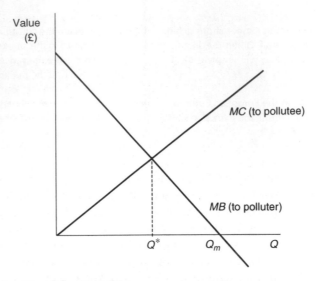

Figure 12.7. A market for externalities.

other parties, there is no market for the pollutant involved, so the producer has no incentive to take into account the costs involved. This insight provides a key to solving the problem, and in order to analyse the situation further the concept of an optimal level of an externality now needs to be considered.

12.4.1 Optimality with externalities

Optimality here refers to optimality in terms of resource allocation. More specifically, we are often concerned with a **Pareto optimum**: this is a situation where *one party cannot be made better off without making another party worse off*. We shall consider the situation of a polluter; this could be a firm or an individual, and the pollution could relate to air, water, land or noise. The costs and benefits in this situation are illustrated in Figure 12.7. The marginal benefit (MB) to the polluter of producing more pollution tends to decrease as they pollute more, through the familiar law of diminishing returns. A smoker, for example, receives less additional satisfaction from smoking more cigarettes. The party suffering from the pollution, the pollutee, tends to have increased marginal costs as the amount of pollution increases.

The level of pollution given by Q^* can be described as the optimal level of pollution from the point of view of the community as a whole, meaning that total welfare is maximized at this point. If more pollution is produced than this amount the additional costs to the pollutee more than offset the additional benefit to the producer, while if less pollution is produced than this the benefits that the polluter forgoes more than offset the costs to the pollutee of suffering more pollution.

What happens if there is no government intervention? The answer depends on the disposition of **property rights**. As we have seen, such rights refer to the legally enforceable power to take a particular action. If the polluter has no legal restraints they will pollute up to the level Q_m, where there is no additional benefit from polluting more. This level is more than the optimum because the polluter does not have to consider the costs to the pollutee. On the other hand, if the pollutee has the right not to be polluted at all, there will be no pollution, again not an optimal situation from the viewpoint of the community as a whole.

However, this assumes that there is still a 'missing market', meaning that the right to pollute cannot be traded. It has long been observed[19] that such market failure need not occur if such property rights can be traded. This is a point that was initially raised in the very first case study in this text, regarding the Kyoto Treaty and the conflict between the US stance and the European stance. If the polluter can trade the right to pollute with the pollutee they can come to some agreement in terms of payment, and the optimal solution will still be reached, without any government intervention. This principle was recognized in the United States with the Clean Air Act of 1990. The issue of who pays whom clearly depends on the disposition of property rights, but regardless of this disposition, an optimal situation can be achieved in terms of the allocation of resources as long as the parties involved can negotiate with each other; this is the Coase theorem again. The situation becomes more complicated in the international situation, where polluters in one country affect the welfare of consumers in another country, and there is some debate regarding the effectiveness of pollution permits in this case.[20, 21]

The main assumption of the Coase theorem, which causes many of the problems on an international basis, is that there are zero transaction costs. As we have seen in the previous section, this is often not a realistic assumption; therefore there are important implications as far as government policy and managerial policy are concerned.

12.4.2 *Implications for government policy*

There are various approaches that a government can take to improve the situation when transaction costs are high. The main options, along with their advantages and disadvantages, are outlined in the following paragraphs.

1. Do nothing. This may seem an overly passive approach, but it represents the best option if the costs of intervention, in terms of administrative costs, exceed the benefits in terms of resource reallocation.

2. Internalize the externality. This involves forcing the producer of the externality to become its consumer also. The main problem here is that it is often simply not possible, or at least practical. A smoker, for example, cannot be made to feel the cost of his activity, nor can a firm polluting a river usually be forced to suffer all the costs of doing so. Essentially, only in the limited case where one firm damages one other firm can a merger of such firms solve the problem.

3. Regulation. If the existence of transaction costs prevents polluter and pollutee from reaching agreement, there will be the amount given by Q_m

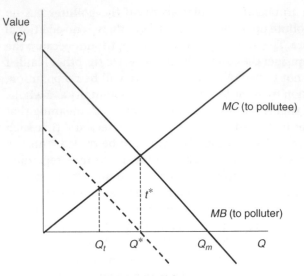

Figure 12.8. Taxes and externalities.

(assuming that polluters have the relevant property right in the absence of any government regulation). In order to prevent this non-optimal situation from occurring the government may regulate the production of pollution, ideally so that the amount Q^* is produced. In effect this policy divides the property rights between producer and consumer. The government then has the not inconsiderable task of estimating the value of Q^* (which in turn involves a cost to the government, and hence the taxpayer).

4. *Taxes and Subsidies*. These have a similar effect to internalization but tend to be much more practical in terms of administration. The principle involved is to tax the producer of negative externalities and subsidize the producer of positive externalities. The effects of this can be seen in Figure 12.8.

Any indirect tax will shift the marginal benefit curve of the polluter down by the amount of the tax; if the externality were positive a subsidy should be used to shift the marginal benefit of the provider upwards. In order to bring about the optimal level of the externality (it is assumed, as in Figure 12.7, that the externality is negative), the level of tax required is t^*. It is obviously very difficult for a government to estimate this amount. Some governments levy a tax based on output or consumption (petrol for example), but this ignores the possibility that the amount of pollution per unit of output/consumption can vary according to the technology in place (whether catalytic converters are used, for example). Even if a tax is based directly on units of pollution produced, this cost may vary according to the level of output.

Three main points need to be made regarding this solution:

● It is not costless; similar transaction costs to those described earlier are now incurred by the government.

- The resulting solution will only be optimal if transaction costs are significant. Otherwise, the parties will still negotiate an agreement, and combined with the imposition of the tax, the result will be that the amount of externality given by Q_t will be produced; this again is a non-optimal solution.
- The welfare of the individual parties involved will not be the same as with other solutions.

In conclusion, there can be no generalization made regarding which type of policy is best. This will depend on the circumstances, in particular on the type and extent of the transaction costs incurred with each policy option. For example, partial regulation is often difficult to enforce compared with a total ban; it is easier to see if a factory is emitting smoke from its chimneys than to measure the amount of this smoke and check whether it is over a certain limit. The general principle involved may be to maximize total welfare of the community taking into account transaction costs, but in practice this can be very difficult to implement. Political factors can make arriving at an optimal solution even more difficult. The introduction of green fuels, in particular liquefied petroleum gas (LPG), has been a case in point in the UK. In 2000 this was touted by the UK government as being the environmental-friendly fuel of the future, and there were generous grants of two-thirds of the cost of conversion, along with a level of fuel duty only about 10 per cent of that on unleaded petrol and diesel. By 2004 there had been a substantial U-turn in policy, with grants being slashed and fuel duty being raised. The justification was that LPG no longer had superior 'green' credentials, since newer fuels are now much cleaner and newer cars are much more efficient.[22]

These political factors are further examined in the next section, along with an account of the government policies that have actually been pursued on an EU and worldwide basis.

12.4.3 Implications for management

Some readers at this point may be saying that the above analysis of market failure and government policy is all very well, though somewhat abstract, but why is it important to managers? There are three points of relevance here.

1. Managers need to know how governments react or are likely to react to market failure, as explained in the introduction, so that they can anticipate government actions and in some cases even influence such actions by using their lobbying power. For example, firms in an industry may get together to lobby for lower indirect taxes on their products or to have a lighter regulatory burden.

2. Managers may try to find ways to reduce the transactions cost involved in reaching agreements that may be more beneficial than government intervention. Improved methods of finding and processing information and methods of enforcing agreements are important in this context.

Case study 12.3: Fuel taxes and optimality

Fuelling discontent[23]

How much should petrol be taxed?

The tax on petrol varies widely around the developed world. America's gasoline tax is currently about 40 cents an American gallon, equivalent to 7 pence a litre. Many Americans are calling for it to be cut, as the summer increase in prices begins to make itself felt, and reflecting a more general alarm about the country's 'energy crisis'. In Canada the tax is half as big again as in America; in Australia it is more than double. In Japan and most of Europe, the specific tax on petrol is around five times higher than in America, standing at the equivalent of some 35 pence a litre. At the upper extreme is Britain, where fuel duty (paid in addition to value-added tax) has risen in recent years to a punitive rate of just under 50 pence a litre, seven times the American levy.

You would expect well-designed petrol taxes to vary from country to country, according to national circumstances – but not, on the face of it, by a factor of seven. In America it is taken for granted that Europe's petrol taxes, let alone Britain's, are insanely high, and presumably something to do with socialism. In Britain, on the other hand, it is taken for granted that America's gas tax is insanely low, part of a broader scheme to wreck the planet. Protests in Britain last year showed that petrol tax had finally been raised all the way up to its political ceiling – but nobody expects or even calls for the tax to be cut to the American level.

America and Britain may both be wrong about the gas tax, but it seems unlikely that they can both be right. So how heavily should petrol be taxed? A paper by Ian Parry of Resources for the Future, an environmental think-tank in Washington, DC, looks at the arguments.

The most plausible justification for taxing petrol more highly than other goods is that using the stuff harms the environment and adds to the costs of traffic congestion. This is indeed how Britain's government defends its policy. But the fact that burning petrol creates these 'negative externalities' does not imply, as many seem to think, that no tax on petrol could ever be too high. Economics is precise about the tax that should, in principle, be set to deal with negative externalities: the tax on a litre of fuel should be equal to the harm caused by using a litre of

fuel. If the tax is more than that, its costs (which include the inconvenience inflicted on people who would rather have used their cars) will exceed its benefits (including any reduction in congestion and pollution).

The pollution costs of using petrol are of two main kinds: damage to health from breathing in emissions such as carbon monoxide and assorted particulates, and broader damage to the environment through the contribution that burning petrol makes to global warming. Reviewing the literature, Mr Parry notes that most recent studies estimate the health costs of burning petrol at around 10 pence a litre or less. The harm caused by petrol's contribution to global warming is, for the time being, much more speculative. Recent high-damage scenarios, however, put an upper limit on the cost at about $100 per ton of carbon, equivalent to 5 pence a litre of petrol. Adding these together, you come to an optimal petrol tax of no more than 15 pence a litre.

JAMMED

High petrol taxes also help to reduce traffic congestion. However, they are badly designed for that purpose. Curbing the number of car journeys is only one way to reduce congestion. Others include persuading people either to drive outside peak hours or to use routes that carry less traffic. High petrol taxes fail to exploit those additional channels. As a result, Mr Parry finds, the net benefits of a road-specific peak-period fee (the gain of less congestion minus the cost of disrupted travel) would be about three times bigger than a petrol-tax increase calculated to curb congestion by the same amount. Still, if politics or technology rules out congestion-based road-pricing, a second-best case can be made for raising the petrol tax instead. According to Mr Parry, congestion costs in Britain might then justify an additional 10 pence a litre in tax.

This brings you to a total petrol tax of around 25 pence a litre. The pre-tax price of petrol is currently about 20 pence a litre, so this upper-bound estimate of the optimal tax represents a tax rate of well over 100% – a 'high tax', to be sure. Yet Britain's current rate is roughly double this. On the same basis, of course, America's rate is far too low (even a lower bound for the optimal rate would be a lot higher than 7 pence a litre).

Britain's rate, judged according to the environmental and congestion arguments, looks way too high – but plainly the British government has another reason for taxing petrol so heavily. It needs the money to finance its plans for public spending. Politically, raising money through the tax on petrol, protests notwithstanding, has proved far easier than it would have been to collect the cash through increases in income tax or in the broadly based value-added tax – or, for that matter, through congestion-based road-pricing (always dismissed as 'politically impossible').

This seems odd. Supposing that actual and projected public spending justified higher taxation, Mr Parry's analysis strongly suggests that the country would have been better off paying for it through income taxes than through a punitive petrol tax. And the petrol tax is not only wasteful in economic terms, if Mr Parry is right; it is also regressive in its distributional effects, increasing the cost of living for poor car-owning households much more than for their richer counterparts.

At last, Britain has found the political ceiling for the petrol tax. What is remarkable is just how high it proved to be.

Questions

1 What are the economic reasons for fuel taxes being different in different countries?

2 What additional factors are relevant in explaining why fuel taxes in the UK are seven times the level in the USA?

3 Why are fuel taxes an inefficient way of reducing traffic congestion?

4 Given that fuel taxes are higher in the UK than the rest of Europe, what implications does this have for UK firms competing with European ones?

3. Managers may also anticipate consumer reactions to externalities and take the necessary actions. Examples of situations where this was not done are the Exxon Valdez oil spill and the Union Carbide disaster in India. In both cases consumers saw these firms as uncaring about the externalities that they had caused and much goodwill was lost, and ultimately customers also.

The final case study in the chapter involves the evaluation of the optimal level of tax for petrol, based on the externalities involved. In practice, products are often taxed for reasons other than externalities: they are convenient sources of revenue. This applies to cigarettes and alcohol in particular. More recently, speed cameras have come into use to target drivers for fines, which essentially amount to a tax. Again, the introduction of cameras has largely been for revenue reasons rather than for safety. All these cases tend to involve inelastic demand; otherwise they would not be so attractive to governments as a source of revenue. However, in their desire to obtain such revenue, governments should not ignore the distorting effects on the market of the taxes involved, even in the case of speeding fines.

12.5 Imperfect information

As seen earlier, there are two main aspects to this, incomplete information and asymmetric information. These are not mutually exclusive categories, but in the first case the main concern of the government is consumers' lack of information, whereas in the second it is the fact that one party to a transaction has more information pertaining to the transaction than the other.

12.5.1 Incomplete information

The fact that consumers, firms and governments do not have complete knowledge is inevitable; it means that either we do not have complete information or we cannot process it correctly or sufficiently quickly, or all of these. The problem is related to that of **transaction costs**, since by engaging in various transactions, for example buying a newspaper or surfing the Internet, we can improve our knowledge. However, there is a cost involved, even if this is only in terms of time. Transaction costs are examined in more detail in the next subsection.

Regardless of cost though, we can never have perfect knowledge. What are the implications of this? People may take drugs, either not knowing, or at least underestimating, their harmful and addictive effects. Thus the benefits obtained may turn out to be considerably less than the costs incurred, for the individuals involved. Externalities also arise, as was explained in an example above. Likewise, people may underestimate the benefits of education and underconsume this product in terms of its benefits and costs; again there are externalities, in this case positive ones. The government may therefore decide that it should discourage the consumption of drugs and encourage the consumption of education, in order to improve the allocation of resources.

What about pornography and prostitution? There is no case here in terms of imperfect information. People who argue against the consumption of these products tend to do so on the grounds that they are demeaning, or 'immoral'. This obviously makes these topics a normative issue, not an issue related to an efficient allocation of resources. While stating that governments frequently do implement policies regarding such issues, such as banning or restricting sales, it is commonly held as a principle of democratic government that governments do not intervene in matters of private habits or consumption, unless these affect other people, in which case externalities are relevant.

12.5.2 Asymmetric information

Governments are also sometimes concerned about the issue of **asymmetric information**. As already seen in Chapter 2, this refers to a situation where *one party in a transaction has more information than the other*, giving them an advantage. This can occur in many markets, particularly secondhand markets and those where specialized knowledge is required, such as the financial markets. The problems created involve adverse selection (hidden action resulting in pre-contract opportunism) and moral hazard (hidden information resulting in post-contract opportunism). Again both problems have already been discussed, and some game theory analysis performed.

What are the implications for government policy? These are best explained by using some examples; the adverse selection situation will be considered first, and then moral hazard.

a. Adverse selection

We have seen that the provision of insurance involves both adverse selection and moral hazard. Adverse selection arises because only those people with poor risk profiles will tend to want insurance at the prevailing rates. This can cause the whole market to collapse, as rates increase more and more, gradually excluding more and more people, until only very high risk persons are left; these people may not be able to afford the insurance at the rates required. Government policy can help to spread the risk by providing universal insurance at fixed rates, as it does in many countries in the case of health insurance. This does not prevent the problem of moral hazard, however, as will be seen.

Another common situation where adverse selection is involved is **insider trading** in the financial markets. This means *trading instruments on the basis of information that has not yet been made public*. In most countries this kind of activity is illegal and is prosecuted with various degrees of enforcement, including fines and jail terms for convicted offenders. There are normative arguments against insider trading, related to taking unfair advantage of one's position, but the main economic argument is that, like private health insurance, it can lead to a collapse of the market. If it is known that insiders are trading on the market, this will discourage people without such information from entering the market, since they will be at a disadvantage and will generally lose money. With only insiders involved, the financial markets will lose much of their depth, breadth and liquidity, and this will ultimately have bad consequences for the economic system as a whole, since financial resources will be inefficiently allocated.

b. Moral hazard

In private medicine there is an opportunity for doctors to overprescribe treatment, in order to increase their incomes, based on the ignorance of their patients. Similarly, there is an opportunity for car repair shops to recommend unnecessary repairs, based on the ignorance of car owners. In the UK in particular there has been considerable scandal in recent years regarding the mis-selling of pensions; financial advisors have seen an opportunity to increase their incomes by selling inappropriate financial instruments to an uninformed public. Unemployment insurance reduces the incentive for unemployed workers to find work. Deposit insurance reduces the caution that depositors exercise before placing funds in a bank, and also reduces the caution with which banks invest these funds. Current systems of corporate governance often lead to senior executives providing misleading information to investors, profiting the executives but at the expense of shareholders, as discussed in Chapter 2. All these examples involve moral hazard, and the relevant markets are therefore often more highly regulated than others. However, it is important to note that regulation does not necessarily solve the problem; in fact it can make the problem worse. In order to see this we shall concentrate on the last three situations.

Many countries have state systems of unemployment insurance, with varying degrees of financial support for unemployed workers, and varying degrees of monitoring effectiveness, in terms of checks to see if the workers really are unemployed and are genuinely searching for a job. It can be seen that the greater the financial support given and the lower the monitoring effectiveness, the greater will be the abuse of the system. Incentives and efficiency are likely to be greater in a private insurance system than a state system.

Deposit insurance, also organized by the state, has caused serious problems in the United States in the late 1980s and early 1990s, with the Savings and Loan crisis. There were many factors involved in this crisis, but certainly the moral hazard created by deposit insurance played a big part. The problem is at an even greater level in the Japanese financial industry, where state support has traditionally been a major pillar of the system. Therefore it must be recognized that state systems of insurance tend to increase moral hazard compared with private systems, by causing a greater distortion of incentives.

The third example above, concerning corporate governance, has been an issue that has attracted the attention of many governments over the last few years. The Sarbanes–Oxley Act in the USA was passed in 2002, while in the UK the Higgs Report has recently been hotly debated by the various affected parties. Governments in Germany, France and Canada are also in the process of changing their rules in this area, largely in response to a variety of corporate scandals that have been reported in the press. These developments are discussed further in the next subsection.

12.5.3 Implications for government policy

We have already seen that governments have to be careful about regulating markets where imperfect information is involved, or they may make the situation worse rather than better. In general there are three types of policy that a government can use, particularly with regard to asymmetric information, and these are now discussed.

a. Disclosure of information requirements

In this case the government requires the party with more information to disclose the relevant information. This has been common in financial markets for decades. For example, the Securities and Exchange Commission (SEC) in the United States requires all public companies to file a prospectus with all the relevant financial information in order to help shareholders and potential investors make better decisions; most countries with well-developed financial markets have similar regulations. These requirements are now being increased in the wake of various accounting scandals. The Sarbanes–Oxley Act, among many provisions in its 130 pages, now also requires the CEOs and CFOs of all the 14,000 listed companies to vouch for the integrity of company reports and financial statements, a symbolic act reinforcing the threat of criminal prosecution for fraud. Executives have to report share ownership more quickly, and company lawyers have a duty to report managerial transgressions to the board.

An interesting variation of a disclosure policy concerns car repair shops; in the UK they are required to give back to the buyer any parts that they have replaced, so that they may be inspected to ensure that they were actually faulty. Such policies are clearly not foolproof, and like all policies they involve enforcement costs.

b. Regulation of conduct

Apart from concentrating on the provision of information the government can also regulate the behaviour of the parties involved. Buyers may be given time to cancel contracts after a sales agreement has been made. This allows buyers to reconsider their situation, maybe in the light of better information. Such time periods generally vary from three to thirty days. This kind of policy is aimed specifically at defusing high-pressure sales tactics. Certain professions may also be prohibited from advertising their services, like doctors and lawyers. This used to be government policy in the USA, but it was found that when the prohibition was dropped the prices charged by such professions fell considerably on account of the increase in information and competition. Thus in this situation the government has to consider the benefits of prohibitions, in terms of the avoidance of unnecessary transactions and exploitation, against the costs, in terms of increased prices and reduced competition.

Again, in the area of corporate governance, managerial conduct is now being restrained in various ways. The Sarbanes–Oxley Act in the USA prohibits subsidized loans to executives and requires bosses to reimburse incentive-based compensation if profits are mis-stated.

c. Regulation of firm and industry structure

The main purpose here is to prevent the conflict of interest that can often arise with asymmetric information. As we have seen, doctors may overprescribe treatments, car repair shops may perform unnecessary repairs, financial companies may sell inappropriate pensions. Structural regulation involves separating the function of analysis and prescription from the function of provision or sale of the product. For example, doctors may be prohibited from selling medicines, financial advisers may be forced to state whether they are independent or not, commercial banking may be separated from investment banking, brokers may be separated from dealers or market-makers by 'Chinese walls'.

In the area of corporate governance there have been a number of changes in the regulations relating to structure. One issue that has arisen recently, in view of the various scandals involving the reporting of profit, concerns the separation of the auditing and consultancy functions of accountancy firms. In the United States, accounting firms are now required to rotate partners supervising audits, but there is no mandatory rotation of auditors at this point. However, the self-regulation of accountants is being replaced by a public accounting oversight board.

The New York Stock Exchange and NASDAQ have also implemented some changes in their rules: all listed firms need shareholder approval for stock-option plans; a majority of independent directors is required on the board; only independent directors are allowed on audit committees and on committees selecting CEOs and determining pay.

In the UK the Higgs Report recommends that chairmen should be banned from heading nomination committees, and that senior non-executive directors should be required to hold regular meetings with shareholders. The report has met with considerable opposition; a recent survey by the CBI indicated that over 80 per cent of large firms opposed some of the proposals. All policies of structural regulation are bound to face serious political resistance from vested interests; Sarbanes–Oxley has been criticized both for doing too little and for doing too much. The accusation of too little action focuses on the facts that shareholders still have no power to put up candidates for the board, and that institutional investors are not required to disclose proxy votes. The main problem of doing too much is that the increase in responsibilities of both executive and non-executive directors will make them too risk-averse. They may have an inordinate fear of lawsuits from shareholders.

12.5.4 Implications for management

Managers are often wary of governmental regulation. They may fear a loss of profits caused by a better-informed public, they may regard the provisions as restricting their practice of free trade, or they may resent the increase in administrative costs caused by the enforcement of the regulation.

In some cases, however, firms can forestall the threat of regulation by subjecting themselves to self-regulation. This is often achieved by the establishment of professional associations, which license all firms in the industry. Such organizations usually regulate aspects such as training, entry standards, code of conduct, and often various marketing practices, like pricing and advertising. Such self-regulation is more common in the UK than in the USA, where a principles-based rather than a rules-based approach is taken to regulation. Self-regulation is common in medicine, law and finance. However, if abuses still occur, the government may well intervene, enforcing its own standards. For example, the London Stock Exchange practised self-regulation for decades, but in view of continuing instances of malpractice the UK government has introduced a variety of regulatory bodies in the financial markets in the last ten years, in particular the Financial Services Authority.

Summary

1 It is important for managers to understand the principles surrounding government policy in order to be able to respond to it in the best possible way, to anticipate it, and even to influence it.

2 Governments have both macroeconomic and microeconomic objectives.

3 The most important microeconomic objectives are to correct market failure and to redistribute income.

4 The main causes of market failure are monopolies, externalities, public goods, imperfect information and transaction costs.

5 The economic principle regarding government intervention is that it should intervene at that point in the economic system closest to the policy objective in order to maximize total welfare. In practice this principle tends to be ignored or overruled by political factors.

6 Governments have an economic reason for intervening in monopolistic markets because of the potential for deadweight welfare loss.

7 Governments tend to have two main strands of policy, one aimed at existing monopolies and one at potential monopolies.

8 Existing monopolies often feature structural barriers while potential monopolies tend to feature strategic barriers.

9 When structural barriers exist, government policies are often aimed at conduct, while the existence of strategic barriers can cause policies to be targeted at structure as well as conduct.

10 There is no one foolproof measure of monopoly power; governments tend to take into consideration a number of measures, in particular the degree of concentration in the industry and the level of profit or rate of return.

11 Government policies towards monopoly tend to depend on the political philosophy of the government, in particular whether it favours the ASM or the ESM.

12 The ESM tends to favour public ownership more, while the ASM tends to prefer privatization.

13 The ESM tends to favour more regulation, while the ASM often favours deregulation and liberalization.

14 The ASM tends to have stricter laws relating to restrictive practices, and stricter enforcement of such Laws.

15 Collusion is usually illegal and causes government intervention, unless it is seen as being in the national interest.

16 Collusion is very difficult to detect; simultaneous price movements by firms do not necessarily imply collusion if such movements accompany changes in demand or cost conditions.

17 In practice, governments often defend monopolies when they represent 'national champions', even though this is frowned on by the European Commission.

18 Externalities occur when the action of one agent affects the welfare of other agents, and these effects do not involve an economic transaction.

19 The existence of tradable property rights can lead to an optimal solution in allocating resources in situations where externalities are present.

20 Externalities only require government intervention because of the incidence of transaction costs that prevent people from negotiation.

21 Governments have various policy options for dealing with externalities: doing nothing, internalizing them, regulation and using taxation and subsidies.

22 Asymmetric information, involving moral hazard, can lead to consumers buying more, or less, of products than they otherwise would and leads to a reduction in total welfare.

23 Asymmetric information also causes many problems in corporate governance, where managers have more information than shareholders and other investors.

24 Governments can implement three different types of policy to deal with the problem of asymmetric information: requiring disclosure of information, regulating conduct, and regulating the structure of the industry.

Review questions

1 Explain the relevance of the SCP model to government policy.

2 Discuss the advantages and disadvantages of public ownership.

3 Examine the different policy options for a government dealing with the problem of traffic congestion, explaining the advantages and disadvantages of each option.

4 Different governments have different policies for determining the level of fuel taxes; what implications does this have for firms in different countries?

5 What is meant by predatory pricing? Why is it a concern to government authorities?

6 Why do governments sometimes protect monopolies from competition?

7 Discuss the various problems associated with regulating natural monopolies.

8 What measures can governments take to reduce price-fixing practices?

Notes

1 M. Hirschey, J. L. Pappas and D. Whigham, *Managerial Economics*, London: Dryden Press, 1995.

2 R. A. Posner, 'The social costs of monopoly and regulation', *Journal of Political Economy*, **83** (1975): 807–827.

3 J. K. Galbraith, *American Capitalism: The Concept of Countervailing Power*, New York: Houghton Mifflin, 1952.

4 J. Gray, *False Dawn: The Delusions of Global Capitalism*, London: Granta Books, 1999, p. 112.

5 R. Layard, 'Clues to prosperity', *The Financial Times*, 17 February 1997.

6 Gray, *False Dawn*, pp. 24–25.

7 'Come back Dr Beeching', *The Economist*, 17 January 2002.

8 http://www.cliffordchance.com/, 'The Enterprise Act 2002: summary of Main competition provisions, July 2003'.

9 http://www.competition-commission.org.uk/rep_pub/reports/2003/481safeway.htm#summary, 'Safeway plc and Asda Group Limited (owned by Walmart Stores Inc); Wm. Morrison Supermarkets plc; J. Sainsbury plc; and Tesco plc: A report on the mergers in contemplation'.

10 http://www.competition-commission.org.uk/rep_pub/reports/2003/index.htm
11 C. Mortished, 'Antitrust chiefs seek common approach', *The Times*, 26 October 2001.
12 R. M. Harstad, and L. Phlips, 'Information requirement of collusion detection: simple seasonal markets', extracts in L. Phlips (ed.), *Competition Policy: A Game-Theoretic Perspective*, Cambridge: Cambridge University Press, 1995.
13 'Europe's last post', *The Economist*, 11 May 2000.
14 http://www.cliffordchance.com/, 'The Enterprise Act 2002'.
15 'Setting the trap', *The Economist*, 31 October 2002.
16 O. Ashenfelter and K. Graddy, 'Auctions and the price of art', *Journal of Economic Literature*, **41** (2003): 763–787.
17 'A state of gloom', *The Economist*, 18 January 2001.
18 'Europe's last post'.
19 R. Coase, 'The problem of social cost', *Journal of Law and Economics*, **3** (1960): 1–44.
20 J. M. Tomkins and J. Twomey, 'International pollution control: a review of marketable permits', *Journal of Environmental Management*, **41** (1994): 39–47.
21 A. Collins, 'International pollution control: a review of marketable permits – a comment', *Journal of Environmental Management*, **43** (1994): 185–188.
22 'Green fuel runs out of gas', *The Sunday Times*, 28 March 2004.
23 'Fuelling discontent', *The Economist*, 17 May 2001.

Index

Lightning Source UK Ltd.
Milton Keynes UK
19 January 2010

148841UK00006B/26/P